THE LETTERS

OF

GERTRUDE BELL

VOLUMES I AND II

SELECTED AND EDITED BY LADY BELL, D.B.E.

PREFATORY NOTE

In the letters contained in this book there will be found many Eastern names, both of people and places, difficult to handle for those, like myself, not conversant with Arabic. The Arabic alphabet has characters for which we have no satisfactory equivalents and the Arab language has sounds which we find it difficult to reproduce. We have therefore in dealing with them to content ourselves with transliterations, some of which in words more or less frequently used in English have become translations, such as 'Koran,' 'kavass,' etc. But even these words (there are many others, but I take these two as an example) which have almost become a part of the English language are now spelt differently by experts, and at first sight it is difficult to recognise them in 'Quran' and 'qawas'--which latter form is I believe in accordance with the standardised spelling now being officially introduced in Bagdad. Gertrude herself in her letters used often to spell the same word in different ways, sometimes because she was trying experiments in transliteration, sometimes deliberately adopting a new way, sometimes because the same word is differently pronounced in Arabic or in Turkish. These variations in spelling have added a good deal to the difficulty of editing her letters especially as reference to expert opinion has occasionally shown that experts themselves do not always agree as to which form of transliteration is the best.

I have therefore adopted the plan of spelling the names as they are found when they occur in the letters for the first time, and keeping to it. Thus Gertrude used to write at first 'Kaimmakam,' in her later letters 'Qaimmaqam.' I have spelt it uniformly with a K for the convenience of the reader; and so with other words in which the Q has now supplemented the K.

The word 'Bagdad' which used to be regarded as the English name of the town, a translation and not a transliteration, was spelt as I have given it in Gertrude's first letters long ago. It is now everywhere, even when regarded as a translation, spelt

'Baghdad' and it ought to have been so spelt in this book. The same applies to the name 'Teheran' which is now always spelt 'Tehran' but of which I have preserved the former spelling.

Dr. D. G. Hogatth has been good enough to read the preceding pages of this Prefatory Note, and to give them his sanction. He adds the following paragraph:

"A more difficult question still in reproducing proper names has been raised by the vowel signs in Arabic, including that for the ain and by the diacritical points and marks which convey either nothing or a false meaning to uninstructed Western eyes."

I have therefore omitted the vowel signs altogether.

My own interpolations, inserted where required as links or elucidations, are indicated by being enclosed in square brackets [ ] and by being "indented," i.e., printed in a shorter line than the text of the letters.

The formulae beginning and ending the letters have been mostly omitted, to save space and to avoid repetition. The heading H. B. at the top of a letter means that it is addressed to Gertrude's father, and the heading F. B. means that it is addressed to me.

I am most grateful to the people who have given me counsel and help in compiling this book: Sir Valentine Chirol, Mrs. W. L. Courtney, H. E. Sir Henry Dobbs, Dr. D. G. Hogarth, Elizabeth Robins, and Major General Sir Percy Cox, who has had the kindness to read and correct many of the Proofs.

I am also much indebted to the following for placing at my disposal maps or photographs, letters or portions of letters from Gertrude in their possession, or accounts of her written by themselves: Captain J. P. Farrar, Vice-Admiral Sir Reginald Hall, Mrs. Marguerite Harrison, Hon. Mrs. Anthony Henley, The

Dowager Countess of Jersey, Mary Countess of Lovelace, Hon. Mildred Lowther, Mr. Horace Marshall, Hon. Mrs. Harold Nicolson, Sir William Ramsay, Mr. E. A. Reeves, Miss Flora Russell, Lady Sheffield, Mr. Lionel Smith, Mr. Sydney Spencer, Lady Spring Rice, Colonel E. L. Strutt. Also for clerical help given me by Mrs. D. M. Chapman and my secretary Miss Phyllis S. Owen.

FLORENCE BELL
Mount Grace Priory,
August 1927.

CONTENTS

INTRODUCTION

Gertrude Margaret Lowthian Bell, to give her all her names, although she rarely used the second, was born on the 14th July, 1868, at Washington Hall, Co. Durham, the residence of her grandfather, Isaac Lowthian Bell, F.R.S., afterwards Sir Lowthian Bell, Bart. Sir Lowthian, ironmaster and colliery owner in the county of Durham, was a distinguished man of science. His wife was Margaret Pattinson, of Alston in Cumberland, daughter of Hugh Lee Pattinson, F.R.S. Gertrude's father, now Sir Hugh Bell, was Sir Lowthian's eldest son; her mother was Mary Shield, daughter of John Shield, of Newcastle-on-Tyne. Gertrude therefore had the possibility of inheriting from both Northumbrian and Cumbrian forbears some of the energy and intelligence of the north.

Gertrude was three years old when she lost her mother, who died when Gertrude's brother Maurice was born.

Gertrude Bell, happily for her family and friends, was one of the people whose lives can be reconstructed from correspondence.

Through all her wanderings, whether far or near, she kept in the closest touch with her home, always anxious to share her experiences and impressions with her family, to chronicle for their benefit all that happened to her, important or unimportant: whether a stirring tale of adventure or an account of a dinner party. Those letters, varied, witty, enthralling, were a constant joy through the years to all those who read them. It was fortunate for the recipients that the act of writing, the actual driving of the pen, seemed to be no more of an effort to Gertrude than to remember and record all that the pen set down. She was able at the close of a day of exciting travel to toss a complete account of it on to paper for her family, often covering several closely written quarto pages. And for many years she kept a diary as well. Then the time came when she ceased to write a diary. From 1919 onwards the confidential detailed letters of many pages, often written day by day, took its place. These were usually addressed to her father and dispatched to her family by every mail and by every extra opportunity. Besides these home letters, she found time for a large =and varied correspondence with friends outside her home circle both male and female, among the former being some of the most distinguished men of her time. But the letters to her family have provided such abundant material for the reconstruction of her story that it has not been found necessary to ask for any others. Short extracts from a few outside letters to some of her intimate friends, however, have been included. The earlier of these letters, written when she was at home and therefore sending no letters to her family, show what her home life and outlook were at the time of her girlhood, when she was living an ordinary life-- in so far as her life could ever be called ordinary. They foreshadow the pictures given in her subsequent family letters of her gradual development on all sides through the years, garnering as she went the almost incredible variety of experiences which culminated and ended in Bagdad. Letters written when she was twenty show that after her triumphant return from Oxford with one of the most brilliant Firsts of her year she threw herself with the greatest zest into all the amusements of her age, sharing in everything, enjoying everything, dancing, skating, fencing, going to London parties; making ardent girl friendships, drawing in to her circle intimates of all kinds. She also loved her country life, in which her occupations included an absorbing amount of gardening, fox hunting--she was a bold rider to hounds--interesting herself in the people at her father's ironworks, and in her country village, making friends in every direction. And when she was wandering far afield (her wanderings began very early--she went to Roumania when she was twenty-two and to Persia when she was twenty-three) she was always ready to take up her urban or country life at home on her return with the same zest as before, carrying with her, wherever she was, her ardent zest for knowledge, turning the flashlight of her eagerness on to one field of the mind after another and making it her own, reading, assimilating, discussing until the years found her ranged on equal terms beside some of the foremost scholars of her time.

To most people outside her own circle Gertrude was chiefly known by her achievements in the East, and it is probably the story of these that they will look for in this book. But the letters here published, from the time she was twenty until the end of her life, show such an amazing range of many-sided ability that they may seem to those who read them to present a picture worth recording at every stage.

Scholar, poet, historian, archaeologist, art critic, mountaineer, explorer, gardener, naturalist, distinguished servant of the State, Gertrude was all of these, and was recognised by experts as an expert in them all.

On the other hand, in some of the letters addressed to her family are references to subjects or events that may seem trivial or unimportant. But Gertrude's keen interest in every detail concerning her home was so delightful, and present her in such a new light to many who knew her only in public that these passages have been included.

Her love for her family, for her parents, for her brothers and sisters, her joy in her home life, has always seemed to those who shared that life to be so beautiful that it is worth dwelling on by the side of more exceptional experiences, and by the side of the world-famous achievements of one whose later life especially might well have separated her in mind and sympathy as well as in person from her belongings. But her letters show how unbreakable to the last was the bond between her and her home, and above all between her and her father. The abiding influence in Gertrude's life from the time she was a little child was her relation to her father. Her devotion to him, her whole-hearted admiration, the close and satisfying companionship between them, their deep mutual affection--these were to both the very foundation of existence until the day she died.

THE LETTERS
OF
GERTRUDE BELL

VOLUME 1

TO GERTRUDE'S FATHER

CHAPTER I

1874-1892 - CHILDHOOD-OXFORD-LONDON

[This is the earliest letter extant from Gertrude, dated when she was six years old. It is addressed to me, at a time when she was not yet my little daughter but my "affectionate little friend." Mopsa, about whom she writes, was a large grey Persian cat, who played a very prominent part in the household.]

Redbarns, Coatham, Redcar, September, 25th, 1874

MY DEAR FLORENCE,
Mopsa has been very naughty this morning. She has been scampering all over the dining-room Cilla says. I had a great Chase all over the hall and dining room to catch her and bring her to Papa. She bit and made one little red mark on my hand. During breakfast she hissed at Kitty Scott. Auntie Ada had her on her knee and Kitty was at one side. As Auntie Ada let Mopsa go down she hissed at Kitty and hunted her round to my side of the table. Please Papa says will you ask Auntie Florence if she will order us some honey like her own. I gave Mopsa your message and she sends her love. I forgot to say Kitty was very frightened. I send you my love and to Granmama and Auntie Florence.

Your affectionate little friend,

Gertrude Bell.

[At the time that the above letter was written, the two children were living with their father at Redcar on the Yorkshire coast. His un-married sister, Ada Bell, was then living with them.

Gertrude was eight when her father and I were married. She was a child of spirit and initiative, as may be imagined. Full of daring, she used to lead her little brother, whose tender years were ill equipped for so much enterprise, into the most perilous adventures, such as commanding him, to his terror, to follow her example in jumping from the top of a garden wall nine feet high to the ground. She used to alight on her feet, he very seldom did. Or she would lead a climbing expedition on to the top of the greenhouse, where Maurice was certain to go through the panes while Gertrude clambered down outside them in safety to the bottom.

They both of them rode from a very early age, and their ponies, of which they had a succession, were a constant joy.

From her early years Gertrude was devoted to flowers and to the garden. I have found a diary of hers when she was eleven. It was an imposing looking quarto volume bound in leather, apparently given her for a Christmas present in 1878 but only kept for a few pages, alas. I have left her own spelling.]

Jan. 11. 1879 Sunday--we played in liberry morning.

Feb. 11. Read Green till 9. Lessons went off rather lazily. We went into the gardin. I looked at flowers. Stilted.

Feb. 14. 1879--St. Valentines Day. I got 12 valentines. The lessons went very badly. The lessons themselves were good. Each got twopence . . . we caught a pigion we put it into a basket.

15 Feb. The pigion was brought into our room it drank some milk Maurice spilt a lot on my bed. So we went into the cuboard. Breakfast. I read all the morning. Dinner. I read all the afternoon. Tea. I played with Hugo. Mother read to us. Taught Maurice geography and read. Went to bed tired, had a little talk not fun and went to sleep.

Feb, 16. . .We now have out some yellow crocus and primroses snodrops and primroses. Primroses and snodrops in my garden. Crocus in Papas.

[The only remaining entry in the diary is an account of her birthday, the day she was eleven, Monday, 14th of July. The record, the celebrations, and all the presents seem amusingly childish for a little girl who was reading Green's history before breakfast, and devouring every book she could find.]

When I woke up I went to see the time. It was a quarter to seven. I woke Maurice. Then I hid my face and he got out his presents. He gave me scales a fireplace with pans kitchen furniture. Then I found under my pillow a book from nurse then we got up. When we were ready we went into Mother's room and there I found a hopping toad from Auntie Bessie dinner set from Mother, watering can from Papa. Then we went downstairs to breakfast Mother and Maurice and I cooked a dinner because it was wet. We had soup fish mince crockets Puding, cheese and butter and desert.

[Gertrude never entirely mastered the art of spelling, and all her life long there were certain words in her letters that were always spelt wrong. She always wrote 'siezed,' 'ekcercise,' 'exhorbitant.' Sometimes she wrote 'priviledge.'

The cooking lessons referred to in the diary and sometimes in the early letters did not have much praftical result. She never excelled in this art.

The two or three years following the time described in the diaries were spent happily at Redcar with Maurice--years of playing about, and studying under a German governess, and having pet animals, of which there were always one or two on hand. There were periodical onslaughts of grief when one of these died, grief modified by the imposing funeral procession always organised for them and burial in a special cemetery in the garden.

Gertrude's and Maurice's earliest and favourite companion from babyhood onwards, was Horace Marshall their first cousin and son of their mother's sister Mrs Thomas Marshall. Then after their father's second marriage the two Lascelles boys came into the circle as intimates and cousins, the sons of my sister Mary spoken of in the letters as Auntie Mary, wife of Sir Frank Lascelles.

Florence Lascelles, my sister's only daughter, is constantly mentioned in the letters. She was a good deal younger than her two brothers and Gertrude, but as she grew up she was always one of

9

Gertrude's chosen friends and companions. She married Cecil Spring Rice in 1904.

When Gertrude was fifteen and Maurice had gone to school, she went, first as a day scholar and afterwards as a boarder, to Queen's College in Harley Street, where a friend of her mother's, Camilla Croudace, had just been made Lady Resident. Gertrude lived at first at 95 Sloane Street with my mother Lady Olliffe, who took her and Maurice to her heart as if they had been grandchildren of her own.

The History Lecturer at Queens College at that time was Mr. Cramb, a distinguished and inspiring teacher. Gertrude's intelligence and aptitude for history impressed him keenly, and he strongly urged us to let her go to Oxford and go in for the History School. The time had not yet come when it was a usual part of a girl's education to go to a University, and it was with some qualms that we consented. But the result justified our decision. Gertrude went to Lady Margaret Hall, in 1886 just before she was eighteen, she left it in June 1888 just before she was twenty, and wound up, after those two years, by taking a brilliant First Class in Modern History.

One of her contemporaries at Lady Margaret was Janet Hogarth, now Mrs. W. L. Courtney, who, in a delightful article contributed to the North American Review, entitled "Gertrude Bell, a personal study" and also in her interesting book "Recollected in Tranquillity," has described Gertrude as she was when she first arrived at Lady Margaret Hall-I quote both from the article and the book.

". . . . Gertrude Lowthian Bell, the most brilliant student we ever had at Lady Margaret Hall, or indeed I think at any of the women's colleges. Her journeys in Arabia and her achievements in Iraq have passed into history. I need only recall the bright promise of her college days, when the vivid, rather untidy, auburn-haired girl of seventeen first came amongst us and took our hearts by storm with her brilliant talk and her youthful confidence in her self and her belongings. She had a most engaging way of saying 'Well you know, my father says so and so' as a final opinion on every question under discussion-[and indeed to the end of her life Gertrude, with the same absolute confidence would have been capable of still quoting the same authority as final].

"She threw herself with untiring energy into every phase of college life, she swam, she rowed, she played tennis, and hockey, she danced, she spoke in debates; she kept up with modern literature, and told us tales of modern authors, most of whom were her childhood's friends. Yet all the time she put in seven hours of work, and at the end of two years she won as brilliant a First Class in the School of Modern History as has ever been won at Oxford."

And many years later Mrs. Courtney who had herself taken a first class (in Moral Philosophy) the same year as Gertrude, writes as follows in the 'Brown Book', which is the organ of Lady Margaret Hall:

"I never lost touch with her for well nigh forty years after we parted in the First Class, as she said the day I went round to Sloane Street to wish her joy when the History List appeared"

The untidiness in Gertrude's appearance referred to by Mrs. Courtney gradually gave place to an increasing taste for dress, and she is remembered by more than one person who saw her during the finals of the History School appearing in different clothes every day. The parents of the candidates were admitted to the 'viva voce' part of the examination, and I have a vivid picture in my memory of Gertrude, showing no trace of nervousness sitting very upright at a table, beneath which her slender feet in neat brown shoes were crossed. She was, I have since been told, one of the first young women at Oxford to wear brown shoes, of which she set the fashion among her contemporaries.

Mr. Arthur Hassall of Christchurch, Oxford, who knew her well, records the following incident of Gertrude's 'viva voce.' I quote from his letter: "S. R. Gardiner, the famous historian of the times of James I and Charles I, began to 'viva voce' Miss Bell. She replied to his first question 'I am afraid I must differ from your estimate of Charles I.' This so horrified Professor Gardiner that he at once asked the examiner who sat next to him (I think it was Mr. H. O. Wakeman) to continue the 'viva voce.'"

The result of the whole examination however did her so much credit that she may perhaps be forgiven this lapse into unparalleled audacity.

Mrs. Arthur Hassall also writes: "Gertrude went to the four balls given at Commemoration that week, of which the last was the night before her 'viva voce,' and danced all the evening looking brilliantly happy." She also writes: "she was the only girl I have ever known who took her work for the schools and her examination in a gay way."

After the happy culmination of her two years at Oxford she rejoined her family in London and then at Redcar. My sister-Sir Frank Lascelles being at that time Minister--at Bucharest--begged me to send Gertrude to stay with them for the winter, after the return from Oxford, opining that frequenting foreign diplomatic Society might be a help for Gertrude "to get rid of her Oxfordy manner." My sister was very fond of Gertrude, whom she called her niece and treated like a daughter: they were the greatest friends. The effect however on Gertrude's "Oxfordy manner" of the society of foreign diplomats was not all that Lady Lascelles had hoped, for it is recorded that on one occasion when a distinguished foreign Statesman was discussing some of the international problems of Central Europe, Gertrude said to him, to the stupefaction of her listeners and the dismay of her hostess: "Il me semble, Monsieur, que vous n'avez pas saisi l'esprit du peuple allemand."

There is no doubt that according to the ordinary canons of demeanour it was a mistake for Gertrude to proffer, as we have been shown on more occasions than one, her opinions, let alone her criticisms, to her superiors in age and experience.

But it was all part of her entire honesty and independence of judgment: and the time was to come when many a distinguished foreign statesman not only listened to the opinions she proffered but accepted them and acted on them.

Gertrude hardly ever dated her letters except by the day of the week, sometimes not even that, so that where the envelope has not been preserved I have had to guess the year by the context. By some mischance none of her letters from Bucharest seems to have been preserved, but we know that she was extremely happy there, and keenly interested in her new surroundings. From Bucharest she returned to London, from London she Went to Redcar, enjoying herself everywhere. At Redcar she shouldered the housekeeping and also various activities among the women at the ironworks, Clarence, Often mentioned, being Bell Bros. ironworks on the north bank of the Tees.

Her letters of this time give a picture of her relation to the Younger children-her step-brother and her two Step-sisters, Hugo, Elsa and Molly. Hugo was ten years Younger than Gertrude, Elsa eleven years younger, Molly thirteen years. Her letters often recount what she was doing with her two little sisters who adored her. Hugo by this time had gone to school. Some letters are here given that she wrote between 1889 and 1892 during the time spent in England in one of our two homes either in London in the house shared with my mother or at Redcar, where we lived until 1904. These letters are mostly about every day happenings, always lifted into something new and exciting by Gertrude's youthful zest. Some of these early letters are to her parents, others of which fragmentary extracts are given, are to Flora Russell who remained her intimate friend all her life. Flora was the elder daughter of Lord and Lady Arthur Russell, who lived in Audley Square. The Audley Square circle, the house, the hosts, the people who used to assemble there, formed for Gertrude, as for many others, a cherished and congenial surrounding.]

To H.B., London, 1889

. . . The little girls spent all day with Hunt [their nurse] at her brother-in-laws. They came home at eight, radiant. Molly says he was a very kind man, he gave them strawberries and cream and lots of flowers but to their surprise he had no servants though he has a conservatory! We suppose he must be a market gardener. . .

To F.B., Red Barns, 1889

I think the reason the books were so high was because of the dinner party-it was before I began to keep house wasn't it, so I am not responsible, though I feel as if I were.

I paid everything but the butcher with what you sent, and had over 1 pound balance which I have kept for next time.

I went to Clarence to-day and arranged about the nursing lecture to-morrow,-there were a lot of things to prepare for it. Then I paid some visits and came home with Papa at 4:35. Molly and I have since been picking cowslips in the fields. It is so heavenly here with all the things coming out and the grass growing long. I am glad I'm here.

To F.B., London 1889

I must tell you an absurd story. Minnie Hope was sitting with an Oxford man. Presently he grabbed her hand and said "do you see that young lady in a blue jacket?" "yes" said Minnie lying low. "Well," said he in an awestruck voice, "she took a first in history!!"

To F.B., London, Friday, 14th February, 1889

. . . In the afternoon Sophie [my younger sister, now Mrs. H. J. Kitcat] and I walked across the Green Park to the London Library where I had a delicious rummage with a very amiable sub-librarian who routed out all the editions of Sir Th. Browne and Ph. Sidney for me to see I took down the names and dates and armed with these I felt prepared to face Bain himself.

To F.B., London, July 5th, 1889

Billy [Lascelles] and I sat in the garden and had a long talk so long that he only left himself a quarter of an hour to catch his train. I expect he missed it. He wanted to take me with him to Paddington and send me back in a hansom, don't be afraid, I didn't go-What would have happened if I had, it was ten o'clock!

Yesterday morning I went to the French Literature class at Caroline's [Hon. Mrs Norman Grosvenor] house, I came back here, dressed, and went to Queen Street for a seven o'clock dinner-we were going to the Spanish exhibition after it.

We drove in hansoms to the exhibition and Captain ---- brought me home, I hope that doesn't shock you; I discussed religious beliefs all the way there and very metaphysical conceptions of truth all the way back-that sounds rather steep doesn't it--I love talking to people when they really will talk sensibly and about things which one

14

wants to discuss. I am rather inclined to think however that it is a dangerous Amusement, for one is so ready to make oneself believe that the things one says and the theories one makes are really guiding principles of one's life whereas a matter of fact they are not at all. One suddenly finds that one had formulated some view from which it is very difficult to back out not because of one's interlocutor but because the mere fact of fitting it with words engraves it upon one's mind. Then one is reduced to the disagreeable necessity of trying even involuntarily to make the facts of one's real life fit into it thereby involving oneself in a mist of half-truths and half-falsehoods which cling about one's mind do what one will to shake them off.

It's so hot this morning, I went into the gardens to be cool, but presently came the babies who announced that they were barons and that they intended to rob me. I was rather surprised at their taking this view of the functions of the aristocracy, till I found that they had just been learning the reign of Stephen. Molly informed me in the pride of newly acquired knowledge that there were at least 11,000 castles in his time! So we all played at jumping over a string, not a very cooling occupation, till fortunately Miss Thomson came and called them in. Did we tell you how Molly puzzled and shocked her dreadfully the other day by asking her suddenly what was the French for "this horse has the staggers"! . . .

To F.B., Red Barns, October 30, 1889

The ladies of Clarence were friendly, and oh, unexpected joy !--their accounts came right. . .

The children and I played the race game in the nursery. They have a great plan but unfortunately they have not hit upon any way of carrying it out, of all catching the measles and being laid up together indefinitely. It seemed to me a gruesome form of conversation and I left them discussing it and their supper very happily. They have expressed no regrets as to your absence. . .

To F.B., Red Barns, November 25th, 1889

My gown came from Kerswell this morning-charming I am so glad I did not have a black one. I had a delightful dancing lesson, learnt two more parts of the sword dance, began the minuet. It is lovely, you must learn it the first dancing lesson you are here. It was so fine this afternoon, a rough sea almost up to the esplanade. I walked a long time and then came in and did history for to-morrow.

[i.e. to prepare the children's lesson for the next day. She was then teaching them history.]

To F.B., Red Barns, December 1, 1889

. . . The little girls and I went out before lunch. They came up into my room and I made them some Turkish coffee After lunch, they then disappeared. I expect to see them again shortly. They had supper with me last night by which they were much amused. . .

I have read Swinburne's Jonson which I will keep for you, it is quite excellent. I should very much like for a Christmas present Jonson's works edited by Gifford in 3 vols. not big ones I think. There are some of his masques I want to read. I don't think they are to be found anywhere else. . .

The little girls think it is a great pity you are coming back so soon, because we are so comfortable. We shall be delighted to have you though, one's own society palls after a time.

We had a capital cooking lesson yesterday, made scones and gingerbread and boiled potatoes . . .

To F.B., London, 1889

About the little girls frocks Hunt would like to have one for Molly made of cambric matching the pattern of Elsa, 16d a yard 40 in. wide: the other two one for each little girl of nainsook which is a shade finer and will she says wash better, 13d. and 38 in. wide. There are two insertions, one at 6d. not very pretty, one at 10d. very pretty indeed.

Would you like to have Molly's cambric frock trimmed with the 6d. insertion and the two nainsook frocks with the 10d or would you prefer them to be all trimmed with the cheaper insertion? The cheap insertion is not at all bad and I think it would not look otherwise than well but there is no doubt that the other is nicer. However it is also 4d a yd. dearer. . .

Mr. Grimston says that he cannot supply us with mutton for 9d a pound, it is so dear now. I have asked the other butchers and find they are all selling it at 10d or 10+ a pound so I think it would be best to pay him 10d for legs and loins-what say you? . . .

To F.B., London, February 12, 1890.

. . .Met Lord ---- in Piccadilly who stopped and said Oh, how do you do? and then of course had nothing more to say. So I told him I was going to the Russells' where he said we should probably meet-and then we went our ways, It is so foolish to stop and talk in the street-one only does it out of surprise.

. . . Miss Croudace gave me tickets for a soirée at the Old Water Colours this evening, but I have no one to take me so I can't go. . .

To F.B., Red Barns, April 2nd, 1890.

I have just returned from Clarence where I found only a few mothers but some very agreeable ladies amongst them. I walked back with a very friendly lady-I wonder who she was. She lives in the New Cottages and only comes up to the other end of Clarence for the Mothers' Meeting and for confinements!

. . . Elsa's cambric frock is quite charming. It fits her perfectly and is most becoming. I never saw her look so bewitching and so grown up too.

To F.B., Red Barns, April 17th, 1890.

. . . I should like to go to the first drawing room if You could because I shall want some evening gowns and shall have none till I can use my court gown.

THE LETTERS OF GERTRUDE BELL

To F.B., Red Barns, April 18th, 1890.

I like the pattern you sent us very much, it is charming. I certainly think a green velvet train would be nicer than a black don't you? I am just going to Clarence so good-bye.

To F.B., Red Barns, Nov. 26, 1890.

. . . The little girls and I had a peaceful evening together. They appeared about half past six and I read them selections from Stanley's letters by which they were much interested.

We looked out his route in the map. Molly was so enthusiastic that she carried the atlas and the Times up to the nurses and expounded it all to Lizzie. Elsa had great difficulty with her knitting. The stitches kept dropping in the most unaccountable way and had to be picked up from the very bottom of the cuff. 3 guinea pigs have been sold! the little girls have realised 2/6 by the transaction.

[Lizzie, first our nursery maid, then lady's maid, was Hunt's daughter. She was with us 38 years and is still in touch with us all.]

To F.B., Red Barns, 1890.

The children rode on donkeys this afternoon but it was not very successful for we refused the assistance of the donkey boy and consequently could not get the donkeys to move! We passed a ridiculous hour and finally left our beasts standing peacefully on the esplanade and came home. I don't think judging by their former activity that there was any fear of their escaping.

To F.B., London, 1890.

This is just a little line to tell you how I am getting on. I had a very nice morning. Lizzie and I went out together and did some delightful shopping in Sloane Street and then walked up Piccadilly and up Bond Street and went on myself in a hansom to the National Gallery where I spent a peaceful hour.

THE LETTERS OF GERTRUDE BELL

To F.B., London, February. 8th, 1892

All the sales are over I'm afraid. I went to Woollands this afternoon for the sashes, they had nothing approaching the colour, but I will find it somewhere. I am much interested about your gown, though as you rightly supposed a little sorry its black!. . .

To-day Flora and I called on Sarah Lyttelton [now Hon. Mrs. John Bailey] and had a delightful long talk with her. I like her so much. . . I want some sashes which are either in a cardboard box or on the high shelf outside my bedroom door. If there are any ribbons I should like them too. . . , I went to Audley Square where Henry James appeared.

To F.B., London, February. 14, 1892

Horace came here about three on Saturday and we walked to Kensington Square, where I took him to call on Mrs. [J. R.] Green. It was pleasant and amusing. . . Mrs. Green told me that Mr. York Powell had said to her-this is not a becoming story, and suited for the ears of one's immediate family only-that I was the only girl he had ever examined who knew how to use books or had read things outside the prescribed course and that he thought I had got into the heart of my subject. What a little daring it takes to deceive his misguided sex!

To F.B., London, February. 16th, 1892

. . . I ordered the buttons today at Woollands. I hope they will prove satisfactory.

I regret to announce to you the death of my trumpeter, under which painful circumstances I'm bound to tell you that Lady Edward [Cavendish] has been very complimentary about me to Auntie Mary. She is pleased to approve of me.-We all dined at Devonshire House on Thursday.

The Lytteltons have invited me to a dance of theirs on the 25th. I shall go if Lady Arthur will take me. I suppose I can ask her.

Feb. 18th. This afternoon I called on the Lushingtons.

[She was at this time staying in London with Lady Lascelles.]

To F.B., London, February. 20, 1892

We dined at Devonshire House. There were there Lady Edward, William Egerton, Alfred Lyttelton and Victor Cavendish [now Duke of Devonshire] who came in from the House announcing that he must be back in 30 minutes but finally stayed till ten. Victor C. is tremendously interested in his politics, talks of nothing else; it is very nice to see, as genuine enthusiasm always is.

To F.B., London, February. 22nd, 1892

. . . Yesterday such an absurd thing happened. Auntie Mary had gone out; Florence and I were walking together; the boys alone here, hear a ring and a voice asking for Lady Lascelles, then for me, then angrily, "Well, it's a very odd thing for I was told particularly to come here this afternoon." Presently we came in and found Lord Stanley's card-now this was very odd for Lord Stanley does not know Aunt Mary--We wondered what could be the explanation until tea time when Auntie Maisie came she said "I hear Henry is giving you Persian lessons!" Then it appeared that Grisel Ogilvie to whom I had related my attempts to find a teacher of Persian had sent him--he is a good Persian scholar. Auntie Maisie had met him at Dover Street at lunch and he had told her he was coming here to teach me--and had asked if he Would be likely to find us in. She had said "no" but he had come all the same. . .

I had another offer of lessons on Saturday afternoon at Miss Green's from Mr. Strong. I feel I shall end by receiving special instruction from the Shah in person. . .

To F.B., London, February. 26th, 1892

I have been paying a visit to Maclagan this morning. Which I think was wise as I have been feeling tired and unenergetic lately. He gave me a tonic and told me to take care of myself and not do too much. . .

It was pleasant at Mansfield Street. Mr. William Peel, Horace, Diana, Harold, Grisel, Mildred Hugh Smith. [Horace Marshall, Diana Russell, Harold Russell, Lady Grisel Ogilvie and Mildred Hugh Smith, now Countess Buxton, G.B.E.]

Uncle Lyulph presently went to sleep; Harold, Mildred and I had a long and amusing talk together which lasted all the evening. She is such a nice girl.

On Thursday I walked in the afternoon with Flora and went back with her to tea. . .

The Stanley dance was extraordinarily successful. There were about 20 little girls and ten big ones and a few young men. We danced wildly with the children and the young men. At eight a kind of elaborate tea was provided for the children and for us a small dinner of soup and cutlets and so on. Uncle Lyulph was quite taken aback by the splendor of his party, "I knew we should have something to eat," he said, "but this gloat I certainly did not expect." He was so much pleased by the success of the evening that Auntie Maisie thinks he will let her give a real grown up ball. . .

["Uncle Lyulph," then Lord Stanley of Alderley, afterwards Lord Sheffield. "Auntie Maisie," now Lady Sheffield.]

[During this year, there are very few letters to her family. I have inserted a few extracts from her letters to Flora Russell, recording some of her doings.]

To Flora Russell, Redcar, January. 4, 1892

My DEAREST FLORA,
* * * *I had a long and delightful letter from Clara the other night, she is a person who charms and interests me immensely
[Clara Grant Duff, now Mrs. Huth Jackson].

To the same., Red Barns, January. 10, 1892

Lady Arthur's approval is very well worth having, and I am grateful to you for telling me of it. . .

THE LETTERS OF GERTRUDE BELL

To the same, Red Barns, January 23, 1892

We have spent a racketing fortnight dancing and acting; I am just beginning to fall back into my usual peaceful frame of mind which is rather difficult to regain. I feel to have got rather behindhand with the whole world during the course of it and that I must hurry along very fast to catch it up again. But it's the old world I really want to catch up. I have just got to an inviting stage in my Latin when I feel there is really no reason I shouldn't read anything-and as a matter of fact I can read nothing without dictionaries and great labour. The slough of despond is nothing to it. But I mean to wade on diligently for the next fortnight and stumble as best I may over the horrid catching briars of prepositions and conjunctive moods. . .

To the same, Red Barns, August 13, 1892

We spent a madly amusing five days at Canterbury, of which nothing remains to tell except that we danced every night, saw a good deal of cricket and talked a little. . .

Do you remember discussing what other girls do with their days? Well! I have found out what one particular class does-they spend the entire time in rushing from house to house for cricket weeks, which means cricket all day and dancing all night; your party consists of an eleven and enough girls to pair off with-you discuss byes and wides and Kemp at the wicket and Hearne's batting and any other topic Of a similar nature that may occur to you. It seems to me to be rather a restless sort of summer. . .

To the same, Red Barns, July 22, 1892

The Lascelles are moved to Teheran which is rather thrilling. They are coming back to England now and my uncle goes to Persia in October, my aunt later, I don't know when. I should like her to take me out with her, Persia is the place I have always longed to see, but I don't know if she will.

I expect my aunt will be rather annoyed for she will hate being so far away, but it is a great promotion. As for me if only I go there this winter everything will have turned out for the best.

I wear a blue-green velvet in my hair which is becoming.

To the same, Red Barns, December 23, 1892

I have been reading Latin with great energy. It's a language of which I know very little but whose difficulties must be mastered somehow for I constantly find myself brought up against a blank wall by my ignorance of it. It is very interesting to learn but I could wish it were a little easier. . .

To the same, Red Barns, 1892

This is for the private eye: Bentley wishes to publish my Persian things, but wants more of them, so after much hesitation I have decided to let him and I am writing him another six chapters. It's rather a bore and what's more I would vastly prefer them to remain unpublished. I wrote them you see to amuse myself and I have got all the fun out of them I ever expect to have, for modesty apart they are extraordinarily feeble. Moreover I do so loathe people who rush into print and fill the world with their cheap and nasty work and now I am going to be one of them. At first I refused, then my mother thought me mistaken and my father was disappointed and as they are generally right I have given way. But in my heart I hold very firmly to my first opinion. Don't speak of this. I wish them not to be read.

To the same, Red Barns, January 28, 1892

I read a certain amount of history with the children's lessons, for exercise, and the works of Balzac for amusement. Dante for edification. It's an agreeable and a varied programme.

CHAPTER II

1892-1896 - PERSIA, ITALY, LONDON

[Gertrude went to Teheran, to her great joy, in the spring of 1892. Her letters from Persia, of which there were a good many, are like those from Roumania unfortunately not to be found. The only one we have is addressed to her cousin Horace Marshall, written from Gula Hek, the exquisite summer resort of the British Legation.]

To Horace Marshall, Gulahek, June 18, 1892

DEAR COUSIN MINE,

Are we the same people I wonder when all our surroundings, associations, and acquaintances are changed? Here that which is me, which womanlike is an empty jar that the passer by fills at pleasure, is filled with such wine as in England I had never heard of, now the wine is more important than the jar when one is thirsty, therefore I conclude, cousin mine, that it is not the person who danced with you at Mansfield St. that writes to you to-day from Persia-Yet there are dregs, English sediments at the bottom of my sherbet, and perhaps they flavour it more than I think. Anyhow I remember you as a dear person in a former existence, whom I should like to drag into this one and to guide whose spiritual coming I will draw paths in ink. And others there are whom I remember yet not with regret but as one might remember people one knew when one was an inhabitant of Mars 20 centuries ago. How big the world is, how big and how wonderful. It comes to me as ridiculously presumptuous that I should dare to carry my little personality half across it and boldly attempt to measure with it things for which it has no table of measurements that can possibly apply. So under protest I write to you of Persia: I am not me, that is my only excuse. I am merely pouring out for you some of what I have received during the last two months.

Well in this country the men wear flowing robes of green and white and brown, the women lift the veil of a Raphael Madonna to look at you as you pass; wherever there is water a luxuriant vegetation springs up and where there is not there is nothing but stone and desert. Oh the desert round Teheran! miles and miles of it with nothing, nothing; ringed in with bleak bare mountains snow crowned and furrowed with the deep courses of torrents. I never knew what desert was till I came here; it is a very wonderful thing to see; and suddenly in the middle of it all, out of nothing, out of a little cold water, springs up a garden. Such a garden! trees, fountains, tanks, roses and a house in it, the houses which we heard of in fairy tales when we were little: inlaid with tiny slabs of looking-glass in lovely patterns, blue tiled, carpeted, echoing with the sound of running water and fountains. Here sits the enchanted prince, solemn, dignified, clothed in long robes. He comes down to meet you as you enter, his house is yours, his garden is yours, better still his tea and fruit are yours, so are his kalyans (but I think kalyans are a horrid form of smoke, they taste to me of charcoal and paint and nothing else.) By the grace of God your slave hopes that the health of your nobility is well? It is very well out of his great kindness. Will your magnificence carry itself on to this cushion? Your magnificence sits down and spends ten minutes in bandying florid compliments through an interpreter while ices are served and coffee, after which you ride home refreshed, charmed, and with many blessings on your fortunate head. And all the time your host was probably a perfect stranger into whose privacy you had forced yourself in this unblushing way. Ah, we have no hospitality in the west and no manners. I felt ashamed almost before the beggars in the street-they wear their rags with a better grace than I my most becoming habit, and the veils of the commonest women (now the veil is the touchstone on which to try a woman's toilette) are far better put on than mine. A veil should fall from the top of your head to the soles of your feet, of that I feel convinced, and it should not be transparent.

Say, is it not rather refreshing to the spirit to lie in a hammock strung between the plane trees of a Persian garden and read the poems of Hafiz-in the original mark you!-out of a book curiously bound in stamped leather which you have bought in the bazaars. That is how I spend my mornings here; a stream murmurs past me which Zoroastrian gardeners guide with long handled spades into tiny sluices leading into the flower beds all around. The dictionary which is also in my hammock is not perhaps so poetic as the other attributes let us hide it under our muslin petticoats.

This also is pleasant: to come in at 7 o'clock in the morning after a two hours' ride, hot and dusty, and find one's cold bath waiting for one scented with delicious rose water, and after it an excellent and longed for breakfast spread in a tent in the garden.

What else can I give you but fleeting impressions caught and hardened out of all knowing? I can tell you of a Persian merchant in whose garden, stretching all up the mountain side, we spent a long day, from dawn to sunset, breakfasting, lunching, teaing on nothing but Persian foods. He is noted for his hospitality every evening parties of friends arrive unexpectedly "he goes out, entertains them" said the Persian who told me about it, "spreads a banquet before them and relates to them stories half through the night. Then cushions are brought and carpeted mattresses and they lie down in one of the guest houses in the garden and sleep till dawn when they rise and repair to the bath in the village." Isn't it charmingly like the Arabian Nights! but that is the charm Of it all and it has none of it changed; every day I meet our aged kalendars and ladies who I am sure have suits of Swans feathers laid up in a chest at home., and some time when I open a new jar of rose water I know that instead of a sweet smell, the great smoke of one of Suleiman's afreets will come out of its neck.

In the garden there are big deep tanks where in the evenings between tennis and dinner I often swim in the coldest of cold water. Before we left Teheran when it was too hot to sleep, I used to go out at dawn and swim under the shadow of the willows. We were very glad to leave Teheran though we liked the house there. It began to be very stuffy and airless; here, though we are only 6 miles away, there is always air, except perhaps between two and four in the afternoon when one generally sleeps. We are much higher up and much nearer the hills and all round us are watered fields where the corn is almost ripe for cutting The joy of this climate! I do think an English summer will be very nice after it.

I learn Persian, not with great energy, one does nothing with energy here. My teacher is a delightful old person bright eyes and a white turban who knows so little French (French is our medium) that

he can neither translate poets to me nor explain any grammatical difficulties. But we get on admirably nevertheless and spend much of our
time in long philosophic discussions carried on by me in French an by
him in Persian. His point of view is very much that of an oriental Gib-
bon, though with this truly oriental distinction, that he would never
dream of acknowledging in words or acts his scepticism to one of his
own countrymen. It would be tacitly understood between them and
their intercourse would be continued on the basis of perfect agreement.
Now this is a great simplification and promotes, I should imagine, the
best of good manners. . .

Goodbye, write to me and tell me how the world goes with
you.

[This letter, bearing the impress of her youth, shows the first
effect on Gertrude's mind of the impact of the East. It practically
summarises her impressions. We have further records of them in a
book she wrote the year after her return, published by Bentley in 1894,
entitled "safar Nameh " i.e., "Persian Pictures," in which the life of the
town and of the bazaars, the desolate places so strangely near them,
the dwellers in the tents, the divine Persian gardens and many other
aspects of her surroundings, are described with the glowing eagerness
of a first experience. The little book attracted attention and was fa-
vourably reviewed.. I have dwelt on it here, for the interest of
comparing it in one's mind with the books of Eastern travel Gertrude
was to publish many years later, when she was no longer a spectator
only, but a sharer to the full in the Eastern life that she described.

She had, as we have seen in many of the letters, a special and
very valuable gift, that of forming extremely vivid impressions,
whether of places or of human beings. She would dive beneath the
surface, estimating, judging, characterising in a few words that were
not often mistaken. She would ride through a countryside and report
on its conditions, human, agricultural, economic, and her report would
be adopted. When she came into contact with human beings, whether
chiefs of the desert or men and women of her own Western world, she
would label them, after her first meeting with them, in a sentence.

I am not pretending that her judgments were always infallible. But on the whole they were correct often enough to enable her to thread her way successfully through the labyrinth of her experiences.

It was characteristic of Gertrude, and it was an inestimable advantage to her, that she insisted on learning Persian before going to Teheran. She arrived there knowing as it is commonly called, the language, i.e., able to understand what she heard and what she read. But she had not yet reached the stage in which the learner of a language finds with rapture that a new knowledge has been acquired, the illuminating stage when not the literal meaning only of words is being understood, but their values and differences can be critically appreciated. It was not long before Gertrude was reading Persian Poetry by this light and with the added understanding brought to her by her knowledge of Western literature.

She was wont when she was at home and someone asked her a question about history to reply with a laugh " Oh! that is not my period," although it must be confessed that an answer to the question was generally forthcoming. But in literature it would be hard to say off-hand what was her " period."

She published a translation of the Divan of Hafiz in 1897. The book includes a life of Hafiz, which is practically a history of his times as well as a critical study of his work. These, and the notes on his poems at the end of the book, show how wide was her field of comparison. She draws a parallel between Hafiz and his contemporary Dante: she notes the similarity of a passage with Goethe: she compares Hafiz with Villon, on every side gathering fructifying examples which link together the inspiration of the West and of the East.

The book on its publication was extremely well received.

I quote here from two of the translations.]

TO HAFIZ OF SHIRAZ
(Two first stanzas)

Thus said the Poet: " When Death comes to YOU, All ye whose life-sand through the hour-glass slips, He lays two fingers on

28

your ears, and two Upon your eyes he lays, one on your lips, Whispering: Silence. "Although deaf thine ear, Thine eye, my Hafiz, suffer Time's eclipse, The songs thou sangest still all men may hear.

Songs of dead laughter, songs of love once hot, Songs of a cup once flushed rose-red with wine, Songs of a rose whose beauty is forgot, A nightingale that piped hushed lays divine: And still a graver music runs beneath The tender love notes of those songs of thine, Oh, Seeker of the keys of Life and Death!"

DIVAN OF HAFIZ xlv

(From poem on the death of his son)

The nightingale with drops of his heart's blood Had nourished the red rose, then came a wind, And catching at the boughs in envious mood, A hundred thorns about his heart entwined, Like to the parrot crunching sugar, good Seemed the world to me who could not stay The wind of Death that swept my hopes away. Light of mine eyes and harvest of my heart, And mine at least in changeless memory! Ah! when he found it easy to depart, He left the harder pilgrimage to me!

Oh Camel-driver, though the cordage start, For God's sake help me lift my fallen load, And Pity be my comrade of the road! He sought a lodging in the grave--too soon! I had not castled, and the time is gone. What shall I play? Upon the chequered floor Of Night and Day, Death won the game--forlorn And careless now, Hafiz can lose no more.

Gertrude, who was an ardent lover of poetry all her life long, and who kept abreast of the work of the moderns as well as of their predecessors, seemed, strangely enough, after the book of Hafiz had appeared, to consider her own gift of verse as a secondary pursuit, and to our surprise abandoned it altogether. But that gift has always seemed to me to underlie all she has written. The spirit of poetry coloured all her prose descriptions, all the pictures that she herself saw and succeeded in making others see.

It was a strangely interesting ingredient in a character capable on occasion of very-definite hardness and of a deliberate disregard of sentiment: and also in a mental equipment which included great practical ability and statesmanlike grasp of public affairs.

But in truth the real basis of Gertrude's nature Was her capacity for deep emotion. Great joys came into her life, and also great sorrows. How could it be otherwise with a temperament so avid of experience? Her ardent and magnetic personality drew the lives of others into hers as she passed along.

She returned to England from Teheran in December of 1892. In January 1893 we find her starting for Switzerland and northern Italy with Mary Talbot, a beloved friend who had been with her at Lady Margaret Hall. Mary Talbot married the Rev. W. O. Burrows, now Bishop of Chichester, in 18 96. She died, to Gertrude's great sorrow, in 1897.

In April she went to Algiers with her father to stay with some of his relations, afterwards going back to Switzerland, and then joining Maurice, who was established in a German family at Weimar that he might learn the language. Needless to say that as soon as Gertrude arrived at Weimar she arranged to have German lessons, and went three times a week to talk with " a delightful old lady living in whose house do you think?--Frau von Stein's!" Her letters all through these travels from the beginning of the year are as usual amusing and full of observation, whether describing the flamboyant setting of the foreign residents at Algiers or the trim traditional life of the ladies of Weimar. But it is not worth while to take up space by accounts of routes already well- trodden, or places and social surroundings well known.

Gertrude came back to England from Germany in the early summer of 1893 and does not seem to have gone abroad again until the spring of 1896. There are no letters of the two intervening years. and unfortunately no records. In the spring of 1896 Gertrude travelled in the north of Italy, first in the company of Mrs. Norman Grosvenor and then of Mrs. J. R. Green, both of whom were her dear friends. Her father was with her part of the time.

They stayed in Venice, they stayed in Florence. As might be expected, on her arrival in Italy, Gertrude at once arranged to have

Italian lessons. She writes from Venice "At 3 I had my parlatrice until 4. "

The Talbots (now General the Hon. Sir Reginald and Lady Talbot) were staying in Florence, which was a great added enjoyment. Lady Talbot was Mrs. Grosvenor's sister.

After Gertrude's return from Italy she was at home until the end of the year.]

To F.B., London, 1896

One line to say we had a most amusing party at the Portsmouth's yesterday. I made the acquaintance of Miss Haldane, whom I have long wished to know, and I am going to tea with her tomorrow. Haldane was most complimentary about my book--which I think he hasn't read by the way. A delightful review in the Athenaeum.

E. and I dined with the Strachey's first--very pleasant, we four, St. Loe had just finished reviewing my book!

Flora lunched to-day and we went out together afterwards. Tomorrow I have a Buddhist Committee lunch.

I wrote my review of Lafcadio this morning, the sort of blissful morning when one suddenly realises at the end of a few hours that one has been quite unconscious of the passing of time. I'm just going to finish it now.

Moll looked charming last night.

To F.B., London, February. 12th, 1896

I studied my grammar this morning and went to the London Library where I looked through volumes and volumes of Asiatic Societies. . .and found little to my purpose.

To F.B., London, Thursday, February. 14th, 1896

I had a very nice evening with the Ritchie's--Pinkie Was there and she played the piano, and we talked (not wile she played) and it was very merry. They are looking very well. I think they are coming to you for Easter.

I came away rather early for I had a lesson at 5. My Pundit was extremely pleased with me, he kept congratulating me on my proficiency in the Arabic tongue! I think his other pupils must be awful duffers. It is quite extraordinarily interesting to read the Koran with him-and it is such a magnificent book! He has given me some Arabian Nights for the next time and I have given him some Hafiz poems to read, so we shall see what we shall see. He is extremely keen about the Hafiz book. . .

To F.B., London, February. 17, 1896

This morning I stayed in and read some most illuminating articles on Sufyism. There's a lot to know but I guess I'll know some of it before I've done. I expect I shall get my reading ticket to-morrow.

To F.B., London, February. 24, 1896

My Pundit brought back my poems yesterday-he is really pleased with them. I asked him if he thought they were worth doing and he replied that indeed he did. He is full of offers of assistance and wants to read all that I have done, which from a busy man is, I think, the best proof that he likes what he has seen. Arabic flies along-I shall soon be able to read the Arabian Nights for fun.

To F.B., London, 1896

My domino is going to be so nice and it will cost me very little for it is all made of a beautiful piece of white stuff Papa gave me in Algiers. Lizzie is making it. . .

Give my love to Lisa. [Elizabeth Robins, the dear friend of us all, and the constant guest--then as now.] I wish I could come and have a long talk with her to-night over the fire.

To H. B., Palazzo Gritti (Venice), Saturday, April 14th, 1896

Mrs. Green went in the morning to see Lady Layard, who offered us her gondola to go out and see the arrival of the Emperor. Meanwhile I went and called upon the Wards who are at the Hôtel de l'Europe and found them all and combined many meetings. Dorothy and Arnold walked me home.

At 2Mrs. Green and I started out in a splendid gondola and went nearly to the Lido amidst a crowd of boats. It was very gorgeous for the Municipio appeared in splendid gondolas hung with streamers and emblems and rowed by 8 gondoliers in fancy dresses of different colours. About 3 the Hohenzollern steamed in through the Lido port, a magnificent great white ship with all the sailors dressed in white and standing in lines upon the deck. The guns fired, the ships in the harbour saluted and all the people cheered. The Hohenzollern anchored nearly opposite the Piazzetta and we saw the King and Queen and a crowd of splendid officers Come up in a steam launch all hung with blue. They went on board the Hohenzollern and presently we saw them all go away again with the Emperor and his two little boys. We were much amused, and for magnificence there never was anything like a festa with the Ducal Palace for background. It was a very imperial way of arriving to steam up in your gorgeous white ship. I only wished it had not been that Particular emperor we were welcoming.

To H. B., Venice, Palazzo Gritti, Thursday, April, 1896

Mrs. Green and I went out in a gondola and saw the sun set behind the Euganean Hills. . . she is a great dear. . .

To H. B., Florence, Sunday, April, 1896

Caroline [Grosvenor] is a delightful companion-we are particularly happy.

To F.B., London, May 7th, 1896

I had a real busy morning and settled all my summer clothes and ordered a gown at Mrs. Widdicombe's. I hope it will be ready before you come as I should like you to pronounce upon it. Tomorrow I intend to spend an hour or two over my Hafiz things and get them all straight.

To F.B., London, Saturday, May 13th, 1896

I went to the British Museum on my bicycle this morning. It adds a great joy to my studies and I feel all the brisker for it. The children have had a tennis court marked in the square. I am just going out to see! them play. They are looking blooming and are such angels! However we will try not to be too foolish about our family.

To F.B., London, Sat., May, 1896

. . . I was invited to Lady Lockwood's dance but I really couldn't be bothered to hunt up a chaperon and go to it. . .

To F.B., London, Monday, May 11th, 1896

. . . About the children's flower gowns--we finally decided that the cheapest and best thing we could do was to trim the gowns with field flowers (artificial of course), buttercups) daisies and forget-me-nots. We have cut a sort of ruche of tulle round the bottom of the skirt with little bunches of flowers tucked into it, and hung flowers from the neck and from the waist in little streams--on the whole I think this plan has made as much show as possible for as little money and the dresses look quite charming . . . I hope I've done right about it. The children were extremely anxious to have their gowns very flowery. Elsa was inclined to think that they didn't look flowery enough as it was, but we all assured her they were very very nice, and I really think 15/- is enough to have spent on this absurd amusement. . .

To F. B., London, 1896

We had a very merry dinner and started out about ten, along the embankment, the Strand and through the City to the Tower Bridge, then home by Holborn Viaduct and oxford Street. The Strand was pretty full but the City quite empty, all brilliantly lighted and the asphalt pavement excellent good going. It was a delicious night with a little moon and I enjoyed it extremely. We went back to supper with the Tyrrells and I was not in till 1:30. However I went off after breakfast to the Museum where I asked for a book they' hadn't got! It is rather funny that I should have exhausted the whole British Museum in a fortnight, but it's also a bore, for I wanted a nice French translation and now I shall have to fall back on the original Persian which they have. . .

I have told Lizzie about the bonnet and cloak so you will find them ready.

To F.B., London, May 15th, 1896

Our party last night was a great success, the babies looked charming. I was much complimented upon their appearance. It was most amusing being a chaperon. I sat on a bench and watched them dancing round and knew just what you felt like at Oxford. . .

To F.B., London, Thursday, May, 1896

Went up to the Museum this morning and read a Persian life of Hafiz with a Latin crib. I think I got at the meaning of it with the help of a Persian dictionary, but a Latin translation is not so clear to me as it might be. . . I didn't go to Lady Pollock's on Tuesday, because I had promised to go to a party at Audley Square and I couldn't combine the two unchaperoned. Audley Square was amusing . .. I am going down to Caroline (in Kent) for Whitsuntide. I want to bicycle down on Saturday if I can get an escort, it's only 17 miles, and send my luggage by train. London is beginning to feel very Whitsunday. Beatrice Clementi came to see me this afternoon just before I went out. She is to be married in November. . . [to Sir Douglas Brownrigg, Bt., now Rear-Admiral, retired.]

To H.B., London, June, 1896

It is very close here and has been raining a good deal think of ordering a tasteful costume for Ascot consisting of a short skirt, a waterproof and a large umbrella. Florence and I arranged the flowers at 95 and did the dinner table at 90 most elegantly--I dine there to-night. The rest of the party are Lady Edward John Cavendish and Mr. Chirol. Then I had a long talk with Auntie Mary, who seems very brisk and well.

I took Florence with me to try on my gown and we walked together in the Square until a storm of rain came on and drove us in.

Auntie Maisie asks me to dine with her Friday and go to a ball, and Maurice is to come to dinner if she can possibly find a place for him, and at any rate to come in directly after dinner and go to the ball too.

To F.B., London, Thursday, June, 1896

. . . We have had a most delightful day. We started about 10:30, Gerald, Florence, Uncle Frank and I, got to Ascot half an hour before the first race, which we saw from the top of the Royal Enclosure Stand; then we lunched in the Bachelors' tent, Billy being our host, and I sat next Colonel Talbot and was much amused. He had a Carpenter niece with him. Then we went back and saw all the races over the railing of the Royal enclosure, which is just opposite the winning post. The family had small bets on, mostly unsuccessful (I didn't bet, I need not say). . .

At the end of all we had tea in the Guards' tent and came home very comfortably, getting in about 7:30. I am going again to-morrow. .
.

My gown was a dream and was much admired. I am going this evening with Auntie Mary and Florence and the Johnsons to sit out of doors in the Imperial Institute and listen to the band-rather nice as it is very hot.

Florence and I did amuse ourselves so much! What a dear Lord Granville is. . .

To F. B., London, July 14th, 1896

Thank you very much for your letter and will you thank the little girls for me, I have no time to write to them to-day. Hugo came up in great form and we started off to Lord's together, but on the way discovered that he had lost the blue tassel on his umbrella, which saddened us dreadfully! So we tried in many shops to get one, and failed alas! However we were Comforted at Lord's when we saw that many

many Eton boys had no tassel! We had the most excellent places, we carried our lunch with us and supplemented it with green-gages, after eating which we both made fervent wishes as they were the first we had eaten this year. I asked Hugo what he had wished, to which he replied, "Why I wished Eton might win--what in the world is there to wish for besides? He was such a darling!

To F. B., London, 1896

I saw Heinemann this morning. He was extremely pleasant. I told him a lot about the book and he expressed a desire to see it. So at any rate it will have a reading. I shall send him the poems and preface from Berlin, Mr. Strong cannot come to town and has not yet finished the preface.

CHAPTER III

1897 - BERLIN

[In January 1897 we find her starting for the British Embassy at Berlin. Her first letter is sent from the station at York.]

To F.B., York, January. 6th, 1897

I can't conceive what I am doing in this station, nor why I am going away. It's too silly. I wish I were stopping quietly at home.

All sorts of smart people on this platform! One begins to realise what the world is like when one gets to York, doesn't one. Never mind, I'll be smart too presently!

To F.B., Berlin, Saturday, January. 1897

The reason why I had not sent the poems to H. was because Mr. Strong has not yet sent me back the preface. . . I hope I may get it by the next bag. Meantime I have sent the 30 poems with their notes to H. and explained to him why the preface is not with them and apologised for the delay.

To her sister, Berlin, January. 22nd, 1897

DEAREST ELSA,
I made my bow to the 'Kaiser Paar' on Wednesday. It was a very fine show. We drove to the Schloss in the glass coach and were saluted by the guard when we arrived. We felt very swell! Then we waited for a long time with all the other dips. In a room next to the throne room and at about 8 the doors were thrown open. We all hastily arranged one another's trains and marched in procession while the band played

the march out of Lohengrin. The Emperor and Empress were standing on a dais at the end of the room and we walked through a sort of passage made by rows and rows of pages dressed in pink. The 'Allerbôchst' looked extremely well in a red uniform--I couldn't look at the Empress much as I was so busy avoiding Aunt Mary's train. She introduced me and then stood aside while I made two curtseys. Then I wondered what the dickens I should do next, but Aunt Mary made me a little sign to go out behind her, so I 'enjambéd' her train and fled!

To F.B., Berlin, January. 24th, 1897

. . . The Princess Frederic Leopold's ladies asked when I was going to be introduced to her . . . we arranged that I should be presented during the first polka of the first Court ball. . .

To F.B., Berlin, Monday January 25th, 1897

. . . We have been skating all the afternoon with surprising energy, A very ridiculous thing happened-I had retired into a secluded corner and put my muff down to make a centre round which to skate a figure, when suddenly I was aware of a short fat German gentleman arriving into the middle of my figure on his back. He picked up my muff and himself and handed them both to me, so to speak, with a low bow. . . We propose if the frost lasts making a big party, sledging down to Potsdam and skating there. I hope it will come off, it would be very amusing. . .

To F.B., Berlin, Thursday, January. 28th, 1897

On Thursday afternoon I went with Aunt Mary to see Florence perform the gavotte. A great 'Probe' at the Kaiserhof to which all the people who were going to dance at the Court Ball came . . . After the lesson was over there were a couple of waltzes, so I offed with my coat and danced too. There is a rather nice sort of variant of the 'pas de quatre' which they call the 'pas de patineur' which I quickly learnt. . .

To F.B, Berlin, Tuesday, 1897

. . .F. and I went to see Henry IV last night, the Emperor having invited all the Embassy to come to the royal box. Uncle F. and

Aunt M. were dining with the Frederic Leopolds so they were obliged to decline the box for themselves but the Emperor said that he hoped we should go as we should be chaperoned by Countess Keller, one of the ladies-in-waiting. Accordingly we went off by ourselves and sat very comfortably with Countess Keller in the second row of chairs-no one might sit in the front row even when the royalties were not in the box. All the Embassy and a lot of the Court people were with us, the Emperor and Empress were in a little box at the side. The play was very well done. The Falstaff excellent and the whole thing beautifully staged. There was no pause till the end of the second act when there was a long entr'acte. Countess Keller bustled away and presently came hurrying back and whispered something to Knesebeck and Egloffstein, two of the Court people, and they came and told F. and me that we were sent for. So off we went rather trembling, under the escort of Countess K. and Egloffstein who conducted us into a little tiny room behind the Emperor's box where we found the 'Kaiser Paar' sitting and having tea. We made deep curtseys and kissed the Empress's hand, and then we all sat down, F. next to the Emperor and I next to the Empress and they gave us tea and cakes. It was rather formidable though they were extremely kind. The Emperor talked nearly all the time; he tells us that no plays of Shakespeare were ever acted in London and that we must have heard tell that it was only the Germans who had really studied or really understood Shakespeare. One couldn't contradict an Emperor, so we said we had always been told so. Egloffstein's chair broke in the middle of the party and he came flat on to the ground which created a pleasing diversion-I was so glad it wasn't mine! Countess K. was a dear and started a new subject whenever the conversation languished. After about 20 minutes the Empress got up, we Curtseyed to her, shook hands with the Emperor. Florence thanked him very prettily for sending for us and we bowed ourselves out. Wasn't it amusing! Florence said she felt shy but she looked perfectly self-possessed and had the prettiest little air in the world as she sat talking to the Emperor. I felt rather frightened, but I did not mind much as I knew I need do nothing but follow Florence's lead. The Empress sits very upright and is rather alarming. He flashes round from one person to the other and talks as fast as possible and is not alarming at all. . . We go again to-night to the second part . . . but we shall not be sent for as Uncle Frank and Aunt Mary will be there.

To F. B., Berlin, February. 5th, 1897

. . .The Court Ball on Wednesday was a fine show. We were asked for eight o'clock and at a quarter past we formed up for waiting. The ambassadresses sat on a line of chairs to the left of the throne in the Weiser Saal, and we stood meekly behind them. After about half an hour someone tapped tapped on the floor with a wand and in came a long procession of pages followed by the 'Kaiser Paar' and all the 'Furstliche Personen.' The whole room bobbed down in deep curtseys as they came in . . . In to supper . . . back to the ball room. The room was almost empty and the few people that were there were dancing the 'trois temps'--one is only allowed to dance the 'deux temps' when the Empress is there. It was a very delicious half-hour for the floor is peer-less and all these officers dance so well. Then followed the gavotte which Florence danced very prettily.

To H. B., Berlin, February. 8th, 1897

I wish you many many happy returns of your birthday and may your children become less and less tiresome with every succeed-ing year!. . .

The house is all upside down for the ball. Wherever one goes one finds lines and lines of waiters arranging tables. We can seat 340 people at supper. There are to be tables in all the ball rooms, the Chan-cery ante-room and even the big bedroom. We all intend to bring our partners up to the big bedroom which makes a delightful supper-room. Florence and I went into the kitchen this morning and inspected the food. I never saw so many eatables together. . .

To F.B., Berlin, February. 10th, 1897

* * * *It was a great success and very splendid. Florence and I were of course (as it was in our own house) covered with bows and loaded with flowers. There were supper tables in all the drawing-rooms--it looked extremely nice. . .

I went to tea with Marie von Bunsen and stayed till past 7. She is most interesting. . .

To F.B., Berlin, February. 12th, 1897

The Court Ball on Wednesday was much nicer than the first one. . . The Emperor wore a gorgeous Austrian uniform in honour of an Austrian Archduke who was there--the brother of the man who is heir to the throne. He will be Emperor himself someday as the heir is sickly and unmarried. The Emperor William is disappointing when one sees him close; he looks puffy and ill and I never saw anyone so jumpy. He is never still a second while he is talking. . .

Uncle Frank is in a great jig about Crete. He thinks there is going to be red war and an intervention of the Powers and all sorts of fine things. I wonder.

To F.B., Berlin, February. 14th, 1897

. . . Florence and I spent the most heavenly morning at the 'Haupt Probe'. . . Since then we have been bicycling round the house for exercise as it is raining and we could not go out. . .

On Friday Mr. Acton, Mr. Spring Rice and Lord Granville dined with us. After dinner we played hide and seek till we were so hot we could play no longer and finished up the evening with pool and baccarat . . . I went to the National Gallery to see the modern pictures . . .I had been reading about modern German painters and knew what I wanted to look at. . . Should like to go out but I mayn't go by myself. So I suppose I can't!

To F.B., Berlin, February. 17th, 1897

[The play referred to in this letter is the second part of Henry IV.]

We had a most exciting evening at the play yesterday. We were all sent for in the entr'acte. We had a very agreeable tea with the Emperor and Empress and her sister. . . It was like an act out of another historical drama--but a modern one. A sheaf of telegrams were handed to the Emperor as we sat at tea. He and Uncle fell into an excited conversation in low voices; we talked on to the Empress trying to pretend we heard nothing but catching scraps of the Emperor's remarks, " Crete . . . Bulgaria . . . Serbia . . . mobilizing," and so forth. The Empress kept looking up at him anxiously; she is terribly perturbed about it all and no wonder for he is persuaded that we are all on the brink of war. . .

CHAPTER IV

1897-1899 - ROUND THE WORLD, DAUPHINIE, ETC.

[Gertrude came back to England at the beginning of March. My sister Mary Lascelles died on April 3rd, after three days' illness. Her death made a terrible gap in Gertrude's life.]

To F.B., Redcar, April 7th, 1897

I have been to Clarence to-day-it was no use sitting and moping so I thought I had better make myself useful if I could. . .

[In August of that year we all went to the Dauphiné, staying at La Grave under the shadow of the Meije, objective of all Dauphin climbers, This holiday makes an epoch, as it was the beginning of Gertrude's climbing experiences, although this year she did nothing very adventurous.

She went over the Brèche with two guides, slept at the refuge, came down over the Col des Cavales and proudly strode back into the village next morning between her guides, well pleased with herself.

She was at home with us all the rest of the year.

On the 29th December 1897 Gertrude and her brother Maurice left home for Southampton, to embark on a voyage round the world.

Gertrude kept a diary letter on the voyage. She posts from Jamaica, Guatemala, San Francisco--wherever she had an opportunity. It is not worth while reproducing all that she and Maurice saw on this well-known route, which has so often been described. They enjoyed it all, taking part in the unpretentious diversions of a voyage. They asked the Captain's permission to mark out a golf course on board, which had a great success.]

"There are a lot of children on board, with whom I have made friends," she writes.

"Eight of us are playing a piquet tournament: I am first-favourite at present."

(Then there was a ball on board.]

"We took a great deal of trouble to make it go, Maurice was the life and soul of it."

[Then we are told of]

"a partial eclipse of the moon, seated in the stalls, so to speak, our deck chairs. It was most luxuriously arranged by nature."

"I won the piquet tournament to the great joy of the other members of the party."

[She and Maurice returned to London in June.

In September, after a delightful two months in the West of Scotland--we had taken the Manse at Spean Bridge for the summer--Gertrude is at Redcar again, enchanted to return to her books.]

To F.B., Redcar, September 2nd, 1898.

. . .Hugo has been playing golf and we are now going to have a game of racquets before settling down to our work. Oh, how I wish I were going to have a month of this. The bliss of being really at work is past words.

Herbert Pease stands for Darlington, I see in the evening papers. . .

To H. B., Saturday 22nd September, 1898

. . .I'm going to Rounton on Sunday . . . having finished a great batch of Arabic and Persian for Mr. Ross. [Now Sir Denison Ross]

To F.B., Redcar, Autumn 1898.

I have been at the Infirmary all the afternoon. I've got another engagement--to lecture at the High School. I've been arranging about my lantern slides. . .

By the way, confided to Lisa that she felt quite anxious about Elsa because she thought we were all so beautiful and so clever that we couldn't all go on living. Elsa won't mind being the 'offer' to the jealous gods, I hope!

To F.B., London 1898

. . . That angel of a Mr. Vaughan Williams has found me a real Persian-at least he is an Afghan and his name is Satdar and he speaks beautiful Persian. I have written to him to-day. Isn't it interesting. . .

[Gertrude begins the year 1899 at Redcar, she and Hugo are left together for a few days at Red Barns.]

To F.B., Redcar, January 6th, 1899

. . . Hugo and I have made an excellent 'ménage'--we get on admirably and I have come to know him much better, chiefly because he has told me all his views as to his future. They are rather a blow to me, I admit. He is one of the most lovable and livable with people I have ever come across.

To her sister Elsa., London, January 1899

. . . I thought the braid a little too braidy. A modification of it would be lovely. I should have no braid on the coat just the seams strapped. 'Tis very smart so. I went to Prince's this morning and skated . . .with Flora and a lot of people. . .Next time I'm in London I shall have a few lessons there. It's silly not to be able to skate well when everybody does.

My new clothes are very dreamy. You will scream with delight when you see me in them!

To F. B., London, January. 1899

I have sent off the purple dress and a grey one which is nine guineas and very nice indeed. It has a dark coat and everything suitable to Elsa. My only doubt is whether the black trimming is not too black. There is another most elegant elephant grey costume strapped with grey, but the coat is quite tight fitting so that it might not be so becoming to Elsa. . . .

To F.B., London, Thursday, Mar. 17th, 1899

. . . I write from a sofa. This morning at Prince's I fell violently on my knees and when I shortly after took my skates off, I found I couldn't walk. . . Maclagan, however, says I must lie up for a few days. Isn't it boring? I'm writing to all the amusing people to come and see me, having dressed the part well in a Japanese tea gown. . .

I shall beguile the time with my pundits while I'm invalided. I've told them all to come.

It is so provoking because I was getting to skate really well.

[In the spring of the year 18 99 Gertrude went abroad again to Northern Italy, by herself, then to Greece, with her father and her uncle Thomas Marshall, a classical Scholar and translator of Aristotle, deeply interested at going to Greece for the fifth time. A most successful tour altogether. In Athens they find Dr. Hogarth and go the Museum, " where Mr. Hogarth showed us his recent finds-pots Of 4000 B.C. from Melos. Doesn't that Make one's brain reel?" Another distinguished archaeologist, Professor Dôrpfeld is there also. They listen with breathless interest to his lecture on the Acropolis: "he took us from stone to stone and built up a Wonderful chain of evidence with extraordinary ingenuity until we saw the Athens of 600 B.C. I never saw anything better done."

She also writes from Athens Papa has bought him a grey felt hat, in which he looks a dream of beauty and some yellow leather gaiters to ride in the Peloponnesus. He will look smart, bless him . . . . .

Then to Constantinople, and back again to England in May.

In August she started with Hugo for Bayreuth, joining on the way Sir Frank Lascelles and his daughter Florence, and Mr. Chirol (now Sir Valentine Chirol). They go to Nuremberg and Rothenburg on the way, enjoying themselves ecstatically everywhere. She writes] " this is really too charming. You never met a more delightful travelling party. Florence is in the seventh heaven all the time. His Ex. a perfect angel, Mr. Chirol, and in fact all of us, endlessly cheerful and delighted with everything." [They hear Parsifal and The Ring at Bayreuth. Gertrude, "tief gerührt", as she tells us, sends home long, vivid descriptions of the performances. These letters on a subject now almost hackneyed are too long to insert here. She was not, and did not pretend to be, an expert on music) but she cared for it very much.

Hugo, who was an admirable musician, was conservative in his tastes and was at first prepared to be on the defensive with regard to Wagner.

Gertrude also records some personal social experiences.]

To F.B., Bayreuth

Frau Cosima has asked us all to a party on Friday evening. Great Larks! . . . The restaurant was crowded when the door opened and in came the whole Wagner family in procession, Frau Cosima first on Siegfried's arm. There was a great clapping as she passed down the room to her table.

To F.B., Bayreuth, Wed. August 16th, 1899

This morning about half past 8 came a message from the Grand Duke [of Hesse] asking us whether we could be at the theatre at 9 as he would show us the stage. We bustled up and arrived only a few minutes late. It was most entertaining; we were taken into every corner, above and below. We descended through trap doors and mounted into Valhalla. We saw all the properties, and all the mechanism of the Rhine maidens; we explored the dressing rooms, sat in the orchestra and rang the Parsifal bells! The Grand Duke was extremely cheerful and agreeable--he's quite young--and of course everyone was hats off and anxious to show us all we wanted to see. It's a very extraordinary place, the stage; the third scene of Siegfried was set. We shall feel quite at home when we see it to-night. Hugo is delighted with it all. He was much impressed by the Walküre though he says it will take a great deal to make him a Wagnerian.

[After Bayreuth the party breaks up, all of them except Gertrude returning to England.]

I'm awfully sorry to have parted with Hugo. He really is one of the most delightful people in the world. The Harrachs, you will be glad to hear, thought him very beautiful . . . when I told you that they were people of discernment!

[After this Gertrude went back through Switzerland to the Dauphiné and fulfilled her year-old purpose of ascending the Meije.)

To H.B., La Grave, Monday, 28th August, 1899

I sent you a telegram this morning [" Meije traversée") for, I thought you would gather from my last that I meant to have a shot at the Meije and would be glad to hear that I had descended in the approved, and in no other manner. Well, I'll tell you--it's awful! I think if I had known exactly what was before me I should not have faced it, but fortunately did not, and I look back on it with unmixed satisfaction--and forward to other things with no further apprehension. . .

We left here on Friday at 2:30, Mathon, Marius and I, and walked up to the Refuge de l'Alpe in two hours. Two German men turned up at the Refuge. . . Madame Castillan gave us a very good supper and I went at once to bed. I got off at 4:30 and got to the top of the clot at 8:10. In the afternoon, there arrived a young Englishman called Turner with Rodier as guide and a porter. I went out to watch the beautiful red light fading from the snows and rocks. The Meije looked dreadfully forbidding in the dusk. When I came in I found that Mathon had put my rug in a corner of the shelf which was the bed of us all and what with the straw and my cloak for a pillow I made myself very comfortable. We were packed as tight as herrings, Mr. Turner next to me, then the two Germans and Rodier. Mathon and the porters lay on the ground beneath us. Our night lasted from 8 till 12, but I didn't sleep at all. Marius lighted a match and looked at his watch. It was ten o'clock. " Ah, c'est encore trop matin," said Rodier. It seemed an odd view of 10 p.m. We all got up soon after 12 and I went down to the river and washed a little. It was a perfect night, clear stars and the moon not yet over the hills. . . We left half an hour later, 1 a.m., just as the moon shone into the valley. Mathon carried a lantern till we got on to the snow when it was light enough with only the moon. . .

At 1:30 we reached the glacier and all put on our ropes. . . It wasn't really cold, though there was an icy little breath of wind down from the Brèche. This was the first time I had put on the rope . . . we went over the glacier for another hour . . . we got into the Promontoir, a long crest of rock and rested there ten minutes . . . we left there at 2:40. . . We had about three hours up very nice rock, a long chimney first and then most pleasant climbing. Then we rested again for a few minutes. . . I had been in high feather for it was so easy, but ere long my hopes were dashed! We had about two hours and a half of awfully difficult rock, very solid fortunately, but perfectly fearful. There were two places which Mathon and Marius literally pulled me up like a parcel. I didn't a bit mind where it was steep up, but round corners where the rope couldn't help me! . . . And it was absolutely sheer down. The first half-hour I gave myself up for lost. it didn't seem possible that I could get up all that wall without ever making a slip. You see, I had practically never been on a rock before. However, I didn't let on and presently it began to seem quite natural to be hanging by my eyelids over an abyss. . . just before reaching the top we passed over the Pas du Chat, the difficulty of which is much exaggerated. . . It was not till I was over it that Mathon told me that it was the dreaded place. We were now at the foot of the Pyramide Duhamel and we went on till we came in sight of the Glacier Catré, where we sat down on a cornice, 7:45. . . The Germans got up a quarter of an hour later having climbed up the rock a different way. . . At 8:45 we got to the top between the Pic du Glacier carré and the Grand Pic de la Meije and saw over the other side for the first time. We left at 9 and reached the summit at 10:10, the rock being quite easy except one place called the Cheval Rouge. It is a red flat stone, almost perpendicular, some 15 feet high, up which you swarm as best you may with your feet against the Meije, and you sit astride, facing the Meije, on a very pointed crest. I sat there while Marius and Mathon went on and then followed them up an overhanging rock of 20 feet or more. The rope came in most handy--! We stayed on the summit until 11. It was gorgeous, quite cloudless. . . I went to sleep for half-an-hour. It's a very long way up but it's a longer way down-unless you take the way Mathon's axe took. The cord by which it was tied to his wrist broke on the Cheval Rouge and it disappeared into space. There's a baddish place going down the Grand Pic. The guides fastened a double rope to an iron bolt and let Mr. Turner and me down on to a tiny ledge on which we sat and surveyed the Aiguille d'Arve with La Grave in the foreground. Then was a very nasty bit without the double rope-how anyone gets down those places I can't imagine. However, they do. Then we crossed the Brèche and found ourselves at the foot of the first dent. Here comes the worst place on the whole Meije. I sat on the Brèche and looked down on to the Châtelleret on one side and La Grave on the other. . . Then Mathon vanished, carrying a very long rope, and I waited. . . Presently I felt a little tug on the rope. " Allez, Mademoiselle," Said Marius from behind and off I went. There were two little humps to hold on to on an overhanging rock and there La Grave beneath and there was me in mid-air and Mathon round the corner holding the rope tight, but the rope was sideways of course-that's my general impression of those ten minutes. Added to which I thought at the time how very well I was climbing and how odd it was that I should not be afraid. The worst was over then, and the most tedious part was all to come. It took us three hours to get from the Grand Pic to the Pic Central-up and down over endless dents. We followed the crest all the way, quite precipitous rock below us on the Châtelleret side and a steep slope on the other. There was no difficulty, but there was also no moment when you had not to pay the strictest attention. . . I felt rather done when we got to the Pic Central. . . There was an hour of ice and rock till at last we found ourselves on the Glacier du Tabuchet and with thankfulness I put on my skirt again. It was then 3 and we got in at 6:30. The glacier was at first good then much crevassed. We skirted for nearly an hour the arête leading up to the Pic de Momme and it was 5:30 before we unroped. . . When I got in I found everyone in the Hotel on the doorstep waiting for me and M. Juge let off crackers, to my great surprise. . .

I went to bed and knew no more till 6 this morning, when I had five cups of tea and read all your letters and then went to sleep again until ten. I'm really not tired but my shoulders and neck and arms feel rather sore and stiff and my knees are awfully bruised.

[After the Meije there is one more letter, too long to insert here, from La Grave, in which she relates her successful ascent of the Ecrins. She comes back to England in the middle of September, well pleased, as shown by her letters, with her progress in climbing.]

CHAPTER V

1899-1900 - JERUSALEM: FIRST DESERT JOURNEYS

In November 1899 she starts for Jerusalem, with many hopes and plans, including learning more Arabic. Dr. Fritz Rosen was then German Consul at Jerusalem. He had married Nina Roche, whom we had known since she was a child, the daughter of Mr. Roche of the Garden House, Cadogan Place. Charlotte Roche was Nina's sister. They made everything easy for Gertrude.

On the way she writes a long letter from Smyrna, where everyone was most kind and hospitable. She describes the "Mediterranean race " to which the inhabitants of Smyrna belong].

It speaks no language though it will chatter with you in Half a dozen, it has no native land though it is related by marriage to all Europe, and with the citizens of each country it will talk to its compatriots and itself as " we "; it centres round no capital and is loyal to no government though it obeys many. Cheerful, careless, contented, hospitable to a fault, it may well be all, for it is divested of all natural responsibilities, it has little to guard and little to offer but a most liberal share in its own inconceivably hugger mugger existence. Kindness is its distinctive quality, as far-as I have sampled it, and I hope I may have many opportunities of sampling it further.

[From Beyrout she writes]
We settled that when I come riding down from Damascus in the spring
. . ..

[The last part of the voyage is made on a Russian boat] all the stewards speak Russian and we communicate by signs, my fellow passengers are an American Catholic Priest and a Russian engineer and 400 Russian peasants who are making a pilgrimage to Jerusalem.

THE LETTERS OF GERTRUDE BELL

To F.B., S.S. Russia, Sunday 10th December, 1899

The pilgrims are camped out all over the deck. They bring their own bedding and their own food and their passage from Odessa costs them some 12 roubles. They undergo incredible hardships: one woman walked from Tobolsk, she started in March.

To H.B., Hotel, Jerusalem, 13th December, 1899

Here I am most comfortably installed. I am two minutes' walk from the German Consulate. My apartment consists of a very nice bedroom and a big sitting room, both opening on to a small vestibule which in its turn leads out on to the verandah which runs all along the first story of the hotel courtyard with a little garden in it. I pay 7 francs a day including breakfast, which is not excessive. My housemaid is an obliging gentleman in a fez who brings me my hot bath in the morning and is ready at all times to fly round in my service. I spent the morning unpacking and turning out the bed and things out of my sitting room; it is now most cosy-two armchairs, a big writing table, a square table for my books, an enormous Kiefert map of Palestine lent me by Uncle Tom and photographs of my family on the walls. The floor is of tiles but they have laid down a piece of carpet on it. There is a little stove in one corner and the wood fire in it is most acceptable. I propose buying a horse! for which I shall pay about 18 pounds and sell him at the end for no less, I hope. The keep is very little, Dr. Rosen says, and you see the alternative would be to use theirs. Now they have only 3 for their 3 selves and I already have all my meals except breakfast with them, so don't think I can infringe further on their hospitality.

We got in soon after 8, and the kind Rosens came on board with a kavass and carried me off to a very nice hotel where we breakfasted. The garden was full of parrots and monkeys which breakfasted also when I had finished. It was a delicious sunny day. We drove round about Jaffa, caught the only train at 1:20 to Jerusalem. It was 5 before we arrived, Charlotte met us. The Consulate is small but very comfy, all the rooms open on to a long central living room which is full of beautiful Persian things. The two boys were much excited by my arrival and greeted me with enthusiasm. They are perfect dears, these people. I feel as if I should love them very much indeed. And so charming about all arrangements, hospitality and kindness itself.

To-day Dr. R. and I went for a long walk, I left a card and a letter of introduction on Mrs. Dickson at the English consulate. One's first impression of Jerusalem is extremely interesting, but certainly not pleasing. The walls are splendid (Saracenic on Jewish foundations), but all the holy places are terribly marred by being built over with hideous churches of all the different sects.

[Gertrude's interest in the holy places was that of the archaeologist only and not that of the believer.

There is no space to insert in extenso her long and interesting letters from Jerusalem, where she was entirely happy learning Arabic, exploring her surroundings, and being admitted into the delightful intimacy of the Rosens. But some extracts from the letters are given here.]

To F.B.

This morning I went out with Charlotte and the children (I have not Yet got my teacher). The two boys rode on a donkey and looked angels. They are delicious children. I saw a charming little horse, a bay, very well bred with lovely movements rather showy, but light and strong and delightful in every way We have embarked on negotiations for him which promise to take some time as they now ask 40 pounds and my price is 18 to 20! He comes of a well-known stock so that I should run no risk of losing on him when I sell him. Charlotte, Dr. R'. and I rode this afternoon, I on a pony belonging to the hotel keeper, very bad, much too small and slow, he wouldn't do at all. My saddle had to be wrapped round him!

This morning I had my first lesson. My teacher's name is Khalil Dughan and he is exactly what I want. I learnt more about pronunciation this morning than I have ever known.

In the afternoon, Nina, Dr. R. and I rode out.

To F.B., December 13th, 1899

My days are extremely full and most agreeable. I either have a lesson or work alone every morning for 4 hours-the lesson only lasts one and a half hours. I have 3 morning and 3 afternoon lessons a week. I am just beginning to understand a little of what I hear and to say simple things to the servants, but I find it awfully difficult. The pronunciation is past words, no western throat being constructed to form these extraordinary gutturals. Still it's really interesting. We lunch at 12:30 and go out about 2, generally riding till 5. Then I come home to my work till 7 when I dress and go in to dinner. I aim at being back by 10 to get another hour's work but this doesn't always happen, especially now when Nina is very busy preparing a Xmas tree and we spend our evenings tying up presents and gilding walnuts, Dr. R. reading to us, the while, all his travel letters from Persia--extremely interesting.

My horse is much admired. My teacher, also, is a success. He has the most charming fund of beautiful oriental stories and I make him tell them to me by the hour as I want to get used to the sound of words. He is a Christian and his family claims to have been Crusaders.

He has given me a lecture of his, written out in English on the customs of the Arabs. It begins "The Arabs are the oldest race on earth; they date from the Flood!!" Comes my housemaid, "The hot water is ready for the Presence," says he. "Enter and light the candle," say I. "On my head," he has replied--it sounds ambiguous in English! That means it's dressing time.

To her sister Elsa, Jerusalem, December 20th, 1899

The days fly here so that I scarcely know how to catch at them for a moment's time to write to you. It is now 11 p.m. and I must go to bed quickly so as to be up early and prepare my lesson before my Arab comes. (I may say in passing that I don't think I shall ever talk Arabic, but I go on struggling with it in the hope of mortifying Providence by my persistence. I now stammer a few words to my housemaid--him of the fez--and he is much delighted.) With Charlotte, who is a most spirited companion, I explored a great part of the inner town. We are quite the family party and I love them all. The boys are angels. Now to bed.

The first night of rain I was awakened by a rushing sound of water and found that it was falling in sheets on to my pillow! I took up my bed and walked and spent the rest of the night in peace.

THE LETTERS OF GERTRUDE BELL

To F.B., Jerusalem, Thursday, December 28, 1899

It has rained quite persistently for 5 days. You may imagine how I say 'Heil dir, Sonne!' this morning when I woke and saw the sun. Yesterday the Rosens had a Xmas tree for all the German children. It was most successful and the children were dears. I am beginning to feel very desperate about Arabic and I am now going to try a new plan. A Syrian girl is to come and spend an hour with me 3 Or 4 times a week and talk to me. I shall take her out walks sometimes, if she is satisfactory, and converse with her. It is an awful language.

To F.B., Jerusalem, January 1st, 1900

Will you order Heath to send me out a wide gray felt sun hat (not double, but it must be a regular Terai shape and broad brimmed) to ride in, and to put a black velvet ribbon round it with straight bows. My Syrian girl is charming and talks very prettily but with a strong local accent. It adds enormously to one's difficulties that one has to learn a patois and a purer Arabic at the same time. I took her out for a long walk on Friday afternoon and went photographing about Jerusalem. She was much entertained, though she was no good as a guide, for she had never been in the Jewish quarter though she has lived all her life here! That's typical of them. I knew my way, however, as every Englishwoman would-it's as simple as possible.

She came with us on the following day on a most delightful expedition. We started at 9 in the morning-it was Sunday and therefore a legitimate holiday-and rode down the Valley of Hinnon and all along the brook Kedron (which is dry at this season) through a deep valley full of immensely old olive trees and rock tombs scarcely older. Then up a long hill and down on the other side into a shallow naked valley, where there were many encampments of the black Bedouin tents, and so into an extraordinary gorge called the Valley of Fire. The rock lies in natural terraces and is full of caves; the Brook Kedron (it had rejoined us in a roundabout way) has cut the steepest, deepest cleft for its bed and on either side rise these horizontal layers of stone. They have been a regular city of anchorites, each living in his cave and drawing his ladder up behind him when he went in. Half a mile or so further on lies the citadel of this cave town, the Monastery of Mar

Saba, itself half cave and half building, its long walls and towers creeping up the steep rock, the dome of its chapel jutting out from it, and the irregular galleries and rows of cells hanging out over a precipice. The rock itself is full of little square windows and these are the cave cells and probably about as old as St. Saba who lived in the 6th century.

To F.B., Jerusalem, January 5th, 1900

What a terrible time it is. I feel such a beast to be writing to you about my pleasant doings in the midst of all this, still I can do no good to you all by being very anxious. On Wednesday we rode down to the Dead Sea, over a long stretch of country on which grew thorny plants, then through a curious belt of hard mud heaps, then along the Jordan valley and finally across a bit of absolute desert, white with salt and plantless. It was a glorious day, bright and hot.

To her sister, Jerusalem, January 11th, 1900

My DEAREST ELSA,
It is sad about Berlin and all your beautiful clothes. I was thrilled by your account of your coat-it sounds too beautiful. But dear, dear! that you should not be going to shine in it in imperial circles! I am extremely happy and much amused, and I am very busy with Arabic. Whenever I can I get Ferideh to come and spend the afternoon with me, but as she teaches in a school, I can usually only get her on a Saturday. She comes to tea with me, however, two other days a week and we converse for an hour. I often go walking alone of an afternoon and explore the surrounding country And nearly always find some exciting flower among the rocks. The earliest flower place is the Valley of Hinnon. I went there yesterday afternoon for starch hyacinths and cyclamen and had a tremendous scramble. As I came back along the Road I met an Arab who greeted me affably and told me he had seen me climbing on the rocks. So we walked home together We had a long talk--my conversations are limited to rather simple subjects. The first thing they always say is, "We have heard that there is a great deal of water in your country." then I expatiate on the greenness of it and the distance and the cold and so forth. It's awful fun.

THE LETTERS OF GERTRUDE BELL

I am just beginning to feel my feet after a fearful struggle. The first fortnight was perfectly desperate--I thought I should never be able to put two words together. Added to the fact that the language is very difficult there are at least three sounds almost impossible to the European throat. The worst I think is a very much aspirated H. I can only say it by holding down my tongue with one finger, but then you Can't carry on a conversation with your finger down your throat can you? My little girl Ferideh Yamseh is a great success. She talks the dialect, but that is all the better as I want to understand the people of hereabouts. I went to visit her and her family after dinner yesterday--they are quite close. It was most amusing. I found the mother a pretty charming woman who has had ten children and looks ridiculously young (they marry at 13). Two sisters and presently a brother came in. The mother talks nothing but Arabic so the visit was conducted in that language with great success Ferideh interpreting from time to time. I was regaled on cocoa, a very sweet Arab pastry and pistachios which I love and shown all the photographs of all their relations down to the last cousin twice removed. . .

My Sheikh has just told me that Ladysmith is relieved I do hope it is true and that this is the beginning of good news. I am sending you a little packet of seeds. They are more interesting for association's sake than for the beauty of the plant--it is the famous and fabulous mandrake. By the way the root of the mandrake grow to a length of 2 yards, so I should think somebody shrieks when it is dug up-if not the mandrake, then the digger.

I took Ferideh for a drive and a walk yesterday and talked Arabic extremely badly and felt desponding about it. However there is nothing to be done but to struggle on with it. I should like to mention that there are five words for a wall and 36 ways of forming the plural. And the rest is like unto it.

To H.B., Jerusalem, January 11th-14th, 1900

Sunday 14. This goes to-morrow. It ought to reach you in a week as it goes by a good post via Egypt. The posts are arranged thus: Sunday and Monday outgoing posts and the rest of the week nothing.

Dr. R. Nina and I rode this afternoon, heavenly weather. We went an exploring expedition through a lovely valley under a place called Malba. The path of course awful. In one place we had to get off, pull down a wall and lead our horses over it. There are no decent paths at all, only the hard high road. I so often wish for you--always when I'm making a nice expedition. Next spring let us come here together. Anyhow let us have a nice travel together soon.

To F. B., Jericho, January 17th, 1900

I rode down here yesterday afternoon with Isa, one of the kavasses. We started at 1:30 and got here at 5, which was pretty good going. It was a most pleasant day for riding, cool and not sunny, today is brilliantly sunny, I came down the last hill in company with a band of Turkish soldiers, ragged, footsore, weary, poor dears ! but cheerful. We held a long conversation. The Russian Pilgrim House we visited last night and found it packed with pilgrims as tight as herrings sleeping in rows on the floor. Even the courtyard was quite full of them and on a tree an eikon round which a crowd of them were praying, Charlotte and I rode off with Isa about 11 and went down to the Jordan, taking our lunch with us. There ,*we found an enormous crowd assembled. Bedouin and fellaheen, kavasses in embroidered clothes. Turkish soldiers, Greek priests and Russian peasants, some in furs and top boots and some in their white shrouds, which were to serve as bathing dresses in the holy stream and then to be carried home and treasured up till their owner's death. We lunched and wandered about for some time, I photographing some of these strange groups--long-haired Russian priests in their shrouds standing praying in the hot sun by the river bank, among the tamarisk bushes and the reeds, every one, men and women, had chains of beads and crucifixes hung round their necks. The sun was very hot and we waited and waited while those who were going to be baptised signed their names and paid a small fee. We found ourselves ensconced on willow boughs just opposite to the place where the priests were coming down to bless the water. We waited for about half an hour, then the crowd opened and a long procession of priests came to the water's edge with lighted candles. The shrouded people clambered down the mud banks and stood waist deep In the stream until the moment when the priest laid the cross three times upon the water, then suddenly, with a great firing off of guns, everyone proceeded to baptise himself by dipping and rolling over in the water. It was the strangest sight. Some of them had hired monks at a small fee to baptise them and they certainly got their money's worth of baptism, for the monks took an infinite pleasure in throwing them over backwards into the muddy stream and holding them under until they were quite saturated. We then rowed back, returned to our horses and got back about 5.

To F.B., Jerusalem, February 18th, 1900

There is a regular commerce apart from all others here to supply the Russian pilgrims with relics, souvenirs and the necessities of Russian peasant life. I bless the typewriter. it is such a joy to open an envelope of yours and find long sheets from the typewriter. It is rather terrible to think that Maurice is off; I hoped he wouldn't leave till the end of the month, Anyhow you will telegraph to me on his arrival, won't you, and all items of news you receive from him which can be conveyed by telegram. He writes in great spirits and it may be that it will be good for him, the out-of-door life there. My last letter I have sent home to be forwarded to him. Do you know the way when something disagreeable happens, that one looks back and tries to imagine what it would have been like if it hadn't happened? That's how I feel about his going.

[Maurice had gone out to the Boer War in command of the Volunteer Service Company, Yorkshire Regiment. He and Gertrude were bound together by the closest affection and her constant anxiety and solicitude about him is shown in her letters.]

Do you know these wet afternoons I have been reading the story of Aladdin to myself for pleasure, without a dictionary! It is not very difficult, I must confess, still it's ordinary good Arabic, not for beginners, and I find it too charming for words. Moreover I see that I really have learnt a good deal since I came for I couldn't read just for fun to save my life. It is satisfactory, isn't it? I look forward to a time when I shall just read Arabic-like that! and then for my histories! I really think that these months here will permanently add to the pleasure and interest of the rest of my days! Honest Injun. Still there is a lot and a lot more to be done first--SO to work!

THE LETTERS OF GERTRUDE BELL

To F.B., Jerusalem, February 28, 1900

Sunday, was too many for me. I did not go out at all but sat It
home and read Aladdin and looked at the streaming rain. Monday was
a little better. Charlotte and I put on short skirts and thick boots and
went for a long walk to a lovely spring she knew of. We walked down
a deep valley which s long as we have known it has been as dry as a
bone and where to our surprise we found a deep swift stream, Ain
Tulma, our object, was on the other side and as there are no bridges in
this country, (there being no rivers as a rule) there was nothing for it
but to take off our shoes and stockings and wade. The water came
above our knees. The other side was too lovely--the banks of the river
were carpeted with red anemones, a sheet of them, and to walk by the
side of a rushing stream is an unrivalled experience in this country.
When we got to Ain Tulma we found the whole place covered with
cyclamen and orchis and a white sort of garlic, very pretty, and the
rocks out of which the water comes were draped in maidenhair. There
were a lot of small boys, most amiable young gentlemen, who helped
us to pick cyclamen, and when I explained that I had no money they
said it was a bakshish to me--the flowers. We had a very scrambly
walk back, waded the stream again and when we got to a little village
at the foot of the hill, we hired some small boys to carry our flowers
home for us. (In this village I lost my way and we found ourselves
wandering over the flat roofs and Jumping across the streets below!) I
hurried on (as it was 5 and I had a lesson at 5:30) with 5 little beggar
boys in my train. They were great fun. We had long conversations all
the way home. It's such an amusement to be able to understand. The
differences of pronunciation are a little puzzling at first to the foreigner. There are two k's in Arabic--the town people drop the hard k
altogether and replace it by a guttural for which we have no equiva-
lent; the country people pronounce the hard k soft and the soft k ch,
but they say their gutturals beautifully and use a lot of words which
belong to the more classical Arabic. The Bedouins speak the best; they
pronounce all their letters and get all the subtlest shades of meaning
out of the words. I must tell you this is a great day--a German post office has been opened, and we expect marvels from it. There is parcel
post and all complete and I advise you to put German Post Office on to
your letters to me. One of our kavasses has gone to be Post Office
kavass and as I passed down the Jaffa Street he rushed out open armed
to greet me and begged me to come in. So in I went and retired behind
the counter and shook hands warmly with the two post masters (they

dined with us a few nights ago) and bought 6 stamps to celebrate the occasion--which I didn't pay for, as I had no money--the kavass saying all the time--"Al! ketear 'al!" which means "It is extremely high," and is the superlative of admiration in Arabic. The tourists who were sending off telegrams were rather surprised to see someone seemingly like themselves come in hand in hand with an old Arab and fall into the arms of the officials behind the counter! It was extremely high!

Friday 2. To-day came the joyful news of the relief of Lady-smith. My horse is extremely well. We are going for a long ride to-morrow. The R's and I have been planning expeditions. We mean to go for 10 days into Moab about the 18th. It will be lovely. We shall take tents, Dr. R. Nina and I. Our great travel is not till the end of April, but I shall go to Hebron some time early in April. Goodbye.

To F.B., Jerusalem, March 6th, 1900

By the way, I hope Elsa clung to the Monthly Cousin article and did not allow it to be published elsewhere. The style of it was only suited to that journal, but I'm glad it pleased. It's a gorgeous day. I'm going riding-in my new hat!

[The Monthly Cousin was a typewritten and handwritten periodical edited by Elsa and Molly, of which the contributors were the wide family circle of the Bells and of their cousins. It appeared regularly from 1897 to 1907, and has been preserved as a precious family record. Gertrude revelled in it, and on occasion contributed to it.]

To H.B., Ayan Musa, Tuesday, March 20, 1900
(From my tent)

I left Jerusalem yesterday soon after 9, having seen my cook at 7 and arranged that he should go off as soon as he could get the mules ready. (His name is Hanna--sounds familiar doesn't it! but that H is such as you have never heard.) I rode down to Jerusalem alone--the road was full of tourists, caravans of donkeys carrying tents for cook and Bedouin escorts. I made friends as I went along and rode with first one Bedouin and then another, all of them exaggerating the dangers I was about to run with the hope of being taken with me into Moab. Half way down I met my guide from Salt, east of Jordan, coming up to meet me. His name is Tarif, he is a servant of the clergyman in Salt and a Christian therefore, and a perfect dear. We rode along together, sometime, but he was on a tired horse, so I left him to come on slowly and hurried down into Jericho where I arrived with a Bedouin at 1-- famished. I went to the Jordan hotel. We then proceeded to the Mudir's for I wanted to find out the truth of the tales I had been told about Moab, but he was out. By this time Tarif and Hanna had arrived and reported the tents to be one and a half hours behind, which seemed to make camping at the Jordan impossible that night. . . I determined to pass that night in Jericho and make an early start.

This morning I got up at 5 and at 6 was all ready, having sent on my mules and Hanna to the Jordan bridge. I knocked up the Mudir and he said he would send a guide to Madeba to make the necessary arrangements for me. The river valley is wider on the other side and was full of tamarisks in full white flower and willows in the newest of leaf, there were almost no slime pits and when we reached the level of the Ghor (that is the Jordan plain) behold, the wilderness had blos- somed like the rose. It was the most unforgettable sight--sheets and sheets of varied and exquisite colour--purple, white, yellow, and the brightest blue (this was a bristly sort of Plant which I don't know) and fields of scarlet ranunculus. Nine-tenths of them I didn't know, but there was the yellow daisy, the sweet-scented mauve wild stock, a great splendid sort of dark purple onion, the white garlic and purple mallow, and higher up a tiny blue iris and red anemones and a dawn- ing pink thing like a linum. We were now joined by a cheerful couple, from Bethlehem, a portly fair man in white with a yellow keffiyeh (that's the thing they wear round their heads bound by ropes of camel hair and falling over the shoulders) and a fair beard, riding a very small donkey, and a thinner and darker man walking. The first one looked like a portly burgher. He asked me if I were a Christian and said he was, praise be to God! I replied piously that it was from God. So we all journeyed on together through the wilderness of flowers and every now and then the silent but amiable Ismael got off to pick me a new variety of plant, while the others enlivened the way by stalking wood pigeons, but the pigeons were far too wily and they let off their breech loaders in vain and stood waist deep in flowers watching the birds flying cheerfully away--with a "May their house be destroyed!" from my Christian friend. A little higher up we came to great patches of corn sown by the Adwan Bedouins-, Arabs' we call them east of Jordan, they being the Arabs par excellence, just as we call their black tents 'houses,' there being no others. Then goodbye to the flowers! Now we saw a group of black tents far away on a little hill covered with white tombs--Tell Kufrein it is called--and here the barley was in ear and, in the midst of the great stretches of it, little watch towers of branches had been built and a man stood on each to drive away birds and people. One was playing a pipe as we passed--it was much more Arcadian than Arcadia. We had now reached the bottom of the foothills, and leaving the Ghor behind us, we began to mount. We crossed a stream flowing down the Wady Hisban (which is Heshbon of the fish-pools in the Song of Songs) at a place called Akweh. It was so wet here that we rode on to a place where there were a few thorn trees peopled by immense crowds of resting birds-they seize on any little bush for there are so few and the Arabs come and burn the bush and catch and cook the birds all in one! On the top of the first shoulder we came to spreading cornfields. The plan is this--the "Arabs" sow one place this year and go and live somewhere else lest their animals should eat the growing corn. Next year this lies fallow and the fallow of the year before is sown. Over the second shoulder we got on to a stretch of rolling hills and we descended the valley to Ayan Musa, a collection of beautiful springs with in Arab camp pitched above them. I found the loveliest iris I have yet seen--big and sweet-scented and so dark purple that the hanging down petals are almost black. It decorates my tent now. Half an hour later my camp was pitched a little lower down on a lovely grassy plateau. We were soon surrounded by Arabs who sold us a hen and some excellent sour milk, 'laban' it is called. While we bargained the women and children wandered round and ate grass, just like goats. The women are unveiled. They wear a blue cotton gown 6 yards long which is gathered up and bound round their heads and their waists and falls to their feet. Their faces, from the mouth downwards, are tattooed with indigo and their hair hangs down in two long plaits on either side. Our horses and mules were hobbled and groomed. Hanna brought me an excellent cup of tea and at 6 a good dinner consisting of soup made of rice and olive oil (very good!) an Irish stew and raisins from Salt, an offering from Tarif. My camp lies just under Pisgah. Isn't it a joke being able to talk Arabic! We saw a great flock of storks to-day (the Father of Luck, Tarif calls them) and an eagle. I am now amongst the Bilka Arabs but these particular people are the Ghanimat, which Hanna explains as Father of Flocks.

Wednesday 21. Well, I can now show you the reverse side of camping. I woke this morning at dawn to find a strong wind blowing up clouds from the east. At 7 it began to rain but I nevertheless started off for the top of Siagheh, which is Pisgah, sending the others straight to Madeba. I could see from it two of the places from which Balaam is supposed to have attempted the cursing of Israel and behind me lay the third, Nebonaba in Arabic. The Moses legend is a very touching one. I stood on the top of Pisgah and looked out over the wonderful Jordan valley and the blue sea and the barren hills, veiled and beautified by cloud and thought it was one of the most pathetic stories that have ever been told. I then rode to Nebo, the clouds sweeping down behind me and swallowing up the whole Ghor. As I left Nebo it began to stream. Arrived at Madeba about 11:30, wet through. As I rode through the squalid muddy little streets, to my surprise I was greeted in American by a man in a waterproof. He is a photographer, semi-professional, and his name is Baker and he is very cheerful and nice. He is travelling with a dragoman. I selected my camping ground on the lee-side of the village and Mr. Baker took me to the Latin monastery where he is lodging to keep out of the wet while my camp was being put up. I sent up to Government House, so to speak, to find out what my Mudir's letter had done for me in the matter of to-morrow's escort. The answer came that this Mudir was away but that the Effendi was coming to see me. He appeared, a tall middle-aged Turk; I invited him into my tent with all politeness and offered him cigarettes (you see a bad habit may have its merits!) while Hanna brought him a cup of coffee. But--the soldier was not to be had! There weren't enough. I determined to wait till the coffee and cigarettes had begun to work and turned the conversation to other matters-with as many polite phrases as I could remember. Fortunately I fell upon photography and found that his great desire was to be photographed with his soldiers. I jumped at this and offered to do him and send him copies and so forth and the upshot of it was that for me he would send a soldier tomorrow at dawn. I think it's rather a triumph to have conducted so successful a piece of diplomacy in Arabic, don't you? The wind has dropped and the sky is clear, but it's cold and dampish. I had the brilliant idea of sending into the town for a brazier which was brought me full of charcoal and put into my tent. I have been drying my habit over it. From my camp I look over great rolling plains of cornfields stretching eastwards.

Thursday 22. This has been a most wonderful day. Hanna woke me at 5:30. By 6:30 I had breakfasted and was ready to start. I sent up to know if my soldier was coming. He arrived in a few minutes, a big handsome cheerful Circassian mounted on a strong white horse, and a little before seven we started off. In a dip we came suddenly upon a great encampment of Christians from Madeba and stopped to photograph them and their sheep. They were milking them, the sheep being tied head to head in a serried line of perhaps forty at a time. We went on and on, the ground rising and falling and always the same beautiful grass-no road, we went straight across country. Another big encampment of Christians. The people were most friendly and one man insisted on mounting his little mare and coming with us, just for love. So we all cantered off together, through many flocks and past companies of dignified storks walking about and eating the locusts, till we came to the road, the pilgrim road to Mecca. Road of course it is not: it is about one-eighth of a mile wide and consists of hundreds of parallel tracks trodden out by the immense caravan which passes over it twice a year. We next came to some camps and flocks of the Beni Sakhr, the most redoubted of all the Arab tribes and the last who submitted to the Sultan's rule--"Very much not pleasant" said Tarif--and now we were almost at the foot of the low hills and before us stood the ruins of Mashetta. It is a Persian palace, begun and never finished by Chosroes 1, who overran the country in 611 of our era and planned to have a splendid hunting box in there. Grassy plains which abound in game. The beauty of it all was quite past words. It's a thing One will never forget as long as one lives. At last most reluctantly, we turned back on our four hours' ride home. We hadn't gone more than a few yards before three of the Beni Sakhr came riding towards us, armed to the teeth, black browed and most menacing. When they saw our soldier they threw us the salaam with some disgust, and after a short exchange of politenesses, proceeded on their way--we felt that the interview might have turned differently if we had been unescorted. We rode on straight across the plains putting up several foxes and a little grey wolf. Unfortunately we did not see the white gazelles of which there are said to be many, also jackals and hyenas. Just as we came to the edge of the corn fields, again two of the Beni Sakhr sprang up seemingly out of the ground and came riding towards us. Exactly the same interview took place as before and they retired in disgust. We got in at 5, quite delighted with our day. Don't think I have ever spent such a wonderful day.

Friday 23. Hanna woke me at 6:30 just in time to see a lovely sunrise across the Madeba plains. At 7:30 I went up to the Sarai to see if the Effendi wanted to be photographed but I found him so busy that he had not had time to get into his swell clothes, so we arranged that it was to be for when I came back. The Effendi insisted on sending a soldier with me to Kerak. It is quite unnecessary, but this is the penalty of my distinguished social position and also, I think, of my nationality for the Turks are much afraid of us and he probably thinks I have some project of annexation in my mind! The Circassian--for he is again a Circassian, is good looking and pleasant. They are an agreeable race. I was off at eight. We were on the Roman road all the day-paved on the flat, hewn out of the rock in the gorges. Oh, my camp is too lovely to-night! I am in a great field of yellow daisies by the edge of a rushing stream full of fish and edged with oleanders which are just coming out. (I have a bunch of them in my tent.) On either side rise the great walls of the valley and protect me from every breath of wind. I have just been having a swim in the river under the oleander bushes and Tarif has shot me a partridge for dinner . . . There is a very pretty white broom flowering. Mashallah! Oh, the nice sound of water and frogs and a little screaming owl!

Saturday 24. Gaisse aus Kerak! Do you know where to find it on the map? it's quite a big place I assure you. . .

I half climbed up on a little plateau near the river--a Roman guard house. The place was remarkable for possessing two trees--terebinths; they are the only trees I have seen for four days. A little hill called Shikan which I can see from my windows in Jerusalem. Ruins of a Moabite town, supposed to be the capital of King Sihon and there-fore very very old. I could see the terraced lines of the old vineyards . . . and the Roman road straight as an arrow, paved and edged with a low double wall, one stone high. There were lots and lots of ruins, villages and towns--what a country it must have been! At 11:30 we reached a place that had been a land mark. Quite suddenly, there opened below us an enormous valley, splitting in the middle to make place for a steep hill almost as high as the plateau on which we were standing, and the top of the hill was set round with great Crusader forts with acres of mud roofs between-it was Kerak. We went down and down and up and up and at 5 o'clock passed under the northern fort and en-tered the town. . . to see the English doctor, Johnson is his name, to whom I had letters. . . After tea Dr. Johnson took me down to my camp where we found an . . . official who had come to find out who I was and whither going. My camp is pitched in the north-west angle of the town. The steep valley goes straight down below me; I am just under the great north-west fort and beyond it I look right down the valley across the Dead Sea to the hills of Judea--and Jerusalem. . .

Sunday 25. I'm going on to Petra! What with giving out that I'm a German (for they are desperately afraid of the English), I have got permission and a soldier from the Governor and this is always difficult and often impossible, and I can't but think that the finger of Providence points southwards! I would telegraph to ask your permission, but there's no telegraph nearer than Jericho! I think a missionary and his wife, Mr. and Mrs. Harding, are coming with me; they are nice people and I shall like to have them. He has gone to see about mules, etc., now, and we are off at dawn. I have Spent a pleasant day here. . . I photographed and came back to my tent determined to penetrate into the south-west fort which is now used as barracks for the Turkish soldiers. Dr. Johnson had told me I could not possibly get permission, so I asked for none, but took Hanna and walked calmly in, in an affable way, greeted all the soldiers politely and was shown all over! As I was walking about I came to the edge of a deep Pit and Whom should I see at the bottom of it but my poor Madeba friends! It was the prison, there were underground chambers on either side of the pit, but they were all sitting outside to enjoy the sun that straggles down at midday. We greeted each other affectionately. I then went down a long outer stair to a lower floor, so to speak, of the forts, and here again was shown great vaulted rooms cut out of the rock. These are all inhabited by soldiers and mules. I felt I had done a good morning's sight-seeing and came back to my tent where I was presently fetched by a little Turkish girl, the daughter of an Effendi, who told me her mother was sitting down in the shadow of the wall a little below my camp and invited me to come and drink coffee. We went down hand in hand and I found a lot of Turkish women sitting on the ground under a fig tree, so I sat down too and was given coffee and as they all but one talked Arabic, we had a cheerful conversation. We had a glorious view down the valley and across the Dead Sea--It is supposed to be the tomb of Noah and honoured as such. It's a glorious hot night. We bought a lamb to-day for a medijeh, . . . which seems cheap. He was a perfect love and his fate cut me to the heart. I felt if I looked at him any longer I should be like Byron and the goose, so I parted from him hastily--and there were delicious lamb cutlets for supper.

My soldier is again a Circassian-his name is Ayoub--job. He appears to possess the complacent disposition of his namesake, but he has little of the Arabic, his native tongue being of course Turkish. We have a beautiful flowery place for our camp and I have been bathing in the stream. The men have shot partridges, and caught fish in a most ingenious way. They put a basin weighted with some stones in the stream with a little bread in it and cover it with a cloth in which there are a few holes. The fish swim in to eat the bread and can't get out. They are very small. My servants are admirable. My own camp goes like clockwork with never a hitch. Hanna is the prop and stay of it all. The two muleteers are also extremely good servants and we have vowed always to travel together. . .

We heard that we were still 6 hours from Wady Musa. One of the great difficulties of this journey is that no one knows the distances even approximately and there is no map worth a farthing. Another is that the population is so scant we can't get food! This is starvation camp tonight, we have nothing but rice and bread, a little potted meat. No charcoal and no barley for our horses.

We have been on the Roman road all day. The men are all in good spirits and we are extremely cheerful. It is a good joke, you know. . .

Thursday 29. Wady Musa--at length we have arrived and it is worth all the long long way. We descended to the village of Wady Musa where we hoped to get provisions, but devil a hen there was, so we despatched a man post haste to the nearest Bedouin camp for a lamb, and as yet--7 p.m.--none has appeared! However, we have got laban and barley and butter so we can support life with our own rice and bread. What the people in Wady Musa live on I can't imagine. They hadn't so much as milk. These things settled, we rode on and soon got into the entrance of the defile which leads to Petra. The Bab es Sik is a passage about half a mile long and in places not more than 8 ft. wide; the rocks rise on either side straight up 100 ft. or so, they are sandstone Of the most exquisite red and sometimes almost arch overhead. The stream runs between, filling all the path, though it used to flow through conduits, and the road was paved; oleanders grew along the stream and here and there a sheaf of ivy hung down over the red rock. We went on in ecstasies until suddenly between the narrow opening of the rocks, we saw the most beautiful sight I have ever seen. Imagine a temple cut out of the solid rock, the charming facade supported on great Corinthian columns standing clear., soaring upwards to the very top of the cliff in the most exquisite proportions and carved with groups Of figures almost as fresh as when the chisel left them all this in the rose red rock., with the sun just touching it and making it look almost transparent. As we went on the gorge widened, on either side the cliffs were cut out into rock tombs of every shape and adorned in every manner, some standing, columned, in the rock, some clear with a pointed roof, some elaborate, some simple, some capped with pointed pyramids, many adorned with a curious form of stair high up over the doorway. . . . The gorge opened and brought us out into a kind of square between the cliffs with a rude cut theatre in it and tombs on every side. We went on and got into a great open place the cliffs widening out far on every side and leaving this kind of amphitheatre strewn over with mounds of ruins. And here we camped under a row of the most elaborate tombs, three stories of pillars and cornices and the whole topped by a great funeral urn. They are extremely rococo, just like the kind of thing you see in a Venetian church above a seventeenth century Doge leaning on his elbow, but time has worn them and weather has stained the rock with exquisite colours--and, in short, I never liked Bernini so well!. . . It is like a fairy tale city, all pink and wonderful. The great paved roads stretch up to a ruined arch and vanish; a solid wall springs up some 6ft. 'A rose red city half as old as Time'--I wish the lamb had come!

Friday 30. I have had a busy day. An hour before dawn Ayoub and I started off riding, with a shepherd to guide us, to the top of Mount Hot--you realise that no daughter of yours could be content to sit quietly at the bottom of a mountain when there was one handy!--we rode up nearly to the top and then dismounted and climbed to the highest summit on which stands, whose tomb do you think! Aaron's! I have never seen anything like these gorges; the cliffs rise for 1000 ft. on either side, broken into the most incredible shapes and coloured!-- red, yellow, blue, white, great patterns over them more lovely than any mosaic. I came back to my tents and found we had bought fifty eggs, some figs and a sheep! but unfortunately the sheep has grown rather old in his long journey to us.

Saturday 31--We left Petra at 7 this morning with great regret. It was looking too exquisite and I longed for another day, but the Hardings were bound to be back. I certainly underestimated the length of the entrance gorge.

Saturday, April 1. We were Off at 7 this morning and rode two and a half hours along our former road across the wide stretching uplands. The monotony was broken by keeping a watch for the Roman milestones. We were going very slowly so as to keep in touch with the mules and we passed one every quarter of an hour the whole way. The paved road was often very well preserved. It was blazing hot. We lunched at the opening of the usual broad shallow valley where there was a very dirty pool at which the mules watered, and one tiny thorn bush under the shade of which we tried to sit, but as it was 1 ft.there was not much shade to be had. In all this country there is practically no water, there are a few cisterns scattered over the hills and, I should think, emptied before the middle of the summer, and where we are camping a couple of wells, and that's absolutely all! I nearly went to sleep on my horse this morning, but was wakened up by hearing Ayoub relating to me tales of Ibn Rashid. One gets so accustomed to it all that one ceases to be bored. We set off again at 12 and Ayoub sighted some Arabs on a hill top so he and I and Hanna and Tarif left the others and rode up and over the hill and found a lot of Arabs watering their flocks at a 'bit' (that's a cistern). It was a very pretty sight. They brought the water up in skins and poured it into the stone troughs all round and the sheep and goats drank thirstily. We followed the Roman road, which runs straight over the tops of the hills. . . our camping place down in the valley at 2:30. It is called Towaneh and was once a big town, the ruins of it stretch up on either side of the valley, but there is nothing now but a cluster of black tents a few hundred yards below us. I paid a call on some Arab ladies and watched them making a sort of sour cream cheese in a cauldron over their fire. They gave me some when it was done, we all ate it, with our fingers, and then they made me coffee, and we drank it out of the same cup, and it was quite good. It was very difficult to understand them for their vocabulary is perfectly different from mine; however, we got along by keeping to simple subjects! These people are gipsies, some of them have just been dancing for me, round my camp fire. It was quite dark, with a tiny new moon, the fire of dry thorns flickered upfaded and flickered again and showed the circle of men crouching on the ground, their black and white cloaks wrapped round them and the woman in the middle dancing. She looked as though she had stepped out of an Egyptian fresco. She wore a long red gown bound round her waist with a dark blue cloth, and falling open in front to show a redder petticoat below. Round her forehead was another dark blue cloth bound tightly and falling in long ends down her back, her chin was covered by a white cloth drawn up round her ears and falling in folds to her waist and her lower lips tattooed with indigo! Her feet, in red leather shoes, scarcely moved but all her body danced and she swept a red handkerchief she held in one hand, round her head, and clasped her hands together in front of her impassive face. The men played a drum and a discordant fife and sang a monotonous song and clapped their hands and gradually she came nearer and nearer to me, twisting her slender body till she dropped down on the heap of brushwood at my feet, and kneeling, her body still danced and her arms swayed and twisted round the mask like face. She got up, and retreated again slowly, with downcast eyes, invoking blessings upon me at intervals, till at last I called her and gave her a couple of besklihs. Near Damascus is their home, and they are going back there from Mecca where they have been near the Prophet (thanks be to God!) and they have seen the holy city (God made it!) and they hope to reach Damascus in safety (if God please!). They talked Arabic to me, but to each other the gipsy tongue which sounded more like Turkish than anything else.

Monday 2. We left this morning at 7. It was very hot, a strong baking wind from the south and a heavy hot mist, most unpleasant. Through this we rode for two hours or more straight on up the side of the valley. The morning's amusement was again the milestones which are wonderfully well preserved, many of them still standing upright in groups of three or four. I have counted as many as eight in one place--I don't know why this is, unless every succeeding emperor who mended the road put up a few milestones of his own. The inscriptions are always visible, but would generally be very difficult to decipher, the letters being much worn. Besides which a mass of Arab tribe marks have been cut on top of them. Many of them, however, have been read by the learned. We went to a tiny village called Aineh where there is a lovely spring and a watermill. We were still six hours from Kerak and Ali black in the face from the heat, so that I thought he was going to have a sunstroke. The Hardings were obliged to go on, but I decided to stay here. They have been very nice. My camp is pitched half way up the hill, with the head of the spring at my door and in front, deep corn fields where the barley is standing in the ear and the storks walking solemnly up to their necks in green. There has been an immense flock of them flying and settling on the hillside, and when I took a stroll I soon found what was engaging the attention of the Father of Luck. The ground was hopping with locusts; on some of the slopes they have eaten every leaf and they are making their way down to the corn. I have just been watching my people make bread. Flour was fortunately to be got from the mill below us; they set two logs alight and when they had got enough ashes they made an immense cake, 2 ft. across and half an inch thick, of flour and water and covered it over with hot ashes. After a quarter of an hour it had to be turned and recovered and the result is most delicious eaten hot; it becomes rather wooden when it is cold. The flour is very coarse, almost like oatmeal. These are the Moments when my camp is at its best--half a dozen ragged onlookers were sitting round in the circle of flickering light and a tiny moon overhead. . .

One of my muleteers, Muhammad, is a Druze. If all his sect are like him, they must be a charming race. He is a great big handsome creature, gentle and quiet and extremely abstemious. He eats nothing but rice 'and bread and figs. it makes me the more keen to go to the Hauran which is the chief centre of then, and I want very much to take these two muleteers with me: they are very capable and obliging, and Muhammad would be interesting to have in a Druze country. One mayn't know or see anything of their religious observances, but he has been telling me a great deal about their life and customs. He says nearly all the people in the Lebanon are Druzes. He himself comes from Beyrout, where he lives next door to Ali. They both talk with the pretty, soft, sing-song accent of the Lebanon. I have a good variety of accents with me for Tarif has the Bedouin and Hanna the real cockney of Jerusalem. They appeal to me sometimes to know which is right. I never was so sunburnt in my life; I'm a rich red brown, not at all becoming! in spite of the Quangle Wangle hat you sent me.

Friday 6. (Jericho again). Madeba, in proportion to its size, must have the largest number of mosquitoes and fleas of any inhabited spot on the globe. Chiefly owing to the mosquitoes, my night was rather a restless one, it also rained a great deal and rain makes an unconscionable noise on a tent, besides the fact is I was troubled to think of my poor people outside. There was still a little rain when I got up at 5, but the clouds lifted and we had no more. I broke up my camp here, and rode myself into Jericho with Hanna. We came down the same road that we had come up-but-the Ghor had withered. In one little fortnight the sun had eaten up everything but the tall dry daisy stalks. It was almost impossible to believe that it had been so lovely so short a time ago. Jericho doesn't look at all nice, all burnt up and withered.

Our plans are these: the Rosens and I start off on Monday fortnight, the 23rd, and go up together to the Hauran. It will take us about a fortnight. They come home and I go straight up to Damascus, a couple of days or so, and so perhaps across to Palmyra, and the rest as before, reaching Jerusalem again about the end of May.

To her sister, Jerusalem, April 9th, 1900

DEAREST ELSA,
It is so amusing to have a letter with photographs in it. I quite understand your impressions of Florence and Venice. To this day I feel more inside Florence, myself, but I went to Venice knowing the East and knowing a good deal of Italy and for those reasons I think I found it easier to become a part of it. Also, I was there a month, nearly, you must remember. But it is very strange--'unheirnlich', some silly German said and it's not as silly as it sounds at first. It's a heavenly feeling when suddenly the thing jumps at you and you know you understand. I daresay you don't, but it doesn't matter, the feeling is there. I don't think you get it out of books a bit, though books help to strengthen it, but you certainly get it out of seeing more and more, even of quite different things. The more you see, the more everything falls into a kind of rough an ready perspective, and when you come to a new thing, you haven't so much difficulty in placing it and fitting it into the rest. I'm awfully glad you love the beginnings of things--so do I, most thoroughly, and unless one does, I don't believe one can get as much pleasure out of the ends. The early Florentines are too wonderful-- there's such a feeling for beauty even in the woodenest of them, and they are so earnest, bless them, that they carry one with them--well, very nearly up into Paradise and down into Hell! Now, rejoice with me! my travel photographs are all right. I've only seen the negatives, but they are lovely and you shall have a Monthly Cousin article, illustrated, on Petra. I was dreadfully nervous about them, for when it was so hot that the chocolate melted in the canteen, I thought the gelatine might have melted in the camera. I have gone into summer clothes, which always feels very festive, don't you think? Tell the ditty Moll, talking of clothes, that I've got a little present for her. It's a complete Bethlehem costume, with the high hat and the veil and everything. She can wear it at the next fancy dress ball if she likes. It was made for her by a dear little Bethlehem woman who comes to the Consulate to do the washing.

CHAPTER VI

1900 - DESERT EXCURSIONS FROM JERUSALEM

To H.B., Jerusalem, April 13th, 1900

To-morrow the Rosens and I are going off after lunch to Neby Musa, where we are to camp for 2 nights. I think it will be immensely amusing. Oh, Father dearest, don't I have a fine time! I'm only overcome by the sense of how much better it is than I deserve! . . .

To H.B., Jerusalem, Sunday, 22nd April, 1900

* * *but perhaps you haven't had time to read it yet! I have had the most madly rushing days since I wrote last. My acquaintance here now comprises a set of the ruggedest, wildest looking Dervishes! but in spite of their appearance they are quite human and eager to stop and have a chat when we meet in the bazaar. I went to call on my teacher in the afternoon and found his pretty wife and four charming children all expecting me. They gave me odd (and nasty) things to eat and a narghileh to smoke, which I hated, but to my relief found that with the best of good will I couldn't keep it alight, so that I didn't have much of it. Saturday was the great day here, the day of the annual miracle of the Holy Fire. Charlotte and I went off to the Russian Consulate, for we were to go to the Russian balcony to see the ceremony in the Church of the Holy Sepulchre. The church was packed, every soul having bunches of candles in his hand to receive the Holy Fire. There was a moment of breathless interest--you know the murmur of a great crowd which is waiting for something to happen; it was intoxicating, I never felt so excited in my life. Suddenly the sound of the crowd rose into a deafening roar and I saw a man running from the corner of the sepulchre with a blazing torch held high over his head. The crowd parted before him, the flying figure and the flaming light disappeared into the dark recesses of the church-he had been the first to receive the heaven-sent fire. Then followed a most extraordinary scene. On either side of the sepulchre the people fought like wild beasts to get to the fires for there were two issuing from the two windows of the sepulchre, one for the Greeks and one for the Armenians. In an instant the fire leapt to the very roof; it was as though one flame had breathed over the whole mass of men and women. Every soul was bearing a light, torch or candle or bunch of tapers--behind us in the Greek church, which is almost dark, there was nothing but a blaze of lights from floor to dome, and the people were washing their faces in the fire. How they are not burnt to death is a real miracle. . . Then came a man from the sepulchre with a whip, bursting through the crowd, and behind him the Patriarch in his mitre holding two great torches over his head and two priests holding up his arms, and they ran, like men carrying some great tidings, through the narrow Passage which had been cleared for them and which closed up behind them like water, and passed below us and up the Greek church to light the candles on the High Altar. I have a vision of looking up into the huge dome and seeing high high up, an open window with men standing in it, and their torches flaming between the bright sun and the dense smoke. Well, I can scarcely tell you about it sensibly, for as I write about it, I am overcome by the horrible thrill of it.

Monday, April 30th. DERAA. 1900. This morning we none of us had a very long way before us so I didn't get up till 6:30, which was most pleasant. When I looked out of my tent door, there was Mount Hermon gleaming all Its snows, right in front of me. It was so beautiful I had the greatest difficulty in not turning my face northwards and rushing straight for it, but the Druze mountains were standing mistily on the eastern horizon and I must try for them first. We breakfasted, as usual, in front of the Rosens' tent, with Hermon occupying the fourth place at our table, and at 8:30 we very sadly parted and I went east and they west. I have two muleteers, Muhammad and Yakoub, and Hanna. I rode for three hours over the great Hauran plain, through streets of corn. There were villages scattered about and the people looked prosperous. There were also tracts of country ploughed and lying fallow for next year's crops. They practically never manure, so that they can't grow barley two years running. The maps mark this country as belonging to the Anazeh, a great tribe which stretches to the Euphrates, but they appear to have withdrawn their black tents further eastward, probably because of the encroaching Turkish government. After three hours' ride we came to a mud and stone built village standing upon a little hill, with a mosque on top. (By the way, it was very curious yesterday returning to the Arab villages after the neat Circassian streets and courtyards.) The people were very busy cutting grass and bringing it home on the backs of camels, laden string after string of them. In these villages they use nothing but camels, with a little donkey to lead the string. There was a strong, cool west wind, but the sun was blazing hot, so hot that one had to put on a coat to keep it out. I wear a big white keffieh bound over my hat and wound round me so that only my eyes show, and they are partly hidden by a blue veil; but the chief comfort of this journey is my masculine saddle, both to me and to my horse. Never, never again will I travel on anything else; I haven't known real ease in riding till now. Till I speak the people always think I'm a man and address me as Effendim! You mustn't think I haven't got a most elegant and decent divided skirt, however, but as all men wear skirts of sorts too, that doesn't serve to distinguish me. Mount Hermon was a great joy all along the road; it looked now like a white cloud hanging in mid air. About two we entered Deraa, built of black volcanic stone it is, all bare and dusty, with a black ruined tower. The mules were behind; Hanna and I rode down to the well at the east of the town and sat there waiting for half an hour in the dust and the sun, watching the countless string of camels bringing in the corn which is ripe here. They don't reap it, but pluck it up by the roots. At last we rode back to see what the mules were doing and found that they had arrived, and that my tents were pitched on a hill by some ruined Roman baths, in sight of Hermon and the Jebel Druze. You wouldn't believe how soon the most unpromising spot changes into a comfy, home-like place as soon as one's tents are up and one's horses tethered. I rested and had tea, and then made an attempt to see an extraordinary underground town there is here, and which is supposed to belong to the times of Og the king of Bashan. But I could not get any one who knew the way, and after grubbing about under the earth for an hour, amongst the remains of hyenas' meals, I came away disgusted.

Wednesday, May 2nd. BOSRAH I am deep in intrigues ! I will tell you all from the beginning. We set off with a soldier for guide across the corn-covered plains; here and there a black village stood out from the green and the ground was covered with black porous stone. The volcanic peaks of the Jebel Druze lay ahead of us eastwards all day. At 11 I got to the first really interesting village, Jizeh, and here I saw the building of this country. You must understand that the peculiarities of it depend on the faft that there was (and is) no wood at all, and when the Romans made a great colony here in the first century, about, they built entirely with stone--the rafters are long bits of stone stretched across from arch to arch over the rooms, the doors are solid blocks of stone with charming patterns carved on them; the windows even are stone perforated with holes and carved between the holes. All this in black basalt; it is curious to see. There was one perfect house in Jizeh, small and four-square, with a cornice running round near the top On the outside, but it had no window at all. There was another, the beautiful walls of which were standing, and the stone roof, but the original door and windows were gone. It was turned into a mosque. Bosrah stood up, black and imposing, before us for miles before we arrived, a mass of columns and triumphal arches with the castle dominating the whole. I went up the square tower of the minaret and looked out over the town-columns and black square towers over every ruined church and mosque, and the big castle and the countless masses of fallen stone. I had been joined by a cheerful, handsome person, the Mamur (the Sultan's land agent) who climbed with me in and out of the churches and the fallen walls and the ruined houses. Such a spectacle of past magnificence and present squalor it would be difficult to conceive. There were inscriptions everywhere, Latin, Greek, Cufic and Arabic, built into the walls of the Fellahin houses, topsy turvy, together with the perforated slabs that were once windows, and bits of columns and capitals of pillars. After two hours of this I began to feel light-headed with fatigue and hunger. At last he took me to the top of the castle to see the view of the town and introduced me to the head of the soldiers, who produced chairs and coffee on his roof-top, and subsequently glasses of arrack and water in his room below. The Mamur is a Beyrouti and talks Arabic, but the other is a pure Turk, and our common tongue is French--most inadequate on his side. At length I induced them to let me go, and retired to my tents below the castle. I found the Mudir (Governor of the town) waiting for me, a handsome, dignified Arab, much looked down on by the whipper-snapper Turkish officials. We exchanged polite greetings and I retired to my dinner and my bed. This morning the Mamur appeared at eight to take me to a ruined village to the north. I went first to see the Mudir, whom I found sitting in his arched and shaded courtyard. He gave me coffee and negotiations began. "Where was I going?" "To Damascus." "God has made it! there is a fine road to the west with such and such places in it, very beautiful ruins." "Please God I shall see them! but I wish first to look upon Salkhad." (This is in the heart of the Druze country, where

79

they don't want me to go) "Salkhad! there is nothing there at all, and the road is very dangerous. It cannot happen." "There has come a telegram from Damascus to say the Mutussarif fears for the safety of your presence." (This isn't true) "English women are never afraid." (This also isn't true!) "I wish to look upon the ruins." And so on and so off, till finally I told him I was going nowhere to-day and he said he would come and see me later. We parted, he saying "You have honoured me!" and I "God forbid!!" and I rode off with the Mamur to a village Khutbet, crossing many beautiful Roman bridges on the Way.-There was nothing of interest there) and we turned east to Jemurrin, where there are some very beautiful ruined houses. They used no mortar, but the walls are built in a most wonderful way, the stones being often notched out and fitted into one another. We got back about 11. I lunched, After which my two Turkish friends came to call, but fortunately did not stay long. While they were with me, a Druze Sheikh was hanging round my tent, but I could not speak to him under the eyes of the officials. A Bedouin has also been to ask if I want to go east, but I prefer to put myself under the protection of the Druzes. It's awfully amusing, and my servants fully enter into the fun of the thing. If only I Could put myself into communication with the Druzes, all Would be Well. If not, I shall try starting very early to-morrow, And making a dash for them; once into their country I'll move quickly and it will be difficult for the Turks to catch me, for they are horribly afraid of the Druzes. I may fail--God is He who knows! I gather that the two Turks would put nothing In my Way to stop me out of jealousy of the Mudir, who is the local authority. But one can't never tell how much they Say is true, and I keep my own counsel as far as possible. & yet I haven't let on that the places I want really to go to are not Salkhad at all but some ruined towns further north, but they know. There are no Druzes living in Bosrah. I took a walk by myself this afternoon. Walking about Bosrah Is like trying to walk about a room on the furniture only. The game is never to get off the house-tops and one generally succeeds. After tea the Mamur came to fetch me and took me up to the military gentleman's room in the castle. They both had their eyes nicely blacked with kohl, but otherwise their toilette was incomplete. The Rais el Askar was being shaved while I sat and drank coffee. We then took a walk about the town which I lengthened out till sunset, because I wanted to miss the Mudir's visit; but he did not come, and I hope this may mean that he doesn't want to know my movements officially. I hope so. Meantime, we all feel like conspirators.

JEBEL DRUZE, Thursday, May 3rd. I've slipped through their fingers, and as yet I can scarcely believe in my good fortune. The story begins last night; you must hear it all. I dined early and as I was sitting reading in my tent, I heard the voice of the Mudir. I blew out my light and when Hanna came to tell me of his coming, I sent him a message that I was very tired and had gone to bed. I heard this conversation: Hanna "The lady has been awake since the rising of the sun--all day she has walked and ridden, now she sleeps." Mudir. "Does she march to-morrow?" Hanna. "I couldn't possibly say, Effendim." Mudir, "Tell her she must let me know before she goes anywhere." Hanna. "At your pleasure, Effendim." And he left, but not without having assured me that he meant to stop me. I hastily re-arranged my plans. He knew I was going to Salkhad and when he found that I had flown, he would send after me along that road as far as he dared; I decided, therefore, to strike for a place further north, Areh, where I saw in Murray that a powerful Druze sheikh lived. Moreover the road lay past Jemurrin, which I knew, and whither I could find my way. Providence watched over me, as you will see, in this resolution. I told my servants. Muhammad tried to dissuade me, saying that if I told the Mudir I was going to Suweidah, north of Areh, he would raise no difficulties as there were Turkish soldiers there; but I knew better, and besides, what was the good of being passed from the hands of one Turkish official to another? I afterwards found out that Muhammad, poor dear! was terrified out of his life and was trying all he knew to prevent my going. I went to bed, but what with excitement and dogs, I didn't sleep much. At two Hanna called me and I got up into the shivering night. By three I was ready, and the packing up began under the stars. It was bitter cold--one felt it after the heat of the days and in our thin summer clothes. I walked backwards and forwards and prayed Heaven that no soldier would look over the castle wall, see our lantern, and come to enquire what was happening. Fortunately the Mudir lived inside the town. The stars began to pale and that darkest moment of the night, when the east whitens, set in. At 4 we were off. It was a ticklish business finding our way in the dark round the walls to the east, I didn't know this bit of the road, having only seen the beginning and the end of it. The houses seemed to finger out towards us, and suddenly we would find ourselves heading inwards and were obliged to retrace our steps. It took us near an hour, but at last we were past the N.E. corner and I hit on the Jemurrin road. We had met only two men driving out their cows. By this time the little band of cloud in the east had turned pink; half an hour later it was gold and we saw the black ruins

81

of Jemurrin in front of us. The sun rose just as we had passed them. Now we had to find our way by my excellent map; it was not difficult for we had the Roman road for our guide, but oh! it seemed long to the first Druze village. Muhammad was trembling lest he should see either a Druze or a soldier. I feared the latter only, but much. I was borne up by the extraordinary beauty of Hermon, with the dawn touching its snows. The road rose gradually; we could see nothing ahead but the top Of the west slope of corn, and a black village where I hoped we should find Druzes, but which turned out to be only a ruin--Deir Zubier was its disappointing name. There was a man among the corn, however, with the white turban and black keffiyeh of the Druze and I greeted him thus (it is the right form) "Peace be upon you! oh, son of my uncle!" He put us into the path, which we had missed. At length we came to the top of the last slope and saw in front of us a rolling fertile, watered country, scattered over with little volcanic hills, and behind it, higher hills and the pointed peak of the Kulieb rising over all-the Little Heart, the highest of the Jebel Druze. In front of us, not half a mile away was the tiny village of Miyemir. I hurried on. At the foot of the hill on which it lay was a pool and fig trees near by. The women were filling their earthenware jars at the water, Druze women in long blue and red robes and white muslin veils drawn over their heads and round their faces, and by the water stood the most beautiful boy of 19 or 20. I dismounted to water my horse; the boy (his name is Saif ed Din, the Sword of the Faith) came up to me, took my hands and kissed me on both cheeks, rather to my surprise. Several other men and boys came up and shook hands with me; they were all more or less beautiful, and so are the women, when you can see their faces. Their eyes look enormous, blacked with kohl, men and women alike; they are dark, straight browed, straight shouldered, with an alert and gentle air of intelligence which is extraordinarily attractive. I asked Saif ed Din if he would show us the way to Areh, but he said he was busy and it was only half an hour off, so we rode on. But we hadn't gone a quarter of a mile before he repented and came running after us to offer his services, touching his heart and his forehead in token of obedience, So we went on through meadows, cornfields and vineyards in this pleasant country of little hills, and the muleteers began to sing and the kindly white turbaned people working in the vineyards stopped to salute as we passed, and I laughed for joy all the way at the thought of the Mudir and the Turks. And so about 8:30 we reached Areh. Some persons of apparent importance were standing by their house doors at the bottom of the hill, so I rode up and gave them the salaam. They took me by both hands and begged me to alight and drink coffee with them. This was just what I wanted, for I needed information. We walked hand in hand, Druze fashion, with our little fingers clasped, not our hands, to the nearest houses. As I entered they said "Are you German?" and when I told them I was English they nearly fell on my neck--you need no other introduction here. With many Mashallahs! they piled all their cushions on to a raised seat for me, brought a stool for my feet and water for me to wash my hands, and then sat round in a circle on the clean matted floor making coffee for me. The nicest of them all, Hamma Hamid, sat by me and laid his hand on my shoulder when he talked to me. I told them all my tale and how I escaped from the government and come to them, interrupted by many interjections of welcome and assurance that there was no government here (Turks, that means), and that I was safe with them and might go where I pleased. The sense of comfort and safety and confidence and of being with straight speaking people, was more delightful than I can tell you. They asked about the war and knew the names of all the towns and generals and were very sympathetic about Maurice--were cultivated, civilised human beings. The coffee finished (very good it was) I asked if I could see the Sheikh. "Sheikh!" said they, "Yahya Beg is the head of all the Druzes in the land, of course you must visit him." So we went off to the top of the little hill on which stands the Beg's veranda-hed house, Hammad and I finger in finger, and as we went he told me that the Beg had been five years in prison in Damascus and had just been let out, three weeks ago, and warned me that I must treat him with great respect. I said my Arabic and not my feelings would be at fault, and indeed I would defy any one not to treat Yahya Beg with respect. He is the most perfect type of the Grand Seigneur, a great big man (40 to 50, I suppose) very handsome and with the most exquisite manners. We walked straight into his reception room, where he was sitting on a carpet with six Or eight others eating out of a big plate. He beckoned me into the circle, and I ate too, using the thin slabs of bread for spoon and fork. The food was laban, and an excellent mixture of beans and meat. I should have liked to have eaten much more of it, but the Beg had finished and I was afraid it wouldn't be polite. The plate was removed and he piled up his cushions for me on the floor and I waited till he sat down, very politely, for he's a king, you understand, and a very good kink too, though his kingdom doesn't happen to be a large one. Then I had to tell my tale over again and the Beg shut his big eyes and bowed his handsome head from time to time, murmuring "Daghy, daghy"--it is true--as I spoke. I told him all I wanted to see

and that I didn't want to see Suweidah because of the Turks in it--
there's a telegraph too, greatest danger of all--and he was most sympathetic and arranged all my travels for me and told me to take Saif ed
Din with me and to count on his protection wherever I went. So we
drank coffee and then someone suggested I should photograph the Beg
(to my great delight) and I posed him in his verandah and very splendid he looked. So we parted, and I walked down to a delicious water
meadow where I found my horses and mules grazing and set off with
Saif ed Din and another gentleman called Aly, whose functions I don't
rightly know, but who seems an agreeable travelling companion. Saif
ed Din, walking along briskly while I rode, his embroidered skirts
neatly buttoned up over a white petticoat. On the way we met a troop
of shining ones, all in their best, carrying guns and lances. They were
going to congratulate the Beg on his safe return. They stopped to greet
me and bid me every kind of welcome--it's a pleasant change after being with people whose one idea is to tell you not to go anywhere! We
went gradually upwards towards the second ridge of hills, Saif ed Din
showing me the plain where the great battle was fought, four years
ago; they say 500 Druzes fell and 1400 Turks. At first we went
through corn and meadows, then up a stony ground with grass between
the stones. The country is thinly peopled, but there are Bedouins scattered about, who come in with their flocks for the pasturage and pay
rent in money and camels. The Druzes use them as servants. The ruined sites are countless. On the southernmost corner of the ridge,
finely situated, is the village of Habran, where I now am. My camp is
pitched by a big pond, in a meadow, with evergreen oaks growing
about in it and the black village behind. Kulieb stands over me to the
north--dear Little Heart! I did not dare to think last night that I should
ever be so near it. We got into camp at 12:30. I washed and lunched
and slept, and at four went off with Saif ed Din to explore. The village
is full of the old stone houses, more or less ruined and built up again.
The best house I saw, with its arches inside and stone rafters and cor-
bels supporting them, is now used as the Druze church--Khelweh, they
call it. The village is beautifully clean, full of fruit trees, and hay drying on the flat roofs. The women were coming down to the various
ponds on all sides with their jars for water on their heads. The Sheikh
of the village took me to his house, spread some carpets and cushions
outside and made me coffee--a lengthy process, as you begin from the
beginning, roast and pound it. I didn't mind, however, as I lay on my
cushions talking to all the pleasant friendly people and watching the
light fade on Kuleib. since dinner I have been swimming in the pond--

it's almost a lake and quite deep. The women are very shy; they don't unveil even to me, but they let me photograph them. They appear to spend most of their leisure time mending their mud roofs, but the men treat them with great respect and affection even when they are muddy up to their elbows. Isn't this all too wonderful? I'm so delighted with it! But I began my day at 2, so good night. The Sheikh of the village invited me to dinner, but I refused on the plea of fatigue. To-day when I was having my first coffee party in Areh, Hammad asked me to tell them something out of the Bible. I translated for them "Love thy neighbour as thyself," which seemed a good all round maxim, and they were much pleased with it.

Friday, 4th. After breakfast this morning, I found the good Sheikh had been waiting round my tents since dawn to take me to his house. I went first to a Mazar close to my tent--a Mazar is generally the tomb of a saint or a sheikh. It was a very well Preserved example of the old type of house building--stone doors and rafters, etc. Nusr ed Din (this is his name, by the Way, not Saif ed Din, as Hanna told me) kissed the threshold and the door posts and all the arches and the corners of the tomb Most devoutly. I then went up to the Sheikh's house and was given a most excellent breakfast--I wished I hadn't eaten before as I should have liked to have breakfasted on it. It consisted of 10 or 12 leaves of their delicious thin bread, a bowl of milk with sugar and a little brown meal in it, and a bowl of laban. Coffee began and ended the meal. It was eight before I was off. Its name was Ayun. I went there and was well rewarded, for in the first place it was a ruined Roman village, which had apparently never been re-inhabited, and one could therefore trace the exact shape and style of the houses; and in the second, there was a Mazar in it and a troop of women and children from a neighbouring village were visiting it, all dressed in their best and the boys carrying branches of briar and long stalks of flowering hemlock. Their religion is most mysterious. They seem to think all saints are equally worshipable except Muhammad, who they say is no saint at all. They have prayers every night, but especially on Friday night. They are divided into two kinds, Initiated and the Uninitiated, but the only difference between them seems to be that the Initiated don't smoke--it would seem an odd religious distinction! They have sacred books which are only read by the appointed elders. From Ayun we rode over a little rise which brought us out face to face with Salk-had. A most wonderful place. A great castle built in, and rising out of, the cone of a volcano. The outside is almost perfect, old foundations (of dateless antiquity they say; it's one of the places that is mentioned as belonging to Og, King of Bashan), then probably Roman work, and all worked over by Saracens. The Castle of Salkhad is the last outpost of the hills which here drop away into a few volcanic tells--and then the desert till the Euphrates. There are one or two inhabited villages at the foot of the hills and a few ruins on the tells, and after that no one knows anything about it and it's white on the map. But from my feet, almost, and running in a straight line south east as far as the eye could see was the track of a Roman road--and the other end of it is at Bagdad. I wished the Mudir could have seen me! The Arabs were pasturing enormous flocks of camels. I found my camp pitched and surrounded by some hundred people, amongst whom two little sons of the Sheikh--he is a nephew of Yahya Beg's, who welcomed me with the most exquisite politeness. After I had had tea and washed--by dint of shutting my tent door--I came out to find two little daughters of the Sheikh waiting for me and we Went off hand in hand to their house, with all the population of the town following me. The Sheikh was not there, but a lot of women and children received me and we sat in an open verandah till I couldn't stand the crowd any longer, when one of the boys took me into an inner room and I sat and drank coffee. The Sheikh's children, boys and girls, are most beautiful creatures, and there were some lovely girls amongst the coffee party. I asked them if they ever unveiled. They said never, not even when they are alone or when they go to bed! There came a lot of Christians to see me; there are many in this country; they come to escape from the oppression of the Turks.

Saturday, 5th. A Christian lady sent me a delicious dish for breakfast-- some flat thin bread with cream rolled up in it, slightly salted.

. . . There is a Mazar outside the town. I went in and found a charming room with a row of columns supporting the dome roof and lots of little children, sitting on the floor, to whom the schoolmaster was teaching reading. The Mazar itself Was an inner domed chamber with a tomb in it. I was off at 7:30 with Nusr ed Din. The barley was most beautiful, but alas! lots of locusts eating it. He begged me to come a little out of the route to Sehweh and honour his mother by drinking coffee with her. It was a charming village, new, but built with old materials brought from El Kafr on the usual volcanic tell. Corn, figs, vines and such a look of prosperity. I sat under a Mulberry tree with Nusr ed Din's family, nice handsome People, and ate fried eggs and bread and drank coffee and milk the whole village crowding round. When one expostulates they say: "We wish to gaze upon you, because you have honoured us." The Sheikh is Nusr ed Din's uncle. I visited him and his wife and tried to please, apparently with success.

I also bought from the wife of Nusr ed Din's cousin a Druze woman's robe, which I intend to present to Elsa. It is very pretty and extremely interesting, for the costume has died out in all places but these hills. An hour's ride up a hill side, prettily wooded with stunted oak and hawthorn in full flower, brought us to El Kafr, where I found my tent pitched. I am just at the foot of Kuleib, but, contrary to my custom, I have not gone up it, because it is Sirocco which makes one feel as if one were made of blotting paper and also spreads a thick, hot mist over the world. Directly I arrived, the Sheikh's son and some other persons of importance came to see me. They were a group of the most beautiful people you would wish to see. Their average height was about 6 ft. 1 in. and their average looks were as though you mixed up Hugo and you, Father.

At 4 I sallied out with Ali, whose native town it is. I don't need him really--it's an absurd luxury to have two guides, but when I tell him to go he replies that he is my brother and must accompany me everywhere--not without recompense, of course! I returned the call of the Sheikh's son and while I was drinking coffee the old Sheikh arrived. He had been to see Yahya Beg, and half expected me because the Beg had asked after me in the following terms: "Have you seen a queen travelling, a consuless?" They offered me a sheep, but I refused it. I hope I did right; one never knows and I'm terribly afraid of committing solecisms. I feel it would be too silly, under these exceptional conditions, not to see all I can in a country which so few people have seen. It's extraordinarily enjoyable too. They took me to see the Khelweh, which was bigger and better than any I have yet seen. It was divided into two parts by a thin black curtain, one being the Harem for the women. The straw objects are for putting the holy books on. . . There came a gentleman with a poem in Arabic which he had composed in my honour. I said I didn't know the custom in his country, but in mine, if anyone wrote a poem about me, I should certainly give him a shilling. He said "Yes, it would happen." I gave him a quarter of a medjideh, and he presented me with a copy of the poem, so we were both pleased. . . I have told them all that I am going to bring you, Father, here next year, and they are much delighted and bid you "relationship and ease."

Sunday, 6th. I sent my mules straight to Busan this morning, with my brother Ali, and rode with Hanna and Nusr ed Din S.E. to a place called Salah. We passed under the foot of Kuleib, where there were delicious pastures, after which we got out on to a very desolate country, stony and quite uncultivated. There is however, water and plenty of grass, and the Arabs pasture their camels here. It seems to extend down all this E. watershed to the desert. Last night was so warm after the Sirocco east wind, that I slept with no blankets; to-day the wind has changed to the W. and is blowing strong and cold. It brought up a lot of cloud with it; Kuleib was wrapped in mists when I got up and there has been light cloud all day and cold all day. I am now wrapped in all my cloaks; it's most odd to be cold

Monday, 7th. When you are travelling in hot countries, the primary rule is always to bring your winter clothes. I have had reason too-day to be glad that I had learnt it. I meant to camp another night in the hills, go up Kuleib and be on the spot for the Druze gathering tomorrow, but when I woke I found the west wind colder than ever and the hills wrapped in cloud. I therefore decided to come straight across the ridge and sleep at Kanawat, much to my servants' delight, for a town is a better camping place in rainy weather than a mountain side. Before I left I explored Busan, which is an interesting place because the old houses are better preserved than usual. Most Of them are not lived in: they have big dark stables beneath and roofless rooms, many windowed, above. Some staircases were standing and I saw one house with a little bath room, the stone conduit for the water being still visible. I got a photograph between the blowing mists. We were off at 8:30 across the hills. My faith! it was cold. I thought the bare Plateau on the top of the ridge would never end. I was truly glad when Nusr ed Din said "Mashallah! Kanawat!" and I saw its ruined temples standing up on a spur of the hills. It is splendidly placed; one looks all down across the great Hauran plain and I got in at 12 and it began to rain in sharp showers. We rode up to the temples, at the top of the town, and I lunched in a Mazar, a little room leading out of a temple and was very grateful to Saint Whatever his name may be, for his roof. I have pitched my camp hard by, with two temples to the right and one to the left, and there's another further down to the west. From my tent door I look out on to great Corinthian columns and a doorway most elaborately carved. The work here is much better than any I have seen to the S. and E. The rain held up more or less till 3, and I had time to explore the town-alone, for a wonder. The streets are paved with the red paving; there is a splendid house in the middle with steps leading up to it. Inside it a big court with a stair, the steps of which were built into the wall on one side and standing free on the other, but so massive that few of them have broken away. They led up to a balcony, made in the same manner, with the stones just standing out from the wall, but all broken. This ran round two sides of the court, and the windows and doors of the rooms opened on to it. On the north side of the town is a deep rocky valley with a stream at the bottom and willows growing in it. There is a tiny theatre among the willows and a charming little building which the books say was a bath, and above a ruined castle and a round tower. I am much tempted to pay a flying visit to Suweidah, but I think perhaps it would be rather silly. I should look such an idiot if I were caught by the Turks and my further progress stopped! You will be pleased to hear that the prophet job is buried at Busan. I visited his Mazar. It is evidently much honoured for the door and some broken columns in front of it were all red with blood. (N.B. This is not true! The prophet job is buried here. I don't know who the much honoured saint at Busan was.) s

Tuesday, 8th. Dawned fine and I was in high spirits. But the clouds blew over after an hour and all the hills were wrapt in the mists, and I spent the day visiting Kenath and her daughters--you know Kanawat is Kenath? I took Nusr ed Din and we rode on to the hills to a place called Sia, once a great suburb of Kanawat and now a heap of stones. From thence we rode over a charming hill through a thicket of stunted oak full of a purple flowering vetch and other pretty things, and when we came to the edge of it there was Suweidah not two miles from us. I was very keen to go to it, but Nusr ed Din shook with fear and said it was inhabited by the Osmanli, the accursed, and why did I want to go? So I turned reluctantly away. I don't see what they could do to me, but I might get some of my kind hosts into trouble.

Wednesday, 9th. Before leaving this morning I went to the house of my friend, Ali el Kady, to drink a cup of tea--these were the terms of his invitation. He was very vague about the tea making, consulting me as to whether he ought to boil the water and the milk together. I said that wasn't the way we did it usually. He gave me an extraordinary variety of foods, a pudding, some very good fried cakes dipped in honey and almonds and raisins, both of them swimming in a sweet syrup--the almonds were excellent, It is fortunate that my digestion is ostrich-like, for I seem to eat very odd things at the oddest hours. I parted here with Nusr ed Din. I am sorry to leave the little hills. Though they are so small, they have quite the air of a mountain district and also the climate. The hot, fine weather has come back today. We went on, skirting the hills, north by east. Mount Hermon was a shining glory across the plain to the west and beyond him, northwards, stretched the long line of the Anti-Lebanus, also snow-topped. The Jebel Druize end in tiny volcanoes the beginning of the purely volcanic Lejah. It all looks black and uncanny--cunheimlich.

It is an extraordinary bit of country, but I decided after taking thought, not to go through it. It is very bad for the beasts., So rocky. I must come back here from Damascus some year and explore it all thoroughly. We rode all day with the Lejah on the left and Mount Hermon in front of us, flanked by the Lebanus. The corn is ripe here and they are plucking it out by the roots, which is their form of reaping. It was excellent going and we made very good time. A little Past 4 we reached the last village at the N.E. corner of the Lejah, and here I camped, it being only a seven or eight hours' ride to Damascus. It is also the last Druze village, alas! The Sheikb and all the swells came to call and took me into the village to look round. Dear, nice people! I am sorry to leave them. I haven't left them yet, however, for the Sheikh, Ibrahim, is still in my tent door as I write. He makes well, I must say, being singularly beautiful. It is a hot, hot night.

Friday, 11th. Damascus, but a long, long day to get to it. We were off at 6, and after an hour's riding we got to Burak and passed the first Turkish garrison without remark. Then came an endless five hours; we never seemed to gain on the scenery. We went on to the River Awaj, where we watered man and beast under the poplars and willows, a charming spot. Here I rode on alone up the Black Mountains a low range of hills separating the Awaj valley from the Abana, and at the top I saw far away in a green plain and ringed round with gardens, Damascus. This is the way to arrive at a great eastern city. I journeyed along with the trains of camels carrying the merchandise of Damascus to and fro, and the Arabs on their pretty mares, and the donkey boys bringing in grass and all the varied population of an oriental road. But the way was very long. It was 4 before I got into the town. I dawdled up through the bazaars and stopped to eat ices made of milk an snow and lemonade from a china bowl half full of snow and half of lemon juice and water-nothing was ever so good. At 5 I reached my hotel, saw that my horse was properly looked after--and went off to the German Consulate to get the box of clothes I had sent from Jerusalem. There I also, to my joy, found letters from you all. A very civil Oriental secretary has been giving me advice about Palmyra, whither I shall go, if your telegram is satisfactory, on Wednesday, returning here In about a fortnight. Dearest Father! you are a perfect angel to let me do all this! I don't see that the Palmyra journey ought to be much more expensive than all the others. It seems I don't have to take more than three soldiers at the outside. I've got so many things to say to you, Mother, that I should have to make my letter as long again if I began saying them. it is at times a very odd sensation to be out in the world quite by myself, but mostly I take it as a matter of course now that I'm beginning to be used to it. I don't think I ever feel lonely, though the one person I often wish for is Papa. I think he really would enjoy it. I keep wanting to compare notes with him. You, I want to talk to, but not in a tent: with earwigs and black beetles around and muddy water to drink! I don't think you would be your true self under such conditions. . . Of course Arabic makes just all the difference. It would be small fun without.

To her family, Damascus, May 14th, 1900

Beloved Family.
To-day came your telegram which it was a great relief to receive.

I'm off to-morrow with an escort Of 3 soldiers and all promises well. I expect to be back in a fortnight. I shall meet Charlotte here, spend another couple of days, and then with her, Over the hills to Baalbec and the Cedars. Beyrout (a week or so), from whence by boat to Jerusalem.

KUREIFEH, May 15th. I got off this morning at 9. After the usual difficulties attending the first day's start, an hour's vigorous activity found us all in the saddle. You never can get off the first day, so what's the good of bothering? I have three soldiers, Ali, Musa and Muhammad. Following Lattiche's excellent advice, I have arranged to give then half a medjideh a day each, and they keep themselves which is a great simplification for us. They seem pleased, and as I believe they levy food and barley on the inhabitants as they go along, it pays them amply! We left the town by the north east gate, and rode for three hours through gardens, orchards, vineyards, the road bordered by big shady walnuts and running water everywhere. We stopped once by a little stream where a gentleman was making coffee on a mud stove and some others were smoking narghilehs under a clump of poplars. We watered our horses and drank little cups of coffee and rested for a quarter of an hour and then rode on to a khan, where I lunched under the trees by the edge of the clearest water. From here the country began to change. An hour or so of corn fields and vineyards, and barrenness and waterlessness began. All the great rivers which flow down from the snows of Hermon seem to die off when they see the bare volcanic hills of the Saffa across the plain. In the map they just end. I don't know what becomes of them. . . At the top of the pass there was a well of rain water, very good, said Ali, and I made Hanna fetch me a cupful. It was, however, full of little red animals swimming cheerfully about, and one must draw the line somewhere, so I did not partake. I heard the story of Shibly Beg's capture from Lüttiche. . . There's a cuckoo here; let me quickly write and tell the Spectator.

Wednesday, 16th. We were off at 5, Ali and I going ahead to see about camels for the desert. To Jarad at about 7:30. We went to the house of one Sheikh Ahmed and Ali went off to see about camels to carry our water for the night, while I lay on his cushions and ate white mulberries and drank coffee. They pressed a narghileh on me, but I firmly refused. Never again; it's too nasty. A boring delay now occurred, for we waited for the mules and they went straight on without calling for us and waited in Nasariyeh. The time was filled in by the good Sheikh's giving us an excellent meal, bread and olives, and dibbis and butter, laban and eggs. The worthies of the village came and talked to me, and very pleasant people they were. Lüttiche says the Arabs settled hereabout are the best people in all Syria, being descended straight from the original invaders. At 9:30 we went on again, muleless, depending on getting our corn for the night in Nasariyeh. We passed through a little village and then on through a desert plain.

At 11:50 we reached Nasariyeh--may God destroy its houses! there was no corn in them. The camels had not come up and anyhow there was nothing to be done but to send back to the village, and accordingly Hanna and Jacoub rode off together. I lunched under a white umbrella, for there was no shade. Nasariyeh is a new place, the property of the Sultan. It lies in the middle of the wide, flat valley between bare hills that we have been following all day, and beyond it there is no water for twelve hours. There was an enormous caravan of camels grazing near their piled up saddles and a little tent in which were seated some merchants from Bagdad, the owners of the caravan. They had been two months on the way, said one of them, who came down to our canal to get water; he walked as slowly as a camel and was about as communicative, answering me in a sort of dazed way as if the desert had got into his brain, and turning slowly, heavily away with his water-skin. Hanna and I, after taking counsel together, had bought eight skins and four leather bottles in Damascus, which was lucky, for we found none here. When they came to fill them, however, they found that one had a big hole in it and came despairingly to tell me. For once I was equal to the occasion. Do you remember, Father, the Greek boy we met as we went over the hills from Sparta, whose skin of oil broke? I had seen him mend it cunningly with a stone and a bit of string and I mended mine with much skill in the same way. It has held, too. The sun was so hot it burnt one through one's boots. I have gone into linen and khaki. The latter consists Of a man's ready-made coat, so big that there is room in it for every wind that blows, and most comfy; great deep pockets. The shopkeeper was very anxious that I should buy the trousers too but I haven't come to that yet. We got Oft at 1:30; having sent the three camels on, and rode till 5, When we just pitched down anywhere, in the desert it's all the same. The road was enlivened by Ali and Muhammad the soldiers, who are both extremely intelligent and who related to me many interesting tales. The soldiers are delighted that I can talk Arabic; they say it's so dull when they can't talk to the gentry. They talk Kurdish together, being of Kurdish parentage, but born in Damascus. Their Arabic is very good. Mine is really getting quite presentable. I think I talk Arabic as well as I talk German (which isn't saying much, perhaps!), but I don't understand so well. It's so confoundingly--in the Bible sense!--rich in words. This is my first night in the desert--the first of I wonder how many dozens, scores-- Heaven knows! There was a great stretch of shining salt to our right as we passed Nasariyeh, and while we rode I saw immense plaques of water on the horizon--always on the horizon, the farther we rode the further they went. We passed a ruined khan half an hour from here--I believe they occur at regular intervals all the way to Palmyra. I meant to be a couple of hours farther on, but the delays prevented it, and start under the moon to-morrow. The smooth, hard ground makes a beautiful floor to my tent. Shall I tell you my chief impression--the silence. It is like the silence of mountain tops, but more intense, for there you know the sound of wind and far away water and falling ice and stones; there is a sort of echo of sound there, you know it, Father. But here nothing.

KARYATEIN, Thursday, 17th. I got up at 1:30 this morning and dressed quickly, but the packing up always takes rather longer by night, and we were not Off till 3:45. Such a night, with a bright moon and the vague, wide desert between the low hills! It was bitter cold; I should think there must be 50 difference between the night and the day. (This is not excessive. Dr. R. has registered up to 70 degrees difference.) My hands and feet were quite numb before the sun rose and for half an hour after. By 8 it was broiling and at mid-day my off foot was burnt through my boot. It was a pretty dull ride. The chief distraction was the catching of a jerboa. He was a darling, but I let him go again and he hopped off on his long hind legs in a futile manner. I am going to travel by night from here. I have two days of from 10 to 12 hours each, waterless both of them, and it's too hard on the beasts to go in the hot sun. It's also hard on me, though I read when I travel by day which I can't do at night.

I can all but sleep in the saddle, however, which passes the time wonderfully. Yesterday I fell off. I was still sitting sideways in my saddle with a map in one hand and a parasol in the other when suddenly my horse began to trot. I hadn't even got the reins in my hands, so I jumped off, much to the amusement of my soldiers. They are a good lot, my soldiers, quite the best I have yet had. This journey is being made much more amusing than I expected. I thought it would be rather tame after my recent experiences, but I'm enjoying it very much. This sort of life grows upon one. The tedious things become less tedious and the amusing more amusing, especially as Arabic grows. It's a cloudy night, hot consequently, and I'm going to bed.

Friday, 18th. And to sleep for nine hours, as it proved. I have made for myself an enormous muslin bag in which I sleep and which protects me from all biting animals down to sand flies. I'm very proud of this contrivance, but if we have a ghazu of Arabs I shall certainly be the last to fly, and my flight will be As one Who runs a sack race.

Sunday, 20th, Palmyra, for I've got here at last, though after such a ride! We left Karyatein on Friday evening at 5:30. At dusk we found ourselves in the desert region. The night closed in very dark, the west being thick with cloud. My rolling stone which gathers moss all the way had picked up another companion, One Ahmed, white robed and perched up on the top of a camel. The Agha had provided him as a guide. I was not on the ordinary road I must tell you, having decided to make a détour to the south in Order to avoid going and coming by the same route. No tourist ever goes this way. It leads to a spring called Ain el Wu'ul, the Spring of the Deer, in the S. hills, which is half way between Karyatein and Palmyra. This we had to make as soon as possible after sunrise for the sake of the beasts for whom we had no water. It was very strange pacing on in the silent dark behind my white robed guide, the three soldiers, black shadows, beside me and the mules tinkling behind. For the first few hours there was a sort of path which one could see white and clear through the scrubby desert plants; when it left off Ahmed turned off resolutely into the broken ground under the hills, guiding himself by the stars in the clear east and by a black hill which stood out in front of us, and from which, he said, the Spring was seven hours away. The ground was very rocky; the horses' hoofs rung out on the rough slabs of stone. We went on and on and I talked first with one of my men and then with another, and at intervals I half fell asleep and woke up to see Ahmed's swaying figure like a kind of beckoning Fate leading us into a grim waterless world. Across the range of hills there is a country that no one ever travels over-right away to Nejd there is not a spring--not a well; 44 waterless days, said Ahmed. He imparted me scraps of information at intervals; he knew the name of every hill and every bare furrow--I was surprised to find that they had names, but it seems they have. This was the sort of conversation. "Where is the Lady;?" "Here, oh, Ahmed." "Oh, Lady, this is the Valley of the Wild Boar." There didn't seem anything to say about it except that it was a horrid sandy little place, so I replied that God had made it. Ahmed accepted this doubtful statement with a "God the Exalted is merciful!" on which Ali, the five times hadgi, would break in with "Praise be to God who is Great! may he prolong the life of the Sultan!" Soon after 3, Ahmed said "Oh, Lady! the light rises." I looked and the east was beginning to pale. I felt as if I had been sitting in my saddle for a lifetime an my horse felt so too. He was so hungry that he began to snatch at the camel's food as he passed--now the names of these plants I know, but only in Arabic, so I think it best not to tell. I was also hungry, and I had a light refection of chocolate and an orange, and then I got off and walked for near an hour, Ahmed walking too to keep me company. The light came quickly across the stony ground in the furrows. We mounted and rode on till 5, when the sun was behind some clouds. We were now coasting along the foot of the hills and Ahmed began to look about and wonder where the spring was. He had only been there once in his life before. The hills consisted of a long range of little stony peaks with a valley running up between them every quarter of a mile or so; in one of these valleys, high up, was the spring; the question was which. Ahmed wasn't sure, so he left me with the camel and set off running into the hills to explore. The others came up, and I made Hanna give me a bit of bread and a cup of milk which had turned into butter and whey (but awfully good) and I fell asleep almost while I was eating it. I had been riding for 12 hours. Half an hour later I heard my men say that Ahmed was beckoning to us. We had gone a good bit too far. We rode back half an hour, entered one of the valleys and climbed up it nearly to the top, and there on a tiny platform between rocks, we found the spring. it was only a very small cup, 6 or 8 feet across, More perhaps, and about 10 feet deep of water the cup being barely half full. The water was clear and cold but covered with masses of weed and full of swimming things of all kinds. The soldiers and the beasts didn't seem to mind, however, and I shut my eyes and drank too. It was past 7 when we got to it. I had something to eat, climbed up to a shady cave, and slept till 1, indifferent to the fact that my bed was thistles and my bed fellows stinging flies. If we had missed this one spring hidden in the hills we should have been hard put to it. The good Hanna gave me an excellent lunch of fried croquettes and a partridge that he had killed, and tea. I had told him to cook nothing but his conscience was too much for him, and he had made a charcoal fire between some stones, and Prepared these masterpieces, bless him! At 3 we were off again. and down into the plain, and then straight east at the foot of the hills. It had never been really hot all day, fortunately; the sun set without a cloud and it began to be very cold. We rode till 7 and then stopped for the animals to eat and for us to eat too. I put on gaiters, a second pair of knickerbockers and a covert coat under my thick winter coat, rolled myself up in a blanket and a cape and went to sleep all the men following my example, rolled up in their long cloaks. The cold and the bright moon woke me at midnight and I roused all my people (with some difficulty!) and at one we were off. Again, you see, we had to reach our water as soon as possible after the sun, so that the animals might not suffer too much from thirst. We went on and on; the dawn came and the sun rose--the evening and the morning of the second day, but I seemed to have been riding since the beginning of time. At sunrise, far away in the distance, on top of one of a group of low hills, I saw the castle of Palmyra. We were still five hours away. They were long hours. Except Petra, Palmyra is the loveliest thing I have seen in this country, but five hours away. They were long hours. The wide plain gradually narrowed and we approached the W. belt of hills, rocky, broken and waterless. It's a fine approach, the hills forming a kind of gigantic avenue with a low range at the end behind which Palmyra stands, and the flat desert, very sandy here, running up to them. My horse was very tired and I was half dazed with sleep. As we drew near Palmyra, the hills were covered with the strangest buildings, great stone towers, four stories high, some more ruined and some less, standing together in groups or bordering the road. They are the famous Palmyrene tower tombs. At length we stood on the end of the col and looked over Palmyra. I wonder if the wide world presents a more singular landscape. It is a mass of columns, ranged into long avenues, grouped into temples, lying broken on the sand or pointing one long solitary finger to Heaven. Beyond them is the immense Temple of Baal; the modern town is built inside it and its rows of columns rise out of a mass of mud roofs. And beyond all is the desert, sand and white stretches of salt and sand again, with the dust clouds whirling over it and the Euphrates five days away. It looks like the white skeleton of a town, standing knee deep in the blown sand. We rode down to one of the two springs to which it owes its existence, a plentiful supply of the clearest water, but so much impregnated with sulphur that the whole world round it smells of sulphur. The horses drank eagerly, however, and we went on down a line of columns to the second spring which is much purer, though it, too, tastes strongly of sulphur. If you let it stand for 12 hours the taste almost goes away, but it remains flat and disagreeable, and I add some lemon juice to it before I drink it. It's very clean, which is a blessing. We pitched our tents by a charming temple in the very middle of the ruins--it was 10:30 before the mules came up, we having got in at 10. I was too sleepy to be very hungry, but someone brought a big bowl of milk and I ate sour bread and dibbis, while the brother of the Sheikh talked to me and the howling wind scattered the sand over us. There seems to be always a wind here; it was such a hurricane in the afternoon and evening that I thought my tent would go, but it held firm. What with one thing and another, it was 11:30 before I could retire and wash and go to bed, but I then slept most blissfully for a couple of hours; after which I had tea and received all the worthies of the town-the Mudir is an old Turk, who talks much less Arabic than I do--and when I had sent them away happy I walked Out and down the street of columns into the Temple of the Sun--the town, I should say, for it is nearly all included within its enormous outer walls. The stone used here is a beautiful white limestone that looks like marble and weathers a golden yellow, like the Acropolis.

Monday, 21st. I got up feeling extremely brisk, and spent the whole morning exploring Palmyra. Except Petra, Palmyra is the loveliest thing I have seen in this country. but Petra is hard to beat.

Wednesday, 23rd. We were off at 5, just as the sun rose. As I rode over the hill, Palmyra looked like a beautiful ghost in the pale stormy light. I am returning by the ordinary tourist route, The old high road across the desert. Last night there arrived from the East a big caravan Of camels belonging to the Agail Arabs, who are going to sell them in Damascus. The chief man of them is one Sheikh Muhammad. I had met him yesterday in Palmyra, and he told me that 'Please God, who is great,' he meant to travel with me. He comes from Nejd, and talks the beautiful Nejd Arabic; there are one or two Bagdadis with him, and the rest of the party are the wildest, unkemptest Agail camel drivers. The interesting part of it is that the Agail are some of the Rashid's people, and I'm going to lay plans with Sheikh Muhammad as to getting into Nejd next year. I found them breakfasting on dates,- camels' milk and the bitter black coffee of the Arabs--a peerless drink. I also made a supplementary breakfast with them and then we all started off together. The reason Sheikh Muhammad wants to travel with me is that he is anxious to have the extra protection of my three soldiers--he has two of his own--fearing a raid of Arabs on his camels on the way to Karyatein. I think it's great sport; I'm not sorry to be able to do a good turn to an Agail, and he and his Bagdadis are very interesting to talk to, with their dragoman on the box and their mules following behind the crowds of tents. We had a very agreeable chat and they gave me some gingerbread biscuits, for which I blessed them and we made plans for meeting in Damascus. I wouldn't really have changed places with them, and I prefer a Sheikh from Nejd to a dragoman from Jerusalem as a travelling companion. We got to our camping place, Ain el Baida, about 11:30---It's a short march, but there's no water beyond. It was again blazing hot. I was glad to get under the shadow of my tent and to lunch and sleep. Since then I've been watching the troops of camels come slowly in, their masters carrying a club or an enormous lance 12 feet long, and all the process of drawing water from the deep well and emptying it into basins hastily scooped out in the ground for the camels to drink. The Agail have pitched a black tent not far from me, and stuck a lance into the ground beside it, and they are now making bread for their supper.

Thursday, 24th. I wish I could manage to travel on the approved lines, but the fates are against me. I had laid all my plans for coming back from Palmyra like a lady, but no! it was not to be. We got off rather late this morning5:30, it was before I left Ain El Baida, and then the mules were not ready. I started without them--a fatal step, as you will see. The Agail were off half an hour before, the good Sheikh Muhammad having put two water skins for me on his camel. Ahmed, my guide, put another two on his camel and I told the muleteers to bring the other four, so that we should have enough water for our beasts and could sleep comfortably in the desert. There is no water between Ain el Baida and Karyatein, three hours on. I caught up the Agail who had stopped to breakfast and were making coffee and baking bread--they eat nothing in the morning before they start. We stopped, too, and had some coffee and dates and my soldiers ate bread new baked--very good, I tasted it--and drank camels' milk. They eat surprisingly little, these Arabs, when they are travelling. Nothing but bread and dates and milk and coffee, and little enough of that. Often the bread runs short, and only dates and milk remain. It was a wild looking party that was gathered round the coffee pot. There's lots of negro blood in them, owing, I think, to their having negro slaves, one of whom was with them. They intermarry a great deal with these slaves and the son of a slave woman is as good as another. Sheikh Muhammad went to and fro, superintending the cooking and bringing food for us all. I had intended to go on another two hours and camp, leaving a short day's march into Karyatein next morning, but at Kast el Khair we found that the two water skins on Sheikh Muhammad's camel had leaked and were quite empty, and Hanna told me that Yacoub, the muleteer, had refused, after I left, to carry his two skins and had poured the water out on the ground. So here we were with two skins and a couple of leather bottles for ten animals and seven people. There was nothing to be done but to make a dash for Karyatein, The Agail were rather distressed at this, being still terrified for their camels, but what was I to do. They had no water, camels needing none and after I had watered my beasts at Kars el Khair, I had none--I couldn't keep my camp 24 hours waterless. we were only seven hours from

99

Karyatein., and we had done barely seven that morning, in fact our horses were so brisk that Ali, Muhammad the soldier, Ahmed the guide and I got into Karyatein in five hours-but we rode for it! I came in the last hour or two on Ahmed's camel--it's the greatest relief after you have been riding a horse for 8 or 9 hours to feel the long comfy swing and the wide soft saddle of a camel beneath you. We got in at 6 and went to the house of one Abdullah the priest. He took us into a big vineyard of his and brought me a carpet and some cushions to lie on, and bread and dibbis to eat. Hanna and my third soldier, Musa, arrived at seven, but my mules didn't get in till 9:30, having done a 16 hours' day. I rolled myself up in a rug and my carpet and made a pretence of going to sleep under the stars, but it was pretty cold and the attempt wasn't very successful. I was glad to get into my tent again and to bed about 11, feeling as if I had had enough of travelling for one day.

Friday. I found my camp pitched in Mahin near the water, and hundreds of camels drinking near it. A big company of the Hasineh Arabs had just arrived, moving from their winter quarters and their black tents were pitched not far from me. Their Sheikh, Muhammad, came to call on me, a boy of 20 or younger, handsome, rather thick lipped, solemn, his hair hanging in thick plaits from under his kef-flyeh. He carried an enormous sword, the sheath inlaid with silver. After he had gone, his sister and some other women appeared in all the trailing dirt of their dark blue cotton robes. Sheikh Muhammad is a great swell. He owns 500 tents and a house in Damascus, and Heaven knows how many horses and camels. After tea, I returned his call and sat on carpets and cushions in the big Sheikh's tent, the Hasineh making a circle round me while I drank coffee. The Sheikh's mother also appeared and was treated with great honour, Muhammad getting up and giving her his place on the carpet and his camel saddle to lean on. After a bit, one of the black browed, white robed Arabs took a rubaba, a single stringed instrument played with a bow, and sang to it long melancholy songs, monotonous, each line of the verse being set to the same time and ending with a drop of the voice which was almost a groan. The murmur of the rubaba ran through it all--weird and sad and beautiful in its way. All the silent people sat round looking at me, unkempt, half-naked, their keffiyehs drawn up over their faces, nothing alive in them but their eyes, and across the smouldering fire of camels' dung, the singer bent his head over the rubaba or looked up at me as he sent the wailing line of his song out into the dark. Sometimes one would come in to the open tent (the front is never closed) and standing on the edge of the circle, he greeted the Sheikh with a "Ya Muham-mad!" his hand lifted to his forehead and the company with "Peace be upon you," to which we all -answered "And upon you peace!" Then the circle spread out a little wider to make room for the new comer.

At last I got up and said good-bye, I hadn't gone more than a few steps than my soldiers told me I had committed a fearful solecism. They had killed a sheep for me and were preparing a dinner, of which I ought to have partaken, and further, said Ali "Muhammad is a great Sheikh and you ought to give him a present." I went back to my tent rather perturbed, what could I give? Finally, after thinking things over, I sent one of my soldiers with Ali's pistol wrapped up in a pocket handkerchief (you can give nothing to an Arab but arms or horses) and a message that I hadn't known he had meant to do me such honour and would he accept this present (net value 2 pounds). He returned answer that he was grateful, that he was doing nothing but his duty and would I honour them? So back I went with Athos, Porthos and What's-his-name, and we all sat down again on the cushions and carpets and waited. We waited till 9:30! I wasn't bored (though I was hungry!). One by one, the Arabs dropped in till the circle stretched all round the big tent; at intervals the talk went round--the politics of the desert: who had sold horses, who owned camels, who had been killed in a raid, how much the blood money would be or where the next battle. It was very difficult to understand, but I followed it more or less. Besides the bitter black coffee, we were handed cups of what they called "white coffee"--hot water, much sweetened and flavoured with al-monds. At length came a black slave with a long spouted water jar in his hand, to me first and then to all the company. We held out our hands and he poured a little water over them. And at last dinner--four or five men bearing in an enormous dish heaped up with rice and the meat of a whole sheep. This was put down on the ground before me, and I and some ten others sat round it and ate with our fingers, a black slave standing behind us with a glass which he filled with water as each guest required it. The food was pretty nasty, saltless and very tough--but it was 9:30! They eat extraordinarily little, and I was still hungry when the first circle got up to make place for the second. More hand-washing, with soap this time, and I bowed myself out and retired to biscuits and bed. It was rather an expensive dinner, but the experi-ence was worth the pistol.

Sunday, 27th. It was interesting this morning to see the Hasi-neh on the move. Sheikh Muhammad had only twenty or thirty of his five hundred tents with him, yet the camels filled the plain like the regiments of an army, each household marching with its own detach-ment of camels. . .

Monday, 28th. Sending my mules by a desert road, I took two of my musketeers and Hanna, and rode to an exquisite place called Mualula. It is interesting as being one of three places--the other two are close by--where the old Syrian language is spoken, the language in which Christ spoke. Most of the inhabitants are Christians--their Christianity dates from the first century--and there are two big con-vents, Catholic and Greek. I spent a charming hour in the Greek convent, where the monks and nuns were delightful people. The Prior is a Greek, pleasant, intelligent and cultured. . .

Tuesday, 29th. I had a very beautiful ride into Damascus. The air was sweet with the smell of figs and vines and chestnuts, the pomegranates were in the most flaming blossom, the valley was full of mills and mill races bordered by long regiments of poplars--lovely, it must be at all times, but when one comes to it out of the desert it seems a paradise. I got to Damascus soon after two and rode through the bazaars, eating apricots, with which all Damascus is full. Now he who has not eaten the apricots of Damascus has not eaten apricots. To my joy I found Charlotte here when I arrived and letters. Telegrams from you and the war news excellent. . . 95 [Sloane St.] will be splen-did I Tell my sisters I love their letters and fly to them as soon as I get my post. . . I do fervently hope to be in London about the 21st. I should like a week there because I am somewhat ragged, as you may well imagine. I wish I were as well stocked with clothes as Elsa, tell her! As for my travelling clothes-'nein!!' Oh, my dear family! I do long to be with you again. I want to have the most fearful long talk about nothing with my sisters and about things with my father and about everything taken together with my mother. By the way, did I mention that Damascus is a singularly beautiful place? I found a delightful let-ter from Caroline here. Much love to her.

[Gertrude's letters until her return to England are very vaguely dated, but it is clear that she remained with the Rosens, making more or less distant excursions with them at intervals. In one of her letters I find:

Nina and Dr. Rosen are perfectly delightful travelling Companions, we have just been agreeing that for a dwelling anything but a tent is merely a kind of makeshift.

[She writes delightful descriptions of the country she passes through, of its wealth of flowers, of its smiling Prosperity alternated with desert wilderness. She describes Baalbek and the Lebanon Range. She and her companions ride to the place where the great cedars flourish.]

To H.B., Arak el Emir, Wednesday, 30th May, 1900

From my camp. (Arabia, suggests Dr. R., in case you shouldn't know where the above important place is). Well, we left yesterday after lunch, after a tremendous getting off, such a packing and saying Goodbye! I never had my hand kissed so often! it was blazing hot, but a furious wind got up as we rode down to Jericho. It made us a little cooler but raised such storms of dust as I have never seen. We could neither speak nor hear nor see, and when we arrived in Jericho we looked as if we had just been dug up from an untimely grave. We spent a very comfortable night and got off at 5 this morning. The wind had gone and had taken with it the heat, and the flies, so that we had a most pleasant ride across the Ghor. We crossed the Jordan by the bridge and then turned away a little further northwards than my former road, getting into the foothills about 8. From thence we rode up a long winding grassy valley, very pretty, with plenty of corn in it and all the fields full of lovely pink hollyhock and flowering caper, which is like St. John's Wort, but with pink stamen and white petals. This valley led us up on to a little col from whence we looked down into the beautiful Wady Sir with Arak el Emir lying in the bottom of it. Heights thinly covered with oak behind. Now this place is very interesting. It was a palace built by an enterprising gentleman called Hyrcamus about 200 years before Christ, and Josephus describes it so accurately that one can to this day trace the lines of the moats and tanks and gardens. Of the palace little remains except a great 'pan de mur' built of enormous stones, the upper ones carved with lions. You can trace a long road leading up some cliffs about a quarter of a mile behind (from these the place takes its name, Arak meaning cliff) in which are cut a regular town of caves, one of them being an enormous stable with mangers for 100 horses cut in its walls. We got here at 1, very hungry and instantly lunched by the stream which is bordered by thickets of oleander. At our feet was a beautiful little blue lake, Yamonneh, with a great spring flowing out of the rocks high up above it and a silvery water flower growing over it in patches. It was such an odd combination to see a mountain lake looking quite civilised, and camels beside it! Both the lake and the spring dry up in summer--there is awfully little water on this side of the hills. We then rode W. up the cleft, a deep valley full of corn and scrubby trees which had expended most of their energy in growing along the ground, and got into our camp at 6. I was glad to see it for had been rather a poor thing all day and hadn't expected nearly such a long ride. The result was that I was dead beat and slept very badly and felt extremely miserable this morning.

Tuesday, 5th June. However, we had a very interesting and a short day before us. We rode up to the crest of Lebanon, and then all along the ridge to the highest point, Jebel Mahmal. It was gorgeous, the sea on one side and the desert on the other, Hermon to the south and Horns to the north. We rode to within an hour of the top and might have ridden all the way, except that it was rather a Pull for the horses. There were no rocks, only Slopes Of gravel, more or less steep, with occasional patches Of snow and a good deal of mud where the snow had just melted--We were 10,000 feet up. There is no glaciation, but they say a little snow lies the summer through. Below us lay the cedar clumps protected by an amphitheatre of hills, and the great gulf of the Wady Kadisha running down to Tripoli with villages scattered along its brink. We sleep in one of them to-morrow. There were some exciting clumpy Alpine things growing--one a very dwarf broom covered with yellow flowers, the others, pink and white and purple, I didn't know. There was also a charming tiny tulip, Purple outside, and white within, with a yellow centre, and a lovely pale blue scilla. We got down to the cedars at 1:30, after a very rough descent; and found our tents pitched under the trees. After having been told so Often that they are ragged and ugly, I am agreeably disappointed in them. There are about 400 of them. Some very fine old trees, grass and flowers growing under them--a heavenly camping ground. At this moment it is too delicious! a low Sun. birds singing in the great branches and the pale brown, snow-sprinkled hills gleaming behind. We are extremely happy.

Wednesday, 6th. There is such an exquisite village in front of me that I can scarcely take my eyes off it to write to you. Its name is Hasrun and it stands perched up on cliffs over the deep valley Kadisha' the stream being 1,000 feet or more below it, and the mountains rise above it, and the whole is a red gold at this moment, for the sun is busy sinking into the sea out Tripoli way. We spent a delicious lazy morning at the cedars, breakfasted and lunched under the big trees and photographed and drew and listened to the birds. The ground is covered with tiny cedars, but they never grow up under the shadow of their parents (how different from the Belgian Hare!) but wither off when they have reached the height of about 2 inches-which is small for a tree. There were, however, outside the big trees a few saplings which had sprung up of themselves and were growing extraordinarily slowly; they were five years old, said the guardian of the wood, but they were not more than 18 inches high. I have brought a lot of cones away with me. Shall we try and make them grow at Rounton? It would be rather fun to have a real Cedar of Lebanon--only I believe they don't grow more than about 20 feet high in 100 years, so we at least shall not be able to bask much under their shadow. We tore ourselves away at 1, the guardian of the woods making us low salaams as we rode off. He was a beautiful creature tall and straight and dressed in a red and gold cotton coat and a white felt scull cap on his curly head. There were pale periwinkles growing on the edge of the wood and a sweet-scented pink daphne inside--well, well, we were sorry to go. . .

[Gertrude brought the cones home, and distributed them to her family and friends--and so there is a real Cedar of Lebanon growing on the lawn at Rounton now. It is about 16 ft. high. Another stands on Sir George Trevelyan's lawn at Wallington.]

Thursday, 7th, We started off at 6:30 this morning. There is very lovely broom in this country with flowers much larger than ours. On the very highest col, from which the snow had just melted, the ground was blue with sweet violets. From this highest col we saw our ultimate destination far away and behind it a great hog's back called Jebel Sunnin, white with snow. Below us was a place called Akurah, to which we descended by an awful road, and lunched, it being then 1. We lay under some mulberry trees and all the population sat round on walls and looked at us--stalls full, dress circle full., upper boxes full!

We reached Aflea, which is one of the wonders of the Lebanon. The river Adonis--for this is the site of the Venus and Adonis legend--springs out of a great cave high up in the cliff and round the cave are several other springs, starting straight out of the rock and foaming down into the valley, falling in 3 or 4 cascades into deep blue pools and hurrying away under planes and walnut trees. The water is ice-cold; I have just been bathing in it. It's a very hot close night. We are going to dine outside my tent. There is such a roar of water! The moon is shining on the great cliffs and the steep steep banks of the valleys and mountain sides, up which climb black companies of cypresses, and there are little twinkling lights on all the hills. . . .

Friday, 8th There came one from the village this morning to tell me about the road. I said You will come with us, oh my uncle?" He replied, "Upon my head and eyes, oh my sister." So I returned to my breakfast well pleased. But when it came to getting on my horse, Hanna told me that the Metawaileh (he belonged to that peculiar Muhammadan sect--please note that in the plural the accent is on the second syllable--Metawaileh; this puzzled me a good deal at first!) had retired, saying that he had business, an excuse so palpably absurd that it was almost rude Of him not to find a better. Well, we had to start Off over the hills alone, leaving our guide of yesterday, Martin, to take the mules straight to Reifun. The result was we went a long 'giro,' an hour or more out Of Our road, Charlotte, Hanna and I, and then we found a charming gentleman called Masa, pasturing his flocks on the hill-side, and he mounted his mare and came with us--a Christian he was, as all the people are in this country, the Metawaileh being merely servants here. At last, after an appalling road, we came into a great amphitheatre of hills and saw the Roda Bridge, our object, in front of us, and all our path, and here Masa left us, after stoutly refusing to be tipped. We got to the natural bridge at 12 and lunched there, and very wonderful it was, with a rushing torrent flowing under it. We set off again at 1 and rode over hill and down valley by road, perfectly indescribable. I have been on worse, but never for so long. The rhododendron was flowering and masses of yellow broom, and the hills were terraced for mulberry and vine right up to the summit. After we had gone about 2 hours I saw that my horse was lame and, on examination, found that he had lost a shoe. Fortunately we were near a village, so that we could stop and put things right-all the horses needed looking to, and no wonder. I talked to the village people while we waited-charming people they all were, Maronites, most intelligent. Lots of them emigrate to America.

Saturday, 10th. And so to-day. We set off about 7-it was already fearfully hot, we walked 3 hours leading our horses, over the

devilish road. Then we got on to the carriage road to Beyrout and followed it all along the coast arriving at 3 about. We shall go to Jaffa to-
morrow, as there is a boat and I am anxious to get home. But you
know, dearest Father, I shall be back here before long! One doesn't
keep away from the East when one has got into it this far.

CHAPTER VII

1901-1902 - SWITZERLAND-SYRIA-ENGLAND

To F.B., Redcar, March 5th, 1901
[She had been on the golf links.]

It was a regular March day with a bitter wind. The pools of water on the links were as blue as the cracks in a glacier and the wind shivered them into steely lines. They reminded me of a simile in an Arab war song--"the folds of their coats of mail were like the surface of a pool which is struck by the pressing wind. . ."

[Gertrude does not seem to have left England again until the late summer of 1901 when she returns to Switzerland for some more climbing.]

To H. B., Grindelwald, Sunday, 1901

. . . I'm enjoying myself madly--I had a very interesting day on the Schreckhorn yesterday. We went up from here on Friday to the Schwartzegg Hut and lunched on the way at a little place called the Baregg. After we had been at the nice comfy hut about an hour (during which time I had seen a friendly marmot--he sat for some time on a rock looking at me and then hopped thoughtfully away) there arrived two young men Gerard and Eric Collier with their guides... We had a most cheerful evening and retired to bed on our shelf at 8:30 BY 11:30 we were off. " Schreckhorn !", said one of the Colliers' guides like an omnibus conductor, and we walked off into the night. Till 4 we climbed up a series of snow couloirs and small arêtes, a little steep cutting, but all quite easy; then we got on to the rocks and sat down to breakfast till the dawn came. It was bitter cold. We then had 2 hours of arête, one or two nice traverses at the top, but the rock very rotten and requiring great care. The Colliers did it in excellent style. At 6 we got out into sunshine on a snow saddle and saw down the other side. I was beginning to think that the Schreckhorn had an absurd reputation, but the hour of arête from the saddle to the top made me alter my opinion. It's a capital bit of rock climbing, a razor edge going quite steep down, snow on one side and rock on the other, not quite solid so that you have to take the greatest care, and with a couple of very fine bits of climbing in it. It raises the Schreckhorn into the first class among mountains, though it's rather low down in its class. After 5 minutes of wondering what was going to happen next, I found my head and my feet and had a thoroughly enjoyable hour. We got to the top at 7 and the Colliers about a quarter of an hour later. . . We parted at the Schrund, they going over Grimsel way. I took the snow couloir, which was rather imprudent; we glissaded down as hard as ever we could go and good luck was with us, for not one stone fell while we were in it. We got down to the hut at 12. Here rather a comic incident occurred. We had left provisions and wood for our return and imagine our feelings at finding 3 Frenchmen burning our wood and making our tea! I said very politely that I was delighted to entertain them, but that I hoped they would let us have some of the tea, since it was really ours. They looked rather black, but made no apologies, nor did they thank me and I went away to change my things outside. When I came back they had gone, but they left the following entry in the visitors' book, "Nous sommes montés au refuge sans guides. Vue splendide! mais quelle faim! Heureusement nous avons trouvé du thé." I completed the entry by adding, "NB. It was my tea! " and signing my name. . . . But for the moment all our thoughts are turned to the virgin arête on the Fingeraarhorn and we are going up to the Schwartzegg to have a shot at it. It has been tried unsuccessfully 3 times; I don't suppose we shall manage it, but we shall have an amusing time over it. We keep it a deadly secret!. . .

To F.B., Kurhaus, Rosenlaui, Berner Oberland, August, 1901

I am established for a day or two in this enchanting spot, having been driven out of the higher mountains by a heavy snowfall on Monday, which renders the big things impossible for a day or two. Here, there is a fascinating little rock range, which can be done in almost any weather. So I walked over on Tuesday by the Great Scheidegg and was at once received into the bosom of the Collier family. . . We spent Tuesday afternoon playing cricket, the whole family and I, with fir tree branches for stumps, and large butterfly nets handy to fish out the balls when they went into the river! Yesterday my guides and I were up at 4 and clambered up on to the Engelhorn range to take a good look round and see what was to be done. It was the greatest fun, very difficult rock work, but all quite short. We hammered in nails and slung ropes and cut rock steps-mountaineering in miniature. Finally we made a small peak that had not been done before, built a cairn on it and solemnly christened it. Then we explored some very difficult rock couloirs, found the way up another peak which we are going to do one of these days. . . I shall probably stay here till Sunday morning which will give the snow time to get right. Then I shall return to my great schemes. . .

To H.B., Rosenlaui, Sunday, 8th September, 1901

I am now going to give you a history of my adventures. Friday: we set out before dawn, the mists lying low everywhere on the sporting chance of finding fine weather above them. We walked up the hour and a half of steep wood which is the Preface to every climb here, and got to our familiar scene of action, a rocky valley called the Ochsenthal. Our problem was to find a pass over a precipitous wall of rock at he S. end of it. Now this rock wall had been pronounced impossible by the two experts of these parts and by their Guide,. We cast round and finally decided on a place where the rock wall was extremely smooth, but worn by a number of tiny water channels, sometimes as much as 3 inches deep by 4 across. These gave one a sort of handhold and foothold. just as we started up it began to snow a little. The first 100 feet were very difficult and took us three quarters of an hour. The rock was excessively smooth and in one place there was a wall some 6 feet high where Ulrich had to stand on Heinrich's shoulder. Above this 100 feet it went comparatively easily and in an hour we found ourselves in a delightful cave, so deep that it sheltered us from the rain and sleet which was not falling thick. Here we breakfasted, gloomily enough. After breakfast things looked a little better and we decided to go on though it was still raining. The next bit was easy, rocks and grass and little ridges, but presently we found ourselves on the wrong side of a smooth arête which gave us no hold at all. We came down a bit, found a possible traverse and got over with some difficulty. A rotten couloir and a still more rotten chimney and we were on the top of the pass, rh. 2000. from the cave. We were pleased with ourselves! It was a fine place; about 2000 feet of arête, less perhaps, between the great peak of the Engelhorn on the right and a lower peak on the left,

110

which is the final peak of that arête of 4 peaks we did the other day. We called this 5th peak of our arête the Klein Engelhorn. . . The whole place up there is marked with chamois paths, no one, I expect, having ever been there before to disturb them. There is, however, an old old cairn on the low slopes of the Engelhorn, made by some party who, having come over the Engelhorn, tried to traverse down the N. side and turned back at this place. We know that neither the N. nor the S. side of the Gemse Sattel, as we have called it, has ever been done. Indeed the S. side may be impossible, but I don't think it is. They say it is, but we know that the experts may be mistaken. It was snowing so hard that we decided we could do no more that day and returned by the way we had come. . . We got down the smooth rocks with the help of the extra rope. It was most unpleasant, for the water was streaming down the couloirs in torrents and we had to share the same couloirs with it. It ran down one's neck and up one's sleeves and into ones boots--disgusting! However, we got down and ran home through the woods. In the afternoon it cleared and at dawn on Saturday we were off again. We went again to the top of the Gemse Sattel; it was a beautiful day and we knew our way and did the rocks in an hour and ten minutes less than we had taken the day before. Here we breakfasted and at 10 we started off to make a small peak on the right of the saddle which we had christened beforehand the Klein Engelhorn. We clambered up an easy little buttress peak which we called the Gemse Spitz and the Klein Engelhorn came into full view. It looked most unencouraging; the lower third was composed of quite smooth perpendicular rocks, the next piece of a very steep rock wall with an ill-defined couloir or two, the top of great upright slabs with deep gaps between them. It turned out to be quite as difficult as it looked. We got down the Gemse Spitz on to a small saddle, did a very difficult traverse forwards and upwards above the smooth precipitous rocks, scrabbled up a very shallow crack and halted at the bottom of a smooth bit of overhanging rock. The great difficulty of it all was that it was so exposed, you couldn't ever get Yourself comfortably wedged into a chimney, there was nothing but the face of the rock and up you had to go. For this reason I think it more difficult than the Simili Stock. Well, here we were on an awfully steep place under the overhanging place. Ulrich tried it on Heinrich's shoulder and could not reach any hold. I then clambered up on to Heinrich, Ulrich stood on me and fingered up the rock as high as he could. It wasn't high enough. I lifted myself a little higher--always with Ulrich on me, mind!--and he began to raise himself by his hands. As his foot left my shoulder I put up a hand straightened out my arm and made a ledge for him. He called out, "I don't feel at all safe--if you move we are all killed." I said, "All right, I can stand here for a week," and up he went by my shoulder and my hand. It was just high enough. Once up he got into a fine safe place and it was now my turn. I was on Heinrich's shoulder with one foot and with one on the rock. Ulrich could not help me because he hadn't got my rope-I had been the last on the rope, you see, and I was going up second, so that all I had was the rope between the two guides to hold on to. It was pretty hard work, but I got up. Now we had to get Heinrich up. He had a rope round his waist and my rope to hold, but no shoulder, but he could not manage it. The fact was, I think, that he lost his nerve, anyhow, he declared that he could not get up, not with 50 ropes, and there was nothing to do but to leave him. He unroped himself from the big rope and we let down the thin rope to him, with which he tied himself, while we fastened our end firmly onto a rock. There we left him like a second Prometheus--fortunately there were no vultures about! So Ulrich and I went on alone and got as far as the top of the first great slab which was a sort of gendarme.

[I must add as a footnote to this letter that when Gertrude came home to us and related the thrilling ascent, still more exciting naturally in the telling, she told us that after it was over Ulrich had said to her, "If, when I was standing on your shoulders and asked you if you felt safe, you had said you did not, I should have fallen and we should all have gone over." And Gertrude replied to him, "I thought I was falling when I spoke.")

Here Ulrich shouted down to me, "It won't go!" My heart sank--after all this trouble to be turned back so near the top! Ulrich came down with a very determined face and announced that we must try lower down. We were now on the opposite side of the mountain from that on which we had left Heinrich. We went down a few feet and made a difficult traverse downwards above a precipice till we came to a chimney. I leant into the crack, Ulrich climbed on to my shoulder and got to the top. It was done! a few steps more brought us to the very top of all and we built a cairn and felt very proud. There was a difficult moment coming down the first chimney. We had left our thin rope with Heinrich, SO we had to sling the thick rope round a rock for Ulrich to come down on. But it was still wet from the day before and when we got to the bottom the rope stuck. He went up and altered its position and came down and it stuck again. Again he went up, and this time he detached it and threw it down to me and came down without a rope at all. I gave him a shoulder and a knee at the last drop. So we got back and rescued Heinrich and after a great deal of complicated rope work we reached the Gemse Sattel again after 4 hours of as hard rock climbing as it would be possible to find. Lunch was most agreeable. Our next business was to get up the Engelhorn by the arête up which I told you we saw the chamois climb the other day. This proved quite easy-it has not been done before, however-and at 3:30 we were on the top of the Engelhorn. Now we had to come down the other side--this is the way the Engelhorn is generally ascended. It's a long climb, not difficult, but needing care, especially at the end of a hard day when you have no finger tips left. . . It was 7 o'clock before we reached the foot of the rocks. It Was too late and too dark to think of getting down into the valley so we decided that we would sleep at the Engen Alp at a shepherd's hut. We wandered over Alps and Alps-- not the ghost of a hut was to be found. It was an exquisite starry night and I had almost resigned myself to the prospect of spending the whole night on the mountain side, when suddenly our lantern showed us that we had struck a path. At 9:30 we hove up against a chalet nestled in to the mountain side and looking exactly like a big rock. We went in and found a tiny light burning. in a minute 3 tall shepherds, with pipes in their Mouths, joined us and slowly questioned us as to Where we had come from and whither we were going. We said we were going no further and would like to eat and sleep. One of the shepherds lighted a blazing wood fire and cooked a quantity of milk in a 3-legged cauldron and we fell to on bowls of the most delicious bread and milk I ever tasted. The chalet was divided into two parts by a wooden partition. The first Part was Occupied by some enormous pigs, there was also a ladder in it leading up to a bit of wooden floor under the roof where the fresh hay was kept. Here I slept. The other room had a long berth all down one side of it and a shelf along another filled with rows of great milk tins. The floors were just the hard earth and there was a wooden bench on which we ate and a low seat by it. I retired to my hayloft, wrapped myself in a new blanket and covered myself over with hay and slept soundly for 8 hours when my neighbours, the pigs, woke me by grunting loudly to be let out. The shepherd gave us an excellent breakfast of milk and coffee--we had our own bread and jam. It was so enchanting waking up in that funny little place high up on the mountain side with noisy torrents all round it, The goats came flocking home before we left: they had spent a night out on the mountains, having been caught somewhere in the dark and they bleated loud complaints as they crowded round the hut, licking the shepherd's hand. It was about 7:30 before Ulrich and I set off down the exquisite Urbach Thal; Heinrich had gone on before. We walked down for a couple of hours discussing ways up the Engelhorn and the Communal System! then we turned into the valley of the Aar and dropped down on to Innertkirchen in the green plain below. This is Ulrich's native place. We went to his home and found his old father, a nice old man Of 70, who welcomed us with effusion. It was an enchanting house, an old wooden chalet dated 1749, with low rooms and long rows of windows, with muslin curtains, and geranium pots in them. All spotlessly clean. They gave me a large--well, lunch, it was 11:30, of eggs and tea and bread and cheese and bilberry jam, after which Ulrich and I walked up through the woods here and arrived at 2 in the afternoon. I don't think I have ever had two more delightful alpine days. To-morrow I go over to Grindelwald; the weather looks quite settled. Wednesday up to the hut, from whence on Wednesday night we try the Finsteraarhorn arête. If we do it we sleep at another hut On Thursday night, and at the Grimsel on Friday and Saturday. Sunday night we bivouac under the Lauteraarhorn and Monday try the arête to the Schreckhorn. Probably I should leave for England on Tuesday. . .

I am very sorry to leave this nice place. What do you think is our fortnight's bag? Two old peaks. Seven new peaks--one of them first-class and four others very good. One new saddle, also first-class.

The traverse of the Engelhorn, also new and first-class.

That's not bad going, is it! . . .

To F. B., Grindelwald, September 12th, 1901

Our tale is a sad one. We went up to a hut for the new Finsteraarhorn arête yesterday morning, in very shaky weather. it shook down, rained all the afternoon, and at 6 a.m. this morning began to snow. By 8, when we left, there were 3 inches of new snow, so we raced back to Grindelwald. . . It is very provoking, when one feels one might do really good climbs! We hope to do a new Engelhorn peak, and we have not yet quite abandoned all hopes of one of the high arêtes. I would like to have one of them to my name! It is a silly ambition, isn't it! Still one does like to have the credit one really deserves.

To F. B., November 27, 1901

Of course I will take the Mothers' Meeting on Wednesday. I will find out about sending out the invitations. Will you tell me what you want read--any of the Health Book?--and if so, where is it? I can look out some story. . .

To F.B., Red Barns, Thursday, December 18, 1901

All has gone off quite well. We had over 200 people. Your telegram arrived and I read it out to them in the middle of my speech! The magic lantern slides are lovely, it was most exciting seeing them. . .

Tell Father I've written to Maurice by every mail all about him! He mustn't get to think there's nothing else to write about! Hugo says Prout's an old fogey--that's what he says! I say Hugo is a great darling!

To F.B., Red Barns, December 29, 1901

I have spent the afternoon in Clarence and Middlesbrough and made all the arrangements for the teas. My slides are announced, so all is well. . .

Hugo sends seasonable wishes. He has retired into Cicero.

[1902. Gertrude, her father and Hugo indefatigably start for another sea voyage after the new year, leaving Liverpool January 14 and going by sea to Malta, then to Sicily and up through Italy. Hugo and his father returned and Gertrude made her way into Asia Minor.

Her letters, full of interesting descriptions, are too long to quote, from Malcajik, Smyrna, Magnesia, Burnabat and finally from Smyrna by sea to Haifa.]

[At Malcajik--"Mr. Van Lennep and his family full of help and hospitality." By Smyrna to Pergamos.]

"You should see me shopping in Smyrna, quite like a native only I ought to have more flashing eyes. At Pergamos I went all over the Acropolis and examined temples and palaces and theatres and the great altar of which the friezes are at Berlin."

[Magnesia and Sardis.] "I was fortunate enough to get a secondhand copy of Herodotus in French."

[Sardis] "I was delighted that I had Herodotus so fresh in my mind. . ."

"It is a madly interesting place."

"Some day I shall come and travel here with tents but then I will speak Turkish, which will not be difficult and I will take only a couple of Turkish servants with me."

[To Butnabat, where she is warmly welcomed by Mr. Whittall and his family.

To Ephesus. She then goes on an Austrian boat from Smyrna to Haifa.

She finds a temporary abode at Mount Carmel.]

"I am now become one of the prophets-at least I make merry in their room so to speak--and it's a very nice room, I may add, and I am sitting writing at my own writing table with everything genteel about me."

To F. B., Mount Carmel, 26th March, 1902

There must be something in the air of Mount Carmel favourable to mental derangement of a special kind--at any rate if you want to commence prophet you take a little house in Haifa, you could scarcely begin in any other way. I have already made the acquaintance of one or two for this afternoon I went down to Haifa--I live on the top of the hill--Haifa is half an hour away--to seek out a teacher. Presently I also approached the window and there was the prophet in his shirt with bare arms working at his trade which I take to be that of a carpenter. . . I distinctly like prophets--Herr Wasserzug is a charming man, most intelligent about Semitic languages. He sent me off to one Abu Nimrud, a native, 'comme de droit,' of Nineveh, who, he said, was the best man he could recommend. On my way I called on Mr. Monahan. offered me books and advice and coffee. . . I took a Persian history of the Babis from him and went off hunting Nimrud all over the town. At last I found him in his shop in the bazaar--he agreed to come up and give me my first lesson to-day, but need I say he hasn't come. The next thing was to get a Persian. My old friend Abbas Effendi. . . I heard that the son-in-law of Abbas, Hussein Effendi, lived here, and I determined to apply to him. Accordingly I made my way to his shop--a sort of little general store like the shop in a small country town--and in this unlikely setting I found a company of grave Persians, sitting round on the biscuit tins and the bags of grain, and Hussein himself leaning over the counter. The upshot of it is that I hope I shall end by getting a Persian to come and talk to me. A horse was the next necessity and horse dealers my next acquaintances--I see one this instant upon the road bringing me up a horse to try. I am excellently lodged in two rooms with a balcony from whence I see all across the bay and Acre at the end of a long stretch of sand, and the Plain of Esdraelon with Kishor, running through it and far away Hermon white with snow,

Later. But for all that I find I shall have to déménager. Abu Nimrud came up this morning and gave me a long lesson but he declared that it was too far for him to come and that he could only get me a Persian on condition that I would come down into the town, so I rode down this afternoon and inspected the two hotels and fixed on one standing in a charming garden where I could get 2 big comfortable rooms; it has the further advantage of being kept by Syrians so that I shall hear and speak nothing but Arabic. . . Hussein Effendi's brother-in-law is going to teach me Persian.

To H.B., Mount Carmel, 30th March, 1902

* * * But mind, if ever you think I'm unbearable, just say it straight out and mention what you can't abide and I'll do my best to mend it. To return to the East. I'm having a comic time, but most amusing. I had a delightful afternoon by myself on Friday and rode out

from 1 to 6 on the worst horse in the world. I rode and rode all along the top of Carmel, and though the prophet declares that if you even flee there the Almighty would certainly find you, I think myself that he is mistaken. I can't find anything, not even a village, of which I am told there are some. But I rode over ridge after ridge of rolling hill, and round the top of valley after valley, rocky slopes covered with wild flowers running steeply down into waterless hollows and the whole mountain was heavy with the scent of gorse and the aromatic herbs that my horse crushed through from time to time to avoid an unusually slippery bit of rock in the path. The whole afternoon I saw only 2 houses and 4 people, shepherds with flocks of lop-eared goats-- ridiculous ears they have, 10 inches long I should say, an absurd waste of skin. . . Sometimes I walked and drove my horse in front of me, and by this means I found out that he really could gallop, for he galloped away from me and I concluded not to let him go loose any more. I gathered 2 scarlet tulips, the lovely little tulips with the curling leaf; it is the same as the one of which Hafiz says thus, doubting the promises of Fate it carries always a Wine cup through the wilderness. . . I am much entertained to find that I am a Person in this country--they all think I was a Person! And one of the first questions everyone seems to ask everyone else is, "Have you ever met Miss Gertrude Bell?" Renown is not very difficult to acquire here.

Monday, 31. To-day I came down into Haifa early with Mr. M. and established myself in my new hotel. I had an Arabic lesson and interviewed a Persian who is to come and teach me every evening after dinner. My hotel is most comfortable, kept by Syrians and I hear and speak nothing but Arabic which is really ideal. I have a large sitting-room--you should see how nice it looks with all my books and things and great pots of mimosa and jasmine and wild flowers.

To H.B., Haifa, April 7th, 1902

This afternoon I paid a long call on the mother and sisters of my Persian--their house is my house, you understand, and I am to go and talk Persian whenever I like. This is my day: I get up at 7, at 8 Abu Nimrud comes and teaches me Arabic--till 10. I go on working till 12, when I lunch. Then I write for my Persian till 1:30, or so, when I ride or walk out. Come in at 5, and work till 7, when I dine. At 7:30 my Persian comes and stays till 10, and at 10:30 I go to bed. You see I have not much leisure time! And the whole day long I talk Arabic.

To F.B., Haifa, April 2, 1902

I love my two sheikhs. It's perfectly delightful getting hold Of Persian again, the delicious language! But as for Arabic I am soaked and soddened by it and how anyone can wish to have anything to do with a tongue so difficult when they might be living at ease, I can't imagine. I never stop talking in this hotel and I think I get a little worse daily . . ..

The birds fly into my room and nest in the chandelier!

To F. B., Tuesday, 22nd April, 1902

On Monday I went to lunch with my Persians. A young gentleman was invited to meet me-he's a carpenter-and he and I and Mirza Abdullah lunched together solemnly while the wife and sisters waited on us. We had a very good lunch, rice and pillau and sugared dates and kabobs. It was all spread on the table at once and we helped ourselves with our forks at will, dilating the while on the absurdity of the European custom of serving one dish after another so that you never knew what you were going to have, also of whipping away your plate every moment and giving you another! The conversation was carried on in Persian which I speak worse than anyone was ever known to do. I told you that there were 2 American Professors of Divinity in the Hotel? One whose name I don't know is a particularly attractive man, oldish, very intelligent and with a sweet goodness of face and I am sure of character which is very loveable. I was telling Mirza Abdullah about him last night and he said he would like to see him and ask him a question. So I went out and fetched my old American, telling him the sort of person he had to deal with, and Mirza Abdullah (I being interpreter) asked him what he considered were the proofs of Christ's being God. The American answered in the most charming manner, but of course could give no proofs except a personal conviction. Mirza A. said, "He speaks as a lover, but I want the answer of the learned." I felt as I interpreted between them how much the philosophic inquiring eastern mind differed from ours. The value my professor attached to the vivifying qualities of Christ's teaching was certainly lost on the Oriental, and on the other hand Abdullah's dialectics were incomprehensible to the western--at least the starting point was incomprehensible. They talked for about an hour and at the end Abdul-

119

lah was quite as much at a loss as before to understand why the Professor accepted one prophet and rejected the others and I'm bound to say I quite sympathised with him. He said to me after the Professor had gone: "You must reject all or accept all, but he chooses and can give no reason. He believes what his fathers have taught him." It was a very curious evening. The professor was a perfect angel all the time. One could not help being immensely impressed with the quality of his faith.

[She returns to England at the end of May. She has a pleasant month at home, and early in July we find her in Switzerland again.]

To F.B., Rosenlaui, July 8th, 1902

I had a most luxurious journey. My 2 guides met me, I dined and made plans and went to bed and slept for 11 hours! . . . We got up to this enchanting place in time for lunch and I was received with rapture by my friend the innkeeper--oh! I must tell you that the guard on the train of the Brünnig line asked me if I were Miss Bell who had climbed the Engelhorn last year. This is fame. There is another climbing woman here--Frl. Kuntze--very good indeed she is, but not very Well Pleased to see me as I deprive her of Ulrich Fuhrer with whom she has been climbing. She has got a German with her, a distinguished climber from Berne, and I sat and talked to them this afternoon when they came in from a little expedition. They have done several things in the Engelhorn but the best thing hereabouts remains to be done and Ulrich and I are going to have an inspection walk the day after tomorrow. Tomorrow we propose to do a new rock which Will probably give us an amusing climb and which will, I hope, be short. . . The flowers are entrancing--piles of things of which I remember the pictures in my alpine book and forget the names. I wish you would send me that book--Alpine Flora, I think it's called--on one of the shelves above MY writing table at Redcar.

To F. B., Rosenlaui, July 11th, 1902

We had a delightful day on Tuesday, did a charming little rock, up one way and down another, both ways new though the point had been made from a third side by some guides. especially the descent which was quite difficult. We got ourselves landed on to the top of some very smooth rocks, down which we slid on an extra rope with the exciting uncertainty as to whether the rope would reach far enough and as to what would lie below. But the rope was exactly long enough to a foot and led us down to some broken cracks and couloirs by which we descended on to the grass slopes . . .. Between the two Wellhorns there is an arête of rocks which has never been attempted--it is indeed one of the 4 impossibles of the Oberland--and we intend to do it and we think we can. . . Accordingly we got up to-day at midnight, a beautifully starry night, and set off with quantities of spare rope up the slopes to the foot of the Vorder Wellhorn. We hadn't been gone more than half-an-hour before a storm began coming up from all sides at once and we called a halt to see how matters were going to turn out. We lay shivering under a rock for some time while the clouds blew up faster and faster, and lightning began and the thunder and the first drops of rain reached us. Fortunately there were some deserted chalets just below us so I sent Ulrich to see if we could take shelter in them. He came back looking rather dubious and I asked whether there was any one in them. "Dere is pig," he replied. Still pig were better than rain, so we hurried down and fortunately found a hut with nothing in it but some clean hay on which we established ourselves luxuriously. It was half-past 2 or 3 by this time and we lay and waited to see what the dawn would bring, Ulrich relating alpine adventures to pass the time. But the dawn brought more rain and more thunder and we gave up hope, and ran down to the inn where we arrived about 5. I went to bed promptly and slept till 12. And if it clears we are going to begin the same game again to-night.

To F. B., Vorder Wellhorn, July 14th, 1902

We have done the first of the impossibles , the Wellhorn arête, and are much elated. We started at 5 yesterday and ran up the Vorder Wellhorn as fast as ever we could, making only a 5 minutes halt while we roped. The arête looked awful from the top of the Vorder Wellhorn. There was a most discouraging bit of smooth rock in it and above that an overhang round which we could see no way. My heart sank--I thought we should never do it. However we set off and when we came nearer we found that these two places were not half as bad as they looked and after 4 hours of very fine arête climbing we lunched at the top of the overhang in the best of spirits. But the worst was to come--a long knife edge of rock so rotten that it fell away in masses as we went along, horrid precipices beneath us so that the greatest care was needed at every step. And it ended in a sharp gap on the further side of which 2 short but extremely exposed chimneys led up to the final slopes. We took nearly an hour over these, I standing most of the time, shivering with cold, at the bottom Of the lowest, while my two guides worked on the tiny ledge above me which was too narrow for us all 3. Finally Ulrich called out "I have hold of it!" and Heinrich and I scrabbled after him with the aid of an iron nail driven in in the worst place and of a double rope. We ended our day by crossing the Rosenlaui glacier under the séracs, a thing we had no business to do for they hung over us in the most threatening manner, but it Saved us at least 2 hours and we got through without their falling On us. I think if the weather holds, I shall go over to the Grimsel, for the second impossible is now on our minds and we want to set about it as soon as we can.

To H. B., Kurhaus Rosenlaui, Berner Oberland July 20, 1902

I came over here yesterday morning, walking over the Scheidegg, and a most delicious hot day. Yseult Grant Duff met me on the top of the pass and walked down with me. . . This morning I started out at 5:30 to--well, Ulrich Calls it examining the movement of rocks, it means that you go up and see if a stone falls On You and if it doesn't you know you can go UP that way. It's a new ascent of the Wetterhorn--a mad Scheme I'm inclined to think, but still we'll see how it goes. We went up the steep slopes and up rocks and under a glacier fall, where I examined the movement of a stone on my knee-- fortunately a small one, but it hurt for it fell from a long way up--and then we hastily turned back. However, on examination we thought we could get up another way and we intend to try it seriously. . .

To H. B., Meiplingen, Sunday, August 3, 1902

For once I must begin by acknowledging that Donmul's gloomy forebodings came very near to being realised, and I am now feeling some satisfaction in the thought that my bones are not lying scattered on the Alpine mountains cold. Don't be alarmed, however, they are all quite safe and sound in the Grimsel and if it were not for a little touch of frostbite in the feet I should be merrily on my way to fresh adventures. . . On Monday it rained and we could do nothing. On Tuesday we set out at 1 a.m. and made for a crack high up on the Wetterhorn rocks which we had observed through glasses. We got up to it after about 3 hours' climbing only to find to our sorrow that the séracs were tumbling continually down it from all directions. We concluded that it was far too risky--indeed it would have been madness to attempt it for we could see from the broken ice on the rocks that the great blocks were thrown from side to side as they fell and swept the whole passage and it was the only place where the cliffs could be climbed at all; we turned sadly back. I record this piece of prudence with pleasure. . . Next day I came up here. It was a most delicious morning. I left Meiringen at 6 and shared my coach with a dear little American couple who were making a walking tour in Switzerland-by coach mostly, I gathered. There was also a pleasant Englishman called Campbell who was coming up with a rope and an ice axe, a member of the A.C. as I found on talking to him at the halting places. He appears later in the story. Well, we lunched here and set off in the afternoon to the Pavillon Dolfuss, of ill omen, where we arrived at 6. But anything more inviting than the little hut that evening it would be difficult to imagine. It was perfect weather, the most lovely evening I have ever seen in the Alps. Until the sun set at 7 behind the Schreckhorn I sat out of doors without a coat and walked over the tiny alp botanizing while My guides cooked the soup Every sort of Alpine plant grows on the cultivated alp; I found even very sweet pale violets under the big stones. I had it all to myself; I was the lord of all mountains that night and rejoiced exceedingly in my great possessions. The matter we had in hand was the ascent of the face of the Finsteraarhorn: it is a well-known problem and the opinions of the learned are divided as to its solution. Dr. Wilson looked at it this year and decided against it. We have looked at it for 2 years and decided for it and other authorities agree with us in what I still think is a right opinion. The mountain on the side facing the Schreckhorn comes down in a series of arches radiating from the extremely pointed top to the Finsteraar glacier. . . The arête, the one which has always been discussed, rises from the glacier in a great series of gendarmes and towers, set at such an angle on the steep face of the mountain that you wonder how they can stand at all and indeed they can scarcely be said to stand, for the great points of them are continually overbalancing and tumbling down into the couloirs between the arêtes and they are all capped with loosely poised stones, jutting out and hanging over and ready to fall at any moment. But as long as you keep pretty near to the top of the arête you are Safe from them because they fall into the couloirs on either side, the difficulty is to get on to the arête because you have to cross a couloir down which the stones fall, not to speak Of avalanches; the game was beginning even when we (crossed it an hour after dawn. We left the hut at 1:35 a.m. Thursday. Crossed the séracs just at dawn and by 6 found ourselves comfortably established on the arête, beyond the reach of the stones which the mountain had fired at us (fortunately with rather a bad aim) for the first half-hour on the rock. we breakfasted then followed a difficult and dangerous climb. It was difficult because the rocks were exceedingly steep, every now and then we had to creep up and Out of the common hard chimney--one in particular about midday I remember, because we subsequently had the very deuce of a time coming down it, or round the face of a tower or cut our way across an ice couloir between two gendarmes and it was dangerous because the whole rock was so treacherous. I found this out very early in the morning by putting my hand into the crack of a rock which looked as if it went into the very foundations of things. About 2 feet square of rock tumbled out upon me and knocked me a little way down the hill till I managed to part company with it on a tiny ledge. I got back on to my feet without being pulled up by the rope, which was as well for a little later I happened to pass the rope through my hands and found that it had been cut half through about a yard from my waist when the rock had fallen on it. This was rather a nuisance as it shortened a rope we often wanted long to allow of our going up difficult chimneys in turn. So on and on we went up the arête and the towers multiplied like rabbits above and grew steeper and steeper and about 2 o'clock I looked round and saw great black clouds rolling up from the west. But by this time looking up we also saw the topmost tower of the arête far above us still, and the summit of the mountain further still and though we could not yet see what the top of the arête was like we were cheered and pushed on steadily for another hour while the weather signs got worse and worse. At 3 just as the first snow flakes began to fall, we got into full view of the last two gendarmes and the first one was quite impossible. The ridge had been growing narrow, its sides steeper as we mounted, so that we had been obliged for some time to stick quite to the backbone of it; then it threw itself up into a great tower leaning over to the right and made of slabs set like slates on the top with a steep drop of some 20 feet below them on to the Col. We were then 1000 feet below the summit I should guess, perhaps rather less, anyway we could see our way up, not easy but possible, above this tower and once on the top could get down the other side in any weather. It had to be tried: we sat down to eat a few mouthfuls the snow falling fast driven by a strong wind, and a thick mist marching up the valley below, over the Finsteraar joch, then we crept along the knife edge of a col, fastened a rope firmly round a rock and let Ulrich down on to a ledge below the overhang of the tower. He tried it for a few moments and then gave it up. The ledge was very narrow, sloped outwards and was quite rotten. Anything was better than that. So we tried the left side of the tower: there was a very steep iced couloir running up at the foot of the rock on that side for about 50 feet, after which all would be well. Again we let ourselves down on the extra rope to the foot of the tower, again to find that this way also was impossible. A month later in the year I believe this couloir would go; after a warm August there would be no ice in it, and though it is very steep the rocks so far as one could see under the ice, looked climbable. But even with the alternative before us of the descent down the terrible arete, we decided to turn back; already the snow was blowing down the couloir in a small avalanche, small but blinding, and the wind rushed down upon us carrying the mists with it. If it had been fine weather we should have tried down the arête a little and then a traverse so as to get at the upper rocks by another road. I am not sure that it could be done but we should have tried anything--but by the time we had been going down for half-an-hour we could see nothing of the mountain side to the right or to the left except an occasional glimpse as one cloud rolled off and another rolled over. The snow fell fast and covered the rocks with incredible speed. Difficult as they had been to go up, you may imagine what they were like going down when we could no longer so much as see them. There was One corner in particular where we had to get round the face of a tower. We came round the corner, down a very steep chimney, got on to a sloping out rock ledge with an inch of new snow on it; there was a crack in which you could stand and with one hand hold in the rock face, from whence you had to drop down about 8 feet on to steep snow. We fixed the extra rope and tumbled down one after the Other On to the snow; it was really more or less safe because one had the fixed rope to hold on to, but it felt awful: I shall remember every inch of that rock face for the rest of my life. It was now near 6. Our one idea was to get down to the chimney--the mid-day chimney which was so very difficult--so as to do it while there was still only a little snow on it. We toiled on till 8, by which time a furious thunderstorm was raging. We were standing by a great upright on the top of a tower when suddenly it gave a crack and a blue flame sat On it for a second just like the one we saw when we were driving, you remember, only nearer. My ice axe jumped in my hand and I thought the steel felt hot through my woollen glove--was that possible? I didn't take my glove off to see! Before we knew where we were the rock flashed again--it was a great sticking out stone and I expect it attracted the lightning, but we didn't stop to consider this theory but tumbled down a chimney as hard as ever we could, one on top of the other, buried our ice axe heads in some shale at the bottom of it and hurriedly retreated from them. It's not nice to carry a private lightning conductor in your hand in the thick of a thunderstorm, It was clear we could go no further that night, the question was to find the best lodging while there was still light enough to see. We hit upon a tiny crack sheltered from the wind, even the snow did not fall into it. There was just room for me to sit in the extreme back of it on a very pointed bit of rock; by doubling up I could even get my head into it. Ulrich sat on my feet to keep them warm and Heinrich just below him. They each of them put their feet into a knapsack which is the golden rule of bivouac. The other golden rule is to take no brandy because you feel the reaction more after. I knew this and insisted on it. It was really not so bad; we shivered all night but our hands and feet were warm and climbers are like Pobbles in the matter of toes. I went to sleep quite often and was wakened up every hour or so by the intolerable discomfort of my position, which I then changed by an inch or two into another which was bearable for an hour more. At first the thunderstorm made things rather exciting. The claps followed the flashes so close that there seemed no interval between them. We tied ourselves firmly on to the rock above lest as Ulrich philosophically said one of us should be struck and fall out. The rocks were all crackling round us and fizzing like damp wood which is just beginning to burn--have you ever heard that? It's a curious exciting sound rather exhilarating--and as there was no further precaution possible I enjoyed the extraordinary magnificence of the storm with a free mind: it was worth seeing. Gradually the night cleared and became beautifully starry. Between 2 and 3 the moon rose, a tiny crescent, and we spoke of the joy it would be when the sun rose full on to us and stopped our shivering. But the sun never rose at all--at least for all practical purposes. The day came wrapped in a blinding mist and heralded by a cutting, snow-laden wind--this day was Friday; we never saw the sun in it. It must have snowed a good deal during the thunderstorm for when we stepped out of our crack in the first grey light about 4 (too stiff to bear it a moment longer) everything was deep in it. I can scarcely describe to you what that day was like. We were from 4 a.m. to 8 p.m. on the arête; during that time we ate for a minute or two 3 times and my fare I know was 5 ginger bread biscuits, 2 sticks of chocolate, a slice of bread, a scrap of cheese and a handful of raisins. We had nothing to drink but about two tablespoonfuls of brandy in the bottom of my flask and a mouthful of wine in the guides' wine skin, but it was too cold to feel thirsty. There was scarcely a yard which we could come down without the extra rope; you can imagine the labour of finding a rock at every 50 feet round which to sling it, then of pulling it down behind us and slinging it We had our bit of good luck-it never caught all day. But both the ropes were thoroughly iced and terribly difficult to manage, and the weather was appalling. It snowed all day sometimes softly as decent snow should fall, sometimes driven by a furious bitter wind which enveloped us not only in the falling snow, but lifted all the light powdery snow from the rocks and sent it whirling down the precipices and into the couloirs and on to us indifferently. It was rather interesting to see the way a mountain behaves in a snowstorm and how avalanches are born and all the wonderful and terrible things that happen in high places. The couloirs were all running with snow rivers--we had to cross one and a nasty uncomfortable process it was. As soon as you cut a step it was filled up before you could put your foot into it. But I think that when things are as bad as ever they can be you cease to mind them much. You set your teeth and battle with the fates. we meant to get down whatever happened and it was such an exciting business that we had no time to think of the discomfort. I know I never thought of the danger except once and then quite calmly. I'll tell you about that presently The first thing we had to tackle was the chimney. We had to fix our rope in it twice, the second time round a very unsafe nail. I stood in this place holding Heinrich, there was an overhang. He climbed a bit of the way and then fell on to soft snow and spun down the couloir till my rope brought him up with a jerk. Then he got up on to a bit of rock on the left about half as high as the overhang. Ulrich came down to me and I repeated Heinrich's process exactly, the iced extra rope slipping through my hands like butter. Then came Ulrich. He was held by Heinrich and me standing a good deal to the left but only half as high up as he. He climbed down to the place we had both fallen from asking our advice at every step, then he called out " Heinrich, Heinrich, ich bin verloren," and tumbled off just as we had done and we held him up in the couloir, more dead than alive with anxiety. We gave him some of our precious brandy on a piece of sugar and he soon recovered and went on as boldly as before. We thought the worst was over but there was a more dangerous place to come. It was a place that had been pretty difficult to go up, a steep but short slope of iced rock by which we had turned the base of a tower. The slope was now covered with about 4 inches of avalanche snow and the rocks were quite hidden. It was on the edge of a big couloir down which raced a snow river. We managed badly somehow; at any rate, Ulrich and I found ourselves on a place where there was not room for us both to stand, at the end of the extra rope. He was very Insecure and could not hold me, Heinrich was below on the edge of the couloir, also very insecure. And here I had to refix the extra rope on a rock a little below me so that it was practically no good to me. But it was the only possible plan. The rock was too difficult for me, the stretches too big, I couldn't reach them: I handed my axe down to Heinrich and told him I could do nothing but fall, but he couldn't, or at any rate, didn't secure himself and in a second we were both tumbling head over heels down the couloir, which was, you understand, as steep as snow could lie. How Ulrich held us I don't know. He said himself he would not have believed it possible but hearing me say I was going to fall he had stuck the pointed end of the ice axe into a crack above and on this alone we all three held. I got on to my feet in the snow directly I came to the end of my leash of rope and held Heinrich and caught his ice axe and mine and we slowly cut ourselves back up the couloir to the foot of the rock. But it was a near thing and I felt rather ashamed of my part in it. This was the time when I thought it on the cards we should not get down alive. Rather a comforting example, however, of how little can hold a party up. About 2 in the afternoon we all began to feel tired. I had a pain through my shoulder and down my back which was due, I think, to nothing but the exertion of rock climbing and the nervous fatigue of shivering--for we never stopped shivering all day, it was impossible to control one's tired muscles in that bitter cold. And so we went on for 6 hours more of which only the last hour was easy and at 8 found ourselves at the top of the Finsteraar glacier and in the dark, with a good guess and good luck, happened on the right place in the Bergschrund and let ourselves down over it. It was now quite dark, the snow had turned into Pouring rain, and we sank 6 inches into the soft glacier with every step. Moreover we were wet through: we had to cross several big crevasses and get down the sérac before we could reach the Unteraar glacier and safety. For we had felt no anxiety having relied upon our lantern but not a single match would light. We had every kind with us in metal match boxes but the boxes were wet and we had not a dry rag of any kind to rub them with. We tried to make a tent Out Of my skirt and to light a match under it, but our fingers were dripping wet and numb with cold--one could scarcely feel anything smaller than an ice axe-and the match heads dropped off limply into the snow without So much as a spark. Then we tried to go on and after a few steps Heinrich fell into a soft place almost up to his neck and Ulrich and I had to pull him out with the greatest difficulty and the mists swept up over the glacier and hid everything; that was the only moment of despair. We had so looked forward to dry blankets in the Pavillon Dollfuss and here we were with another night out before us. And a much worse one than the first, for we were on the shelterless glacier and in driving drenching rain. We laid our three axes together and sat on them side by side. Ulrich and I put our feet into a sack but Heinrich refused to use the other and gave it to me to lie on. My shoulders ached and ached. I insisted on our all eating something even the smallest scrap, and then I put a wet pocket handkerchief over my face to keep the rain from beating on it and went to sleep. It sounds incredible but I think we all slept more or less and woke up to the horrible discomfort and went to sleep again. I consoled myself by thinking of Maurice in S. Africa and how he had slept out in the pouring rain and been none the worse. We couldn't see the time but long before we expected it a sort of grey light came over the snow and when at last I could read my watch, behold it was 4. We gathered ourselves up; at first we could scarcely stand but after a few steps we began to walk quite creditably. About 6 we got to where we could unrope--having been 48 hours on the rope--and we reached here at 10 on Saturday.

They had all been in a great state of anxiety about us, seeing the weather, and had telegraphed to Meiringen, to Grindelwald, to know whether we had turned up. So I got into a warm bath and then discovered to my great surprise that my feet were ice cold and without any sensation. But having eaten a great many boiled eggs and drunk jugs of hot milk I went to bed and woke about dinner time to find my toes swollen and stiff. Frau Lieseguay then appeared and said that a S. American doctor had passed through in the afternoon and had seen Ulrich and Heinrich and had bound up their hands and feet in cotton wool and told them to keep very warm; so she bound up my feet too- my hands are nearly all right but I think my feet are worse than theirs. Still they seem better now and I don't expect I shall be toeless. They are not nearly as bad as my hands were in the Dauphiné, but the worst of It is that with swollen toes bound up in cotton wool one can't walk at all and I shall just have to wait till they get better. I slept for about 24 hours only waking up to eat, and it's now 4 in the afternoon and I'm just going to get up and have tea with Mr. Campbell, who has, I hear, been an angel of kindness to my guides. They seem to be none the worse except that Ulrich had a touch of rheumatism this morning, and as for me, I am perfectly absolutely well except for my toes-not so much as a cold in the head. Isn't it remarkable! I do wonder where mother is and whether she is anywhere near at hand; if she were I should like to have nursed my toes in her company but I expect I shall be all right in a day or two. I don't mean to move till I am. Isn't that an awful dreadful adventure! It makes me laugh to think of it, but seriously now that I am comfortably indoors, I do rather wonder that we ever got down the Finsteraarhorn and that we were not frozen at the bottom of it. What do you think?

[Captain Farrar of the Alpine Club writes as follows respecting this ascent :

"The vertical height of the rock face measured from the glacier to the summit of the mountain is about 3,000 feet. There can be in the whole Alps few places so steep and so high. The climb has only been done three times including your daughter's attempt, and is still considered one of the greatest expeditions in the whole Alps."

The following In Memoriam notice of Gertrude, Written by Colonel E. L. Strutt, now editor of the Alpine journal, appeared in the A.J. for November, 1926, at which time Captain Farrar was the editor.

"I do not know when Miss Bell commenced her mountaineering career. It was, however, in the first years of this century that her ascents attracted attention, and about the period 1901-1903 there was no more prominent lady mountaineer. Everything that she undertook, physical or mental, was accomplished so superlatively well, that it would indeed have been strange if she had not shone on a mountain as she did in the hunting-field or in the desert. Her strength, incredible in that slim frame, her endurance, above all her courage, were so great that even to this day her guide and companion Ulrich Fuhrer---and there could be few more competent judges--speaks with an admiration of her that amounts to veneration. He told the writer, some years ago, that of all the amateurs, men or women, that he had travelled with, he had seen but very few to surpass her in technical skill and none to equal her in coolness, bravery and judgment.

"Fuhrer's generous tribute on what was probably the most terrible adventure in the lives of all those concerned. 'You who have made the climb will perhaps be able to correctly appreciate our work. But the honour belongs to Miss Bell. Had she not been full of courage and determination, we must have perished. She was the one who insisted on our eating from time to time. The scene was high up on the then unclimbed N.E. face of the Finsteraarhorn, when the party was caught in a blizzard on that difficult and exposed face and were out for fifty-seven hours, of which fifty-three were spent on the rope. Retreat under such conditions, and retreating safely, was a tremendous performance which does credit to all.' The date was July 31 to August 2, 1902; the occasion was a defeat greater than many a victory. 'When the freezing wind beats you almost to the ground, when the blizzard nearly blinds you, half paralysing your senses . . . when the cold is so intense that the snow freezes on You as it falls, clothing you in a sheet of ice, till life becomes insupportable. . ..' then, indeed, was Miss Bell preeminent.

"The Lauteraarhorn-Schreckhorn traverse was probably Miss Bell's most important first ascent, July 24, 1902. It is related that she and her guides, meeting on the ridge another lady with her guides making the same ascent from the opposite direction, were not greeted with enthusiasm. In the seasons 1901-1902 Miss Bell was the first to explore systematically the Engelhorner group, making with Fuhrer many new routes and several first ascents. An extract from a letter of the chief Alpine authority, dated December 10, 1911, may be quoted. . . 'You ask me for some notes on Miss Bell's ascents, and I send all I have. . . she was not one to advertise, and yet, or probably because of it, they tell me that she was the best of all lady mountaineers. . . (Signed) W. A. B. Coolidge.'

"The notes contain the following, all relating to the different Engelhorner and all new routes or first ascents

Similistock, August 30, 1901. King's Peak & Gerard's Peak August 31, 1901. Vorderspitze & Gertrude's Peak & Ulrich's Peak & Mittelspitze September 3, 1901. Klein Engelhorn & Gemsenspitze & Urbachthaler Engelhorn September 7, 1901 Klein Similistock, July 8, 1902.

"For the reasons stated above, it is difficult to name her other expeditions in the Alps, but a well-known climber has stated that his most vivid recollection of an ascent of Mont Blanc was the effort required to follow Miss Bell.

"Such, briefly and inadequately tendered, are some of the Alpine qualifications of her who must ever be regarded as one of the greatest women of all time., E. L. S."]

To F.B., London, August 11th, 1902

I am quite perfectly well. I left Grimsel on the Monday after my adventure and returned to Rosenlaui, walking up, although on rather swollen toes. There I stayed 2 days and then, my time being up, returned home via Bruges where I spent a charming 74 hours. I met the Frank Pembers and the Albert Grays there. . .

My toes are nearly well; I'm still just a little lame, but it's nothing. I walk about gaily. My best love to Amy. it's horrid cold here.

To F.B., London, August 13th, 1902

I am so dreadfully sorry to gather that you have been anxious about me. . . I am now in boisterous health, as I hope this finds you.

I had a very pleasant dinner with Domnul en tête-à-tête on Monday. We drew out maps and discussed his Persian journey and our hidden plans. He has just been to tea with me--we want to meet in Delhi! I've got a letter from Colonel Baring saying that we are to be put up in the Viceroy's camp. It will be the greatest joke in life. I lunched yesterday with the Storrys. He wants me to write a book for him in a series on art he is bringing out for Gerald Duckworth. He gave me my choice of subject. I think if I did it I would write on Florentines between Giotto and Donatello--the great moment of upspringing when art threw off Byzantium and took on Greece. But I feel very doubtful as to whether I could do it and then when! However, I am to think it over. What do you think? I must tell you the other writers are Furtwangler and people of his sort! Charlie Furse is to do Tintoret, Mrs. Strong Rome, Strzygowski, the greatest living authority, the period before mine. It is very alarming.-----

['Domnul,' the Roumanian word for 'gentleman,' is an affectionate nickname for Sir V. Chirol, dating from the Bucharest Days.]

CHAPTER VIII

1902-1903 - ROUND THE WORLD THE SECOND TIME

[At the end of 1902 Gertrude and Hugo started off to go round the world together, their route being India (including the Delhi Durbar), Burma, Java, China and America.

Shortly before their departure the present Bishop of St. Albans, then the Rev. Michael Furse, came to stay with us at Redcar. He was a Don at Trinity College, Oxford, when Hugo was an undergraduate there, and they became great friends. Hugo was devoted to him for ever afterwards. The Bishop now sends us these notes of a talk he had with Gertrude at that time.

"I remember well a walk which I took one evening on the sands at Redcar with his very remarkable and Charming sister Gertrude; it was just before she and Hugo were going off round the world together. In her delightfully blunt and provocative way, she turned on me suddenly and said in a very defiant voice, 'I suppose you don't approve of this plan of Hugo going round the world with me?' 'Why shouldn't I?' I said. 'Well, you may be pretty sure he won't come back a Christian.' 'Why do you say that?' I asked. 'Oh,because I've got a much better brain than Hugo, and a year in my company will be bound to upset his faith.' 'Oh, will it?' I said. 'Don't you be too sure about that. If I Was a betting man I'd give you a hundred to one against it. But even if things do pan out as you think, I am tremendously glad Hugo is going with you, for I should much rather he came to the conclusion that the whole thing was nonsense before he took orders than afterwards! You do your hardest' (which I fear was not the actual word I used, but something much stronger!) 'and see what happens.'"

The Bishop was right. Hugo returned unchanged, and in due course he was ordained in 1909. In 1909 Mr. Furse became Bishop of

Pretoria. Hugo followed him to South Africa in 1912 and was with him as his chaplain until the Bishop came back to England for good in 1920.]

To F.B., December 4th, 1902

* * * Hugo is the most delightful of travelling companions. We spend a lot of time making plans with maps in front of us. We are chiefly exercised as to how many of the Pacific Islands we shall visit. It is immensely amusing to have the world before us . . .

[So many descriptions have been written of the Delhi Durbar, and of the well-trodden route which Gertrude and Hugo took afterwards, that it is not worth while giving her letters in extenso, though I have included a few of her comments on her daily personal experiences.]

[Arrival in India]
To F.B., S.S. "China," December 12th, 1902

Mr. [Leo F.) Schuster went off by himself and had coffee in Asia, the first time he had set foot on that continent. You can't think how charming and amusing and agreeable the Russells have been. It's added a great deal to the pleasure of the voyage having them. Our servant met us at the quay; he seems a most agreeable party and he's going to teach us Hindustani.

[These lessons seem to have been a success as far as Gertrude at any rate was concerned, because more than once in her subsequent travels she rejoices in being able to talk Hindustani.]

To F. B., December, 1902

We have become almost unrecognisably Indian, wear pith helmets--and oh! my Hindustani is remarkably fluent! We no longer turn a hair when we see a cow trotting along in front of a dogcart and we scarcely hold our heads an inch higher when we are addressed as "Your Highness." I called on a Persian to whom my Haifa friends had given me letters,! A Babi. I found him asleep on his verandah (he keeps a printing press), woke him up and had a long conversation with him in Persian. He regarded me with suspicion but treated me with the utmost consideration. I asked him to sell me some Babi books, but he wriggled out of it politely, so I turned to indifferent subjects and had an amusing talk about the plague and things of that kind.

(They go to Government House.]

Lord Northcote is charming, delightful to talk to, and she is even more charming and they were both extremely friendly. My Hindustani is quite enough to carry us through without an interpreter, it's really most convenient.

To H. B., Jeypore, December 22nd, 1902

We had a most cheerful dinner in the station with Mr. Schuster. I feel a considerable affection for him. He is so Cheerful and so equable and he travels about in the lap of luxury. I shared his good fun, his salad, and his delicious coffee. I wish we had been at the last Thursday party. I told You Sir Ian [Hamilton] was a fascinating person.

To F.B., Delhi Durbar, December 31st.

A cotton gown, a sun helmet and a fur coat was my simple costume, the only one, I find, which meets the variety of the Indian climate. No one can be dull on an Indian road because Of the birds and beasts. They are so tame that they scarcely get out of the way of your carriage. There is a delightful sort of starling called a maina, with white barred wings, the fat contented bourgeois of the bird hierarchy; the flocks of green parrots are the gay smart people, the vultures sitting--rather huddled up in the early morning cold are the grave Politicians. As for the grey crow, he is the ubiquitous vaut rien [sic] Without which the social system would not be complete. Arthur [Godman] appeared before lunch; he is such a darling, looking older and thinner, and very wise about the country and the people, having seen and observed a great deal and drawn conclusions which are well worth hearing. . .

[Arthur L. Godman, now Group Captain, R.A.F., was Gertrude's first cousin, being the eldest son of Ada Bell referred to on page 7, who married Colonel Arthur Fitzpatrick Godman.]

The function began with the entrance of the Delli siege veterans--this was the great moment of all, a body of old men, white and native, and every soul in that great arena rose and cheered. At the end came some twenty or thirty Gurkhas, little old men in bottle green, some bent double with years, some lame and stumbling with Mutiny wounds. And last of all came an old blind man in a white turban, leaning on a stick. As he passed us, he turned his blind eyes towards the shouting and raised a trembling hand to salute the unseen thousands of the race to which he had stood true. After that Viceroys and Kings went by almost without a thrill. But still it was a great show. . .

To F.B., Delhi, January 2nd, 1903 Visitors' Camp

We went to tea with Lady Barnes (she has just been knighted) the sister of the Vanbrughs and a most charming woman with whom I have sworn friendship. She is coming to see us in London some day and I'm going to stay with her in Burmah some day. We also made the acquaintance of her husband, Sir Hugh, who is very nearly as charming as she is. Then we went on to congratulate the Lawrences and met Sir Walter Lawrence outside his tent, and he sent us home in one of the Viceroy's carriages, so we were the howling swells. The Russells told me that the first night they were disturbed by the sound of continuous mewing, so much so that Lady A. got up and looked out of her tent and called " Puss, puss!" What do you think would have come if what she had called had really come? The elephants! isn't it deliciously ridiculous! They make a funny sort of mewing sound which from a distance sounds just like cats. I went to a Muhammadan Conference to which I had been invited by Mr. Morison, the head of the Aligarh College. I stepped on to the platform as bold as brass (in my best clothes!) and sat down by Morison who is an enchanting person. . .

In the train from Alwat to Delhi.

To F.B., January 18th, 1903

My thrice blessed Hindustani, though it doesn't reach to any flowers of speech, carries us through our travels admirably and here we were able to stop where no one has a word of English, without any inconvenience.

[They send for an elephant.]

An elephant is far the most difficult animal to sit that I have ever been on. You feel at first rather as if you were in a light boat lying at anchor in seas a little choppy after a capful of wind--but the sensation soon wears off and you learn to dispose yourself with ease and grace upon the hoodah, and above all U learn not to seize hold of the side bars when the elephant sits down, for they are only hooked and jerk out, landing you, probably (as they nearly landed me) in the dust a good many feet below. We soon discovered that the great tip for good elephantship is to grasp the front bar the moment you get on, for he gets up from in front (and very quickly too for he doesn't like kneeling at all) and the problem is how not to fall over his tail. It's a little disconcerting to find that an Indian, when he wishes to ascribe ideal movement to a woman, calls her "elephant gaited." "An eye like a gazelle, a waist like a lion, and a gait like an elephant."

To H.B., Peshawar, Friday, January 23, 1903

[At Peshawur they stop to photograph a group of people who are singing to the lute a sort of hymn of praise.]

There were two men outside playing on a sort of lute and singing praises of the Granth, but they can't have been very serious worshippers, for when I stopped to photograph them I heard them interpolate into the song "and the Memsahib came and took a picture "-- all in the same squeaky tune.

Aligarb. And here we are safely installed in the Morisons' house. He is one of the most charming of men--a son of Cotter Morison.

[Then follows a description of the Muhammadan College] the only residential College in India.

To H.B., in the train--as usual! February 2, 1903

. . . I liked Mrs. Morison on further acquaintance. They swear by her in the College and she was very kind to us. Mr. Morison is without doubt the most charming of men. We had an early tea to which he had invited an old Nawab who is a great personage in the College. He was a delightful old man; we conversed in Persian, though I found I could quite well follow him when he spoke Urdu with Mr. M. and Mr. M. can understand, though he cannot speak Persian. . . Hugo's attitude to his friends is too comic. We heard that one X. was at Hong-Kong. " Good old X. " said Hugo, "I must look him up." I asked who he was. "Oh, he was at oxford with me." "Did you know him well?" "No." I asked whether he liked him. "No--no, I didn't like him. He's not at all an attractive person. Good old X! I'll tell you what--I'll write and let him know we are coming." . . . I got two lovely gowns of Madras muslin, embroidered from the foot to the knee, for 23 rupees, and an old man with a white beard is making them up for me at 4 rupees apiece. I think I shall go to him in future, he is so much cheaper than Denise. Hugo meantime bought flocks of white ducks and a silk coat Of which he is very proud . . .. I wrote letters to all the people in the Straits Settlements, to tell them we're are coming--lucky dogs!

[At Darjeeling they go up into the Himalayas. They find the Russells and have a cheerful evening with them. . . and then to bed, meaning to get up in the dawn.]

"At 4:30 Hugo came into my room and said, "Get up, get up! the Moons shining on all the snows!" And I jumped out of bed and into a fur coat--for it was bitter cold--and there they were,, white, evanescent, mysterious and limitlessly high dreamy mountains under the moon. We ought to have been wakened at 4, it was most lucky Hugo woke, however we set ourselves to it with some purpose, got into riding clothes, bolted two eggs--I ate my first with sugar, which they had brought in instead of salt, in the hurry of the moment! and some tea, had our horses saddled, and at 5 we were dashing up the road behind the hotel, with two Nepalese saises panting behind us. That was a ride! We dashed on to the top of Tiger Hill, which is about 9,000 ft. high.

As we got to the top, I saw the first sunbeam strike the very highest point of Kinchinjunga--Nunc Dimittis--there can be no such sight in the world. Away to the west, and 120 miles from us, Everest put his white head over the folded lines of mountains. . . The old women of these parts have a plan of lacquering their noses and cheek bones with a brown lacquer, it looks like a frightful skin disease. . . Our servants on our expedition were as good servants as you could wish to have. We made great friends with them and I vowed I would take them all with me next time, when I come to climb Kinchinjunga.

To H.B., S.S. "Tara," Bay of Bengal , February 22, 1903

Thanks to your good wishes, we have hitherto escaped from the 96 diseases, the 24 dangers and the 11 calamities. (I'm commencing Buddhist, you see, before I get to Rangoon, and this is the proper Buddhist way of beginning a letter.)

[They travel from Rangoon in a gorgeous railway carriage of which Gertrude enumerates and describes the furniture. In the middle of a description of the scenery: "we have just discovered nine more cupboards."

They stop at a village and go for a walk while their carriage waits for them on a siding].

. . . At one of the little shops there was a basket of Pineapples, of which we wished to buy one. The lady of the shop was having her midday sleep; her small and entirely naked son roused her when he saw us fingering the pineapples. She just woke up enough to say " Char, anna " (which is 4d.) and then went to sleep again. We paid the 4 annas to the small boy and walked off with the pineapple.

*To F.B., March 2, 1903, o*n the Irrawaddy

We came to a very small steam boat. We said "To Pakukku," very loud and clear and our guides seemed to assent. A steep and slippery plank led out to the boat. I took my courage in both hands, crept along it, lifted the awning, and received a broadside of the hottest, oiliest, most machinery laden air, resonant with the snores of sleepers. I lit a match and found that I was on a tiny deck covered with the sheeted dead, who, however, presently sat up on their elbows and blinked at me. I announced firmly in Urdu that I would not move until I was shown somewhere to sleep. After much grumbling and protestations that there was no place to sleep there (which, indeed, was obvious) one arose, and lit a lantern; together we sidled down the plank and he took us back to one of the mysterious hulks by the river bank. It was inhabited by an old Hindu and a bicycle and many cockroaches. We woke the Hindu, and, at the suggestion of our guide, he climbed a stair, unlocked a trap door and took us on to an upper deck where, oddly enough, there were deck cabins with bunks in them. In these we made our beds--it was now 11:30--and went to sleep. What the place was, we haven't to this hour the least idea, but we believe it to have been Maya, pure illusion, for directly we left, it hid itself behind another barge, which was not there before, and has been no more seen. Next morning we caught the small and smelly ferry, and in company with a party of Burmese, steamed down the river to Pakukku . . .

[They go down the Irrawaddy.]

. . . and into the monasteries, where I was hailed by an old monk on a balcony, who begged me, by sign and gestures, to come up and take a picture of the pagoda. By great good luck a little monk appeared, who had a smattering of English. I explained to him that I would go and fetch my brother and that we would then take pictures. We had the funniest visit. The monks haven't enjoyed anything so much for a long time; they laughed till their yellow robes fell off their bare shoulders. We all sat cross-legged together under the carved roofs and discussed our various ages and the price of Hugo's watch, while an immense concourse of children gathered round close and closer. I was of no account at all when Hugo appeared, until it came to the picture taking. We had to drive the children away while I photographed the monks, but, at my friend's request, I then took a consolation picture of all the children sitting in a row. The camera may be a horrid modern invention, but it's a universal letter of credit in strange parts. H. questioned the little monk closely as to what he did all day. He replied blandly "Nothing!" One of them was sewing the silk wrapper of a Pali book. They showed us the books, palm leaf books written in gold lacquer, and we made the monk read us a sonorous Pali sentence. He asked us if we could understand and we were obliged to admit that we couldn't, but I don't think he could either. The little monk took us into a second monastery, where we found an extremely old party in yellow, asleep on a chatpoy. He was enchanted to see Us, however, and had all the doors opened that we might see the frescoes on the walls. H. taught the little monk to shake hands when we came away, but he wouldn't shake hands with me. He oughtn't even to have looked at me, according to the rules of the order. . . Hugo bought a whole orchestra of Musical instruments from a gentleman almost naked except for a pair of spectacles. Our tastes then drew us irresistibly to the monasteries, where we spent a happy twilight hour walking about on gilded balconies and teaching the monks the names, in English, of the beasts carved upon their doors. They can't pronounce the consonants at the end of our words--but we can't pronounce the consonants at the beginning of theirs, so we're quits.

[Gertrude was anxious to see the dancing and was taken by a learned Chinaman to the house of a charming old Burman who had been Theebaw's private secretary. The dance is described. The host produces some of his old court dresses, and the insignia of the Minister's rank, gold ornaments of various kinds. A travelling companion of Gertrude's had accompanied her on this visit.]

"A 12-stringed chain was sent to Mr. Gladstone. I wonder what he did with it?" said the unknown man. "Mr. Morley will tell us that," replied the Chinaman, cheerfully. You might have knocked me down with one of the Burmese lady's tail feathers: the last time I had talked of John Morley's Life of Mr. G. was in the Pollocks' drawing room at Hind Head. One dancer retired to appear as a boy. The change was not overwhelming, for instead of one tight trouser she now wore skirts rather voluminous in front.

To F.B., Batavia, March 16, 1903

We have at last got out of England and are now travelling on the Continent. No one knows what comfort on the sea can be till he travels by a Dutch boat. . .

[They go to Singapore where they stay with Sir Frank Swettenham. Hugo was very ill here with some sort Of malaria. Sir Frank Swettenham was endlessly kind to him, and kept him and looked after him until he was well enough to go away.]

THE LETTERS OF GERTRUDE BELL

To F.B., Astor House, Shanghai, April 4th, 1903

The hotel is most comfortable, when we arrived we found a note left for us by the kind Russells giving us some introductions to people here. It really was very thoughtful of them. We landed on Easter Sunday and had to do all our own getting ashore. The Chinese natives surrounded us and offered to carry our luggage, to carry us, to carry the ship, I fancy, if we would give them a long enough bamboo pole. I adore Chinamen with a passion that amounts to mania. They are the most delightful people in the world. They do everything to perfection. They'll make you a shirt in three hours, a petticoat in two, wash your clothes before you can wink, forestall your every wish at table, fan you day and night When you have the fever--you should have seen the Chinese boys sitting by Hugo's bedside at Singapore and fanning him all day long. . .

(Please give my love to Sir Ian, when you see him next!)

So we went to a silk shop, and the most delightful gentleman in China showed us for two hours the loveliest stuffs I have ever seen. Kings will leave their thrones in the hope of catching sight of me when I wear a brocade I bought there, and crown princes will flock after Elsa and Moll when they are clothed in some Chinese crêpe I design for them. Hugo addresses all Chinamen as Gnome, but as they don't understand they aren't offended. I like travelling in China. Hugo nods and becks to everyone he meets and they nod back delighted.

[They travel northward through China, sight seeing on the way and being much interested all the time.]

To F. B., PEKING, 26th April, 1903

[To Peking, where Claude Russell was then at the Legation, also Sir Walter and Lady Susan Townley.

Gertrude gives a detailed and very interesting description of Peking, of which however so many descriptions have been written already by other travellers that it is not worth while reproducing hers here. She also gives details of the Boxer Rising and contrasts it with the peace of China at that moment (1903). It is Of interest to read this passage in 1927, with an intensified sense of contrast.]

You can't conceive what the horrible fascinating streets of Peking are like. Full, full of people, a high mud causeway down the middle, crowded booths on either side and a strait and uneven way between them and the shops. Your rickshaw dashes in and out, bumps over boulders, subsides into ditches, runs over dogs and toes and the outlying parts of booths and shops, upsets an occasional wheelbarrow, locks itself with rickshaws coming in the opposite direction and at a hand gallop conveys you, breathless, through dust and noise and smells unspeakable to where you would be.

[They see the Temple of Heaven. They dine with the French Minister, M. Dubail, a great connoisseur, and then go shopping with him. Gertrude remarks in her letter to me " I'm so glad I speak French so well, aren't you?]

To H.B., Tairen, March 20th, 1903

We may as well back out. I've seen Dalny and I know. We may just as well back out. Five years old and a European town. Roads--you don't know what that means in China--fine streets of solid brick houses, a great port, destitute of shipping as yet, but that will come, law courts, two hotels, factories in plenty, six lines of rails at the station, a botanical garden in embryo, but still there. It contains some deer, an eagle and two black bears--note the symbolism! Do you remember a story of Kipling's in which a Russian officer is well entertained by an English Regiment? He gets up after dinner to make a speech. "Go away, you old peoples," he says. "Go away you--old--peoples!" and falls drunk under the table. That's the speech Dalny is making and I feel inclined to take its advice. In fact there is no alternative. We arrived at 7 a.m. on Thursday, went ashore and breakfasted at the Gastinnea Dalny where the proprietor fortunately spoke German. They take nothing but roubles, being in Russia, and we had to go to the renowned Russo-Chinese bank to change our notes--having paid for our breakfast, our friend, the proprietor, put us into a droschky--a pukha droschky--and we drove round the town. Our driver was a cheerful Kurlander who knew a little German too. He came out last autumn and meant to stay 2 years. "Business is good?" said I, observing his fat and smiling face. "Recht gut," said he, "sometimes one earns 18 roubles a day." No wonder he smiled and grew fat. The railway cutting is being widened, the station is not yet finished. Both were black with thousands of Chinese coolies working for dear life. How long is it, therefore, between project and completion in Russian hands? Hugo gnashed his teeth, but I did nothing but admire. They deserve to rule Asia-and they mean to rule Asia. Go away, you old peoples!

[They sail for Japan.]

To H.B., Tokyo, May 23rd, 1903

I spent my time in the train learning Japanese so that when we arrived at Miyajima I was able to explain that we wanted to leave our heavy baggage at the station! (At this moment came in a gnome with a most exquisite grey alpaca gown he has just made me an exact copy of one of Denise's but that cost 6 pounds and this 3! I am glad to have it, for Peking dust put a final touch to my dilapidated toilette.) I was delighted to have Lord Lovelace's enchanting letter. He writes like someone in the beginning of last century, touches of politics, social anecdotes, all with a perfect style and in an exquisite hand.

[Gertrude's friendship with Lord Lovelace was always a great pleasure to her. Their companionship ranged over literature, gardening, mountaineering,--whatever else came to hand. I include here one or two extracts from her letters to him, in reply to those she describes.]

To the Earl of Lovelace. August 5, 1902

What a series of successes you have had! . . .. isn't it delightful and wonderful to step on to a hilltop where no one has been before! you have had this sensation very often, I know.

To the same, July 12, 1902
[Writing of Alpine flowers.]

No other flowers have the same delicate exquisiteness except indeed those that Fra Angelico puts beneath the feet of dancing saints; but then they are dream flowers. And so are these, I believe growing in delicious dream gardens that exist only for us mountain people.

145

To the same, September 28th, 1903

Oh the tariff--I cannot keep so philosophically remote as you do though I have enough self-control to realise that I value one couplet of Imrul Kais above all the fiscal pamphlets in the world.

To the same, April 22, 1904

I have been reading the Buddhist scriptures and making the 'école buissonnière' between and I don't know which is the more profitable occupation.

To H.B., Tokyo, Sunday, 24th May, 1903

I spent a delicious morning wandering about temples and gardens under the charge of my rickshaw man. In one of the temples, a wonderful place all gold lacquer and carving set in a little peaceful garden, a priest came up to me and asked if I were an American. I said no, I was English. He bowed and smiled: "So--is that how it is? the English are very good!" I replied in Japanese, in which tongue the conversation was being conducted--"English and Japanese are one." This was greeted with great satisfaction to judge by the expression of my friends, the priests; what they said I could not understand. Aubrey Herbert came to lunch and we all went sightseeing together afterwards, but we were so busy talking that we didn't pay much attention to the sights.

To H. B., Thursday, 28th May, 1903

(They meet the Colliers, and Reginald Farrar, "who is a great gardener."]

They and Mr. Herbert all came to see us, and carried Hugo to a tea house to spend the evening in the company of geisha! I wonder how he comported himself. Eric said he appeared to be quite at his ease. . .

[To Yokohama, then across the ocean to Vancouver. Gertrude's first experience of America.]

THE LETTERS OF GERTRUDE BELL

To F.B., Lake Louise, Rocky Mountains,

June 30, 1903

Need I tell you that I am now climbing the Rocky Mountains!

We arrived at Glacier after a wonderful morning through the great canyons of the Selkirks. And at Glacier whom do you think I found, pray? 3 Swiss guides from the Oberland, ropes and ice axes and everything complete. So we fell into one another's arms, and they said, "Ach wass! it was Fraulein Bell! how did the Gracious Fraulein enjoy the Finstetaarhorn?" We discussed politics at dinner with our waiter at Vancouver. Says he: "There's only one man understands the Colonies: that's Chamberlain." G.B. loq.: "I think you'll have to pay some of the cost if you want to call so much of the tune." Waiter, loq. "I guess that's so, but they don't seem to think so out here." And he handed me the potatoes.

To H.B., July 8th, 1903, On the train.

[On the way to Chicago they stop at Moose Jaw--they are delighted with the strips of green, the prairie dogs, the people " A Lancashire man recently come out who is prospering and pleased with everything." They stop to photograph a widow's house and fall into talk with the owner of it.]

She wouldn't live in Moose jaw for worlds; it's to crowded for her. If you could only see Moose jaw, You would realise the force of that statement. It's Just a little more crowded than the desert.

[So to Chicago.] . . . Raymond Robins came to see us. He talked uninterruptedly for one and a half hours. He is rather like Lisa, talks like her, throws back his head and speaks with bursts of eloquence. . . Hugo and I listened to him, breathless for an hour, and a half. He is a very striking person; I fancy he is going to be a big power. Hugo was so enthralled by his accounts that he is actually going back to Chicago to spend four days with him. I encouraged this notion, for Raymond is exactly the kind of person Hugo ought to be with. He is so entirely outside the bounds of any stereotyped creed. But he was desperately busy the next three days, so we decided that

147

Hugo should come with me to Niagara. as arranged, and then return, by which time R. will be free to show him about. . .

[They go to] a sort of Earl's Court called Sans Souci, where we dined and saw the shows and enjoyed ourselves. I may say we had then the experience of a lifetime, for we went on a switchback that looped the loop. I can't say it was nice. Hugo says he was distinctly conscious of being upside-down--which we were for the fraction of a second--but I only knew a rush and a scramble and my hat nearly off. Now Hugo and I part company. Lisa meets me in Boston to-morrow afternoon and Hugo goes back to Raymond. . .

[Gertrude and Hugo landed at Liverpool on July 26th of this year. She was then in England until the following February, when we find her and her father staying at the Embassy in Berlin, after which she returned home.]

CHAPTER IX

1903-1909 - ENGLAND, SWITZERLAND, PARIS

[Our youngest daughter Molly was married to Charles Trevelyan on January 6th, 1904. As Gertrude was then at home with us and also during most of the preceding year, there are no letters to us concerning Molly's engagement in the previous November, or her marriage. Some letters are included here which Gertrude wrote at this time to a young cousin, Edward Stanley, second son of the 4th Lord Stanley of Alderley, afterwards Lord Sheffield.

Edward Stanley went out to Nigeria as Civil Commissioner in 1903. He was a boy of great ability, keen about his work and ready to shoulder responsibility and to face danger. Gertrude cared very much about this young cousin, and kept in touch with him. He was not gregarious, he had not many intimates, and at times when the life in front of him, with its ambitions and possibilities, seemed to him bewildering, he found in Gertrude the most sympathetic of confidantes and correspondents. As usual, none of her letters have the date of the year, and the envelopes of these letters have not been kept, but they seem to have been written between 1903, when he went out to West Africa, and 1908. His early death at his post in the summer of 1908 was one of the great sorrows Of Gertrude's life.]

To N. J. Stanley,

Yes Marcus Aurelius is a good counsellor, if one can follow his advice. I mostly find myself rebelling against it, with an uncanny sense of being too hopelessly involved in the mortal coil to profit by it. What is the use of bending all one's energies to the uncongenial thing? One is likely to do little enough anyway, but if half one's time is taken up persuading oneself one likes it or at least conquering distaste there is very little left to achieve success with.

Find the thing that needs no such preparatory struggle and then do it for all you are worth if you can. There will always be black or grey moments when it is sufficiently difficult to do even the thing you like.

To the same,

Elsa and I had a delicious day this week in the Eske Valley, at Glaisdale. The woods were full of flowers. We both fell into the river and were wet through and we agreed it was very nice to have reached an age when you can't be scolded and yet still like doing the things you would be scolded for.

To the same,

Last night I went to a ball at your house--a very exceptional thing for me to do and enjoyed myself so much that having gone for a moment, I stayed for three hours. A most pleasant party not too crowded, pretty people, a charming hostess and a most cheerful host. London has become very hot and I am glad to think that I shall leave it next week. . .

I had an amusing dinner the other day sitting between Lord Peel and the Agha Khan. Do you know who he is? He is a direct descendant of the Prophet, supreme head of half the Shiah world, an English subject, enormously rich (his sect allows him 190,000 pounds a year) and a pretender to the throne of Persia. We talked of travel and I said I might be in Bagdad next year. "If you go " said he, "do let me know, I should like to give you letters to my uncles, who look after the shrine at Kerbela. The Marlborough Club always finds me." Isn't that a fine jumble. He explained to Gilbert Russell, whom he knows very well, that he was so rich that 2,000 pounds was to him, as 6pence is to other people. Then," said Gilbert, "could you change me a shilling?"

To the same,

. . .Sargent came to dinner this week. Did I tell you I made friends with him last summer? He is delightful, I think. I should like to have about three hours talk on end with him, for one keeps getting into things one can't discuss at a dinner party because there is not time.

Last dinner we embarked on composition as understood by the Greeks, which is a most thrilling theme. I think he is wrong, far too modern in his idea of composition. He sets too much store on complexity which is not at all necessarily an admirable quality and may be very difficult to handle--must be. But he is catholic and he has thought things out with a mind that can do a deal of thinking, and to some purpose, and he is extremely keen, so it is interesting to hear his views . . ..

[In August Of 1904, she again went to Switzerland.)

To H.B., Riffelberg, Thursday, August 11th, 1904

I came up here this morning and found Geoffrey Young and a cousin of his. Mr. Young gave me much good advice and a general introduction to all the mountains that can be seen from here. He is a very nice creature, charming to look at and I am sorry he is going away. This morning when I was looking at maps outside the Monte Rosa hotel, there came up the old porter and said how gratified they were that I had come to climb in these parts. They had heard so often of my doings in the Oberland and were wondering when I should be coming to Zermatt!

To F.B., Zermatt, Sunday, August 21, 1904

Yes, as you say, why do people climb? I often wonder if one gets most pleasure out of the Alps this way. Some year I shall try the other and come and wander over grass passes and down exquisite Italian valleys and see how I like it.

To F.B., Zermatt, Wednesday, August 31st, 1904

We got our climb yesterday. It is a much better climb than I expected. I left Breuil early on Monday morning. It was very delightful walking up to the hut over the Matterhorn meadows and up easy rocks below the Dent du Lion. The mountain is full of story--here the great Carrel died of exhaustion, there so and so fell off from the rocks above, and when we got on to the little Col du Lion, which separates the Dent from the main mass of the mountain, we were on historic ground, for here Tyndall and Whymper bivouacked year after year when they were trying to find their way up. There is a difficult chimney just below the hut, but there is a fixed rope in it so that one has not much trouble in tackling it. We got up to the hut about 11:15, a tiny little place on a minute platform of rock, precipices on either side and the steep wall of the Matterhorn above. It is very imposing, the Matterhorn, and not least from the Italian hut; the great faces of rock are so enormous, so perpendicular. Unfortunately the hut is dirty, and smelly, as I had occasion to find out, for I spent the whole afternoon lying in the sun in front of it, sleeping and reading. The guides went away for an hour or two to cut and find steps on the snow above and I had the whole Matterhorn to myself--no, I shared it with some choughs who came circling round looking for food about the hut. At 7 we went to bed and I slept extremely soundly till about 1:30, when the guides got up and reported unfavourably of the morning. There was a thin spider's web of cloud over the whole sky, a most discouraging sign, but the moon was shining and we made our tea and observed the weather. By 3 it had distinctly cleared and we started off, without even a lantern, the moon was so bright. I knew the mountain so well by hearsay that every step was familiar, and it gave me quite a thrill of recognition to climb up the Grande Tour, to pass over the little glacier of the Linceul, the snow band of the Cravate, and to find oneself at the foot of the Grande Corde which leads back on to the Tyndall Grat. It was beautiful climbing, never seriously difficult, but never easy, and most of the time on a great steep face which was splendid to go upon. The Tyndall Grat leads up to a shoulder called the Pic Tyndall; it was dawn by this time and a very disquieting dawn too, SO we hurried on for it's no joke to be caught by bad weather on this side of the Matterhorn. However, the sky gradually cleared and we had our whole climb in comfort. The most difficult place on the mountain is an overhanging bit above the Tyndall Grat and quite near the summit. There is usually a rope ladder there, but this year it is broken and in consequence scarcely any one has gone up the Italian side. There is a fixed rope, which is good and makes descent on this side quite easy, but it is a different matter getting up. We took over 2 hours over this 30 or 40 ft.--the actual bad place! & not more than 15 or 20 ft.-and I look back to it with great respect. At the overhanging bit you had to throw yourself out on the rope and so hanging catch with your right knee a shelving scrap of rock from which you can just reach the top rung which is all that is left of the ladder. That is how it is done. I speak from experience, and I also remember wondering how it was possible to do it. And I had a rope round my waist which Ulrich, who went first, had not. Heinrich found it uncommonly difficult. I had a moment of thinking we should not get him up. We got to the top at 10 and came down at a very good pace. The Swiss side is all hung with ropes. It's more like sliding down the banisters than climbing. We got to the Swiss hut in 3 hours and were down here by 4 o'clock. We have heard that two parties who tried to do the Matterhorn from the Italian side this year have turned back because they do not tackle the ladderless rock, so we feel quite pleased with ourselves.

[Gertrude returned to England till November, when she went to Paris to study with Reinach again.]

To F.B., Paris, Monday, November 7th, 1904

it is being extremely pleasant. Yesterday morning I break-fasted with the Stanleys and went with Sylvia to see the Wintter Salon. After lunch I drove out, left some cards and went to see Salomon Reinach, whom I found enthusiastically delighted to see me. There were 2 other men there, an American from the Embassy and one Ricci, who appeared to be terribly learned. We sat for an hour or more while Salomon and Ricci piled books round me and poured information into my ears. It was delightful to hear the good jargon of the learned, and all in admirable English, for they know everything. But bewildering. This morning I read till 11 about Byzantine MSS. which I'm going to see at the Bibliothéque Nationale; then I went shopping with the Stanleys and bought a charming little fur jacket to ride in in Syria--yes, I did! Then I came in and read till 2 when Salomon fetched me and we went together to the Louvre. We stayed till 4:30--it was enchanting. All empty, of course, for it is a Monday; and I think there is nothing more wonderful than to go to a museum with my dear Salomon. We passed from Egypt through Pompeii and back to Alexandria. We traced the drawing of horns from Greece to Byzantium. We followed the lines of Byzantine art into early Europe and finally in the dusk we went and did homage to the Venus, while Salomon developed an entirely new theory about eyelids--Greek eyelids, of course, and illustrated it with a Pheidean bust and a Scopas head. It was nice.

To F.B., Paris, November 8th, 1904

I had the most enchanting evening with Reinach. I got there at 7:30 and left at 11:30 and we talked without ceasing all the time. After dinner we sat in his library while he showed me books and books of engravings and photographs and discoursed in the most delightful manner. He does nothing but work--never goes out, never takes a holi-day except to go and see a far away museum. And the consequence is he knows everything. I like him so much. This morning, I went to the Bibliothèque Nationale. Reinach had given me a letter to one of the directors and I was received with open arms. They are most kind. I looked at 2 wonderful Greek MSS.--illuminated--from 12 to 3:30! and I am going back there to-morrow to see ivories and more precious MSS. which they will have out for me. It is perfectly delightful. I should like to do nothing else for 6 months . . ..

To F.D. Paris, Thursday, November 10, 1904

Yesterday I read all the morning in the Bib. Nat. where I might well spend a great many more mornings. I lunched at home and went afterwards with Reinach and Ricci to a Byzantine Museum not yet open to the public. Most interesting it was. I don't begin to know, but I begin to see what there is to know. I dined with the Stanleys and went with Aunt Maisie to the new Donnay play--absolutely charming. We both enjoyed it. To-day I went to the Louvre in the morning then at 12 with Reinach to St. Germain (NB. I had no lunch at all!), where I read while he was busy and then was shown over it by him and intro-duced to several large domains of art of which I hadn't suspected the existence! Now I'm going to dine with him and spend the evening in his library. He wishes me to review a new book of Strzygowski's for the Revue Archaeologique--I think I might as well try my prentice hand as it happens to be a Syrian subject which I do just happen to know a very little about. Anyhow it is a jolly task. So to that end I'm going to consult his admirable books.

St. Germain is a nice place, isn't it? I had never been there. Re-inach is director of the Museum.

To F.B., Friday, November 11, 1904

I have spent the whole day seeing ivories at various museums. As far as Paris is concerned I've seen all the ivories that concern me, and I find to my joy that I'm beginning to be able to place them, so that this afternoon at Cluny I knew a good deal more than the catalogue--

which I'm bound to add was very bad. They have some wonderful things here.

This happy result is a good deal caused by having looked through such masses of picture books with Reinach. Last night he set me guessing what things were--even Greek beads--it was a sort of ex-amination--I really think I passed. Reinach was much pleased but then he loves me so dearly that perhaps he is not a good judge. He has sim-ply set all his boundless knowledge at my disposal and I have learnt more in these few days than I should have learnt by myself in a year.

But You can't think what odd things they made about the 3rd and 4th centuries in Gaul. It's a most fascinating study.

CHAPTER X

1905 - SYRIA-ASIA MINOR

To F.B., London, January 4, 1905

I have given Smith & Sons the following addresses--British Consulate, Jerusalem, for 3 weeks beginning from next week, British Consulate, Damascus, for the 3 weeks following; but I will let you know from Jerusalem by telegram. . .

Aren't I going a long way off? It is not nice at the beginning.

To F.B., S. S "Oatoxa," Wednesday, January 11th, 1905

Days spent at Port Said are certainly not red letter days. The last I spent here was with Hugo and I wish he were with me now, though I can't think he would desire it, But it is a pleasure to be speaking Arabic again. I feel it coming back in a flood and every time I open my lips expecting toads, pearls come out, at least seed pearls!

To H.B., Beyrout, 18 January, 1905

I'm deep in the gossip of the East! It's so enjoyable. I thought to-day when I was strolling through the bazaars buying various odds and ends what a pleasure it was to be in the East almost as part of it, to know it all as I know Syria now, to be able to tell from the accent and the dress of the people where they come from and exchange the proper greeting as one passes. A bazaar is always the epitome of the East, even in a half European town like Beyrout. I also went to the big mosque and photographed the doors which are rather pretty and made friends with the Imams--great fun it was ! I feel a very fine fellow now that I am the lord of two horses.

THE LETTERS OF GERTRUDE BELL

To H. B., from my camp, near Dumeir, January 20th, 1905

You see I'm off! I got off finally this morning at 12-the first day's start is always an endless matter and I'm thankful to have it over. It was blazing hot and I, having like a prudent traveller kept to my winter clothes, had to push my coat away in my saddle-bags and ride in a shirt. The road is all along the coast, one has a broad blue sea on one side and mulberry orchards on the other. I have a charming camping ground near a river and a full moon besides, and I am dining out of doors at the front of my tent. I mention all this in the hope of giving pain--I strongly suspect you are in the middle of a fog if you are in London. It is a great thought that I shall be many months under this little green roof.

AIN EL KAUTARAH, January 21st. To-day we have had a full day's ride and all goes well. I began by bathing in the river at dawn-a mighty cold business. I left the servants packing up and rode on alone to Saida where I spent an hour. But the port is charming, with a ruined castle built on an island in the sea and connected with the town by a narrow bridge. I got permission from the chief officer, who was busy having his head shaved completely bald at the time, to lunch there and very agreeable it was. I am beginning to rejoice again in the comfort of my saddle. The first day I generally feel it's rather a toss up whether I remain in it or not. N.B. The horse does the tossing up. He was rather fresh yesterday morning and bucked about through the streets of Beyrout. A strong sense of what was fitting alone kept me from biting the dust of Beyrout.

Sunday, 22nd. A strong wind rose in the night and blew up clouds. In the morning it looked very threatening and was blowing hard. So I jumped up in order to get my tents pitched before the rain came and at 7:30 we were ready. It's no wonder the Phoenicians were seafarers, for it would be difficult to find a more barren stony country than theirs. There is an extraordinary charm in these stony hills and valleys. They look like a land of dead bones,-grey limestone rocks and a few grey fig (you know the whitish colourlessness of them when they are leafless) and a few grey-green olives. But when you come near, the valleys are full of tiny niches which are gardens of anemones and cyclamen, and the rocks are full of beauty, the high-perched villages have an air of romance and the naked hills a wild and desolate splendour.

157

HAIFA, Wednesday, 25th.

. . .Oh, I've had such a day ! I've lunched with my Persians, I've drunk tea with my horse-dealer, I've spent hours in conversation with my landlord, I've visited everyone I know in Haifa. I'm off tomorrow morning. I doubt if it will be very nice in tents tomorrow, but still!

To F.B., February 1, 1905

I had a ride full of vicissitudes from Haifa. The first day was extremely and unavoidably long, 31 miles which is more than one can comfortably take one's animals. Moreover the road lay all across the Plain of Esdraelon (which is without doubt the widest plain in the world) and the mud was incredible. We waded sometimes for an hour at a time knee deep in clinging mud, the mules fell down, the donkeys almost disappeared ("By God!" said one of the muleteers, "you could see nothing but his ears!") and the horses grew wearier and wearier. I got in to camp after dark, at a place called Jenin it was, feeling very tired and head-achy and wondering why. Next day I was worse and by the time I had ridden for an hour I realised that I had a sharp attack of Acre fever, a thing I invariably catch here. It was extremely disagreeable, but I rode on for 6 hours through the most beautiful country-not that I paid much attention to it! till I got to Samaria and then I determined I could go no further. The mules and baggage had gone by another road to Nablus and I had only my cook with me. At the entrance of the town is a great ruined Crusader church, one corner of which has been built up into a mosque. A single bay of the aisle is converted into a room, and hard by in a sort of lean-to there lives the Imam of the mosque. He hurried out and said he could put me up in the aisle room for the night, there was a bed of sorts in it and a few quilts, more or less clean, and then I dropped down and went to sleep. I wish you could have seen the Imam. . . He was dressed in a long blue robe and had a white turban round his tarbush. He bustled about softly in his ragged socks and made me tea and filled a bottle with hot water to make me warm and finally left me to an uneasy repose. However next day I was almost well. I got up about noon and went out to see the town, which has had great days, and after lunch rode cheerfully into Nablus, which is Shechem. It was bitterly cold and there was a mighty keen wind blowing so I decided not to camp and put up at the Latin Monastery, which was inhabited by two Syrian monks. On

Sunday 30, I started off at 8 and walked into the town which is supposed to be the most fanatical Moslem town in all Syria. There are the remains of a beautiful Crusader church in it. Then I went to the top of Mount Gerizim where the Samaritans hold their Passover and such a view from it too--and then rode to Jacob's well, which is the scene of the interview with the woman of Samaria. The Greeks have built a wall round it and made a little garden in which narcissus were flowering; bits of carved mouldings and capitals lay about between the flowers, all that is left of a mediaeval church, and the grey olives were growing up between the stones. It was very peaceful and charming the most impressive, I think, of all the sacred sites in Palestine. The road lay all down Samaria, over hills and rocky valleys and through olive groves. . . I got into camp late and had a coldish night; there was ice everywhere when I got up next day. Then 2 hours ride into Jerusalem. In the afternoon I paid some calls and had a long call from Mr. Dickson the consul. He told me that Mark Sykes and his wife were here., so I went off to see them and found them half encamped and half in a Syrian house. They received me with open -arms, kept me to dinner and we spent the merriest of evenings. They are perfectly charming.

I've got a dog, an extremely nice dog of the country. it sleeps in my tent and he is perfectly charming. He is yellow. His name is Kurt, which is Turkish for Wolf.

To F.B., Rameleh, Friday, February 3, 1905

As regards the children's books: it is a pity to send them all away, I think. I remember what a joy ours were to us. Could not they be stored on a shelf in the long gallery? There are not so very many and I think they would be a joy to future children.

[The books were kept, and as Gertrude foresaw have been a great joy to the successive children of the family.]

I have had a few very busy days in Jerusalem. First I have engaged a new cook. The last was not capable enough for me. I was forced to fall back on my muleteers for all service. (One of them, Habib, who is about 25, is turning out an admirable servant, trustworthy and willing and intelligent. He is a Christian from the Lebanon. I have also his father, Ibrahim, who is a good old soul, and a Dorn,

Mahmud, who knows the country into which I am going. They are all good men and I am keeping them on.) The question of a cook was very serious and I had to set about looking for one with great care. Finally I hit on one who seemed satisfactory and learnt from him that he had accompanied Lord Sykes into Asia Minor. So I went off to Lord Sykes and lunched with him and heard a very good account from him. He said he was trustworthy and extremely brave, and on these qualifications I engaged him at once. Mark Sykes also says he can't cook, but it's 5 years since he was with him and we will hope he has learnt. So far I am very well satisfied with him. He has taken over all the arrangements with great skill and I find he never has to be told a thing twice. I hope my camp is now in its final shape and quite complete. I look forward to being very comfortable in a modest way. Not like Lord Sykes! I've seen a great deal of the Sykeses and like them very much.

I have discovered in Jerusalem a German who has started a market garden and collected all the bulbs of the country. I have ordered from him 6 wonderful sorts of iris and a tulip which he is to send to Rounton in the summer. It will be most delightful if they grow. I learned them nearly all for I have seen them flowering at different times. One is the black iris of Moab, and another a beautiful dark blue one, very sweet scented, which grows in Gilead.

To F.B., Jordan Bridge, February 5, 1905

We got down to Jericho about 2, but I had resolved not to camp there as I had always had a desire to pitch a camp down by the great Jordan Bridge, the Bridge of the Desert. We stopped to buy corn and straw for our beasts and went on with the muleteers. After about an hour a sharp shower followed and overtook us. By this time we had got to the edge of the strangest bit of all this strange Jordan Valley; it consists of mud hills about 100 ft. high cut into very steep slopes and ravines, and the road--save the mark!--winds on and along the precipitous sides of them. With a very little rain they are turned into hills of soap, inconceivably slippery and quite impassable. We hurried on and fortunately the rain stopped, but only just in time. We had to get off and lead our horses--mine slipped, began to slide down the bank but regained his feet almost miraculously. It lasted only about Half an hour, but it was with many thanks be! that we came to the end of it. People have been known to have been caught in rain in that Sodom and Gomorrah--it's about the site of them, I believe--and to have remained there all night, quite unable to move. We got to the Jordan at 4 and pitched camp in a delightful open place with a little grass and a few tamarisk bushes, just this end of the bridge. A little shrub of spina Christi bushes divides us from the river. The muleteers had made a great fire and we collected round it under the stars listening to the tales of a negro who has appeared from Lord knows where, like a dog turning up where there may be food, and is a bit of a wag in his way. There passed through this morning 900 soldiers on their way to help Ibn Rashid in Central Arabia. It's good luck to have missed them.

At Salt I was busy looking about for some place where I could sleep, and there came to me a charming old party who said I must without doubt be his guest. So here I am installed in the house of Yusef Succur who with his nephew and children waits upon me most attentively and is now going to give me dinner! I have also some other friends here, the sons and daughters of the old man who taught me Arabic at Haifa, and they have all been in to see me and fallen on my neck.

To F.B., February 7th, 1905

I passed the funniest evening yesterday. My host was a well to do inhabitant of Salt, Yusef Succur by name (upon him be peace!) He established me in his reception room, which was well carpeted and cushioned but lacking in window panes, and therefore somewhat draughty. He and his nephew and his small boys held it a point of hospitality not to leave me for a moment, and they assisted with much interest while I changed my boots and gaiters and even my petticoat, for I was deeply coated in mud. That being accomplished they brought me an excellent dinner, meat and rice and Arab bread and oranges. When I had finished it was placed before my cook who had joined the party. Then I held an audience. Paulina, the daughter of the old man at Haifa who used to teach me Arabic her brother-in-law, Habib Effendi Faris, the schoolmaster and the doctor all "honoured themselves" ("God forbid! the honour is mine!" is the answer). We drank lots of bitter Bedouin coffee, and at last settled down to business, which was this: How am I to get into the Jebel ed Druze? Finally, Habib Effendi, who was kindness itself arranged to send me out to his brother-in-law Namoud, who inhabits a ruin on a tiny hill called Tneib three hours east of Madeba. Now Madeba is east of the Dead Sea, and you will find it on a map. At 9:30 they left me, and my host, who was a magnificent looking old man, began to lay down the quilts for my bed. Then came my hostess, though they are Christians, her husband keeps her more strictly than any Muslim woman, and she sees no men. She was a very beautiful woman, dressed in the dark blue Bedouin clothes, the long robe falling from her head and bound round the forehead with a dark striped silk scarf. Moreover, her chin and neck were closely tattooed with indigo after the Bedouin fashion. At 10 they left me, and I went to bed and slept like a top till 6. The only drawback to my comfort was that I could not wash at all. You see, I was lodged in the drawing room, and naturally there were no appliances for washing there-if there were anywhere. This morning Yusef gave me a very good breakfast of milk and eggs and bread and honey. Habib provided me with a guide and I set off about 8:30 for a long day's ride. It was fortunately heavenly weather. It had rained last night and rained itself out, we had a perfectly clear sky all day. I love this East of Jordan country. We rode through wide shallow valleys, treeless, uninhabited and scarcely cultivated. Every now and then there were ancient ruined sites, once or twice we met a rider coming from the Bedouin, now and then we saw a flock of goats shepherded by an Arab with an immensely long gun. About 4 we came out Into the great rolling plain that stretches away and away to the Euphrates. The first few miles of it are all under corn. A mile or two in front of us lay the little hill round which my friend Habib has his property. We got in at 5:15 and pitched camp on the edge of the hill, looking south. Namoud was away, but he has been sent for. There are some 50 inhabitants of the ruins who work in Habib's corn land, and a few of the black Arab tents are scattered over the plain. A gorgeous sunset over it all, a new moon and absolute stillness. And I have just enjoyed the greatest luxury of my camp--my evening warm bath! It is all too delightful for words.

Wednesday, 8th. All is well. At 10 last night came Namoud. We fell on each other's necks, metaphorically speaking, and swore friendship and he left with the prospect of good talks next day. It was awfully cold in the night. After waking several times I had to get up and put on all my clothes. To-day was delicious, cold but fine. Namoud appeared after breakfast we had our maps--but my next three or four days Journey appears on no map--and stated exactly how I should get to the Jebel Druze. I am now waiting for my Arab guide and praise be to God! I think I have slipped through the fingers of the Government a second time. It was delightful having a day in camp with this wonderful plain stretched out before me like the sea. Namoud knows every Sheikh of all the Bedouin for miles and miles round, and we had lots of interesting talks about them. He is about thirty-five I should think, a Christian, by origin from Mosul and he is the man I have been looking for for long. We have planned an immense journey for the winter after next, no less than to Ibn Rashid. I think it will come off this time.

Thursday, 9th. To-day we are weather-bound. The rain began this morning on a strong south wind which turned into a real storm-- such rain as we seldom have in England and it was absolutely impossible to move. However, we are not badly off. All the horses and mules have been put into a big cave, and as for me, my tent is without doubt the most remarkable edifice that has ever arisen from the mind of man. Though it has streamed all day with a raging wind, not a drop of water has come in; the servants have a big Egyptian tent through which the rain has come a little on the weather side, but not much. This afternoon there arrived half a dozen Bedouins or more, of the tribe of the Beni Sakhr, the biggest tribe here abouts, driven out of their black tents by the rain. N.B. They had left their women behind in the black tents. They came to Namoud for hospitality, and he has lodged them in the big cave in which he and all his people live. I went in for an hour or two this evening and sat with them talking and drinking the bitter black coffee of the Bedouin. The dark fell we were lighted by the fire over which two women were cooking the guests' meal. ("They eat little when they feed themselves, but when they are guests, much--they and their horses," said Namoud).

We sat round the embers of another fire by which stood the regulation three coffee pots and smoked and told tales, and behind us, with a barrier of bags of chopped straw and corn between, some twenty-three cows moved and munched. We made great friends, the Beni Sakhr and I. "Mashallah! Buit Arab," said they: "As God has willed: a daughter of the desert."

Saturday, 11th. And I am still at Tneib. Yesterday it stopped raining, but the weather was still so very doubtful, that we decided not to risk matters by setting out for the desert. For ourselves it does not much matter, but our beasts have to stand out in the rain all night and it is bitter weather for them. So I sent into Madeba for more corn, and myself employed the afternoon in riding out across the plain to a Roman camp called Kartal. On My way home I stopped at the tents of the Beni Sakhr and dined with them. It was a charming party. We sat round the fire and drank tea and coffee and were presently joined by three of the Sherarat, raggeder and dirtier even than most Arabs. They had come from a day or two out in the desert to buy corn from Namoud, much as Joseph and his brethren must have come down into Egypt. The Sherarat are a very big and powerful tribe, but of base blood. The high born Arabs like the Sakhrs won't intermarry with them; but their camels are the best in Arabia. They were very cold--it was a bitter evening--and crouched round the fire of desert scrub. Then came dinner, rice and meat and sour milk, very good. Mahmoud and I ate out of one dish, and all the others out of another. While we were eating we were joined by a fair and handsome young man whom all the Sakhrs rose to salute, kissing him on both cheeks. He was Gabtan, son of one of the Sheikhs of the Daja, the tribe to which I am going as soon as the weather clears. He had heard that Namoud was looking for a guide for me and had come in to take me to his uncle who is the head of all the tribe. He sat down in a corner , ate little and spoke little and very soon after we had finished eating, one of our hosts called Namoud aside and talked long in a whisper to him. He came to us, and said we had better go so we gave the salaam and rode off with Gabtan home to Tneib. It then appeared that there was blood between the Sherarat and the Sakhrs, and the three Sherarat had not known who Gabtan was, but he knew them, and feeling the situation to be strained, our hosts the Sakhrs had hastened our departure. To-day however, the Sherarat have come up for their corn and have spent the morning sitting peaceably enough with Gabtan in Namoud's cave. To-day it has poured nearly all day and is still at it. So we were obliged to remain here--it is boring, but unavoidable. Meantime, I am entirely acclimatised. It's very cold, you understand, and everything in my tent feels damp, bedding, clothes, everything. The match boxes are so damp that the matches won't strike. I feel perfectly warm, and as for catching cold, I don't dream of it. I live in my fur coat, and at night I have a hot water bottle in my bed, a most excellent luxury. To-day Namoud lunched with me that he might eat curry, a delicacy he had never tasted. Then Gabtan and one of the Sakhr came in and drank coffee and smoked. I fortunately have a brand of Egyptian cigarettes they don't like much so the smoking is limited. We laid plans for my journey and Gabtan asked me whether I thought I should have to fight the Turkish soldiery, as if so he would take his rifle. I assured him I did not intend to come into open conflict with the Sultan and I hoped to avoid the soldiers altogether. But he has decided to take his rifle, which I daresay is as well. There was a gleam of fine weather and I went out to -watch the Sherarat buying corn. The corn lives in an ancient well, a very big deep cave underground, and is drawn out in buckets like water--only the buckets are of camels' hair. Then it has to be sifted for it is stored with the chaff to protect it from the damp. This is a mightily long business and entails an immense amount of swearing and pious ejaculations. We all sat round on stones and from time to time we said "Allah! Allah!" "Praise God the Almighty." Not infrequently the unsifted corn was poured in among the chaff. Namoud loq: "Upon Thee, Upon Thee, oh boy! may thy dwelling be destroyed! may thy life come to harm!" Beni Sakhr: "By the face of the Prophet of God, may he be exalted!" Sherarat (in suppressed chorus): "God! God! and Muhammad the prophet of God, upon him be peace!" A party in bare legs and a sheepskin: "Cold! cold! Wallah! rain and cold." Namoud: "Silence, oh brother! Yallah! descend into the well and work."

At four I went into the servants' tent to have tea over their charcoal fire. Namoud joined us and remained till seven telling us bloodcurdling tales of the desert. The muleteers and I listened breathless and Mikhail cooked our dinner, and put in an occasional comment. He is a most cheerful travelling companion is Mikhail. Namoud gave us a warning which I will tell you as it is an indication of the country we are travelling in. Between the Beni Sakhrs and the Druzes there is always blood. There is no mercy between them. If a Druze meets an Ibn Sakhr, one of them kills the other. Now, one Of MY muleteers is a Druze. He has to pass for a Christian till we reach the Jebel Druze, "for," said Namoud, "if the Sakhr here" (my hosts of last night, you understand) "knew he was a Druze, they would not only kill him, but they would burn him alive." Accordingly, we have rebaptised him for the moment, and given him a Christian name.

Sunday, 11th. It was still rather stormy, but I decided to start whatever happened. We got off a little before nine, Namoud, Gabtan and I riding together. In about half an hour we crossed the Mecca railway which is the true boundary between towns and tents. We rode for some two hours across the open plain till we reached the foot of a low circle of Hills, and here we found Gabtan's people, the Daja, a group of six or seven black tents, and were made welcome by his uncle, Fellah Al'Isa, who is a very great man in these parts and a charming person. We went into his tent and coffee making began. It takes near an hour from the roasting of the beans onwards. By this time the mules had arrived, I lunched hastily and rode off with Namoud and Gabtan to see a ruin in the hills. . ..I came back to tea in my own tent and at six o'clock Gabtan summoned me to dine with the Sheikh Fellah. I hope you realise what an Arab tent is like. It's made of black goats, hair, long and wide, with a division in the middle to separate the women from the men. The lee side of it is always open and this is most necessary, for light and warmth all come from a fire of desert scrub burning in a shallow square hole in the ground and smoking abominably; we had had a discussion as we rode as to the proper word for the traces of former encampments, and at dinner I produced the Muallakat (preMuhammadan poems) and found three or four examples for the use of various words. This excited much interest, and we bent over the fire to read the text which was passed from hand to hand, then came dinner, meat and sour milk, and flaps of bread, all very good. All my servants were "guests" too, but their meal was spread for them outside the tent. I had left one of the muleteers to look after our tents in my absence, and to him too was sent a bowl of meat and bread "for the guest who has remained behind." Dinner over, we drank coffee and smoked cigarettes round the fire, and I spent a most enjoyable evening listening to tales of the desert and of Turkish oppression, and telling them how things are in Egypt. Egypt is a sort of Promised Land, you have no idea what an impression our government there has made on the Oriental mind.

Monday, 13th. To-day the weather has turned out lovely, so we were right to wait those tedious four days. After many farewells and much coffee, I set out with Gabtan a little before eight, and we rode up the low hills across the rolling tops of them. The country was rather like our own border country, but bigger and barer. From time to time we came across little encampments, first of our friends the Daja, then of the Beni Hassan. There was sorrow in the tents of the children of Hassan. Yesterday a great ghazu, a raid, swept over this very country and carried Off 2,000 head of cattle and all the tents of one of the small outlying groups. In one tent we found a Man weeping, everything he had in the world was gone. I could not help regretting a little that the ghazu had not waited till to-day that we might have seen it. Five hundred horsemen, they say there were. We ourselves rode all day till past three, up and down the great sweeps of the hills with the Jebel ed Druze always before us, far, far away to the north. And Gabtan told me tales of ghazus as we went. We are now camped near a big village of houses of hair--the Arabs never say tents--belonging to the Hassanieh. It is a heavenly evening and looking west from my tent door I can see the country, which, if I were in it, I could not have left, and I laugh to think that I am marching along the Turkish frontier, so to speak, some ten miles beyond it, and they can't catch me or stop me. It is rather fun to have outwitted them a second time. I must tell you what will happen to the destitute of the Beni Hassan. They will go round to the rest of the tribe and one will give a camel, and one will give a few sheep and one some pieces of goat's hair for the tent, until each man has enough to support existence--they don't need much. So they will bide their time until a suitable moment when they will gather together all the horsemen of their allies, and ride out against the Sakhr and the Howeitat who were the authors of their ills; and then if they are lucky they will take back the 2,000 head of beasts and more besides. It seems a most unreasonable industry this of the ghazu--about as profitable as stealing each other's washing, but that's how they live. Meantime Gabtan is rather anxious, for the Daja and the Hassanieh are close friends, and the Sakhr are the foes Of both, and this latest exploit may lead to a general commotion. To-Morrow is the great feast of the Mohammedan year, the Feast of Sacrifice. They are going to kill and eat three camels in this encampment. One of these (i.e.the Camels) is walking about outside my tent, all dressed up. And there has been a great washing--it occurs once a year I have reason to believe. All the tents are hung with white shirts, drying. After sunset there was a mighty firing off of guns. I too contributed--by request--in a modest way, with my revolver, the first, and I expect the only time I shall use it.

BEIT Umm Ej JEWAL, Tuesday, 14th. The Mother of Camels, that is where we are, in short we have arrived, praise be to God. But our ride to-day was not without excitements. The first was a river which the rain had filled very full and which was running with some speed. The water came well up on to the horses' girths and the donkeys almost disappeared. Moreover, the banks were deep, steep mud. Gabtan was invaluable, he put his mare backwards and forwards through the stream and brought each mule safely over. I was truly thankful to see them across. From this point we got into the black volcanic rock of the Hauran, the tents of the Beni Hassan grew scarcer and scarcer, and finally we came out on to a great plain, as flat as could be, stretching away 2 days' Journey to the Druse mountains. Gabtan was anxious, he more than half expected to encounter enemies, for the Arabs of the mountains and the Daja are never on comfortable terms. Moreover we did not know exactly where in that immense plain the Mother of Camels was. So we rode on and on and at last on a little mound we saw some shepherds. At the same moment, two came running across the plain towards us from the right, and as they came they fired--at us-- which is the customary greeting to anyone you don't know. Gabtan rose in his stirrups, and threw his fur cloak over his arm and waved it above his head--we riding slowly towards the two as he did so. This reassured them and we were presently exchanging salutes on the best of terms. They directed us on our way, and before long we saw the towers and walls of Umm ej jewal before us. It looks like a great city and when you get near you find it is an empty ruin, streets of houses, three stories high, all of solid beautiful stone, with outer Staircases of stone and arched windows. I have pitched my camp in an open space in the middle, and there are a few Arab tents near me, the Arabs of the mountains. At sunset I was climbing about the ruined streets at some distance from my tents when Gabtan came running after me in a terrible state of mind, saying that if any of the Arabs were to see me in my fur coat, in the dusk, they would take me for a ghoul, and shoot me. Gabtan leaves us here, I am sorry to say. He has been a delightful companion. A gentleman called Fendi, from here, guides us tomorrow.

UMM ER RUMAMIN, Wednesday, 15. (The Mother of Pomegranates-but there aren't any.) We are encamped in the first Druze village, where we have been warmly welcomed. We had a tedious six hours' ride across the endless stony plain, enlivened by a little rabbit shooting. They were asleep under the stones, the rabbits, it was not a gentlemanly sport, but it fills the pot. The sheikh of this town is an old man called Muhammad and he is of the great Druze family of Atrash, who are old friends of mine. I've just been drinking coffee with him and having a pleasant talk. The coffee was made and served by a charming boy, Muhammed's only son. His mother, too, was an Atrash, and he looks as if he came of a great race. It is very pleasant travelling in this weather, but the nights, after midnight, are bitter cold. This morning the water in my tent was frozen. It is no small matter, I assure you, to get oneself out of bed, and dress before sunrise with the frost glistening inside one's tent.

Thursday, 16th. Without doubt this is a wonderful world. Listen and I will tell you strange things. I began my day in a most peaceful manner by copying inscriptions and was rather fortunate for I had found several Greek, one Cufic and one Nabathaean-Lord knows what it means, but I put it faithfully down and the learned shall read. Then I breakfasted with Sheikh Muhammad at Atrash. Then I rode off with a friend, name of Sakh, and we had a most pleasant journey to Salkhad. He was a remarkably intelligent young man, and questioned me as to every English custom down to the laws of divorce which I duly explained. He was also very anxious to know what I thought about the creation of the world, but I found that a more difficult subject. So we reached Salkhad and I went straight to the house of the Sheikh, Nasib el Atrash--he is another of the great family--and was made very welcome. Now I must tell you that there is a Turkish garrison here and a Kaimmakam 'et tout le bataclan.' I have not yet had a word in private with Nasib for whenever we begin to talk a Turkish official draws quietly near till he is well within earshot-and then we say how changeable is the weather. When I went to his house again I found the Turkish Mudir who lives side by side with Nasib and acts as a sort of spy upon him. The case is this--I want to go out east to a wild country called the Safah and under the protection of the Druzes I can go, but the Turks don't like this at all, and spend their time telling me how horribly dangerous it is, not a word of all which talk I believe. Salkhad is a little black lava town hanging on to the southern slope of a volcano, and in the crater of the volcano there is a great ruined castle, most grim and splendid. This evening as I dined, deeply engaged in thinking of the intrigue which I am about to develop, I heard a great sound of wild song, together with the letting off of guns, and going out I saw a fire burning on the topmost top of the castle walls. You who live in peace, what do you think this meant? It was a call to arms. I told you the Beni Sakhr and the Druzes were bitter foes. A month ago the Sakhr carried Off 5,000 sheep from the Druze folds in the plain. To-morrow the Druzes are going forth, 2,000 horsemen, to recapture their flocks, and to kill every man, woman and child of the Sakhr that they may come across. The bonfire was a signal to the country side. To-morrow they will assemble here and Nasib rides at their head. There was a soldier sitting at my camp fire. He wears the Turkish uniform, but he is a Druze from Salkhad, and he hates the Turk as a Druze knows how to hate. I said: "Is there refusal to my going up?" He replied: "There is no refusal, honour us." And together under the moon we scrambled up the sandy side of the mountain. There at the top, on the edge of the castle moat we found a group of Druzes, men and boys, standing in a circle and singing a terrible song. They were armed and most of them carried bare swords. "Oh Lord our God! upon them! upon them!" I too Joined the circle with my guide. "Let the child leave his mother's side, let the young man mount and be gone." Over and over again they repeated a single phrase. Then half a dozen or so stepped into the circle, each shaking his club or his drawn sword in the face of those standing round. "Are you a good man? are you a true man? Are you valiant?" they shouted. "Ha! Ha!" came the answer and the swords glistened and quivered in the moonlight. Then several came up to me and saluted me: "Upon thee be peace!" they said, "the English and the Druze are one." I said: "Praise be to God! we too are a fighting race." And if you had listened to that song you would know that the finest thing in the world is to go out and kill your enemy. When it was over we ran down the hill together, the Druzes took up a commanding position on the roof of a house--we happened to be on it at the time, for one always walks for choice on the roofs and not in the streets to avoid the mud--and reformed their devilish circle. I listened for a little and then took my leave and departed, many blessings following me down the hill. . .

Friday, 17th. I've spent an 'appy day with Nasib. The Ghazu is put off for a day or two by reason of some difficulties between various Druze Sheikhs, and I'm afraid I shall not see the assembling Of the Druzes. . . Nasib was going to ride out to a village to the south, and I wanted to visit a shrine on a neighbouring hill, so we rode part of the way together, he and I, and some twenty Druze horsemen, all armed to the teeth--including me.

Saturday, 18th. To-day was bitter cold, with some snow. I determined therefore not to move till to-morrow, and this evening is clear and promising. I spent some time making close friends with the Turkish officials, especially with the Mudir who is a charming and intelligent man, a Christian from Damascus. The upshot of which is that I may go wherever I like, and no one will lift a finger except to help me. I hear that Mark Sykes has come into the Jebel Druze with an official escort, so that I might probably have got permission if I had asked for it. But I am very glad I came up through the desert for it has been a most amusing journey and a very valuable experience for a future expedition. You see I have laid the foundations of friendship with several important people--of desert importance that is.

Monday, 20th. We had the devil's own ride yesterday. It was a bright morning with a bitter wind, and I determined to start. So after prolonged farewells I set off with a Druze zaptieh, name of Yusef, and we plodded through the mud and the stones gradually rising into the hills. All went well for the first three hours or so, except that it was so cold that I rode in a sweater (Molly's, bless her for it!) a Norfolk jacket and a fur coat; then we began to get into snow and it was more abominable than words can say. The mules fell down in snow drifts. the horses reared and bucked, and if I had been on a sidesaddle we should have been down half a dozen times, but on this beloved saddle one can sit straight, and close. So we plunged on, the wind increasing and sleet beginning to fall, till at last we came out on to a world entirely white. The last hour I walked and led my horse for he broke through the deep snow at every step. Also I was warmer. By the time we reached Saleh, our destination, it was sleeting hard. The village was a mass of snow drift and half frozen mud and pond. There wasn't a dry spot. So I went up to the house of the Sheikh, Muhammad ibn Nassar, and there I found a party of his nephews who took me into the Makad, which is the reception room, and lighted a fire in an iron stove and made tea. The Makad was a good sized room with closely shuttered windows, by reason of there being no glass, felt mats on the floor and a low divan all round on which carpets were spread for me. Rather a fine place as Makads go. As I sat, drinking my tea and conversing with the nephews--who were delightful intelligent young men--in came the Sheikh, a tall, very old man, and offered me every hospitality he could in the most charming way. Some interest surrounds me, for I am the first foreign woman who has ever been in these parts. Sheikh Muhammad insisted that I should spend the night in his house, and I gladly agreed, for indeed even for a lover of tents,, it was not a promising evening. All the family (males) came in one after another, he has six sons and more nephews than I ever saw, and I established myself on the divan, all the Druizes sitting round in rows, and answered all their questions about foreign parts, especially Japan, for they are thrilled over the war, and explained to them how we lived. They asked particularly after Lord Salisbury and were much saddened to hear he was dead. They knew Chamberlain by name--the real triumph of eloquence was when I explained to them the fiscal question, and they all became Free Traders on the spot.

Two of the sons had been to school in Cple (transcriber's note: Constantinople), and the Sheikh had been honourably imprisoned there

171

for three years after the War, so that they were all a little acquainted with the world, and, as is the habit among the Druzes, wonderfully well informed as to what was passing. Presently came dinner on a big tray, bowls of rice and chicken and a curious sort of Druze food, made of sour milk and semen (which is grease) and vegetables, a kind of soup, not very good. My Zaptieh Yusef and I being the guests, ate together; then the others sat down round the tray. So we re-established ourselves on the divan, drank coffee and continued the conversation till nine o'clock when wadded quilts were brought and spread in three beds, on each side of the Makad--and Yusef, the Sheikh and I coiled ourselves up and went to sleep. But I wish you could have assisted for a moment at that evening party and seen all those white turbans and keen handsome faces of the Druzes, and their interest and excitement at all I said. For my part I slept sound and woke a little before sunrise. The Makad felt rather stuffy so I slipped on my fur coat and went out into the silent frozen village. There is a very attractive old fountain down by the khan, and there I stood in the snow and watched the sun rise and said a short thanksgiving appropriate to fine weather. My servants slept in the khan, they and the horses, all together under the dark shelter. They seemed happy, oddly enough. So I breakfasted with the Sheikh on tea and Arab bread and a sort of treacle they make from grapes, dibbis is its name, and I like it particularly.

We rode off with one of the nephews as a guide, Fais, we are fast friends. We plunged for half an hour or so through snow and ice, and then suddenly left the winter country behind us and had a charming ride all along the eastern edge of the Druze mountains.

Thursday, 23rd. Oh, my dear mother, such a travel I've had! I often wished you could have seen me at it, and wondered what sort of a face you would have made. Listen, then. On Tuesday morning I rode off with my invaluable cook, Mikhail, and the best of my muleteers (and he is as good as anyone could wish) Habib, on the best of his mules, and six Druzes. I left my tents behind, took some rugs, five chickens and plenty of bread, a fur coat and a camera. This was our modest all for three days. We rode down the Druze mountains for an hour, then for an hour through a shallow winding valley of volcanic rock, then we came out on to the wide desolation of the Safah. It is all covered with black stones. How they got there I can't think. The earth they lie on is yellow like sand, but quite hard, and nothing grows but a few plants of desert scrub, of which there are many kinds, but I won't trouble you with their names at the present time. Once in a while you see a small flock of goats or herd of camels quarrying their dinner, so to speak, and from space to space a few black tents belonging to the Ghiath Arabs, who are a very poor tribe that spend the winter in the Safah and come in spring to the Druze hills. Through this wilderness of stones we rode for three hours and then we met one in rags whose name was Hound of God--it sounds like a pretence mystery tale, but it's the real thing. He was exceedingly glad to see us, was Hound of God, having been a friend of the family for years--at least eighty I should judge. He told us there was a pool of water near, and Arab tents two hours away--we found the water and lunched by it, sharing it with a herd of camels, but in the matter of the Arabs he lied, did Hound of God. We rode on over all the stones in the world and at last, half an hour before sunset, just as we were deciding that we should have to sleep out, waterless, one of the Druzes caught sight of the smoke of some Arab tents. We got there in the dusk and stumbled in over the stones with the camels and the goats which were returning home after a laborious day of feeding. Very miserable the little encampment looked. They have Nothing but a few camels, the black tents and the coffee pots. They eat nothing but bread and all their days they wander the stones in fear of their lives, for the Safah is swept by the ghazus of the big tribes from north to south and they harry the Ghiath as they pass. We scattered, being a big party, Ghishghash, my servants and I went to the house of the Sheikh, whose name was Understanding. His two sons lighted a fire of desert thorns and we all sat round watching the Coffee making. And the talk began to the accompaniment of the coffee pounding, a great accomplishment among them. They pound in a delightful sort of tune, or rather a sort of tattoo. We dined on flaps of fresh bread and bowls of dibbis and then I curled myself up in a blanket and went to sleep In a corner of the tent. The smoke of the fire was abominable but it blew out after a bit, one side of an Arab tent is always open, you know. The fleas didn't blow out. I woke in the middle of the night. There was a big moon shining into the tent, the Arabs and the Druzes were all sleeping round the cold hearth, a couple of mares were standing peacefully by the tent bole and, beyond them, on the stones, a camel lay champing. Then I slept till dawn. Half an hour after the sun was up we were off, the party increased by one of our hosts. . . And presently I discovered that the narrow track we were riding in was a road as old as time. It was marked at intervals by piled up heaps of stones and at one place there was a stone which had been a well stone, for it was worn a couple of inches deep with the rub of the rope--it must have served a respectable time, for this black rock is extraordinarily hard--and in another there was a mass of rock all covered with inscriptions, Nabathaean, Greek, Kufic, and one in a babel which I did not know, but it was very like the oldest script of Yemen Sabaean; and last of all the Arabs had scrawled their tribe marks there. So each according to his kind had recorded his passing. At the back of the lava hills we came out into a great plain of yellow clay which stretches for many miles and is called the Ruhbe . . . The second night in Arab tents was rather wearing, I must admit, and I felt quite extraordinarily dirty this morning. We started early and I got back to my tents at 4--the bath that followed was one of the most delightful I have ever had. It was an interesting journey, however, hard work but well worth the trouble. I refused a very pressing invitation to dine with my Druze friends, feeling that I really must have a Christian meal, but I went up and drank coffee with them afterwards and we had a long talk which ended in their declaring that they regarded me as one of the family.

BATHANIYEH, Friday, 24th. There must have been quite ten degrees of frost last night. My sponges were frozen together into a solid mass so that I could not use them, and though there was a bright hot sun the world did not begin to unfreeze till mid-day. I had a charming ride down from the Druze mountains into the Damascus plain.

Saturday 25th. I got out of the Druze country about four o'clock in the afternoon. Just before I left it I met two Druzes with laden mules coming from Damascus. They gave me a very friendly greeting and I said, "Are you facing to the Mountain?" They said, "By God! May God preserve you!" I said, "I come from there, salute it for me!" They answered, "May God salute you; go in peace." To-night I am camped on the edge of the volcanic country in a village of Circassians and in the matterof pens I don't think there is much difference between me and Caroline Herschell. I wish the weather would be a little warmer.

DAMASCUS, Monday, 27th. Here we are. I arrived yesterday afternoon, alighted at the most fascinating hotel, with a courtyard.

I find the Government here has been in an agony of nervousness all the time I was in the Jebel Druze, they had three telegrams a day from Salkhad about me and they sat and wondered what I was going to do next. The governor here has sent me a message to say would I honour him by coming to him, so I've answered graciously that I counted on the pleasure of making his acquaintance. An official lives in this hotel. He spent the evening talking to me and offering to place the whole of the organisation of Syria at my disposal. He also tried to find out all my views on Druze and Bedouin affairs, but he did not get much forrader there. I have become a Person in Syria!

To F. B., Damascus, March 3rd, 1905

I was greeted when I arrived by a distinguished native of the Lebanon, a Maronite Christian, who has constituted himself my cicerone, and has been very useful, though he is rather a bore. He was directed by the Governor to look after me during my visit and he has fulfilled his instructions to the letter! I wrote to you on Monday, I think. That afternoon I went to tea with the American archaeologists. . . One of them, Dr. Littman who is an old acquaintance of mine, is a real learned man and I won his esteem by presenting him with a Nabathaean inscription which he had not got, and one in the strange script of the Safah, which he said I had copied without a fault. That was rather a triumph, I must tell you, for I remember as I did it all the Druzes and my Bedouin guide on his camel were standing round impatiently and crying "Yallah, yallah! oh, lady!" . . . . . Having evaded all the obliging people who offer to escort me everywhere, I dawdled off into the town. I made my way at last to the great mosque-- which was a church of Constantine's--left my shoes at the door, with a friendly beggar and went in. It was the hour of the afternoon prayer. In the courtyard, men of all sorts and kinds, from the learned Doctor of Damascus down to the raggedest camel driver--Islam is the great republic of the world, there is neither class nor race inside the creed-- were washing at the fountain and making the first prostrations before they entered the mosque. I followed them in and stood behind the lines of praying people some two or three hundred of them, listening to the chanting of the Imam. "Allah!" he cried, and the Faithful fell with a single movement upon their faces and remained for a full minute in silent adoration, till the high chant of the Imam began again: "The Creator of this World and the next, of the Heavens and the Earth, He who leads the righteous in the true path, and the evil to destruction. Allah!" And as the name of God echoed through the great colonnades, where it had sounded for near 2,000 years in different tongues, the listeners prostrated themselves again, and for a moment all the church was silence. . . Every afternoon I hold a reception and Damascus flocks to drink my coffee and converse with me. That day I lunched in the bazaars, in the fashionable restaurant, unknown to foreigners, and ate fallap and the delicious dishes for which Damascus is renowned. And in the afternoon came the Governor, returning my call, and the usual stream followed him, so that I sat in audience till dinner time. Yesterday I spent the whole morning in the house of the Emir Abdullah. The Abdul Kadir family has a traditional friendship with the Beni Rashid, which is kept up by yearly presents to and fro. They are going to help me in my journeys thither and perhaps I shall take one of them with me. And after dinner I went to an evening party. It was in the house of a corn merchant who is the agent of the Druzes of the Hauran. I found there a Druze of a famous Lebanon family, the Arslan; he is a poet--have I not been presented with his latest ode--and a man of education and standing. I wish I could picture the scene--some eight or ten of the corn merchants, dressed in blue silk robes and embroidered yellow turbans, my friend the poet in European dress, and me, all sitting on the divan in a room blessedly empty of everything but carpets and the brazier. And then coffee and talk and talk and talk till I got up and took my leave about ten o'clock, and went away laden with thanks and blessings.

This has been a visit to Damascus that I shall not easily forget--I begin to see dimly what the civilisation of a great Eastern city means--how they live, what they think; and I have got on to terms with them.

To F. B., Baalbek, March 5, 1905

I have made some curious observations, but think it better to keep them to myself. There is an Arab proverb which says: "Let him who talks by day take heed." And it applies to those who talk by post, The Vali, when he heard I was going to ride to Baalbek, was all for sending a large escort with me, so I hastily declared I should go by train--only pretence. Such are the penalties of greatness. I do trust I shall now be allowed to relapse into the position of a modest traveller of no importance to anyone. I have found out that while I was in Damascus, every time I went out alone I was followed by a man who was commissioned to watch over my safety--it was merely solicitude on the part of the Government and as there were no secrets about my coming and goings it was harmless. So I was followed to the house of

Naksh Pendi and was introduced to his favourite wife. She is quite young, a pretty woman, but shockingly untidy with her hair all over her eyes and a dirty dressing-gown, clothing a figure which has already, alas! fallen into ruin. The view from Naksh Pendi's Balcony is, however, immortal. The great splendid city of Damascus with its gardens and its domes and its minarets, lies spread out before you, and beyond it the desert--the desert almost up to its gates, and the breath of it blowing in with every wind, and the spirit of it passing in through the city gates with every Arab camel driver. That is the heart of the whole matter.

To H. B., Baalbek, March 6th

I had almost forgotten how beautiful this place is. Except Athens, there is no temple group to touch it, and I have looked at it with new eyes now that I know a little more than I did about the history of decoration and the genesis of pattern and ornament. But I wish I knew a great deal more still.

To F.B., Kuseir, March 8, 1905

We set off at 8 on our way to Homs. We had a terrible adventure: as we were about to start I found that my dog, Kurt, was missing. I sent Mikhail and Habib looking for him through the town and Habib presently discovered him tied up in the house of one who thought to steal him. Chained up, and Habib with some promptness claimed the dog and appropriated the chain, and upon the thief's protesting, he knocked him down and came away. I can't say I regret Habib's action. It will learn our friend not to be a dog stealer.

To F.B., Homs, March 9, 1905

I took a walk through the bazaars, but that was not as pleasant as it might have been on account of the interest my appearance excited. It was an interest purely benevolent but none the less tiresome, for I was never without the company of fifty or sixty people. When I returned, the Kaimmakarn came to see me, and we had a long talk, his secretary piecing out his Arabic and my Turkish. One of the principal inhabitants of Homs, Doury Pasha, to whom I had a letter of introduction from Damascus, has also sent to ask if he may call tomorrow. Oh, Merciful! what fun I am having! Don't you think so?

Friday, 10th. Homs is not Much of a place, but such as it is it has a character of its own. It is all built of black tufa and the best houses have inner courtyards, with a simple but very excellent decoration Of white limestone let into the black either in patterns or in straight courses like the Pisan building. Moreover, the minarets of the mosques and tall slender towers, or Spire, for all the world like an Italian campanile, like the towers of San Gimignano, except that they are capped With a whole cupola, very Pretty and decorative. I spent the morning sight-seeing, with a soldier in attendance so that I was not bothered by the people. Sight-seeing takes a long time in these parts, for when anyone of importance meets you in the streets, he invites you in to drink a cup Of coffee. this happened to me 3 times and gave me the opportunity of seeing the inside of some of the big houses. After lunch I rode down to the river, the Orontes, to see the fashionable lounge, a delicious stretch of meadow and willow trees by the water side. But the trees are not yet in leaf nor the flowers out.

They are all wildly Japanese in this country. There are perhaps 400 people round about my tent.

To F. B., Kalaat el Husn, March 12

I am now staying in perhaps the largest castle known--no, it's not so large as Windsor Castle, but very nearly. It is Crusader--but I must tell you how it all came about. I left Homs at an early hour yesterday--not early enough however to prevent my having a large, eager crowd to watch my departure. It is one of the most difficult things I know to keep One's temper when one is constantly surrounded and mobbed. The aggravation is quite as great when they are friendly; it is the fact of not being able to move without hundreds of people on every side that is so irritating. Only a fixed determination not to afford more amusement than I could help to the inhabitants of Homs kept me outwardly calm. My escort consisted of two mounted Kurds and two prisoners whom the Kaimmakam was sending to the Prison of Husn-- my journey afforded a good opportunity Of conveying them. They were hand-cuffed together, Poor wretches! and they trudged along bravely through dust and mud. I proffered a few words of sympathy, to

178

which they replied that they hoped God might preserve me, but as for them it was the will of their lord, the Sultan. They were deserters. we had a very long day, 10 hours, but when we left the carriage road that goes to Tripoli our way lay through such delicious country that every step of it was delightful. It was beautiful weather. The great castle on the top of the hill was before us for five or six hours. The sun shone on it and the black clouds hung round it as we rode up and up through flowers and grass and across running streams. But it was a long way and the animals grew very tired. At sunset we came to the dark tower. I rode through a splendid Arab gateway into a vaulted corridor which covered a broad winding stair. It was almost pitch dark, lighted only by a few loop-holes; the horses stumbled and clanked over the stone steps--they were shallow and wide, but very much broken--and we turned corner after corner and passed under gateway after gateway until at length we came into the court in the centre of the keep. I felt as if I were somebody in the Faery Queen, and almost expected to see written upon the last arch, "Be not too bold." But there was no monster inside, only a crowd of people craning their necks to see me, and the Kaimmakam very smiling and friendly, announcing that he could not think of letting me pitch my tents, and had prepared my lodging for the night. So we went up into the round tower in which he lives and he took me into his guest room, which was commodiously fitted with carpets, a divan and a bed--I supplied the washing appliances and the table-and he offered me weak tea while he engaged me in conversation. He is a man of some distinction, a renowned poet, I believe--but his hospitality outweighs all his other qualities. My men and my horses and me, he has taken us all in and provided for us all. There were two other guests besides me, one an old Moslem woman and the other a Christian lady, the wife of a government official. . . The Moslem woman was a nice old thing. Her son has recently been murdered in the mountains by a casual robber, and our talk turned mostly upon similar incidents which are very common here. The old lady crouched over a charcoal brazier murmured at intervals: "Murder is like the drinking of milk here. God! there is none other but Thee!" The talk seemed to fit the surroundings. My tower room must have Heard the like of it often. "Murder is like the drinking of water," muttered the old woman. "Oh, Merciful!" At nine they all left me--and one offered to spend the night with me, but I declined, politely, but firmly. To-day is devilish weather, a strong wind and hailstones and thunder storms. . . I spent a very agreeable evening in the company of my host and hostess. We all dined together and he and I talked. We got on to such terms

179

that he ended by producing his latest copy of verses-and reading it aloud to me. We then fell to discussing the poets with much satisfaction, and he forgot his sorrows, poor man, and became quite brisk and excited. As we have often remarked, there is no solace in misfortune like authorship, be it ever so modest. I could have laughed to find myself talking the same sort of enjoyable rubbish in Arabic that I have so frequently talked in English, and offering the same kind of sympathy and praise to my friend's efforts. Yes., it might just as well have been London, and the world is, after all., made of the same piece.

BURI SAFITAH, Monday, 13. At dawn it was raining for all it was worth, and I got up and breakfasted in the lowest of spirits. And then of a sudden Someone waved a magic wand, all the clouds cleared away and we set off at half past seven in exquisite sunshine, loaded with the blessings of our host and parting gifts of a more substantial nature, for he insisted on supplying us with our food for the day. At the bottom of the steep hill on which the Castle stands, there lies in an olive grove a big Greek monastery. I got off and went in to salute the abbot, and behold! he was a friend of five years ago, for I had seen him in a place on the road from Palmyra. Great rejoicing and much jam and coffee to celebrate the occasion. Late this evening, just as I was beginning to write to you, there appeared two high officials sent up by the Kaimmakam of Drekish, where I go to-morrow, to welcome me and to put the whole of the forces of the Kaitylmakanilik at my disposal. I hereby renounce in despair the hope of ever again being a simple, happy traveller. The Turkish Government has decided that I am a great swell and nothing will persuade them to the contrary. It is boring to tears, and also very expensive, but what can I do? The only blot on my happiness is that Kurt has finally disappeared. I suppose he was tempted away by someone who offered him food and then stole him. . . . My Arabic is becoming very fluent, thank heaven! but I wish I talked with more elegance. . .

HAMAH, Thursday, 16. A long and tedious ride to-day, across the foothills and the plain to Hamah. I have just had a struggle with the authorities, who insisted on giving me eight watchmen for the night. I refused to have more than two, which is all one ever has anywhere, and the rest have gone away. It is a perfect pest having so many, for in the first place they talk all night and in the second one has to tip them all.

KALAAT EL MUDDIH, Sunday, March 19, 1905. Apamea, one of the many and a most beautiful place, standing on a great bluff over the Orontes valley. Seleucus Nicator built it and a fine thing he must have made of it, for there is near a square mile of fallen columns and temple walls and Heaven knows what besides. Now think how Greece and the East were fused by Alexander's conquests. A Greek king, with his capital on the Euphrates, builds a city on the Orontes and calls it after his Persian wife, and what manner of people walked down its colonnades, keeping touch with Athens and with Babylon? That is the proposition in all the art hereabouts. The chief characteristics of the person that walked down them to-day-scrambled down them over the huge column boles--was that she was wet. It has rained in heavy showers all day and the deep grass and flowers were dripping wet and I was soaked up to the knees and drenched from time to time from above. One of the difficulties of searching for antiquities is that most of the people don't recognise any sort of picture when they see it, that if you ask a man if there are any stones with the portraits of men or animals on them, he replies, "Wallahi ! we do not know what the picture of a man is like." And if you show him a bit of a relief, however good it is he hasn't the least idea what the carving represents. Isn't that curious?

EL BARCH, Monday, 20th. I photographed and explored and when I got back to my horses I realised that I had lost my coat. I had taken it off some half an hour after we reached Khirbet Hass and fastened it on to my saddle, it had dropped off and was gone. Mahmud went back to look for it and after an hour and a half came back without it. By this time it was past 6, we had an hour and a quarter's ride over very rough country and clouds were blowing up. So we rode off, picking our way through the stones by an almost invisible path. As ill-luck would have it just as the night fell, the storm came upon us--it became quite pitch dark with drenching rain and we missed our Mecca thread of a way. At that moment Mikhail's ears were assailed by the barking of imaginary dogs and we turned off to gain the spot from which the sound came. So we stumbled on and the moon came out a little and it was clear the path we were on led nowhere. . .

The Sheikh is a very sprightly old party who was guide de Vogûé 40 years ago and to every archaeologist since his time. He knows them all by name or rather by names his own very far removed from the original. He rode with me this morning. I made a détour with

181

Mahmud and visited two villages, one more beautiful than the other. We had an 'impayable' conversation by the way. It began by my asking Yunis whether he ever went to Aleppo. "Oh, yes," he said, he was accustomed to go when his sons were in prison there. I edged away from what seemed to me delicate ground by asking how many sons he had. Eight; each of his 2 wives had borne him 4 sons and 2 daughters. I congratulated him warmly on this. Yes, he said, but Wallahi! his second wife had cost him a great deal of money. "Yes?" said I. "May God make it Yes upon thee, oh lady! I took her from her husband and by God (may His name be Praised and exalted!) I had to pay him 1,000 piasters (about 10 Napoleons) and to the judge 1,500." This was too much for Mahmud's sense of decency. "Wallahi!" said he, "that was the deed of a Nosairiyeh or an Ismailiyeh!" "Does a Muslim take away a man's wife? It is forbidden." "He was my enemy," replied Yunis in explanation. "By God and the Prophet of God! there was enmity between him and me even unto death." "Had she children?" said Mahmud, "Ey wallah" (i.e. of course), said Yunis, a little put out by Mahmud's disapproval. "By the face of God!" exclaimed Mahmud, still more outraged, "it was the deed of a heathen." "I paid 1,000 piasters to the man, and 1,500 to the judge," objected Yunis--and here I put an end to the further discussion of the merits of the case by asking whether the woman had liked being carried off. "Without doubt," said Yunis, "it was her wish." At noon I came to a wonderful village called Ruweika and lunched in a tomb like a small temple-there was a violent thunder-storm going on all the time.

Sunday, 26th. On Friday I rode east across a rolling plain covered with débris of towns but uninhabited except by half settled Bedouin. It's a curious and interesting thing to see them all along the western edges of the desert taking to cultivating the soil and establishing themselves therefore of necessity in a given place (in some distant age there will be no nomads left in Arabia-but it is still far off I'm glad to think). In the early stages these new-made farmers continue to live in tents, only the tents are stationary and the accompanying dirt cumulative.

To F. B., Kalaat Sinlan, March 31st

Aleppo, is a town where it always rains--at least that is my 2 days' impression of it. It has been a great great Arab town. . ... An endless barren world stretches round, uninterrupted by hill or tree--you can see the Euphrates from the castle in clear weather; you might see Bagdad for anything there is between. I called on the Governor who received me in his harem, of which I was glad, for his wife is one of the most beautiful women I have ever seen. He returned my call in the afternoon. And finally I spent an amusing evening with a native family and talked the most fluent Arabic till a quarter to 11 by the clock! All my leisure moments were occupied in changing muleteers, getting new ones and saying goodbye (with much regret) to the old. It was a necessary step for I could not take Syrians talking nothing but Arabic into Asia Minor. I have got 3 bilingual natives of Aleppo and so far I like them very much. Yesterday morning, what with new muleteers and what with the numbers of people who came to bid me farewell I did not get off till 10 o'clock. When we got Into the low rocky hills the mules went one way and my soldier went another. We reached the place where I had intended to camp at about 4 in the afternoon. There were a few ruined walls there,--the tents of some Kurdish shepherds. We waited an hour and the mules did not turn up. Then the Kurds announced that it was dinner-time and invited us to come and eat. I was very hungry and not at all sorry to share their cracked oats and meat and sour milk. At 6 o'clock there Came in a little boy who stated that he had seen my mules an hour before and that they had gone on to Rahat Simian, a good hour and a quarter away. So I said goodbye to my delightful hosts, who were much concerned at my case, and by dint of riding as hard as we could over the rocky ground we got in just before it became black dark. To our great joy as we got in we heard the mule bells; the others had arrived just before us. We rode through the huge silent church and found them pitching the tents by the light of 2 candles. And now I must tell you where I am. This is the place where St. Simon lived upon a pillar. While the servants pitched my tents I went out and sat upon St. Simon's column--there is still a little bit of it left-- and considered how very different he must have been from me. And there came a big star and twinkled at me through the soft warm night, and we agreed together that it was pleasanter to wander across the heavens and the earth than to sit on top of a pillar all one's days.

I have had the most delightful day today, playing at being an archaeologist.

Monday, April 3 rd, 19 o 5. I shall not forget the misery of copying a Syrian inscription in the drenching rain, holding my cloak round my book to keep the paper dry. The devil take all Syrian inscriptions, they are so horribly difficult to copy. Fortunately they are rare, but I've had two to-day. Elsa will sympathise with my desperate attempts to take time exposures in a high wind. Heaven knows what they will be like--something like pictures of an earthquake I should think. By this time even my archaeological zeal had flickered out and I rode into my tents at Basuran, arriving at 2 o'clock, chilled to the bone. I have an enchanting camp tonight in the ruins called Debes. It is quite uninhabited and I have pitched my tents in a big church. I can very seldom induce my servants to camp far from habitation. They pine, not unnaturally, for the sour curds and the other luxuries of civilization. I rather miss the sour curds myself but the charm of a solitary camp goes far to console me!

Wednesday, 5th. We have had such a day's mountaineering! I must say I prefer doing my rock climbing on foot and not on horseback. Today, indeed, I was on foot most of the time, but dragging my unfortunate beast after me up and down walls of rock terrific to the eye. This is no exaggeration. I am pretty well versed in bad roads but till today I did not know what a horse could do. We climbed up and down two mountain ranges. At the second I confess my heart failed me. it was awful--indescribable. I didn't for the moment think we should get up with whole limbs. I jumped and tumbled up the stones and my horse jumped and tumbled after me, and all the time we were on the edge of little precipices quite high enough to break us to bits if we fell over. And when you get to the top of these terrible hills, behold a beautiful country. I lunched and photographed and made friends with the few families of servants who live in some cottages near by and imagine my delight when they turned out to be Druzes! I knew there were a few families of Druzes in these hills and had been looking for them. So we fell on each other's necks, and I gave them all the latest news of the Hauran and one of them insisted on guiding me on my stoney way through the hills. We had a remarkable climb down into the great plain through which flows our old friend the Orontes. And then a no less memorable ride along the base of the hills to my camping ground. It was more exquisitely beautiful than words can say, through gardens of fruit trees and olives with an unbelievable wealth of flowers everywhere.

To Florence Lascelles. Konia, April 9

Darling, You can't think how delighted I was to find your long interesting letter awaiting me here. And the best part of it was the news that you are to be in London in June--Florence, we will arrange for some 6 solid hours, when no one shall interrupt us, and talk without stopping, both of us at once, and then perhaps we shall have got through about one-thousandth of what we have to say. For we have to talk out a whole year, and since you came back from Persia I don't believe we have ever been separated for so long. . .

What a country this is! I fear I shall spend the rest of my life travelling in it. Race after race, one on top of the other, the whole land strewn with the mighty relics of them. We in Europe are accustomed to think that civilization is an advancing flood that has gone steadily forward since the beginning of time. I believe we are wrong. It is a tide that ebbs and flows, reaches a high water mark and turns back again.

you think that from age to age it rises higher than before? I wonder--and I doubt.

But it is a fine world for those who are on the top of the wave and a good world, isn't it. . .

To F.B., Payas, April 14, 1905

The hot weather has come with a rush. When I got back from Seleucia--in blazing weather--I stayed a day at Antioch in order to see a collection of antiquities in the house of a rich Pasha. He had a MS of the Psalms in Armenian which he showed me and of which I photographed a page or two for the benefit of Mr. Yates Thompson--you might tell him if you see him. He had also some beautiful little bits of Greek bronze which I photographed for Reinach. Yesterday I rode down to Alexandria, :rather a long day-furiously hot. We were on the Roman Road most of the day, crossing the great Pass of Bailan where were the Syrian gates of the Ancients. It was from this pass that Alexander hurried back to meet the army of Darius at Issus--I have been following the line of his march to-day and am now camped on the edge of the Plain of Issus. . . The plain is very narrow here and fine great mountains rise fteeply up from it. My impression is that the battle must have been fought just about here for the books say that Darius had not room to display his cavalry. . . I never tell you of the difficulties of camp organization because I think they may be tedious. They are however many, especially now that half my servants talk only Turkish. But to-day a really singular thing has happened. The head muleteer from whom I hired all the baggage horses from Aleppo, has simply not turned up. I haven't the least idea what has become of him-- the others suggest that he has either been murdered or imprisoned! He went down into the bazaar after we left Alexandretta and has not been seen since. Fortunately I have the animals nearly up to Konia. I shall go on whether he turns up or not and let him retrieve his beasts from Konia as best he may. I don't regret him at all; he is most incompetent and he treats his subordinates so badly that they leave us at every stage, which is an insufferable nuisance as I have to teach the new men their work--in fragmentary Turkish. The good Mikhail is rather gloomy this evening but I fancy we shall pull through.

April 15th. It rained floods in the night and continued to do so until this morning. The tents were soaked, the water ran in under the tent walls and I was obliged to retire on to my bed which was the only dry place. Thunder and lightning and all complete. In the middle of it all the good Kaimmakam strolled down to invite me to his house, but I did not go as I should have got wet through on the way. When the rain stopped we had to let our tents dry and by that time it was too late to start and I was obliged very reluctantly to resign myself to a day in camp. In the course of the morning, the missing muleteer turned up. He had in fact been detained by difficulties with a creditor. How he got off I don't know--not by paying I'll be bound--but the incident has had the worst effect on the discipline of the camp, for he re-appeared so overflowing with joy, and I was so much excited and amused that I received him as a sort of prodigal father (he's 60 if he's a day) and his shortcomings are all forgiven for the moment. The Kaimmakam sent a present of 6 oranges and 2 small bottles of Russian beer to console me for my enforced stay!

April 17th. Oh, but I've had a tiring 2 days! What it's like to travel in A roadless and bridgeless country after and during heavy, not to Say torrential, rains you can't imagine. We started off yesterday in pouring rain, the path was under water, the rivers roaring floods. In the middle of the day we came to a village buried in lovely gardens, the air heavy with the smell of lemon flowers--and here the heavens opened and it rained as I hope never to see it rain again. We had stopped at the house of a Turk to buy a hen--he invited us in till the rain stopped and I took the opportunity to lunch. Meantime a furious roaring stream which we had succeeded in fording, brought the baggage animals to a stand, and while we, unknowing, went gaily on, they made a détour of nearly 2 hours to find a bridge. . . I was tired and wet and hungry and bad weather travelling is exhausting to the mind and to the body. It was 7:30 before they arrived and we pitched camp in a downpour amid the mutual recriminations of all the servants who had had a hard time too and vented their displeasure On each other. There was nothing for it but to hold one's tongue, do the work oneself, and having seen that the horses were fed, I went to bed supperless because no one would own that it was his duty to light the fire! It was miserable I must say and this morning was just as bad. All the ropes were like iron after the rain and the tents weighed tons and as I splashed about in the deep grass (for I had to watch and encourage every finger's turn of the work) I thought I was a real idiot to go travelling in tents. Then the march--fortunately a short one--through the floods of yesterday's rain. It was very interesting historically for we were going through the Amanian Gates, through which many armies had passed in and out of Cilicia. I was determined not to lose touch with my baggage animals today and when we came to a wide deep river I waited for them and rode backwards and forwards twice through the floods to help them over. When they saw me riding in and out gaily (the water was above my boots I may mention) they took courage and plunged through. And now I hope our troubles are over. We are camped at a place called Osmaniyeh in most lovely country and the sun has come out and our tents are drying and our tempers mending. I think if the rain had lasted another day I should have died of despair--and of fatigue. I'm really in Asia Minor--a most exciting thought. And I have to talk Turkish. There's nothing else for it. I've just been entertaining (in more senses than one) the Kaimmakam in that tongue. I make a preposterous mess of it, but it has to be done. I hope in a week or so I shall begin to scrub along. The chief difficulty now is that though I can put a few questions I cannot easily understand the answers! You know there are moments when being a woman increases one's difficulties. What my servants needed last night was a good beating and that's what they would have got if I had been a mail--I seldom remember being in such a state of suppressed rage!--but as it is I have to hold my tongue and get round them. However as long as one gets through it doesn't matter.

April 18th. The chief interest of this journey is that I find myself talking nothing but Turkish. It's the greatest lark. . . I've learnt piles to-day. I started off this morning with a soldier who could speak nothing else and I had to make the best of it. It was a lovely shining morning and this country is beyond comparison beautiful. We cantered across a wide delicious plain set round with the great snows of Taurus and the Giaour Dagh--it was an hour after dawn, more heavenly than words can say. Then we came to a deep river across which we went in a ferry boat. I lent a hand to some shepherds who were trying to get a herd of goats onto the ferry--I hope it counts as a virtue to help obstinate goats into a ferry; it's certainly difficult any way. A charming gentleman called Mustapha had attached himself to my party and rode with me all day. So we came to a place called Budsian, which is Hierapolis Cartabala, And here I spent 3 hours. It lies among wonderful crags, the acropolis perched up on top of a great rock and below it a fine theatre, there was a street of columns and 2 very lovely churches. These last I photographed with great care and measured, Mustapha holding the end of the tape. By the time I had finished it was near midday and I eat my lunch at a village near by, where they gave me the most excellent milk and curds, for which they would not let me pay. And so we rode on for 5 hours through charming country to Kars Bazaar, which lies under Taurus and here I have camped. I paid a visit to the Kaimmakam and was further invited to tea with some notables who were sitting in the street Outside the café. There was no one to interpret so I had to do my own talking. I must say they are very clever at understanding. And now I must study the Turkish participles--there are some 30 of them. I don't handle them with any skill.

ANAVARZA, April 20th. . . . Yesterday morning I found there were lots of inscriptions to be copied at Kars and a church to be photographed, so what with one thing and another it was getting late before I got off. The mules had gone on ahead--we had to make an immense détour to the north, under the hills, to avoid floods and get to bridges, the rivers being all unfordable. The mules being for once far ahead, missed their way and have gone up on the wrong side of Anavarza with an unfordable stream before them. We were certain something had gone wrong since we did not overtake them but after some indecision I determined to ride on, and following the line of an immense aqueduct, we splashed through the wet plain at sunset into Anavarza. The castle stands on a mass of rock, 2 miles long, which rises like a great island from the sea of plain--it's really a sea at this moment for it is all under water. The rock is some 300 ft. high and in places quite perpendicular; the castle runs all along the top of it and the top is in some places a knife edge, dropping absolutely sheer on either side with just room for a single fortification wall to connect fort with fort. At the western foot of this splendid acropolis lies the city with a double wall of turrets round it buttressed up against the cliff. It was a Greek storing place, a treasury of Alexander's, then Roman, then the capital of the Armenian kingdom-and now a mass of ruin, deeply overgrown with grass. So I rode through the northern gateway of the town not having the faintest idea where I was going to sleep or eat. By good fortune there was a guard-house in the middle of the ruins with a couple of Turkish soldiers in it who supplied me with milk and sour curds. On them and sour native bread I dined: then I spread my cloak on the floor of a little empty room and slept till 6 this morning; in spite Of innumerable mosquitoes. It wasn't really nice however. Roughing it in this weather is more difficult than in the cold. After the long hot day one longs incredibly for one's evening bath and change of clothes. I was most thankful when at 10 this morning the baggage turned up. I shall take great care not to run any risk of its going astray again. I have spent the whole day exploring and photographing and I am going to have another day here in order to have a shot at measuring and planning 3 churches, an extremely difficult business because they are very much ruined and very deeply buried in grass-

April 21st. Remembering the heat of yesterday I got up at dawn and at 6 o'clock started out to grapple with my churches. The whole plain, my tents included, lay under a thick white mist, but the sun was shining on the earth rock and as I climbed up I saw the great white peaks of Taurus all glittering. It was most beautiful. I took my soldier with me and taught him to hold the measuring tape. He soon understood what I wanted and measured away at doors and windows like one to the manner born. After 5 hours very hard work I found I had arrived at results--more interesting than I had expected. In a word, the churches here are not of the Syrian type which they ought by rights to be, but of the Central Asia Minor type--and I think they will surprise Strzygowski not a little. One very delightful thin happened. One of the biggest of the churches is razed to le ground-nothing but the traces of the foundations remain. I looked round about for any scraps of carving that might give an indication of the style of decoration and found, after much search one and one only--and it was dated! It was a big stone which from the shape and the mouldings I knew to have been at the spring of two arches of the windows of the apse and the date was carved in beautiful raised Greek letters between the two arch mouldings--"The year 511." I don't know if they used the Christian era here but it must be pretty close to it anyway, for that's about the date one would have expected. Wasn't it a great piece of luck! Two things I dislike in Anavarza. The mosquitoes and the snakes; the mosquitoes have been the more hostile of the two: the snakes always bustle away in a great hurry and I have made no experiments as to what their bite would be like. There are quantities of them among the ruins. They are about 3 ft. long--I wonder if they are poisonous. "Rira bien qui rira le dernier": I have had the laugh of the vultures. After tea I rode round the rocks on the eastern side and met a shepherd boy. So we tied my horse to a stone and the shepherd and I climbed together up the only path which leads to the castle keep. It was rocky enough in all conscience and it wound cheerfully in and out of precipices and led us at last to a little hole in the wall through which we climbed to the highest tower. Like all ruined castles it was more beautiful from without than from within; but the position is glorious and worth climbing for; the walls built on the edge of a straight drop of a couple of hundred feet or more, the great plain all round and the ring of snows beyond. We dislodged the vultures who were sitting in rows on the castle top-they left a horrid smell behind them-and in a small deep window I found a nest with 2 evil-looking brown eggs in it. It is not often that one finds vultures' nests. I have fallen a hopeless victim to the Turk; he is the most charming of mortals and some day when I have a little more of his language we shall be very intimate friends, I foresee. It's blazing hot weather; the wild hollyhocks are out and today I saw the first fat old pomegranate bud. That means summer.

Saturday, 22nd I shall not soon forget the Cilician plain. The heat of it is surprising and as I told you 'passim' it is most of it under water. We plunged today for ten hours through mud and swamp and sluggish waters, and at last we have come out onto a rather higher bit of country on which the barley is standing in the ear. In a month everything will be burnt up and all the people will have fled to the hills. I don't wonder Anavarza had such a fine necropolis--all the inhabitants must have died off regularly every summer from marsh fever, mosquitoes and snakes. In the blazing middle of the day we came to two very small trees outside a village and I sat down in the shade of them to lunch. No sooner was my coming observed than one of the inhabitants appeared with a large tray of fried eggs, curds and bread for me and my servants. It was pure hospitality-I might give no tips. I could only thank my host sincerely and eat heartily. But though they are the most delightful of acquaintances they are the worst of servants. They will take any amount of trouble for you for nothing, but once you hire them to work, not a hand's turn will they do. At the hands of Turkish mule-teers I suffer tortures. They get into camp and when they have unloaded the mules they sit down on one of the packs and light a ciga-rette with an air of impartial and wholly unconcerned benevolence. I've gone to the length of dislodging them with the lash of my crop, freely applied. It makes no difference; they stroll on to the next pack and take up a position there smiling cheerfully the while.

ADANA, Sunday 23rd I rode in here early this morning leav-ing camp at 3 a.m. to avoid the heat. There was a moon and a high-road and the going was far pleasanter than by day. I got into Adana about 10--there is absolutely nothing of any interest in the town. I went to the house of the Vice-Consul, a very able Greek, and he directed me to the best hotel. . .The other inhabitants of the hotel are strange Greeks and Turks and parties in turbans and Circassians with rows of cartridges set in their brown frock coats--Oh, the oddest crowd! It doesn't surprise me when I am in tents and part of it, but when I come into an hotel and put on civilised clothes, my surroundings astonish me at times. In the afternoon I called on the Vali, an obliging Kurd who promised me all facilities for my journey and gave me a little bronze lion, Greek I think. I have sent on my camp and tomorrow I am actu-ally going to Tarsus by train! Mr. Lloyd comes too and we spend the day together.

Monday, 24th we carried out our programme with immense enjoyment. The railway journey which took an hour and a half was quite an excitement to both of us--I haven't been by train since Mar-seilles. We had a delightful conversation with the station master before we started. He talked English and told us among other things that there were no works of art on the line, only one bridge. We were so busy talking on the journey that we forgot to notice even that work of art. Tarsus is nothing of a place, beautifully situated at the gates of the hills. Mr. Lloyd and I rather enjoyed ourselves however and we fin-ished the day by a dinner-party together in my tent at which Mikhail distinguished himself in the matter of cooking. I have taken on from Mr. Lloyd one of his servants whom he does not want any longer. His name is Fattuh and he is to be general director of the transport and

191

spare hand all round. I think I am wise in taking him for he seems very capable and has an excellent character from Mr. Lloyd, and my transport arrangements have not been going well for the last fortnight.

KARAMAN, May 7th. I daresay it does not often occur to you to think what a wonderful invention is the railway, but it is very forcibly borne in upon me at this moment for I am going to Konia in 3 hours instead of having a weary two day's march across a plain of mud. Yesterday I rode in here some 35 miles. The mountains have no other side, if you can understand me. The road I have come by rose some 6,000 ft. from the sea and did not descend more than 600 on the north side. Inside, the country is exactly what I have often pictured it to myself-a great barren upland with abrupt hills rising out of it. One of my soldiers and I rode on ahead and did the journey in 7 hours. We arrived in a thunderstorm and I went to the hotel and slept for 3 hours till my mules came in. I don't remember having been so tired for a long time. The hotel of Karaman is in the first stage of development from the primitive Khan. Your host provides the roof and every man is his own cook and housemaid. . . I wonder what the Kaimmakam thinks of the hats of English travellers of distinction. I have worn mine for 4 months in all weathers-you can scarcely tell which is the crown of it and which the brim. . .

To H. B., Bustbirklisse, May 13th, 1905

If you had read (and who knows? Perhaps you have the very latest German archaeology books you would be wild with excitement at seeing where I am. I must begin at the beginning and tell you about Konia. I stayed 4 days. My friend the German Consul (name of Loytved) is extremely intelligent and his wife very agreeable. The day after I arrived he took me out to see a Greek village in the hills about an hour from Konia, where he said there was a church. It was exceedingly interesting, with a tradition that it had been founded by the Empress Helena. There was a rock cut church in the same village as old if not older, but as it was Sunday and prayers were going on I could not map them, so I came back next day. It was a carpet making village. Loytved and I Went and had jam and water with a delightful Greek family and inspected their carpets on the looms. The old priest told me of another church in a second Greek village and I spent another morning mapping it, it was just as interesting as the first. These villagers have, I should think, been Christian since the days of St. Paul and the Greek population in them is no doubt descended from Greek settlements before the Christian era.

[Then follow descriptions of splendid Seljouk Mosques in ruins.]

Konia contains the mother house of the Dervishes and the founder of the order, Jelal ed Din Zumi the great Persian, is buried there. My visit to his tomb was a real pilgrimage for I know some of his poems and there are things in them that are not to be surpassed. He lies under a dome tiled with blue, bluer than heaven or the sea, and adorned inside with rich and Sombre Persian enamel and lacquer and on either side of him are rows and rows of the graves of the Chelebis, the Dervish high priests and his direct descendants--all the Chelebis who have been ministers and over each is the high felt hat of the order with a white turban wrapped round it. Beyond the tomb are two great dancing halls with polished floors and the whole is enclosed in a peaceful garden, fountains And flowers set round with the monastic cells of the order, so he lies, Jelal ed din Zumi, and to my mind the whole quiet air was full of the music of his verses: "Ah listen to the reed as it tells its tale: Listen, ah, listen, to the plaint of the reed." "They reft me from the rushes of my home, my voice is sad with longing, sad and low." (But the Persian is the very Pipe, the plaintive pipe of the reed, put into words and there is nothing so invades the soul.) I dined or lunched with the Loyeds daily, and he invited selections of banished Pashas daily to meet me. The result was some most interesting talks, for the best intelligence of Turkey is in exile and being in exile speaks out. Some day I will tell you some curious tales. So I have now an enormous circle of acquaintances in Konia and I spent my last afternoon there sitting in the Ottoman Bank and receiving the town. It was almost like Damascus over again. And my clothes arrived from Smyrna! If you had roughed it for 4 months with 2 tiny mule trunks you would realize what that meant. All things are by comparison and one evening when I put on a skirt that originally came from Paris I felt almost too smart to move. I sent my horses On 3 stations down the line and next day took train myself with my camp furniture and some food and Fattuh. We joined the horses on a blazing hot morning and packed our single load onto a hired beast and set off across the plain to Binbirklisse. The name means The Thousand and one Churches and the learned have tried to identify it with the classic Barala, but as then the learned knew nothing of Barala but the name, it doesn't seem to me to matter much whether the identification is correct or no. It lies at the foot of the Kara Dagh, a great isolated mountain arising abruptly out of the plain and whatever it was in classic times, it must have been a very important early Christian city for it is full of churches dating back Strzygowski thinks to pre-Constantine times. There is a lower town down at the foot of the hills and an upper town about an hour from it on a shoulder of mountain, and fate and my zaptieh ordered by good luck that our road should lead us to the upper town first. I fell in love with it at once, a mass of beautiful ruins gathered together in a little rocky cup high up in the hills--with Asia Minor at its feet. We arrived at mid-day and I established myself in a ruined church to lunch and then the brilliant idea seized me that I could make my headquarters up in the hills and not at Maden Sheher, which is the real Binbirklisse down in the plain. I had no tents with me and it was necessary to find out whether there was a possible place to sleep. The village consists of some 15 Turkish families who have built themselves shanties out of the ruins, but it is Turkish custom that any village however small shall contain a guest room for travellers and we went off to inspect. Yes, of course, said the sheikh of the village, there was an'oda'in his own house and I was most welcome to it. As soon as I saw it I knew that my best dreams were fulfilled. It was a little bare mud built room, with the name of God scratched up on the walls and before the door a platform looking out over the great plain and the slopes of Kara Dagh. I turned out the felts and mats in it put in my own furniture and it has proved ideal. It has had the further advantage that while the lower town has been thoroughly mapped, the upper was almost untouched and I have had the pleasure of doing it myself. The first day I rode down to Maden Sheher and spent the day there, photographing and learning from Strzygovski's book what was the nature of the architecture here. The churches were most interesting, but the place horrid, intolerably hot and with execrable water, so that it was a real delight to come back to my mountain and my beautiful spring in the evening. This was a fortress city of churches and monasteries. It has been most fascinating to work through a whole town and find the same architectural features occurring or being slightly modified by the originality of the builder. And then it has been very amusing to be for 4 days a Turkish Villager. It gives me great pleasure when I come in to tea to find my friend and host, the sheikh, saying his afternoon Prayers on a felt mat spread out at his door (he has got his orientation wrong; he prays looking west which can't Possibly be the direction of Mecca, but I daresay it's all one), and the women weaving coarse cloth in the shadow of the wall and the men driving their wooden ploughs through the stones that are the arable land of the village. Everyone takes me as a matter of course but the dogs who still bark furiously whenever I pass. And then my house is so nice with its mud walls and the name of God written up on them: Allah Allah. And my servants are so charming. And then Fattuh, bless him! the best servant I have ever had, ready to cook my dinner or push a mule or dig out an inscription with equal alacrity--the dinner is what he does least well--and to tell me endless tales of travel as we ride, for he began life as a muleteer at the age of ten and knows every inch of ground from Aleppo to Van and Bagdad. This morning I ascended Kara Dagh, and on horse back! It's a huge volcano the crater of which is about half a mile across, a ring of rocky peaks round the lip of it and the great plain stretching away to snow ranges behind. There were patches of snow still on Kara Dagh with crocuses on the edges of them and there were snowdrops in the oak scrub of the higher slopes, and a whole hillside of orange red tulips lower down and the most beautiful frittillary in the world, a bright deep yellow with brown spots. So you see it has made a delightful end to my travels, Binbirklisse. I do regret that I must go down to-morrow, but my work is finished and we have eaten up all our food. To-day we succeeded in buying a hen from the Sheikh--there are only 4 in the whole village and I thought it rather greedy of me to eat one of them, but Fattuh said stoutly that they would have 3 left and that was enough. The hen thought otherwise. It took sanctuary in every ruined church in turn and was finally run to earth in a tomb where Fattuh shot it with my gun!

May 15th. To-day I came down from my mountain top. I left at the first streak of dawn and rode for an hour before the sun rose. . .

May 16th. I was up at 4 to-day and at 5 I rode off to the hills to see one of the great sights of Asia Minor, the Hittite sculptures at Loriz. It was delicious riding at dawn up towards the snow of Taurus and more delicious still when after a couple of hours we entered a wonderful valley with a rushing stream flowing that I did not know, until we came to the village of Loriz at the mouth of a splendid rocky gorge. Above the village the river rushes out from under the rocks, a great stream as clear as crystal and just below its source there is the famous rock on which the sculptures are. Two figures, a god with curly hair and beard and pointed shoes and Phrygian cap adorned with a crown Of horns, in his hands the fruits of the earth, corn and bunches

195

of grapes, which he offers to a smaller figure, a king standing before him with hands uplifted in prayer. Behind the two run several lines of that strange script which no one can read, and beneath the rock rushes the clear water of the river. So I sat down under the walnut trees and considered that fine piece of symbolism of 5000 years ago: the river bursting from the mountain side and bearing fruitfulness to all the plain below and the god standing at its source with his trails of grapes and his swathe of corn. And then one came from the village and brought me eggs and milk and honey and the biggest nuts in the world and I feasted by the edge of the river. And if I had known the Hittite language I would have offered up a short thanksgiving in that tongue to the god with the curly hair and the tiara of horns who had brought such good things out of the naked earth. And then I rode back to Eryli--blazing hot it was--and took the train and came back to Konia. The Consul and his wife met me at the station and dined with me at the hotel and I found there besides Professor Ramsay, who knows more about this country than any other man, and we fell into each other's arms and made great friends. .

[This was Gertrude's first meeting with Sir William Ramsay, and it led to their interesting partnership in Asia Minor two years later.]

(Extract from Sir William Ramsay's Preface to "The Tbousand and One Churches."

"In 1905 Miss Gertrude Bell was impelled by Strzygowski's book to visit Bin Bir Kilisse; and, when I met her at Konia on her return, she asked me to copy an inscription on one of the churches, in letters so worn that she could not decipher it, which she believed to contain a date for the building. Her belief proved well founded and the chronology of the Thousand and One Churches centres round this text. I sent her a copy of the text, the imperfect--result of four hours' work, but giving the date with certainty; longer study was prevented by a great storm; and I printed in the Athenaeum the impression made on me by a hurried inspection of the ruins, mainly in order to reiterate in more precise form my old hope that an important architectural and historical investigation might be performed by an architect and an epigraphist, combining their work for a month or two on the site. This letter attracted her attention; she wrote suggesting that we should undertake the task; and as no one else seemed likely to do so, my wife and I arranged to join her in 1907. . ."

Sir William Ramsay, once more home from Asia Minor in 1927, writes me this further letter of appreciation of her work with him.

13 Greenhill Terrace, Edinburgh.
24 June, 1927.

DEAR LADY BELL,
. . . I should be glad if you would add an expression of my admiration for the thoroughness and alertness of Miss Gertrude Bell's examination of Bin Bir Kilisse on her first short visit. The important inscription was almost totally concealed in a little cave. During our work in 1907 I spent about a fortnight on that inscription and finally succeeded in deciphering it completely, and it appears in our joint work with the help of her eyes.

I am, Yours faithfully,
W. M. RAMSAY)

CHAPTER XI

1905-1909 - LONDON-ASIA MINOR-LONDON

(In the following June Gertrude was in London again, enjoying herself there as usual. She spent the summer at Rounton. She was extremely keen about the garden and especially greatly absorbed in starting a rock garden which afterwards became one of the show gardens of the North Riding. It was exquisitely situated, formed round a lake, from the shores of which was a view of the wide amphitheatre of the Cleveland Hills.

In the autumn she went to Paris to study with Reinach again.]

To F. B., Paris, October 24, 1905

On Saturday I came over by the 10 o'clock train and arrived rather late, so I sent a word to S. Reinach that I would appear after dinner. . . I went in and found him and Mrs. S. R., who extremely friendly. She is a pleasant woman. After a bit Reinach and I went into his library and I showed him my plans And photographs and we settled some details about publication and illustrations. I came back to my hotel at 11--it's only a step from the Reinach's. This morning, a heavenly bright frosty day, I went to Reinach's at 9:30 and waited till 11:30 when Dussaud the Syrian traveller came to see me, we had a most delightful hour's talk. I'm going to his house to-morrow to look over some Nabathean and Safaitic inscriptions and discuss what is to be found in Nejd. After he went we lunched, I then took a little stroll with the two Reinachs in the bright sunshine. We walked towards the Bois. R. and I came back at 3 and I looked through travel books and inscriptions till 6. It is perfectly enchanting having everything at one's hand, and R. to suggest and lay more books before me. He is delighted with the first article and is going to send it to press at once. To-night he has asked Yves Guyot to dinner because I said I wanted to see him, so we shall have a little 'relâche' from archaeology. . .

I don't feel I could be doing this work under better conditions.

[Gertrude and her father left Plymouth on December 16th, 1905--Gibraltar, Tangiers, Spain, Marseilles, Paris, etc., and so to London.

We have no letters from Gertrude in 1906. That year she seems to have spent between London and Rounton, enjoying mightily having people to stay during the summer, seeing the rock garden grow and writing her book of travels--The Desert and the Sown--which came out the following year.

Among her special friends who stayed with her that summer were Major (now Sir Frederick) O'Connor, Aubrey Herbert, Sir Hugh and Lady Barnes, Lady Arthur Russell, Elizabeth Robins, the William Tyrrells, Sir Valentine Chirol and Mr. and Mrs. Wilton Phipps.

On December 20th of that year she and her father left London and went via Marseilles to Cairo. There her father was ill. They returned to England at the beginning of February, 1907, and early in April she is in Asia Minor again

The technical results of Gertrude's work with Sir William Ramsay were shown in the book they wrote together, " The Thousand and One Churches," published in 1909, in which the plans and measurements of the more important churches and architectural remains were given.

From her letters from Asia Minor in 1907, therefore, I have taken extracts relating to her personal experiences only, on the road. Although travel in Asia Minor is not so adventurous as crossing the deserts of Arabia, it has an adventurous and picturesque side of its own. In Asia Minor she was again befriended by the kind Whittall family.]

To F.B., Cairo, Tuesday, January 1, 1907

The great event is Hugo's arrival yesterday. [Hugo had been to Australia.] He is extremely cheerful and full of interesting tales. We talked all the afternoon and he came up into my room and talked till dinner time. It's quite delightful .having him. We dined with the Cromers--Lady C., Lady Valda [Machell] and I were the only women so I sat on the other side of Lord C. and had a quite enchanting talk with him. He is the nicest person in the world, without doubt. He was very eager to know if there was anything I wanted and when I said I wanted to have a good talk with a learned sheikh, he was much concerned about it, saying to Mr. Machell across the table, " Look here, Machell, you must find us a good sheikh. Just think who is the best." So they are thinking. The immediate result was that they arranged that we should see the Azhar to-day. It is the great university of the Mohammedan world, where they are sometimes rather tiresome about letting women in. However, I found a friend on the doorstep, and we fell into one another's arms and he took us all over. Indeed, we were invited to dine there by an old party from Bagdad who lives there and I'm invited to breakfast on Saturday if I like, so anyway I feel I may come and go as I Please in the Azhar. Hugo talked to Lady Valda all the morning yesterday, and I to Sir W. Garstin, who is very pleasant and interesting, so we all enjoyed ourselves. Father and I had a charming dinner with the Machells, too; Sir W. G. was there also. Yesterday we lunched with the Bernstorffs and we are going to their box at the opera to-night. On Friday, Father and I spent the whole morning with Ernest Richmond, seeing Coptic churches--most pleasant.

To F.B., Cairo, Friday, 12th January, 1907

I had an interesting talk with Moritz while he was teaching me to take squeezes of inscriptions after a manner of his own (an excellently simple one, by the way).

To F.B., Smyrna, April 4th, 1907

I hope I shall get off on Monday. My preparations are really all finished but I have to wait and hear about the head man for my diggings whom Mr. Richard Whittall is engaging for me. As this is the most important matter of all I cannot leave without settling it. Then to call on all my Whittall friends. They have the bulk of the English trade in their hands, bran offices all down the southern coast, mines and shooting boxes and properties scattered up and down the S.W. coast of Asia Minor and yachts on the seas. They all have immense quantities of children. The sons, young men now in the various Whittall businesses, the daughters very charming, very gay. The big gardens touch one another and they walk in and out of one another's houses all day long gossiping and laughing. I should think life presents itself nowhere under such easy and pleasant conditions.

To F.B., Magnesia ad Meandrum, Wednesday, April 9, 1907

I've just been visiting the ruins of this town in the company of a pleasant Greek who talked Turkish, so we managed to have a little conversation. But it is such a bore not talking the language properly. I must hurry up and learn. Of course, one ought to know Greek too, but for the moment I feel one new language is a good deal more than I can manage. I've just been giving my friend the Greek tea in my carriage. The station master came in and joined the party. The station masters on this line are supposed to know English and accordingly as he entered he said cheerfully, " Goodbye!"

To F.B., Miletus, Friday, April 12, 1907

Often when one sets out on a journey one travels by all the roads according to the latest maps, one reaches all the places of which the history books speak. Duly one rises early and turns one's face towards new countries, carefully one looks and laboriously one tries to understand, and for all one's trouble one might as well have stayed behind and read a few big archaeology books. But I would have you know that's not the way I have done it this time. I said to myself: I will go and see the Greece of Asia, the Greece Grote didn't know. And I have found it. The seas and the hills are all full of legends and the valleys are scattered over with the ruins of the great rich Greek cities. Here is a page of history that one sees with the eye and that enters into the mind as no book can relate it.

THE LETTERS OF GERTRUDE BELL

To F. B., Miletus, April 12, 1907

In this sort of travel one goes on very short commons. One starts early and one gets in late; there is no time to cook, and there is no meat to be had if one could cook it. So I have lived mostly on eggs and rice and sour milk, not a bad diet of its kind if you have enough of it, and to-night's dinner (soup and a chicken) was the best meal I have had for some days. . .

I gave up thinking .. . . . for the crossing of that river was itself sufficient matter for thought. There was no bridge--if there had been one it would have been broken--the water was deep and the ferry-boat was a buffalo cart. The river came nearly over the buffaloes' backs; we had to take everything off the horses and lead them behind us--the buffaloes didn't care, they plodded steadily on and held up their noses to keep them out of the water. Now a buffalo can't hold up his nose very far; a little more and they would have been drowned, but they did not think of that. At the other side we changed horses and rode 25 miles into Aidin, all good going till we came to the Meander valley where it was the very devil. Before we reached it, as we rode along the high road, there came a sound of crying and presently we saw a heap of something on the broad road. It was a dead man, lying as he had fallen with a tattered coat thrown over his face, and beside him a ragged child, a little girl sitting all alone in the sun, and wailing, wailing--you have never heard the east Mourning, it is always the same and always more melancholy than any other sound. A man passed just before we reached the child, he merely drew his horse aside and rode on. Eh! a man more or less in the world, and a gypsy at that. We stopped and questioned her. They had sent on news to Aidin, her brother had gone, she didn't know when they would come. And so she took up her dirge again. We rode on to the ferry over the Meander and tried to hire a cart to bring in the dead man's body, but no one would go--no, he must stay there till his people came, that was the custom. The girl? She could stay too to keep the dogs off and if night fell and she was afraid she would come in to the nearest village. Yes, someone would go and watch with her if I would give him two mejidis. But I knew that was no good as he would come away the moment my back was turned. So I rode on too; the child will come into the village at nightfall and the man is dead and does not care how long he lies alone. But I felt a beast, all the same. We crossed the Meander in a ferry--the bridge was broken, I need scarcely say, and the high road beyond was all under water. So we splashed for an hour along a narrow cobbled path running between bottomless swamps. We came to Aidin about 5, it is against the hills and all shining in the sun. But what makes it chiefly memorable is that I got Elsa's telegram here saying she was engaged to Herbert Richmond, and am thinking of it with such mixed feelings. But there it is, and there's nothing else for it but to put up with it and try not to think what a difference it will make. I can't come home now because I can't leave Ramsay in the lurch and I shall hear no more from you till I get to Konia, bother it! I've written to Elsa since there is no way of telegraphing.

To F.B., Bodjeli, April 24th, 1907

I have got your letter telling me of E.'s engagement. Yes, in a way it's easier perhaps not to be at home. it is unsatisfactory for the family rather, still I rather wish I were with you all the same. Meantime I shall continue to tell you of my adventures, if you have time to think of them! One rides for hours over beautiful well watered country without seeing an inch of ploughed ground. We are riding towards a high Snowy range of mountains, at the foot of which Aphrodisias lies. The town must have been distinguished above all other places for the elaborate beauty of its architecture; every doorway was covered with scrolls of fruit and flowers with birds and beasts entwined in them.

I slept! Oh, if you could have seen where I slept! It was in the khan, a tiny room separated by a rough wall of planks from the 30 or 40 muleteers and camel drivers who were lodging there for the night. It was quite empty, however, and I put my camp bed in and was as happy as possible, --One wall was all window--I closed half of it with a shutter when I went to bed, and until then I sat and watched the village unloading its camels, cooking its evening meal over wood fires lighted in earthenware bowls, saying its evening prayer on a little raised platform in front of the khan and after having seen the temple under the moon I went to bed and no number of talking, smoking muleteers could have kept me awake. Fattuh, however, was not at all happy. He did not think it a suitable lodging for my Excellency. . .

THE LETTERS OF GERTRUDE BELL

To F.B., Isdarta, April 28th, 1907

I don't suppose there is anyone in the world happier than I am or any country more lovely than Asia Minor. I just mention these facts in passing so that you may bear them in mind. We rode and rode over the hills and down to the edge of a great lake of Buldur. Bitter salt it is and very blue, and mountains stand all round it, white with snow, and the fruit gardens border it, pink and white with peach and cherry. And SO we Came to Buldur, a fine town standing in a rich land, and there we pitched camp in a green field at the edge of the town. All the authorities came down in turn--begged me not to spend the night in the wilderness and entreated me to share their flea-y houses and told me that my next day's journey was quite Out of the question because of the snow and the mountains and I don't know what, till finally I said I was going to bed and sent them all away. Said Fattuh: "What sort of Soldiers are these? They fear the cold and they fear the mountains and they fear the rivers-perhaps they fear the rabbits and the foxes." And he went away shaking his head mournfully over the degeneracy of the Turkish army and muttering in Turkish "Nasl arkar! nasl arkar! what sort, what sort of soldiers!" To-day I started off at 5:30 and, leaving Fattuh to bring the camp by the straight road, I took a soldier and rode into the hills, a wonderful, wonderful ride. . .

It is now night and the moon has not yet risen. Fattuh has gone to look for horses and I am left with the soldier who is our guard to-night. I think he feels rather anxious at being left alone here in the dark for he has crept in close to the light of my tent and has been telling me, half in Turkish and half in broken Arabic, of his 10 years in Yemen and of how, praise be to God! he did not die there though he was wounded twice.

Tuesday, April 30th. We have not made much way to-day as the crow flies because the road along the eastern shore of the lake is not yet finished and we had very rough going which delayed the baggage animals. It was instructive to see how road making is conducted in Turkey. It's a very hilly road, up and down and in and out over the mountains. They had one old man and three younger ones with a few little boys working at one end and at the other unfinished end there were some 30 men who were engaged in baking and eating bread on the hill-side. Also they take no count of the streams that cross the road continuously, the country being mountainous as YOU Will understand. These streams therefore wash away the work as soon as it is done. I think it will be some time before this road is joined up.

Wednesday, May 1st. I haven't really done much to-day though I have taken a good deal of trouble about it. I had to find a fountain with a Latin inscription of which Ramsay wanted a new copy. I found it, inscription and all complete, and worked two hours at the latter without a very satisfactory result as it was much broken and lay too near the splash of the fountain so that I could not take a good rubbing. The oldest and most decrepit soldier in the world was told off at Egerdir to bear me company. He knows nothing of the country and our intercourse was confined to something like the following: Me: "Where does this road go to?" He: "Effendim, I do not know." Me: "What is the name of that village?" He: "Effendim? I could not say." Me: "How far is it to so-and-so?" He: "Effendim, I have not been." The result of which is that I have to find all my own routes by asking the people by the wayside. . .

I started at 5:45 taking with me an intelligent villager of Tokmajik the place where I had spent the night. He knew the country and was a satisfactory guide and an agreeable companion. He had been a soldier and had served mainly in Crete, an island of which he thought highly. We took a path hitherto untravelled over the hills, past two villages unknown to Kiefert (there were unfortunately no inscriptions in them though there were old worked stones) and dropped down on to the northern end of the Lake of Egerdir. There was a place which Ramsay had begged me to try and visit on the eastern shore of the lake. It is a place of pilgrimage where the Christians come once a year, in September, from all the countryside, and the probability is that it was a holy site long before the Christian era, sacred to Artemis of the Lake who was herself a Pisidian deity re-baptised by the Greeks. I found the Place, about 2 miles down the lake, and a very striking place it Was. The rocks drop here straight into the lake and at their foot there is a great natural arch some 15 feet wide through which glistens the blue water of the lake. In the rock above is a small rock-cut chamber into which I scrambled with some difficulty and found a slab like a loculus in it. It may have been a tomb at some time but I think more probably the slab was sacrificial; at any rate the Christians use the chamber now to celebrate their yearly mass. So we rode back along the beautiful grassy shores of the lake, where the Yuruks were watching their flocks and herds, and all round the swampy northern end of the lake. Almost joined to the shore by beds of immensely tall reeds there is a little island which no one had yet succeeded in visiting. I, however, found a fisherman's hut in the swamp and near it a very old and smelly boat, so I hired the three fishermen for an infinitesimal sum and rowed out to the island with Nazmi, my Tokmajik man. it was completely surrounded by ruined Byzantine walls dropping into the water in great blocks of masonry; here and there, there was a bit of an older column built into them and they were densely populated by snakes. There was only one thing of real interest, a very curious stele with a female figure carved on it, bearing what looked like water skins, and two lines of inscription above. She might have been Artemis of the Lake itself and perhaps the inscription said so, but unfortunately the whole stone was covered by 18 inches or more of shimmering water. It had fallen into the lake and there it lay. I did all I knew to get the inscription. I waded into the water and tried to scrub the slime off the stone, but the water glittered and the slime floated back and finally I gave it up and came out very wet and more than a little annoyed. It was provoking after I had taken so much trouble, wasn't it? However at any rate now we know that it's there and someone can go and fish it out. So we punted back through the reeds. One of my boatmen had been through the Russo-Turkish war--Nish, Pleven, he rambled on about all the things he had seen and done while we brushed through the reeds, looking sometimes for fish in the traps they had set, and sometimes for birds' eggs, and I sat in the sun and dried myself. It was so hot that I was quite dry before I got into camp. Then we rode north up the plain and explored a village for inscriptions as we went. There was a large farm here left by an agreeable Greek who helped me in my search and invited me into his house where his wife gave me milk; and at last at a quarter to seven we got to Mundanely where I found my camp pitched and my dinner ready. In and around Mundanely have been found (mainly by Ramsay) a very curious series of inscriptions relating to an anti-Christian Society of the second century. It was called the Society of those who showed the Sign, and the Sign was probably some act of worship of the Emperor and the old gods. I had all the published inscriptions with me and I hunted round this morning for a couple of hours and found a new one in a Turkish house--very short and I fear not very important, but I took a rubbing to the surprise and joy of the inhabitants, and shall give it to Ramsay. It was very hot again to-day. Got into camp at 3, since when I have done nothing but sleep and eat and write my diary. To-morrow is an off day and I can't say I regret it. It's very laborious being the careful traveller I don't think I do it well either. There are probably lots of things that I don't see because I don't know how to look. I remember Ramsay's telling me that the first journey he made in Asia Minor he found nothing at all. And you see I only find things under water! Fattuh loq: "Never in my life did I see such a town! May God send them to their fathers and may their women be taken captive! I paid 5 pilasters for your Excellency's beans. No meat in all the town and may it be destroyed!" I: "And the chicken is less good than the chicken of Tokmajik." Fattuh (with indignant reminiscence of his culinary experiences at Tokmajik) "That chicken she eat 4 pilasters of fire wood and then I cooked her 3 hours at Mundanely--God send all chickens to their fathers!"

In the afternoon I called on the Kaimmakam--I must tell you about the Kaimmakam. Fattuh went down into the town early. The barber's shop is as you know the fashionable lounge and there he found the Kaimmakam, the Bengasi, the Imam the Kati and a few more all sitting together. In the afternoon I go to the Kaimmakam; the Kaimmakam, the Bengasi, the Imam the Kadi, etc., are still all sitting together drinking coffee and smoking. An hour later comes a message to say that the Kaimmakam, the Binbashi, etc. wish to call on me. SO up they came, six of them, all in a serried row and sat in my tent and drank more coffee and smoked more cigarettes. It's my private conviction that that's all they can do, any of them, and they all do it together every day. They appear to have given their advice collectively as regards the hiring of a cart for my luggage and even the buying of candles and rice, so to-day they have been unusually busy. I've bought another horse, this time for 10 pounds, which is not dear. I like the look of him very much. The first one has turned out excellently, and I think this one is even better. Now I'm provided. In this transaction I did not seek the advice of the Kaimmakam, the Binbashi, the Imam or the Kadi.

Tuesday, May 7th. We've had laborious travelling, but it has all ended successfully. We left Yalorach early on Sunday, 6 a.m. I had hire a cart for my luggage. I had always been told by the authorities on the subject that that was the proper way to travel in Asia Minor. Now I know it isn't. One has to learn these things for oneself. So we set out, and I was riding my new horse which was as wild as a hawk and as timid as a lizard, so I had enough to think of for the first hour or two. (He is settling down now he has got into good hands and is becoming a capital little animal, I think the best horse for travel I have ever had.)

In four and a half hours we came to a dullish place called Karagash. We went to the khan and determined to wait anyhow till the cart arrived and then set out again. We waited and waited and at noon we lunched and then there came a most furious thunderstorm with sheets of rain and batterings of hail and at length came news that the cart had broken down and the man had gone back to fetch another. By this time the road was deep in water and mud, and the end of it was that the luggage arrived at 5 and there was no more thought of travel for that day. On the whole perhaps it was as well, for it rained without stopping till 7 so that we should have got very wet. So I ate some of the curious soup that Fattuh makes out of the Lord knows what and went to bed. I may mention that my room was crowded with bugs and fleas, but I had my own bed at least. There were no horses to be got at Karagash, no horses, so there was nothing for it but to hire another cart next day and again we set out at 6 o'clock full of hope. For the first hour or two the road was deep in mud but presently we came to a little pass and the ground hardened and cleared. Here Fattuh stopped to wait for the cart and I rode on with my soldier. At 10:15 I got to Kassaba, another miserable little hole, again I went to the khan and again I waited. This time after an hour and a half came a message sent by Fattuh to say that the cart had stuck in the mud and he had gone back to Karagash for another. I ordered eggs and bread and curds and lunched and did my best to be patient and at 1:30 up came Fattuh triumphantly with two carts, having pulled the first out of the mud with buffaloes and then driven it into Kassaba. But I was not going to be put off again with half a day's journey, so I left the carts and Fattuh to rest for an hour and rode on over the flat plain by Bey Sheher lake. It is not so fine as the other lakes though the mountains drop steeply into it on the W. side, but it is very typical of this country and of no other. A melancholy land, in spite of its lakes and mountains, though I like it. You leave the bright and varied coast line which was Greece, full of vitality, full of the breath of the sea and the memory of an active enterprising race, and with every step into the interior you feel Asia the real heart of Asia. Monotonous, colourless, lifeless, unsubdued by a people whose thoughts travel no further than to the next furrow, who live and die and leave no mark upon the great plains and the barren hills-such is central Asia, of which this country is a true part. And that is why the Roman roads make so deep an impression on one's mind. They impressed the country itself, they implied a great domination, they tell of a people that overcame the universal stagnation. It was very hot and still and clouds of butterflies drifted across the path and there was no other living thing except a stork or two in the marshy ground and here and there a herd of buffaloes with a shepherd boy asleep beside them. At the end of the lake a heavy thunderstorm gathered and crept along the low hills to the east and up into the middle of the sky. And so we came to the earliest record of what was probably one of the earliest trade roads in the world and the forerunner of the Roman road; and here the clouds broke upon us in thunder and lightning and hail and rain and I saw the four Hittite kings, carved in massive stone, against a background of all the fury of the storm. They are seated at the edge of a wide pool, a spring bubbling out of the hillside, from which a swift river flows away to the lake; and above them are figures with uplifted hands, as though they praised the god of Gotat waters.

KONIA, Saturday 11th. . . ..I'm writing to Elsa about plans (I can scarcely bear the idea of not being at her wedding). Ramsay arrives in three days and I've got a hundred thousand things to do so I'll write no more now.

To F.B., Maden Sheher, May 21, 1907

My donkey goes at dawn to-morrow to fetch the post and I must write you a word, though 10 hours hard riding, which is what I have been doing to-day, is not a good preparation for letter-writing. The habit of building everything on the extreme top of hills is to be deprecated. It entails so much labour for subsequent generations. It was very hot to-day. I lunched in the house of a charming Circassian, who lives in a Circassian village on the other side of the hills. He gave me coffee and some curds to add to my own lunch and we made great friends. He has invited me to come and stay. All the other Circassians sat round the while. Yesterday I had a hard day. I had found the afternoon before, a ruined site with a very perfect church on the top of a hill near my camp, and in the church was a half-buried stone which I thought was probably the altar. So I took up some of my men with picks and crowbars and had it out and it was the altar. Then I photographed and planned the whole site, a good 5 hours' work. I came back my tents for lunch and an hour's rest and then we rode off to another further hill and there I found a church and chapel, much ruined but of an interesting plan, so I worked at them all the afternoon. I meant to draw them out to scale when I came back but I was too tired and they are still waiting to be done. The truth is there is too much work here for one person, but I am very much enjoying my solitude, and the work is mighty fun too if one could only do it a little better. As yet I haven't touched this place, thinking that Ramsay had better have the responsibility. If he doesn't come there are one or two things I must do and the rest I shall leave to someone cleverer. My Cast! oh my cast! it's more professional than words can say. I'm longing to do another when I can find time. My larder is splendidly supplied with hares and partridges which the villagers bring me. It's as well, for they won't sell their lambs as nearly all their sheep died in the cold winter they have had. Fattuh rode out to a village 5 hours away and brought back a lamb across his saddle bow. We kept it against accidents, such as the Ramsay family appearing unexpectedly, and it browses round my tents in a charming fashion.

To F.B., Maden Sheher, Saturday, May 25, 1907

I really must begin a diary to you. The Ramsays arrived yesterday. I was in the middle of digging up a church when suddenly 2 carts hove into sight and there they were. It was about 3 in the afternoon. They instantly got out, refused to think of going to the tents, Lady R. made tea (for they were starving) in the open and R. oblivious of all other considerations was at once lost in the problems the church presented. It was too delightful to have someone as much excited about it as I was! . . . They have brought their son Louis with them who is deeply learned on birds and beasts and has a commission from the British Museum to collect the small mammalia of these parts.

Now I must tell you something very very striking. The church on the extreme point of the Kara D., at which I worked for 2 days before R. came, has near it some great rocks and on the rocks I found a very queer inscription. The more I looked at it the queerer it became and the less I thought It could be Christian or anything that I knew, so I took it down with great care, curious rabbit-headed things and winged sort of crosses and arms and circles, and with some trembling I showed it to R. The moment he looked at it he said, "It's a Hittite inscription. This is the very thing I hoped most to find here." I think I've never been so elated. We now think nothing but Hittites all the time.

Now this is the manner of Asia Minor: there is never a shrine of Christian or Moslem but if you look long enough you will find it has been a holy place from the beginning of history and every church on the top of the hill stands on a site where the Hittites worshipped. We began to find queer things, a tower of a very ancient sort of fortification, and then we found cuttings in the rocks which puzzled us for a long time till I, who had seen the same before in Syria, discovered that they were winepresses, and the long and the short of it is that we think we have a Hittite settlement at Maden Sheher and that this was the entrance fort. Of course we may get no more evidence and the thing will have to remain as a supposition, but the inscription on the top of the Kara D. is a fixed point.

[Then followed excited days of visiting churches, planning, deciphering, guessing.]

. . ..I haven't told you half enough what gorgeous fun it's being! You should see me directing the labours of 20 Turks and 4 Kurds! We are going to get something out of it, you'll see.

To F.B., Maden Sheher, May 29, 1907

I got a long letter from you today dated May 19, enclosing some photographs from Hugo (for which I am deeply obliged) and describing the plans for Elsa's wedding. I fear I have definitely given up all hope of coming back for it. I am in for this business and I must carry it through. I get up at 5 and breakfast before the Ramsay family have appeared and go off before 6 to wherever we are digging, and stay there till 12 superintending and measuring as we uncover. Then I come back to the tents for an hour, for the men have an hour off in the middle of the day and after lunch I go back to the diggings and stay there till 5 or later. R. generally appears on the scene about 7 or 8 in the morning and about 3 in the afternoon Then he has inscriptions to find and read and the map to make and he can't physically do more. I shall have all the measuring and planning to do and I'm at it some 12 hours a day on and Off. Nor can it be otherwise for that's the part that I have undertaken. Of course it's great great fun, but it's also very hard work, you understand. And there is no one to do it but me. Therefore I can't leave and that's an end.

To F. B., Maden Sheher, May 29th, 1907

One of the difficulties of the commissariat here is the water. I have to send 2 hours up the hill for it daily and I find I can't supply the needs of the whole camp with one donkey load and the poor donkey can't go more than once a day. So Fattuh is going to Karaman to morrow to buy another donkey and more water tins. Housekeeping in the wilderness takes a great deal of thinking about! But I must say the difficulties are considerably alleviated when all your guests are as amenable as mine are.

Friday, May 30th. We've had a very long day clearing out a round church which is a difficult architectural problem, and oh! Horrible to measure. I'm tired now and I shan't write any more.

To F. B., Maden Sheher, June 4, 1907

I haven't kept to my good resolutions in the matter of a diary letter but the fact is I'm so very busy.

I've been working all today from dawn on the big apse on which I first began. It still remains a complete puzzle and one I fear will not be elucidated. I shall give it a day off so as to think about it and then do another day's work on it. The walls we have uncovered seem to have no meaning and they are such bad work that it's a stretch of the imagination to suppose that there is any consecutive idea in them. Anyway it's not a church, of so much we are certain; and the guesses of all our Predecessors have been wrong, but what to guess ourselves is the problem. The learned world is agog about my Hittite inscription. We shall have to go up and do some more work there. It's all very, very nice-I'm enjoying it thoroughly.

To F.B., Daile, June 8, 1907

Today we have had the greatest exodus known since the days of the Jews. We have moved all our camp up to the yaila, the summer quarters. It took 11 camels and 4 donkeys to transport us. Now this is the place that I first came to two years ago. It is on a shoulder of the Kara Dagh, 1000 ft. above Maden Sheher and it is entirely composed of churches, chapels and monastic foundations. A few Turkish hovels are' accommodated in the ruins-in one of them I stayed two years ago. The people are overjoyed at my return and gave me a most cordial welcome. They sent down to me while I was at Maden Sheher to say they hoped I was coming up and I hired from them all the camels for the transport. One of the most interesting parts of our job has been the tracing of the first settlement of the mountain. It began with my Hittite High Place; there we found several vestiges of an ancient town at Maden Sheher and today Sir W. has seen 3 Hittite inscriptions on an outlying spur of the mountain-he went there while we were moving camp. Of these and of the High Place we are going to take casts so as to have absolutely perfect impressions of them. Isn't it a good thing I learnt to take casts, by the way! Without that we could not have got perfect impressions of these things for the stone is so rough that it is extremely difficult to get anything like a good rubbing. We are getting so much material that it will certainly make a book. Our plan is that Sir W. shall write the historic and epigraphic part and I the architectural. I think it will be well worth doing, for this is the first time that an accurate study has been made of any one district in these parts, hitherto people have only travelled through and seen what they could see and gone On. We shall certainly be able to contribute a great deal to the knowledge of such settlements as this must have been. I look forward to a delightful winter at home drawing my plans and writing my part of the book. I should have been helpless here without Sir W. and the more I work with him the more I like him and respect his knowledge. In fact, it's being a magnificent success, quite everything I hoped it would be.

It will be a very dull book, you understand, but I intend it to be magnificently illustrated. I wonder if Heinemann will do it for me!

It will be very pleasant to have the Barneses at Mt. Grace-I hope they will come.

To her brother, Daile, June 14, 1907

I must answer at once your delightful letter with the descriptions of Penrhos all so characteristic! His Lordship! I can see him with the Times Atlas listening to my letter! You would be surprised to see the scene in the middle of which I am writing. Thirty-one Turks are busy with picks and spades clearing out a church and monastery. At intervals they call out to me " Effendim, effendim! is this enough?" or "Come and see this-this is good!" or something. They are perfectly charming people up here and I have got the pick of my men from Maden Sheher and we are all on the most friendly terms. It is about 7 a.m. and I have been at work for an hour. If you find some earth in my letter it's the dust of Byzantines which flies round me.

To H. B., Daile, June 14, 1907

I'm charmed to hear the rock garden looks nice. I'm glad we have an addition to the stable. I hope the foal will turn out well. I am horribly bored at not being at E.'s wedding. I shall always regret not having seen her married, but I think I am right in deciding to stay and finish this job. I hope You think so. I really haven't a moment to think of anything but my work and it accumulates with an almost malignant rapidity. I tremble to think of the amount of drawing I have before me now.

To F. B., Karadagh, June 17, 1907

Of course you can't write to me much. I'm busy too in a modest way. . . I believe this is the very first time anyone has set Bout to explore thoroughly a single district in central Asia. See what we have got out of it! Two great sites and a vast amount of unexpected Byzantine remains. We spend much time discussing our book, which is to be a great work, please God! Oh, it's delightful, delightful! I only do so hope you think I was right to stay Out here, I could scarcely bear it if you didn't--at a breath from you I would come back by the next train. I hate being away, you understand, but I am deeply absorbed by this work. it grows more and more exciting as one gets further into it.

To F.B., Daile, June 21, 1907

Torrents of rain are streaming down onto my tent, the first heavy rain we have had for 5 weeks and more. I hope it won't go on very long or it will probably run in under my bed where I keep all the long rolls of my big plans. We have had rather a disagreeable few days as regards weather; first 2 days of great heat (I was digging with 30 men on one of them and had to be out the whole day long in the sun). Then we had 2 days' wind which is the most intolerable thing possible and almost prevents us from working at all, as one can scarcely dig or measure and if one goes to one's tent to draw, one finds it a kind of dust heap inside. Last night the wind brought up a thunderstorm and it rained a good deal in the night and this morning it was quite grey and cool. Sir W. and I profited by this to go down to Maden Sheher to finish up some odds and ends. I think we have still about a week's work here and it's the most important work of all for we are now beginning to get our views and our information into some kind of shape. This consoles me a little for I should have had to have been going away now to get home in time for Elsa's wedding. I am become quite the architect I must tell you. I have pages and pages of mouldings all beautifully drawn out and MY plans are most elaborate, I don't think anyone has ever published any of these Anatolian mouldings before-- our book will be very 'bahnbrechend,' you'll see! . . . I'm so glad the new motor is a success. Dear me! it will be very pleasant to be back again in the bosom of my family. Still, I'm very happy.

I propose to stay at home for a good long time after this.

To F.B., Daile, Tuesday, June 24, 1907

We are coming to the very end of our time here. The Ramsays leave on the 26th and I on the 28th. Well, we have accomplished a great deal. This last week has been the most useful of all. It makes me quite sad to think that in all probability I shall never come back here. We have been a sort of small providence, what with our work and the market we have offered. I don't suppose so much money has passed hands in the Karadagh since the time of the Byzantines.

My simple annals must seem very paltry to you in the midst of all your festivities. Yes, it is very very nice to be completely absorbed in the thing one is doing and to have no interruption in it. I rather shiver to think what a tremendous work it will be writing all this. It will take months, I think. I am not going to lecture at all--I've refused to go to Redcar. I must get this book done or someone else will nip in and take the wind out of our sails. I'm afraid I shall not be back till the beginning of August, but as I've stayed so long it would be silly to scamp things for the sake of a week more or less. . .

THE LETTERS OF GERTRUDE BELL

To F.B., Karapuna, June 30, 1907

Yesterday I took the road again. A great plain is a wonderfully beautiful thing. It stretched away and away from my tent door as far as the eye could see, as level to the horizon as it was level under my feet. It looked like an immensely wide floor made ready for some splendid spectacle. To-day we rode over it again for 3 hours to Karabanar, a small town at the foot of the Karajadagh. There lives on the plateau the largest beetle I have been privileged to see. Black and green is his colour and he is the size of a mouse.

I lunched in the khan, waiting for my luggage cart. They gave me quite a nice bare room to myself; publicity, however, was ensured by a window which opened into the room next me. Then the Kaimmakam and another came to call. Thank Heaven I can now talk enough Turkish not to be left speechless with Kaimakams and the rest. We were in the thick of making arrangements to go straight on into the hills.

When I arrived I had asked if there were pack horses. "As many as you like can be found," said the innkeeper. Presently he returned to say there were none. "Then," said I, "I will take a cart to the village at the edge of the hills." Most excellent," said the surrounding company, "the cart will draw you to the hills and then you will get camels." "Camels are to be found, then?" said I. "Many," said they. Then arrived the Kaimmakam and the Other, and I explained that I was leaving at once for Salur with my luggage in a cart. They heartily approved this plan. Over the coffee the Other let fall a remark to the effect that I should find no people at all as they had all gone up to yaila. "Then how shall I find camels?" said I. "Effendim ," said he, "there will be no camels." Finally I resolved to take camels from him and after waiting for 4 hours the camels have appeared. An incident similar to this occurs daily when travelling in Asia Minor; the wonder is that one gets through at all. . . There go the camels with a Haide! father! pull, my soul! hasten, hasten!" from all onlookers.

They pulled very well and we got in here at 5:30. . .

I must tell you that this expedition into the Karajadagh is rather an adventure. No one has as yet explored the mountain. We

216

have come into the heart of it and pitched tents and so far all is well. The whole of the upper part of the mountain is entirely deserted. It's extraordinarily lonely. There are said to be robbers about.

I have no less than 6 men here, including the 2 camel drivers, so I don't feel at all anxious even if they should be still in these parts.

Wednesday, July 3 I am so dreadfully torn this week by considering exactly what you are doing and wishing I were doing it too. I feel terribly outcast when I think of you and long 50 times a day to be at home. However, there it is and next week I shall feel better, after it's all over and done with. Yesterday I had a very long day. We started out, Haidar and my gipsy, Aziz is his name, and I, and rode up to a hill on the top of the crater above us. It was cold, absurdly enough, a north wind which increased all day till it became a horrid nuisance. There were two men on the uplands above the crater, one with a herd of deer and one with a herd of cattle from the villages below--we saw no other living soul all day. And there was a cruciform church with monastic buildings and fortifications and all complete! I do not doubt that this is the chief and central shrine of the Karajadagh so I am content. No one has been here before--it's a most curious sensation to step into these great ruined places and to be the first person of the same civilization which they stand for since the last monk fell or fled before the Seljuks. Up in the mountains there was the absurd cuckoo which shouted all day above my camp. I don't like hearing the cuckoo in deep summer; he is sadly reminiscent of the delicious beginnings of things--"where are the joys of spring? Oh, where are they!" The kite who screams above my tents here is better.

Friday, July 5. Yesterday I had a long, hot and tiresome day. We spent the whole morning going from village to village along the side of the Karajadagh looking for ruins and inscriptions. The manner of proceeding is this: you arrive in a village and ask for inscriptions. They reply that there are absolutely none. You say very firmly that there are certainly inscriptions and then you stand about in the hot sun for 10 minutes or so while villagers gather round. At last someone says there is a written stone in his house. You go off, find it, copy it, and give the owner two piastres, the result of which is that everybody has a written stone somewhere and you have to look at them all, 99 per cent. of them being only a lintel with a cross on it. As you leave they all tell you that though there are not many written stones here, in the next village, or in the village on the next mountain 10 hours away, or in the one you have just left behind you there are at least a hundred. I know this village of the hundred inscriptions so well now that I hear of it without any emotion, even when I have left it behind. At 11 o'clock I determined that I would do no more of this pottering work, so we rode down to a village in the plain, where we expected to find the tents and lunch in the shade. No tents, no shade, no people, for they had all gone to the yaila. At last we found a deaf old man who told us that there was a magnificently cold place to lunch in by the mosque and thither we went. It was the mosque porch. I distinguished myself by climbing wearily on to a sort of erection of planks in the corner. Haidat arriving with the lunch looked horrified at seeing me there and begged me to come down at once for it was the village hearse. So I came down, thinking that it probably hadn't been much disinfected since the last man who died of smallpox was carried on it to his grave, and for the evil omen that I had brought upon the party Heaven sent a sacrifice in the shape of a young swallow who dropped out of his nest above me on to the pavement and died at once, poor little dear.

Transport is rather difficult in this country. The camel drivers we had brought from Karapuna declared last night that they were going no further than the Karajadagh, but as we had no other means of carrying our packs but their camels only, we put force upon them and insisted that they should take us across to Hassan Dagh lest nameless evils should befall them. So they went, and they went 8 hours, poor people, the usual camel march being 5. We started before 5 in the morning so that it might be cool for them, and by great good luck it was a grey cloudy day with scarcely a glimpse of sun, and we rode across the waterless flat plain without any trouble and up the low foot hills that lie before Hassan Dagh.

Saturday, July 6th. An aged man appeared this morning at the tents and professed to know all the ruins round about, so Fattuh engaged him as guide-in-chief for the day. His name was Ali as I had presently cause to know. After breakfast I went down to the village and drew the church and by dint of wading about in dark and horrible stables and poking into the dark and horrible houses that had been built in the aisles and apse I got it out all complete and it proved extremely interesting. Then I came in and changed all my things, for the houses and the stables were, as always, alive with fleas. Very great travellers would no doubt think nothing of this, but I find it an almost intolerable vexation, yet one can't leave a church unplanned because there are fleas in it. Then I questioned the aged man as to what I should ride out and see. He said: "Many churches there are, a very great many." "Where?" said I. "over there," said he, "that side," waving his hand vaguely round the mountains, "there is one ." "What is his name?" said I (there's no neuter in Turkish). "Ali," said he. "Not your name, the church's name." "Chanderlik," said he. "Aren't there any in the other direction?" said I, for the way he seemed to be pointing was my route for to-morrow. "Not any at all," said he. A bystander, "Many, a great many; over there, there is one." "What is his name?" said I. The bystander, "Ali." "Not his name, the church's name?" "Uleuren there is, and Karneuren and Yazlikisle a. . ." so on and so on. (Euren means ruin and kisle means church.) Ali indignantly, "No churches! Ruins muins" (you repeat the word changing the first letter to 'm' when you want to say "and so forth") "euren meuren,"said he louder and louder, "all destroyed, mestroyed pulled down, broken, all ruins." "It's ruins I want to see," said I. "All ruins," he said, "all broken, moken, no marble churches, all marble and so forth, not any at all." "My soul," expostulated a fellow townsman, "there are two at Uleuren." "No marble churches," said he (there aren't any, anywhere, I may mention)" all ruins, all broken." However we went to Uleuren and I found two churches and a long inscription. Ali was not a success as an archaeologist and I declined to employ him further. Nor did he want to come.

We are now going round to the north side of the mountain where I am told there are a million if not a billion churches or something of the kind. I hope there may be one or two. I know how you are spending this Sunday -how I wish I were with you! I also wish so many flies were not spending Sunday with me.

Wednesday, July 11th. I thought of you a great deal on Monday and very much longed to see Elsa looking as pretty and as happy as I am sure she did look. I shall love to see the wedding photographs and hear all the tales. Now that it is all over I am glad I did not come back, for you see I should have been landed with my work half done and a horrible feeling that I could not go ahead properly for want of knowledge.

The long-expected robber turned up in the night and I was awakened by my servants' firing at him. They missed him, but he missed our horses.

The following preposterous conversation has just occurred:

G.B. loq: Oh! Fattuh, to whom does this poplar garden belong?
F.--To a priest, my lady.
G.B.--Doesn't he mind our camping in it?
F.--He didn't say anything.
G.B.--Did you ask him?
F.--No, my lady.
G.B.--We must give him some backshish.
F.--At your Excellency's command.
A pause.
F.--My lady.
G.B.--Yes?
F.--That priest is dead.
G.B.--!!! Then I don't think we need bother about the backshish.
F.--No, my lady.

The trouble is they don't use speech for the same purpose in the East as we do in the West.

It was piping hot, and we rode over barren rocky uplands and made our horses go their best pace--so good a pace that in 3 hours instead of the promised 4 we got to the great church that I had heard of. I should think it is 10th Cent. All round it the rock is honeycombed with the rooms and halls of a monastery with columbaria and churches. MY heart sank when I saw it for I knew I could do nothing at it under 3 hours and it was the hottest day we have had. However, I eat my lunch under the dome and then we set to work and we got it done in the three hours, the church only, I had not time to touch the rockcut things though they ought to be properly examined. And then we rode down the hills and across an endless plain.

Saturday, July 13. I was very glad to have a day off. I spent the whole morning in my tent drawing out some of all the work that has collected in the last few days. It was blazing hot.

Sunday, July 14. From Akserai we had 3 days of absolutely uninteresting travel across the great plains to Konia. I resolved that nothing should induce me to ride, it's too boring and too hot, so we sent the animals on with Haidar and my Turkoman, very early in the morning and Fattuh and I started off with the baggage at 5:15 in two carts. They are springless wooden carts covered with a hood of plaited straw with a cloth thrown over it. I should think less luxurious carriages do not exist. We packed all the luggage into one and put a quantity of rugs and waterproof sheets on to the floor of the other in which we journeyed, and it really wasn't so bad. At any rate! we were out of the glare and much less hot than we should have been riding.

Tuesday, July 16th. Everything comes to an end, even the road from Akserai to Konia. We got in at 10 o'clock this morning. I found quantities of letters from you and Father and Hugo and Moll, and was delighted to have them.

Domnul gives me the first description of the wedding. It Sounds all very very successful.

On Board the "Imogen", off Constantinople, July 27, 1907

I'm having a mighty fine time, I must tell you. The Ambassador was more than cordial. Then he insisted on carrying me off to Therapia with him--the Embassy is there now. So I flew back to my Hotel and packed and went down to the quay. Up came Hugoenin, the Director of the German Ryl. So I introduced myself to him, and he pushed me and my box into his launch and steamed up the Bosphorus till we met Sir Nicholas coming down to fetch me. This morning I went into C'ple and did a lot of business and then came back to Therapia to lunch. Now I have gone off with the O'Conors on their yacht to sail about these waters till Monday. It is perfectly delightful and they are both extraordinarily kind.

To H.B., Pera Palace, Constantinople, Thurs, August 4, 1907

Today I accomplished the most important object of my visit here--I saw the Grand Vizier. He is a very great man, is Fetid Pasha. . .

There are troops of professors and people of that kind here who have all been to see me. I find it vastly entertaining.

I expect I shall be in London about the 7th or 8th and I should be most grateful if Marie could be sent up to meet me there. I shall have to stay a day or two to get some clothes.

To F.B., London, Friday, August 9, 1907

Today I lunched with Sir Edward and Mr. Haldane--Willie [Tyrrell] told Sir E. I was here and he quickly asked me to lunch. It was most interesting and delightful. I'll tell you about it.

Sir Frank [Swettenham) is coming to tea and I dine with Domnul and spend the balance of the evening, after he goes to the office, with Willie T.

Sir Henry C. B. hasn't sent for me yet--I'm a little surprised, aren't you? So different from my habits in Constantinople.

To F.B., Cambo, Northumberland, Wed, September 4, 1907

I don' think I ever saw anything more adorable than Moll's children. There's no question about Pauline's being pretty, I think she's quite charming. We have just been spending an hour with them in their garden trying to photograph them. I don't know that it will be a great success for there was no sun an one of them was always crawling busily out of the picture, so that all you saw was the end of its legs. Then I photographed Moll with them, she looks so beautiful with them hanging about her. Now we are going to take Pauline with us and look at the Wallington garden.

To H.B., London, Saturday, October, 1907

I have had a wild 24 hours. I worked at the Geog. Soc. All yesterday and in the evening I went to Red Hill, getting there at 8. A young man (one of my fellow students-I think his name is Fairweather) met me at the station and we walked up on to the Common where we met Mr. Reeves. Then we took observations on stars for two hours. It was wonderfully calm and warm but the moon was so bright even the big stars were a little difficult to see. However, I took a number of observations and shall work them out on Monday. I got back after midnight, very hungry, and this morning I was back at Red Hill before 10 and spent three hours taking bearings for a map with Mr. Reeves. That has to be plotted out too on Monday at the Geog. Soc.

[I wrote to Mr. Reeves in May, 1927, asking him to tell me something of Gertrude's studies with him. I give here an extract from his reply.

ROYAL GEOGRAPHICAL SOCIETY, May 21st, 1927

Dear Lady Bell,
". . .She came to me for instruction in surveying and astronomical observations for determining positions just before starting on her great journey in Arabia 1913-14. I have never had anyone to teach who learned more rapidly and took a more intelligent interest in the subject, we had to deal with. . .

"Miss Bell's prismatic compass route traverse Made on her remarkable journeys after she left me, was Plotted from her field books, and adjusted to her latitudes here by our draughtsmen. I need not say that her mapping has proved of the greatest value and importance. Her field books are here in our possession and will be greatly treasured."

All the following year, 1908, she was at home absorbed in writing "A Thousand and One Churches," the work she wrote in collaboration with Sir William Ramsay recording their architectural experiences in Asia Minor.

Early in 1909 she made one of her most important desert expeditions, to the castle of Ukhaidir. It is deplorable that there are no letters from her to be found about her very important undertaking of the reconstruction by plans and measurements of this immense castle. She subsequently wrote a book published by the Clarendon Press in 1914. The book is a quarto volume 13 inches by ten inches of 168 pages of letterpress, two maps and 93 plates which included 15 ground plans of her own planning and 166 photographs taken by herself besides photographs and plans from other sources. It is dedicated to Dr. Walther Andrae.

As there are no letters remaining about Ukhaidir I quote from Gertrude's preface. it is too important an enterprise for her record of it to be omitted altogether. M. Massignon, the French traveller, was the first to make any record of Ukhaidir, although it had been visited by other travellers several times.]

"The next visitor to the palace was myself. I left Aleppo in February, 1909, and reached Ukhaidir on March 25, travelling by the East bank of the Euphrates and across the desert from Hit via Kubaisah and Shethathâ. . . I published a paper on the vaulting system of the palace in the Journal of Hellenic Studies for 1910 and I gave a more detailed account of the building, in the following year (Amurath to Ammrath, p. 140). I returned to the site in March, 1911, in order to correct my plans and to take measurements for elevations and sections. Going thence to Babylon, I found that some members of the 'Deutsche Orient-Gesellschaft' who were engaged upon the excavations there had been to Ukhaidir during the two years of my absence and were preparing a book upon it. Their book appeared in 1912 and is referred to frequently in this volume. For their generosity in allowing me to use some of their architectural drawings, I tender my grateful thanks, together with my respectful admiration for their masterly production.

"I feel indeed, that I must apologize for venturing to offer a second version. . . But my excuse must be that my work which was almost completed when the German volume came out, covers not only the ground traversed by my learned friends in Babylon, but also ground which they had neither leisure nor opportunity to explore; and further, that I believe the time has come for a comparative study of the data collected by myself and others such as is contained in this book. . .
.

"With this I must take leave of a field of study which formed for four years my principal occupation, as well as my chief delight. A subject so enchanting and so suggestive as the Palace of Ukhaidir is not likely to present itself more than once in a lifetime, and as I bring this page to a close I call to mind the amazement with which I first gazed upon its formidable walls; the romance of my first sojourn within its precincts; the pleasure, undiminished by familiarity of my return; and the regret with which I sent back across the sun drenched plain a last greeting to its distant presence."

[She was in England during the latter half of 1909 and again enjoyed at Rounton the company of a succession of congenial visitors among them Sir Frank Lascelles, Sir George Lloyd, P. Loraine, Lady Arthur Russell, Sir Edwin and Lady Egerton, G. W. Prothero, Sir Valentine Chirol, Sir Ernest Shackleton, etc.

Gertrude, as may well be imagined, was the pivot of these gatherings and was always inventing exciting things to do, sometimes, indeed, too exciting for some of the guests. I have a vivid recollection of her insisting when the Egertons were with us on having a picnic on the top of the hill behind Mount Grace. Sir Edwin Egerton, a retired Ambassador, no longer very active, perhaps, had protested against going for a picnic and declared there was nothing he disliked more than sitting on the ground. Gertrude however insisted on his going. But she made many arrangements for his comfort, and when Sir Edwin arrived at the hill top, he found a table and chair awaiting him, his cover laid, and everything complete. . .

But in spite of the influx of guests that came and went, and her absorption in her own work in the intervals, she managed to go away on one or two visits.]

To F.B., August 17th, 1909 [P.S. only]

I'm drawing my castle [Ukhaidir] and it is coming out beautifully. I can scarcely bear to leave it for a moment.

To F.B., September 13th, 1909

I've finished the chapter for Strzygowski-only blocked out of course, there is a lot more work to be done on it, but the worst part is over and what is more I think it's rather neat. I've been so absorbed in it that I haven't had a moment to think of anything else. Now I'm going for a walk on the moors to forget about it till after tea.

I fear I shall have to come straight home and not go to Moll yet. Next week I must write an article for Mr. Prothero and even if I get home on Friday it leaves me very little time. I would rather go to her after it's done, when I shall be through this overwhelming batch of work that has to be done in such a hurry.

She writes from Ardgowan, Greenock, in September, she was staying with Sir Hugh and Lady Alice Shaw Stewart.]

To F. B., Ardgowan, September 15th, 1909

Mr. Prothero, would rather not have my article till Jan. an immense relief to me, especially as the Hellenic Soc. want me to lecture on November 9th and that will take a vast preparation. By the way Mr. P. talks of being in Yorkshire early in October, and I've asked whether he cannot come to us, saying I know you would endorse the suggestion. He is in Scotland This is one of the most beautiful places I ever saw. There is an amusing party, the Gerald Balfours, Rayleighs, Bear Warre and others. The men go shooting every day. As for Lord Rayleigh I think he is very alarming, but he took me in to dinner yesterday and told me most exciting things suited to my understanding about radium. He opens doors into a wonderful unknown world which I shall never be able to walk in however. My hostess is delightful. . .

[Hugo was ordained at Ripon on September 19th, 1909.)

I don't think I shall go to Ripon. I do feel so entirely out of that atmosphere. Of course don't say that to Hugo, I would not wound his feelings for the world, and if you think I shall do so by not going, I will.

To F.B., London, October 5th, 1909

I went straight to the office and had an interview with a very capable lady who used to be the organising secretary of one of the Suffrage societies and has seen the error of her ways and wants to work for us. I fancy she will make an excellent and very sensible speaker and I intend to follow the matter up.

When I came in I found a telegram from George Lloyd Asking me to lunch to-day so I rang him up and asked him to dine with me. He came back yesterday. I asked Willie T. to come too but he was busy and is coming in after dinner. So I shall have a good all round view of the crisis.

[During this year the women's suffrage agitation took greater proportions. Gertrude was strongly opposed to it. I have found no letters from herself about it but Lady Jersey who was Chairman of the Women's Anti-Suffrage Committee sends me the following note, respecting Gertrude's connection with it.

From the Dowager Countess of Jersey.

"In the summer of 1908 Gertrude became interested in the movement against the extension of the Parliamentary Franchise to Women, and joined Mrs. Humphry Ward, myself and others in the formation of a Women's Anti-suffrage League. The women received throughout practical assistance from men, among whom Mr. John Massie was the able advisor and Hon. Treasurer. After two or three years Lord Curzon and Lord Cromer formed a larger League into which the Women's Society was ultimately merged.

"In the initial steps and until her departure for her great Arabian journey, Gertrude displayed her usual delightful energy and powers of organisation. . . It is impossible here to name the many keen women who rendered devoted assistance. It was soon realised that defence was harder than attack. . . But in Gertrude at least there was never any want of spirit, and her unfailing good temper and direct common sense encouraged and inspired those who sometimes felt the task of opposition a hard one.

"In the Great War Gertrude's unrivalled experience of the East immediately marked her out for important spheres of action and her colleagues in the Anti-Suffrage cause had regretfully to abandon the hope of welcoming her back to their counsels; they however are among the many who, while mourning her death, are proud of her life of achievement."]

CHAPTER XII

1910-1911 - ITALY-ACROSS THE SYRIAN DESERT

(In these letters from Rome, Gertrude is again in places too well known to make it worthwhile to give her descriptions of them. I quote however some personal extracts, which show her keenness and thoroughness of study.

She goes from Rome to Spalato.

She goes to Dalmatia and then back to Spalato where she is shown the palace of Diocletian by Monsignor Bulic, Director of Antiquities, "the most charming old man imaginable."

She goes to Zara, Polo, Ravenna, deep in study everywhere with experts, and then feels she must turn homewards.]

To F.B., Rome, February 28th, 1910

I have decided to stay on here another week with Eugénie (Mrs. Arthur Strong]. I have got a very nice room in her pension. But I shall miss Father dreadfully. We have had the most interesting ten days together and I hope he has enjoyed them as much as I have. He is such an ideal companion. With the archaeologists he is in his element, and he disconcerts the learned by extremely perdinent questions! but they are all delighted with him and I think he puts them upon their mettle and that they are far more interesting when he is there. We have made several new friends. The head of the German school Dr. Delbrück is extraordinarily able and we are going to spend a long morning together on Thursday in his library and discuss vaults. But our chief friends are the dear Wyndhams, who are darlings both of them. Robert Hichens turned up. at my lecture this afternoon--Oh, I think the lecture went quite well and I had a very distinguished audience of professors.

Dr. Ashby at the head of the British School spends his time in trotting round with us.

Well it's all being quite as amusing as we meant it to be.

To F.B., Rome, March, 1910

It is most kind of you to agree to my staying here, and I want to tell you that I feel an awful beast about the dinner party. But at the same time I do think another fortnight here will be of immense value to me. Even in this last week I have begun to get hold of things. Today I worked at Architectural decoration all the morning, partly out of doors and partly in the German Institute where I went to read for an hour before lunch. In the afternoon I joined Miss Van Demen at the Baths of Caracalla and looked at them all the afternoon. They are very difficult and I have not got them quite straightened out so I shall have another day at them tomorrow. I can't tell you what a delightful sensation it is to begin to understand these things. I feel so excited about them that I can scarcely bring myself to come in to lunch. I came back at 5 for Eugénie's lecture, a very good one and very helpful to me.

To F.B., Rome, March, 1910

When my literary remains come to be published the letters from Rome will not occupy an important place.! ween have not a minute to write but I must seize spaces between archaeologists to tell you what I am doing. . . Yesterday morning I spent three hours with Delbrück who gave me the most wonderful disquisition I have ever heard on the history of architecture. It was a regular lecture. He had prepared all his notes and all his books to illustrate what he was saying. He is a very remarkable man and as he talked I got the hang of things that had always remained mysteries to me. He ended by saying that it was absurd that I should be so ignorant of the Roman monuments and by telling me that I ought to come here for 6 weeks to study. He is perfectly right and I'm contemplating quite seriously whether I will not come in Oct. and Nov. and study. I would like to do it before I go back to the East. It is a bore but after all 2 months is a short time in one's life. If it would give one a real hold of Roman problems it would be infinitely well spent. We'll talk of this when I come home.

To F.B., Rome, 1910

. . . I went to the Capitol Museum and worked at ornament over which I grew so excited that I flew up to the Terme and went through all the ornaments there with immense satisfaction. . . . .

To F.B., 1910

You were really very kind not to mind my staying in Rome. I felt when I got your letter about the dinner party that I ought to come home at once, and I shall think of you tomorrow evening. Meantime my regrets are tempered by having learnt so much. I have been working like a slave and have got to the bottom of Diocletian's baths this last day or two. I have also been working at ornament and find to my joy that the moment one begins to look at it with care a regular sequence is apparent and the things that all seemed an immense muddle fell into a quite comprehensible history. All this has left me very little time for anything else. . .

To F.B., Rome, 1910

I called on a delightful old Italian, Signor Sordini. We sat and talked of East and West with the completest accord and made great friends--all in Italian, mind you. I talk it disgracefully badly however and I know I constantly call people Thou in my anxiety to call them It [sic.]

To H.B. and F.B., Ravenna, 1910

. . . As for London, no, I don't expect I shall be there much. I must fall back to the book and I think that can be written best at home. You see I don't want to waste any more time than I can help--the book!
. . .

[This was 'Amurath to Amurath.'

Before going to England she goes to Munich to See the exhibition of pictures. There she receives a letter from W. Heinemann.)

To F.B., Munich, 1910

. . . Then I came in to grapple with a letter from Heinemann who wants me to reply by telegram to the terms he offered me for my book and to agree to have it ready early in November. I have agreed, but I expect we shall have the devil's own hurry over it and so I have written to him.

The exhibition is wonderful. I am very glad that I am alone here so that I can really work at it.

To F.B., Munich, 1910

I have had these evenings when I have been alone to write an article on the Persian and Arab Poets for Mr. Richmond. I hope it is all right. I think it is, and I am glad to have it off my mind.

To F.B., January 9th, 1911

Two things I want in Rome.

You know the round church of Santa Costanza) outside the walls? Next to it is the little basilica of St. Agnese which has in the inside a double storey of columns on either side of the nave. The capitals of the lower story are acanthus capitals with tiny garlands hung over the corners. I want a photograph of one of these, showing the garland clearly, for it is the only example I know in Rome of the garlanded capital of the early Christian monuments at Diarbekr and in the Tur Abdin. The photograph does not, I think, exist. But Eugénie's photographer would take it for me for a few francs. I shall want it as a point for comparison when I write my forthcoming work about the Tur Abdin.

The second thing is in the Museum of the Terme. I was shown it by the curator, Paribene, who took Eugénie and me around. It is Part of some architectural fragments from a tomb of the Antonines found some way out of Rome, near Tivoli, I think. When I saw these fragments, they were not yet being exhibited to the public. Paribene said they had to be sorted and set up. The interesting thing about them was that some of the decoration was the acanthus spinosus, the fat jagged acanthus, not the broad, flat-leaved one. Now the earliest example I know of the acanthus spinosus, except this tomb, is at Spalato--50 years later than the fragments at the Terme. It is undoubtedly an Asiatic motive (the plant itself is Asiatic) and it points to a school of Asiatic stone-cutters having existed in Rome in the time of the Antonines--so I think. If Paribene would be so kind, I should like to have a good photograph of one of these fragments, showing exactly that particular kind of acanthus decoration. It is rather an important point which I should like some day to use. Here again, the photographs would probably have to be taken specially for me. Eugénie knows the fragments in the Terme--we saw them together--and she could get permission from Paribene to have them photographed, if she would be so good. . .

(this letter from Gertrude was written on board ship on her way to the East on February 9th 1911. Her father and I were in Rome. It shows her thoroughness of study, and her determination to verify every detail of architecture. The photographs she asked for were sent to her.)

To F. B., Beyrout, January 16th, 1911

. . ..I went off to the Jesuit College where I was received with open arms by the two librarians. We had a long talk and I told them all I was going to do, and they gave me some useful introductions to bishops in the Tur Abdin. And then we went over the printing establishment. I found one compositor setting up the Arabic text which Sir Charles Lyall is bringing out, much perplexed over some indecipherable English words which I succeeded in reading for him. He only knew Arabic you see. They are sending me a lot of their publications, the two fathers of the library (I always send them my books) so they will arrive at Rounton some time and must be kept for me. With all this I have spent a most delightful morning, as you may imagine. You remember I told you that my delightful Sheikh was in prison on a charge of murder. Fattuh tells me they succeeded in getting him out, by a free use of my testimony to his character! I'm delighted. He'll be able to murder someone else now. What a country! Already I feel my standards of virtue entirely changed.

THE LETTERS OF GERTRUDE BELL

To F.B., Damascus, January 18, 1911

. . . I thought I had better begin to see about my journey so I went off to the quarter where the sons of Abdul Kadir live. They are the great people here and if any one knows the desert, it is the Amir Umar, Abdul Kadir's son, and the Amir Takir, his grandson. I found them both in the Amir Takir's house, and we had a long talk, the up-shot of which is that the Amir Takir is going to seek out a sheikh of the Wahed Ali, who is now in Damascus, and we are all to meet and discuss matters. The Emir Ali is the eldest son of Abdul Kadir. He is a great big splendid looking man with hair and beard as black as coal, and that directness of address which is very typical of the Abdul Kadirs.

Now I must tell you another old friend has turned up, Selim Tabit. I found him waiting for me when I came in and we went to a neighbouring hotel where he lodges and found there the Amir Umar and the Amir Takir whom I presently took aside and conversed at length about my journey. All is going well, and in a day or two I hope we shall see our way clear. It's still pretty cold, but the weather is im-proving. I have just come in from dining with Selim Tabit. He is, I must say, a very amusing companion. He told me the gossip of Syria by the yard and as the dinner drew to a close it occurred to me to ask after my old friend, Muhammad Pasha Jerudi.

"Oh," said Tabit Bey, "he has just come in from Jerud--shall we go and see him?" So we stepped round to old Jerudi's house. He was sitting all alone in a great coat, running a rosary through his fin-gers and with nothing else to amuse him. The night was bitter cold and the room, which was all window, was warmed by a charcoal brazier. So we sat down and Tabit Bey talked uninterruptedly for an hour and a half. I doubt if Jerudi can read, but anyway Selim is better than any newspaper. He related what was happening in Macedonia and what in the Yemen, the latest news from the Jebel Druze and from Persia. It interested me just as much as it interested Jerudi and by the time we left I found that I had even forgotten that I was shivering with cold.

So you see Damascus is as delightful as ever.

THE LETTERS OF GERTRUDE BELL

To F.B., Damascus, January 27th, 1911

I shall not be able to post a letter to you for a long time because I shall not be in the way of a post-office, but when I get to Hit I
will send word to our consul in Bagdad and ask him to telegraph to
you, "Arrived Hit." then you will know that all is well and that I shall
be in Bagdad about a fortnight later.

To F. B., Damascus, February 1st, 1911

. . .The first reviews of my book have come. . . But now the
reviewers all stick at the archaeology (well, they will have to bear it)
and not one of them has said anything about my fellow travellers,
Cyrus and Julian, whom I think I treated rather well. There is little satisfaction to be got out of reviewers, whether they praise or blame,

To F. B., Damascus, February 7th, 1911

We have been blocked up by snow on all sides, all the
rlys.stopped, no posts, no nothing. At last the spring has come and we
are off. I'm glad you did not send a photograph to the Daily Graphic. I
have had an interesting time, though too much of it. I've done some
work at inscriptions, for van Berchem and I've seen all the world. The
best of all is the delightful old Arab Sheikh who has helped me with
my journey. I pay him calls at his house after sunset and find always
some twenty or thirty people there from every corner of the Moslem
world. One night I was sitting there as usual when he rose and said to
the company: "Will you pray?" It was the hour of the evening prayer.
His great nephew brought out white felts from an inner room, spread
them on the floor facing Mecca and all the guests stood up and prayed.
After telling me all the news of the desert he asks me whether I think
there are diamond mines there and whether gold--questions difficult to
answer.

To F.B., Dumeir, February 9th

We're off. And now I must tell you the course of the negotiations which preceded this journey. First as you know I went to the sons
of Abdul Kadir and they called up Sheikh Muhammad Bassam and
asked him to help me. I called on him the following evening. He said it

was too early, the desert camels had not come in to Damascus, there was not a dulul (riding camel) to be had and I must send out to a village a few hours away and buy. This was discouraging as I could not hope to get them for less than 15 pounds apiece, I wanted five and I should probably have to sell them for an old song at Hit. Next day Fattuh went down into the bazaar and came back with the news that he and Bassam between them had found an owner of camels ready to hire for 7 apiece. It was dear but I closed with the offer. All the arrangements were made and I dispatched the caravan by the Palmyra road. Then followed misfortune. The snow closed down upon us, the desert post did not come in for three weeks and till it came we were without a guide. Then Bassam invented another scheme. The old sheikh of Kubeisa near Hit (you know the place) was in Damascus and wanted to return home; he would journey with us and guide us. So all was settled again-

But the sheikh Muhammad en Nawan made continuous delays, we were helpless, for we could not cross the Syrian desert without a guide and still the post did not come in. The snow in the desert had been without parallel. At last Muhamma en Nawan was ready. I sent off my camels to Dumeir yesterday (it is the frontier village of the desert) and myself went to sleep at the English hospital whence it was easier to slip off unobserved. For I am supposed to be travelling to Palmyra and Deir with four zaptiehs. This morning Fattuh and I drove here, it took us four hours, and the Sheikh came on his dulul. The whole party is assembled in the house of a native of Kubeisa, I am lodged in a large windowless room spread with felts, a camel is stabled at my door, and over the way Fattuh is cooking my dinner. One has to put on clogs to walk across the yard, so inconceivably muddy it is, and in the village one can't walk at all, one must ride. I got in about one and lunched, after which I mounted and went out to see some ruins a mile or two away. It was a big Roman fortified camp. And beyond it the desert stretched away to the horizon. That is where we go tomorrow. It's too heavenly to be back in all this again, Roman forts and Arab tents and the wide desert. All the women here address me as Hajji. It is very gratifying. Every few minutes someone comes into my room and enquires after my health. I reply politely: "Praise God!" and he leaves me. We have got for a guide the last desert postman who came in three days ago, having been delayed nine days by snow. His name is Ali.

Syrian Desert February 10th. There is in Dumeir a very beautiful temple, rather like one Of the temples at Baalbek. As soon as the sun was up I went out and took some photographs of it, but I was ready long before the camels were loaded; the first day's packing is always a long business, Finally we got off soon after nine, a party of fifteen, myself, the sheikh, Fattuh, Ali and my four camel men, and the other seven merchants who are going across to the Euphrates to buy sheep. In half an hour we passed the little Turkish guard house which is the last outpost of civilisation and plunged into the wilderness. Our road lay before us over a flat expanse bounded to the N. by the range of barren hills that trend away to the N.E. and divide us from the Palmyran desert, and to the S. by a number of distant tells, volcanic I should think. I rode my mare all day, for I can come and go more easily upon her, but when we get into the heart of the desert I shall ride a camel. it's less tiring. Three hours from Dumeir we came to some water pools which are dry in summer and here we filled r skins, for where we are camping there is no water. There was a keen wind, rising sometimes into a violent storm which brought gusts of hail upon us, but fortunately it was behind us so that it did not do us much harm. Late in the afternoon another hail storm broke over us and clearing away left the distant hills white with snow. We had come to a place where there was a little scrub which would serve as firewood, and here we camped under the lee of some rising ground. Our companions have three big Arab tents, open in front, and we our two English tents, and oddly enough we are quite warm in spite of the rain and cold wind. I don't know why it is that one seldom feels cold in the desert; perhaps because of the absence of damp. The stony, sandy ground never becomes muddy. A little grass is beginning to grow and as you look over the wide expanse in front of you it is almost green. The old sheikh is lamenting that we are not in a house in Damascus (but I think one's first camp in the Hamad is worth a street full of houses); "By the head of your father!" he said, "how can you leave the garden of the world and come out into this wilderness?" Perhaps it does require explanation.

February 11th. But to-day's experiences will not serve to justify my attitude. When I went to bed a hurricane was blowing. I woke from time to time and heard the good Fattuh hammering in the tent pegs, and wondered if any tent would stand up in that gale and also what was going to happen next. an hour before dawn Fattuh called to me and asked if I was cold. I woke in surprise and putting my hand out found the waterproof valise that covered me wet with snow. "It is like the sea," cried Fattuh. Therefore I lighted a candle and saw that it had drifted into my tent a foot deep. I dug down, found my boots and hat and put them under the valise; I had gone to bed as I stood and put all my extra clothing under the Wolsey valise for warmth so that nothing came to harm. At dawn Fattuh dragged out the waterproof sheet that covers the ground and with it most of the snow. The snow was lying in great drifts where the wind had blown it, it was banked up against our tents and those of the Arabs and every hour or so the wind brought a fresh storm upon us. We cleared it out of our tents and settled to a day as little uncomfortable as we could manage to make it. In the afternoon seven Arabs of the Heseneh rode in, in a furious sleet storm. I was busy cutting firewood at the time. We built up the fire in Sheikh Muhammad's tent, gave them coffee and dates and sent them on a little comforted. They had spent the night out, on the way to a distant camp. At last, at sunset the wind dropped, the barometer rose and we pray for the weather to-morrow. Most of the snow has melted already, and left the desert spongy.

February 12th. We have got out into smooth waters at last. You can imagine what I felt like when I looked out of my tent before dawn and saw a clear sky and the snow almost vanished. But the cold! Everything in my tent was frozen stiff--yesterday's damp skirt was like a board, my gloves like iron, my sponges--well, I'll draw a veil over my sponges--I did not use them much, Nor was my toilette very complicated as I had gone to bed in my clothes. The temperature after sunrise was 30, and there was a biting wind blowing sharply from the west. I spent an hour trudging backwards and forwards over the frozen desert trying to pretend I was warm while the camels were loaded. The frozen tents took a world of time to pack-with frozen fingers too. We were off soon after eight, but for the first hour the wet desert was like a sheet of glass and the camels slipped about and fell down with much groaning and moaning. They are singularly unfitted to cope with emergencies. For the next hour we plodded over a slippery melting surface, for which they are scarcely better suited, then suddenly we got out of the snow zone and all was well. I got on to my camel and rode her for the rest of the day. She is the most charming of animals. You ride a camel with only a halter which you mostly tie loosely round the peak of your saddle. A tap with your camel switch on one side of her neck or the other tells her the direction you want her to go, a touch with your heels sends her on, but when you wish her to sit down you have to hit her lightly and often on the neck saying at the same time:

"Kh kh kh kh," that's as near as I can spell it. The big soft saddle, the 'shedad,' is so easy and comfortable that you never tire. You loll about and eat your lunch and observe the landscape through your glasses: you might almost sleep. So we swung on through an absolutely flat plain till past five, when we came to a shallow valley with low banks on either side and here we camped. The name of the place is Aitha, there is a full moon and it is absolutely still except for the sound of the pounding of coffee beans in the tents of my travelling companions. I could desire nothing pleasanter.

February 13th. Don't think for a moment that it is warm weather yet. At 5:30 to-day (which was the hour of my breakfast) the thermometer stood at 20, but there was no wind. We were off soon after six. The sun rose gloriously half an hour later and we began to unfreeze. It is very cold riding on a camel, I don't know why unless it has to do with her extreme height.

We rode on talking cheerfully of our various adventures till after ten which is the time when my companions lunch, so I lunch too. The camels were going rather languidly for they were thirsty, not having drunk since they left Damascus. They won't drink when it is very cold. But our guide, Ali, promised us some pools ahead, good water, he said. When we got there we found that some Arabs had camped not far off and nothing remained of the pools but trampled mud.

The extraordinary folly of Bedouin habits is almost past belief. They know that the pools collect only under a sloping face of rock; if they would clear out the earth below they would have good clear water that would last them for weeks; not only do they neglect to do that but they don't even clear out the mud which gets deeper and deeper till there is no pool at all. So we had to go searching round for another pool and at last we found one about a mile away with a very little water in it, but enough for the riding camels, my mare and our water skins. It is exceedingly muddy however. We got into camp about four not far from some Arab tents. This is our plan of action: first of all we all set to work to put up our tents, my part of the proceeding being to unpack and set up my camp furniture. By the time I have done that and taken off my boots Fattuh has tea ready. My companions scatter over the plain with axes to gather firewood which is a little dry plant called Shik, six inches high at the highest. We speak of it as the trees. A few strokes with the pick makes the square hearth in the tents and in a

238

moment a bundle of shik is blazing in it, the sheikh has settled down to his narghileh and coffee making has begun. We never stop for five minutes but we pile up a heap of shik and warm our hands at the bonfire. We seek out for our camping place a bit of low ground. When we get near the place Ali purposes to camp in, the old sheikh is all for stopping. "This room is fair," says he looking at a little curve in the bank. "Wallahi oh sheikh," says Ali "the next room is better; there are more trees." So we go on to the next allotted chamber. It is a wonderfully interesting experience this. Last night they all sat Up half the night because my mare pricked her ears and they thought she heard robbers. They ran up the banks and cried out "Don't come near! we have soldiers with us and camels." It seemed to me when I heard of it (I was asleep at the time) a very open deceit but it seems to have served the purpose for the thief retired. As we rode this morning Ali detected hoof marks on the hard ground and was satisfied it was the mare of our enemy.

February 14th. What I accuse them of is not that they choose to live differently from us: for my part I like that; but that they do their own job so very badly. I told you of the water yesterday now I will give you another instance. Everybody in the desert knows that camels frequently stray away while feeding, yet it occurs to no one to put a man to watch over them. No when we get into camp they are just turned off to feed where, they like and go where they will. Consequently yesterday at dusk four of our baggage camels were missing and a riding camel belonging to one of the Damascene sheep merchants and everyone had to turn out to look for them. I could not do anything so I did not bother and while I was dining the sheikh looked in and said our camels had come back--let us thank God! It is certain that no one else could claim any credit. But the riding camel was not to be found, nor had she come back when I was ready to start at 4:30 this morning. We decided to wait till dawn and that being two hours off and the temperature 30 I went to bed again and to sleep. At dawn there was no news of her, so we started, leaving word with some Arabs where we were gone. She has not yet appeared, nor do I think she will. I was very sorry for the merchant, who now goes afoot, and very much bored by the delay. For we can't make it up at the other end because the camels have to eat for at least two hours before sunset. They eat shik; so does my little mare, she being a native of the desert. At ten o'clock we came to some big water pools, carefully hollowed out "in the first days" said Ali, with the earth banked up high round them, but now half filled with mud and the banks broken. Still they hold a good deal of water in the winter and the inhabitants of the desert for miles around were driving their sheep and camels there to drink. We too filled our water skins. We got into camp at three, near some Arab tents. The sheikh, a charming old man, has just paid us a long visit. We sat round Muhammad's coffee fire and talked. It was all the more cheerful because the temperature is now 46--a blessed change from 26. My sponges have unfrozen for the first time. We have got up into the high flat plain which is the true Hamad, the Smooth, and the horizon from my tent door is as round as the horizon of the sea. The sharp dry air is wonderfully delicious: I think every day of the Syrian desert must prolong your life by two years. Sheikh Muhammad has confided to me that he has three wives, one in Damascus, one in Kubeisa and one in Bagdad, but the last he has not seen for twenty-three years. " She has grown old, oh lady--by the truth of God! and she never bore but one daughter."

February 15th. We were off at five this morning in bitter frost. Can you picture the singular beauty of these moonlit departures! the frail Arab tents falling one by one, leaving the camp fires blazing into the night; the dark masses of the kneeling camels; the shrouded figures binding up the loads, shaking the ice from the water skins, or crouched over the hearth for a moment's warmth before mounting. "Yallah, yallah, oh children!" cries the old sheikh, knocking the ashes out of his Narghileh, "Are we ready?" So we set out across the dim wilderness, Sheikh Muhammad leading on his white dulul. The sky ahead reddens, and fades, the moon pales and in sudden splendour the sun rushes up over the rim of the world. To see with the eyes is good, but while I wonder and -rejoice to look upon this primeval existence, it does not seem to be a new thing; it is familiar, it is a part of inherited memory. After an hour and a half of marching we came to the pool of Khafiyeh and since there is no water for three days ahead we had to fill all our empty skins. But the pool was a sheet of ice, the water skins were frozen and needed careful handling for if you unfold them they crack and break-and we lighted fire and set to work to thaw them and ourselves. I sent the slow baggage camels on, and with much labour we softened the skins and contrived to fill them. The sun was now up and a more barren prospect than it revealed you cannot Imagine. The Hamad stretched in front of us, flat and almost absolutely bare; for several hours we rode over a wilderness Of flints on which nothing grew. It was also the coldest day we have had, for the keen frosty wind blew straight into our faces. We stopped once to wait for the baggage camels, and warmed ourselves at a bonfire meanwhile, and again We stopped for half an hour to lunch. We watched our shadow catch us up and march ahead of us as the sun sank westward and at three o'clock we pitched camp in the stony waste. yet I can only tell you that we have spent a very pleasant day. The old sheikh never stops talking, bless him, he orders us all about when we pitch and break up camp, but as Fattuh and I know much more about the pitching of our tents than he does, we pay no attention. "Oh Fattuh," said I this evening when he had given us endless advice, "do you pity the wife in Bagdad?" "Effendim," said Fattuh, "she must be exceedingly at rest." Still for my part I should be sorry not to see Sheikh Muhammad for twenty-three years.

February 16th. After I had gone to bed last night I heard Ali shouting to all whom it might concern: "We are English soldiers! English soldiers!" But there was no one to hear and the desert would have received with equal indifference the information that we were Roman legionaries. We came to the end of the inhospitable Hamad to-day and the desert is once more diversified by a slight rise and fall of the ground. It is still entirely waterless, so waterless that in the spring when the grass grows thick the Arabs cannot camp here. All along our way there is proof of former water storage-I should think Early Moslem, marking the Abbassid post road. The pools have been dug out and banked up, but they are now full of earth and there is very little water in them. We are camped to-night in what is called a valley. It takes a practised eye to distinguish the valley from the mountain, the one is so shallow and the other so low. The valleys are often two miles wide and you can distinguish them best by the fact that there are generally more "trees" in them than on the heights. I have made great friends with one of the sheep merchants. His name is Muhiyyed Din. He is coming back in the Spring over this road with his lambs. They eat as they go and travel four hours a day. "It must be a dull job," said I. "Eh wallah!" he replied, but if the spring grass is good the master of the lambs rejoices to see them grow fat." He travels over the whole desert, here and in Mesopotamia, buying sheep and camels; to Nejd too, and to Egypt, and he tells me delightful tales of his adventures. What with one thing and another the eight or nine hours of camel riding a day are never dull. But Truth of God! the cold!

February 17th. We were running short of water this morning. The water difficulty has been enhanced by the cold. The standing pools are exceedingly shallow so that when there is an inch of ice over them little remains but mud; what the water is like that you scrape up under these conditions I leave to the imagination Besides the mud, it has a sharp acrid taste of skins after forty-eight hours in them--not unhealthy I believe, but neither is it pleasant. So it happened that we had to cut down rather to the south today instead of going to the well of Kara which we could not have reached this evening. Sheikh Muhammad was much agitated at this programme. He expected to find the camps of tribes whom he knew at and near the well, and he feared that by coming to the south of them we might find ourselves upon the path of a possible raiding party of Arabs whom he did not know coming up from the south. Ali tried to reassure him, saying that the chances were against raiding parties (good, please God!) and that we were relying upon God. But the Sheikh was not to be comforted. "Life of God! what is this talk! To God is the command! we are in the Shamuyyeh where no one is safe--Face of God!" He is master of a wonderful variety of pious ejaculations. So we rode for an hour or two (until we forgot about it) carefully scanning the horizon for ghazus; it was just as well that we had this to occupy us, for the whole day's march was over ground as flat as a board. It had been excruciatingly cold in the early morning but about midday the wind shifted round to the South and we began to feel the warmth of the sun. For the first time we shed our fur coats, and the lizards came out of their holes. Also the horizon was decorated with fantastic mirage which greatly added to the enjoyment of looking for ghazus. An almost imperceptible rise in the ground would from afar stand up above the solid earth as if it were the high back of a camel. We saw tents with men beside them pitched on the edge of mirage lakes and when at last we actually did come to a stretch of shallow Water, it was a long time before I could believe that it was not imaginary. I saw how the atmospheric delusion worked by watching some gazelles. They galloped away over the plain just ordinary gazelles, but when they came to the mirage they suddenly got up on to stilts and looked the size of camels. It is excessively bewildering to be deprived of the use of one's eyes in this way. We had a ten hours' march to reach the water by which we are camped. It lies in a wide shallow basin of mud, most of it is dried up, but a few pools remain in the deeper parts. The Arabs use some sort of white chalky stone--is it chalk?--to precipitate the mud. We have got some with us. We boil the water, powder the chalk and put it in and it takes nearly all the mud down to the bottom. Then we pour off the water.

February 18th. We were pursued all day by a mad wind which ended by bringing a shower of sleet upon us while we were getting into camp. In consequence of the inclemency of the weather I had the greatest difficulty in getting the Sheikh and the camel drivers to leave their tent and they were still sitting over their coffee fire when we and the Damascene merchants were ready, to start. Inspired of God I pulled out their tent pegs and I brought their roof about their ears--to the great joy of all, except those who were sitting under it. So we got off half an hour before dawn and after about an hour's riding dropped down off the smooth plain into an endless succession of hills and deep valleys--when I say deep they are about 200 feet deep and they all run north into the hollow plain of Kara. I much prefer this sort of country to the endless flat and it Is quite interesting sitting a camel down a stony descent. The unspeakable devilish Wind was fortunately behind us--Call upon the Prophet! but it did blow!

February 20th. We marched yesterday thirteen and a half hours without getting Anywhere. We set off at five in a delicious still night with a temperature of 36--it felt quite balmy. The sun rose clear and beautiful as we passed through the gates of our valley into a wide low plain--we were to reach the Wady which is the father of all valleys in this desert, in ten hours, and the little ruin of Muheiwir in half an hour more and there was to be plentiful clear water. We were in good spirits as you may imagine; the sheikh sang songs of Nejd and Ali instructed me in all the desert roads. We rode on and on. At two o'clock I asked Ali whether it were two hours to Muheiwir? "Nore," said he. "Three?" said I. "Oh lady, more." "Four?" I asked with a little sinking of heart. "Wallahi, not so much." We rode on over low hills and hollow plains. At five we dropped into the second of the valleys el Ud. By this time Fattuh and I were on ahead and Ali was anxiously scanning the landscape from every high rock. The Sheikh had sat down to smoke a narghileh while the baggage camels came up. "My lady," said Fattuh, "I do not Think we shall reach water to-night." And the whole supply of water which we had was about a cupful in my flask. We went on for another half hour down the valley and finally, in concert with Ali, selected a spot for a camp. It was waterless, but, said he, the water was not more than two hours off: he would take skins and fetch some, and meantime the starving camels would eat trees. But when the

243

others came up, the Father of Camels, Abdullah, he from whom we hired our beasts, protested that he must have water to mix the camel meal at night (they eat a kind of dough) and rather against r Judgment we went on. We rode an hour further, by which time it was pitch dark. Then Muhiyyed Din came up to me and said that if by chance we were to meet a ghazu in the dark night, it might go ill with us. That there was reason in this was admitted by all; we dumped down where we stood, In spite of the darkness Fattuh had my tent up before you could wink, while I hobbled my mare and hunted among the Camel loads for my bed. No one else put up a tent; they drew the camels together and under the shelter they gave made a fire of what trees they could find, Fattuh and I divided the water in my flask into two parts; with half we made some tea which he and I shared over some tinned meat and some bread; the other half we kept for the next morning When I shared it with the sheikh. We were none of us thirsty really; this weather does not make you thirsty. But my poor little mare had not drunk for two days, and she whinnied to everyone she saw. The last thing I heard before I went to sleep was the good Fattuh reasoning with her. "There is no water," he was saying. "There is none. Ma fi, ma fi." Soon after five he woke me up. I put on my boots, drank the tea he brought (having sent half to the poor old sheikh, who had passed the night under the lee of his camel) and went out into a cheerless daybreak. The sky was heavy with low-hanging clouds, the thermometer stood at 34, as we mounted our camels a faint and rather dismal glow in the east told us that the sun was rising. It was as well that we had not tried to reach water the night before. We rode to-day for six and a half hours before we got to rain pools in the Wady Hauran, and an hour more to Muhei-wir and a couple of good wells in the valley bed. For the first four hours our way lay across barren levels; after a time we saw innumerable camels pasturing near the bare horizon and realised that we must be nearing the valley: there is no water anywhere but in the Hauran and all the tents of the Deleim are gathered near it. Then we began to descend through dry and stony watercourses and at midday found ourselves at the bottom of the great valley, and marched along the edge of a river of stones with a few rain Pools lying in it. So we came to Muheiwir which is a small ruined fort, and here we found two men of the Deleim with a flock Their of sheep--the first men we have seen for four days. there camp is about three miles away. Under the ruined fort there are some deep springs in the bed of the stream, and by them camped, feeling that we needed a few hours' rest after all our exertions. The sheikh had lighted his coffee fire while I Was taking a first cursory view of the ruin. "Oh lady" he cried "honour us." I sat down and drank a cup of coffee. "Where" said he, looking at me critically, "where is thy face in Damascus and where thy face here?" And I am bound to say that his remark was not without justification. But after ten days of frost and wind and sun what would you have? The clouds have all cleared away--sun and water and ruins, the heart of man can desire no more. The sheikh salutes you.

February 21st. We got off at four this morning and made a twelve hours' stage. It was freezing a little when we started, the moon rode high on the shoulder of the Scorpion and was not strong enough to extinguish him--this waning moon has done us good service. It took us two hours to climb up out of the Wady Hauran. I was talking to Muhiyyed Din when the sheikh came up, and said "Oh lady, speech before dawn is not good." He was afraid of raising some hidden foe. Reckless courage is not his characteristic. We have camped under a low bank, selecting carefully the east side of it so that our fires can be seen only by the friendly Deleim to the east of us. We are nowhere tonight--just out in the open wilderness which has come to feel so homelike. Four of the sheep merchants left us yesterday hearing that the sheikhs with whom they deal were camped near at hand, for each man deals every year with the same sheikh. If you could see the western sky with the evening star burning in it, you would give thanks--as I do.

February 22nd. An hour's ride from our camp this morning brought us to the small desert fortress of Amej. . . But Muhiyyed Din and the other sheep merchants found that their sheikhs were camped close at han and we parted with much regret and a plentiful exchange of blessings. So we rode on till at four o'clock we reached the fortress of Khubbaz and here we have camped beneath the walls where Fattuh and I camped two years ago. It feels almost like returning home. It blew all day; I must own that the desert would be nicer if it were not so plagued with wind. The Sheikh and Ali and one of the camel drivers sang trios for Part of the afternoon to beguile the way. I have written down some of the sheikh's songs. They are not by him, however, but by the most famous of modern desert poets, the late Emir of Nejd.

February 23rd. The morning came grey and cheerless with an occasional scud of rain. We set off about six and took the familiar path across barren watercourses to Ain Zaza. The rain fell upon us and made heavy and sticky going, but it cleared before we reached the Ain and we lunched there and waited for the baggage camels till eleven. Kubeisa was only an hour and a half away, and it being so early I determined to refuse all the Sheikh's pressing invitations that we should spend the night with him, and push on to Hit, three and a half hours further. The baggage camels were informed of the change of plan and Fattuh and I rode on in high spirits at the thought of rejoining our caravan that evening. For you remember the caravan which we despatched from Damascus was to wait for us at Hit. But before we reached Kubeisa the rain came down again in torrents. Now the ground here is what the Arabs called 'sabkha,' soft, crumbly salt marsh, sandy when it is dry and ready at a moment's notice to turn into a world of glutinous paste. This is what it did and since camels cannot walk in mud I was presently aware of a stupendous downfall and found myself and my camel prostrate in the sticky glue. It feels like the end of the universe when your camel falls down. However we both rolled up unhurt and made the best of our way to the gates of Kubeisa. And here another misfortune awaited us. The rain was still falling heavy, Abdullah, Father of Camels, declared that his beasts could not go on to Hit across a road all sabkha and even Fattuh admitted that, tired and hungry as they were, it would be impossible. So in great triumph and with much praising of God, the Sheikh conducted us to his house where I was seized by a pack of beautiful and very inquisitive women ("They are shameless!" said Fattuh indignantly) and conducted me into the pitch dark room On the ground floor which is the living room. But the sheikh rescued me and took me upstairs to the reception room On the roof. Everyone we met fell on his neck and greeted him, With a kiss on either cheek and no sooner were we seated upstairs and a bonfire of trees lighted in the middle of the room, than all the worthies of Kubeisa began to assemble to greet him and hear the news. At the end they numbered at least fifty. Now this was the room in which I was supposed to eat and sleep--there was no other. I took Fattuh aside--or rather outside, for the room was packed to overflowing--and said "The night will be troublesome." Fattuh knitted his brows and without a word strode down the stairs. I returned to the company, and when the room grew too smoky with trees and tobacco, sat outside talking to the sheikh's charming son, Namân. The rain had stopped. My old acquaintances in Kubeisa had all been up to salute me and I sat by the fire and listened to the talk and prayed that Fattuh might find some means of escape. He was as resourceful as usual. After a couple of hours he returned and said "With your permission, oh Muhammad. We are ready." He had found a couple of camels and a donkey and we were off. So we took a most affectionate leave of the Sheikh and left him to his narghileh. Half the town of Kubeisa, the female half, followed us through the streets, and we turned our faces to Hit. The two camels carried our diminished loads, Fattuh rode the donkey (it was so small that his feet touched the ground and he presently abandoned it in favour of one of the baggage camels and sent it back) and I was supposed to ride my mare. But she had a sore heel, Poor little thing, and kept stumbling in the mud, so I walked most of the way. We left at 2:30 and had two and a half hours before sunset. The first part of our way was hard and dry; presently we saw the smoke of the Hit pitch fires on the horizon and when we had passed between some low hills, there was the great mound of Hit and its single minaret in front of us. There remained an hour and a half of journey, the sun had set and our road was all sabkha. The camels slipped and slithered and tumbled down: "Their legs are like soap,,, explained the camel boy. If the rain had fallen again we should have been done. But it kept off till just as we reached Hit. The mound still loomed through the night and we could just see enough to keep more or less to our road-less rather than more-but not enough to make out whether stone or mud or sulphur pools lay in front of us. So we three great travellers, Fattuh, the mare and I, came into Hit, wet and weary, trudging through the dark, and looking I make no doubt, like so many vagabonds, and thus ingloriously ended our fine adventure. The khan stands outside the town; the khanji is an old friend. "Ya Abud!" shouted Fattuh "the caravan, our caravan, is it here?" "Kinship and welcome and may the earth be wide to you! They are here , The muleteers hurried out, seized my bridle, seized my hand in theirs and laid it upon their forehead. All was safe and well, we and they and the animals and the packs. Praise God! there is no other but He. The khanji brought me tea, and various friends came to call, I dined and washed and went to bed. And so you see, we have crossed the Syrian desert as easily as if it had been the Sultan's high road, and we have made many friends and seen the ruins we went out to see, and over and above all I have conceived quite a new theory about the mediaeval roads through the desert which I will prove some day by another journey. And all that remains is the hope that this letter, which is the true history of all, will not be lost in the post.

February 24th. We have repacked our loads and are off this day on the road to Ramadi.

To F.B., Ramadi, February 27th.

We did not leave Hit yesterday till one o'clock, having a good deal of repacking to do. Then I rode off with a Zaptieh over the sandy wastes that surround Hit and presently Came in view of Euphrates and put up a thanksgiving at the blessed sight of him. We rode on for three hours til we came to a little valley, full of water after the rains, and then we stopped to direct the baggage animals to the bridge and I heard for the first time the sound of my own caravan bells. We camped a quarter of an hour further under a cliff by the river's edge near a few mean huts of the Dulaim and a patch of green Corn, with the sound of the water wheels in our ears, and the Euphrates lying big and calm under the sunset. There is no river to be compared to him. Neither is it possible to describe the comfort of a fully appointed camp. Praise be to God! as Fattuh frequently exclaims, there is nothing that we lack. we had a march of about seven and a half hours-not very interesting, the familiar barren landscape of the lower Euphrates. All the palm trees have been killed by the snow; there are miserable brown patches instead of the old vivid green. Kubeisa and Hit were scarcely to be recognised. It is a great misfortune. We camped about half a mile outside Ramadi on the Rakkahyyeh road (which we take to-morrow) and Fattuh went off into the town to buy corn and things. I was sitting reading in my tent when suddenly I heard unusual sounds and stepping out saw my muleteers in the grip of about fifteen rascally young men who had picked a quarrel with them, thinking they were alone, I rushed into the fray, feeling rather like the lady in the Nonsense Book (only I had no stick) and soon put an end to the business, for the roughs were alarmed when they saw a European. But after they had gone Mahmud discovered that his watch was missing and Fattuh, presently returning with Government in the shape of a couple of officials, found that a revolver had been taken from one of the saddle bags. So we lodged a complaint but whether the things will be recovered or not I don't know. It is a bore, but wasn't it surprising? A Deleim sheikh who is camped near us came down to offer his assistance and we have two of his men as watchmen to-night as well as two soldiers. So we ought to be all right. Anyhow I shall be less prompt by night for I shall be asleep.

February 26th. There were no suites to last night's incident except that the Commissaire Effendi (whatever that post may be) paid me a second visit and after offering me his watch and revolver-this was merely formal--begged me not to lodge a complaint with Nazim Pasha of whom they are all mortally afraid, I gave the promise the more readily as I never had any intention of pursuing the offender-no more copy for the Daily Mail if I can help it! Moreover, the combined value of the two things did not amount to thirty shillings. We have taken a short cut to Ukhaidir via Rakkahyyeh; it saves at least a day, probably two. Our path lies through the most pitiless desert I have ever seen, a pebbly sand like a hard sea beach, and sometimes not even hard. The pebbles are all water worn; I expect this waste was once the bottom of the sea and I can't help thinking that it had better have remained there, for it is unfit to meet the eye of the sun. The reports about water were extremely varied, there was said to be a salt well at Abu Furukh which the horses would drink and plenty of fresh water in the valley of Roda. We fortunately met a caravan from Rakkahyyeh which said there was no water at Roda (this left me indifferent, for I had made Fattuh fill a skin with Euphrates water, and when we got to Abu Furukh we found a good fresh pool in the sandy water course. I relate this tale in full so that you may realize how difficult it is to get trustworthy information, our two zaptiehs were as ignorant as ourselves. But I am now instructed; I always carry water. So we watered our horses at Abu Furukh and filled five skins for their evening provision. We came into camp among sandhills near Roda and since we have marched nine and a half hours today I think we can only have about eight before us, so we need not fear. It is impossible to get meat; I subsist entirely upon the hen, sometimes in the form of eggs and at other times in that of boiled chicken.

February 27th. We got up at six this morning and reached Rakkahyyeh at noon. Bidding farewell to our two soldiers, who had been bidden to accompany us only to Rakkahyyeh, we pushed on to Shethatha and got into camp at 4:30--a long march. While we were pitching our tents the Sheikh of the town sent us an invitation to pass the night in his house and I replied that I was exceedingly grateful, which means No thank you. There is a hot wind and the temperature was 70 at sunset, the highest we have had. We bought a wild duck of a man in Rakkahyyeh marsh, the same appeared for dinner to-night. I said: "Oh, Fattuh this duck is very good. May God conquer her women!" He replied: "how much we laboured With her! She would not cook." "She has turned out well," said I. "A double health!" said Fattuh, "May God destroy her dwelling!"

March 1st. Yesterday morning broke grey and threatening and presently it began to rain. My men went off to buy necessary provisions in the bazaar while I devoted an hour or two to the darning needle. By the time my caravan was ready it was near noonday and the rain was coming down in torrents. Ukhaidir was only three hours off and I would not stay. It took us however an intolerable four and a half hours, mostly in streaming rain. We plunged for an hour through the slippery paths of the oasis, in mortal danger of tumbling into the irrigation streams, and for the rest of the time we plodded through the Soppy desert, heavy going for man and beast. The rain had almost stopped when we reached the beloved castle, but we were wet through. I carried a letter to Sheikh Sukheil of the Zagarit, a subtribe of the Shammar, who was camped near the castle, and sent out news of my arrival to his tents. He came at once with some twenty others and found us pitching our tents in the dusk outside the castle gate. We stabled our horses in the great hall, and the Sheikh and three others stayed with us all night as watchmen. This morning we moved our tents into the inner court and put our horses into two vaulted rooms that lead out of it. The pair of Arabs who were our guides yesterday have gone back to Shethatha and we are left with the men of the Zagarit who are extremely friendly and agreeable. I have had a hard day's work correcting a few details in my old plan and beginning the measurements for an elevation. We have three men to watch over us tonight and being within the castle walls I think we are safe from attack--at least I hope so; one is never very safe at Ukhaidir. My friends of last time have left and the castle is empty of all but us. I wish they had cleaned up a little before they went away; it is very dirty.

March 3rd. I worked for eleven hours yesterday at elevations and had therefore little time to think of anything else. The Zagarit are thoroughly enjoying our visit. They sit in an expectant circle round Fattuh's tent, waiting for any stray handful of dates or cigarettes that he may give them. They bring their needlework and establish themselves for the afternoon. I found the men of the tribe employed upon some new shirts (of which they stood in great need) when I came in for a hasty lunch. "Don't your women make your shirts?" said Fattuh. "Wallahi, our women do nothing but keep quiet" they replied. And I'm not sure that one can ask more of woman. They came down in the morning, a few of them, to look at me, but they don't interrupt me--I just go on working. This morning we rode out with the Sheikh at 6 o'clock. I went castle hunting and he rabbit hunting. His equipment

was the more picturesque for he came hawk on wrist, with his greyhound at his heels. While we were saddling our mares the greyhound
foraged about for stray bones; when the hawk saw her eating he was
very angry and screamed to her for food, but the sheikh would not let
me give him any till we came back. He was a most charming bird. Unfortunately we found no rabbits, but as far as I was concerned the
expedition was quite successful, for about an hour from Ukhaidir we
came to the old plaster factory, from which I make no doubt they
brought the plaster for the building of the castle, all standing and quite
interesting. So I planned and photographed it and we got home at ten.
The quarry is said to be about an hour in the other direction. The
Mudir of Shethatha came with a large party to see how I was getting
on--very friendly of him. I handed him and his friends over to Fattuh
who entertained them in the proper manner with coffee, After lunch
the Mudir came and sat with me for a little and then they all rode
away. It was a delicious day, the first fine day we have had here. I
made a map of the site with a plain table and though it isn't amazingly
good I feel unreasonably proud Of it. You see it is the first. My plan of
two years ago, on the other hand, is wonderfully accurate. I have cor-
rected one or two mistakes, but they are so insignificant that really
they do not matter much. However I have the satisfaction of feeling
that one or two points on which I did not feel quite clear are now explained. Also I have done a lot more work at details of construction.

March 4th. We left Ukhaidir this morning. I wonder whether I
shall ever see it again and whether I shall ever again come upon any
building as interesting or work at anything with a keener pleasure. We
are now bound for Nejef, but you are not to think that we are taking
any common road to it. On the contrary, we have cut straight across
the desert, for I had heard of a couple of ruins, one at least unvisited,
which I longed to see, Sukheil and Nasir. We rode for three hours over
intolerable sand, then climbed a low hill and got on to an immense
level which was a little better going. At the top of the hill I looked
back and saw Ukhaidir for the last time. An hour or so further on we
came to the first ruin, Mujdeh which proved to be a very interesting
round tower, built of brick and finely wooded. I expect it was a beacon
and I should date it somewhere in the 9th century. It did not take long
to plan it, and I caught up the baggage horses, lunching on my mare as
I went to save time. We saw standing up above the horizon the next
ruin, Khan Arsham, so flat is the plain. All the desert was scattered
over with the flocks and tents of the Beni Hassan and we found some

of the tribe camped under the ruined khan. It was hot, the first hot day
we have had, and I was feeling rather tired after eight and a half hours
hard marching--but the khan brought back my energies. For it is a
really Splendid ruin of I should think the 9th century, about The time
of Samarra, and it opens up all kinds of interesting questions as to old
roads and as to the date of Ukhaidir itself. I set about the plan without
delay and worked on till the light failed and the camp fires of the Beni
Hassan gleamed out red all over the plain. It is a wonderful sight the
desert in the spring. And this is our last sight of it. To-morrow we return to high roads and soldiers and the rest of it. Well, even high roads,
when you must take them, have their advantages, especially in the
matter of water. We brought ours from Ukhaidir to-day and the horses
are so thirsty after their hot march that there is not enough for me to
have a bath. A misfortune! tomorrow, please God. All the Zagarit were
very smart this morning in their new shirts. They do not, however hem
them up at the bottom, which makes them look rather ragged round the
ankles. As we crossed the desert to-day the deserted encampments
where the snow had fallen a month ago were marked by the corpses of
sheep and donkeys. None of these Arabs had ever seen snow. The
Mudir of Shethatha told me that the people there when they woke and
saw it lying on the ground, thought it was flour.

March 5th. The day broke grey and threatening and I was in
mortal dread of rain which would have made the heavy desert sand
quite impassable. I don't know what we should have done, for we had
neither oats nor water, but I suppose we should have got through
somehow. However we were not put to the test, for the rain held off. I
had still an hour's work to do at the Khan and we did not get off till
seven. We parted with two men of the Zagarit and took as guides two
men of the Beni Hassan. The map was of course a "perfect and absolute blank" and I had only a hazy idea where we were--and how long it
would take us to reach the road. I guessed we must be five hours from
the first khan and I was only a quarter of an hour wrong-it took us four
and three quarters of an hour to reach it. Our land-mark after the first
hour was the Tower of Babel. One of the Arabs sighted it first, an almost invisible speck on the North East horizon, it grew and grew till
we could see it rising above a sea of palms, and finally when they were
still three hours away we saw the palm trees round Hamad which was
an objective. I confessed I breathed a sigh of relief when we reached it
and found ourselves upon the Nejef road. Here we parted from the
Beni Hassan who had been most cheerful companions. They are better

by day than by night. The men of the tents near Khan Arsham roved round our camp all last night and if my men had not kept good watch we should have found ourselves with seriously diminished possessions this morning. The road was almost as sandy and barren as the desert. Nejef and Kerbela are you know the greatest Shiah shrines in the world and the whole of Persia comes on pilgrimage to them. The inhabitants (mostly Persian) are exceedingly fanatical; no Sunni is allowed to live within the walls of Nejef, nor may he enter the great mosque where the Khalif Ali is buried. The road between the two towns is provided with immense khans for the accommodation of pilgrims and by one of them we have camped. Its name is Muzalla; there are a few houses near its walls in a dry canal, soldiers, chickens and most of the other luxuries of civilisation--at least so it seems to us who come to it fresh from difficult travel in the desert. I warned my Sunni muleteers to be on their guard and found that they had forestalled my prudence by becoming Shiahs for purposes of convenience. "My lady " said they, "we heard the men here call upon Ali as we call upon Allah, and when they asked us what we were, we said we were Shiahs come from Aleppo to pray at the grave of our Lord." Muleteers, having a wide experience of men and customs, are generally able to cope with new conditions, and since they don't mind passing as Shiahs, I do not think that my soul need feel the weight of the deception. We are all very cheerful at having got safely through the last few days. They were not easy. And do you realise that I have only been one day on a road since I left Damascus? Fattuh and I feel some satisfaction when we look back on the events of this journey. "We are," says he, "Praise be to God, skilled in travel--God made us!"

March 6th. We were premature when we rejoiced last night over the end of our desert journey. I had determined to send my caravan into Nejef and to ride out myself to see some curious caves cut in the cliff that forms the western boundary of our old lake, now dry but still called the sea of Nejef. Accordingly I took an Arab as a guide, Sheikh Selman of the Beni Hassan. As we rode out across the desert, he said: "Do you want to go to Rakban?" "What is Rakban?" said I. "it is a castle of the first time" said he "but you cannot reach Nejef from it to-day." In a flash my mind ran out to the Lakhrnid castles which none of us has been able to trace; in another flash I had turned round, stopped my caravan, told the men to buy corn at the khan and to come out with me into the desert. They accepted the order as cheerfully as if I had invited them into a garden. The golden dome of Nejef gleamed at us invitingly on the horizon, but even more invitingly gleamed those delusive castles of Ibn Mundhir. There was a high wind and by the time we reached the cliffs of the Sea of Nejef, it had raised a dust storm. We climbed down them and crossed the floor of the sea in driving sand. Five hours from Musella we reached some water pools, bitter salt but the horses drank there. I meantime lunched hastily and grittily in the unspeakable sand. An hour further we came to a pool less bitter and I left my men to fill the water skins and rode on with the Sheikh. Presently the black mass of the castle appeared in front of us. I plunged on through the sand, reached it and found it to be nothing but a mud-built enclosure, not 50 years old. "Oh, Selman," said I "this castle is not old."

"Oh lady," he said, "before my beard was grown I saw it here." It said much for the temper of my camp that when my men came in and I told them we had had all our trouble for nothing, no one was angry. So we camped-it was half past three-and I can see that the Lakhmid castles, if any of then, still exist, are not for me. But what was I to do? I could not leave a ruin unvisited.

To H. B., Babylon, Friday, 10th

I have been so busy travelling the last three days that I have put off letter writing till I got here. On the 7th We retraced our steps through the sand as far as Amm el Gharrof and then journeyed by a good firm path along the bottom of the sea to Nejef which we reached at mid-day. It is a walled town standing on the edge of the cliff of the dry sea and surrounded on the other sides by a flat plain. Above the walls rises the golden dome of Ali's tomb which is the place of pilgrimage of all the Shiah world and outside the walls the town is encompassed on two sides by the graves of the Faithful who are brought from far to be buried here. We pitched our tents on the third side and after I had lunched I went to call upon the Kaimmakam who instructed the chief of the police to take me sight-seeing. But there was little to be seen; I might not go into the mosque, nor even pass very close to the doors of it (even as it was the people eyed me angrily and one man jumped out of the crowd and tried to stop me from going nearer the mosque); the bazaars were without interest, and presently I returned to our tents where I received a number of visitors, sheikhs of the mosque and official personages. At night, however, I came into conflict with the officials who wished to place a guard of thirty soldiers round my tents. I protested with oaths and the guard was withdrawn. The reason for these precautions was that there are nightly disturbances in the cemeteries. The Arabs bring in their dead by night and try to bury them without paying the sum of 10 s. which the town exacts as a fee for every grave; the soldiers shoot at them and they shoot back. We heard this shooting going on, together with the vibrating cry of the women, but we were far from the cemetery and no one troubled us.

Next day I sent my caravan direct to Kifil and taking an aged soldier with me (he was useless as a guide for he knew The way to nowhere) I rode out for an hour or two south to the ruins of Khawarnek which really was one of the Lakhmid castles. Nothing remains but mounds, but I was interested to see the site. My old zaptieh, Abbas, was extremely conversational, but as he was also toothless it was difficult to understand all that he said. I rode off with a guide, and lunched on top of the Tower of Babel. You know what it was? It was an immense Babylonian temple dedicated to the seven spheres of heaven and the sun god. There remains now an enormous mound of sun-dried brick, with the ruins of a temple to the North of it and on top a great tower of burnt brick, most of which has fallen down. But that which remains stands up, like a finger pointing heavenwards, over the Babylonian plain and can be seen from Nejef to Babylon. I left Babylon with many regrets, then I rode on to Hilleh, meeting my caravan at the gates of the town. And as we rode through the bazaar an officious policeman took upon himself to seize my rifle from Fattuh, saying that the carrying of rifles is forbidden. I went at once to the head of the police and Pointed out that every Arab in the desert carries a rifle and that as we had come through the desert I had to carry arms; Moreover I had permission to do so. But he would listen to no reason so I betook myself to the Kaimmakam and found him to be an intelligent and cheerful soldier from Bagdad who Promised at once to have the rifle restored.

Sunday, 12th. Bagdad lies on the east side of the river but the bridge had been swept away by the floods, so Fattuh and I having left our horses at the khan with the baggage horses (which had come in hours before) stepped into a 'guffa' and floated down the Tigris to the Residency. The Lorimers were most friendly and gave me a large and very welcome tea. I think it possible that I may not be able to get letters again till Diatbekr, but you will hear pretty regularly from me and if I am a long time on the road I will send you a telegram through the Diarbekr Consul.

To H.B., Bagdad, March 18, 1911

(This for the private ear of my family). Mr. Lorimer says that he has never met anyone who is in the confidence of the nations in the way I am, and Mr. Lorimer, I should wish you to understand, is an exceptionally able man!

To F.B., 21st March, 1911

. . . Mr. Lorimer and I steamed up the river in the launch and called on Sir William Willcocks. He is a twentieth century Don Quixote, erratic, illusive, maddening--and entirely loveable. . . I left Bagdad early on Sunday morning. I do owe an immense debt of gratitude to the Lorimers. No two people could have been kinder. The road to Khanikin, which I am now following, is the quickest way to the Persian frontier. We had a journey of 11 hours the first day to Bakuba (it is 35 miles from Bagdad and very dull it was: absolutely flat, barren country, a waste of hard sand on which little or nothing grows. Moreover there was a strong wind). We reached Bakuba at nightfall and camped outside the village not far from the banks of the Diala river. Next morning I rejoiced to see those banks set thick with blossoming fruit trees and when we had crossed the river, by a bridge of boats, and ridden through the town, we found the plain on the other side of it a great stretch of young spring wheat and the irrigation trenches deep in grass. So that day's ride, though the country was as flat as ever, was a great deal pleasanter. And it was only 9 hours. We camped in a green field outside the village of Shabraban--you realize that during our whole journey we have never yet seen grass covering the earth? Before us stretched the low range of the Hauran, nearer akin to real mountains than anything we have met since the Syrian snows dropped down below the lip of the Hamad. To-day we crossed the Hamrin; there were flowers in its dry watercourses; at noon we reached the village of Kesrabad (Kizil Robat the maps call it) and rode on another 3 hours into a second stretch of low hills wherein we camped by a big guard house. It is a delicious camp, all green with grass and flowering weeds, and I have a cup full of yellow tulips on my dinner table.

Tuesday, March 28th. Most wonderful of all were the mountains of Persia, range beyond range and white with snow. So we rode gaily along the broad road scattered with tiny mud-built huts where you can drink tea and buy bread and dates and hard-boiled eggs, and towards noon we came to Khanikin which lies on either bank of the Heliwan river. The storks had arrived before us; they were nesting on every house top. Sami Pasha's relations in Bagdad had given me a letter to a Kurdish chief of high repute, Mustafa Pasha, and to his house I went. I accepted his invitation--there was nothing else to be done--and was lodged in a tiny room at the top of the house side by side with a pair of storks. Mustafa Pasha was sitting in his reception room when I arrived, with a number of friends. They most of them spoke Arabic, but between themselves they spoke Kurdish, which bored me for I wanted to hear what they were saying. We spent a couple of hours in this fashion, the Pasha transacting business from time to time and receiving innumerable letters. This is also typically oriental. Every man would appear to carry on an unlimited correspondence with the other inhabitants of his town or village, which is the more surprising as they all seem to visit each other every day. I was beginning to feel rather hungry when fortunately the Pasha called out to his servants to bring food. Some 8 of us went into the next room where we found a table spread bountifully with a variety of meats and we ate from the dishes with our fingers as best we might. It was all very good, if messy. I nearly had a 'fourire' in the middle, when looking round upon the party with which I lunched I remembered Herbert's picture of me, so wonderfully exact was the likeness. . .

Towards sunset the Pasha invited me to come into the harem and I spent some time with his two wives and his other female relations. They were extremely pleasant and I don't doubt that they were glad to see me, for they never go out of the house. " We are imprisoned in the courtyard)" they said. Their furthest excursion is to take the air on the roof. When the Pasha was exiled he left them behind and they spent all those years alone in Khanikin. Next day I was talking to one of my muleteers, a Moslem, and I told him how Mustafa Pasha's ladies never went beyond the courtyard. "Wall' ahi!" said he, "that is how it should be." And then he told me that his mother (his father is also a muleteer) had never been outside their house in Aleppo until last year, when she went to Mecca with her husband. What a great adventure the Hajj must seem to them, who see the world for the first time! . . .

257

(She then rides north again with a man Mustafah Pasha had sent to them with directions to see to their safety.]

About 1 o'clock we reached Kasri Shirin which stands beautifully on the river Helwan, a straggling street climbing the hillside, the great fort of Kerim Khan standing on top. It was to Kerim Khan that I was specially recommended, and I took a short cut up to his fortress, forgetting that I ought to pass through the Persian custom house which is managed by a Belgian. You see I had become so accustomed to neglecting custom houses. I interviewed the Khans (there were a great many of them) and told them I was going to work in the ruins. They bade me very welcome and I galloped after my caravan. The ruins, I must tell you, are a couple of great Sassanian palaces and it was these that I had come all this way to see. I found my servants camping near the first palace and a little upset because two bullets had whizzed past their ears while they were riding up to it. However, I told them that Kerim Khan would look after us, and after that I forgot all else in the excitement of working at the palace. A good many people came out to see me in the course of the afternoon and they all assured me that we should be greatly troubled by thieves if we spent the night there. I remained sceptical as to the thieves, but there was no doubt about the rifle bullets, and it is almost as annoying to be shot by accident as on purpose. The last incident of this eventful evening was the arrival of a mild-looking man with a message from Kezim Khan. He said that the Serkar had heard that I had had some dispute with the head of the Custom House and desired to know whether I was in any difficulty for he would be glad to settle it by having all the custom house people shot. It was merely a complimentary expression of good will, though so picturesquely couched. I sent back my salaams and thanks and said there was no need for extreme measures as I had made It up with the head of the Custom House. I worked for the next two days at the palaces without so much as turning round. I went out to the ruins at 6 a.m. and remained there till 9 p.m. and I never stopped for a moment drawing, measuring and photographing except when Fattuh sent or brought me lunch and tea. It is almost more than the human frame can bear when you have got to struggle through such an undertaking single-handed and I wished several times that the Sassanians had never been born. . .

I'm glad I've seen Kasri Shirin; it is one of the most beautiful places I have ever been in and I shall never forget the exquisite look of it all as I worked from dawn till dusk. . .

Next morning we had a difficult job to tackle, the crossing of the Diala, bridgeless and in flood. We rode through the first arm of it; it was not very deep, up to a tall man's waist; but it was very swift. In the middle I heard shouting above the turmoil of the waters and looking round caught the terrified eye of my donkey who had been swept off his feet, thought his last hour was come. One of the ferrymen with us rescued him, as well as the muleteer whom he had spilt in mid stream, and they were both brought safely over. The second arm was too deep to ford. We crossed in a craft called a kelek, 19 inflated skins tied together and floored over with reeds. It looked very frail in those swift waters but it served our purpose and in 4 journeys took us and our loads over. The last kelek load was the donkey, bound hand and foot, with Fattuh sitting on his head and one of the muleteers on his tail. The horses had to swim. Two of the ferrymen stripped naked and got on to the 2 bare-backed mares--the others were driven in behind them and I watched, with my heart in my mouth, while the rushing water swept them down. May God be praised and exalted! they all clambered out safely on the other side. . .

(She crosses the Zab again, where she changes Zaptiehs and buys provisions.]

. . .We rode off with our new Zaptieh but once outside the town I found that he was heading for Mosul, whereas I wanted to go to Kalat Shergat. I protested and he declared that he knew no other road to K. Shergat. So I rode back to the mayor and with the aid of a very imperfect map (War Office!) I explained that I did not wish to go a day's journey out of my way. He came with me, good man, to the Mudir, and I restated my case. The Mudir was much perplexed; one day more or less seemed to him a small matter to fuss about. He asked to see the map, but since he looked at it upside down we were not much further forward. He got more satisfaction out of my permit from Kerkuk which was the next thing he asked to see. It stated in the clearest language that I was to do anything I liked--the officials treat me with unparalleled generosity and kindness--and that everyone was to help me to that end. I then suggested that I should take the Zaptieh and add to him a man of the town as guide. The Mudir agreed with relief and told the mayor to find a guide. The mayor and I went down into the street and there met an aged party whom the mayor clapped on the back and taking him by the hand ticked off on his fingers all the places to which he was to lead me, ending with Shergat. The old man did not seem to be the least surprised---it is a two days' journey, you must re-alise. He tucked up his skirts, made A suitable reply in Turkish and marched off down the street, I following. "In the peace of God! and give him two mejidehs (7s.) when you get to Shergat," said the mayor. "Upon my head!" said I, "We salute you," and rode away.

Sunday, April 2nd. My old guide is a great source of satisfac-tion to me. He has no visible means of support: he does any odd job that turns up and if someone happens to need a guide he is always ready to meet their wishes. "Khanum Effendi" (we talk Turkish), "I had not a penny left. And then you came. God is merciful; you came! There is no God but God!" When we began our march this morning he repeated the profession of faith uninterruptedly under his breath for an hour, and he never neglects the appointed hours for prayer, though he has to run with all his might to catch us up afterwards. I make the caravan go slowly while he prays, so that he has not to run so far. He has a wife and two small children. How they live is not stated. We had a 9 hours' march to-day and it was hot, but he walked all the way with unceasing cheerfulness except when my kind muleteers mounted him on their animal for an occasional half hour. He takes special pride in telling me the names of all the villages. "Khanum Effendi, that so-and-so--write, write!" So I get out my map and put it in.

Monday, April 3rd. Safely arrived at Kalat Shergat where Dr. Andrae and his colleagues have given me a very warm reception.

To F.B., April 14, 1911

I spent three enchanting days at K. Shergat and would gladly have stayed longer. Three of the four who were there two years ago I found this year and two others whom I had not seen before. One of them, Herr Preusser, had visited two of my Tur Abdin churches and is publishing them, so we had a great time comparing plans. But chiefly I found this year, as I found two years ago, great profit from endless talks with Dr. Andrae. His knowledge of Mesopotamian problems is so great and his views so brilliant and comprehensive. We went over the whole ground again with such additional matters as I had brought from Kasri Shirin, and as he had derived from two more years of dig-ging. He put everything at my disposal, photographs and unpublished plans, and his own unpublished ideas. I don't think that many people are so generous. Also they taught me to photograph by flashlight-provided me with the material for doing so, which I shall find very useful in some of my pitch-dark churches. And we went over the last two years' work stone by stone and discussed it in all its bearings. K. Shergat was looking its best. I love it better than any ruined site in the world. The only drawback of my visit was that I was so reluctant to go away, and I carried a heavy heart over the high desert to Hatra--which is a long way! But one can't be heavyhearted at Hatra; it is too wonderfully interesting. It was (perhaps you know?) the capital city of the Parthian kings about whom we know so little. The Parthians were an eclectic folk; their arts sprang up on ground that had already been strongly Hellenised by the Alexandrids; and they learnt, no doubt, from the Romans, with whom they were always at war. They worked out these new ideas upon old oriental foundations, and the palace at Hatra is the one building left out of all their cities where you can see the results at which they arrived, for it stands to this day. We arrived late on a gray and stormy afternoon and were received with acclamations by the Turkish army. I shall write a long article for some leading journal when I get home, and call it "Pacification of the Desert," for it should be known how well and wisely the Turks are handling matters here.

After I had done my work we paraded the army--cavalry, infantry, and artillery, and I photographed them all, to their great satisfaction and to mine. The drawback of Hatra is the water; it's all salt. The town stands about half an hour from the river Tharthar, which is so bitter salt that no one drinks it but the Arabs: we drank from wells, but they were exceedingly nasty. When I left I was escorted for a couple of hours by half-a-dozen officers, who galloped with me across the beautiful grass plains; we drew up on a mound and waited for the caravan, and then we took a tender farewell of one another, and I went on more soberly with my own men. We followed the Tharthar valley and fortunately in an hour or two came to a rainwater pool, at which we filled a skin. It was even more horrid than the Hatra salt water, sticky, greasy standing water, tasting strongly of decayed grass. But we had nothing else. There were Arab camps and flocks all along the shallow valley and we camped at evening near some of these. There was abundant grass, but we had no fresh water for the horses, and all but my mare refused to drink the Tharthar water. I could not wonder, for it tasted like the sea. We had a difficult journey next day. Fattuh was very ill and we had a march of nearly 11 hours which we could not shorten because there was no fresh water. We passed a rain pool in the morning, watered our horses and took a skinful with us, but the day was hot and the men thirsty, and by five o'clock there was scarcely any left. At last we saw Arab tents ahead and knew that there must be drinkable water near at hand. We put up our tents near them, boiled water and made hot compresses for Fattuh and forced him to lie down while the muleteers made shift to cook some sort of dinner. The Arabs were very sympathetic and brought us some curds and milk, but the water they had was next to undrinkable, drawn from standing rain pools. We joined company with a body of the Shammar who Were on their way northwards from Riza Bey's gathering of the clan at Hatra. They were moving camp when I came up to them and the whole world was alive with their camels. Now the Shammar are Beda; only the Shammar and the Anazeh are real Bedawin, the others are just Arabs. Akh-el bair we call the Beda, the People of the Camel. They never cultivate the soil or stay more than a night or two in one place, but wander ceaselessly over the inner desert. It was delightful to see their women and children travelling in the camel howdahs and their men carrying the long spears that are planted before the tent door.

Fattuh having called in a native doctor who bled him copiously he rather surprisingly recovered. . .

We got back to our tents just as a very heavy shower of rain fell and congratulated ourselves on having escaped the worst of it, when suddenly a hailstorm battered on to my tent roof. I began hastily to fasten the door and before you could wink a hurricane of wind swept down upon us and every tent was flat. My books and papers went flying out into the universe, Fattuh and Abud flying after them, while I, half blinded with wind and hail, strapped up our open boxes. It only lasted for a minute or two, but we were all wet through, We gathered ourselves together and began putting up the tents again. The casualties were extraordinarily small: a tent pole, an eyeglass and a comb, and a good many odds and ends of papers--nothing very important. The two muleteers came running down from the town where they (fortunately for themselves!) had been buying corn, the tents were got up again, the sun came out and we changed and spread out our wet things to dry. It was an extremely disagreeable experience, but what we should have done if it had happened at night, I can't think! You may imagine how we lay awake and listened to every gust of wind!

Monday, April 17. There is a charming passage in Sir Edward Grey's book on fly-fishing in which he praises the various moods of Nature. "Rain," says he, "is delightful," and I remember when I read it, thinking of warm May rain on our opening beech leaves at home and thoroughly agreeing with him. But one begins to feel rather differently about it when one is camping in pitiless torrents. It rained like the devil on Saturday night and like ten thousand devils on Sunday. The wind howled through my tent ropes till it sounded like a hurricane on board ship and the rain thundered against the canvas. I thought my tent would go down more than once, but my excellent servants kept the pegs firm by piling stones on to them. The storks were less fortunate: their house was blown away. . .

[She then goes on by Nisibin to Mardin, and so into the mountainous region of the Tur Abdin, exploring ruins, planning, photographing, over the rocky ridges of the Tur Abdin across the valley and down into a rocky gorge.]

. . .And at the foot of the cliff rolled the Tigris, in full flood, between the broken piers of a huge stone bridge. The first thing we learned was that there could be no crossing of the Tigris till it had run down. The ferry boat is a raft on skins, on which you can't put horses and neither raft nor the horses could cross in that flood. We were delayed for two days, but they were not wasted days . . .

[More photographing of inscriptions in fifteenth century mosques and minarets.]

I managed to piece together a very pretty piece of Arab History. . ..

On the afternoon of the second day the river had dropped so far that I gave the order to cross. The landing place on the opposite side was nearly a quarter of a mile below the bridge--it looked a very long way off and the rush of the water against the piers of that bridge was anything but encouraging. So the horses thought, for when we drove them into the water they struggled about in the deep backwater by the bridge and eventually returned to us. Then we devised another scheme. We tied two of them to the raft, which was loaded with the pack saddles, and drove the rest in again They, seeing the raft swirling down the stream, and two of their companions with it, swam after it, all but 2 who again were swept back to our bank. These 2 we tied to the raft on its final journey, when I also crossed, and so we all got over in safety--but I shall long remember the rather too exhilarating sensations of that ferrying, the raft darting down the flood and the two horses panting and groaning in the water beside it.. . .

[After 12 hours' ride she reaches Mayafarkin where she makes a day's halt.]

I found, first, the most splendid ruined mosque I have ever seen, secondly, the remains of a huge basilica of the fifth century and thirdly, a great domed church of the sixth or seventh century. I have had two days' hard work at these three. I feel very triumphant over them. They have not been published, and no one knew any more than I did when I arrived, what a wealth of material there was at Mayafarkin. Moreover, the mosque will never be done again as I have done it, for they are busy rebuilding it and the old work will disappear under the new, and under whitewash and other abominations. I felt as if I was receiving its dying will and testament as I worked at it, and I only hope I have written down every word. We have suddenly jumped into summer. The temperature is 70 in the shade, the trees have all rushed into full leaf, and the corn stands high in the fields. The ruined bastions of Mayafarkin, walls, towers of unrivalled Arab masonry rise out of all this sea of green; the storks nest in every tower and the world is full of the contented clapping of their beaks. The Kaimakam's wife sent a special message asking me to visit her, and when I arrived she greeted me, rather disconcertingly, with "Addio!" It was the prelude to a very voluble conversation in Turkish, of which I picked up what I could, and was much amused. A native Protestant pastor gave me great help in reading the inscriptions. He had learned a little English at Mardin, so from time to time I talked English laboriously. G.B.-"Is it more cold here or at Mardin?" Pastor.-"Yes." It then became very difficult to take up the thread of the dialogue.

Saturday, May 6th. When the 1st of May came I had a great 'sehnsucht' for the daffodils and the opening beech leaves at Rounton-- it's not all beer and skittles travelling, you know. The splendid finds at Mayafarkin consoled me a little, but I still have an overpowering desire to see my family. However the work here must be done first--one does not pledge oneself to ancient buildings for nothing. I feel out here more like the Heathen than ever, for the passion for stocks and stones becomes a positive worship. . . Poor Maurice! his collar bone is really too brittle. I have the most delicious post-card from Pauline--angel!

To F.B., Sunday, May 14, 1911

I left Diarbekr on Thursday and had 2 long days' journey to Wirausheber. Wirausheber was the headquarters of Ibrahim Pasha the famous Kurd who was in league with Abdul Hamid. Before I left Wirausheber I called on Ibrahim Pasha's widow--or one of his widows--Khanza Khatun, a very remarkable woman. She was renowned for her beauty-though she is now old, you can see the traces of it in the fine shape of the face and in the splendid carriage of the head. Her deep-set eyes have some of the old fire in them and as she came out to greet me she looked like "one who wins and not like one who loses." We sat together on a carpet outside the house by the edge of a spring, among willow trees: it was early morning, the women were cleaning the sour curds in skins hung from the willow branches. The men of her household stood back while we discussed her position, and the possibility of the sons' return. She manages all the estates, which are still very large, during their absence. She wore a long European man's coat over her dress, and an Arab cloak over that; on her head the male keffiyeh, silk kerchief, bound over the head with a thick roll of black silk. I looked back, after I had bidden her farewell and mounted. She stood under the willow trees with shrouded head and gazed after me with her deep-set eyes--a very striking figure. "Thijah!" murmured Fattuh, as we rode away, "She is a man!" I must relate to you another silly talk with Fattuh. He made for me in Diarbekr some very good little mutton sausages. "Oh, Fattuh," said I, thinking to improve my Arabic, "What is the name of these?" "Effendim," said Fattuh, "these? Their name is sossigio."

URFA, Thursday 18. We had two long and rather difficult days from Ras al Ain to Harran. We could get no corn at Ras al Ain and therefore had to do the journey on grass, which meant stopping 2 hours in the middle of the day to let the horses feed-and there was really nothing for them to feed on. Then there was also trouble about a guide; my soldiers knew nothing of the desert way and I set out from Rasal Ain with only a compass to direct me, and a map. But the good old head of the Circassians, Hassan Bey, sent a boy after me and it was as well he did, for though we should probably have found a way

265

through, the water was scanty in the extreme and not easy to find. The first day we met no people and saw only the very smallest traces of former habitation. The second day we passed a very interesting fortress. Lack of food obliged us to push on. Then we came to a large ruined town, quite deserted and full of dead sheep. There was a large encampment of Arabs not far from it and near there we stopped and pastured our horses. Soon afterwards we reached the Crest of the high ground and saw the great mound of Harran before us, two or three hours away in the fertile plain. We got into camp at 7 p.m. having started that morning soon after 5 a.m. It is said to be the place where Abraham met Rebecca, at any rate, it was out of this origin that the Jewish tribes migrated to Canaan and the huge village mouns scattered over the plain are an indication of its early importance. I had come there to see the ruins of a very splendid mosque of the early Abbassid period. We camped in the great court and I spent nearly 3 hours next morning photographing it stone by stone. It was wonderfully interesting. There is no town now, only a collection of mud-built huts inhabited by half-settled Arabs, and the mound with an immense ruin field round it, all enclosed by the remains of a fine stone wall. There was a very ancient moon cult here, as old as Abraham probably; the Emperor Julian came to propitiate the goddess before he set out on his fatal campaign. So we rode into Urfa over the fertile plain, and were not sorry for once to have done with desert and with marches 12 hours long. The town lies on the lower slopes of the hills and I camped above it in a terraced garden which was once a café but has fallen into disuse, fortunately for us. I have spent the day here: it's a beautiful place and like Harran and Hierapolis it goes back into the dimmest mists of Oriental history, of which it preserves the memory in the sacred pool stocked with unmolested fish which may not be caught.

It has become really hot and this morning we set out before sunrise, while it was still cool. But we did not avoid heat and it is still at 6 p.m. 87 in the shade. I do not mind it, but it makes the horses languid. Birejik is one of the most famous of the Euphrates passages. Here Crassus passed over the river to his defeat at Harran: the eagles of the 5th Legion turned backwards from the bridge of boats, but he would not heed the omen. To-morrow I go to Carchemish in the hope of finding Mr. Hogarth there.

Just after I had written to you the Kaimmakam came over to call on me and told me that Mr. Hogarth had left but that Mr. Thompson was still at Carchemish. Accordingly I went there-it was Only 5 hours' ride--and found Mr. Thompson and a Young man called Lawrence (he is going to make a traveller) who had for some time been expecting that I would appear. They showed me their diggings and their finds and I spent a pleasant day with them.

[This is Gertrude's first meeting with T. E. Lawrence. She then returns to Aleppo and is back in England in June.]

CHAPTER XIII

1913-1914 - JOURNEY TO HAYIL

To H.B., London, October 28th, 1913

Last night I went to a delightful party at the Glenconners' and just before I arrived (as usual) 4 suffragettes set on Asquith and seized hold of him. Whereupon Alec Laurence in fury seized two of them twisted their arms until they shrieked. Then one of them bit him in the hand till he bled. And when he told me the tale he was steeped in his own gore. I had a great triumph on Monday. I got Edwin Montagu to lunch to meet Major O'Connor and the latter talked for one and a half hours of all the frontier questions--admirably E.M. sat and listened For one and a half hours and then summed up the whole question with complete comprehension. I was enchanted. He is not only able, E.M., he is the real thing--he's a statesman. . .

[On November 13th she starts for the East via Marseilles.]

To F.B., Alexandria, November 20, 1913

Alexandria is not much of a place but it makes me feel as if I were dropping back into the East. Oh my East! My cab driver yesterday showed all the solicitude of one's oriental servants, took me for a drive along a very smelly canal because I was tired of looking at catacombs and insisted on my drinking a cup of coffee under the trees to fortify me before I went to the museum! It did fortify me, or else he did.

To F.B., Damascus, November 27th, 1913

Yesterday I sent round to Muhammad al Bassam to tell him I was here. . . he came to see me at once and spent half the morning with me. He is my great support in all plans and arrangements. It looks as though I have fallen on an exceedingly lucky moment, everyone is at peace. Tribes who have been at war for generations have come to terms and the desert is almost preternaturally quiet. Bassan knows Of some good desert camels, riding camels, going cheap it Damascus, an almost incredible stroke of good luck as I thought I should have to transport myself somewhere into the wilds and haggle for camels there. In short I scarcely like to trust to all this good fortune but I hope it will turn out to be true. I am not quite certain yet whether I shall go to the Druzes or the Anazeh first. I shall have no difficulty in going to either but there may be some little complication in passing from one to another; nothing however that cannot be overcome. Muhammad says that it is perfectly easy to go to Nejd this year. If I found it so I should certainly go. I will let you know anyhow from Madeba--look for it on the map east of the north end of the Dead Sea. Go on writing here and I will keep in touch with you as long as possible.

Now Fattuh and I must go and talk about camels. It is heavenly weather.

To H.B., Damascus November 29th, 1913

I sent you to-day a telegram which I fear will rather surprise you asking you to make the National Bank telegraph 400 pounds to my credit through the Ottoman Bank London to the Ottoman Bank here. I telegraphed to you because I did not know whether if I telegraphed straight to the National Bank they would think the request sufficient without receiving it in writing, but I hasten to explain to you (which I could not do in the telegram) that this is not a gift for which I am asking. I wish to borrow the money from the N. Bank The position is this: As far as I can make out and I have had a good deal of information from many sides, there never was a year more favourable for a journey into Arabia than this. The desert is absolutely tranquil and there should be no difficulty whatever in getting to Hayil, that is Ibn al Rashid's capital and even much further. Moreover I have got to-day exactly the right man as a guide. He was with Mr. Carruthers 3 years ago. I heard of him with the highest praise from him. To-day he turned up at Bassams and Bassam at once told me that I could not have one who is better acquainted than he with all the Arab tribes. To have got him is a piece of extraordinary good luck. He is the man of all others whom I should have chosen. So much for the chances of success in this business. As for the expenses, you see this time I have to begin by buying everything I shall need here. As far as I can make out we shall need 17 camels (we have bought one or two already) and they cost an average Of 13 pounds a piece including their gear. Bassam says I must reckon to spend 50 pounds on food to take with us, 50 more for presents such as cloaks, keffeyehs for the head, cotton cloth, etc. It is obvious that this is wise advice because the things are worth much more there than they are here and a kerchief which costs only 5 shillings here is a respectable present in the desert. That comes altogether to 321 pounds. Bassan says I ought to take 80 with me and to give 200 to the Nejd merchant who lives here in return for a letter of credit which will permit me to draw the sum in Hayil. I think both these sums are reckoned very liberally but I don't like to provide myself with less money lest when I get into the heart of Arabia (Inshallah) I should not be able to do anything for want of funds. You will see that I have now come to a total of 601. I could not possibly explain all this in my telegram so I attempted to explain nothing but I hope you will not say No. It is unlikely that you will because you are such a beloved father that you never say No to the most outrageous demands. Perhaps it is a pity that you don't. I am practically using all my next year's income for this journey, but if I sit very quiet and write the book of it the year after I don't see Why I shouldn't be able to pay it all back. And the book ought to be worth something if I really get to Nejd and beyond. On the whole I hope you will think it is worth it since the conditions are so good. I shall try to keep in some sort of touch with you. At the end of the first 3 or 4 weeks I shall have no difficulty in sending you letters by the Hadj railway, and I shall make arrangements to have my letters sent to me from here. After that I fear I shall not be able to hear from you though I shall try to get one lot of letters at Hayil. I think there is no doubt I shall be able to get news out to you, It ought to take about a month from my station near the Hadj railway to Hayil that is to say you will hear from me after the lapse of some 2 to 2 and a half months. And if I go further South I will try to send out news from somewhere on the Persian Gulf. Anyway wherever I can possibly find a messenger I will send a letter. I must tell you that there have been very good autumn rains so that we ought to find plenty of surface water and also grass.

I feel much better after four days here and I am beginning to drop into the East.

One thing more I must tell you. I have arranged with Mr. Cumberbatch that if I reach anywhere where I can I will telegraph to him and he will communicate with you. But of course there is no such place till I get to the coast somewhere. Also I shall write to him from here and tell him exactly what I intend to do and let him know that if at any time you or he want information about me the best person from whom to get it is Bassam. M.C. could communicate with him privately. He has all the news of the desert, he knows exactly what I am doing and he is sure to know more or less where I am. But don't go to him with questions unless news of Me is greatly overdue.

Dearest beloved Father don't think me very mad or very unreasonable and remember always that I love you more than words can say, you and Mother.

You know things are working out much better than I expected they would but don't talk about Nejd to outsiders in case it does not come off.

To F.B., Damascus, December 5th, 1913

I don't think I shall be off till next Friday, 12th, so that puts all the dates I gave Father a week later. There are such a lot of things to buy and arrangements to make. Meantime I spend my days quite pleasantly. To-day was fine and I worked with my theodolite all the morning on the roof and went for a walk in the afternoon. We walked up on to a hillside and climbed to a top of an eminence whence we had a glorious view over Damascus and its gardens, still brown and gold with autumn leaves and then straight into the desert where I am going. I saw the little volcanic hills to the S.E. where I shall make the first stages of my journey and I wished I were already among them.

I have called on a good many of my Mohammedan friends and have been received with open arms. They are all extremely kind and cordial. There are one or two I still want to see but the mud has made visiting difficult except in houses near at hand. I have got much fatter than when I came, idleness partly, I suppose, and partly an abundant diet of sour curds which is without doubt the best food in the world.

I wonder what you are doing and where you are--it is difficult to think of you making preparations for Xmas. My love to Maurice.

To F.B., Damascus, December 12., 1913

My camels should have got off to-day but we were delayed by a tiresome contretemps. Fattuh has an attack of malaria and I shall be obliged to wait another day or two. . . I dined in the native bazaar quarter the Maidan with my old guide Mohamed al Mardwi. An enormous party was assembled to meet me including the agent of Ibn al Rashid. The latter was a curious figure, young very tall and slight, wrapped in a gold embroidered cloak and his head covered with an immense gold bound camel's hair robe which shadowed his crafty narrow face. He leant back among his cushions and scarcely lifted his eyes, talking in a soft slow voice the purest classical Arabic, but after a bit roused himself and told marvellous tales of hidden treasure and ancient wealth and mysterious writings in central Arabia of which you may believe as much as you please. The men on either side of me murmured from time to time "Ya Satif! Ya manjud," Oh Beneficent, oh Ever Present! as they listened to this strange lore. Finally we ate together that bread and salt might be between us and then-why then we all came back together on the electric tram!

To F.B., December 15th, 1913

A misfortune has befallen us. Fattuh fell sick a week ago and we fear it is typhoid. Fortunately his wife is here. I have put off my departure from day to day and now I'm going-my camels left to-day and I sleep with the Mackinnons and start to-morrow. I still hope that in three weeks or so when I near the railway F. may be able to join me and he of course never doubts for a moment that he is coming. But it is a horrible bore. I've got a boy to take his place--take his place indeed! He seems bright and quick, I like him and I do not doubt that after a day or two my camp will fall into order. . .

To F.B., 20th December, 1913

I got off safely on the 16th from the kind Mackinnons, drove out a couple of hours, picked up my camels, loaded water and went off into the desert. We camped early about an hour or more S. of Dumeir and it was as well we did so, for the first night in camp always means a good deal of sorting out, and when you have no single man with you who has ever travelled with a European you can guess what it Is like. I had to show them everything, and find everything myself, Fattuh not being there, who had packed all. They did not even know how my English tents went up, nor how to boil an egg. But they are all most anxious to please me and most willing to learn, and by dint of patience and timely instruction I am getting things into shape. It rained and blew the night of the 16th and all the day of the 17th, impossible to travel if the devil had been behind us (and I was a little afraid that the Damascean authorities might look for us) so there we sat and shivered and overhauled our packs. I've learnt by now to bear rainy days in camp when you are never for one moment warm or dry and the hours seem endless. We sent to Dumeir for firewood for the men, chopped straw for the camels and cotton cloth for me, with which I sat at my needle and made bags for all our provisions. It is long since I have sewed so diligently. Next day was fine, but what with wet tents and unaccustomed men we took 2 and a half hours to break camp--I de-spaired, but kept silence until later, and the second morning we were under one and a half hours from the time I woke till the time we marched and that is as good as anybody can expect. I have good ser-vants, you see, and besides I know the job and they soon find that out. We struggled on the 18th for an hour through the mud and irrigation canals of the Dumeir husbandry--a horrible business with the camels slipping and falling. At last we were out in the open desert, with the rising ground of the stony volcanic country, the region of Tells, under our feet, and mud forgotten. We marched through it all yesterday and all to-day, a barren region Of volcanic stones and tells. We have sighted but one camp of Arabs in all our Way. A man rode out from it to see who we were and we found them to be one of the half-cultivator tribes from near Damascus. For water we have an occasional rain pool, very muddy, but I still have drinking water with me from Damascus, and bread and meat and eggs and butter, so that hardships have not yet begun. It was bitter cold last night; the temperature fell to 28 and I woke several times shivering. When we set off to-day in a dense mist the sparse grass and shrubs were all white with frost and we ourselves blue with it. But one takes no harm. The mist did not lift till near mid-day, which made mapping most tedious as I could take no long bear-ings, but we came into camp early in the afternoon (having started early) in glorious sunshine and I am now writing in the long afterglow of a cloudless sunset. Already I have dropped back into the desert as if it were my own place; silence and solitude fall round you like an impenetrable veil; there is no reality but the long hours of riding, shivering in the morning and drowsy in the afternoon, the bustle of getting into camp, the talk round Muhammad's coffee fire after dinner profounder sleep than civilization contrives, and then the road again. And as usual one feels as secure and confident in this lawless country as one does in one's own village. We have a Rafiq, a comrade of the Ghiyatah with us--we fetched him from Dumeir to stand surety for us if we met his tribe. We ought by rights to have a man of the Beni Hassan, with whom our Ghjyatah is useless since they are deadly foes and if we come across the B. Hassan we will take one along. Good, please God! the earth is ours and theirs and I do not think we shall trouble one another. Such good mushrooms grow here. I have them fried for dinner.

December 7th, JEBEL SAIS. We have reached our first goal and a very curious place it is, but I will begin at the beginning. It was horribly cold last night. The temperature dropped to 19 and it was impossible to keep warm in bed. N.B.-I am not cut out for Arctic Exploration, it is clear. Anyhow I kept waking up to shiver. The men's big tent was frozen hard and they had to light fires under it to unfreeze the canvas, otherwise it would have torn when they packed it. But the sun rose gloriously, clearing away the mists, just as we marched, and in half an hour we were all warm. We sighted J. Sais at 8 and reached it at 12, marching over almost flat ground covered with volcanic stones--a desolate country which must be a furnace in summer. But the rains have filled all the water pools and the grass and shrubs are growing. On our way Muhammad saw two men in the distance and was much perturbed, but they were probably only, shepherds of the Saiyadand--anyway I did not bother about them. I have got men enough with me who will recognise or be recognized by all these tribes. J. Sais is a big and very perfect volcano with a sort of deep moat round the W. and S.sides, ending to the S.E. in a lake, now full of water. I took some photographs while the men pitched camp and then climbed with my Ghiyatah guide to the lip of the volcano to take bearings. "Oh! Hammad," said I, as we breasted the stony slope, "who can have lived in this strange place?" "By God," "we would learn from you. But, indeed, oh lady, there is no guide to truth but God." It was a wonderful view from the top--desert, desert and desert; wide stretches of yellow earth, great shining water pools, and miles and miles of stones. We scanned the whole world for Arab tents, but saw none anywhere. With that I ran down the hill and had just time to plan all the ruins before sunset. There remains a little photography and taking of angles for to-morrow morning. I have not for a long time enjoyed anything so much as this afternoon's work. Content reigns in my camp and all goes smoothly.

December 22nd. A preposterous and provoking episode has delayed us to-day. We had marched about 2 hours when we sighted camels and the smoke of tents. We took them to be (as indeed they were) Arabs of the Mountain, the Jebel Druze, with flocks. I told you that we tried in Dumeir to get one of the Jebel Druze Arabs as a companion and failed--and we suffered for it. Presently a horseman came galloping over the plain, shooting as he came, into the air only. He wheeled round us, shouting that we were foes, that we should not approach with weapons, and then while he aimed his rifle at me or other of us Muhammad and Ali tried to pacify him, but in vain. He demanded of Ali his rifle and fur cloak, which were thrown to him, and by this time a dozen or more men had come galloping or running up, some shooting, all shouting, half dressed--one of them had neglected to put on any clothes at all--with matted black locks falling about their faces. They shrieked and leapt at us like men insane. One of them seized Muhammad's camel and drew the sword which hangs behind his saddle with which he danced round us, slashing the air and hitting my camel on the neck to make her kneel. Next they proceeded to strip My men Of their revolvers, cartridge belts and cloaks. My camel got up again and as there was nothing to be done but to sit quiet and watch events that's what I did. Things looked rather black, but they took a turn for the better when my camel herd, a negro, was recognised by our assailants, and in a minute or two some sheikhs came up, knew Ali and Muhammad, and greeted us with friendship. Our possessions were returned and we rode on together in quiet and serenity. But to avoid the occurrence of such events, or worse, we are to take with us a man from their tents, and to that end we have been obliged to camp near them that a suitable companion may be found. The sheikhs have drunk coffee with me, enjoyed a long conversation with all of us and been so good as to accept my backsheesh in token of our gratitude in being rescued from the hands of the shepherds. And they have given us a comprehensive letter to all the Arabs of the Mountain. Good, please God, but I feel not a little impatient at the delay.

December 23rd. It rained hard till 8 o'clock this morning and the desert turned into paste. But it dries quickly and by 10 we were off, at the bidding of my impatience. All went well, however. We had no more rain though it remained cold and grey. We have with us to guard us against the Arabs of the Mountain the oldest old man you could wish to see. He crouches upon a camel by day and over the camp fire by night. He seldom speaks and I can scarcely think that any one would respect a party introduced by so lifeless and ragged a guarantor. We are camped in a strange bleak place under a gloomy volcanic hill.

Winter travel has its trials. We got off an hour before dawn in a sharp frost. No sooner had the sun risen than a thick mist enveloped the world and hung over it till 10:30 faith, but it was cold! far too cold to ride so I walked for some four hours, the mist freezing into a thick hoar frost on my clothes. We had passed out of the black hills before sunrise and we walked on and on over an absolutely level plain with the white walls of the fog enclosing us. It was not Unpleasant--though I wonder why? One turns into nothing but an animal under these conditions, satisfied with keeping warm by exercise and going on unwearied and eating when one is hungry. But I was glad when the sun came out and we could see our way again. I got bearings back to the hills of our camp so that my map will not suffer. This business of mapmaking, far from being a trouble, is a great amusement, and alleviation in the long hours of riding and walking. The light came upon us just as we entered a wide and shallow valley up which we shall march until we reach our goal--the fort of Burqa which has been heard of but never seen.

BURQA, December 24. We sighted the keep of the fort at 10 this morning and reached it at 1 o'clock--I with an excitement scarcely to be kept in bounds. Burqa has proved most interesting. There is a good Kufic inscription which I have deciphered--it is dated in the year 81 A.H. and as inscriptions of the first century A.H. are very rare, it is exceptionally important..

December 25. What part of Xmas Day have you been spending? I have thought of you all unwrapping presents in the Common Room and playing with the children. But you were certainly not breakfasting out of doors in a temperature of 28, which was what I was doing at 7 a.m. It was so cold that I could not take rubbings of my inscriptions till late in the morning, because it was impossible to keep the water liquid, I have worked hard all day, planned, photographed, taken a latitude. Late in the afternoon I discovered that the boulders were covered with Safaitic inscriptions and I copied them till night fell. They are pre-Muhammadan, the rude inscriptions of nomad tribes who inhabited these deserts and wrote their names upon the stones in a script peculiar to this region. So you can picture the history of Burqa-- the Byzantine outpost with Safaitic tribes camping round it; the Muhammadan garrison of the 7th century; then a gentleman who passed along in the 8th century of the Hejira and wrote his name and the date upon the walls; then the Bedouin laying their dead in the courtyard of the fort (it is full of graves) and scratching their tribe-marks on the stones; and lastly we to read the meagre tale. Well, I have had a Profitable day. I have not had time to think whether it has been merry. Bless you all.

December 26. I should like to mention that it was 25 when I breakfasted this morning. The wonder is that one minds it so little. I walk for an hour or two every morning so as to unfreeze after the painful process of getting up and packing before dawn. We have been doing to-day the very thing I dreamt of doing. We have been following an ancient road, not metalled, but marked all the way by Safaitic inscriptions.

Heaven be praised, it is 10 degrees warmer to-night than it was last night. What with sun and frost I am burnt out of all knowledge and, as you may imagine, feel like the immortal gods for health. Nor do I believe that they sleep half so well as I, nor eat so much.

December 27th. I copied inscriptions for another two hours this morning and then we broke up camp and set off. But the devil took possession of the old old man who is my rafiq and he set off independently or went to sleep somewhere or I don't know what. Anyhow after half-an-hour's searching we discovered he was not with us, and having spent an hour in looking for him, he turned up from quite a different direction, and we all cursed him, poor old thing, for wasting our time and energies. It was a horrid march to-day in the teeth of a wind and over endless stones with no apparent path through them. Heaven send us better ground to-morrow.

December 28th. The last prayer was not answered. We marched over stones all day, and marched far, being waterless. At 4 in the afternoon we reached a khabra nearly dry and after some time we espied the smoke of Arab tents far off and camped hastily, hoping that they would not notice us. At night we watched their distant fires flickering and sinking. No doubt they watched ours for we had not been more than a couple of hours on our way to-day before we heard sounds which meant our neighbours were stirring. We left Abu Ali, my old old man--on top of a stony ridge to tackle them and ourselves descended into low ground and halted. Presently a horseman topped the ridge and greeted us with the customary rifle shot, but Abu Ali met him and found him to be of his kin. So all was well. Meantime we had lighted a fire, round which we sat with the newcomer, gave him food and tobacco and exchanged with him information as to the movements of tribes. He told us we should meet the Serdiyyeh moving camp and half an hour later we did meet them and went through the usual formulae. It happened to be the chief Sheikh, Ghalib, whose people we had met, and he joined us and insisted on our camping with him that night. There was no help for it since we shall have to take a rafiq from him to guarantee us with his tribe further on. So I have spent the afternoon sitting with him, sitting with the women, drinking coffee, doctoring a man with a horribly bad foot--my only remedy was boric ointment which can work neither harm nor good, but if I had said I could do nothing they would not have believed me. And now I am going to dine with Ghalib, who has killed a sheep for us. In return for which I shall give him a cloak. The new moon is just setting in a wonderful clear sky, the fires are all alight in the Arab tents; it's all very lovely and primeval, but I prefer a solitary camp.

December 31st. Yesterday we rode all day over stones. At noon we reached a Roman outpost, a little fort on a hill top. I sent my camels on, and keeping two men with me planned and photographed the place. We got into camp late, but since we were without the baggage camels we trotted our camels wherever the ground permitted. It was a nice camp by some springs-the joy of clean water! This morning we moved into Qasr Azraq, which stands among palm trees, surrounded by a multitude of springs. I had ridden on with one man, whom I left with my camels while I went into the castle alone. It is inhabited by Arabs, but in the front room I found a Druze who greeted me with the utmost cordiality and gave me coffee I then began to plan the castle when immediately I was surrounded by Arabs all shouting at the top of their voices that if I wrote a line they would burn my book. I took them all down to my Agent, Ali, the postman of 3 years ago (they had shut the great stone gate of the castle to keep me prisoner the better while they haggled with me). We sat down under the palm trees and I smoked and left Ali to explain, with the result that before long they declared themselves to be entirely at my service. I've worked at this place all day and shall have another day at it to-morrow. I really don't know if it was worth the trouble, but I dislike leaving things undone in far away places. I rather think I have got one new Greek inscription. I must take a rubbing of it to-morrow and see what can be made of it. So the year ends.

January 2, 1914. They were all outlaws and outcasts at Azraq and, as Ali observed, as we rode away this morning "The world would be more restful if they were all dead."

It was really warm to-day for the first time. I dined after sunset with my tent all open. But there seems to have been no rain here and the question of water may present difficulties. We can carry--and are carrying to-day--water for 4 nights, if we are careful with it--no baths and very little washing, I fear! After dinner I sit for an hour or so at the men's camp fire and they tell tales of raiding and of desert journeying. The fire lights us as we sit in a circle and one after another takes up his story. The negro camel herd, if he is not asleep in a corner (for he takes the first watch at night), looks Over the shoulders of us gentry with his face one gleaming smile as the detailed adventures grow more and more blood curdling. When I get up to go they all rise and send me away with a blessing. I often look round the circle and think how closely I resemble Herbert's picture of me.

January 5th. I have had 3 days of very hard work at Kharaneh, another of the Umayyad pleasure palaces. Nothing so interesting has come into my way since Ukhaidir. It is not my discovery, but I have done much more at it than anyone else; in fact, it has not been studied at all as yet. Besides the wonderful architectural details I have got heaps of Kufic graffites which I hope Moritz will be able to study from my copies and photographs. One at least is dated A.H. 92. The difficulty here has been water, as we feared. My men have scoured the country round, but 4 waterskins was all the neighbourhood offered. But with what we brought with us we had enough for three nights here which was all I wanted and we still have to-morrow's supply in case we come across none on our march. Lack of water has unfortunately frustrated my admirable plan of sending in to Madeba while I worked here. As we don't know when the next supply will be found we could arrange no rendezvous. It means, too, no washing and I begin to feel that I shall never be clean again. However Karaneh is worth it all-- delays and dirt and everything. I have worked these days from 6:30 a.m. till 5 p.m. with an hour off for lunch at 11. Darkness at either end prevented longer hours. But it has been glorious. So now we march west, towards Madeba, and camp where God ordains.

January 6th. My letter goes and I fetch letters.

To H.B., January 9th, 1914

As I said before, paf! I'm caught. I was an idiot to come in so close to the railway, but I was like an ostrich with its head in the sand and didn't know all the fuss there had been about me. Besides I wanted my letters and Fattuh. Well, I've got both. Fattuh turned up yesterday morning, just arrived from Damascus, still looking pale and thin (and no wonder), but with a clean bill of health from Dr. Mackinnon. And do you know I really believe that his coming makes up for all the mis- adventure? I have missed him dreadfully, my faithful travelling companion. Never in the world was anybody given more devoted friendship and service than he gives me. He was in the seventh heaven at being with me. Well meantime none of the 4 men whom I had sent in to Madeba and Ziza to buy stores had returned. In the Middle of the morning one of the camel drivers arrived with chopped straw, and af- ter the camels and I had lunched on all the luxuries Fattuh had brought from Damascus) I rode off to Mshetta, which is only an hour from my camp. As we came back Ali, the camel driver, looked up and said "Are those horsemen or camel riders going to Our tents?" I looked, and they were horsemen and, what is more, they were soldiers, and when we rode in they were sitting round our camp fire. More and more came, to the number of 10, and last of all a very angry, rude (and rather drunken) little Jack-in-Office of a Chaowish, who said they had been looking for me ever since I left Damascus. There it was. We put on a good countenance and when the Chaowish stormed we held our tongue. I sent off at once telegrams to Beyrout and Damascus to the two Consuls, but I had to send a man with them to Madeba and the Chaowish intercepted them--and put the man, one of my camel driv- ers, into the Ziza castle, practically a prisoner. Thither he presently sent Fattuh also, on some imaginary insult (F. had said nothing) and then he ransacked our baggage, took possession of our arms, and posted men all round my tent. All this which he had not the slightest right to do I met with an icy calmness for which God give me the reward; and later in the evening he began to feel a little alarmed himself and sent to ask me whether I would like Fattuh back. But I refused to have Fattuh routed out again for the night was as icy as my demeanour and I shivering in bed, had some satisfaction in thinking of how much those unwelcome guardians of ruins were shivering outside. The temperature was 22. There was a frozen fog. To-day we have waited for the Kaimmakam of Salt to turn UP or send permission for us to go elsewhere. He is the nearest authority and I only wish he would come. The Chaowish left us in the early morning to the care of 6 Or 7 soldiers and turned up in the evening very affable. We have spent the day not unpleasantly, gossiping with the soldiers, mending a broken tent pole, and also in very long periods of gossip in Fattuh's tent, one member of the expedition or another dropping in to share in the talk. And I am busy forging new plans for I am not beaten yet. But I fancy this road is closed and I shall probably have to go up to Damascus and start afresh via Palmyra. The Bagdad Residency is the best address for me. It's all rather comic. I don't much care. It's a laughable episode in the adventure, but I do not think the adventure is ended, only it must take another turn. I have done some interesting work in the last 3 weeks--just what I meant to do, but I have not enjoyed the thing much up to now and my impression is that this is not the right road. I think I can do better. Anyhow I will try. God ordains. Fattuh observes cheerfully, "I spent the first night of the journey in the railway station, and the second in prison, and now where?"

Saturday, January 10th. So far all is well. The Kaimmakam not having arrived I came down to Amman and here I found him on his way to me, a charming, educated man, a Christian, willing and ready to let me go anywhere I like by any road I please. The Commandant here, a Circassian, ditto. But there comes in a question of conscience. I do not want to get the Kaimmakam into any trouble by taking advantage of his kindness so I have telegraphed to Damascus for permission to visit the ruins round Ziza and if I get that (I see no reason why I should not), I shall have relieved my friend of all responsibility and shall be free, as occasion offers, to go my own way. I am bound to say that I shall be glad when the permission comes. It was curious riding through hilly ways and cultivated country to-day after three weeks of desert. But such weather! Wind and sleet and it's blowing like the devil to-night. They wanted me to sleep in the serai, but I preferred my tent. This is such a wonderful place. If only it is fine to-morrow I shall like seeing it again. I was here with the Rosens 14 years ago. But it has been a heavy road for the laden camels, up and down hill. The camel is not a mountain bird in this part of the world. They all know me in these parts. I have met here a nephew of Namoud, the man who helped me into the Jebel Druze in 1905--vide "The Desert and the Sown." And they are all as nice as can be. Altogether the misadventure is rather fine so far. What will Damascus say? Well, I shall know to-morrow. But I can take no other course than that which I have taken.

January 11th. The reply has not yet come from Damascus, but the Kaimmakam thinks they can't refuse the permit so I wait with an easy mind. I am sending letters up to Damascus to-night and this shall go with them. I have spent the day receiving--and returning)--visits from the notables of Amman and it has been very amusing. Also I took a long walk with the Kaimmakam in the afternoon and had an interesting talk with him. He is a very nice man, but these Christians always give me a hopeless feeling. They walk blindfold and won't look facts in the face. It is not easy for them to work with the Muhammadans, but if you think they meet them half way--well, it isn't so. Yet this is a capable man and intelligent. I have liked being with him and with the good old Circassian magnate. I expect I shall be here to-morrow too. There was no sun to-day, but to-night it is fine again and I have a good deal of photography to do to-morrow.

To F.B., Amman, January 14, 1914-

My troubles are over. I have to-day permission from the Vali to go when I like. The permission comes just in time for all my plans were laid and I was going to run away to-morrow night. They could not have caught me. However, I am now saved the trouble--and amusement! of this last resource. The delay has had the advantage of giving Fattuh a few days to pick up strength. He looks and is much better than when he joined me but one does not recover from typhoid in a twinkling of an eye. Now I think he will be able to travel without fatigue. To-morrow I camp again at Ziza in order to pick up two rafiqs--one of the Beni Sakhr and one of the Sherarat who will serve us

282

as guarantors when we meet their tribes as we probably shall in a few days.

I have made the acquaintance of all the leading inhabitants of Amman! To-day I attended a Circassian wedding and drank tea with the protestant congregation which numbers 15 families.

To H.B., January 19th, 1914

I must begin a chronicle, though Heaven knows when it will be sent off. We left Amman on the 15th, I have given the authorities at Amman an assurance that the Ott. Government was not responsible for me. This amounted to little, for wherever I went without gendarmes the government had the right to wash its hands of me. And I could not take gendarmes into the desert. I rode up that day to the farm of some Christians in the hill above Lina, where I was given a regal entertainment. Also Nimrud, the man who helped me in 1909, came up and spent the night there. I was delighted to see him.

I must tell you that I was in some trouble about my muleteers. The men I had brought from Damascus were very uncertain as to whether they would come on with me--I think they really dreaded the perils of the road. While we were at Amman we had fetched another man from Damascus a nephew of my old guide, Muhammad, his name is Said. It Was as well we did so, for on the 16th, just as I was starting, the three Agail threw down their camel sticks and declared that they would not come. I had Said and my negro camel herd, Fellah, an excellent boy. My hosts pressed into my service a fellah, a peasant, on their farm (his name is Mustafa), and I engaged as third man an Agaili, who had followed us from Amman in hope of getting work. His name is Ali, not to be confused with Ali Mausar, the postman guide of 1911, who is still with me and will never, I think, leave me. Besides these, I have Salim, another nephew of Muhammad's, whom I took at first in Fattuh's Place; he is an admirable servant and a very nice, well-educated man, I like him immensely. And finally, I have Fattuh, the lynch pin of the whole party.

So we set out. My hosts provided me with two Rafiqs a man of the Sherarat of whom I have not seen much, and a man of the Beni Sakhr, Sayyah, who is a delightful companion. They themselves rode with me till beyond Lina and then by the Mecca railway, they, Nim-rud, and I, and various slaves and retainers made a hearty lunch and I Parted from them with a feeling of gratitude. They clasped me by the hand, embraced Muhammad and Fattuh, and sent us forth with many deep voiced blessings. I crossed the Mecca railway and turned my face to Arabia.

We rode next day across the undulating country of the Beni Sakhr and passed occasional herds of camels and flocks of sheep. A young sheikling of the Sikhur joined us, he and his slave, and spent the night with us as guests, the sacred word. He was a charming boy, cousin to the great Sheikh Hathmel, and he was very anxious to come on with us, he and his slave.

Next day we went on our way over hills and wide shallow val-leys, entirely covered with flints, and came in the afternoon to the palace of Tubah. It had been sufficiently planned by Musil, but very insufficiently photographed, and I spent a very profitable afternoon working at it. We camped among the ruins and found a good clear wa-ter pool in the sandy bed of the valley on which they stand, but the men were rather anxious that night, as the desert to the east of us was "empty" i.e., there were no Sukhur beyond us, and they feared the pos-sibility of an Anazeh raiding party, making for the grazing camel herds we had passed in the morning. This thought did not, I need scarcely tell you, keep me awake-I should sleep but little in the next few weeks if I were to be disturbed by such things--and when I woke I found there had been no raiding party and my goods were safe and sound.

It was 34 when we started before dawn, and 70 when we camped at two o'clock. It is difficult to adjust one's toilet to a ther-mometer which behaves in this fashion. We have ridden through flint country all day, no water in the valleys, and consequently no people. We brought our water with us from Tubah. We are camped in a dry valley bed, not far from the great land-mark of all this country, the three pointed hills which are called the Thlaithuwat: the blessing it is to have a point for my compass bearings is more than I can say! Since there is no water there is not much fear of raiders, but we keep watch for casual robbers, who, if they found us watchful, would turn out as guests, and if they found us sleeping, would lift our camels. "Beni Adam!" as Muhammad says, "Sons of Adam!" I listen all day as we ride to tales of raid and foray. But it is a fine country, this open desert, and I am enjoying myself mightily.

January 21st. We rode all day across flint strewn desert on the 20th. About mid-day two camel riders came up behind us and proved to be Jadan, the great Sheikh of the Agaili, and one of his men. They had spied us as we passed under the Thlaithuwât, and taking us for a raiding party, had followed us to see where we were going.

"We took you for foes," said he.

"No, praise be to God," said I, " we are friends."

he rode on with us for an hour, for company, and then turned back to reassure his people. And we came at two o'clock to the last of the castles, Bair, as yet unplanned and unphotographed. The plan is a very old type and the place may be 8th century. It is very famous on account of its wells, and in summer and autumn, if the Sukhur are not camped here, all the ghazus pass this way. I have therefore heard more raiding stories here than ever before, and I will tell you one.

Muhammad, Sayyah (my rafiq) and I were sitting on the top of the biggest well, which is about twenty meters deep, and M. observed that when he first knew Bair this well was filled in. A party of the Isa had fallen here on the Sukhur and killed a horseman. The Sukhur killed Of the Isa two camel riders. The Isa were thirsting and the Sukhur, before they made off, threw the two dead men and their camels into the well and rolled in a few big stones on top, so that the Isa might not drink and follow them.

"Haram," said I, "it is forbidden."

"No," said Sayyâh, "their thought was good."

"The Arabs are devils," observed Muhammad.

"Devils," said Sayyâh.

"They are the very devil," said I, and with such conviction that Sayyâh looked up and laughed. You may take that as an example of our usual conversation.

Friday, 23 rd. We have marched for two days across exceedingly featureless country, indeed, for most of to-day there was nothing on which to take a bearing, but my camel's ears, which are not a good line. We march for an hour or two across flintstrewn uplands, glistening black, and then down and up the banks of a deepish valley--dry, of course--and then into the upland again. All the valleys here run approximately East and West.

Last night we had some rain, and the first deep valley to which we came there were small standing pools, which the camels drank greedily. We are carrying water, and since we are rather uncertain whether we shall reach pools to-morrow, we are using it sparingly, No baths and little washing of any kind. It has turned cold after the rain, not frosty, but a nipping wind--rather nice, however.

Yesterday we picked up a stone with a Safaitic inscription, a great deal further south than I expected to find such things. It is a desolate land--barren beyond all belief. But in the valleys we find dry bushes, on which the camels Pasture-

Sunday, 25th. We changed our course a little yesterday, for seeing how dry and barren the world was, we decided that the Sukhur must have moved off east and that it was no good looking for them. We reached the western edge of the flint plateau.

Then we dropped down into a sandy valley and saw in the sand many foot-prints of camels, coming and going. But what Arabs had passed this way we did not know.

We camped in a hollow, where our fires could not be seen, and Ali, Sayyâh, and I went off scouting for Arabs. We climbed very cautiously up a high tell and from the shoulder surveyed the landscape through my glasses. But there was no soul in sight

To-day we set off in a frosty dawn and marched on down the valley. Ali and I walked on for an hour and waited in a sandy hollow for the camels, and the foot-prints were all round us in the sand. "They are fresh," said Ali. The valley ended in A wide, open plain, set round with fantastically riven hills black and rusty red as the volcanic stone had weathered. The light crept round them as we marched across the plain. They stood in companies watching us, and in the silence and emptiness were extraordinarily sinister. Suddenly Sayyâh called out "There is smoke." A tall spire of smoke wavered against a black hillock. I must tell you that we were waterless and thirsty--the camels had not drunk for four days. We were not at all sure when we should find water, neither did we know in the least what Arabs had kindled the fire whose smoke we watched, but the consensus of opinion was that it was a ghazu--raiders. These are the interesting moments of desert travel. We decided that it was best to go up and see who was there; if they were enemies, they would be certain to see us and follow us anyway; if they were friends they would give us news of the tribes and water. The latter question, however, we solved for ourselves--we found the pool for which we had been looking. We watered the camels, leaving the men to fill the water skins, Muhammad, Ali, Sayyâh and I went on to examine that questionable smoke; we crossed a little ridge, and on the farther side saw flocks of sheep and the shepherds of the Howaitât who came up and greeted us and gave us news of their sheikhs. All was safe and we went on into the hills and camped. To-morrow I hope we shall be guests of the Howaitât. The big camps cannot be far away, for the only water in this district is the pool we found this morning, with the exception of one small well in the hills to the east. The Howaitât are great people. They raid all across to the Euphrates and have a resounding name for devilry--reckless courage.

Tuesday, 27th. Yesterday we rode into the hills. On our way back we met a camel rider who told us that a very regrettable incident had occurred the night before. A man who was camping with the Sukhur had attacked a small camp of the Howaitât--he had an old grudge against the dwellers in it--and carried off sheep. The Howaitât pursued him and killed him; in revenge his brother shot three of the pursuers and fled to the tents of the Sukhur. This news caused my Sukhur rafiq, Sayyâh, to feel very anxious as to the reception he might meet with in the tents of the Howaitât and I tried to comfort him (with some success) by assuring him that under no circumstances would I desert him. But all turned out well. We reached the tents of Harb, one of the sheikhs of the Howaitât, and were received with all kindness, Sayyâh included. Harb killed a sheep for us and we all dined with him that night. To-wards the end of dinner another guest arrived, who proved to be Muhammad Abu Tayyi-the Abu Tayyi are the great sheiks of the Howaitât. He is a magnificent person, tall and big, with a flashing look--not like the slender Beduin sitting round Harb's fire. He carried the Howaitât reputation for dare-devilry written on his face-I should not like to Meet him in anger.

To-day we have sent the camels down for water; all this country drinks from the pool at which we filled our water skins on Sunday, and we dare not go on without a good provision. Accordingly, I have had rather a long day in camp, sitting and talking to Harb and his people, drinking coffee, talking again, photographing--they love being photographed--I took a latitude at noon, which is much to the good. Muhammad al Marawi and his nephew, Said, my camel driver Sayyâh, goes back from here, and I shall send this letter in the hope that it will ultimately reach a post and give you assurance that I am safe and flourishing. We take a Howaitât from here, and as the Howaitât are all along our way, we reckon we ought to be sufficiently protected. I have decided to go to Taimah--you will see it on the map--so as to get news of Nejd there. It is a town of the Rashids. I count it some eight easy marches from here. I expect I shall be able to write you from there.

I've bought an ostrich skin and two eggs! They live about here but I haven't seen a live one yet.

To H.B., February 4, 1914

I have really delayed too long in beginning my next letter To you. Since I sent off the last by Sayyâh (I wonder if you will get it?) we have changed our plans several times and I still hesitate to pronounce that we are on the road to Nejd, though I think we are. At any rate we are in Arabia, in the very desert and no doubt about it. But you must hear. When it came to the point of leaving Harb's tents I found that the question of who was to come as our new rafiq was by no means settled. On the contrary, all the Arabs and all my men were gathered round the camp fire with faces the one longer than the other. It seemed that the desert before us--the way to Taimah--was "khala," empty, i.e., there were no tribes camping in it. It would be, they all assured me, infested by ghazus who would fall upon us by night and undoubtedly rob us, if not worse. Whether this were true or no I had

288

no means of judging, but I take it to be against the rules of the game to persist in taking a road against which I am warned by all; moreover there was the conclusive difficulty that we could get no rafiq to lead us along it. Therefore, after prolonged consultations, it was decided that we should strike east, go to Jof, throw ourselves on the kindness of the Rualla and make our way south, if possible, and, if not possible, east to Bagdad. We set out next morning with Harb's brother, Awwad, as rafiq, for Jof and the Wadi Sirhan in pursuance of this plan. I did not add anything to my letter, though Sayyâh was not yet gone, because the future seemed so doubtful, and it was as well I did not. I should have said we were going to Jof and it would have been no truer than that our way lay to Taimah. Riding over the last hills--they were very delicious, full of herds of camels--we came presently to the big tent of Audah, the great sheikh of the Howaitât; Audah was away, as we knew, raiding the Shammar, but we stopped for coffee and photographs and then rode on east. But it happened that a man who was among the coffee drinkers had given Awwad the information that some of the Ruwalla were camped in the Wady Sirhan. Now as any man of the Ruwalla whom he might chance to meet would cut his throat at sight it was clear that he could not conduct us to the Wadi Sirhan and I was again rafiq-less. I sent him off to the tents of Muhammad, Audah's brother (he turned up in Harb's tents the first night we were there--a formidable personage) to fetch a Sherari of repute who had no blood feud with the Ruwalla, and we came into camp and waited results. He returned in an hour accompanied by Muhammad himself and several others who all stayed to dine and sleep. Muhammad brought in a lamb and a very beautiful ostrich skin, and further, over the coffee cups, he told me of a ruin in the Jebel Tubaiq which, if I would come back with him to his camp, he would take me to see. Now I was very reluctant to turn back, but a ruin is a ruin, and moreover it is my job to determine what kind of ruin it may be. So next day we rode back with Muhammad, my men inclined to grumble and I not a little inclined to doubt my own wisdom. We had got our Sherari guide, Musrud, and might have gone on if we wanted. But after all I was right. In the first place the ruin was worth seeing. It has a Kufic graffito and all complete and to get to it I rode five hours across the Jebel Tubaiq, saw and photographed a pre-Muhammadan High Place (so I take it to be) and got a far better idea of these exceedingly interesting hills. They are full of wild beauty and full of legend; they deserve a good month's study which I may perhaps give to them some day, and we such friends With the Howaitât. For I made great friends with Muhammad. He is a good fellow and I like him and trust him. In the 3 days I spent with him--one, indeed, a very long one, was spent in riding over the hills and back--I saw him dealing out justice and hospitality to his tribe and found both to be good. Of an evening we sat in his big tent--he is an important person, you understand--and I listened to the tales and the songs of the desert, the exploits of Audah, who is one of the most famous raiders of these days, and romantic adventures of the princes of Nejd. Muhammad sat beside me on the rugs which were spread upon the clean soft sand, his great figure wrapped in a sheepskin cloak, and sometimes he puffed at his narghile and listened to the talk and sometimes he joined in, his black eyes flashing in question and answer. I watched it all and found much to look at. And then, long after dark, the "nagas," the camel mothers, would come home with their calves and crouch down in the sand outside the open tent. Muhammad got up, drew his robes about him, and went out into the night with a huge wooden bowl, which he brought back to me full to the brim of camel's milk, a most delectable drink. And I fancy that when you have drunk the milk of the naga over the camp fire of Abu Tayyi you are baptised of the desert and there is no other salvation for you. I saw something of the women, too--Muhammad's wives and sister. Yes, those were interesting days. They were prolonged beyond my intention for this reason. The day I visited the ruin we had sent our camels to water at a khabra and bring us water. Do you know what khabra is? It is a rain pool. Now this khabra proved to be so far away that the camels took 18 hours on their way there and back, and one never came back at all. It sat down and it would not get up and they left it 6 hours away. That's what camels do; if they are tired and don't mean to move, nothing in this world or the next will induce them to stir. It was clear that we could not abandon a camel. We despatched a man in the middle of the night to feed and fetch her and waited another day. During that day we changed all our plans once more. Muhammad al Marawi came to see me and said he thought if we went to Jof we should have great difficulty in getting on to Nejd, since the Ruwalla are foes of the Shammar, moreover Musrud, our Sherari rafiq, was prepared to take us south--to Taimah, if we liked, or if we liked better, S.E. and direct to Nejd. The ghazus, the perils, the rifle shots at night, seemed to have vanished into thin air. I questioned Musrud very closely, made up my mind that the scheme was feasible and told my men that the less said about it the better. Nominally we were still going to Jof--one becomes very secretive in these countries. The camel messenger came back that night and reported that he had persuaded the

290

camel to move on three hours--we did not mind her non-appearance, for our new road lay in her direction. The real danger ahead, as I made out, was the lack of camel food. If we found no pasturage in the desert to the south (we had only six days' aliq with us--aliq is fodder-) we should be faced by starvation for the camels and with I did not know--what for us. But the reports, if they were to be believed, of the country ahead were good and as all other chances of getting to Nejd seemed so remote I resolved to take the risk. Muhammad gave us half a load of corn, his crowning act of hospitality, and I gave him a Zeiss glass in return for all his kindness. We set out and rode 3 hours to the southern edge of the Jebel Tubaiq, dropping down by a rocky gorge into the plain below, where we camped. Here we found our camel, more or less recovered, and fit to go on next day. The " trees " were greening and there was plenty of good pasturage. Before us lay the country in which we now are, a country of red sandstone and the resulting sand. But the early winter rains have been good and the sparse thorny bushes grow-ing in the sand have sprouted into green, all the rain pools are full and (so far) raiders non-existent. We have with us not only our Sherari rafiq, but still better a man to conduct us into the heart of the Shammar country--not a man, a family. We met them in our last Tubaiq camp, at the foot of the hills, a Shammar family who wanted to return to Nejd. Without us for company they would not dare to take this direct road, and we are no less grateful than they, for if we meet a Shammar ghazu we are guaranteed against them. So here we are, camped in red gold sand among broken hillocks of red sandstone, with all the desert shrubs grey green and some even adventuring into colourless pale flowers. They smell sweet and aromatic. "Like amber" said Ali, sniff-ing the wind as we came into camp this afternoon. And the camels have eaten their fill. We march slowly, for they eat as they go but I don't mind. I never tire of looking at the red gold landscape and won-dering at its amazing desolation. I like marching on through it and sometimes I wonder whether there is anywhere that I am at all anxious to reach.

February 7th. Three days' journey have not brought us along very far. There is such abundance of green shrubs and flowering weeds that the camels stop and graze as we go, and yesterday we came into camp very early so as to give them a good feed. A day or two more of this sort of country will make a wonderful difference to them. Yet it is nothing but sand and sandstone, long barren hills and broken sandstone tells. But the early rains have been good and to-day there

were places where the bare desert was like a garden. It is very delightful to see. Also the rain which fell upon us the day we left the J.
Tubaiq was very heavy over all this land. We find the sandstone hollows full of clear, fresh rain water and scarcely trouble to fill our water
skins, so plentiful is the supply each night. It is wonderfully fortunate.
Yesterday we had an absurd adventure. Besides the Shammar family
we have a couple of Sherarat tents with us, the people miserably poor
(they seem to be kept from the ultimate starvation which must overtake them by small gifts of flour from us) possessing nothing but a few
goats and the camels which carry them. These goats had gone on with
their herd before dawn; just before the sun rose the Shammar and
Sherarat followed on their camels and I went behind them on foot for I
Wanted to take bearings from a little ridge ahead. We had been camping in a very shallow valley. Musrud was with me. We may have
walked about 100 yards when all those in front of us turned round and
hurried back to us. " They are afraid," said Musrud. "They have seen
an enemy." Ghadi, the chief Sharnmari came riding up. "What is it?" I
asked. "Gom," he answered, "foes." "How many?" said I. "Twenty
camel riders," he answered, and shouted to my men "To the valley, to
the valley!" We crouched all the camels behind the sand heaps and
tamarisk bushes, got out our arms and waited. Nothing happened.
Presently Ghadi crept back to the ridge to scout. Still nothing happened. Then Fattuh, Musrud and I went across to the ridge and swept
the world with my glasses. There was nothing. We waved to the others
to come on and marching down the hills in complete security, came to
the conclusion that the 20 camel riders could have been nothing but
the Father of goats who was found presently pasturing his innocent
flock ahead of us. At night I announced that I intended to take a rafiq
of the Beni Maaz, the Goat Tribe, and this not very brilliant witticism
threw the whole company round the coffee fire into convulsions of
laughter.

February 10th. On Feb. 8 we fell among thieves-worse than
the goats. An hour or two after we had struck camp we met some of
the Howaitât who told us that Sayyah, Sheikh of the Wadi Sulaman
was camped a few hours to the east. Since it was pretty certain that he
would hear of our presence we thought it wiser to camp with him that
night and take a rafiq from him, -otherwise, you understand, he would
probably have sent after us in the night and robbed us. He received us
with all courtesy, but it was only pretence. Presently the one-eyed ruf-
fian came into our camp, examined all our possessions and asked for

everything in turn. We thought at first to get off with the loss of a revolver, but it ended by my having to surrender my Zeiss glass also to
my infinite annoyance. He swore that no Christian had ever visited this
country and none should go, that he would send no rafiq with us so
that he might be free to rob us, and finally he proposed to said and Fattuh that they should aid him to kill us and share the spoil. He got no
encouragement from them and I do not know that any of the threats
were more than words. I clung to my glass as long as I could, but when
at last Said, who knows the Arabs, advised me to yield lest things
should take a worse turn, We got our rafiq, Sayyâh's cousin, and are
therefore assured against "the accursed of both parents." We took also
two men of the Faqir, another tribe whom we may meet. They are said
to be still more unfortunate in their ancestry than the Wadi Sulaiman.
One of their sheikhs was camping with Sayyah and he sent his brother
and another with us. This brother, Hamid, is a very pleasant fellow
traveller, and I have no fault to find with Sayyah's cousin Zayyid. But
Sayyah has a name for roguery. It was typical of him that he mulcted
our Shammar companions Of 3 mejidehs before he would let them go
on with us. They had no money and could not pay, but Muhammad al
Marawi stood surety for them and I shall of course give them the ran-
som, poor souls. We had a very dull day's journey yesterday over
rolling pebbly sandhills, nothing whatever to be seen, except that once
we crossed the tracks of an ostrich. To-day has been rather more varied, hills on which to take bearings, and we have come into camp in a
valley bottom full of green plants for the camels. We have recovered
from the depression into which Sayyah's conduct threw us and we are
in good hopes that we shall not meet any more sheikhs.

February 12th. We rode yesterday over a barren pebbly waste
and came down through sand hills to a desolate low lying region
wherein we found water pools. We watered our camels and filled our
water skins and then turned our faces S.E. into the Nefad which lay but
an hour from us. The Nefud is a great stretch of sandhills, 7 or 8 days'
journey across. Our path lies through the S.W. corner and I am glad to
see this famous wilderness of sand. It is the resort of all the tribes during the winter and spring when an abundance of vegetation springs
from the warm sand, but there is no permanent water except at the extreme borders and in summer it is a blazing furnace. This is the right
moment for it. All the plants are greening and putting forth such flowers as they know how to produce and our camels eat the whole day as
they march. But the going is very heavy--up and down endless ridges

of soft pale yellow sand. occasionally there are deep gulleys hollowed out by the wind and we make a long circuit to avoid them, and from time to time the sand is piled up into a high ridge or head--a 'tas,' it is called in Arabic--which stands out yellow over the banks for its precipitous flanks are devoid of vegetation. Towards midday we came to a very high tas and I climbed to the top and saw the hills near Taimah to the west and the first of the mountains of Nejd to the S.E., Jebel Irnan. When I came down Fattuh greeted me with the news that one of the camels had sat down and they could not make her stir. Muhammad, Fellah and I went back with some food for her, thinking she might be weary with walking in the deep sand and that with food and coaxing we could get her on, but when we reached her we found her rolling in the sand in the death agony. Muhammad said "She is gone. Shall we sacrifice her?" I said "It were best." He drew his knife and said "In the name of God. God is most powerful." With that he cut her throat. She was, he explained, sick of a malady which comes with great suddenness. Fortunately she was one of the 3 weak animals we have with us. I should have been obliged to sell her at Hayil and she would not have fetched more than a pound or two. She is no great loss as far as that goes, but I am deeply attached to all my camels and grieve over the death for reasons of sentiment.

February 15th. We continue our peaceful course through the sands of the Nefûd, for according to all the information which comes to us from the Arabs we meet encamped it is the safest road, and I, who am now so close to Hayil, have no other desire but to get there without being stopped. We are now skirting Within its southern border and from every sandhill top we see the mountains of Nejd. Yesterday we camped early in order to water. We had seen no water since the khabra. The well Haizan was an hour and a half from our camp and I rode down with the camels to see the watering. Wells are very scarce in the Nefûd. They are found only on its borders and are very deep. Haizan lies at the bottom of a great depression enclosed by the steep sandbanks of the Nefûd. Our well rope was 48 paces long. We carried two stout sticks with us and a little wheel with which we made a pulley for the rope. There was an Arab camp near ours and the Sheikh, Salim, was there with some of his people watering their camels. They used a pulley like ours. It was interesting to watch and I took a lot of photographs. There were some who objected at first to my photography and asked what it was for. I asked the Shammar who was with us and the two brothers who have come with us from the J. Tubaiq whether I ought to stop, but they said no, it did not matter. And so I went on and no word was said. When you consider what a strange sight I must be to these people who have never seen a European it is remarkable that they leave me so unmolested. Desert manners are good.

February 19th. Marching through the Nefûd is like marching through the Labyrinth. You are for ever winding round deep sand pits, sometimes half a mile long, with banks so steep that you cannot descend. They are mostly shaped like horseshoes and you wander along until you come to the end and then drop down into low ground, only to climb up anew. How one bears it I don't know. I should think that as the crow flies we barely covered a mile in an hour. But there is something pleasant about it too; the safe camping grounds among the Sands, the abundance of pasture, the somnolent monotony. But we have done with it. We came out of it to-day. Two days ago we were held up by heavy rain. It began just as we broke up camp. We marched for two hours, by which time all the men were wet through and I was far from dry. The clouds stay on top of the sandhills like a thick fog and at last my rafiq declared that he could see no landmarks and could not be sure of our direction. No Arabs march in rain and I had to give way. We pitched camp and dried ourselves at an immense wood fire. It rained and hailed and thundered most of the day and night and all the world rejoiced. "To-day the sheikhs will sacrifice a camel," said my rafiq. The camels will pasture in the Nefûd for 3 months after this rain. Last night we got to the first Shammar camp--the Shammar are the Arabs of Nejd--and took as a rafiq the oldest and raggedest sheikh in the world. Beduin are not noted for strong and steady judgment, but he is one of the most birdwitted whom I have met. And this morning we reached the barren sandstone crags of Jebel Misma, which bound here the Nefûd, and passed beyond them into Nejd. As we topped the last sand bank the landscape which opened before us was more terrifyingly dead and empty than anything I have ever seen. The blackened rocks of Misma drop steeply on the E. side into a wilderness of jagged peaks set in a bed of hard sand and beyond and beyond stretches the vacant plain, untilled and unpeopled and scattered over with isolated towers and tables of sandstone. We have camped once more on the skirts of the Nefûd for the sake of the pasture, and tomorrow we go down into the plain.

Sunday, February 22nd. It proves to be a very pleasant place that dead country. The sandstone hollows were all full of water and there was plenty of pasturage. We marched gaily over a hard floor all day and camped in the midst of hills on a sandy floor between high cliffs. We had some Shammar for neighbours about a mile away. Yesterday we had a dull journey over an interminable flat and up sandbanks to another little camp, but this time high up in the heart of the little range. Somewhere in the sandbanks we passed the boundary between the sandstone country and the granite. I had noticed that the strange shapes of the sandstone hills were not to be seen before us and when we came to our camp in Jebel Rakkam behold the rocks were granite. I climbed into the top of one of the peaks and found flowers growing in the crevices, small, white and purple weeds and thistles and a dwarf asphodel-not a great bounty, but it feasted the eyes in this bare land. And to-day we passed a tiny village with corn plots round it--the first we have seen since Ziza. There were only 6 Or 7 Of them. And thereafter we were overtaken again by the Nefûd which puts out a long finger to the south here, and marched by hollow ways of sand in a very hot sun. We are camped in sandhills to-day.

February 24th. We are camped within sight of Hayil and I might have ridden in today, but I thought it better to announce my coming and therefore I sent on Muhammad and Ali and have camped in the plain a couple of hours or so from the town. We finished with the Nefûd for good and all yesterday, and today we have been through a charming country--charming for Arabia--of great granite rocks and little plains with thorny acacia trees growing in them and very sweet scented desert plants. We passed a small village or two, mud houses set in palm gardens and all set round with a mud wall. I hope the Hayil people will be polite. The Amir is away and an uncle of his is left in charge.

March 7th. And now I must relate to you the strange tale of my visit to Hayil. I broke up camp at sunrise on the 25th and rode towards the town. When we had been on the road for about an hour we met Ali on his camel, all smiles. They had seen Ibrabim, the uncle in charge. He was most polite, said I was welcome and there were three slaves of his household come out to receive me. With that he pointed to 3 horsemen riding towards us, one of whom carried a long lance. So we came up to the walls of Hayil in state, skirted them and entered the town by the S. gate. At the doorway Of the first house stood Muham-

mad al Rashid, great uncle of the present boy. I walked up a long sloping passage--not a stair, a ramp--to an open court and so into a great
room with a roof borne on columns and divans and carpets round the
walls. It was the Roshan, the reception room. Here I sat and one of the
slaves with me. These slaves, you must understand are often very important personages. Their masters treat them like brothers and give
them their full confidence, Also when one of the Rashids removes the
reigning prince and takes his place (which frequently happens) he is
careful to murder his slaves also, lest they should revenge the slain.
The men then went away to see to the lodging of the camels and the
pitching of the tents in the wide courts below. (There are five courts to
my domain, all mudwalled and towered. It was here that in the old
days, before the Mecca railway, the Persian Hajj used to lodge.)
Thereupon there appeared upon the scenery two women. One was an
old widow, Lu-lu-ah, who is caretaker here, as you might say. The
other was a Circassian, who was sent to Muhammad al Rashid by the
Sultan as a gift. Her name is Turkiyyeh. Under her dark purple cloak--
all the women are closely veiled here--she was dressed in brilliant red
and purple cotton robes and she wore ropes of bright pearls round her
neck. And she is worth her weight in gold, as I have come to know.
She is a chatterbox of the first order and I passed an exceedingly
amusing hour in her company. She had been sent here to spend the day
and welcome me. After lunch Ibrahim paid me a state visit, slaves
walking before him and slaves behind. He is an intelligent and (for an
Arab) well educated man. He was clothed in Indian silks and carried a
gold mounted sword. He stayed talking till one of the slaves announced that the call to afternoon prayer had sounded. Then he rose
and took his leave. But as he went he whispered to old M. al Murawi
that as the Amir was away and as there was some talk in the town
about my coming, a stranger and so on, he was bound to be careful and
so on and so on--in short, I was not to leave the house without permission. I spent most of the afternoon sitting in the women's court and
talking to Turkiyyeh who was excellent company. My camels badly
wanted rest; there is no pasturage near Hayil and we decided to send
them away to the Nefûd with one of my men and a couple of Hayil
Men whom Ibrahim had provided. I sold 6 camels--the Amir being
away raiding and with him all available camels, they are fortunately
much in request at this moment--6 which were badly knocked up by
the journey, and sent the remaining 13 away next morning. And then I
sat still in honourable captivity and the days were weary long. On the
27th Ibrahim invited me to come and see him in the evening--I had

expressed a wish to return his call. After dark he sent a man and a couple of slaves and I rode through the silent empty town to the Qasr, the fortress palace of the Amirs. I rode in at the gate, and was conducted by troops of slaves to the Roshan, the great columned reception room, where I found Ibrahim and a large company sitting on carpets round the walls. They all rose at my entrance. I sat at Ibrahim's right hand and we talked for an hour or more while the slaves served us first with tea and then with coffee. Finally they brought censers and swung them before each one of us three times and this is the sign that the reception is ended. So I rode home, tipping each of the many doorkeepers as I left. I had sent silken robes to all these people,-- Ibrahim and the chief slaves and the absent Amir--to him a Zeiss glass and a revolver also. I was now living upon the money which I had received for my six camels and it became necessary to ask for the 200 pounds which I had deposited with the Amir's agent in Damascus. It was met by the reply that the Letter of Credit was made out to the Amir's treasurer who was away raiding with him and that the money could not be paid to me till he returned. Now the Amir will in all probability be away for another month. I did not contemplate remaining in Hayil for a month; even if I had been free to go and come as I chose. Moreover I was persuaded that the Amir's grandmother, Fatima, who is a very powerful person in his court, had been left in charge of the treasury and could give (or withhold) as she pleased. But I could not risk being left here penniless. I had just 40 pounds. I told my men that it must suffice, that I should call in my camels, take the 8 best and go with Fattuh, Ali and Fellah to Bagdad, while the rest of the men would wait another week till the camels were rested and return to Damascus via Medina and the railway. The money I had would just suffice for all of us and for the tips in the house here. So it was agreed and after two more days I asked for a private audience with Ibrahim, went again to the Qasr at night, saw him and again heard from him that no disbursement could take place in the Amir's absence. I replied that if that were so, I much regretted that I should have to leave at once and I must ask him for a rafiq. He said the rafiq was ready and anything I wished should be given. That morning I must tell you, he had returned the gifts I had sent to him and to his brother Zamil, who is away with the Amir. Whether he did not think them sufficient or what was the reason I do not know. I took them back with me that evening, said I had been much hurt and must request him to receive them, which he did. He had lent me a man in the morning and I had ridden out with one of his slaves to a garden belonging to him and beyond the town. For this I thanked him and we parted on the best of terms. Next day I sent a messenger out for my camels--they proved to be two days away-and again I sat still amusing myself as best I might and the best was not good. I had no idea what was in their dark minds concerning me. I sat imprisoned and my men brought me in rumours from the town. Ali, in particular, has two uncles here who are persons of consideration; they did not care to come and see me, but they sent me news. The general opinion was that the whole business was the work of Fatima, but why, or how it would end, God alone knew. If they did not intend to let me go I was in their hands. It was all like a story in the Arabian Nights, but I did not find it particularly enjoyable to be one of the 'dramatis personae.' Turkiyyeh came again and spent the day with me and next day there appeared the chief eunuch Said--none more powerful than he. He came to tell me that I could not leave without permission from the Amir. I replied that I had no money and go I must and would, and sent this message to Ibrahim and Fatima. But he answered that going and not going was not in our hands. I sent hasty messages to Ali's uncles and in the afternoon one of their nephews came to see me--an encouraging sign. That night I was invited to the Qasr by the women. The Amir's mother, Mudi, received me and Turkiyyeh was there to serve as introducer of ambassadors. It was more like the Arabian Nights than ever. The women in their Indian brocades and jewels, the slaves and eunuchs, and the great columned rooms, the children heavy with jewels--there was nothing but me myself which did not belong to medieval Asia. We sat on the floor and drank tea ate fruits--vide, as I say, the Arabian Nights passim. Thereupon passed another long day. At night came Turkiyyeh-the women only go out after dark. We sat in the big Roshan here and drank tea, served by one of my slaves--for I also have two or three. A single lamp lighted us and the night wind blew through the chinks of the shutters. No windows are glazed. I told her all my difficulties, that I had no money and could get none, that I sat here day after day and that they would not let me go. Next day I was invited by two boys of the sheikhly house--I won't tell you all the relationships, though I heard them all--to spend the afternoon in a garden near at hand. I went and there were the two boys and all the other Rashid male babies--all that have not been murdered by successive usurping Amirs, and of course many slaves And the eunuch Said. We sat on carpets in a garden pavilion, as You may see in any Persian miniature you choose to look at, and I again put forward my requests, which were again met by the same replies on the part of Said. I ended by declaring that I wished to leave the next day and asked for a rafiq.

Thereat we wandered through the gardens and my hosts, the two boys, carefully told me the names of all the fruit trees (which of course I knew) and the little children walked solemnly hand in hand in their long brocade robes. And then we drank more coffee and at the afternoon prayer I left. After prayers came Said and told Muhammad al Murawi that I must understand that nothing could be done till permission came from the Amir. I went to the men's tent and spoke my mind to Said without any Oriental paraphrases and, having done so, I rose abruptly and left them sitting--a thing which is only done by great sheikhs, you understand. The camels came in at dusk and I, thinking that in the end I should have to stay here for another indefinite time, was beginning to plan where to send them out to graze, when after dark came Said and another with 200 pounds in a bap, and full permission to go where and when I liked. The rafiq was ready. I replied with great dignity that I was very much obliged and that I did not intend to leave till the next day for I wished to see the Qasr and the town by daylight. And today I have been shown everything, have been allowed to photograph everything and do exactly as I pleased. I gave 10 pounds in backshish in the Qasr. As I was returning I was given an invitation from Turkiyyeh and I went to her house. She says she explained the whole position to Fatima and I think that the 'volte-face' is due to her, but however it may be I am profoundly thankful. I go to Bagdad. After careful enquiries I feel sure that the road south is not possible this year. The tribes are up and there is an expedition pending from here. They would not, therefore, give me a rafiq south and I should have considerable difficulty in going without their leave. So Hayil must suffice for this year. Moreover I have learnt a good deal about travel in this country and I know that none of the southern country can be travelled 'a la Franca.' If ever I go there I must go with no more baggage than I can carry on my own camel.

Sunday, March 22nd. We are within sight of Nejef. I have camped an hour from the town because I know there is no camping ground near it and I should probably have to put up in the Government sarai, which is tiresome. Also I very much want to get through to Bagdad without questions or telegrams. Oh, but it is a long dull way from Nejd! I wanted to come up by the old pilgrim road, which has a certain historic interest and is also the shortest, but the morning I left Hayil came a slave with a message to say I was to travel by the western road as the eastern was not safe. As I did not much mind the one way or the other I acquiesced. Two days out we met the Amir's messengers bringing in a tale (which they served up to us) of a highly successful raid, the flight of all the Anazeh before the Amir and the capture of Jof. They said the Amir was a few days further on. But when we had crossed the Nefûd for 4 days and come near the place where he was reported to have been he had left and crossed over to the eastern road and was said to be off raiding some tribes further east. I did not intend to turn back for him and it would have been useless for I might have taken days to find him so I went on my way in all tranquillity. We rode for ever over immense levels not a valley or a hill to be seen and so little water that we were almost always too short of it to spend it in washing. As long as we were with the Shammar and that was for the first 10 days, we were perfectly safe with a rafiq from Hayil. He rode with us for 8 days and we took on another Shammari for the next 2 days. Then the fun began. We had to get through the Shia tribes of Iraq, all out in the desert now for the spring pasture and all accursed of their two parents. The first we reached were the Beni Hasan and we spent a very delicate hour, during which it was not apparent whether they meant to strip us or to treat us as guests. Ultimately they decided on the latter course. We camped with them, they killed a lamb for us and gave us two rafiqs next day. That day luckily we saw no one and camped in solitude. Early on the following morning we sighted tents and our rafiqs were reduced to a state of quivering alarm for they will kill each other just as gaily as they kill you. One of them, however, was induced to ride up to the tents, which he found to be those of an allied tribe. He brought back two new rafiqs for he and his companion flatly refused to go on. So We rode on for 6 hours or so and then again we sighted tents and-'même jeu!' The rafiqs even talked of turning back and leaving us. But again we made one of them go up and en-quire what Arabs they were and as great good luck would have it they were the Ghazâlat who are the only people of any real importance and authority in these parts. We camped with them and took on an excel-lent rafiq--a well-known man--his name is Dawi. With him we have felt comparatively safe, but if we had not had him with us we should have been stripped to the skin twice in these last two days. The first morning we came down to water at some horribly stagnant pools we found a large company of the Madan filling their water skins there. The Madan are possibly the worst devils known. They offered Dawi 30 pounds if he would abandon us for they could not touch us as long as we had a sheikh of the Ghazalat with us for fear of the Ghazalat, you understand. And yesterday afternoon we met a large caravan of Madan coming up from Meshed and in a moment we were surrounded by stalwart armed men who laid hold of our camels and would have made them kneel. But Dawi called out to them and when they saw him they let go and drew off. This morning a casual person who was tending flocks sent a rifle bullet between the legs of our camels. Dawi ran out and expostulated with him before he sent another and we protested loudly at the treatment he had accorded us. "An enemy does not come riding across the top of the plain in full daylight!" said Ali " and if you feared us the custom is to send a bullet over the heads of the riders till you have found out whether they are friends or foes." He admitted that he had broken the rules and, for my part, I rejoiced that he had broken none of the camels' legs. Even to-night I don't upon my honour know whether we are safe camping out here two hours from the town, but the men seem to think it is all right, and anyhow here we are! The edges of the desert are always stormy and difficult. The tribes are not Bedu but Arab, a very important distinction, for they have not the code and the rules of the Beduin. But these Shia people are a great deal worse than any one we have met upon our whole way. Having penned these lines it occurred to me to go and ask Ali whether he thought we were safe for the night. He replied that he did not and that his mind was far from being at rest. (He had chosen the camping ground himself, I mention.) I enquired what he thought we had better do. He thought we had better go on to a village. It was then two hours before sunset. We packed the dinner, which was cooked, into our good camp saucepans, struck camp and loaded all in half an hour and off we set! It was a most absurd proceeding, but I thought it would be still more absurd to have a regrettable incident on this last night of our desert journey. Just at sunset we reached a small village of wattle huts and here we have camped. The villagers have received us with much courtesy and to the best of our belief we are in security at last.

To H.B., Bagdad, March 19th

Yes, we were safe and we got here without further incident. I drove from Meshhed to Ketbela--Nejef and Meshhed are the same-- dined and spent the evening with our vice-consul and drove into Bagdad next day. I have fallen on my feet with some new acquaintances, Mr. Tod, the head-man of Lynch's company and his darling little Italian wife. I am going to stay with them when I come back from Babylon. I go to Babylon for a couple of nights to-morrow. They wanted me to come to them at once, but I thought I would have a few days of complete freedom here first. I have seen all my native friends;

they precipitated themselves and gave me a welcome which warmed my heart. Bagdad has grown a 'weltstadt!'

I may stay here another week or so when I come back from Babylon. Then across the Syrian desert to Damascus--quite safe and easy. . . I have written to Louis Mallet suggesting myself to him. I should like to tell him my tales and hear his. I love Bagdad and this country much better than Damascus and Syria and I do not know when I shall be here again so that I gladly stay a day or two longer. Besides I shall get another mail, which is good--perhaps 2. It's queer and rather enjoyable at first, the sense of being in perfect security, but one soon loses the realisation of it.

To H.B., 23rd April, 1914

Behold I'm 11 days out from Bagdad and I have not begun to tell you my tale. I have been put to it to get through the long days and I have been too tired at the end of them to write. I drove out from Bagdad to Feluja, on the Euphrates, having arranged that my camels were to leave Bagdad the previous day and meet me at Feluja. The day they left Ali made an unjustifiable request--that I should take a cousin of his with us, the cousin wishing to escape military service. I refused and Ali struck. Fattuh got him and the camels off with great difficulty late at night; in consequence they had not arrived when I reached Feluja, and when they came Ali had brought the cousin with him! Ali was very angry, Ali was in the Devil's own temper and I dismissed him on the spot to find his way back to Bagdad with the cousin. He has given me a great deal of trouble. I have put up with a great deal for the sake of long acquaintance, but gross insubordination I won't stand and there is an end of him. MY party therefore was Fattuh, Sayyif and Fellah (the negro) and I was left without a guide for the Syrian desert. I am travelling very light with two small native tents, a bed on the ground, no furniture, no nothing--for speed's sake. We pitched our tiny camp half-an-hour out of Feluja in the desert by your Dulaim tents--it was blazing hot, and what with the heat and the hardness of the ground (to which I have now grown accustomed) I did not sleep much. Next day we rode along the high road to Ramadi on the Euphrates, where lives the chief Sheikh of the Dulaim. I went straight to him. He received me most cordially, lodged me in his palm garden, gave me a great feast and a rafiq from his own household, Adwan, a charming man. It was blazing hot again and noisy, dogs and people talking, and I slept less than ever, We were off before dawn and struck south west into the desert to the pitch springs of Abu jir. We arrived in a dust storm, the temperature was 90 and it was perfectly disgusting. The following day was better, as hot as ever) but no dust storms. We rode on west into the desert. Two days more, west and slightly north, with the temperature falling, thank Heaven, brought us up on to the post road and here we fell in with the sheikh of the Anazeh and I took a new rafiq from him, Assaf is his name, and very reluctantly said good-bye to Adwan. We rode down the following day to muhaiwir in the Wadi Hauran, where I had been 3 years ago. The world was full of Anazeh tents and camels--a wonderful sight. It meant, too, that with my Anazeh rafiq I was perfectly safe. And in two more days we came to the great Sheikh of these eastern Anazeh, Fahad Bey, and I alighted at his tents, and claimed his hospitality. He treated me with fatherly kindness, fed me, entertained me, and advised me to take a second rafiq, a man of the Rwalla, who are the western amazeh. I spent the afternoon planning a ruin near him--a town, actually a town in the heart of the Syrian desert! Only the fortified gate was planable, the rest was mere stone heaps, but it throws a most unexpected light on the history of the desert. There was most certainly a settled population at one time in these eastern parts. We had violent thunderstorms all night and yesterday, when I left Fahad, a horrible day's journey in the teeth of a violent wind and through great scuds of rain. To-day, however, it has been very pleasant. I have been following the old road which I came out to find and am well content to have my anticipations justi-fied. We came to a small ruin in the middle of the day which I stopped to plan. Fahad told me that the desert from the camp to Bukhara is 'Khala,' empty, i.e., there are no Beduin camped in it. I like solitary camps and the desert all to myself, but it has the drawback of not being very safe. With our two rafiqs no Anazeh of any kind will touch us, but there is always the chance of a ghazu. Very likely they would do us no harm, but one can't be sure. However, so far I have run my own show quite satisfactorily and it amuses me to be tongue and voice for myself, as I have been these days. But I am tired, and being anxious to get through and be done with travel, we are making long marches, 9 and 10 hours. Oh, but they are long hours, day after day in the open wilderness! I have come in sometimes more dead than alive, too tired to eat and with just enough energy to write my diary. WE are now up nearly a couple of thousand feet and I am beginning to feel better.

On the24th we began the day by sighting something lying on the desert with an ominous flutter of great wings over it. Assaf observed that it was 3 dead camels and 2 dead men, killed ten nights ago--ghazu met ghazu, said he. . . On 25th we came at midday to an encampment of Seubba, a strange tribe of whose origin many tales are told. We halted at their tents to buy some butter and I was glad to see and photograph them. They are great hunters; one man was clad in a lovely robe of gazelle skins. They pressed us to camp with them, but we rode on for a couple of hours and camped by ourselves. On the 26th . . . In the middle of the morning we met a man walking solitary in the desert. We rode up to him and addressed him in Arabic, but he made no answer. Assaf, my rafiq, said he thought he must be a Persian dervish. I spoke to him in Turkish and in what words of Persian I could muster, but he made no reply. Fattuh gave him some bread which he accepted and turned away from us into the rainy wilderness, going whither? But we rode on towards the mountains and missed our way, going too far to the north, till at last we came upon some tents and herds, an Anazeh tribe, and they directed us. We were in sight of Palmyra, lying some 10 miles from us in a bay of the hills. Seeing it thus from the desert one realizes the desert town, not the Roman,-- Tadmor, not Palmyra. We are terribly bothered by wind, both marching and in camp, when it sheets us in dust. We march very long hours, and oh, I'm tired!

May 2nd. We rode through the mountains, a beautiful road but I was too tired to enjoy it much. Also we made very long hours, ten and twelve a day. On the 30th we went in to Adra an camped there, on the very spot where I mounted my camel the day I set out from Damascus, four months and a half ago. Next morning, yesterday, through gardens and orchards to Damascus. I rather think I shall catch a boat to C'ple on the 8th, getting there on the 12th, stay there a week or less and come on by train, getting to London about the 24th.

[This arrival at Damascus on her return journey marks the end of Gertrude's travels in the desert with her caravan.

Dr. David Hogarth, President of the Royal Geographical Society, gave an account on April 14th, 1927, before the Society, of Gertrude's adventurous expedition to Hayil from which I quote the following.

"Her journey was a pioneer venture which not only Put On the map a line of wells, before unplaced or unknown but also cast much new light on the history of the Syrian desert frontiers under Roman, Palmyrene, and Ummayad domination. . . But perhaps the most valuable result consists in the mass of information that she accumulated about the tribal elements ranging between the Hejaz Railway on the one flank and the Sirhan and Nefûd on the other, particularly about the Howaitât group, of which Lawrence, relying on her reports, made signal use in the Arab campaigns Of 1917-1918.

"Her stay in Hayil was fruitful of political information especially concerning both the recent history and the actual state of the Rashid house, and also its actual and probable relations with the rival power of the Ibn Sauds. Her information proved of great value during the war, when Hayil had ranged itself with the enemy and was menacing our Euphratean flank. Miss Bell became from 1915 onwards, the interpreter of all reports received from Central Arabia."

Dr. Hogarth also said in reference to her return across Hamad to Damascus from Bagdad:

"To another European woman, in the days before desert motor services had been thought of, such a journey would have seemed adventurous enough. But to Miss Bell, who had been into Nejd, the crossing of the Hamad seemed something of an anti-climax.

". . .The jaded traveller, writing in April 1914 her diary and letters at Bagdad, had no suspicion that, in little more than a year, the knowledge and experience acquired during the past four months would become of national value. Nor could she foresee that, even after the war Northern Nejd would return to the obscurity from which she had rescued it. Up to this year of grace, 1927, her visit to Hayil, thirteen years ago, remains the last that has been put on scientific record by a European traveller . . . . ."

CHAPTER XIV

1914-1915-1916 - WAR WORK, BOULOGNE, LONDON, CAIRO

To F.B., Embassy, Constantinople, May 15, 1914

I ought to have telegraphed yesterday for I arrived on the evening of the 13th. . . I have entirely recovered from the exhaustion of the Syrian desert. . . If you are at Rounton I should come straight there. Sir Louis is perfectly delightful. He is tremendously full of his job and we have talked for hours.

[Gertrude was then in England for the rest of the summer. At the outbreak of war she was at Rounton. During September 1914 she went round to various places in the North Riding of Yorkshire giving addresses on the war, and cheering people on. She was an admirable speaker, and her addresses always aroused enthusiasm.

After this she went for a time to Lord Onslow's Hospital at Clandon, and afterwards, by the initiative of Lord Robert Cecil (now Lord Cecil), to Boulogne, where she worked with Flora and Diana Russell in the office for tracing the Missing and Wounded.]

To H.B., Boulogne, November 26, 1914

Ian Malcolm has brought a motor over with him so for the moment that's all we want. But I can't be certain that we may not want one later, for this whole thing is merely in course of organisation, a new branch is in prospect and I wish you could hold your hand till I see what happens. It Is fearful the amount of office work there is. We are at it all day from 10 till 12:30 and from2 to 5 filing, indexing and answering enquiries. Yesterday after five I went to see Mrs. Charlie Furse at the central Ry. station where she has her out station and afterwards we went together to one of the big hospitals at the Casino and talked to some of the men of the wards. A lot came in with frost bite last week; now it's warm and that won't occur. The Red X won't let any women make the enquiries at the hospitals, which is very silly, as it would give us all occasional change of work, but of course I shall gradually make friends with C.O.s and sisters and go in after to wherever I like. Mrs. Furse lunched with Diana and me to-day, an interesting woman, she is doing her job awfully well. Will you ask General Bethune to send us out as complete a list as he can of the Territorial Battalions--something corresponding to the Army List for Regulars. Also can I have some sort of London Address book for the office? An old telephone directory would do.

To F.B., Boulogne, November 27, 1914

. . . I sometimes go into our big hospitals and talk to the men. It is immensely interesting to hear their tales. There are a good many Germans to whom I talk. Our men are exceedingly good and kind to them and try to cheer them as far as they can with no common language. I generally go for a walk by the sea from 8:30 to 9 a.m.--it's the only time I have. We lunch in a tiny restaurant with soldiers of all sorts and kinds, the oddest world. Everybody takes everybody else for granted.

To F.B., Boulogne, November 28, 1914

I hear to-day that you have your convalescents 20 of them (where have you put them all). Now would you like me to come back? I am quite, quite ready to come. I don't approve doing other things when you are wanted in your own place. If you send me a telegram I will return at once and no more said. I should not be happy here if I thought you needed me.

Please telegraph and I'll come home at once.

To F.B., Hotel Meurice, Boulogne, November 30, 1914

. . . We are very busy to-day making up double card catalogue which has to be done over and above our work mostly in the luncheon hour and after tea when the office is supposed to be shut. It will take days I fear but when it is done the office will be in far better order. . .

To F.B., Boulogne, December 1, 1914

In time I think we ought to have one of the best run offices in France we are already scheming to get into closer touch with the front which is our weak point. Lord Robert asked the Adj. General to let us have a representative and he refused categorically. Now we have a great plan for getting lots of Army Chaplains for it is quite clear we shall have to make our own channels for ourselves. Also I have several other ideas in my head to put into execution gradually. I'll tell you about them as they evolve.

We have had the most pitiful letters and we see the most pitiful people.

Don't let all this discourage you at all from bringing me home if you want me.

To H.B., Boulogne, December 5, 1914

. . . Would you please ask the County Association office to send me the latest arrangements about Soldiers and Sailors allowances--what is given to the widows and orphans if the man is killed and what to the man if he is disabled. The orders have been so many that I have not kept them in MY head and we want them for reference.

To F.B., Boulogne, December 6, 1914

I've got a great deal of work done these last days and I very nearly cleared away the mountain of mistakes which I found when I came.

To H. B., Boulogne, December 19th, 1914

You know we have a head office in London under Lord Roberts at 83 Pall Mall. Sometime when you are near there you might go in and see him and find out if he is satisfied with the way we run the office here.

To H.B., Boulogne, December 26, 1914

Diana and I took a half holiday yesterday and walked along the coast in frosty sun.

To H. B., Boulogne, December 30 1914

. . . Do you mind my being here, dearest father. I feel as if I had flown to this work as one might take to drink, for some kind of forgetting that it brings, but, you know it, there is no real forgetting and care rides behind one all the day. I sometimes wonder if we shall ever know again what it was like to be happy. You sound terribly overworked. . . . . ..

I try to look in the face the thing that may be before us-but it won't bear speaking of. I shall see Maurice when he comes over and before he goes to the front. I may very likely have a day or two with him, that's what I hope.

To F.B., Boulogne, January 1, 1915

A happier New Year. What else can I wish you? Diana and I caught ourselves wondering last night whether the next 31st Dec. would find us still sitting at our desks here. We saw the New Year in after all. It happened this way.

Yesterday morning there 'débouchéd' in our office Mr. Cazalet, who is working with Fabian Ware out at the front. Mr. Cazalet brought a tangled bundle of letters and lists which we had been working to compare with ours and to be put straight for him. We had 24 hours for the work before he returned to the front. It was just like a fairy story only we hadn't the ants and the bees to help us in a mountain of work. Diana ran out got a great ledger and proceeded to make it into an indexed ledger which we couldn't find here.

We had two hours off from 7 to 9 to dine with her cousin who has come out to look for a missing son--dead I much fear. At 9 we went back to the office. By 9:30 everything was sorted out and I began to fill in the ledger, Diana keeping me supplied, we could not have done it if I had not prepared all that was possible beforehand. At midnight we broke off for a few minutes, wished each other a better year and ate some chocolates. At 1 a.m. a young man of an acquaintance seeing our lights burning came up to know if he could help us but he could not and so sent him away with thanks. By 2 a.m. we were within an hour or two of the end so we came home to bed I was back at 8:15 prepared the ordinary days work, shortened it a little, the rest will stand over for tomorrow got through my part with the men when they came in and leaving Diana to clear up the rest returned to the ledger. BY 12:30 it was finished with just an hour to spare and I took it to Mr. Cazalet. It had been an exciting time but we won it and now this really important thing is set going. There now remains a card index of names to write for him but we have a week for that.

To H.B., Boulogne, January 6th, 1915

We are going to start an office at Rouen I think and hope. The Russells will take charge of it and I am to have Tiger Howard here. I had a long talk with Mr. Fabian Ware tonight--he appears to be very grateful for our lists and things and delighted to heap all his information upon us which is the one thing I want. As for Lord R. he is quite delightful. And he is satisfied with the way things have been done here-I think more than satisfied which is a great relief to my mind. He contemplates making this more and more of a centre and I think it will become the real distributing place of information for which, geographically it is best suited. They all seem to want that and I need not say I'm ready to take it all. The more work they give me the better I like it.

To F.B., Boulogne, January 12, 1915

. . . The Rouen office is settled. Flora and Diana are together taking charge of it alternate fortnights . . ..

To H.B., Boulogne, February 10, 1915

. . . Katie Freshfield turned up. She is a V.A.D. part of a detachment which is going up as orderlies to the Cross Hospital at G.H.Q. They are delayed here for the moment and she and another girl came in at an early hour to dust our office.

[From Boulogne Gertrude was summoned back to London by Lord Robert Cecil. The office in London for tracing the wounded and missing was in a state of chaotic confusion and Lord Robert opined that Gertrude would be the best person to put it straight-which she did, and succeeded in organising it on efficient lines.

In November she was sent for to Cairo. Dr. David Hogarth, then in close connection with Col. T. E. Lawrence, who was taking an active part in the Revolt in the Desert, felt that Gertrude's knowledge of the tribes of Northern Arabia would be invaluable. Through his intervention therefore and that of Capt. Hall (now Vice-Admiral Sir Reginald Hall) in London, it was Proposed to Gertrude that she should go to Cairo at once. She went there in November 1915.)

To F.B., Cairo, November 30th, 1915

I telegraphed to you this morning after my arrival and asked you to send me by Lady B. another gown and skirt. I have not yet been to see the MacMahons but I must leave a card on them to-day. For the moment I am helping Mr. Hogarth to fill in the intelligence files with information as to the tribes and sheikhs, It's great fun and delightful to be working with him. Our Chief is Col. Clayton whom I like very much. This week Mark Sykes passed through and I have seen a good deal of him. I have just heard that Neil Malcolm has arrived from Gallipoli--I think he is chief staff officer here; I have written to him and asked him to dinner if he is not too great for such invitations.

We had a horrible journey--almost continuous storm. Helen Brassey and I survived triumphantly and took comfort in one another's society. She is a very charming creature. We reached Port Said after dark on Thursday night. Capt. Hall, the brother of our Capt. Hall (he is head of the Railway here) made every possible arrangement for my comfort and Capt. Woolley, ex-digger at Carchemish and head in the Intelligence Dept. at P. Said came on board to meet me. Next morning I came up here. Mr. Hogarth and Mr. Lawrence (you don't know him, he is also of Carchernish exceedingly intelligent) met me and brought me to this hotel where they are both staying. Mr. Hogarth, Mr. Lawrence and I all dined together; at our table sit two Engineers Col. Wright (brother of Hagberg) and very nice and Major Pearson. Occasionally we have Mr. Graves into dinner--he was Times Correspondent in Constantinople in former days. I knew him there. Now you know my circle-it is very friendly and pleasant, but Mr. Hogarth leaves next week which will make a terrible gap in it. You will write to me here in future Won't you and will you have the Times sent out to ne--the edition which appears three times a week. I'm glad I came but I long for news of you.

To F.B., Cairo, December 6th, 1915

Mr. Hogarth leaves tomorrow, to my great sorrow. He has been a most friendly support and I have scarcely Yet found my own feet yet. They have given me some work to do on Arab Tribes their numbers and lineage. It is a vague and difficult subject which would take a lifetime to do properly I should think it will be about a month before I can get it into any sort of shape, but it rather depends on what information one can collect. I haven't begun yet for I have been doing odds and ends of jobs for Mr. Hogarth which have taken all my time. Far the nicest people who I have met are the MacMahons with whom I dined last night. They are both charming, so pleasant and agreeable. They gave me a standing invitation to come in whenever I liked and I am going to have a long talk with him one of these days.

To F.B., Cairo, December 13th, 1915

. . .. The days pass quickly here. I am quite happy and beginning to feel a little more as if I were getting hold of things. I do the same thing every day all pleasant but not matter for good letter writing. I have an Arabic lesson from 8:15 to 9:30 then I walk up to the office and work at tribes or annotate telegrams--the latter is great fun. Back to lunch and then to the office again and I seldom get home much before 7. . . . but usually I dine here with Col. Wright, Mr. Lawrence and a party of people, we all share the same table. And it is not till after dinner that I go back to Arabic and do a little work for next morning. I wonder if you sent me out a purple evening chiffon gown by Lady Brassey--I telegraphed for it, but I haven't heard anything of it or her yet. Also a new white skirt from Ospovat which I found I hadn't got. I am rather short of clothes for a prolonged stay in Cairo. It is heavenly weather--almost too nice for wartime I feel. Still I think I'm right to be here. . .

[She stayed in Cairo for 6 weeks, during which time she met one person after another who interested her, either old friends or new acquaintances.]

To F.B., on the Nile, December 25th, 1915

You don't mind my staying, do you? as long as they have a job for me. Of course if you want me I will come home. I rather wish I had brought out more clothes. Could you possibly send out to me the blue shot silk gown with a little coat and its own hat trimmed with feathers? And if you are sending anything I should like too the purple satin day gown with a cape--Marie knows which I mean--and a mauve parasol, I have lots I know. I don't know whether things sent by parcel post would be likely to reach me. Both gowns would fold up so small that they could almost be sent by letter post--not a hat however. Perhaps if you were to ask the kind Captain Hall he could contrive to send out a small box for me, by bag even. I should be very grateful--and the sooner the better.

To F.B., Cairo, January 1, 1916

A second year of war--and I can only wish you as I wished you last first of January that we may not see another. Never another year like the last. Its probable that I may go on for a few days to India towards the end of the month. I have had long and very interesting letters from Domnul and an invitation from the Viceroy who wants to see me. it comes rather conveniently for there are certain matters on which we should like to have the V's sympathy and co-operation. I should not stay more than a week. It seems a long way to go from Saturday to Monday but my chiefs are inclined to think it would be worth it. I will telegraph to you if this plan takes form. Mr. Hogarth writes to me that he is coming back as soon as possible which will be very nice. Also he might bring me out some clothes!

To H.B., Cairo, January 3, 1916

My tribe stuff is beginning to be pulled into shape and will make quite a respectable book when finished-a respectable basis for further work at any rate. I love doing It--you can't think what fun it is. In fact I have come back to it with such renewed zest that I can scarcely tear myself away from it. . . . They are immensely kind all these people and it is most useful to be able to draw on their knowledge and experience. I'm getting to feel quite at home as a Staff Officer! It is comic isn't it.

To H.B., Cairo, January 16th, 1916

I rather hope I may hear this week from Domnul in reply to a cable I sent him saying I might come out to India at the end of the month. My chief here is warmly in favour of the idea. They would very much like me to stay a fortnight or so at a halfway point on my way back--I won't 'préciser' further and if Lord H. views the idea with favour as I believe he might I should certainly do so and I think it would be very useful in many ways. There is no kind of touch between us except telegrams and it would be a great advantage if we could establish more direct and friendly relations. I feel a little nervous about being the person to carry it out, but the pull one has in being so unofficial is that if one doesn't succeed no one is any the worse.

To F.B., Cairo, January 19th, 1916

Here is the letter about my summer clothes. It seems a great deal but I know it isn't more than I had last year--they only just lasted me through. Lady MacMahon sent me a lot of things from Egypt. I'm feeling awfully tired and done up. I don't know what's the matter. I've been working a great number of hours and getting through dreadfully little, having anamia of the brain. I'm going to try a course of morning rides to see if exercise will do any good. I feel just like I was before I had jaundice, yet it would be unnatural to have jaundice again! Its jaundice of the imagination this time.

To H.B., Cairo, January 24th, 1916

I can't write through censors and I must therefore send you a private word by bag enclosed to the Hogarths to tell you what I'm doing--it is of course only for you Mother and Maurice. . . When I got Lord H's message through Domnul I suggested that it might be a good plan if I, a quite unimportant and unofficial person were to take advantage of the Viceroy's invitation and go out to see what could be done by putting this side of the case before them and hearing that. My chief has approved. I cabled to Domnul and received from him an enthusiastic reply. So I'm going. I don't suppose I shall be in India more than ten days or a fortnight. I shall go straight up to Delhi to Lord H. If they will let me I would very much like to go to Basrah for a week or two on my way back. I shall very probably spend a few days at Aden before I return here as there is a good deal of information about tribes and the people which we want from them and don't seem to get. I feel a little anxious about it, but take refuge in my own extreme obscurity and the general kindness I find everywhere. I shall find Domnul at Delhi which will make everything easy, otherwise I don't think I should have the face to set out on a political mission.

To F.B., Cairo, January 25th, 1916

Your news about Maurice filled me with such immense relief that I can scarcely believe anything so fortunate should be true. It seems odd to regard an operation in that light. The knowledge that he is safely at home makes me feel indifferent as to going to India which did seem a fearfully long way from home. . . I don't much like going away from here. I've fallen into the way of it, friendly and pleasant._ 11 days of solitary journey is a formidable prospect but I've no doubt it will be very nice when I get there and I'm looking forward to seeing Domnul. Anyhow I think I ought to go and that's an end. I have practically finished the Tribal book I have been doing as far as it can be finished here, but I look forward to getting lots of fresh material in India.

To H.B., Cairo, January 18, 1916

I'm off finally at a moment's notice to catch a troop ship at Suez, I really do the oddest things. I learnt at 3 p.m. that I could catch it if I left at 6 p.m. which did not allow much time for thought. I'm charged with much negotiation--and I hope I may be well inspired.

[An officer who was at Cairo at the time said afterwards that he "never saw anyone mobilise as quickly as Miss Bell."]

CHAPTER XV

1916-1917 - DELHI-BASRAH

To F.B., S.S. "Euripides," February 1, 1916

We reach Karachi on the 6th and I'm cabling to Domnul to let him know. It is an extraordinary quick voyage. The cat and I are the only two people not in uniform on board. There is a chaplain called Wood who is a friend of Hugo's and was ordained on the same day. I have foregathered with him a little. He has asked me to come and talk to the troops this afternoon about Arabia or anything--they get so bored poor dears, I shall love to do anything to amuse them. The adjutant has also asked me to give a conference on Mesopotamia to the officers which I shall like less. They are the 23rd and 24th Rifle Corps coming out to do Garrison duty in India in order to relieve younger troops. I'm luxuriously comfortable with a large cabin and a big room next to it usually the nursery where I go and work all the morning and again after dinner. It's the first time I've ever succeeded in doing any work on the sea, the weather is deliciously warm.

To F.B., Vice-Regal Lodge, Delhi, February 11th, 1916

. . . But in order properly to appreciate dust you must go by train across the desert of Sinde. We reached Delhi at 7:30 a.m. I hadn't an idea what was to happen to me, nor whether anyone knew I was coming and behold when I got out coated in dust on an icy cold morning, there was Domnul On the platform and a Vice-Regal motor waiting outside. YOU may imagine my joy.

[Then followed some very interesting days at the Vice-Regal lodge discussing the situation with the Viceroy, seeing Mr. Baker and Mr. Lutyens, hearing of the new Delhi.]

Later. I've just come in from another dinner party at Vice-Regal Lodge. At the beginning of dinner the V. sent me a scribbled card to say that it was all settled about my going on and that I was given permission to go much further up the river than I had originally thought of doing. It is interesting, deeply interesting, but oh, it's an anxious job. I wish, I wish, I knew more--and was more. And I am rather overwhelmed at meeting with so much kindness and confidence.

I shall be here another week, I suppose, but as to that I shall do what I'm told.

I know you will both think that this is right. Tell Maurice and Herbert. Otherwise I always think the less said the better.

To H.B., Vice-Regal Lodge, Delhi, February 18th, 1916

. . . No one has helped another as you helped me, and to tell you what your love and sympathy meant is more than I know how to do.

. . . As at present arranged I leave Delhi on the 23rd, and spend a day or two at Lahore and start from Karachi on the 27th. What will happen after that I have no idea. The V. is anxious that I should stay at Basrah and lend a hand with the Intell. Dept. there, but all depends on what their views are and whether I can be of any use. That hangs on me, I feel--as we have often said, all you can do for people is to give them the opportunity of making a place for themselves. The V. has done that amply. He has been extraordinarily kind, and indeed all the people here have been delightful. Mr. Grant has placed all their archives at my disposal and I have spent my time reading the Arabian files--and learning much from them. Besides reading the files I have seen all the people concerned with Indian Foreign Affairs and talked to them about Arabia till I am weary of the very word--they must be too, I should think. I think I have pulled things straight a little as between Delhi and Cairo. But nothing will ever keep them straight except a constant personal intercourse-it ought not to be difficult to manage and I am convinced that it is essential.

THE LETTERS OF GERTRUDE BELL

To F.B., Vice-Regal Lodge, Delhi, February 18th, 1916

. . . The Viceroy took me one afternoon, to see the new Delhi. It was very wonderful seeing it with him who had invented it all, and though I knew the plans and drawings I didn't realise how gigantic it was till I walked over it. They have blasted away hills and filled up valleys, but the great town itself is as yet little more than foundations. The roads -are laid out that lead from it to the four corners of India, and down each vista you see the ruins of some older imperial Delhi. A landscape made up of empires is something to conjure with.

[Extract from letter written to Captain R. Hall (now Vice-Admiral Sir Reginald Hall, G.C.B.) from the Vice-Regal Lodge, Delhi, Feb. 20th, 1916.)

DEAR CAPT. HALL,

. . . Before I went to Basrah I remember your putting your finger on the Bagdad corner of the map and saying that the ultimate success of the war depended on what we did there. You are one of the people who realised how serious are the questions we have to face. . . I have had a most useful fortnight here. . . I have got on terms of understanding with the India F.O. and the I.D. It is essential India and Egypt should keep in the closest touch since they are dealing with two sides of the same problem. . .

Gertrude Bell

To H.B., Karachi, February 26th, 1916

I can't remember where I left off in my last letters. I spent the remaining days at Delhi ardently reading all their files and got through the most important of them. A man came down from Simla to see me and spent a long day discussing how we should best co-operate intelligence work, so that the same ground should not be covered twice over by Egypt and by India. That was most profitable and I sent my scheme to Cairo for an approval which I think I shall get. It seems obviously reasonable that we should not work in watertight compartments but it's not an idea which dominates official dealings though I find everyone curiously ready to accept it when once it's mooted. The result is that I'm now enrolled as one of the editors of the Gazeteer of Arabia which is being compiled at Simla and I very much fear that I shall have to come back and see Col. Murphy there before I return to Egypt-- whenever that may be. My last night at Delhi I dined with Mr. Grant of the Indian F.O., and had a long evening's talk with him which was very useful. He also would like to see me on my way back and he wants me to come with a sort of informal report for the benefit of the new Viceroy. If I have anything to say, therefore, I expect I shall have to go back and say it, but it depends on how long they keep me at Basrah and on how much they let me see and hear.

To H.B., March 3rd, 1916

We are within half an hour of Basrah. I've come on a transport. It interests me immensely coming into this country from this direction, which I have never done before. We have been steaming up the river all the morning through a familiar landscape of palm groves and Arab huts, with apricot trees blooming here and there in untidy mud-walled gardens--I'm so glad to see it all again and I feel as if I were in my own country once more and welcome it, ugly though it is. Now it remains to be seen whether they find a job for me or send me away without delay.

I wish I knew how Maurice is and were certain that he is not going back to France yet.

To F.B., Basrah, March 17, 1916

Monotonous days pass so quickly that I never realize it's mail day till it is upon me. I am still with the Coxes but I only dine, sleep and breakfast here--for I go in to lunch next door to G.H.Q., which saves time and trouble. Next week I am to be lodged there also. Sir Percy is most charming, Well read and interesting. But I can't decently impose upon their kindness much longer--I've been with them a fortnight already. Mr. Dobbs also is a great standby. I go walking with him of an evening.

I'm still wading through the stuff which they have got here but tomorrow I have a man who is coming to see me and give me information, an Arab of Central Arabia, and I expect to have rather an amusing talk with him.

No mail in yet. One pines for news.

To H.B., Basrah, March 18th, 1916

. . . And I fall to asking myself what I am really doing here-- really nothing, though I work at it like a nigger all day long. At the end of a week I look back and think I've perhaps put in one useful word- and perhaps not; I can't be certain. And if I went away it wouldn't matter, or if I stay it wouldn't matter. However I've thrown in my lot with it--and I would as soon be here as anywhere. They are fussing in Egypt to know how long I'm going to stay. I don't know whether they want me to come back, but I've written to say I think I had better stay on a bit till we see what happens. But I don't mind either way. I have an unhappy feeling all the time of trying to take a hand in things which are too big to be guided. They move on inevitably and you can't stay them with your little knowledge and your feeble will.

To F.B., Basrah, March 9, 1916

I wish I ever knew how long I was going to stay in any place or what I were likely to do next. But that is just the kind of thing which one never can know when one is engaged in the indefinite sort of job which I am doing. There is, however, indeed a great deal of work to be done here. I have already begun to classify the very valuable tribal material which I find in the files at the Intel. Dept., and I think there are pretty wide possibilities of adding to what has been collected already. It is extraordinarily interesting; my own previous knowledge though there was little enough of it, comes in very handy in many ways--as a check upon, and a frame to the new stuff I am handling. And I can't tell you how wonderful it is to be in at the birth, so to speak, of a new administration. Everyone is being amazingly kind. I have been given a lodging next door to Headquarters in the big house on the river which belongs to Gray, Mackenzie & Co. That is most convenient, for I have only to step across the bridge a little creek to get to my work. To-day I lunched with the Generals--Sir Percy Lake, General Cowper, General Offley Shaw and General Money, and as an immediate result they move me and my maps and books onto a splendid great verandah with a cool room behind it where I sit and work all day long. My companion here is Captain Campbell Thompson, ex-archaeologist--very pleasant and obliging and delighted to benefit with me by the change of workshop, for we were lodged by day in Col. Beach's bedroom (he is head of the I.D.), a plan which was not very convenient either for us or for him. The whole of Basrah is packed full, as u may understand when it has had suddenly to expand into the base of a large army. Finally I have got an Arab boy as a servant. His name is Mikhail. Sir Percy Cox came back last night--he has been away at Bushire--and he also is going to help me to get all the information I want by sending on to me any Arabs whom he thinks will interest me. Therefore if I don't make something of it, it will be entirely my own fault. I'm thankful to think that M. won't be back in France at any rate till the end of April. The relief it is to know that he is not fighting! The situation night develop very rapidly here and there is a feeling of changing tide which is exciting and disturbing. My days are, however, very uneventful. I work at G.H.Q. from 8:30 to 12:30, come in to lunch, and go back there from 2 till near 6. Then, it being sunset, wonderfully cool and delicious, I walk for half an hour or so through palm gardens-it's more like a steeplechase than a walk for the paths are continuously interrupted by irrigation channels, over some of which you Jump while over the others you do tightrope dancing across a single palm trunk. I shall fall in some day, and though I shall not be drowned, it will be disgustingly muddy.

To H.B., Basrah, March 24, 1916

. . .I sometimes try to picture what it will be like when we are all at home together again and daren't think of it lest the Gods should be taking heed. We are now on the edge of important things and we hold our breath. If we don't succeed it will be uncommonly awkward. I don't know that there is much point in my being here, but I'm glad I came because one inevitably understands much more about it. And I'm glad I have got to know Sir Percy Cox. He is a very remarkable person, not the least remarkable thing about him being his entire absence of any thought about himself. He does his job-a gigantic job-and thinks no more about it. I wonder if Elsa is back at Rounton yet. Very soon the wild daffodils by the little pond will come out and nod their heads to the east wind. It is 3 years since I saw them.

To F.B., Basrah, April 9, 1916

. . . This week has been greatly enlivened by the appearance of Mr. Lawrence, sent out as liaison officer from Egypt We have had great talks and made vast schemes for the government of the universe. He goes up river to-morrow, where the battle is raging these days. . . I have nearly finished my tribe handbook, but I want go up to Nasariyeh before it is put into it's final form, for I know it needs checking from there. For that I must Wait to see the result of Kut.

To H. B., Basrah, April 16, 1916

How Kut holds out still I can hardly guess, but it does and we may yet get through in time. But one feels dreadfully anxious. . . Even Basrah has a burst of glory in April. The palm gardens are deep in luxuriant grass and corn, the pomegranates are flowering, the mulberries almost ripe, and in the garden of the house where I am staying the roses are more wonderful than I can describe. It's the only garden in Basrah, so I'm lucky.

To F.B., G.H.Q., Basrah, April 27, 1916

Nothing happens and nothing seems likely to happen at Kut-- it's a desperate business, Heaven knows how it will end. Meantime I have been having some very interesting work and as long as it goes on, I shall remain. One is up against the raw material here, which one is not in Egypt, and it is really worth while doing all these first hand things. I don't mind the heat-there has been nothing to speak of the thermometer so far seldom above 90, and I rather like it. But I wish I had some clothes; my things are beginning to drop to pieces; I wonder if you are sending me out any, and if they will ever arrive. I think I shall write to Domnul in Bombay for some cotton skirts and some shirts. One wears almost nothing, fortunately, still it's all the more essential that that nothing should not be in holes. I generally get up nowadays about 5:30 or 6 and when I haven't got to mend my clothes, bother them I go out riding through the palm gardens and have half an hour's gallop in the desert which is Very delicious. Then back to a bath and breakfast and across the road to G.H.Q. by 8:30, I work there till about 5:30, with half an hour off for lunch after which if I haven't been out in the morning I go for a little walk, but it's getting rather too hot to walk comfortably much before sunset. Then read a little or do some work which I have brought in with me, have another bath, dine at a quarter to 9 and go to bed.

The days pass like lightning. Last week I went out for a night to Zubair. We have a political officer there, Captain Marrs, very nice and intelligent. I was put up at the post office in a room with a mud floor furnished with my own camp bed a chair a bath and a table lent by Captain Marrs, but the Sheikh of the town insisted on entertaining me and we went in to him for all our meals-and unlimited gossip about the desert with which he is always in the closest touch since the caravans come in to Zubair. . .

I was also much obliged to Father for his very interesting statistics about the falling mark, and for the article on the Mesop. campaign in the Economist. I fear the latter is nothing short of the truth, but the blame needs a good deal of distribution. I don't hold a brief for the Govt. of India, but it is only fair to remember that K. drained India white of troops and of all military requirements, including hospitals and doctors, at the beginning of the war, that the campaign was forced on them from England, and that when it developed into a very serious matter--far too big a matter for India to handle if she had had command of all her resources--neither troops, nor artillery, nor hospital units, nor flying corps, nor anything were sent back in time to be of use. And what was perhaps still more serious was that all their best generals had gone to France or Gallipoli many of them never to return.

Politically, too, we rushed with the business with our usual disregard for a comprehensive political scheme. We treated Mesop. as if it were an isolated unit, instead of which it is part of Arabia, its politics indissolubly connected with the great and far reaching Arab question, which presents Indeed, different facets as you regard it from different aspects, and is yet always and always one and the same indivisible block. The co-ordinating of Arabian politics and the creation of an Arabian policy should have been done at home--it could only have been done successfully at home. There was no one to do it, no one who had ever thought of it, and it Was left to our people in Egypt to thrash out, in the face of strenuous opposition, from India and London, some sort of wide scheme, which will, I am persuaded, ultimately form the basis of our relations with the Arabs. Well that is enough of

Politics. But when people talk of our muddling through it throws me into a passion. Muddle through! why yes so we do--wading through blood and tears that need never have been shed.

To H.B., G.H.Q., Basrah, May 14, 1916

You will tell me, won't you, if you think I ought to come home. I will do exactly what you think right and what you Wish, but if you do not send for me I shall stay here as long as they will let me-I might be recalled to Egypt, where they are fussing to have me back, but I am persuaded that for the moment I am much more useful here and indeed I am beginning to feel that I am being really useful. I should have to go a long way back to tell you how many gaps there were to fill. I have got hold of the maps and am now bringing them out in an intelligible form, but that is only one among the many odd jobs which I do. Also the natives here are beginning to know me and drop in with news and gossip. Finally, and I think most important of all, there is the difficult gap between Mesop. and Egypt to bridge and I hope I am going to be the person who is charged with the task. Sir P. Cox wants me and as I have a great respect and admiration for him and get on with him excellently I believe I can keep the matter going without friction. There is so much, oh so much to be thought of and considered-so many ways of going irretrievably wrong at the beginning, and some of them are being taken and must be set right before matters grow worse. I know these people, the Arabs; I have been in contact with them in a way which is possible for no official, and it is that intimacy and friendship which makes me useful here That is why I want to stay; but when I have letters from home telling of sickness and sorrow I can scarcely bear to be away from you.

George Lloyd [now Lord Lloyd] has just come out to work with Sir Percy. It will make a great difference to me to have him. I hope he will find time to ride with me sometimes in the morning, when we can talk things over and help each other. But if I become the Egyptian link, I shall probably go into Sir Percy's office too, and that is where I ought to be. MY work is political, not military. The sole drawback is that it is a quarter of an hour from where I live and one can't come backwards and forwards in the middle of the day. Also it is not so luxurious as G.H.Q., where we sit under electric fans all day and really don't feel the heat. The moment you get away from a fan you drip ceaselessly, but I suppose one will get accustomed to that. I am absolutely fit, and don't suffer at all from the climate.

To H.B., G.H.Q., Basrah, May 4th, 1916

for some days before it actually happened it was clear that Kut must fall. . . Aubrey [Herbert] is, I gather, helping to arrange the exchange of prisoners, his knowledge of Turkish being very useful. The Admiral has just come down here; I have not seen him yet. And to-day the Army Commander and all G.H.Q. staff return from up river. I must then find out what they wish me to do. If they will let me, I shall stay for the work is extremely interesting and I think I can make a good deal more of the sort of jobs I have been doing if they give me a free hand to re-cast a lot of their Intelligence publications. I am now engaged in getting into communication with Ibn Rashid, whom it is rather important to preserve as a neutral if we can do no more. He is only about 4 days off and Sir Percy Cox has approved warmly of my sending him a letter. A curious game, isn't it, but you can understand that it is exciting to have a hand in it. The climate is, of course, infernal, but oddly enough I don't mind it. I ride 3 or 4 mornings a week, going out about 5:30, and then come in to a room with all doors and windows closed and electric fans spinning--really quite comparatively cool. The temperature hasn't run up to 100 yet, but it is very close and stuffy with a perpetual south wind--if you can call it a wind, it seems to me perfectly still. This is always the weather in May and they say it is more trying than the hotter months when the N. wind sets in.

To H. B., G.H.Q., Basrah, May 21, 1916

The question of my position with regard to the correspondence with Egypt is not yet definitely settled but I think it is practically certain that I shall be appointed. I shall have to come more strictly under official control and I should not be able to leave this country without very good cause shown, like any other person with a Job here. But I should have no hesitation in giving undertakings of that kind, knowing that you would approve. The thing is to be of the best use one can and I feel certain that this position would give me far greater opportunities and that I can put them to profit. Things are moving very quickly here as you will probably learn long before this letter reaches you and the political side has become of immense importance, and will be of more importance still.

Well, I come back to your pamphlet and find I haven't said half enough how good and witty and wise I think it, and God bless your soul how can any born man think otherwise?

To F.B., G.H.Q., Basrah, May 26th, 1916

. . ..I have a lace evening gown, a white crape gown, a stripy blue muslin gown, two shirts and a stripy silk gown, all most suitable, and the last superlatively right. Thank you so very much. I ride pretty regularly in the mornings for an hour and a half setting Out at 5:30, and feel much better for plenty of hard exercise. One comes in wet through, has a bath and breakfast, and begins work at 8 or a little before. After that You can't with any comfort go out in the sun till towards evening. The shade temp. is not much over 100. You keep all doors and windows shut and electric fans spinning, and except for about an hour in the afternoon you don't feel it. One sleeps on the roof. The temp. drops to a little above 90 and probably to 80 or so before dawn. It is quite comfortable.

I went yesterday afternoon, after 5, in an electric launch up the Shatt-al-Arab turned into the new Euphrates channel a few miles above Basrah. The floods are out, and the whole country is under water. We left the channel and went across several miles of shallow water with occasional Palm groves standing in it, derelict villages made of reed matting, and even the reeds themselves sticking up where the water was very shallow. All stewing in the blazing heat. And in the middle of it was a solitary buffalo, knee-deep in mud and water, eating the reed tops. Whether he was there because he liked it, or whether he was there by mistake, I don't know. He looked quite happy, but if ever he wanted to lie down, he would have to walk for days-it is slow going-to find a dry place to lie on. The Ark and all the rest become quite comprehensible when one sees Mesopotamia in flood time. . .

[She goes up to Nasariyeh by river with Generals McMunn and Cooper--describes the flooded country on the banks of the Euphrates, always in a burning heat with a scorching wind.]

To H.B., June 12, 1916

. . . . .I could wish Maurice were not so well. The thought of his going back to France--he is probably there by now--is horrible. How dreadfully you will miss him.

Much as I enjoyed my little journey I was very glad to get in under a house roof again, for the last few days were very hot. I found a great deal of work when I returned. It's not easy here--some day I'll tell you about it. But the more difficult it is the more I feel I ought to stay.

To H.B., G.H.Q., Basrah, June 15th

I'm delighted to hear that M. doesn't go back to France yet, but how will he like a Welsh regiment, I wonder. your encouragement to me to remain here came just at the right moment and I have decided to let them appoint me official Correspondent to Cairo. A routine order is now to be issued ,making me part of I.E.F. "D," the Indian Expeditionary Force "D," and I believe I'm am to have pay, but fortunately I need not wear uniform! I ought to have white tabs, for I am under the Political Department. It's rather comic isn't it. It has its disadvantages, but I think it's the right thing to do. The news this week has been of Mecca, deeply interesting, and one up to Egypt and my beloved chiefs there, from whom I am now entirely detached for the moment. I expect the immediate results will not be very great--we must beat the Turkish army before anything very striking can happen--but the revolt of the Holy Places is an immense moral and political asset. I've had a busy week and I expect I shall be busier when I take up my new work. I shall like very much coming into closer contact with Sir Percy Cox. He is going to give me a room in his office where I shall go two or three mornings a week--as often as is necessary. The other days I shall go on working at G.H.Q., which is next door to where I live. Sir Percy's office is a quarter of an hour away-you can't realize what that means until you've stepped out into the sun here anywhere near the middle of the day. The heat from the ground burns you like the breath of a furnace. We've had a very hot and heavy fortnight, and the north wind, long overdue, doesn't come, curse it. The result is that there's an astonishing amount of sickness, all the clerks and typists going down first so that you can't get your work done. I am absolutely well. I never have the smallest touch of fever or even feel tired--a little slack at the end of the hot day, which isn't surprising seeing that one gets up soon after 5. I sleep like a top, My bed is on the roof; I've discarded all mattresses and sleep on a bit of fine matting with a sheet Over it. After midnight it gets cooler and one wakes for a moment and pulls a second sheet over oneself.

Mr. Dobbs has come back. He's a great addition to my small world. I like him so much and he is so interesting and so clever. George (Lloyd] is still here, but I fear he has nearly finished his job. He will be a great loss. It's the queerest life, you know-quite unlike anything one has ever done before. I love the work, and the people are all very kind. On the Whole I like it all.

But I feel rather detached from you--I wish I could sit somewhere midway and have a talk with you once or twice a week.

To H.B., Basrah, July 3, 1916

I have entered on my new duties, to my great satisfaction and amusement. I go every morning at 9 to the Political Office--it's about 10 minutes' walk--and work there till 12:30. They give me a cup of coffee in the middle of the morning. Then I have a cab to fetch me and come back to lunch, after which I rest for half-an-hour and go to G.H.Q., where I either find some job waiting for me, or I write things from the notes I have made during the morning. I hope that it will all work out very well and that it will be satisfactory to the Egyptians. There's no denying that the weather is confoundedly hot. We have had some bad days, temperature over 111, and very damp. Hot nights, too. One swears at it, but I'm perfectly well so I haven't any business to complain. There is a terrible amount of sickness, however, among people who have to be out of doors and who are not luxuriously lodged and fed. To carry on a campaign under these conditions is no small matter, for not only are your soldiers enduring more casualties than in the worst battle, but your staff vanishes like sand before the sun--clerks, typists, servants, they go down before you can wink, and you are left to do the things for yourself.

THE LETTERS OF GERTRUDE BELL

To F.B., G.H.Q., Basrah, July 9, 1916

. . . You both tell me of Maurice's new command and Father of his attempts to get him out to the front, which I devoutly hope will prove fruitless. My work at the Political Office continues to be delightful, and I think it will prove valuable. I had a touch of fever this week and was off for a day, but am now perfectly recovered-it was no more than the attack which I was nursed through by the old man in the mosque, you remember, and I may congratulate myself on having got through half the hot weather with quite exceptional immunity from all ills. Oh, but it's a great game we're playing here, or we will play, and some day I shall have so much to say about the general principles of it. They are so simple and so obvious-and so apt to be neglected.

We've had some rather better days this last week; temp. something over 100 instead of something over 110, which makes a great difference. It's Ramadhan and the Mohammadans are abstaining from food and water all through the daylight hours. It must be awful in this weather, for scarcely any work can be got through. How can you unload ships and tow boats up stream when you are starving and athirst?

To H.B., and F B. G.H.Q., Basrah, July 15th, 1916

. . ..Last night I woke at 1 a.m. to find the temp. still over 100 and myself lying in a pool, My silk nightgown goes into the bath with me in the morning, is wrung out and needs no more bother. Yes, it has been deuced hot, and will be for another 6 weeks at least. I'm all right, but its trying, there's no denying it. It's the first hours of the night, absolutely still, damp and close which I find the worst. But sometimes I think it Pretty horrid to be wet through all day. It's uncommonly difficult to tackle one's clothes! Don't forget, Father, to let me have your paper on Trade Unions. I've always time and the greatest interest for your observations on these matters. But I don't think you can argue Free Trade now on its economic merits--there's bound to be too much passion in the whole question now and for some time to come. Perhaps some day the world will come back to common sense. It won't be yet. I must tell you in confidence that I'm being useful here, more useful than I could be anywhere else because I've got better qualifications for this sort of job than for any. It's not of a world shaking character, but for all that it's worth doing and it would not be done if I didn't stay. That's what holds me up every now and then when I think the nights and days really almost too disagreeable. I'm going to be rather desperately solitary next month. George will be gone, Mr. Dobbs is going on leave, Mrs. van Ess and her husband to Nasariyeh and elsewhere for a month to see about schools. That sweeps away nearly all my circle at one stroke, but General McMunn remains and I find him a great standby and a mighty comfort. There are times when one gets into a sort of impasse, a helpless feeling that there's so much to be pulled straight in human affairs and so little pulling power. One permanent source of satisfaction is my chief, Sir Percy Cox. He is so delightful to work with, so generous to me about all I want to do and so kindly appreciative. I have a very real affection for him. But he is taking on too much, more than any mortal man could accomplish and though it's wonderful how evenly good his health is, I'm always afraid that he may break down under it. After Mr. Dobbs goes there'll be no one capable of taking his place. . . The administration here owes him a very great deal. Upon my soul, it's a comfort to come up against real sound good sense combined with administrative capacity. One needs it in a country of this kind which is all beginnings. The real difficulty under which we labour here is that we don't know, and I suppose can't know till the end of the war, exactly what we intend to do in this country. You are continually confronted with that uncertainty. Can you persuade people to take your side when you are not sure in the end whether you'll be there to take theirs?

To H.B. and F.B., G.H.Q., Basrah, July 23rd.

I had a letter from Maurice besides the one enclosed by Father. Thank Heaven he's out of it for the moment. And still more thanks that he is not out here. it's Hell at the front and nothing short of it. Sir Victor Horsley's death will make people realize perhaps that the climate is warm whereas the daily death from heatstroke of people who are not 'de connaissance' doesn't filter through. The precautions which might have been taken to mitigate the fury of the summer, such as the supplying of plentiful ice machines, were not taken. Even here we are short of ice, at Amarah or the front, God help you. And it's difficult to do anything now for there's barely enough transport to keep the troops supplied with food. There has been a little breath of north wind on and off for the last few days, but not enough even to keep the nights cool. One comforts oneself by thinking that in 6 weeks or SO we shall be through the worst of it. At least in Sep. it's said to be cool at night. George has gone and I miss him bitterly. He has done good work but even better than his work is the atmosphere of sanity he brings with him. It's difficult at times to see straight and to think straight. One gets bewildered--and there are enough materials for be-wilderment--and when the thermometer is persistently over 110 one can't pull oneself together, with the result that things won't fall into scale and the prospect is blocked by a molehill. If you knew what it's like running offices here, with all your clerks and typists going sick and no one to replace them.

Goodbye, my dearest parents. I'm liking my work with Sir Percy very much and indeed I like it all, as well as I should like any-thing. But I shan't be sorry when the temp. drops 20 degrees.

To H.B., G.H.Q., Basrah, July 29th, 1916

. . . As for Free Trade, you know what I think. The question must for the moment cease to be a purely economic one and the wise thing is to 'reculer pour mieux sauter.' At least if not to draw back, to draw in. Is this too much the wisdom of the serpent to suit you? You're too good to play the part of Don Quixote, you know--don't break your lance on the windmill wings of passion; it will be wanted strong and bright when the tempests have ceased to turn those wheels round. But whatever you do I shall continue to think you the most beloved Father.

Lord! it's been hot here. The actual temperature is hotter up river but they say that the dryness there makes it more bearable. It's bearable all right here, but so nasty. Everything you touch is hot, all the inanimate objects--Your hair--if that's inanimate--the biscuit you eat, the clothes you put on. The temp. of the river is 94 and one's bath water, drawn from a tank on the roof, never under 100 except in the early morning. But it doesn't steam--the air's hotter.

To F.B., G.H.Q., Basrah, August 9th, 1916

I've been, I'm ashamed to say, on the shelf with fever this week. I'm all right again but feeling like a limp rag. The stiffening will come back in a day or two. I shall not let this happen again if I can help it. A small daily dose of quinine ought to keep it off. We really have got the north wind at last, which means cool nights even if it doesn't much alter the temperature of the days. Cool nights make a world of difference; the temp. before dawn drops sometimes to 77. One feels deliciously frozen! A fall Of 30 from the daytime temperature isn't bad. The dates are all yellow; they will be ripe very shortly. I'm a great deal too woolly to write.

To H.B., and F.B. G.H.Q., Basrah, August 11th, 1916

How warmly I shall welcome Richard Pennessy! [Colonel Pope-Hennessy.] It's almost too good to be true. We have had a north wind for the last 10 days, with cold nights, though it doesn't seem to make much difference to the days. I'm much better, nearly well--I'm thankful it's not a week ago when I felt too ill even to write to you. I have been steadily at work ever since and am now beginning to feel like a person again.

Yesterday we had a most entertaining man at the Political Office. He is a famous camel doctor and I had heard of him up and down Arabia. He knows every man in the desert and every man knows him. He can go anywhere with perfect security thanks to his remedy for mange, whatever it is. We had a most amusing gossip about the desert. A man Of that kind is a great asset as a bearer of news--or a carrier of messages. I think the Turks are not having much of a time in Mesopotamia. Ottoman Govt. seems to have vanished from every place except Bagdad and a few of the other towns. The tribes do exactly what they like and there is no attempt to control them. We ought to have a look in one of these days. But I wonder what it will be like trying to bring back some kind of order when there has been nothing but the wildest license. I hear from the front that things are much better, more food and more variety of it, cooler nights and the health of the troops greatly improved; heaven be praised! We are through the worst of this summer now, but when I look back on July I fall to wondering how the army weathered it. It was awful.

I rejoice in the thought that M. is still in England and I am glad to hear he's happy.

To H.B., G.H.Q., Basrah, August 19th, 1916

I write to one parent, but it's meant for both. I'm heartily well again and enjoying immensely a bout of cooler weather, the temp. 101 instead of 107 (you can't think the difference it makes) and cool not to say cold nights. It's heavenly. Even if we go back to another spell of great heat it can't last long. Meantime I've taken to riding again which is very delicious.

My paper on labour met with Sir P. C.'s approval and he sent it up to the W.O.-not of course as coming from me but as a memorandum from his office. I was pleased, however. I've been engaged this week in drawing up a memorandum about Musqat where the political situation is both curious and interesting. That's the sort of job I do, sandwiched in with tribe notes and things I pick up from Arabs who come in to see us. It's all very amusing work. The I.G.C. asks me what part I intend to play in the future administration of this country! I think I shall have to keep an eye on it, you know, from time to time! I suppose I shall be able to keep an eye on all the developments in the Near East through the Arab Bureau. . .

To F.B., G.H.Q., Basrah, August 27th, 1916

I went out last week along the light railway 25 miles into the desert--it's the Nasariyeh railway--and found myself in the middle of a big Shammar encampment, hearing all the desert gossip in the familiar manner. It was so curious to travel 50 minutes by rail and find yourself in another universe. General Maude, our new Army Commander, has just arrived. I've made his acquaintance, no more.

I continue to like my work very much and to be extremely thankful for it.

To F.B., Basrah, September 20th, 1916

I didn't write last week because I was having jaundice and truly miserable. It was a mild bout and I'm better but I am going this afternoon for change of air to a sort of big rest house attached to our officers' hospital a few miles down river. It seems a sensible thing to do and I hope a few days will set me on my feet again and restore me to my usual complexion.

It's so provoking to be laid up when there's such a lot of work to do. The thing is growing and this week came a letter from the W.O., to whom I send articles through the Intell. Dept., saying I was sending just what they wanted and would I send more. So that's all right. It makes me want to be back more than ever. Everyone is immensely kind; the Consulting Physician of the Force comes to see me and the woman who is Inspector General of all the hospitals looks after me. I'm ashamed of bothering them about such a silly little ailment.

Will you please send me a winter hat. Something of this kind in dark violet. Either of these would do. Also I would immensely like a soft black satin gown which I could Wear either by day or night-crossed over in front, skirt down to the ground. I would like Marte (Conduit St.) to make it because she will make me something pretty. She doesn't usually make anything but evening gowns, but if you told her it's for me and where I am I know she would do it for me.

To H.B., Bait Namah, 10 September, 1916

I'm still in hospital but I've made a very rapid cure (I was pretty bad when I came) and I hope they will let me go back to Basrah in a day or two. I've been quite extraordinarily comfortable and the kindness of everyone is past belief. It really was very pleasant to find oneself here with all the trouble of looking after one's own self lifted off one's shoulders. I've done little or nothing but eat and sleep and read novels, of which I found plenty here. Oh yes and I've read all Gilbert Murray's translations of Greek plays--glorious they are--which I also found, one of the doctors being brother to Charles Roberts! I must tell you this hospital is in a great huge modern Arab house which we commandeered, very beautiful and splendid. There are two large courts with orange trees in the middle of them, and in one of them they have set aside a ward for convalescent nurses from the other hospitals. That's where I am. There are always 5 or 6 other people in my ward but I have a corner bed with a screen round it, and for the last few days I have scarcely been in the ward at all. I sit all day in the verandah (and for the last 3 days I've been working all the morning). After lunch I have a bath and read till tea and then I go down and sit in the shade by the water's edge. I dine on the verandah and sleep on the roof under the stars.

Do you know I've never been so ill as this before. I hadn't an idea what it was like to feel so deadly weak that you couldn't move your body much nor hold your mind at all. When once I began to mend and to eat I didn't mind it. . .

Would you give Bain the bookseller an order for me. He is to send me every month from 4 to 6 new books, novels and poetry, nothing very serious, he knows exactly the kind of thing I like. Tell him I left England last November and have read nothing that has come out since so he will have plenty to go on with. He might send one or two regularly every week. New poetry I love to have and Bain knows perfectly well the sort of novel I like-Anthony Hope at one end of the scale and the Crock of Gold at the other

To H.B., c/o Base Post Master, M.E.F., Basrah,
November 4th. 1916

I've just been out for a long walk with Mr. Bullard (Revenue Dept.)-the first time I've walked a step since May. It is still too dusty to be a very nice form of exercise; riding is better. At the Political Office I am beginning to reap Profit from the long slow collecting and classifying of information--a job I'm always busy with. They send me down all the telegrams and reports that come in from the provinces with a request for a note on the people, tribes and places mentioned. With any luck I can find and place most of them now-it's a great satisfaction. It's so nice to be a spoke in the wheel, one that helps to turn, not one that hinders.

To F.B., Basrah, November 16th, 1916

I had a pleasant 5 days away from Basrah. I went up to Qurnah and made that my headquarters, living on my launch but spending most of the day in the A.P.O.'s home. I saw innumerable sheikhs and got all the information I wanted. The weather is perfection. The rain hasn7t come yet--it ought to have come but I'm in no hurry for it. The temperature hangs about 80, with cool damp nights. This morning I was out riding as the sun rose and in the desert half an hour later--the air clear as crystal, you count the tamarisk trees at Shaaibah, 8 miles away. It was wonderfully beautiful. From all of which you may gather that I am extremely well, as indeed I am. I wonder what letters of mine went down in the Arabia and whether I asked for anything in them! I know I did ask about that time for a winter hat, smallish, felt, dark blue or purple, and for 4 thick white silk shirts, turned open at the neck.

To H.B., Basrah, November 23rd, 1916

As a fact I am not writing from Basrah but from somewhere on the Shatt al Arab below Qurnah after what seems to Me, looking back on it, to have been an immense journey-but I'll begin at the beginning. I left Basrah on a Saturday night-the I.G.C. motored me down to what we call the terminus station. I found the night train making itself ready, with a small guard's van hitched onto it for me. This I furnished with a camp bed, a chair and the station master's lantern and off we started about 6 into the desert. If ever years hence I come back into this country and travel to Bagdad by the Basrah express, I shall remember, while I eat my luxurious meal in the dining car, how first I travelled along the line in a guard's van and dined on tinned tongue, tinned butter and tinned pears by the light of the station master's lantern. What happened after that I don't know, for I went to bed and except for an occasional vague consciousness of halts in a wide desert dim with starlight, I didn't take note of anything in particular till the dawn crept in at my windowless window and I woke to find my van standing outside rail head camp in the middle of Arabia, so to speak. All this country was Sadun headquarters, the desert home of the ruling family in Southern Mesopotamia who came up from Mecca in the 14th century and are now immensely multiplied, the great aristocracy of the Iraq. Here they come in spring with their camel herds, for they are not only powerful landowners along the rivers, but also real Bedu, nomads of the open wilderness, a wide, flat, sandy land, good desert from the point of view of the camel breeder, for it grows much thorny scrub and plentiful tufts of coarse grass, eaten down now almost to the toot, an unbroken circle of horizon except where to the north it was intercepted by the palms of the river bank, ghostly through the mirage though they were only a few miles away. The eye doesn't travel far over a level waste.

At 8 o'clock there rolled in General Brooking's motor car and a motor lorry and we bumped over the grass tufts and over the sun-split mud of what had been flood water in the spring, to Khamiseyeh, where we have had troops ever since Ibn Rashid came filibustering round last summer. For Kharniseyeh is one of the markets of Central Arabia and he who holds these holds the tribes, as Ibn Rashid found to his cost and perhaps has related by now in Hayil. A mud-built, dirty little place is Khamiseyeh, watered by a small and evil looking canal from the Euphrates which runs into the town up to the walled square where the caravans lodge when they come up from Jebel Shamman. I drove straight into our camp, picked up General Tidswell, who is in command, and made him take me round the town. And there we met the Sheikh of Khamiseyeh, who is a friend of mine and on his pressing invitation went to his house and drank a cup of tea. He had a guest, Sheikh Hamud of the Dhafir, one of our friendly Beduin, and we sat for a while listening to the latest desert news, which I translated for the General. I hadn't met Hamud before, though he was one of the Sheikhs of whom I had heard much talk when I was riding up from Hail. And so on, over the desert, some 25 miles to Nasariyeh, putting up gazelle and sand grouse as we went. I never thought to watch them from a motor.

To F.B., Basrah, December 9, 1916

The winter isn't really very nice here. One is usually sneezing, when not coughing, and one wishes one had a nice warm comfortable place to sit in. To think that I was once clean and tidy! However, these are things of the past. I've been busy with a long memorandum about the whole of our central Arabian relations, which I've just finished. It will now go to all the High and Mighty in every part. One can't do much more than sit and record if one is of my sex, devil take it; one can get the things recorded in the right way and that means, I hope, that unconsciously people will judge events as you think they ought to be judged. But it's small change for doing things, very small change I feel at times.

To H.B., Basrah, December 15, 1916

* * * *Do you know I was thinking yesterday what I would pick out as the happiest things I've done in all my life, and I came to the conclusion that I should choose the old Italian journeys with you, those long ago journeys which were so delicious. . . except only in that

very big thing, complete love and confidence in my family--I've had that always --and can't lose it. And you are the pivot of it. But for that I don't care much one way or the other what happens, except that sometimes I should very much like to see you. But I'm quite content here, interested by the work and very conscious that I couldn't anywhere be doing things that would interest me so much.

The world continues to look autumnal-scarcely wintry yet--in spite of the eternal green of the palms. There is a yellow mimosa in flower, fluffy, sweet-smelling balls, a very heavenly little tree, albeit thorny. Yes, there's always plenty of small change, isn't there!

To F.B., Basrah, December, 1916

The cold weather is just as uncomfortable here as the hot, or nearly as uncomfortable. The houses are so unsuitable for winter. We live in semi-darkness, since all the windows are screened from the summer light and in perpetual cold in rooms that all open on to a court or a verandah. My working room at the Political Office is nice--dark, of course, but I have a little oil stove in it which keeps it warm. Still I feel I've almost forgotten what it is to be really comfortable--not that it matters much.

This is the 4th Xmas I've spent in foreign parts--Arabia, Boulogne, Cairo, Qalat Salih. The last is where I expect to be on Xmas Day and I'm truly thankful to escape any attempt at feasts here.

To H.B., Amarah, January 1, 1917

I will begin the New Year before breakfast by writing to you and sending to you and all my dear family all the best of good wishes.

I must tell you I felt dreadfully depressed on Xmas Day thinking of other Xmas Days when we were together and used to be so absurdly happy a long time ago. I hope Maurice has been with you this year. However, I'm a monster of ingratitude to complain, for I have had a very interesting ten days and enjoyed them. Mr. Philby (Acting Reserve Commission) and I left Basrah on his launch on the 22nd, got up to Qurnah in the evening and spent the night with the A.P.o. We were off early next day and went up river to Qulat Sabib--it was a delicious warm day and the river was delightful. I don't know why it should be as attractive as it is. The elements of the scene are extremely simple but the combination still makes a wonderfully attractive result. Yet there's really nothing--flat, far-stretching plain coming down to the river's edge, thorn covered, water-covered in the flood in the lower reaches, a little wheat and millet stubble in the base fields, an occasional village of reed-built houses and the beautiful river craft, majestic on noble sails or skimming on clumsy paddles. The river bends and winds, curves back on itself almost and you have the curious apparition of a fleet of white sails rising out of the thorny waste, now on one side of you, now the other. And by these you mark where your cruise must be, where the river divides wilderness from wilderness. We passed Ezra's Tomb and its clump of palms and got out to look at it. There's a very ancient tradition which is probably true, that the Prophet is buried here, but the actual shrine is new. . .

Two of these days we spent in riding out over the great farms on either side of the river. These rides brought us into a Mesopotamia which was quite new to me. Behind the high land by the river, the thorny scrub and the millet fields, lies the rich rice country watered by the canals from the Tigris. And here the land is densely populated, village after reed-built village standing on the canal banks, and everywhere the evidences of the great harvest in mounds of straw and garnered fields and grain laden boats panting up the canals. The farms we rode over were not very large as farms go here; the outer edge of the largest, that is to say, the point where the land sloping down from the Tigris runs into the huge marsh, was some 12 miles from the river; but the sheikh pays 11,000 a year in rent to the Govt. from whom he leases the ground. The calculation is nominally on the basis of half the profits, but in reality it is about one-third and the produce of the farm is about 33,000 pounds a year--a respectable output. . . I spend my time in seeing local people and getting lots of information about tribes and families which had baffled me in Basrah, a satisfactory occupation.

To F.B., Basrah, January 13th, 1917

I came back to find the most delightful pile of letters. . . if you have no time to die, as Maurice says, I wonder you have time to write me such splendid long letters! You really must not do it when you feel dreadfully run. Still, I won't deny that I do enjoy having news from you both.

I feel so much ashamed of having bothered you about clothes, etc., especially as all the trouble you've taken has been fruitless, as far as I'm concerned, for nothing has arrived! But I still hope the things may be in time for next winter, when I shall doubtless be glad of them. I don't want any books on Persia, thank you, and as I never seem to have time to read anything, even books on Mesopotamia are unnecessary. I have written straight to Batsford at various times for essentials, and perhaps some day they will come. The failure in winter clothes makes me anxious for the summer, and I've thought of a plan which will spare you trouble. I shall write long and full directions (next mail) to the Ladies' Shirt Co., telling them exactly what I want in cotton gowns. But since the shop might perhaps have ceased to exist (one never knows) I shall send the letter under cover to you and, if they have by chance died out, the letter can be given to Harvey & Nichols as it stands. It's clear the only plan is to send things by post in small parcels, as you did last spring. One absolutely can't be without masses of summer things in this climate, as one needs a clean gown almost daily, and the constant washing destroys everything. So I'll be beforehand with my orders, and perhaps Moll, if she is in London, would just step into the shop and see that they are carrying out my requirements reasonably.

I'm going to move into a tiny suite of two rooms, which Sir Percy has been such a dear to allot to me in the Political Office. It will be much more convenient. What it's like plunging through winter mud to my work!--it's just as bad in the summer being far away, because one can't go backwards and forwards in the middle of the day without acute discomfort. I have two servants of my own, so I shall be self-contained. I'm busy furnishing now, no easy matter, but I have a tower of strength in the angelic I.G.C., who produces everything with a wave of his sword, so to speak, the moment I ask for it. There really never was anybody so kind, and I don't know what I should do without him. He is so cheerful and competent. He is deeply interested in the development of the country. And we truly are doing something behind the battlefields. I have capital material in the local reports sent up to the head office, and I've just drawn up a little memorandum about administrative progress, which I think ought to give satisfaction to the High and Mighty at home. (Happy to tell you that I hear my utterances receive a truly preposterous attention in London.) just at this moment, this is the only theatre of the war where things look rather bright.

The only thing that keeps one going is to have lots of work. At times I feel as if I wasn't worth my keep here, and then at other times I think I'm doing a certain amount of good, but fundamentally, I am sure it is no good bothering as to whether one is or isn't useful, and the only plan is to apply oneself steadfastly to what lies before one and ask no questions. And at least there's plenty before me here. I like it, too, in spite of occasional depressions, generally caused by the sense of not knowing enough and of general inefficiency.

I hope you think I'm right to stay. I don't much enjoy the prospect of another summer in Basrah. There are still some pleasant months before us; it doesn't begin to be hot till May.

I must go to bed, for I'm going to try my new pony at dawn tomorrow.

To F.B., Basrah, January 20th, 1917

A box has just arrived from Marte, through T. Cook & Sons-it ought to have contained a black satin gown, but it has been opened (probably in Bombay, it was sent by Cook to his agents in Bombay) and the gown has been abstracted. Isn't it infuriating? All that was left was a small cardboard box inside, containing the little black satin coat Marte sent with the gown, some net, and a gold flower. These, by reason of their being in the small box, the thief couldn't get out, for he only opened a part of the nailed-down lid, and made a small hole in the interior cardboard lining, through which he pulled the gown. I hope Marte insured it so that Cook will have to pay-but that thought does not console me much at this moment! Marte had better repeat the gown as quickly as possible and send it in a small box by post. That is the only way of getting things. If it can't possibly go by post it must go through the military forwarding officer, but it takes 6 months Will you tell Marte.

THE LETTERS OF GERTRUDE BELL

To F.B., Basrah, January 26th, 1917

In case my letter of last week didn't reach you, I send an abstract of my directions to the Shirt Co., which it contained. I feel, however, pessimistic as to receiving anything, and I expect I shall have to take to Arab dress next summer. I wrote to you a very doleful letter last week-happy to tell you that I'm better physically but I'm suffering from a severe attack of softening of the brain, which I don't know how to master. It makes all work horribly difficult, as well as valueless when done. I feel so useless that I wonder they don't turn me out, perhaps ultimately they will. But what I should do next I can't imagine. Beyond struggling with this devil I've done nothing for the last week, except ride occasionally in the morning. I don't wonder the Arabs are sick of us--I am too. And oh, how weary we all are of the war! Are we going to be beaten do you think, at the end of everything, or practically beaten? I suppose it would mean abandoning this country and that practically means backing out of Asia. Meantime would you be so very kind as to send me a new Swan Fountain pen, large size and broad nibbed. I've broken the sheath of mine. But if you could teach it to write interesting things before it sets out I should be all the more grateful. This one won't.

To H.B., Basrah, February 2nd, 1917

The news this week is overshadowed by Lord Cromer's death. I've turned to him so many times this last year for advice and help. He and Sir Alfred [Lyall] were the two wise counsellors to whom I never went in vain; now they're both gone and I can't replace them.

I'm getting over the attack of softening of the brain of which I told you, at least getting over it a little. I ride pretty regularly in the mornings, going out soon after dawn. I get back to the office about 9 o'clock in better heart, and above all in a better temper. War is very trying to that vital organ, isn't it. I've been doing some interesting bits of work with Sir Percy which is always enjoyable. To-day there strolled in a whole band of sheikhs from the Euphrates to present their respects to him, and incidentally they always call on me.

I've been sorting out all the material which I gathered when I was up the Tigris, and I have written a good deal about it, confidential

343

and unconfidential, but not as well as it might have been done, I'm sorry to say. However, I feel I've begun to see what the people are like in those parts. My acquaintance with tribes and with Ottoman conditions is a great help, but there's an immense amount to learn. You'll see a piece of mine in the papers about Ibn Saud. I gather the India O. are going to publish it. No, after all I don't suppose you will for they usually publish those things in papers which no one reads, which seems to me rather a waste of energy on all sides, and I wish I could have a free hand with Geoffrey Robinson who wouldn't need to be asked twice about some of them. If he would batter at the doors of Govt. offices he might get them to change their mysterious ways. It's not the setting forth that's of value, but the stuff is so new--a new bit of construction work in the midst of the waste of war.

I must make another attempt to get shoes. I'll write to Yapp again. Otherwise I shall presently go barefoot. Isn't it a tragedy about my black satin gown. Of course it's just the very gown most wanted.

To H.B., Basrah, February 16th, 1917

It was the finger of Providence that led me to get into my new abode, for we have had five days of rain and Basrah is a unique spectacle. It is almost impossible to go out. I put on a riding skirt and a pair of India rubber top boots--which I had fortunately procured from India--and stagger through the swamp for half-an-hour after tea and it's all one can do. Yesterday the sun shone, and the I.O.C. and I managed to get down to the desert in a motor and walked along the top of some mounds on the edge of the palm gardens, which so much encouraged me that I jumped up at sunrise to-day hoping to be able to ride. But no sooner was I donned than down came the rain again, through the mud roof of my room too and there was nothing for it but to change sadly into ordinary clothes--and write to you. We haven't had anything like our proper allowance of rain this winter, so we shall probably get it all now in unmanageable quantities. They don't seem to have had it on the Tigris front, and so far operations continue-but very slowly. I doubt whether much more will happen there and we shall probably spend this summer besieging the Turks in Kut. I hope they'll like it-I feel sure we shan't. But it will be better this year than last owing to the fact that the mud deters even those who desire favours--with the result that I've got through a lot of work and blocked out an article on administration which I've long had in my mind. I hope it will see the light somewhere. All the tribal and other material on which I've been busy for a year has now reached the point of publication for official circulation, and I'm beginning to reap a harvest of proofs from India. When once it's printed and put on record I shall feel that the first goal is attained. It's not history, but it will furnish an exact account of the country as we found it. In and out of all other work it has been, and is still, a constant thread which gives me increasing satisfaction as I get a better grasp of it. On the whole it's the work I've liked best here.

Presently I shall have to ask you to send me a nice wig. I haven't got enough hair left to pin a hat to. I don't know what happens to one's hair in this climate. It just evaporates. A momentous event took place this week--the clothes Sylvia [Henley] bought for me arrived, hat and gown and everything. I feel it to be nothing short of miraculous and rejoice accordingly.

I'm so luxuriously comfortable in my mud rooms.

To F.B., Basrah, February 17th, 1917

. . . The box and the umbrella have come too ! Isn't it great. I am so thankful for shoes, skirts, umbrella (we are in the middle of rain) silk coat and everything. If only that rogue hadn't stolen my black gown I should be well supplied till the hot weather comes.

You have taken such a lot of trouble-thank you so very much.

To H.B., Basrah, March 2, 1917

I had a grand post at the beginning of the week with 2 letters from you (Jan. 11th and 18th) and 3 from Mother. I really was starved for letters from home and consequently fattened on them. . . We really have got the Turks shifted this time, how far shifted we don't yet know. If they make a stand before Bagdad I suppose we shan't go on; in any case, I don't know that we shall go on--the line of communication is immensely long. But no matter; what we have already accomplished will make a difference and we may expect developments in other directions. Congratulatory effusions are coming in from Basrah--I wonder what the real thought is at the bottom of most of them. But up country the people who have come in to us will be content, for they will feel greater security; and the people who haven't come in will have grave doubts as to whether they " backed the right horse "-- they're having them already. The Turks thought the crossing of the Tigris in the face of opposition a sheer impossibility. We have that from the prisoners. Let's hope, in consequence, that they are not so well prepared for the achievement as they should be--indeed their headlong flight seems to indicate as much. My own belief is that they won't be able to hold Bagdad for long if we are close up.

Work has been slack for the last few days, at which times I get rather bored, but I've taken to reading Arabic history every morning, with one of our native secretaries, and at the worst I can always put in as much time as I like, and profitably, on Arabic, till things begin again. To-day I've been asked to write a brief outline of recent Arabian history for the Intelligence Department (the sort of thing I really enjoy doing), so I've turned to that. The amount I've written during the last year is appalling. Some of it is botched together out of reports, some spun out of my own mind and former knowledge, and some an attempt to fix the far corners of the new world we are discovering now, and some dry as dust tribal analyses, dull, but perhaps more useful than most things. It comes to a great volume of material, of one kind and another, and I know I have learnt much if I haven't helped others to learn. But it's sometimes exasperating to be obliged to sit in an office when I long to be out in the desert, seeing the places I hear of, and finding out about them for myself. At the end of the war, there's one favour I'm going to ask of the Authorities and that is that they will give me facilities, so far as they can, to cross Southern Arabia. I would like to do one bit of real Arabian exploration, or attempt. But I shall come home first to see you and get theodolites and things. Dearest, I shan't come back this summer. Anyway, we are all begged not to travel more than we can help under present conditions. If I feel the summer too long I may go up to some hill place in India for a week or two, but it wouldn't amuse me at all.

To H.B., Basrah, March 10th, 1917

We are now hourly awaiting the news of our entrance into Bagdad. I had a letter from Sir Percy to-day, from the Front, full of exultation and confidence. I do hope I may be called up there before very long. It's a wonderful thing to be at the top of the war after all these months of marking time, and say what you will, it's the first big success of the war, and I think it is going to have varied and remarkable consequences.

We shall, I trust, make it a great centre of Arab civilisation, a prosperity; that will be my job partly, I hope, and I never lose sight of it.

I had one foot in the grave for five days with a shocking cold in the head--it's now better, and I'm riding again before breakfast. . . I never saw anything so beautiful as the kingfishers--flocks of them whistling through the palm groves, two kinds, a big and a little blue kind, and I rather think a third brown, but I have not been able quite to spot him yet.

I have been seeing something of a very charming General Lubbock, Mr. Percy's brother.

To H.B., Basrah, March 17th, 1917

Since last I wrote the goal has been reached; we have been a week in Bagdad. I've had no news actually from Bagdad, but I hope I shall get letters this week. I need not tell you how much I long to hear exactly what it is all like. Just 3 years ago I was arriving there from Arabia--3 lifetimes they seem as I look back on them. I went to tea last week with the Matron-in-Chief, the notable Miss Jones, whom I like, and afterwards she took me to see the wounded Turkish prisoners. I stammered into Turkish, which I haven't spoken for 7 years, and they were even only too delighted to hear even a few words of Turkish spoken. There they were, the round-faced Anatolian peasants-I could have laughed and wept to see them--from Konia, from Angora, from Cxsarxa, even from C'ple, and we talked of their houses and what far country they lay in. Most of them were well content to be done with war for ever.

I long to go up to Bagdad, but it is no good bothering yet. Everyone is too busy and there is plenty of time, but I should like to have seen the first moments. Also there's very little work here now. I've finished all the outstanding things with a great effort this week so as to have the road clear when the moment comes. And now I'm wearily doing rather dull office jobs and receiving the countless people who come in with congratulations and petitions. The congratulations are not more than skin deep I fancy.

To F.B., Basrah, March 30th, 1917

I'm sitting with my hands in front of me, practically, and shall remain in that attitude till I go up to Bagdad. It is the first time I have been idle since the war began. However, it is not my desire, and Heaven knows that marking time is far worse than working. Of course it's too late now for gray tweeds-nor have they come!-but I shall be truly thankful for tussore, and above all for cotton gowns. Heaven waft them on their way! All I've got now is one thin woollen gown--made, if you can call it making--in Egypt, which is very dirty from much wear. One can get nothing cleaned, made or even mended here. The temp. is already 80 so that the blue clothes Sylvia sent me are too thick to wear any longer. Happy to tell you I'm now extremely well, partly the rest, perhaps, and partly the exemplary habit of riding before breakfast. I feel ready to take on any amount of new work and am longing for it.

In spite of the drawbacks of Mesop. summers I do feel the people who are working at home are shouldering much the heaviest part of the business. I would far rather be in the East among surroundings which are a perpetual interest to me, places and people which have no sharp edge of memory. But here again I didn't choose, did I? The best one can do is to do what one's told, for as long as one is told to do it. It has not been easy, in many ways. I think I have got over most of the difficulties and the growing cordiality of my colleagues is a source of unmixed satisfaction.

To H.B., Basrah, March 30th, 1917
[Before this letter arrived we had a telegram from Gertrude saying "address Bagdad," and knew that her ardent wish to go there had been gratified.]

Until they let me go up to Bagdad, I have nothing to do. I have telegraphed to my chief asking if I may come up to him and await his reply. I read Arabic, do various odd jobs in the office and see people-and that's all. The centre of gravity has shifted up river and my job with it. This last week has been made very pleasant by having Sir Arthur Lawley here.

To H.B., Sheikh Saad, April 10, 1917

I think I might get a letter posted to you from here. It's the fifth day we have been on the way, and we have another four days before us--a long journey, but the river is full and the current strong. My companions are two nurses, two doctors and the ship's officer. And do you know one of the doctors is Brownlie of Middlesbrough! He is out here for a year. We have 600 troops on board, so closely packed on deck that one has to step over them to reach one's cabin, Indians almost all.

All day yesterday we ran through the wide, level lands of the Bani Lam, not much cultivation, but a great deal of grazing ground, and the tents drawn down to the river and surrounded by flocks. Horses too, the Bani Lam are noted horse-breeders. In the afternoon the Persian hills loomed out of the haze, quite close to us really; the foothills are only 16 miles from the river, but partly hidden in heat mist and looking all the taller, for eyes unaccustomed to anything taller than a palm tree, for the veil through which you sought for their summits.

THE LETTERS
OF
GERTRUDE BELL

VOLUME 2

CHAPTER XVI

1917 - BAGDAD

To F.B. and H.B., April 15th, 1917

We are within two hours of Bagdad and I'm free to admit that coming up this river gives one a wholesome respect for our lines of communication. This is the 9th day we've been at it, tying up for a few hours at night but steaming 17 or 18 hours a day notwithstanding. It's well that it wasn't a month later for already the temperature is 90 and on a crowded ship it's hot. We passed Kut before sunrise, but I got up to see it--poor tragic little place--it's shelled walls and shattered palm trees catching the first flash of day. It is quite empty still, but we are going to clean it out and build it up as soon as possible.

We anchored last night just above Ctesiphon. I know the river banks well, for I've ridden up them more than once. Our big camps are the only unfamiliar objects. It's exactly three years to-day since I last set out from Bagdad across the Syrian Desert on my way back from Arabia.

To H.B., Bagdad, April 20th

Such an arrival! Sir Percy made me most welcome and said a house had been allotted to me. I went off to see it and found a tiny stifling box of a place in a dirty little bazaar. It was absolutely empty-- what furniture I had was with my heavy luggage and not yet landed, and I hadn't even a boy, as I had left my servant to look after the heavy luggage. Fortunately, like a good traveller, I had not parted from my bed and bath. These I proceeded to set up and further unpacked my box which had been dropped into the Tigris, and hung out all the things to dry on the railings of the court. It was breathlessly hot. I hadn't so much as a chair to put anything on, and when I wanted water for washing I had to open my front door and call in the help of the bazaar.

Fortunately they responded with alacrity. I dined with Sir Percy, armed myself with a loaf of bread for breakfast and returned to my empty house to sleep. By good luck my servant turned up late that night, so that there was someone to water tea for me next morning.

I confess, however, that after having done my hair and break-fasted on the floor I felt a little discouraged. It was clear that something must be done at once, and I proceeded to hunt for one. The first thing I tumbled on to was a rose garden with three summer houses in it, quite close to the Political Office and belonging, fortunately, to an old friend of mine, Musa Chalabi. I decided at once that this was the thing, but a kitchen had to be built and a bath room, and sunblinds to be put up--a thousand things. I got Musa Chalabi to help me and summoned in an old man, a servant whom I've known for ages, and after five days' work I'm in--'tant bien que mal' and it promises very well. My old man Shamao has engaged me a cook and the Englishman who runs all the supplies Col. Dixon is my faithful friend, having been charged by the I.G.C. to look after me. And my roses I must tell you are glorious. Oh, but it is hot! I'm longing for my thin summer clothes. I wonder when they will reach me here.

Meantime all my acquaintances and friends have flocked in to see me. I've visited the Naqib, the head religious man and an ally of many years' standing, and have been received with open arms. And it is all wildly interesting--War Office telegraphing for signed articles from me, etc., etc. I'm going to have an exciting summer. Sir P. gives me lots of thrilling things to do and is the kindest of chiefs. Bagdad is a mass of roses and congratulations. They are genuinely delighted at being free of the Turks. The rest for another time, I am so busy.

To H.B. and F.B., Bagdad, April 27th, 1917

I'm never here, that's the pity of it, but I intend, when I write my War Office articles, to retire here solidly for the afternoons; other-wise I'm so terribly interrupted by visitors. I love seeing them and they are most useful for purposes of information, but they eat up the hours. I have the most amusing reunions with gentlemen I met at Hayil and Najaf and Heaven knows where besides. It's immense fun, and also it's a great pride to be provided with so many acquaintances. But the heat! It's 90 in my coolest room to-night after dinner, and of course that's nothing really. Next month it will be 10 degrees hotter at least. My programme is to ride from 6 to 7:30, come in and have a bath and breakfast and then straight to the office. I don't get away till Past 7 or sometimes nearly 8. Very shortly I shall begin the day an hour earlier and try to come in at 7 for dinner. I'm conscious of an unworthy rejoicing at the material comfort of existence. At Basrah one could get nothing--lived on tinned milk and butter for a year, and at last I lived without them because one grew so sick of tinned things. Here I have fresh milk and butter and sour curds every day. A bowl of sour curds is my lunch, and it's the nicest possible meal in this weather, that and a cup of Arab coffee. And then masses of roses everywhere. My duties are of the most diverse kinds. We are very shorthanded. I take on everything I can to spare Sir Percy--interview representatives of innumerable creeds, keep an open door for tribal sheikhs and messengers from the desert whose business I discover and send up in brief to Sir Percy, and then behind all this there's my real job, the gathering and sorting of information. Already the new tribal maps and tribe lists are getting into shape, and the first big batch of confidential notes on Bagdad personalities will be issued to Our Political Officers tomorrow--that's not bad going. Presently all the new surveys will begin to come in and I shall have the revision and correction of the place names, a thing I like doing because in the first place it's so nice to get them right, and in the second it teaches me so much geography. The head survey man is an enthusiast, and gives me a free hand. And then I'm going to be Curator of Antiquities or at least I'm going to show the Revenue Commissioner all the old buildings and scraps of buildings that are left here, and he has promised to keep guard over them...It's a thousand times more interesting than Basrah, you understand. To-day there arrived by miracle two charming black satin gowns from Marthe which makes me hope that my new cotton gowns may presently arrive also. I'm very badly in need of them. It's almost too hot already for unwashable clothes, even in the evening. I shall rejoice when I hear that muslin gowns are on their way...

Oh if it were as near the end in France! Is Maurice still out of it? Every time a post comes in I dread to hear that he has gone back.

[Maurice (now Colonel Bell, C.M.G.) had gone to the front in the beginning Of 19 15 in command of the 4th Battalion, Green Howards. He was invalided home the following year and then had a command in England.]

THE LETTERS OF GERTRUDE BELL

To H.B., Bagdad, May 3rd, 1917

* * * *Please will Mother have sent to me by post six pairs of thin white thread stockings, and the same of brown--rather dark brown.

The days melt like snow in the sun. But it's just as well, for I've been realising this evening that if I weren't so very busy I should be very lonely. To-day I was in the office from 8:30 to 8, and had scarcely anything to show for it by reason of the reams of odds and ends that take up all the time. I can't write any of the interesting and pre- occupying things, so you must put up with small change. I spent a couple of hours yesterday before breakfast inspecting an exquisite 14th century mosque and a tomb of the same date and seeing what repairs were immediately essential. The two learned men who dwelt in the respective mosques were my enthusiastic guides. I took the Revenue Commissioner with me, Mr. Garbett. We must have a trained architect out as soon as possible. Fortunately Mr. Storrs from Cairo (Sec. to the High Commissioner) is on his way up on a short visit. He'll give me a hand over getting out the man I want and over several other things.

The Bishop of Nagpur wants me personally to conduct him to Babylon, which I'm well qualified to do I may say! I hope the plan will materialize. I would like to go back there, though it will make my heart ache a little. They were all so kind to me, the German excava- tors, and no war can put an end to the affectionate esteem in which I hold Koldewey.

We have not got nearly enough clerks and typists, one never seems to roll the stone finally to the top of the hill--it rolls back for want of mechanical appliances. I suppose it will all straighten out in time, meanwhile it's laborious. Thank Heaven my house is finished, so that I don't have to begin the day by interviewing carpenters and brick- layers-- it was the last straw! Still on the whole, in spite of the rush and scramble, it's so deeply interesting that one doesn't bother about a straw more or less.

THE LETTERS OF GERTRUDE BELL

To F.B., Bagdad, May 11th, 1917

This week's post is drifting in--a very welcome one from Moll announcing the sending Off Of my summer clothes. The patterns are charming--it's to be hoped they'll wash. But Lord how glad I shall be to have them. my present appearance is that of a hobbledehoy in straitened circumstances who has outgrown her wardrobe--only it's my gowns which have diminished (from much washing) not I who have increased. The event of the week has been the arrival of Mr. Storrs from Egypt. He's here for a fortnight. He brings a perfect hurricane of fresh air from outside and I'm jigged if we shan't send him back on the wings of a similar storm which will blow open their eastern-facing doors and windows. An admirable plan it is having such interchanges. I've taken him round to all my religious dignitaries and learned men, Who delight in him and his Arabic also--the comfort it is to go about in the company of a Father of Tongues! Unfortunately I'm too busy to go about with him much, but such interludes are very reviving and the result is I've applied and outlined a reasonable scheme for the Government of this country--'pas dégoûté!' which I really think may be useful as something to bite upon. There's nothing like a spice of audacity.

* * * *I'm getting to be rather a dab at Arab politics--but it doesn't make them seem the easier. We've shouldered a gigantic task, but I can't see what alternative there was.

This is how I pass my days : I'm out riding before 6, sometimes through the gardens by the river bank, sometimes round the old line of the city wall, a gallop in the desert and home through the bazaars. Occasionally I inspect an ancient monument on the way back--I did so this morning. A bath and breakfast and so to the office before 9. I'm there till after 7. I have a cup of coffee and a bowl of sour curds at 12:30 and tea with Sir Percy at 4--it's the only time I peaceably see him. People drop in all day. Occasionally one has a clear hour or two--generally there's a lull between 12 and 2 and one tries to straighten out all the information one has acquired. But the end of the day finds me with two or three unfinished things and no hope of getting at them the day after. They are piling and piling up and I can't think when I shall be able to clear them off. That's the only bother--there's always just a bit too much to do. I come back to dinner in my garden at 8 and I generally go to bed at 9:30, at which time I begin to fall asleep. It's gloriously cool still but that must certainly end in a day or two.

I must tell you I love Bagdad, and the people are so outgoing-- partly propitiatory no doubt, but they are glad to have us.

To H.B., Bagdad, May 18th, 1917

...I couldn't possibly come away from here at this moment. It's an immense opportunity, just at this time when the atmosphere is so emotional; one catches hold of people as one will never do again, and establishes relations which won't dissolve. It is not for my own sake, but because it greases the wheels of administration--it really does, and I want to watch it all very carefully almost from day to day, so as to be able to take what I hope may be something like a decisive hand in final disposition. I shall be able to do that, I shall indeed, with the knowledge I'm gaining. It's so intimate. They are beyond words outgoing to me. What does anything else matter when the job is such a big one? Incidentally I may tell you--so that you won't be surprised when you see me--that this summer will turn my hair quite white. it is one of the results of this climate. However, that won't matter to gentlemen like one I had in to-day, who was so holy that he couldn't look an unveiled woman in the face! It didn't prevent him from desiring to have a long talk with me on his private affairs, and at the end I'll admit be tipped me a casual wink or two, just enough to know me again. General Wauchope has been here, Mr. Philby has come up from Amarah, he's so quick and intelligent...There never was anything quite like this before, you must understand that--it's amazing. It's the making of a new world. You see I couldn't come away. The W.O. has telegraphed for a series of signed articles on Mesop. and Asia Minor. I shall have to set about them, but it's a wide order.

I never get through my work, but that's better than having no work to get through. Only it makes my letters Scrappy. And I feel so ashamed when I get splendid screeds from You two who are just as busy. It's not really hot yet, seldom up to 100, but it must begin soon. I ride daily in the early morning on MY love of a pony, and keep fit thereby. I really must have another copy of Amurath; will you please send me one. It's in great request, there being nothing else so modern.

It is 8 o'clock, and I have been in the office uninterruptedly since 9, with 20 min. for lunch!

To H.B. and F.B., Bagdad May 26, 1917

...The post brought me a letter from Mother this week--and also, what do you think? Two muslin gowns! I hope they are swallows, so to speak, announcing all my summer clothes. But I regret to say that one of them which according to Moll's pattern was intended for me to wear in the evening was no more an evening gown than it was a fur coat, and won't do at all for that purpose. It's rather a blow, for I had a vision of some nice trailing muslin gowns with floating sleeves, and far from it. However, I shall just have not to dine out when it gets hot. It really hasn't reached that yet. We're almost through May and the breeze has never slackened. It's wonderful. Of course you would think it warm in England--it's got to 100, but that is nothing here.

[Gertrude's disappointment expressed in this letter about the evening gown is explained by the fact that the fashion in London dresses had changed and that there were no 'trailing muslin gowns with floating Sleeves.']

Mr. Storrs leaves next week. He has done us an infinite amount of good. One becomes so provincial seeing no one from outside. The great event in our circles is the arrival of Fahad Bey, paramount sheikh of the Amarat, an almighty swell and an old friend of mine. I stayed with him in the desert three years ago on my way back to Damascus. I hope that with his help we shall get a move in among the tribes. Anyhow, it's a great 'coup' getting him to burn his boats and come in to us. We had the most tenderly affectionate meeting I assure you. Now I'll tell you a sweet story. There came in a couple of old sheikhs, hopelessly ragged and very sorry for themselves, for their tribe happens to be just in the borderland and first they had been harried by the Turks and then by us, and finally making the best of a bad business, they had sought refuge with us, and we, after our truly idiotic manner, had clapped half their followers into gaol, and they couldn't find them, so they came to me and I said I would ask Sir Percy what could be done. At that they almost wept with gratitude and declared that they would forthwith send me a beautiful mare. But I said no, it was a kind thought, but I could not take presents and therewith I went down to talk to Sir Percy. When I came back I found them with their two old heads together and as soon as they saw me they said, "Khatun--if you won't take the horse we're going to send u-- a gazelle!" The gazelle hasn't materialized yet, and I rather hope it won't, for gazelles eat everything including your most important papers, but wasn't it nice of them to hit on such small change for mares. The great pleasure in this country is that I do love the people so much.

We revel in fruit here. The excellent oranges are nearly over, but the apricots have come in, in masses and small sweet greengages, and now the good little melons have begun.)next we shall have grapes and figs--truly a bountiful country. I'm. loving it, you know, loving my work and rejoicing in the confidence of my chief. One morning last week when I was out riding I paid a very early call on my way home on the son of a celebrated old warrior a Circassian whom I knew in the old days. And I found, too, a great man of letters, a native of Bagdad, who is writing leaders for me which I send to the Egyptian papers, and we sat round and sipped tea and coffee and talked and I went away feeling that I really was a part of Bagdad. You know I'm growing into it terrifically fast-- taking root; what do you think of it? I don't think I shall ever be able to detach myself permanently from the fortunes of this country. But I don't bother to look ahead. It's enough that my job is here now. But it's a wonderful thing to feel this affection and confidence of a whole people round You. There are so few of us, you see, that each one is absolutely salient and each is a focus for so many hopes and fears. But oh to be at the end of the war and to have a free hand!

To H.B. and F.B., Bagdad, June 1, 1917

Dearest Parents, I had finally to take desperate steps to cure the above mentioned cold. I lay flat on a bed in a draught in my nice cool room in the office for 3 days and saw no one, and curious as the treatment seems it has now restored me to rude health. I told You about Fahad Bey, didn't I. We had a conference with him one morning, in which he ended by describing the powerful effect produced by a letter from me last autumn--I wrote to him from Basrah. "I summoned my sheikhs" he wound up (I feeling more and more of a person as he proceeded) "I read them your letter and I said to them, Oh Sheikhs,"-- we hung upon his words--" This is a woman--what must the men be like!" This delicious peroration restored me to my true place in the twinkling of an eye. We took him to see an exhibition of flying yesterday to his immense delight. He said he had never enjoyed anything so much. He even ventured into an aeroplane--so that he might tell the Arabs, he explained; but once there he turned to me anxiously and said "Don't let it go away!"

Oh my dearest ones it's so wonderful here--I can't tell you how much I'm loving it.

To H.B., Bagdad, June 8, 1917

I must write to you because I've been reading with profit your papers on dumping and the future of trade. The former appears to me to be unanswerable and the latter both brilliant and moderate. My compliments.

I'm completely recovered--no further bulletins will be issued. But I've retained the excellent habit of sleeping for an hour after lunch, which, though a terrible waste of time, brings a remarkable increase of energy. I'm busy at spare moments with the W.O. articles of which I told you. I've written 4 and I think they will run to 7. It's no light task in the midst of so many other things. They are as good a plea as I can make for the Arab race and I want people to listen. Frankly, who knows if I don't? Life has been 'égayée' by the coming of a harmless old lunatic from the Syrian side of the desert. The motive of his journey was as follows: he met in the desert a woman of stupendous stature and luminous countenance. On being questioned she declared that she was the sun, but this reply did not, apparently, satisfy our friend and pressing her further she admitted that she was the British Government. Thereat he resolved to come straight to Kokus (Sir Percy Cox) seeking the sun, as he reasonably explained.

The word Kokus is rapidly passing into the Arabic language, not as a name but as a title. You are a Kokus, just as once upon a time you were a Chosroes or a Pharaoh. I'm currently described as a Koku-sah, i.e., a female Chosroes. Isn't it delicious!

THE LETTERS OF GERTRUDE BELL

To F.B., June, 1917

I've been dining out frequently. Sir Percy and I dined with General Cobbe. Next evening I dined with General Gunning. The matron of the hospitals was of the party, a nice woman. And it's so pleasant to meet a woman. My chief female friend is the Mother Superior of the Dominican Convent, a charming French woman from Touraine. She comes in often to the office to see me on business of one sort and another, and I have often, to my great pleasure, been able to help her. It's something to be a " Kokusah " you see. Last night--to continue--I dined with the head of the police, Major Gregson, and spent the evening talking to a General called Edwardes. Let me announce to you the arrival of 2 charming hats-- for which many thanks to Moll-your chiffon veils, brown stockings. Of the gowns 2 arrived a fortnight ago and no more since.

The gazelle has materialized and now inhabits my garden. It lives chiefly on the little wizened dates which fall at this season from the unripe bunches on my date trees, and on cucumbers both Of which for a child of the desert must be acquired taste. But it seems to flourish on them. It is a darling little animal. I'm on the look out now for a mongoose.

To F.B., Bagdad, June 22nd, 1917

Ramadhan began last night and everyone is fasting. We keep Ramadhan in state here with big guns at sunset and an hour before dawn. I was awakened to-day by the latter. It is to warn people that they must hasten with their last possible meal. And as I lay wondering over it all I was aware of a bright light through my garden. I sleep on the roof of My central Summer House, and looked up to see a blazing palm leaf fire in the still hot air near my gardener's tent. It was his wife cooking the last meal which must be eaten while it is light enough to distinguish a white thread from a black. Strange isn't it? to be so much in the midst of it all--strange and delightful for I love it.

It has become to me more than a second home now--it's a new life a new possibility of carrying on existence. Only I'm afraid of my personal perspective melting. I'm so flattered, so absurdly over-estimated by my chiefs in England by my colleagues, and of course the

Arabs.--If I become too egregious do call me smartly to attention. It is so immensely difficult to preserve the values...

The sand flies are outrageous to-night. I stop in every sentence to engage them in mortal combat but they carry out a strategic retirement after inflicting some casualties. The flying ants are as numerous but they don't bite Heaven be praised. Still I hate the way they cock their tails in the air.

No more muslin gowns! I have telegraphed to Basrah to make enquiries.

To H.B., Bagdad, June 29th, 1917

All my colleagues are enchanting to work with--they make our collaboration delightful, and best of all is Sir Percy's kindness and consideration. He treats me with what I can only describe as an absurd indulgence. Anything that I want done--anything reasonable--he puts at once into execution. This week, really to please me he has rushed through this arrangement for a local Arabic newspaper for which we have all been longing. We have been held up till now for lack of paper, but it would have dawdled on through many official stages but for my great desire for it. Mr. Philby is official editor and my principal friends in Bagdad, Arab friends, have posts on the staff, and we bring out this first number with a flourish of trumpets on July 1st. We are going to make a great splash. It is called The Arab because it is the first paper published under the new order of Arab liberty. I have, as indeed I ought to have, with the opportunities I am given, a growing sense of mastery in my own work, of familiarity with country people and conditions which is very enjoyable.

There is always an immense amount to learn, but one knows how to learn which is the main thing.

To F.B., June 30th, 1917

May I ask you to oblige very kindly with 4 shirts? 'Crèpe de chine' if you please, 2 ivory and two pink. I enclose some advertisements of Harrods which look nice, specially the cross one.

I should also be very grateful if Lizzie could find and post me a green silk woven jacket thing with silver buttons.

To H.B. and F.B., July 6th, 1917

I have no letters from you as yet by this mail, but Oh my parents, everything is blotted out by the fact that I have two muslin gowns from the L.S.C. Now isn't that great? I was beginning to wonder what I should do and whether I should ask the nuns to make me some clothes and one really hasn't energy to bother about these things now, for its damned hot. I can't conceal it from you. I'll try not to repeat that observation. You may take it as a marginal note passim in my letters for the next two months. I've been very unsociable this week for I've been writing--I have written my five articles on Turkey after dinner. I can't well get the time by day for these things in the press of other work. I've been arranging and getting out the mass of tribal stuff collected since I've been here and have now got all the tribes to the N. and N.E. alphabetically tabled and beautifully typed in many copies for Members and all generals with whom I'm friends. It's really a great work and most useful--to judge by the use we make of It at our office, and I'm busy with this huge confusion of the Euphrates tribes I hope to have reduced to a similar order by the end of next week. I've seen every Sheikh when he has come in to Pay his respects to Sir Percy and got this information about his tribe direct from him so that this body of stuff I have is not a bad beginning...I don't know whether it is a scientific truth but its undoubtedly in accordance with facts--full moon nights are by far the hottest and the stillest. Two nights ago I was completely defeated. I tried to work sitting outside in my garden after dinner, but after half an hour the few clothes I was wearing were wringing wet and I so much exhausted by a day similarly spent that I went to bed helplessly and fell asleep at once on my roof. I hadn't been asleep long when I woke up to find the Great Bear staring me in the face. I lie looking north. It was very strange to see the Great Bear shining so brilliantly in the full moon of Ramadhan and while I wondered half asleep what had happened I realized that the whole world was dark, and turning round saw the last limb of the moon disappearing in a total eclipse. So I lay watching it, a wonderful sight the disc just visible, a dull and angry copper colour. In the bazaar a few hundred yards away everyone was drumming with sticks on anything that lay handy, to scare away the devil which hid the moon, and indeed they ultimately succeeded, for after a long, long time the upper limb of the

363

moon re-appeared and the devil drew slowly downwards, angry still with deep red tongues, and wreaths projecting from his copper coloured body and before I had time to sleep again the Ramadhan moon had once more extinguished the shining of the Bear.

But as for people who read of these things in their almanacs and know to a minute when to expect them, I think nothing of them and their educated sensations.

We've got our treaty settled with my friend Fahad of the Anazeh.

To H.B., Bagdad, July 13th, 1917

We have had a week of fierce heat which still continues, temperature 122 odd and therewith a burning wind which has to be felt to be believed. It usually blows all night as well as all day and makes sleep very difficult. I have invented a scheme which I practise on the worst nights. I drop a sheet in water and without wringing it out lay it in a pile along my bed between me and the wind. I put one end over my feet and draw the other under and over my head and leave the rest a few inches from my body. The sharp evaporation makes it icy cold and interposes a little wall of cold air between me and the fierce wind. When it dries I wake up and repeat the process. This evening Sir Percy and I went out motoring at 7 but it was too hot. The wind shrivelled you and burnt your eyeballs. They say it does not last very long like this-- inshallah! at last the sand-flies have given up the ghost. Also you get an immense satisfaction out of iced lime juice and soda, usually rather an anaemic drink. There is a pleasant hour just after dawn when I usually ride. My room in the office I shut up all day long and have it sluiced out with water two or three times a day. By these means I keep the temperature just under 100. Yes, that's what it is like.

To H.B., Bagdad, July 20th, 1917

I shall undoubtedly revert to the weather, so I may as well begin with it. We've not had the temperature under 116 by day for a fortnight. At night it drops to 82 just for the dawn hour. My room at the office is 99 all day, by dint of keeping it hermetically shut. Yesterday I went in the evening to one of the big hospitals, to see General

Gunning. I went into the first ward to ask my way. It happened to be the ward where they treated the acute heat stroke cases, men with a temperature of 109 and 110--the latter don't often live. You don't consciously suffer with fever like that, but it is awful to see and hear. Today there hasn't been a flicker of air. Mr. Philby and I motored a little after sunset --the dust hung in the streets like a dense fog, and in the desert it lay in Mysterious wreaths, marking, I Suppose, the track of some motor or cart. People here say they haven't had such a burst of heat as we had last week since 1882, but now I imagine, it's normal, and we have six weeks more of it to wear through. Well! ...

There came in the other day a tribesman who had been my guide on the last four days into Najaf when I came up from Hayil. They were the worst days of all the road, and he served me well. He is a grave silent man, well known in the desert. Twice to my knowledge he saved me from being stripped to the skin--on one occasion, though accursed of their two parents, the Iraq tribes had surrounded my caravan and couched the camels before they saw him. On his rebuke they left us. I had sent word to him that I was here and bidden him to come. Besides the usual present from Sir Percy which they all get when they come for the first time, I gave him Rs. 100, and clothed him. He stood solemnly while I flung round him a thick cloak, heavily woven with gold--such wear in this heat!--and draped an orange coloured silk kerchief over his head. I owed him a costume in return for that which remained on my back thanks to him. Another nice thing happened this week. One of my Damascenes who came down with me to Nejd, has turned up here. He heard I was at Basrah, " and I come to your service," he said. Sir Percy is delighted to have him; we shall put him to use.

The hot silence has been broken by 20 big gun shots, which announce the end of Ramadhan. Even I hear them with thankfulness. It has been oppressive to think of people thirsting through these long days.

A Reuter says that Edwin has gone to the India Office. It's splendid. He will be my chief, you realize. Won't that be fun. I wish you would go and see Sir A. Hertzel, the Permanent Under--Secretary. He is a friend of mine, and an ally.

THE LETTERS OF GERTRUDE BELL

To H.B., Bagdad, July 27, 1917

Another week--it's less hot. I don't think we're likely to have a second bout such as we've had. It has caused as many casualties as a battle and what is tantamount to another breakdown in the hospital arrangements. I have a long letter from Beatrice [Lady Brownrigg]--will you please thank her for it if you're seeing her...I can't pick up the thread where I dropped it two and a half years ago; I can't. And it becomes more, not less difficult. Oh if one could look forward and see a time when thought should stop, and memory, and consciousness, I'm so tired of struggling on alone.

Still I'll do it, as you know. At least it's easier here than in England.

On the feast day after Ramadhan Sir Percy and I paid the Naqib a congratulatory visit. Our personal relations with him are useful as well as pleasant. Sir Percy is so charming with the people of the country, grave and kind and attentive. I don't wonder they respect and trust him. He never himself realizes how strong his personal hold is, but we count it one of our best assets. The satisfaction that it is to work for a Chief who is always at the height of the situation ...

I paid another before breakfast call yesterday, on the Jamil Zadah family, some of my oldest friends here. They are landowners, very rich, upright, honest people, staunchly pro-English. Their friendship is worth having. I sat for a long time talking to Abdul Rahman Effendi, the head of the house, --and then with him and his wife and sisters whom I also visited--I knew them before--and came away with a warm sense of cordial and even affectionate companionship. It's when one gets that that one gets the best that can be had. Abdul Rahman's friendship takes also an agreeably tangible expression! He sends in weekly a great basket of fruit from his estate--at this season it's filled with huge white grapes.

Oh and more muslin gowns came last week:--a red letter week! That makes 7.

To H.B., Bagdad, August 3, 1917

I must tell you I've been on the sick list this week and am not off it yet. Having survived the heat I caught cold with the first chill morning and a cold in this country reduces me at once to a state of maddening and unconquerable feebleness. It's no good forgetting it; -- one has to knock under. So for 4 days I've done absolutely nothing and am still much as before, confound it. But the first day when I was lying in my comparatively cool room in the office and cursing, in came Col. Willcox to pay me a friendly call--I could have embraced him, his visit was so Opportune. So now he comes regularly to see if I have pneumonia or consumption--but I never have. Well, he told me some interesting things about the heat wave and its consequences. (It began on July 10 quite suddenly with a temperature of 112 and ended on July 20 with a temperature of 122.8. In between it was frequently over 120. He notes that 115 is the limit of human endurance. The moment the temp. rises above that point, heat strokes begin, and when it drops below, they end. We could have saved many lives if after the crisis was over there had been any cool place to put the men in. But there wasn't and after fighting through the heatstroke they died of heat exhaustion. I suppose if we had had masses of ice we could have made cool places, but ice was lacking. It happened once or twice that we well people went without it because the hospitals needed all there was. I don't think I shall stay through the whole of next hot weather unless there is any very strong reason for it. I shall come to England for a month and return in September. But who knows what we shall be all doing by then. I don't believe we shall still be fighting. Some way or other peace will have to come about.

To H.B., Bagdad, August 10, 1917

I've had rather a slack week getting gradually better and I now consider that I'm returned fit for duty...

The worst of the extreme physical weariness which is apt to attack one in this climate is the mental weariness, not to say desperation, which accompanies it. You feel as if you never again would lift a finger without exhaustion and for all the iron and arsenic you are taking three times a day you're persuaded you'll not get well--not that you want to get well, far from it. However I hope I'm through it now for the moment. ...

The thermometer rarely goes much over 110 and is sometimes below that.

The truth is that we are living in a rather exasperated state, concerning which I refer you to Edwin, to whom I have just been writing a long letter on Mesopotamian economics.

I've invested in a cock and four hens, for to lay me eggs, but so far without any very marked success. They don't lay many more eggs than my gazelle, or to be exact they've laid exactly one more. I never liked hens and I'm contemplating the conversion of these into roast chicken. On the other hand the dates in my garden are ripe and very good. The fresh date is a thing apart.

To H.B., Bagdad, August 31st, 1917

I am coming out of hospital to-morrow. I am perfectly sound but very slack. I don't suppose I shall be much better till the weather begins to cool down, which it ought to do in the latter half of Sep. It is still damnably hot.

There have been some very good articles in the Spectator lately on War Economies, sound common sense about attempts to fix prices and regulate markets. Will you tell St. Loe [Strachey] if you see him that I've found them most useful as propaganda. Every economic mistake that could be made has been made here, with the result that all trade is at a standstill and food prices have quadrupled. I turned up a document the other day in which one of these announced blandly that he felt no anxiety at the rise in the cost of living, because nothing would be easier at any moment than to fix a maximum price. As a cure for scarcity. I ask you! Doesn't it rouse 'Nôhnisch' laughter.

To H.B., Bagdad, September 3, 1917

I didn't go to Samarra after all, Doom struck out, as the poet says, like a blind camel and he caught me straight and full. For with my box and bedding packed, my dinner almost carried to General

Lubbock's hospitable board--I was going to dine with the Father of Railways On my way to the train--I began to feel curiouser and curiouser and anyhow very certain that I had fever. And then Col. Willcox drifted in (Providence always directs the angelic man to my door just when I want him) took my temperature and shattered my Plans --I held out for two miserable days in my own house, too achy and above all too headachy to stir, and then came into hospital with a temperature Of 102. Sandfly fever. Everyone has it. I don't know how I've escaped it so long. They don't know what it is really; they haven't caught its microbe yet. But you get your money's worth out of it, if only from the intolerable headache. Quinine is no good. They give you febrifuges and phenacetin and feed you only on slops, all of which things being unfit, so to speak, for human consumption, you find yourself pretty ragged when at last the devil thing goes.

I'm really over the thing--its gone. But there's no doubt I shall feel cheap for a bit and as soon as I can I shall go away for a fortnight. Col. Willcox is very keen that I should do this and I think it will be salvation. Its so beautifully cool now that one can go any-where. They are extremely kind to me in this hospital. They treat me as if I were a Major General.

Damnable as sandfly fever is it isn't a matter for the smallest anxiety so please feel none, you and Mother. I feel ashamed of behaving like this.

To F.B., Bagdad, September 6, 1917

There's one thing I forgot to answer in some old letters from you and Father. Please, please don't supply information about me or photographs of me to newspaper correspondents. I've said this so often before that I thought you understood how much I hate the whole advertisement business. I always throw all letters (fortunately they're not many in number) asking for an interview or a photograph straight into the waste paper basket and I beg you to do the same on my behalf...

I've been five days out of hospital and I feel much better though still rather weak in the knees and imbecile in the mind. But another day or two will put me right. My quiet leave hasn't been quite as peaceful as might have been wished for the second night after my

return I found a large wasp in my bed. I found him by the simple process of lying on him, upon which he retorted after his kind. The next
night when I came back from the office I went to look at my pony and
found him having a bad fit of colic. We had some restless hours doctoring him and walking him about, and finally he recovered.

It's still very hot, but the temperature is falling, though very
slowly. The nights are quite pleasant, but in the middle of the afternoon it's usually about 112. I won't deny that when you come to
September here you feel you've reached about the limit of human endurance. I shan't stay through the whole of next summer.

To H.B., Bagdad, September 15, 1917

I've got a day out with the week and find suddenly that it is
Saturday morning and mail day instead of Friday as I fondly hoped.
Fortunately the most important letter--to Bridget [Richmond)--I wrote
last night. I asked the kind Red X Commissioner, Major Stanley, about
your launch. He says it is the best on the river, never sick or sorry. I
went to a party this week--the first party I've been to since Delhi.
There was a regatta on the Tigris and G.H.Q. entertained us all at tea. I
think, by the way, I was one of the hosts, since we're included in G.H
*Q. I didn't see much of the regatta because there was a glaring sun an
the river, even at 5 p.m. but I sat under an awning and talked to all the
Major Generals and felt that I was seeing life. It resulted in my going
to tea next day with General Marshall, he commands the 3rd Corps, a
very interesting man whom I had just met as he passed through Basrah
last summer and hadn't seen since. I went to see some carpets and
china which he had bought, very pretty and I should think one or two
of the rugs very good, but I know less and less about rugs I find. He is
coming to see two of mine which are also rather pretty. But I no longer
buy any on account of the War Loan--that was a little burst when I
came to Bagdad. It's really getting cooler; my room at the Office is
never above 91 and these last two days I haven't needed a punkah till
10 O'clock. Its so blessed. Apropos of the Red X I can't tell you how
beneficent they are here. I get my money's worth--or yours--out of
them, for Major Stanley is always supplementing my needs with various odds and ends otherwise unprocurable. However, as I served them
for a whole year I feel less reluctance in sponging on them for comforts. I'm much better, almost quite well. Its time too. This country is a
desperate place for recovering from anything. You go staggering on

feeling like a worm long after there has ceased being anything the matter with you. But its all the more pleasurable when at last the worm begins to turn.

To H.B., Bagdad, September 21, 1917

We are having deliciously cool weather, between 70 and 80 and quite cold at night. I want nothing better but I think the moment of sudden transition is rather trying even if it is enjoyable. One doesn't know how to adapt oneself at first. I had an afternoon out this week-- General Cobbe and I went to Kadhimain, 2 or 3 miles above Bagdad, a sheikh town with a very sacred mosque. I remember last time I was there, in 1909 it must have been, how I hurried past the gateway of the mosque with a sidelong glance into the courtyard. Turbaned gentlemen did us the honours and escorted us well within the gates to the very edge of the courtyard. Except as an unexampled privilege there wasn't much in it, for it's all the worst modern work, gimcrack and hideous, with tiles 30 years old already peeling from the walls and no loss either. Nevertheless I was vastly entertained, having been nowhere since I came to Bagdad.

Kermit Roosevelt turned up this week with letters of introduction to me and to Sir Percy. We both liked him--a very pleasant creature, quite unostentatious. He is serving here as an engineer and has three brothers in the American army in France. They are doing their bit, aren't they? I still dine out of doors, but I sit indoors afterwards, with all doors and windows open. It's most pleasant. I'm longing to begin riding again and indeed I did begin a few days ago, but it wasn't a great success--I felt too tired afterwards. So I shall be very prudent and wait a little longer. It isn't a time of year to play pranks; nearly every one has little goes of fever when the heat begins to drop. I've escaped that luckily. My dear love to all my family. I write indifferently to you and Mother as the letters are equally to you both.

To F.B., Bagdad, September 25, 1917

I'm writing this week because I'm going to Samarra for a day or two. It will be very nice and I think it will do me good for I've not been very flourishing this last month since I came out of hospital and it will be a pleasant change of air and scene. I haven't stirred out of Bagdad since I got here in April. But its amazing how unmonotonous it has been. ...

To think that I've been nearly two years without a maid! but I'm exceedingly tidy, thanks to your good supply of clothes. Oh would you please send me a pair of plain tortoiseshell combs. There's a lizard walking about my walk and catching, I suppose, sand flies. God prolong its existence!

To H.B. and F.B., Bagdad, October 12, 1917

I'm better and going to-morrow to the Convalescent Hospital, a mile down stream from Bagdad...

Maurice doesn't sound very flourishing, which worries me. I do hope he'll come back to R'ton now to set about his own work. Its very difficult not to feel a growing depression. Perhaps I'm rather influenced by being so slack still and certainly the last two months have been horrid. However I expect the winter will set me right and I shan't stay here all through next summer, war or no war. It wouldn't be profitable. -

I can match you at food--we've had no butter all the summer and when we have it its turned and I would rather be without it. I've forgotten what potatoes taste like--the meat is almost too tough to eat., chickens ditto milk turned--how sick one gets of it! Bread I never eat what one gets is fairly good, quite good indeed, but that doesn't affect me--much. Its all right when one's well, but when one's feeling rather a poor thing one does hate it all.

Well,--well--I daresay I'll write from Samarra in a different key.

To H.B. and F.B., October 18th, 1917

Yesterday came your telegram through Admiral Hall enquiring after my health. I'm afraid you will be rather agitated when you come to hear that I've been ill again which I haven't told you in my present reply. But I'm now very nearly well of my fever which I don't suppose I should have had if I hadn't been rather run down before. I've been for the last 6 days at the Convalescent Hospital, a delicious place on the river about 2 miles below Bagdad. They have taken immense care of me and I've got well with great rapidity. In 3 days' time I'm going up to Samarra for a week to stay with Gen. Cobbe. I hope to return in far more flourishing health than I've been since August and since the cold weather is now definitely beginning and the winter climate is delicious I'm as well here as anywhere. Whatever happens I shall not stay here all through next hot weather. I spend my days very peacefully, breakfasting in bed, reading and doing a little work afterwards. I spent this morning in Bagdad getting warmer clothes from my house and doing various odd jobs. The mail had just come in. Bless you both. I can't tell you what it is to have your love and sympathy always with me...

I might be able to see Mrs. Taggart's grandson if he's at Bagdad. I'll try anyhow.

[Mrs. Taggart was a woman at the Clarence ironworks, a very old friend.]

It's bad hearing that there's no more parcel post to Mesop. You don't seem to be aware--indeed I only knew of it by letters of congratulation received this mail from Sir Reginald Wingate and others--that I'm a C.B.E. I am, however. Its rather absurd...

I have a delightful letter from Beatrice Chamberlain which I really must answer, but time is too short this week.

To H.B., Bagdad, October 18th, 1917

You know your friendship is more to me than anything. What a thing it is to be able to talk of friendship with one's parents. Those who haven't got it don't know what it means.

I'm much better. Even after my racketty morning at Bagdad I don't feel a bit tired, and I've been writing letters all this afternoon. But oh, I do long to be back at work! However, I'll be patient this time and take the Samarra time to get really well in.

To F.B., Bagdad, October 26th, 1917

Thank you for your congratulations--I don't really care a button about these things. As for Samarra, I've no luck with it, for just as I was starting--actually stepping into the launch to go and dine--with General Lubbock on my way to the station, came a telegram from General Cobbe putting me off. Turks had heaved into sight and there was a possibility of active operations. They've since heaved out of it again, and I may after all go up presently, but I've ceased to believe it. I'm very much enjoying being back in the office though I'm not much more than a half timer as yet. Still I'm getting better every day. The weather is delicious but it is extraordinary how one feels the cold. My room at the office is now under 70, but after sunset I sit wrapped up in a thick coat and add to it a woollen comforter to walk home in. It's a way the human frame has of showing resentment for having been called upon to endure a temperature of 122. I find that this is the season for gardening operations; I've some vegetables, peas, lettuce, onions and a local sort of mustard and cress--the latter I've not only sown but eaten. And in order not to be too utilitarian, I've bought 7 Pots of geraniums and 4 Of carnations besides sowing carnations and eschscholtzia. I wish I had snapdragon seeds. A clump of chrysanthemums is coming into bloom, and my rose trees are flowering. Everything comes to life when the summer is over, even the washed out European. And one forgets at once how infernal it was. I hope my bijou residence won't prove too damp in winter; it's so nice being quite away by oneself. Anyhow it's particularly pleasant now.

The shirts haven't arrived but I expect they'll turn up and I've enough to go on with for the moment. And oh I'm so sorry to bother you, but would you send me 8 pairs of white thread stockings--they will go by letter post at the worst, and they'll arrive just about the time the warm weather begins again. Those I have are worn out beyond mending.

To H.B., Bagdad, November 2, 1917

You sent me a lot of interesting pieces which I read with much satisfaction and agreement. I always feel when I read your works such an admiration for your style as well as your matter. Its so lucid and so pointed, so entirely unstrained. I hand on some of your works to Sir

Percy who reads them with grave attention, not unmixed with surprise. It is all new to him.

For my part I'm quite well. I've even taken to riding again of an early morning, with great profit to my health and spirits. It's ideal now at that hour. The sting has gone out of the sun which has become a cheerful and companionable luminary. Samarra is off for the present...

We have now got a judicial Officer, Mr. [now Sir Edgar] Bonham Carter from the Sudan. A highly trained man with a very level head is just what we want and I do welcome him sincerely.

To H.B., Bagdad, November 9th, 1917

No mail as yet this week. Happy to tell you I'm much better and have felt to-day quite a zest in life--for the first time. Partly, I think, because yesterday I spent the whole day, nearly, out-of-doors, for Sir Percy and I motored to Baquba. It was 6 years since I went along that road--I say 6 years because it was in 19 11, but really it's a lifetime-- when I was on my way to plan Rasawan palaces at Qasr-i-Shirin, over the Persian frontier. I remember it as a long and tedious day's ride; we did it yesterday in 2 hours. It's 32 miles of bumpy desert road. Baquba is a nice little place set in palm gardens and olive groves on the Diala. I looked at my camping ground near by the river bank and tried to remember the sort of person who pitched tents there, but I couldn't. I hadn't been out of Bagdad since April, nor Sir Percy since March, So you think what a pleasant sense of irresponsible holiday it gave both of us. I only wished we could have gone on further. I am beginning some nice new jobs. One is the taking over of the editorship of Al Arab, the vernacular paper we publish. I'm full of schemes for making it more alive by provincial correspondents and a local news-writer. I feel certain my public will take more interest in hearing that Ibu so and so was fined for being out without a lantern after dark than in the news that an obscure village in Flanders has been bombed. PPère Anastase, the sub-editor comes weekly to read our leading articles, which I censor. He's an Arab from the Lebanon, straight out of Chaucer --all the same; very learned in his own tongue, he speaks and writes French like a Frenchman...

In my garden there's the most gorgeous mud pie I've ever been privileged to see. It's not, however, for frivolous persons; we're busy mending my roofs against the rainy season, and mud is what you do it with. I'm credibly informed that when there's a high flood my garden is under water and that objects from the house I inhabit have been observed to float down the neighbouring street. It's a gloomy thought. I don't know whether to wish for a dry season for my comfort, or to hope for the rain which is essential for our next harvest. If I'm obliged to move out I shall no doubt manage to get a lodging for the necessary two months. Sir Percy would put me up, In any case, but I do very much prefer living alone. It's a comfort to get away from the Office and think of other things which it is morally impossible to do if you remain in the Place you've worked in all day.

To F.B., Bagdad, November 15th, 1917

You all sound over-strained. I don't know how you can be anything else. You know we are out of that atmosphere here; I Often feel ashamed of escaping it, but it is so. There are not the Perplexities and the worries that assail you in England, and then the work is all of one kind and runs naturally along its Own groove.

I have quite recovered and have polished off a lot of things that had got into arrears. We have all moved into winter quarters in the Office, out of dark, cold rooms into sunny ones. It is strange to welcome the sun again. My room is charming, warm and comfortable, with some delightful rugs which I've bought here on the floor, and all the new maps of Mesopotamia pinned up on the walls. Maps are my passion; I like to see the world with which I'm dealing, and everyone comes round to my room for geography.

To F.B., Samarra, November22nd, 1917

I wrote to you last week the day before I was to come up here with the I.G.C. We all dined that evening with Col. Dixon, the Director of Local Resources; the C. in C. was to have been there also but sent a message at the last moment to say he wasn't well. At the beginning of dinner Colonel Willcox was called away--an urgent case of illness, it didn't occur to anyone to ask who it was. Next morning before breakfast the I.G.C. came to my house and said that our departure must be postponed, the C. in C. was dangerously ill of cholera and was not expected to live. I flew round to Sir Percy--it was still very early--and found that he had not yet been informed. It was almost incredible to us all. There had been a little cholera in the town for some weeks past, nothing very serious but very widely distributed. There were a few cases among the troops and one officer had died last week. We had all been inoculated and thought no more about it. Certainly the last person likely to fall a victim was the C. in C. who saw no Arabs and scarcely ever went into the town. He had been at the entertainment at the Jewish school the night before, but we all went there, drank coffee and ate cakes and no one else was any the worse. So there it was--where he got the infection it is impossible to say. He rallied in the afternoon and was distinctly better next morning, well enough to receive a telegram from his wife and dictate an answer. Then his heart failed, he became unconscious and died in the evening. The I.G.C. came in after dinner and told me. It has had for him a tragic ending, the conquest of Bagdad, and yet how fortunate it is when the man dies before the name. There is a splendid sentence in Ammianus's Marcellinus history of that other conqueror who was mortally wounded, N.E. of Ctesiphon,--the Emperor Julian, and "praised the Almighty God that he should die in the midst of glory fairly earned." General Maude was, I should think, a greater Commander, but the epitaph might be his ...

...It's a wonderfully picturesque little walled town with the golden dome of the shrine closing the vista, incongruously enough, in the narrow tumble-down streets...

Oh, there is such a good smell of rain--the first rain, this dry year, since February. If only we have a good plash of it, it will mean a good harvest next spring. An early rain is the most important thing in this country; it sets all the desert growing and starts cultivation--the people can't begin to plough till it comes.

To her family, Samarra, November 30th, 1917

I'm still here though I wanted to go back a day or two ago. The Corps Commander (my kind host) insisted however on my staying till the end of the week to "complete the cure." I'm really most briskly well and longing to get back to work. I'm going back to Bagdad the day after to- morrow. Col. Willcox came up this morning for a change (it's looked upon as a health resort, Samarra) and brought me a bag of letters. I was rather pining for news of you. It's a great comfort to think of Maurice back at home but what with household and industrial difficulties, present or ahead, you don't any of you seem to be having an easy time. We score over you now in weather--day after day of bright sun and exhilarating N. wind. It's perfect and in this empty desert one gets the best Of its advantages. I've been out all day, usually riding the whole morning and motoring somewhere in the afternoon--if you can call it somewhere when it's just desert with the scoring of old canals and mounds of dead villages far out in what is now uninhabited wilderness. It's almost impossible to picture what the country must have been like when it was irrigated by loop canals from the Tigris and (to judge by the village mounds) thickly peopled ten miles out on either bank of the river. It is now cultivated only in the low ground by the river edge, a mile, perhaps, deep on one bank or another, but after last week's rain (we had 18 hours of it) the people are all busily ploughing and the turned up earth looks a live brown instead of a sandy yellow.

To F.B., Bagdad, Office of the C.C., December 7th, 1917

I wish to announce the arrival of 6 pairs of white and ditto of brown stockings which I found here when I got back a week ago...

I was very glad to get back. I plunged at once into a mass of accumulated work and have scarcely lifted my eyes from maps and files. But the pleasure of being well and able to work the whole day long! The truth is that one can't do without that narcotic. To be idle means having time to think and no thoughts are bearable...

The new régime promises well. I haven't seen General Marshall since I came back but he gives signs of being sympathetic towards our side of the game. It's as well, for we were running fast on to rocks, in my opinion. We are now in the middle of operations on our R. flank which seem to have been very successful so far, and that's very encouraging too, though I don't believe we can accomplish anything very dramatic while the Turk holds off as far as he can. The presence of an enemy is an essential element in battle. And we can't walk after him indefinitely because an army walks on its stomach. Vigorous steps have been taken to ensure a good harvest next spring-- but that is not till the middle of April and meantime we are going to be hard put to it to get the civil population fed. This morning I was riding in the desert, out on the Diala road, when I met Arabs from the Diala bringing in donkey loads of brushwood to sell. As soon as I had opened the conversation with a God- save-you they began to tell me how hungry they were out there, and I to explain what we were doing to bring the hunger to an end. I expect they don't usually live in the lap of luxury, those mean tribes on the Diala river, but with prices what they are they must be well pinched this year. We had a very bad harvest this year, what with lack of rain and neglect of canals. They are all being dug out now, seed corn distributed and advances given in money. But it is a big job. To-night it's warm and windy, we might have rain.

My dear pony which I bought up from Basrah is lame. But kind Captain Lupton, who is at the Remounts, has let me send it up to be blistered and meantime he has let me have a charming little mare, a little pocket mare which I feel sure would be up to nobody's weight but my diminished stones, so I'm harming no one. But what she lacks in height she makes up in spirit and we had a delightful gallop this morning out on the Diala road--road, I call it but it's just desert--with the sun rising and a Warm wind in our face. It's everything to see a little of the world outside of a morning I see plenty of the world inside--a succession of callers all with some axe or another to grind and one's task generally being to remove the grindstone gently out of their reach!

To - , Bagdad, December 13th, 1917

...My only news of the outer world is derived from the egregious Reuter and that not good, and one begins to consider what the end will be. Till the Americans can bring in great reinforcements--and can they across all the seas?--it's clear that we shall be put to it to hold our own. It's like the first year of the war over again. Well, it's no good guessing, and we know too little even to guess. Here War is at an end, but administration goes on apace. We are taking hold of the Euphrates valley to the S.W. and getting into lands unmapped and tribes little known. I want to go down there at the end of the month. Meantime I'm puzzling over Euphrates geography and writing a sketch of it as best I can. It's the sort of job which is almost impossible to do in the Office, where one is constantly interrupted, and I generally bring home books and maps and work at it after dinner. The days fly and the weeks hurry after them; it's terrible to think that we're nearly at midwinter. The desired rain hasn't come but we have had a week of delicious cold. The water basin in the middle of my garden has been iced over the last two mornings. It's amazingly invigorating. Yesterday I was out in the desert at dawn in a frosty air which was quite delicious, even though I came in after nearly an hour's brisk riding, with numb hands and feet. I went one afternoon to see the Remount establishment outside the town. Capt. Lupton presides over it. A clearing place with the horses playing about in great paddocks under the palm trees, and a model farm attached where they grow their own maize and barley and vegetables. Capt. Lupton offered me a very handsome Arab mare if the General (Holdsworth) consented. I met the latter next day in the Street and he approved the suggestion. So, in the official phrase, I'm issued with her--Heaven prosper me for writing such horrible English.

To - , Bagdad, December 21st, 1917

Bagdad, and, indeed, most of Mesopotamia is immobilized by mud. My daily walk to and from the office is a real feat of gymnastics, but, as I stumble and reel through the swamp which was once a road, I return thanks for the rain which has gone far to assure next year's harvest. We had about 24 hours of it. I woke after the first night to find my garden a lake, from which emerged a few islands, but I had been provident enough to construct a brick causeway between my bedroom and sitting room--they are at opposite ends of the garden--and along it I was able to get to breakfast high and dry. The water has vanished today and a smoothly hard bed of mud remains. I'm rather disgusted to see in Army Reuter Orders that on the days when we thought the weather so shockingly cold the max. temp. was never below 52. One loses all sense of proportion about climate.

The new régime has ordered the Force to take a holiday on Sunday afternoon, and in obedience to their decree I dragged Sir Percy out riding last Sunday. The immortal baked clay preserves the trace of human habitation when all else has returned to the dust it was; as soon as the canal dries up, the village is deserted, the roaming Arab pulls out the roof beams and breaks up the doors for firewood, the mud walls disintegrate and nothing remains but the imperishable pot. You may break him up as much as you choose, but unless you take a hammer to him and reduce him systematically to powder, he will continue to bear witness to the household which he served. Usually this rough peasant pottery is undatable; you know it isn't of yesterday, however, when you find masses of it in places which have not been irrigated for the last 400 years.

To H.B., Bagdad, December 29, 1917

I am very glad to hear that Maurice is better and congratulate Mother on her pleasant nights with Zeppelins...On Xmas Day I dined with General Stuart Wortley, a Ladies' Dinner, the other guests being matrons and nurses, a quite agreeable evening, but I've crept, on the whole, into a very long shell and seldom care to be pricked out of it by anybody's pin. Also I've got a temporary (let's hope) anaemia of the brain which makes me work SO Slowly that I never get through my jobs and bring work home every night to finish after dinner. Incessant interruption at the office adds immensely to the fatigue Of Putting together reports or compiling information. I've no sooner got hold of the thread than it's broken by someone with a petition or a complaint or what not, and my slow mind must laboriously gather it up again. Perhaps a fortnight's absence in the Euphrates will make me a little less imbecile. There are times when I can scarcely find words to talk or write in French, much less in Arabic. And memory is a lost art. Though half-witted I'm physically well. I've liked this cold weather and not felt cold as I did last Year, though it's much colder here than in Basrah. But it's the general sense of being too much driven through not working quickly enough--because I can't--which is tiresome. I would like to take a month off, learn Arabic and see people --but the awful amount one would have to catch up at the end of it deters me. I'm almost reluctant to go away because I know what a task it will be to write the next fortnightly report when I have to look everything up instead of jotting it down as it happens. But I very much like doing the fortnightly reports, which are the record of our work here, and though I haven't leisure to do them as well as they should be done, they will still be valuable.

Did I tell you of a visit I paid to the home for Armenian girls? Over 100 of them have been collected here, from all places and of all ages. There's an American fund to provide for them. Some had lived for months with the Arabs and were tattooed like Beduin women, some had just borne children and some were such children themselves that they could not remember whence they came. The Beduin coming down to our frontiers from the north bring hundreds of these girls with them. One woman when she first saw the Tigris burst into tears. "Ah," she cried, "the mass of water here! and my sister died in the desert of thirst." And ah! the rivers of tears, the floods of human misery that these waifs represent. What is life worth in this age of violence?

I write every week and if you don't get letters it is not because I don't send them.

CHAPTER XVII

1918-1919 - BAGDAD

To F.B., Karbala, January 3rd, 1918

I'm having a little holiday which is very pleasant and benefi-
cial. I was beginning to feel terribly caged and stale and, though I
haven't stepped out of the cage very far, or for very long, it's agreeable
to be knocking about a tiny corner of the world again. It's a corner so
full of associations. So many times I've come over the Bagdad-Karbala
road after long desert expeditions, with a sense of accomplishment,
and, at the same time, with that curious sense of disappointment which
one nearly always feels with the accomplished thing. The best time, I
think, was when I came back with the plan of Ukhaidir in my pocket--
the worst when I came up from Arabia. I find myself forever stepping
back into a former atmosphere--knowing with my real self that it has
all melted away and yet half drugged with the lingering savour of it,
and chiefly what I miss is the friendly presence of my good Fattuh,
who smoothed all the way of travel and is now where? dead, I fear. I
hear there are no men left in Aleppo; all have been taken for the War
and Turkish soldiers have a poor chance. However--I'll tell you of my
adventures, very modest ones, not like the old days. I left Bagdad on
the 31st, a beautiful sunny morning, and motored out to Musaiyib on
the Euphrates. We spun over the first three-quarters of the road, but
the last eight miles, over low ground, unspeakably muddy, were not so
advantageous to motors. We stuck once badly and I called in some 10
or 15 Arabs who were removing the mud from one part of the road to
another--that seemed to be the extent of their activities--and made
them haul us out...

[The fortnight's holiday takes her motoring through familiar
places full of memories.]

Yesterday, I motored out along the sandy road, the very familiar road, to Karbala, and reached Major Pulley's house about midday. He had put me up close at hand in Col. Leachman's house, the latter being out in the desert with the Arabs, my very own Arabs, Fahad Bey's tribe, but I can't go to them. And then out through mud and swamp on to the edge of the Syrian Desert, which lifted its yellow shoulder in front of me in a manner so inviting that I could scarcely bear to turn away from it... I had tea in my own house before a wood fire and afterwards received a visit from one of the desert merchants one of the Agail who had somehow heard I was here. I knew one of his brothers in Damascus and another in Bagdad. They come, like all Agail, from Central Arabia, and we sat talking desert gossip for a long time--until I felt again that I could scarcely bear to be so close and not to go in to the tribes. What a welcome Fahad Bey would give me. He's about 2 days away.

To H.B., Hillah, January 16th, 1918

I wrote to you almost at the beginning of my fortnight's holiday and now that I've come almost to the end of it I'll begin another letter. I get back to Bagdad to-morrow and feel very much like one going back to school. I'm not sure that it's a good plan to get out of the cage for a fortnight and enjoy the illusion of days that were almost like a former existence. Certainly I've never realized more keenly than I do now the chains and bonds which war draws about one. I wrote from Karbala, didn't I? I spent three days there, saw many people, was greeted by friends from the desert and had the wildest desire to escape into it and be heard of no more...

On my way home yesterday I stopped at Babylon, having been asked by Sir Percy to advise about the preservation of antiquities. 'Tempi passati' weigh very heavy there--not that I was thinking of Nebuchadnezzar, nor yet of Alexander, but of the warm welcome I used to find, the good company, the pleasant days spent with dear Koldewey--it's no good trying to think of him as an alien enemy and my heart ached when I stood in the empty dusty little room where Fattuh used to put up my camp furniture and the Germans and I held eager conversation over plans of Babylon or Ukhaidir. What a dreadful world of broken friendships we have created between us.

THE LETTERS OF GERTRUDE BELL

To F.B., Bagdad, January 25th, 1918

Yesterday I went all over the Civil Hospital with the Municipal doctor, Capt. Carey Evans--he is a son-in-law of Mr Lloyd George. He is doing his work with real intelligence and is full of schemes for the future. ...Medical organization is of the very first importance, not only because there is so much to be done but also because it is so deeply appreciated. It is an invaluable political asset if you choose to look at it from that point of view. Hospitals and dispensaries are the first things the people ask for, and they flock to them, men and women, and don't hesitate to undergo operations or any treatment you please. Capt. C. E. says the standard of vitality is much higher than in Europe; the people here pull through operations which he would not dare to attempt at home. Their nervous system is much more solid. They don't suffer from shock ...

To H.B. and F.B., Bagdad, January 31st, 1918

I have your letters. Also Father's very good and wise piece about Capital and Labour, which I read with profit. A remarkable writer, there can be little doubt.

...The price of living here is enormous, and, though I'm rationed, a great many of the necessaries of life have to be bought, such as soap, rice, eggs and sugar, and they are all at preposterous prices. This also means that one has to raise wages. Kind Musa Chalabi, my landlord, has got me out of difficulties with regard to my gardener's family. There have been living in a single mud room, my gardener, his aged father and mother, two brothers, a wife, a sister and all of them came piteously to me for help and support. I couldn't help feeling that my garden was overcrowded, but, with feeble compassion, I didn't like turning them out into the mud. But there came a day when they quarrelled, and I called in Musa Chalabi as arbitrator. He arbitrated with some vigour and the aged father and mother, together with other members of the family, have found other lodgings. I relinquish any personal share in their fortunes.

I found some irises and some verbenas in a market garden which I used to frequent here, and transferred them to my flower beds. They were very dear, but the joy of them will be worth the price. I have a few pots of violets which provide a tiny bunch for my writing table. Their little blue faces are very friendly and cheerful. I now pursue a happy plan of going out riding or walking every afternoon, generally alone but sometimes in company...There is a great bend in the Tigris below the town which is my favourite resort. It makes a huge peninsula full of gardens and cornfields, and almost empty of soldiers, and there I go and remember that I am really part of Mesopotamia and not part of an army of occupation. The spring is there and colour and life and sound have come with the rains, the sound and colour of the reviving world. We had a tidy drop of rain this week, enough to make 2 days of mud, but we want more. Heaven send it! we are barely up to 2 in. yet and I'm afraid we shall not get our average 6.

The days I don't ride I generally find myself in the bazaar a mildly expensive form of exercise. To-day, after I had been to see additional houses taken on for the Armenian refugees, I dropped into the new shop of an old acquaintance--he used to have a much nicer poky room in a khan--and came away with a very charming Chinese bowl, a little copper incense burner 300 years old (it has a dated Arabic inscription, a thing I can never resist) and a metal water bottle, not old, but such a good shape. All these metal water jars are lovely, traditional shapes which you may see in any 16th Century Persian miniature. The bowl was cheap for it's good Chinese stuff --no bowl would have been cheaper, but there! even the bowl and the verbenas don't run extravagance into a high figure.

I rather fear that my friend Thomas Effendi (he's an Armenian) will send me round a pair of rugs to-morrow. Let's hope they won't be good. Talking of rugs, I'm hatching a plan which, though it isn't directly concerned with rugs, touches their place of origin. I have been thinking about schemes for the summer and am rather inclining towards a 3 months' travel in Persian mountains, I should take tents and might very likely land up in Teheran ultimately, and home by Ispahan. The journey home takes at least five weeks, four of them through heat and the monsoon, whereas I can motor in 2 days to Kirmanshah and reach at once a temperate climate. Then motor through great hills to Urumiah perhaps, which is a paradise. Col. Willcox gives the plan his warm approval from a health point of view, but it's great drawback is that I shan't see you this summer. At any rate, when you get this letter, you might telegraph and say what you think, and meantime I'll consider things more closely. I like the Persian idea much better than Baluchistan, for to get there one still has the terrific journey down river and across the Indian Ocean--terrific in June or July heat. It's the thought of getting into camp once more, and being out of doors among mountains that attracts me and also the possibility of being away from people for a while.

One Of the worst drawbacks of the occupation, from the Point of view of the inhabitants Of the country, is the requisitioning of houses. I don't see what's to be done, for we haven't time to build and we must be lodged, but it's a terrible hardship to the luckless ejected ones ... I have a clean sheet myself, for my house isn't a house and probably no one but me would think of living in it. (They would be wrong, for it is quite comfortable and the space and freedom of my garden are invaluable boons.) It's certainly very difficult to be popular rulers in war time.

With which reflexion I'll close, merely adding that I'm very well now and much less thin.

To H.B., Bagdad, February 8th, 1918

It is getting quite perceptibly, but pleasantly warmer. I've begun to discard some of the innumerable wraps I wear by day and coverings by night. To-day, with the soft air blowing into my room, I thought of R'ton in February and wondered whether by chance it were snowing with you...It is curious to find how many of the Bagdad notables are tribesmen, often only settled in the town for the last generation or two. Some sheikh builds himself a town house, sends his sons to school and starts them in a learned profession leading to Government employment. And at once they settle down into citizens. But the tribal links are unbroken. Any sheikh with business in the town looks by right to his kinsman's house for entertainment in the matter of daily meals--a pretty expensive duty it is--and if a member of the town family gets into trouble he will seek sanctuary with the tribe, safe in the assurance that he would never be given up. Several men I know fled to their tribe during the year before the Occupation, when the Ottoman hand was heavy on the Arabs of Bagdad. Most of these are now in our service and their tribal connection makes them all the more useful. We have a few really first-class Arab officials, just as we have found a few really first- class sheikhs who will assume responsibility and preserve order. There are not many of them, but such as there are, are invaluable. And we in our turn have an immense responsibility towards them...We are pledged here. It would be an unthinkable crime to abandon those who have loyally served us. But there! if I write of Arabs I shall write all night.

To H.B., Bagdad, February 15th, 1918

...All the telegrams prepare me for a terrific assault in France. I've also got your address at the Horden meeting which is excellent. It is so full of ideas and of wise appreciations. When I feel stale I think of your wonderfully fresh mind. There's no doubt you are a very remarkable person and I say it quite without prejudice...

The peace with the Ukraine is the worst thing that has happened, it seems to me. I agree with Lady Macmahon who said she thought the Almighty had shown Himself disappointingly neutral...

To-day I combined business with pleasure and paid a call on Père Lion, abbot of the French monks, and Père Anaftase who is a Syrian. I went to discuss the buying of MSS. for the Indian Government and the translation of the Shiah traditional books, which is a hobby of my own that I'm pressing on the India Office. You see, the first thing in this Shiah country is that we should have a real understanding of the things that lie at the bottom of the Shiah mind. We all 3 sat together in the parlour overlooking the quiet little monastery court which lies in the heart of Bagdad; we had a delightful talk and as I came home through the incredibly narrow crooked streets--the leaves almost touch overhead and the streets wind in and out of them--I had a warm feeling of being part of it all. And so I am, you know; just as much as I'm part of English surroundings. It's a curious sense to have two native lands and to be wound into this one as with that by long links of associations. It made me content with a decision which I've just taken, not to accompany Sir Percy to Cairo and Jerusalem, where he is going for a Conference. He invited me to come too, and though it would have been most interesting, I'm not necessary and I think I had better stay here now when the weather)s so good and we can work. I shall have to go away in the summer for reasons of health. I'm rather discouraged about Persia because people coming in from there give such terrible accounts of the destitution of the country. You can't travel in a place where there's nothing to eat. England, with Palestine on the way, is another idea, but anyhow there are 3 months still before I need decide. The truth is I have a great longing to see you...

However many native lands I may have I've only one father and mother anyway and I'm therefore ever your devoted daughter.

To H.B., Bagdad, 22nd February, 1918

You will get this letter quicker than all the others because Sir Percy carries it. He is coming home on a hasty mission and will probably only be in England a few days, but I have asked him to communicate with you on his arrival, because I feel sure you will want to see him. Also he will discuss with you my plans for the summer...Anyhow, he will be able to tell you what it is like, and, if I can get home without an unreasonable delay, I think I will probably come...

Springy's [Sir Cecil Spring Rice] death is just another piece of the old life gone--a life which I can't in imagination carry on into the future...

Well now, I will finish by writing you an ordinary letter of my doings...

On Monday afternoon, I had a funny, charming expedition. I borrowed a motor and took my old friend and landlord, Musa Chalabi, with his wife and daughter, to their garden outside Bagdad, five or six miles away. Musa's brother, Shakir, lives there and looks after the farming. It was a ramshackle place, with a couple of big single-storied mud-built houses; refuse heaps scattered around and even inside the courtyard; a dirty, smelly, Arab village, half tent, half reed hut under their walls; but the sun shone on the river bank and growing things and the palm trees, and there were three most darling little children of Shakir's to show me the hens and the puppies and the other wonders... And then we motored home. Musa and his ladies were in the seventh heaven, never, I think, having motored before...

You know Sir Percy has been an angel of kindness to me always, but he absurdly exaggerates the value of anything I've done here...

I knew I had another story to tell. To-day there came in to see me one of my travelling companions Of 1914. An Arab of the Dulaim tribe, who rode with me for four days when I was going back to Damascus. He was a good guide, and I was glad to see his pleasant face again--as glad as one can be when one of these ghosts of an independent past rises up before one. He set me longing for the desert. The grass is springing there and the black tents flowing with milk, and man and beast prosper.

To F.B., Bagdad, March 1st, 1918

We had a day or two of wind and rain this week after which the world burst into loveliness. I rode directly after the rain through the gardens S. of the town and found them a vision of apricot and peach blossom and brilliant green cornfields. Everything grows together, fruit tree and palm and corn, with a marvellous luxuriance. If only it weren't going presently--and very soon--to be so infernally hot. I have been very busy this week, contributing some chapters to the review of administration here during 1917. It makes a most remarkable story, the truly remarkable part being the way the people have accepted it. The immense energy with which agricultural development has been pushed forward has been of incalculable political value...There is nothing easier to manage than tribes if you'll take advantage of tribal organization and make it the basis of administrative organization. And our people, with their natural inclination to deal with men on their merits, at once establish familiar relations with sheikh and headman and charge them with their right share of work and responsibility. And the men so treated respond wonderfully well--but then they are men, they've got stuff in them and that's all that is necessary...The European news is terribly bad and I see no prospect of an end. The strain on you at home is more than I like to think of. Don't you wonder often when you wake in the morning, how you are to carry on through the day? I wonder often enough how you bear it...

Yesterday afternoon I went to see one of our new primary schools where the headmaster is a friend of mine. There wasn't a very large attendance. I went round the 3 classes and asked them questions. In the smallest class we held a kind of general intelligence examination and I began by asking who was king of England. One student of history (aged about 7) replied unhesitatingly Chosroes, and another with a better grasp of modern politics amended with Lloyd George. (I don't know whether Father will be able to bear that story!)...The roses in my garden will be out in a week or two and I'm eating my own lettuces, but I'm sorry to say the cabbages have burst into luxuriant yellow flower before they ever became cabbages, so to speak.

To F.B., Bagdad, March 6th, 1918

I'm going away the day after to-morrow down Euphrates again to gather up the remaining threads of tribal information which I want in order to complete my monumental work on Mesopotamian tribes. So if I don't catch a mail next week you'll know why. I'm looking forward to it very much and I hope I shall be able to get the material I want, but it's a difficult job and if one thing's more certain than another, it is that all one writes on tribes is sure to be full of mistakes. One ought to live for a month or two in each district in order to understand them.

This afternoon I attended a small function, the opening of a Civil Dispensary in the heart of the town. It has been the darling wish of Capt. Carey Evans to have a dispensary on this side of the river, and it will be infinitely valuable. There's a ward with 6 beds besides accommodation for seeing outpatients. All the notables came, secular and religious; it was most gratifying as well as being most agreeable. I sat in a row with the Qadhi, the Mudir of Church Lands (Muhammadan), the judge of Appeal and so on and so on, and we had tea and talked and were pleased to see one another. The Grand Rabbi, the Prior of the Dominicans, the Mother Superior and representatives of other Christian denominations were there too.

That's not the only party I've been to, but the other was improvised. Mr. Bullard and I were riding last Sunday through the exquisite fruit gardens S. of the town and I insisted on paying a call on their owner. We found him in his orchards, a hale old man who owns 2 square miles, or thereabouts, of the richest gardens near Bagdad and plants his seedling potatoes with his own hands. He led us through his fruit trees, showed us where he was laying out a new orange grove and where transplanting spring onions. Apricot and peach, apple and greengage are all in white and pink flower, and the thick grass lines the water channels, as it does only in exceptionally good years. Therewith he took us to his house and gave us an excellent tea of fresh bread and butter --the latter a rare luxury--and preserved fruits. We sat on a wide wooden bench in his mud-built guest room and listened to his shrewd talk. As a sequel to the visit he sent me to-day a present of eggs and fresh beans, wrapped up in a red cotton handkerchief.

With Sir Percy away, I have even more visitors than before and most of my morning is taken up with interviews. The Naqib's water pipe has been the question of the hour. I may say it has devastated my prospect as well as swamping the Naqib's quarter, for nothing in this world will keep it in repair. Yet you can't treat it like an ordinary pipe, for it is a religious bequest and must therefore be approached with the utmost circumspection. At length the Naqib, after much heart searching, has agreed to let the Municipality be responsible for its upkeep and a load is slipping from my shoulders.

Yet it's because matters like this one have been so tactfully handled by Sir Percy that all the notables come to tea at the Civil Dispensary...

[In March she again leaves Bagdad to motor among the Sheikhs and] " got a lot of tribal stuff."

[I include here some extracts from letters written by Gertrude at this time to Mildred Lowther (daughter of Lord Ullswater) with whom her friendship had become very close during 19 15 when Mildred helped in the work for tracing the wounded and missing.]

To Hon. Mildred Lowther. March 6th, 1918

I want to see you so very much, beloved Milly. I feel as if I had jumped into old age during the last two years. You would scarcely believe from outside I am the same person, but inside I am not changed.

To the same, Bagdad, March 18, 1918

My Father eagerly desires me to leave this summer but I can't settle myself to making plans while the fate of the world swings in the balance.

To the same, July 6th, 1918

No, I'm not coming back yet, darling. Do not forget me. When I come back I shall want your help and understanding so much. It will be so difficult to pick up life in England I dread it. You must give me a hand as you did before.

It is too hot to write more. I shall go up on the roof and lie on a hot sheet while the sandflies drift through the meshes of the mosquito net-- that's the Arabian night if the truth were known.

To H. B., Samawah, March 17th, 1918

At kufah while I was standing on the high point aforesaid I saw some black tents and camels in a hollow to the S. and presently the owners crept up to us and laid their difficulties before me. They were men of the Ghazzi, a semi-nomadic tribe near Nasiriyeh, and they had been out in the desert since October. Now they wanted to go back to their own people by the river for the summer, but when they got to Shinafiyah where they meant to cross the river, behold there were soldiers and people riding about and the devil's own puzzlement. And they wanted to know whether there was permission for their crossing or what was to happen to them if they might not come down to the river. I said their Sheikh was a friend of the Govt. and bade them go in peace where they liked, but they were not happy till I wrote them an order to say they might cross and continue on their way. With that they kissed my shoulder and departed reassured, I hope, but think what bewilderment all these strange happenings must cause to camel folk who don't know what the intention of the soldiers and the Govt. may be. Next day was disgusting, a high wind and terrific rain. Fortunately my tent stood - (by a miracle) and my roof didn't leak much. There was nothing to be done but to continue sitting under it. I wrote up my tribal notes, and in the afternoon was visited by various sheikhs and saiyids and had some interesting talk, the net result of which was that they too were a little bewildered and anxious like the camel people. We have only been in effective occupation in these parts for the last three months; we are new and strange to them, and they to us. I've had in masses of sheikhs to see me and I think I've made a pretty good tribal register...

It's immensely interesting seeing this bit of the Euphrates and making acquaintance with its inhabitants. No doubt I've only got the vaguest outline of what there is to know, but at any rate it is an outline of a very complicated bit of tribal country, concerning which we were, a few months ago, in complete ignorance...

To F.B., Bagdad, March 28th, 1918

...A terrible cloud has fallen on our work here in the murder at Najaf of one of our Army Political Officers [this was Captain Marshall]. He was a brilliant creature--I personally was very fond of him, and spent a delightful afternoon with him three weeks ago when I was at Kufah. He had I thought a great future, and I do most bitterly regret him...

This tragedy cast a great storm over the end of my journey, but I must tell you the remainder of my tale. I wrote to you from Samawah the day before I left. I came up the Hillah branch of the Euphrates in a motor launch from Samawah to Diwaniyeh. Capt. Goldsmith, a young Surrey officer, came with me for the first couple of hours, with a party of mounted Police--for honour you understand, not for safety. I could have done with less but in spite of them all the ride over the desert green with aromatic plants was delicious. The smell of a desert in spring is like nothing in this world. Each night I held a levy of notables after dinner. The second night when I had listened to the praises of myself, my government and my host, I was fortunately relieved by the entrance of an aged worthy whose appearance and conversation I must describe to you. His face was black with age, his beard scarlet with henna; the black and red were enfolded in a gigantic white turban. As he entered we all gave him salutations which were repeated when he had sat down. Talk then flagged until he took up his tale. "As I came in," said he. "As I entered the very door, without a pen I composed a verse." "Without a pen!"--ejaculations of surprise and admiration fell from the company and we begged to be acquainted with the production. He raised his ancient bony hand as though he would bid the world listen, and in a cracked voice recited three times running, an egregious couplet to the effect that all had learned humanity from the high Government, and that the coming of the Khatun (me) had filled the universe with joy. After the third recital I felt it my duty to write it down--seeing that he had no pen. The rest of the hearers overflowed with praise and a general hope was expressed that "Please God" and with His help the Haji would that night be able to complete the ode so felicitously begun. But whether he did or he did not I don't know, for I fled from Diwaniyah in a motor very early before the notables were awake.

The I.G.C. has been up for a couple of days cheerful and cheering as ever. Also whom do you think I have seen? Driver Woodcock, Mrs. Taggart's grandson. I gave him some cigarettes and a book of mine, which he asked me for, and to-day I've got him some razors and things from the Red Cross.

I must tell you, I'm a person of consequence, for Father's launch is beating all records.

Father's letter of Jan. 15th came also with my last mail. I wish you wouldn't write me such splendidly long letters. Though I love them, Father's account of his week's work is really appalling. His billiard table groaning with his papers! I also got your wire about the Geog. Soc. Medal. It was an absurd thing to give me; they must have been hard up for travellers this year.

To her family, Bagdad, April 5th, 1918

Mr. Bullard and I rode miles up the Tigris and dropped in to call on a charming old gentleman who owns a large garden by the river bank. We were received by his servants with enthusiasm and led out into the garden where we found Faik Bey budding orange trees. He then took us through his fruit garden and cornfields, out to the edge of the desert. It was all green and wonderful with the barley in the ear and deep grass under the fruit trees. So we went back with him to tea, which consisted mainly of dates and oranges. My other gardener host, Haji Naji, came in to see me this week. He was dressed in beautiful purple cloth and looked very imposing: "Do you sit here all day and work?" said he, inscribing imaginary epistles in the air with his fore-finger. "Very laborious!" and he tapped his forehead to indicate his sense of my mental effort. "You must come out again to my garden and be happy among the fruit trees."

A raging south wind, which brought that night a wild storm of rain--rain which lasted intermittently for 3 days and that's unusual at this time of year--but very fortunate, for it keeps the world cool and fresh. On the second afternoon the rain held up a little and I, not being able to bear sitting in the office any longer, waded out through the mud and had tea with the French nuns, darling creatures, whom I found trembling with anxiety about the news of the battle--as who is not? ...

Behind all one's doings lies the terrible sense of these days in France. The first assault seems to have spent itself--at what cost!--and we now, with deep anxiety await news of the second.

Goodbye, my beloved family...

To H.B., Bagdad, April 10th, 1918

I am sending home 50 little black sheepskins in 5 parcels. My fur coat is in holes and some day they will do to make a new one, be-ing both pretty and cheap.

The Willingdons are here on a short excursion from Bombay, staying with the C. in C. It is very nice having them, they are so cheer-ful and pleasant. If the hosts enjoy a party you may be pretty sure the guests are happy too. Among the latter were two wise men from Najaf, crowned with gigantic white turbans, and it was assuredly the first time in history that Najaf Ulama [the doctors of divinity, the learned clerics of Islam] had been seen at such a gathering...

If I can concoct a suitable telegram I shall telegraph to you saying that if you want me to come home this summer you must make arrangements from your end. Women aren't allowed to cross the Medit., but I should think they'll make an exception for me. If I can't come to England I shall go on leave to Baluchistan.

THE LETTERS OF GERTRUDE BELL

To H.B., Bagdad, April 18th, 1918

I've just got a four weeks' mail with your letters of Jan. 27, 31, Feb. 12 and 26, and Mother's of Jan, 30, Feb. 6, 20 and 23. It's an immense comfort to have them. Three days ago I telegraphed to you about plans, saying I doubted whether coming home was advisable. I received next day a wire from you approving all my plans of Jan. 3 1 - but Lord knows what they were! However, I've left it at that, because you will certainly see Sir Percy in a day or two and I shall have your final decision. My own feeling is that it's no good attempting to make plans while everything in France hangs in the balance. While things are very critical I don't want to leave this country for, naturally, it will make people here extremely jumpy as to their future--and I, in a small way, am one of the people who can help to comfort them. If I went, I fear they might think I was deserting them, and that would make them more nervous still.

Except for the fear of your disappointment if I can't come, I don't worry. I'm perfectly well, better than I've been for a year; and escape in the middle of the summer to high ground in Persia is always possible. Two easy days' motoring lands one 5,000 feet up, just think of it 1 So as regards health I'm all right.

First the accounts of Springy. I'm really glad he hadn't had long months of failing health, as I had feared. I do grieve so much over the loss of s him. He did his part splendidly, none better. We've just had the Willingdons here. I saw a great deal of them and loved them both. The Chief insisted on my coming with them to Babylon. We had a delightful two days. We motored to Hillah, where we lunched...We went to Babylon; this wonderful spring had clothed the ruin mounds in flowering weeds and cast a fresh beauty over the dust of palaces. I took them on to a high place, spread out a map, and told them all the long tale, down to Nebuchadnezzar, and then down to Alexander, who died there in the palace on the northern mound. The Willingdons were the most enchanting audience, so was the Chief, and one of the staff said that though he hated ruins (i.e., the staff man hated them) he really had liked Babylon. Lady W. and I agreed that I really had slung quite a good scalp on to my belt!...

I jumped up at 6 and walked for an hour along Euphrates bank --the beloved river--under palms and willow trees, talked with the peasants who were driving their oxen up and down the long slopes of the water lifts, heard the Mesopotamian nightingale and remembered that' these were the same sights and sounds that Nebuchadnezzar had known and even Hammurabi. Were they, I wonder, comforted and sustained by the eternal beauty of the earth and the simple country life of field and river? We motored that day to Birs Nimrud which is supposed to be the Tower of Babel, and I need not say isn't (because, partly, there wasn't one, and partly because the one there wasn't was not in that place --but I fear you'll fail to understand me!) and home to Bagdad. I motored always with Lord W. and told him all we had done--irrigation, agriculture, pacification of the tribes--with illustrations drawn from the country we passed through, and he was the most sympathetic listener. He is so delightfully full of interest and eager that I don't think he can have been bored, for if you care for administration it was a tale worth hearing.

To H.B., Bagdad, April 19, 1918

This evening I have a telegram from Sir P. saying that you and he in consultation had agreed that I had better not come. I feared he would warn you that the journey is now very difficult and I think the decision is a wise one but I can't help feeling a dreadful tightening at the heart at the thought of not seeing you within measurable time. I do sometimes want you so much that I can scarcely bear it. You could always get me home by making the India Office or the F.O. telegraph that they want me and asking the Admiralty to give me facilities. We'll see how things turn; it may be easier in a month or two. I've almost forgotten about France in thinking of you and Mother and Maurice...

This is becoming a sort of diary letter--it's because you are so much in my mind that I want to talk to you. To-day it has been positively cold. I was dressed in a silk coat and skirt and shivered so much that I had to get into a white serge gown which was fortunately hanging up in my dressing-room at the office. Amazing, isn't it? Last year we were grilling at this date.

I've brought out a work on Euphrates geography and tribes which has given satisfaction. I shall have to revise it now, for I learnt so much more when I was down the river last month, but at least it's a beginning. I must tell you that I know a great deal about the Euphrates and nothing about the Diala. That's the next task when I can get at it.

The nuns are making me a muslin gown--it will be a monument of love and care, for I really believe they lie awake at night thinking what new stitches they can put into it. I often go in to see them after tea; we sit on the balcony in their courtyard and talk of France and Bagdad. And then they all troop down in a body to the door to wave me farewell down their narrow, curling street--it's not 6 feet wide, nor are any streets wider in the heart of Bagdad. Yesterday I rode with the O.C. of one of the big hospitals, Col. Crossley, and think of it! he had been for 2 years at Richmond, had taught and examined many of our R. Cross detachments and been to our field day in 1912...

Good-bye, darling Father. I think and think of you. However long I'm away from you, your love and Mother's is like the solid foundation on which all life rests. But I don't feel as if I could bear not seeing you for very much longer.

To H.B., Bagdad, May 4th, 1918
[Received June 22nd, 1918]

The river has been in great flood this week. We trembled for our sown fields, but it's a wonderful sight. The great wealth and bounty of water. All the little water courses flowed in spate through the fields and gardens, things grew as you watched them and the Mespot nightingales shouted through the orchards.

The event of the week was a tea party which I gave to the ladies of Bagdad in Sir Percy's house. I asked no one but the big People, mainly Moslems, and to my surprise they came in flocks. An Armenian family (Madame Sevian and her daughters, whom I like very much), the Mother Superior and some of the nuns came to help and it was an immense success. I've heard that the ladies said that not even in a Mohammedan house would so much care have been taken to exclude all males--it's odd isn't it, that the success of a party should depend on the absence of that element! One woman, the wife of the Director of Religious Bequests (Moslem of the Moslem), said as she went away that if only they could see one another and meet more in company life would be quite different. So now I'm concocting a scheme to hire the cinematograph for an evening and have a ladies' night. They never see anything or go anywhere, think of it!

To F.B., Bagdad, May 9th, 1918

I've had a charming little jaunt Of 5 days. I motored to kamadi in about five hours and stayed there with General Brooking.

Next morning I motored on to Hit over a barren desert road which not even this year's rain can bring to life. We walked about Hit which is the strangest place, unlike any other in Mesop.--set on a high steep mound, made of some 6,000 years' of former Hits... And then we went on into the edges of the desert, flower strewn, struck the Kubaisah road, where I met several dead people who were once me, riding on camels, and gave them greeting with mixed feelings--And so I came home to breakfast.

To H.B. and F.B., Bagdad, May 24th, 1918

Will you forgive me if I write in pencil--it's not really a bit hot, but hot enough to make a fountain pen rather a nuisance; it dries up so fast. Here we are at the end of May and the temperature rarely over 100--it's wonderful...

Oh dear, how much I would like to have you just for an hour to show you our office. I'm accustomed to it now, but it's a wonderful place. We occupy two big houses built round courtyards on the river. Capt. W. and I have rooms next door to one another on the first floor. Mine is all shielded with mats and blinds against the sun and is beautifully cool. It has a writing table and a big map table, a sofa and some chairs with white cotton covers and lovely bits of Persian brocade over them, 2 Or 3 very good rugs on the brick floor and a couple of exquisite old Persian glass vases on top of the black wood bookcase. The walls covered with maps. It's a nice place. On the verandah, which runs round the inside of the court, sit our kavasses--office servants in khaki uniform--to fetch and carry files and papers for us, run messages and so on. They are mostly Arabs, some Persians, with immensely high bulbous felt hats. Opposite is the room of the Financial Adviser, Major May; the peacock mostly sits with him; and in between the map room, the cypher room, the room of the P.O. Bagdad, Captain Gillan, with a crowd of people waiting always to see him. In the next house all the clerks, British N.C.O.'s, capital men, Eurasians doing the confidential work (and they are first rate too), two vernacular departments, Arab and Persian--I love them all; they are so delightful to work with. But a medley, isn't it! And though I'm accustomed to it, I never quite get over the amusement and interest of it. I spend an entertaining time every morning learning Persian, which I've almost forgotten. But it comes back quickly, and during the first week I've already begun to chatter an amazing jargon, three parts Arabic, I'm afraid. I have the complete illusion of speaking Persian, for my teacher (one of our vernacular clerks) instructs me in Arabic and understands what I'm trying to say, but I fear the natives of Persia won't. However, it's great fun.

To her family, Bagdad, June 14, 1918

I've now got a Persian cook, who, besides being able to cook (an art none of my former cooks have possessed), knows no Arabic, so I'm forced to do my housekeeping in Persian, which amuses me--doubtless amuses the cook also at times. The nuns have made me some muslin gowns which are really quite nice--also cheap. The 'essayages' are not like any other dressmaking I've ever known. I go in after riding before breakfast and stand in practically nothing but breeches and boots (for it's hot) while the Mother Superior and the darling dressmaking sister, Soeur Renée, hover round ecstatically and pin on bits of muslin. At our elbows a native lay sister bearing cups of coffee. We pause often while the Mother Superior and Soeur Renée discuss gravely what really is the fashion. The result is quite satisfactory. Soeur Renée isn't a Frenchwoman for nothing

My roses are flowering anew, rather dusty in the face, poor little things, but very sweet.

To H.B., Bagdad, July 5th, 1918

...Two splendid long ones from you. And the first and most interesting thing in them is your suggestion that you might come here next spring. I can't imagine greater pleasure than showing you this world of mine. I hate your not knowing what has meant so much to Me.

I'm going to Persia on Tuesday night. I really feel as if a judgment ought to fall on me for doing anything so nice. It has been very hot this week. The temp. danced up one day to 118 and I can't keep my office under 100. I'm still very well, but I don't feel as if I could bear 3 uninterrupted months of it.

(The holiday in Persia was all that she had meant it to be. She writes from camp on her way to Kirmanshah.]

I jumped up at dawn and climbed to the top of the hills, 2,300 feet above the camp--a tough scramble up limestone rocks. But it was magnificent. The gentians and tulips were seeding--I send you some tulip seed which will you kindly give Hanagan--but the dianthus was still out, and gorgeous thistles and pediculatis--all the great garden of mountains. I came in at 10 to breakfast, a little footsore--I haven't walked for 4 years--but feeling like a new-born creature. It's about 100 in the tents at noon, but one doesn't feel it because there's a cool wind. The country is almost uninhabited here. I met a few woodcutters on the lower slopes this morning, with whom I stopped and talked, but from the top you can see no sign of human habitation--just mountain stillness. To-morrow I go on to Kitmanshah.

It's worthwhile to sit 2 years in an office in Mesop. in order to do this at the end with such enjoyment!

To H.B., Kermanshah, July 13th, 1918

It's a desert, this country; there's little difference between Persia and Mesopotamia, except that in the one the wilderness is set upright and in the other it's laid flat. We ran up 1,000 feet between steep and narrow mountain slopes. The road is a switchback, up and down over low passes, snow-blocked in winter. It's nothing short of a miracle that we can put it to use.

[She then goes to Gulahek, full of memories of her youth--and so back to Bagdad.]

To F.B., Bagdad, August 30th, 1918

if Sir Percy had been here this winter I think they could have done quite well without me, but the moment I got back Capt. Wilson told me the staggering news that he had been appointed to Teheran. But his absence makes me feel that it wouldn't have been right for me to have been away this winter. But it is a disappointment, isn't it! I was looking forward so much to having him here after all these months. However, Capt. Wilson and I are excellent colleagues and the best of friends and I know I can do a good deal to help him by seeing people and being ready to sit and talk as much as they want. It will probably be my main job. But first I'm going to compile an Intelligence book on Persia, for which I've collected materials while I have been away, and I rather think I can make a passable bit of work. It's the sort of thing I love doing. I've rather lost my heart to Kurdistan, country and people. My Persian was enough to carry me through most interesting conversations-- Persian is extraordinarily easy, you know, and I learnt more in that 3 weeks of riding through the country than I could have learnt in months of motoring. But it was hard work--unspeakably bad tracks and very hot in the middle of the day. There were many moments of deadly weariness which are not mentioned in my diary but remain in my memory. Still, I have come back extremely fit. We are now at what I think almost the worst moment of Bagdad, the stuffy autumn heat, temp. 104, and absolutely still and airless.

The two months in Persia have made me much more efficient-that's rather satisfactory. I have got roughly the hang of things there and can judge much better how they affect us here. Quite apart from the enjoyableness, it has been well worth doing.

To F.B., Bagdad, September 5th, 1918

Why, yes, of course I wrote all the Arab of Mesopotamia. I've loved the reviews which speak of the praftical men who were the anonymous authors, etc. It's fun being practical men, isn't it. Oh, I do so agree with you as to the great luck of having something to do during the war--no matter if it's much too much to do. It would be far greater suffering to stand outside it all. Father sends me the most delightful accounts of the Geographical Society meeting and dinner. How glad I am that it was he not I--firstly because he did it much better than I should have done it, thereby keeping up the credit of the family, and secondly because he liked it much better. I really should have been ashamed to receive that medal; it's far too great an honour.

I've had an uneventful week, but a busy one. Lots of people coming in to see me, and then lots of strings to pick up, and a report to write covering the whole time of my absence--fortunately not many things had happened--and then the Persian Intelligence book which is fairly under way. I've been making a Persian tribal map to-day and wishing I knew as much about Persian tribes as I do about Arab. Sir Percy goes to Teheran in 3 days' time.

To F.B., Bagdad, September 19th, 1918

I must announce the good arrival of some gloves and a felt hat, just what I wanted, and General Cobbe tells me that Richard is bringing me some clothes, which is splendid. Woad is the only suitable wear at present. It's infernally hot, 113 and absolutely airless. I don't think I've ever felt the climate more. Also I've had a cold and though I'm taking every means to be better until the weather changes I don't look forward to much vigour. At sunset the dust and mist lie in thick bars over the world and you gasp for breath. When this reaches you I shall probably be shivering, so I write untrammelled--two l's?--by any fear of causing you anxiety.

We have had a tremendous function this week--a Durbar of Sheikhs held by the C. in C. It really was rather wonderful. We had all the leading men of the country, sheikhs and tribal saiyids, from Samawah to Tikrit--the Chief had seen the Basrah people there the week before. There were about 80 of them, only the very biggest from each district had been selected. The Durbar was held in the public gardens and all the notables of Bagdad attended to see it, an immense concourse. It was terrifically hot, but I fortunately was in the shade on the platform, with Consuls and distinguished foreigners, French and American, who happened to be here. At 5 o'clock the C. in C. came up in procession through the garden with all his Major-Generals behind him, very splendid it looked. The sheikhs filed past him by districts, each group introduced by its Political Officer and the Chief.

THE LETTERS OF GERTRUDE BELL

To H.B., Bagdad, November 28th, 1918

I am having by far the most interesting time of my life and thank Heaven I am now well and can grapple with it adequately. The Franco-British Declaration has thrown the whole town into a ferment. It doesn't happen often that people are told that their future as a State is in their hands and asked what they would like. They are all talking and mercifully they all come in to me with the greatest eagerness to discuss what they think. On two points they are practically all agreed, they want us to control their affairs and they want Sir Percy as High Commissioner. Beyond that all is divergence. Most of the town people want an Arab Amir but they can't fix upon the individual. My belief is (but I don't yet know) that the tribal people in the rural districts will not want any Amir so long as they can have Sir Percy--he has an immense name among them--and personally I think that would be best. It's an immense business setting up a court and a power. The whole situation requires very delicate handling. We can't be too wary at this moment when the public mind is so fluid that anything serves to divert it in one direction or another. I always speak quite frankly and they believe me, I think. They know I have their interests more deeply at heart than anything else and they trust me in the same sort of way that they trust Sir Percy.

I'm so thankful to be here at this time, whatever happens I must remain till Sir Percy is brought back. We've telegraphed very fully, A. T. Wilson and I, and I think we have given a just view of the state of things...

...I'm quite sure that I prefer Generals to Bps. Two days later I went with Generals Lubbock and Stuart Wortley to Baqubah to see the Nestorian refugees in camp. We have 80,000 of them; they tramped down from Urumiah to escape from the Turks. The camp is wonderful--like a huge town. Then I walked with my generals in the orange gardens on the other bank, made friends with one of the proprietors and came away laden with oranges. Baqubah oranges are certainly the most beautiful in the world. The gardens are an amazing sight now--5 and 6 huge yellow globes hanging clustered on & boughs--all the groves aglow with them.

405

To H.B., Bagdad, December 6th, 1918

We have had a day's rain this week and the world is pretty muddy. Luckily my first Tuesday party took place the day before. I had about 50 ladies, mostly Moslems--they flock now, and I shall get them all in time. We had tea in the garden and sat talking for nearly 2 hours most cheerfully. I talk Arabic perhaps not quite as well as French, but nearly. The younger men are trooping in now of a morning to give me their views on the political future.

A. T. Wilson and I spend a considerable part of our time laying down acceptable frontiers--by request. It's an amusing game when you know the country intimately, as I do, thank goodness, almost all of it. Was ever anything more fortunate than that I should have criss-crossed it in very nearly every direction.

To H.B., Bagdad, December 27th, 1918

...About Arab rule. In Mesopotamia they want us and no one else, because they know we'll govern in accordance with the custom of the country. They realise that an Arab Amir is impossible because, though they like the idea in theory, in practice they could never agree as to the individual...

To F.B., Bagdad, January 3rd, 1919

On the chance of an outgoing boat I make haste to write you and wish all yours a good new year...

But more interesting was a lecture given one afternoon last week by Prof. Margoliouth. He lectured for 50 minutes by the clock on the ancient splendours of Bagdad in classical Arabic and without a note. It is the talk of the town. It's generally admitted that he knows more of Arabic language and history than any Arab here...

To H.B., Bagdad, January 10th, 1919

We have been having rather a difficult time here. The East is inclined to lose its head over the promise of settling for itself what is to become of it. It can't settle for itself really--we out here know that very well, because it might hit on something that certainly wouldn't simplify state government and that we can't allow in the interests of universal peace. But it is not going to be an easy job to hold the balance straight. I'm thinking of leaving in the last week of February, something like that.

Meantime I'm hard at work at the log book of Iraq Personalities, a gigantic task. I think I shall get it into shape by the end of this month. Further I'm seeing a great many people and incidentally a good many of the women. We have got a lady doctor. I'm taking her to see some of my friends and arranged a series of lectures for her in the home of a Pasha's wife. The ladies seem to be very keen about the classes.

The last day or two I've had a feverish cold--it is curious how everything turns to fever and knocks you out.

To H.B., Bagdad, January 17th, 1919

I was deeply grieved about Beatrice [Chamberlain]; I've written to Mr. Austen. There were few people who were her equal in fair sanity and I realise now how much I always counted on her friendship. It's Possible that I may come home a little earlier. A. T. Wilson shows signs of wanting someone at home who can help to give a guiding hand, if that's possible, keep him closely informed of how things are shaping and at the same time represent the experience we have gathered here. I really don't mind one way or the other myself. I should like to be back here in October, but we'll see what happens. I think on the whole I'm more useful here than in England, but just at this moment I might be able to help to keep things straight--if they'll let me...We are having rather a windy time over self-determination. I'll tell you some day. I wish very much that Sir Percy were here...

I flew with a young man last week--literally not figuratively. We flew for about three-quarters of an hour up and over the Tigris. For the first quarter of an hour I thought it the most alarming thing I had ever done and eagerly wished that that good young man would return to the ground. It was a windy day, the aeroplane wobbled a good deal. However, I presently became accustomed to it and was much interested and excited. I shall go up whenever I have an opportunity so as to grow quite used to it.

To F.B., January 25th, 1919

...The best thing this week was a lecture of Prof. Margoliouths on Abbassid history. I asked him the other day what he thought of the Bagdadis, to which he replied, "You will I trust forgive me for quoting a sentence of the Prophet's of which I am often reminded by the people of Bagdad: seek the advice of women in order to do the contrary."

To F.B., January 31st, 1919

Col. Wilson telegraphed home this week saying he would like to send me to England more or less as his liaison officer while so much is under discussion there. My own view is that he will get no answer.

If we get a permanent form of Government established here by this time next year I think we shall be lucky... It is an immense job, the conversion of a military organisation into a civil administration, all the technical part of it is so overwhelming, forts, telephones, medical and sanitary organisation, etc.; and it means that you cannot demobilise wholesale as if you did there would be a sudden breakdown in all the functions of Government. I haven't anything to do with these things, but I can see how intricate they are...

I have planted my garden most beautifully with hedges of chrysanthemums --it ought to be a sight next Autumn ...I'm sorry I shall not see the country here this Spring it will be wonderful after such a winter of rain.

But I shall see you and I'm immensely looking forward to it. I can't quite believe yet that in 6 weeks or so I shall be in England. I expect I shall be pretty busy, you know. Anyhow I think it will be good for me to go away for a bit. I feel I've become very provincial. How can one help it when one's whole time and thoughts are given to one's province? But it is not a good plan to get quite out of touch. One is more useful here for knowing what the pulse is like at home. I would like to do some propaganda for my province--lectures perhaps, though my mind rather shrinks from the idea at this moment. The Geog. Soc. would perhaps be a good platform but it will probably be too late in the year for them-- they don't, if I remember, have meetings after Easter. Heaven knows I shan't regret it personally; it's only that I want to advertise my province, you understand.

And do you know what I look forward to very much? A leg of mutton! That's not poetic, is it, but you should see and try to eat the meat I live on. I can't think what part of an animal it grows on. I must learn to cook mutton chops while I'm at home--and then see if I can't get them here.

[She goes to the Conference in Paris.]

To H.B., Hotel Majestic, Paris, March 7th, 1919

You must have been surprised at not hearing from me before, but I've dropped into a world so amazing that up to now I've done nothing but gape at it without being able to put a word on to paper. Our Eastern affairs are complex beyond all words, and until I came there was no one to get the Mesopotamian side of the question at first hand. The magnates have been extremely kind... They have all urged me to stay and I think for the moment that's my business. I'm filling up the time by getting in touch with the French and finding out for myself what their views are...I would love above everything to come motoring with you but it depends on how busy I am seeing French people. If I can keep a day or two clear of course I'll come and in any case I'll manage to come to Boulogne and see you for an hour or two there. I hope you'll think I'm right to stay. I can't do anything else.

To F.B., Paris, Sunday, March 16th, 1919

It will be quicker to send a letter by Father than to post it. I can't tell you what it has been like to have him for these two days. He has been more wonderfully dear than words can say, and in such good spirits looking so well. I can scarcely believe that three years of war have passed over his head since I saw him...I'm deep in propaganda though I don't know that it does much good, I don't feel is if I can ne-glect the chance of doing something. Except for the interest of the things which lie in the melting pot I'm not really liking it much and I should be very glad to get away. But one has got to such a state of tension that I don't believe I could at this moment come quietly home and rest.

We had a very delightful lunch to-day with Lord Robert and T. E. Lawrence--just we four. Lord Robert is I think the salient figure of the Conference and T. E. Lawrence the most picturesque. I spend most of my time with the latter and the former is unfailingly helpful.

I think that after A. T. Wilson has arrived and I've put him into touch with my friends, that I can leave matters in his hands. He comes next week, I hope. General Allenby arrives on Tuesday and Mr. Hogarth with him, so that we shall be in force. I can't write or think of anything else but what we are doing with the East---afterwards I wonder what I shall think about.

[On April 13th Gertrude starts for a motor tour with her father through Belgium and the north of France, Paris, then to Marseilles and so by sea for Algiers. Back via Paris in May.

Gertrude is in England for the rest of the summer and leaves again for the East in July.]

To H.B., 26th September, 1919

...We reach Port Said on the 28th so I'll begin to write to you. The weather beautiful, the ship excellent. And Marie [Delaere, her devoted maid] is proving an admirable traveller, and wonders why everyone who can doesn't do this all the time. For my part I've never been so well dressed on a ship for she digs into the boxes and produces a fresh costume daily.

[Gertrude writes from Damascus the account of her journey from Cairo,-- of her halt in Jerusalem, where she stays with Lady Watson wife of the chief Administrator General Sir Harry Watson, and sees a good deal of Sir Ronald Storrs.

"There is practically no question but Zionism in Jerusalem."

From Jerusalem via Beyrout to Aleppo.]

THE LETTERS OF GERTRUDE BELL

To her family, Aleppo, October 17th, 1919

I've been doing the usual thing here, seeing people, but the chief person I've seen is Fattuh. He looks older and as if he had been through an awful time as indeed he has. He has lost everything he had--he was beginning to be quite a well-to-do man and now he has only a horse and a small cart with which he brings in wood to sell in Aleppo. He was chiefly suspect because he was known to have been my servant. I went to see his wife--they live now in a tiny house which they have hired. He used to have two big houses of his own, Poor Fattuh. I was very very glad to see him. He is preparing food for me to take on my Motor journey and he still has some of my camp kit, cups and plates and things, so that I need not buy anything. We have had such happy times together--I called to mind joyous departures from Aleppo, and looking at his haggard face I said, "Oh Fattuh before the war our hearts were so light when we travelled, now they are so heavy that a camel could not carry us." He smiled and said, "Big lady, no, a camel couldn't carry you." My poor Fattuh.

To F.B., Bagdad, November 2, 1919

I have been to pay a visit of condolence on one of the big families, the head of which, an old friend of mine has died. I'm very sorry he's dead but I'm glad he won't have the opportunity of dying again so that I shall not have to pay another visit of condolence... All the women of the family met me on the threshold of the harem, dressed in the blackest black, their hair cut short and tears streaming down their cheeks. N.B. He has been dead a month. They cried uninterruptedly for ten minutes and again at intervals whenever they remembered to do so...I have also attended a meeting for the promotion of a Public Library for the native population. The scheme was started by the wife of one of the judicial Officers, Mrs. Forbes. She seems a nice woman. The proceedings were in Arabic and I made a speech. It was not extempore, I had been asked to do it the day before and had carefully prepared it with the aid of a native, for one has to make speeches in high falutin literary Arabic. Everyone else was much more high falutin. The chief man of letters recited an ode specially written for the occasion. It had an immense success. After any specially eloquent couplet the audience cried out "True, true," and sometimes "Repeat."...The enthusiasm lasted to the end and I made some valuable mental notes as to the right way of making further

411

meetings agreeable to Bagdad audiences. The rules are quite different from ours...

To F.B., Bagdad, November 9th, 1919

I've done very little this week except sit in the Office. I went to tea with the wife of Mustafa Pasha--she is the nicest of women. Also I went to tea with the Pachahji ladies whom I'm very fond of-- he's the owner of my garden and lets me live in it. And I've been to a Jew tea party--you see I'm visiting all my acquaintances--and to a tea party of the wives of some of my colleagues, Mrs. Wilson, Mrs. Waller and Mrs. Bill, I liked them all. Brides come out in swarms to be married here. We've had two weddings in my service since I came. Mr. Bonham Carter dines with me to-night. He had a big function, to which I went as a P.O., for the opening of the new School of Law. Practically all the big people of Bagdad were present. Our greatest man of letters made a speech which it was a privilege to hear. He is a born orator and the rolling Arab periods are magnificent when he declaims them...If only my furniture and crockery would come from Maples I could widen the circle of my dinner parties. I've telegraphed to Maples to ask when they were sent off. And when Marie is here she can look after the arrangements of my household and make it tidier and nicer, a thing I can't do when I'm at the office all day.

To F.B., Monday, November 30th, 1919

Another thing came in to-day, quite as important as the post-- two most beautiful Arab greyhounds sent to me by my old friend the paramount chief of the Anazeh, Fahad Beg. They had walked ten days down the Euphrates with two tribesmen to conduct them, and came in half starved. They are sitting beside me on my sofa as I write, after wandering about the room for half an hour whining. They are very gentle and friendly and I hope they will soon get accustomed to living in a garden instead of a tent. They are perfectly lovely and of course of the finest Arab breed. We have named them Rishan and Najmah--the feathered (that's because of his feathered tail) and the star ...

I lead the life of a hermit, if a hermit could spend all his days in an office. Sir George has provided me with a pony On which I've been riding for three quarters of an hour after 4. I then come back to my house and work at my big Mesopotamian Report till dinner and after dinner until I go to bed. I can rarely get at it in the office because of constant interrupters. One day this week I went to a tea party in the house of a notable who is very far from being pro-British. His wife is a friend of mine and I think it's as well to conduct one's personal relations without regard to politics.

To-day I motored out with Sir George to pay a visit on my dear friend Haji Naji the owner of the best fruit gardens near Bagdad. He gave us coffee and delicious preserved nectarines and offered some very feasible suggestions as to the management of the police force, which here as everywhere is one of the most thorny questions. His gardens were looking lovely, the fruit trees just beginning to turn yellow in our late autumn.

I am sending you a copy of my Syrian Report. It is of course confidential but I have permission to let you have it, and I wish you would tell me what you think of it, I can't judge and nobody offers any criticisms except that on the whole they don't agree with my conclusions. Nevertheless I think I'm right.

To H.B., Bagdad, December 7th, 1919

...If you leave in the middle of February you should be here towards the end of March. But don't be later because by the end of April it may be quite hot. I must break to you that I shan't come back with you. I really can't go away from this country, with which I'm so closely identified, while it's going through such a crisis in its fortunes as all next year it is sure to do. When you see the relations I'm on with the people you'll understand I feel sure. My idea is to go to George and Blanche [Lloyd] for a month or so in the middle of the summer, but we'll see about that later...

I'm gradually getting my house furnished and its going to be very nice. Maple writes that my things were sent off in October. I ordered them in July! In the mean time I've bought a charming black cupboard and chest in the bazaar, very cheap too. Marie has been invaluable in making curtains and generally seeing to things. She is the greatest comfort! don't know how I did without her. Also my new cook--Oh father you'll F love to see him. When he trails about in an abba he gives 'cachet' to my garden, I can tell you! Only, though he can cook a good deal and makes excellent cakes, he can't read or write and as his memory is deficient the morning accounts are a trial. They run as follows:

G.B.: Fallah! Mahdi! the accounts. I must go to the office.
M.: Oh your servant, Khatun. I bought what's its name
G.B.: Well, what is its name.
M.: Rice. Two krans.
G.B.: Eight annas. What next?
M.: Then I bought what's its name.
G.B.: What? Fallah!
M.: Bread, 6 annas.
G.B.: Go on.
M.: And then I bought what's its name.
G.B.: Merciful God! What?
M.: Sugar, two rupees.
G.B.: Two rupees. Fallah!
M.: And then--Khatun, I forgot the eggs yesterday, one rupee.
G.B.: All right. Go on.
M.: And then I gought meat, one rupee.
G.B.: What next?
M.: Wallah, I bought--Khatun shall I prepare for your Excellency this evening efter? (stew).
G.B.: What you like. Finish the accounts.
M. On my head. And then what's its name...

and so on, and so on till I'm hysterical between impatience and laughter...

By the way, will you please send my Syrian Report to George Trevelyan, confidentially. I think it would interest him after a talk he and I had in the Summer...

Do You know what they call me here? Umm al Muminin, the Mother of the Faithful, and the last person who bore that name was Ayishah, the wife of the prophet. But you see why I can't leave.

Would you let Milly see this letter?

I wholly forgot to tell you the main feature of the week which was the Prophet's birthday, Sunni style, make no mistake, the Shiahs celebrate it a week later ... The Pious Bequests Dept. gives an official celebration at Muadhdham, a much frequented Sunni shrine 3 miles above Bagdad. It consists of a square meal and prayers, and for the first time we were invited to the meal. I went and so did Frank Balfour with all his staff. It had rained heavily the night before--our long expected first rain which has come at last--and to motor out to Muadhdham was a ticklish business. The party began at 9 a.m. However we all arrived safely and found a gathering of all the men of religion sitting in the house of the Curator of the Mosque. We sat round and chatted for an hour or so, very pleasantly, and then we had a lunch of excellent Arab food, provided in incredible quantities. Some thought the hour 10:20 a.m., untoward, but I never mind how early I lunch. Then we all went back to our offices. I can't tell you how friendly and nice it all was; I loved it.

To H.B., Bagdad, December 16th, 1919

Don't be later here than the middle of March--I don't think I would be able to meet you further away then Bastah. You must bring a camp bed with bedding which all does up in a Wolsey Valise. As for clothes, it is usually delicious here at that time, temp. rising towards 70 at midday, but we sometimes have rain which means that it would be colder. In mid April you must expect 80 or upwards. You are most likely to want here lightish woollen clothes or flannel, but a silk suit or two would not be amiss. A topee you must have--I advise a sun umbrella...

I have had somehow rather a difficult week. First of all Allah afflicted me with a pain in my inside, but he has now taken it away. Next the Powers that be (on earth) got across the Sunni Vatican and they all tumbled in on me. It was very embarrassing because of course it is not my business and I'm always so dreadfully afraid of (a) misleading my visitors and (b) of annoying my colleagues whose job it is. If the latter weren't such angels (b) would be inevitable. It wouldn't have happened I think if Mr. Bonham Carter hadn't been away for a fortnight. First the Naqib sent round his son with a very special warning. Then next morning the door of my office opened and the room was filled with white turbaned Sunni Divines. I listened and begged them to betake themselves to Capt. Cooke, the Director of Pious Bequests, but no, they wouldn't go. If I hadn't been so bothered I could have laughed to find myself set up as an arbitrator of religious administration. However, all has turned out well. I sent for dear Cooke and after begging him to box my ears expounded the matter and he went straight to the Naqib to put things right. Meantime Mr. Bonham Carter, wisest of men has returned, thank heaven and I've got full absolution from him. What they (i.e. he) was doing was, I am convinced perfectly right, but by a series of accidents it hadn't been properly explained. And when that kind of thing happens they the Bagdadis always let off steam by coming to me.

...We are in the middle of a very difficult situation which you will see in the papers--the seizing of Deir al Zor on the Euphrates by an Arab force. We don't yet know the rights of it.

To H.B., Sunday, December 20th, 1919

Mr. Bonham Carter dined with me one night and we had a delightful long croak about Arab things and politics. To-day we been riding with Major Bullard through Haji Naji's gardens. I delight in our strange winter landscape. The apricots and mulberries dropping golden leaves into the green carpet of the springing barley...

Who so angelic as my two dogs who are curled up beside me on the carpets as I write. I'm beginning to persuade them that sofas and chairs are not meant for greyhounds...

CHAPTER XVIII

1920 - BAGDAD

To H.B., Bagdad, January 4th, 1920

I'll tell you my life and times. On Xmas day I went to an enormous dinner party given by A.T. to all the Political Service and their wives. I came home early, when they began to dance. I dance no longer.

Next morning before eight I caught a special train for Babylon and went there with the Lubbocks and General Hambro and some others, I acting as guide. We had a delicious two hours there after which General H. and Captain Bacon, and his A.D.C. and I went on to Hillah. There we lunched with my dear Major Tyler, the P.O. The lunch was gorgeous because Major Tyler had told the leading citizen that I was coming and he had insisted on sending in the whole meal. The table groaned with delicious Arab foods, the chief dish being a stuffed lamb roasted whole with its tail in its mouth like a whiting...

Here I parted with General Hambro and went on by motor to the other branch of the Euphrates where I found two young men, Captain Mann and Captain Wigan waiting with a launch to take me to the Camp of my host, Major Norbury, P.O. of Shamiyeh...Next morning when I woke and stepped out of my tent into the bright sun and saw all the trees and things I wondered how anyone could live in Bagdad.

The camp was pitched quite near the little village which is the headquarters of the principal Sheikh of the district, Tbadi al Husain. So after dinner he invited us to his Mudhif, his guest house. Now a Mudhif you can't picture till you've seen it. It's made of reeds, reed mats spread over reed bundles arching over and meeting at the top, so that the whole is a huge, perfectly regular and exquisitely constructed yellow tunnel 50 yards long. In the middle is the coffee hearth, with great logs of willow burning. On either side of the hearth, against the reed walls of the Mudhif, a row of brocade covered cushions for us to sit on, the Arabs flanking us and the coffee maker crouched over his pots. The whole lighted by the fire and a couple of small lamps, and the end of the Mudhif fading away into a golden gloom.

We spent next day in camp...It's a rice country and they have had this year a bumper crop. The yellow reed villages lay fat and comfortable in the winter sun, banked up with rice straw. The great golden heaps of rice were not all housed or shipped away but lay on the harvest floors. When we reached the Hor we got into tiny sajahs, the canoe-like boat, and rowed out by passageways through the reeds to the open water. There were thousands of duck, teal and other water birds. The osprey breeds here. The water was covered with the dying leaves of a small water lily on which buffaloes were peacefully browsing, standing belly-deep in the Hor. Of all incongruous diets for a buffalo water lilies are certainly the most preposterous...

Next day we all went to Najaf ...I am amused to find that my status in Najaf is rising. As a rule the great religious leaders, the Mujtahids, don't see me--I don't propose it. because they never look on an unveiled woman--but this time one of them, a first class Mujtahid, but an Arab, not a Persian, sent to ask me to come. He is an imposing figure... Najaf, mysterious, malign, fanatical, but drawing you with wonder and reluctance, by its beauty and unfathomableness.

The last time I had been there I was lunching with Captain Marshall who was murdered 8 days later. And we walked the same path round the town and said just these things about Najaf--alas, too truly...

To F.B., Bagdad, January 12th, 1920

First--and it clouds all other things--Reuter brings the news of Uncle Frank's death. I do grieve so much--there is a figure gone from our landscape, full of dignity and kindliness, which can never be replaced. When I remember how much I owed him, how many delightful experiences and how much sympathy, my heart aches with the thought that I didn't give him enough in return [this was Sir Frank Lascelles]...

And this country, which way will it go with all these agents of unrest to tempt it? I pray that the people at home may be rightly guided and realize that the only chance here is to recognize political ambitions from the first, not to try to squeeze the Arabs into our mould and have our hands forced in a year--who knows? perhaps less, the world is moving so fast-- with the result that the chaos to north and east overwhelms Mesopotamia also. I wish I carried more weight. I've written to Edwin and this week I'm writing to Sir A. Hirtzel. I'm so sure I'm right that I would go to the stake for it--or perhaps just a little less painful form of testimony if they wish for it!

To F.B., Bagdad, January 25th, 1920

I've telegraphed to Father saying I hope he'll come. I would love to show him my world here and I know if he saw it he would understand why I can't come back to England this year. If they will keep me, I must stay. I can do something even if it is very little to preach wisdom and restraint among the young Bagdadis whose chief fault is that they are ready to take on the creation of the world to-morrow without winking.

To F.B., Bagdad, January 25th, 1920

I had an interesting day on Monday. First of all we had the formal opening of the Girls' School--our first. I had invited the important native ladies and to my pleasure the Mohammedans turned up better than I expected. Miss Kelly, the Directress of Education, had made the school look very nice...I made a long speech in Arabic explaining the arrangements of the school and the way the children would be educated. The Muhammadan ladies took their share in it, chiming in with assent and approval. It was most exhilarating.

Then Mrs. Howell declared the school open after which we showed them round and then gave them tea. A most successful performance. That evening I had two young Arabs to dinner and a very interesting officer in the police service, Captain Morgan, to meet them. They came at 7 and stayed till 10:30 talking as hard as they could go, about education and the reform of religious endowments and all sorts of things. We were all on the most cordial terms when they left. I'm going to repeat the entertainment weekly, with different couples of my young men, the Arab young men I mean. I feel certain it's a good plan.

Next day Mrs. Leslie, the wife of the acting C. in C. came to tea, a most attractive woman. Then I had a tea party for my favourite monk, Père Anastase, he is exactly like a monk in Chaucer...

I'm afraid there's going to be no rain. We have had practically none this winter, it's most serious. The birds are famished because there is nothing growing. It's not that I watch the sparrows falling to the ground--I wish I could, confound them. My interest in the matter is that they devour the seedlings in my garden and strip my carnations to the bone.

To F.B., Bagdad, February 1st, 1920

I have been having rather an uphill week with a chronic cold that won't go. The result is that I feel too slack to amuse myself and I do nothing but write. not a' good plan as I feel so very tired at the end of the day...The reason why I've been so busy is that people are beginning to come down the Aleppo road with news of Syria and Turkey, and I, having now rather a satisfactory network of informants, hear of the arrival of most of these and send for them. What With getting their information and writing it out my mornings have been pretty full. It's a distressing story Which they bring. We share the blame with France and America for what is happening--I think there has seldom been such a series of hopeless tangles as the West has made about the East since the armistice...

I have had two more little Arab dinner parties, both very friendly and successful. Sometimes we talk politics and sometimes we just talk about the country but anyhow we talk, exchange views and learn from one another. And it gives us the sense of being all part of the same game which is the main thing.

I have had to drop my India Office report--after writing two chapters on relations with the Kurds, a most thorny and difficult subject--for the annual reports are now coming in and I must read and digest them before I can complete my own chapters on administration. These will run to two or three chapters, after which a chapter on social and political conditions of which I've written half, and then a general revision of the whole will bring me to the end of the task. It has been a big job; I can't yet judge whether I have covered the ground satisfactorily.

Frank [Balfour] and I were agreeing this evening that we feel happier about the whole position here. We feel we are getting into closer touch, that antagonism is melting and cooperation growing. I hope we are right-- it's a thing I don't think we can be mistaken about. He and I and the Howells dined at an immense Arab dinner party last week given by Fakhri Jamil in honour of the birth of a small cousin, the posthumous son of my poor friend, Abdul Rahman Jamil...After dinner I went round to the women's quarters to see the new baby, 3 days old and the mother's up and walking about how they survive I can't think. I must tell you I am honorary head of the Jamil family-- that's how the Jamil profess to regard me ...

To F.B., Bagdad, February 14th, 1920

I had a really delightful 3 days in Hillah, where I arrived feeling half dead and recovered steadily. I was staying with the Political Officer, Major Tyler, and all his staff, some 10 young men; great fun it was. Our job was to inspect the first beginnings of the land survey, the agrarian settlement which lies at the root of all our tribal problems--a gigantic task it's going to be, but if we get it done right it will mean agrarian peace for ever and a day. So we met the surveyors and looked at maps and boundary marks--heaps of earth in this country, not stones, for there are none. And then we rode back and half-way stopped and lunched at the mudhif of the chief sheikhs of the district. He had gathered in representatives of all neighbouring tribes concerned in the settlement, but being a poor man he had let it be understood that he intended to provide only for us and the Bani Hasan, his nearest neighbours. So when our great tray of foods had been set before us, another was laid in the end of the mudhif and the Bani Hasan summoned to it. The rest of the company contented themselves with cigarettes and coffee. After lunch there was a great talk--this is how business is conducted in the provinces, and there's no better council chamber than a sheikh's mudhif ...It was a delightful scene. Our host had fought against us at Kut, having mobilized his tribe at the order of the Turks. "What was it like," I asked, "when you fought with the Turks?" "Khatun," he replied solemnly (that's what they call me--

Madam), "we had nothing to eat. Mind you, they had plenty, but they gave us nothing." "Did you fight hungry?" I asked. "Wallahi no," he answered. "We returned home."

Next day Major Tyler and I motored to Diwaniyah. I hadn't been there for 2 years and I shouldn't have known the place again. Clean and tidy, with widened streets and a good hospital--it was a miracle. So is Hillah, which I spent the following morning in inspecting, after a couple of hours' talk with the two leading inhabitants. School, hospital, gaol, bazaars--like a rose, as we say in Arabic.

To F.B., Bagdad, February 29th, 1920

It's too exciting to think that Father is already on his way here. It's also the first spring day after bitter cold and drenching rain, and being Sunday I'm not going to the office. I've installed myself in the verandah of my garden having brought all my work here for a good morning, which I shall begin by writing to you.

I took the whole Goschen family to Babylon this week...They are charming people to take sight seeing because they are so much interested...I'm very busy trying to get a private hospital for women of the better classes--they have already organised an excellent ward in the Civil Hospital for poor women. It was when we showed them this that the well born women asked if they would collect the money to pay for the building. It will cost, 'tout compris' Rs.45,000, and they must pay for it if they want it--an 8 bed hospital Of 4 rooms with a bathroom and nurses room, 6 rooms in all. We had an immense tea party at Aurelia Tod's whose house is more convenient than mine, being in the middle of the town. She did it beautifully for us. I explained the matter of the hospital to the ladies and they were all very enthusiastic. I am now sending a personal letter to 10 of the richest men in this town asking them each to give Rs.3,000. The rest I think we should have no difficulty in collecting in small subscriptions.

To F.B., Bagdad, March 7th, 1920

It's wonderful to think that by this time Hugo is back. I hope it will console you for Father's absence. I really do think it will do him all the good in the world to be away for a long spell, and the account he and you give me of his doings confirms that view.

I've just written a very long letter to Lord Robert giving an exhaustive criticism of the dealings of the Conference with Western Asia...

We've had torrents of rain and the world a sea of mud...I went off at noon with the Hambros in a launch up river and we found a delicious place in the sun where it was dry and basked in the barley fields under palm trees. After which I made friends with the peasant proprietors and we had a long talk about the dealings of governments. They were darling people and when I went away they gave me five carrots and a fish, just caught...And now my room is full of pots of wild mustard and green rye which we gathered in the fields and I'm reflecting on the recurring miracle of spring.

I told you about my hospital, didn't I? The Rs.3,000 subscriptions are beginning to come in...

I went to tea on Monday with Saiyid Daud. He has a wonderful house, the finest I've seen here. You go out of a tiny narrow street into a big court with beautiful stucco rooms on the upper floor, ceilings of vaulted Persian stucco and looking-glass work 100 years old; and then into another still bigger court full of orange trees and Olives 40 feet high and lovely rooms and balconies, and best of all a stork's nest in the corner.

To F.B., March 14th, 1920

I'm glad it's not this week I was going to Basrah for I've had and have got an unspeakable cold and feel as if my chest were a solid mass. I did not make it any better by going to Kadhimain yesterday and returning late, but the visit was worth making. I've been describing it to Lord Robert as a justification 'pro vita mea'--he cast up against me my love for the horrible Easterns--so to save trouble I'll tell you the same story.

It's a problem here how to get into touch with the Shiahs, not the tribal people in the country; we're on intimate terms with all of

them, but the grimly devout citizens of the holy towns and more especially the leaders of religious opinion, the Mujtahids, who can loose
and bind with a word by authority which rests on an intimate acquaintance with accumulated knowledge entirely irrelevant to human affairs
and worthless in any branch of human activity. There they sit in an
atmosphere which reeks of antiquity and is so thick with the dust of
ages that you can't see through it--nor can they. And for the most part
they are very hostile to us, a feeling we can't alter because it's so difficult to get at them. I'm speaking of the extremists among them; there
are a few with whom we are on cordial relations. Until quite recently
I've been wholly cut off from them because their tenets forbid them to
look upon an unveiled woman and my tenets don't permit me to veil--I
think I'm right there, for it would be a tacit admission of inferiority
which would put our intercourse from the first out of focus. Nor is it
any good trying to make friends through the women--if the women
were allowed to see me they would veil before me as if I were a man.
So you see I appear to be too female for one sex and too male for the
other,

There's a group of these worthies in Kadhimain, the holy city,
8 miles from Bagdad, bitterly pan-Islamic, anti-British 'et tout le bataclan.' Chief among them are a family called Sadr, possibly more
distinguished for religious learning than any other family in the whole
Shiah world. A series of accidents led them to make advances to me to
which I replied that if they would like me to visit them I should be delighted to honour myself ...The upshot was that I went yesterday,
accompanied by an advanced Shiah of Bagdad whom I knew well. I
rather fancy he is secretly a free-thinker. We walked through the narrow crooked streets of Kadhimain and stopped before a small dark
archway. He led the way along 50 yards of pitch-dark vaulted passage-
-what was over our heads I can't think--which landed us in the courtyard of the Saiyid's house. It was old, at least a hundred years old, with
beautiful old lattice-work of wood closing the diwan on the upper
floor. The rooms all opened on to the court--no windows on to the
outer world--and the court was a pool of silence separated from the
street by the 50 yards of mysterious masonry under which we had
passed. Saiyid Hassan's son, Saiyid Muhammad, stood on the balcony
to welcome us, black robed, black bearded and on his head the huge
dark blue turban of the Mujtahid class. Saiyid Hassan sat inside, an
imposing, even a formidable figure, with a white beard reaching half
way down his chest, and a turban a size larger than Saiyid Muham-

mad's. I sat down beside him on the carpet and after formal greetings he began to talk in the rolling periods of the learned man, the book-language, which you never hear on the lips of others. Mujtahids usu-ally have plenty to say--talking is their job; it saves the visitor trouble. We talked of the Sadr family in all its branches, Persian, Syrian and Mesopotamian; and then of books and of collections of Arabic books in Cairo, London, Paris and Rome--he had all the library catalogues; and then of the climate of Samarra which he explained to me was much better than that of Bagdad because Samarra lies in the third cli-matic zone of the geographers. He talked with such vigour that his turban kept slipping forward on to his eyebrows and he had to push it back impatiently on to the top of his head...And I was acutely con-scious of the fact that no woman before me had ever been invited to drink coffee with a mujtahid and listen to his discourse, and really anx-ious lest I shouldn't make a good impression.

So after about three-quarters of an hour I said I feared I must be troubling him and I would ask permission to take my leave. "No, no," he boomed out, "we have set aside this afternoon for you." I felt pretty sure then that the visit was being a success and I stayed another hour. But I tackled this next hour with much more confidence. I said I wanted to tell him about Syria and told him all I knew down to the latest telegram which was that Faisal was to be crowned. "Over the whole of Syria to the sea?" he asked, with sudden interest. "No," I an-swered, "the French stay in Beyrout." "Then it's no good," he replied, and we discussed the matter in all its bearings. Then we talked of Bol-shevism. He agreed that it was the child of poverty and hunger, "but," he added, "all the world's poor and hungry since this war." I said that as far as I made out the Bolshevist idea was to sweep away all that ever had been and build afresh. I feared they didn't know the art of building. He approved that. Then as I made signs of going, he said, "It is well known that you are the most learned woman of your time, and if any proof were needed it would be found in the fact that you wish to frequent the society of the learned. That's why you're here to-day." I murmured profound thanks for the privilege (with a backward glance at the third climatic zone), and took my leave in the midst of a shower of invitations to come again as often as I liked.

On my way home I went to see Frank Balfour who was in bed with a touch of fever and heard from him the afternoon's news which was that Faisal had been crowned king of Syria and Abdullah king of the Iraq...

Tell darling Mrs. Wilson [Mrs. Gerald Wilson, of Mansfield, near Darlington] that the yellow hollyhock seeds have come and I've sown them in my garden and in all the gardens of my Arab friends. I may mention I've got daffodils in flower --the first daffodils seen in Mesopotamia.

To F.B., Bagdad, Sunday, April 10, 1920

I'm leaving it to Father to describe an experience which I'm sure he'll do at length. This is only a word to tell you that it's wonderful having him. It is most interesting to see him sizing up our problems and he happens to have arrived at a very crucial time. I think we're on the edge of a pretty considerable Arab nationalist demonstration with which I'm a good deal in sympathy. It will, however, force our hand and we shall have to see whether it will leave us with enough hold to carry on here...

What I do feel pretty sure of is that if we leave this country to go to the dogs it will mean that we shall have to reconsider our whole position in Asia. If Mesopotamia goes Persia goes inevitably, and then India. And the place which we leave empty will be occupied by seven devils a good deal worse than any which existed before we came.

With these few words, I remain your affectionate daughter.

To H.B., Bagdad, Thursday, 6th May, 1920

It was a delightful surprise to have a letter from you this morning. I wonder how anyone can complain about anything when they have a father like you. I can't tell you what it was like to have you here. One takes for granted where you are concerned that no matter how unfamiliar or complex the things may be that you're seeing and hearing, you'll grasp the whole lie of them at once, and it's only when I come to think of it that I realise what it is to have your quickness of intelligence. Anyhow, I feel certain that you know the general structure here as well as we know it ourselves and I'm enchanted that you should, not only because it makes my job so much more interesting knowing that you understand it, but also because it's good for us all that you should be able to put in a word for us at home...

Says Mizhir: "Some people have faces so heavy that they make the world dark; and some faces so light that everyone rejoices to see them." Hadhrat al Walid has a light face, God bless and preserve him.

To H.B., Bagdad, Sunday, 9th May, 1920

With what different feelings I write to you now that you've been here! All the news seems to be of the utmost moment now you know all about it. The first and chief is Frank's engagement to Phyllis Goschen. I'm very very glad about it. I like her.

Captain A. L. Smith [Lionel] came to dine. We had a long and satisfactory talk about the education of Arabs. I'm not quite happy about what we're doing; nor is he. It's all very well to say we mustn't start secondary schools till we have really first-rate material, both in teachers and pupils, but we can't wait for that. We must get a move on and be content with second best, for the people here are so immensely keen to be provided with higher education and if we hold back they will think we are doing it on purpose to keep them back. You have to look at it from the point of politics as well as of education.

On Friday I went to tea with the ladies of the Jamil family to see my small "son," the little boy who was born after the death of his father, my friend Abdul Rahman. He's a quite beautiful baby...

Rishan [her dog] is in terrible disgrace. First he jumped on to the pantry table and broke all the crockery on it, including my dear little Persian jam-pot. He was looking for something to eat of course. Next he thought fit to roll in a beautiful bed of nasturtiums and destroyed half of them. He was terribly beaten--by me--and goes about with an extremely penitent air.

Before all these unfortunate occurrences we were riding in the desert and the dogs had a magnificent stork hunt. Everyone was pleased; the dogs were wild with excitement and the old stork flapped along just over their heads and laughed aloud...

To F.B., Bagdad, Sunday, May 23rd, 1920

...A.T. has been given a K.C.I.E.--I'm very, very glad. He well deserves it and I'm so specially glad of the recognition of his work by H.M.G...

Another very nice thing has happened this week--Fattuh has turned up, driving a man down from Aleppo...

I am so glad to have my dear Fattuh. He wants to go back to Aleppo as soon as we can devise a safe way to get him back. His first words when he came in were, "Is His Excellency the Progenitor still with you?" I said, "How did you know he had been here?" "Oh," said Fattuh, "one of the Beduins in the desert told me that the Khatun was well and her Father was with her."

So I suppose it's the talk of Arabia...

Next morning I rode out with Frank and Major Hay to Kadhimain to see the Shah make his pilgrimage there. We started about 6, a gorgeous morning-- you can't think what it's like here in the early mornings, not hot and golden clear--getting to Kadhimain about 7... I looked through the gateway of the mosque into the sacred court-- Father knows the gate. The courtyard, into which we might not go, was full of rows of mosque servants in green turbans with groups of divines in white or dark blue turbans and long robes--it looked like a picture by Gentile Bellini. The Shah came up by launch. We rode down to the river where we found the mayor, Saiyid Jafar (with whom Father had tea) and two other magnates. We waited there under palm trees--the landing stage was just opposite the Sunni town of Mua dhdham. The river ran blue and silver, the air was like liquid gold, the gardens and houses of Muadhdham glittered on the opposite bank, with the tall minaret of the Sunni shrine rising out of them--what a setting for a king's pilgrimage, I thought...

It's Ramadhan and everyone is fasting. I had my first Ramadhan party last Thursday evening. Five young Arabs came and 5 of my colleagues. We had very interesting talks about the Turkish treaty. After the Arabs had gone, towards 11, we all had a cold supper in the garden. I'm going on with these parties and I hope they'll be a success...

Another petition story of Frank's: A gentleman who was harbourmaster at Port Sudan sent in a request that he might be granted a week's leave, as his wife was about to be delivered of a buoy.

The more you think of it, the nicer it is.

To H.B., Bagdad, June 14th, 1920

I have your letter from Aden and a word from Mother also tell her, the shoes from Yapp, most welcome. Did I ever announce to her the arrival of my linen riding habit? It's perfect, I've wired for another, 'wegen' the wash. But though linen habits are essential we're having a remarkably cool year. It has rarely been 110 as yet. I've become such a salamander that this is the sort of temp. I like.

We have had a stormy week. The Nationalist propaganda increases. There are constant meetings in mosques where the mental temp. rises a great deal above 113. The extremists are out for independence without a mandate. They play for all they are worth on the passions of the mob and what with the Unity of Islam and the Rights of the Arab Race they make a fine figure. They have created a reign of terror; if anyone says boo in the bazaar it shuts like an oyster. There has been practically no business done for the last fortnight...

I've written 3 articles at the request of A.T. about the League of Nations and the Mandate. Both A.T. and Sir Edgar are much pleased with them and they are to be published here in English and Arabic.

Major Clayton has arrived to take a job here. He is Sir Bettie Clayton's brother. I like him particularly.

To H.B., Bagdad, Sunday, June 20th, 1920

Ramadhan ended...On Friday morning I rode out before breakfast round the suburbs of Bagdad where I knew people would congregate, and saw the whole world making merry over the great

429

feast of Islam, "Id-al-Fitr," the festival of fast breaking. There were numberless booths of sweetmeat sellers, merry-go-rounds with children swinging in them, groups of women all in their best clothes, and the whole as little revolutionary as anything you can imagine. The East making holiday...

On Sat. morning when I got to the office, Ghallal (head Kavass, you remember) met me with beaming smiles and told me Sir Percy had come. I went to the Mess and found him breakfasting with Lady Cox and Major Murray, and I felt as if a load of care had been lifted. To-day, according to my custom, I didn't go to the office. Sir Percy sent me a note in the afternoon saying that he wanted to come and have a talk. He came after tea. We talked a great deal about how to bridge over the next 4 crucial months till he comes back. H.M.G. have telegraphed to him to return to England at once and he leaves to-morrow. Though, of course, I hate his going, I'm thankful that he will be there to appeal to. For I can write everything to him as I can do to no one else, he being my real Chief, and he will be able to take direct action. At 7 he went to see the Naqib taking me with him. It was touching to see the Naqib's joy. We sat in the courtyard--it was fearfully hot and stuffy--and had an hour's talk...It has been such an infinite comfort to be able to talk of public affairs here without committing an indiscretion, as I can to him. Lady Cox also has been most friendly and affectionate. I'm going to keep the parrot while she is away. I should feel easier in my mind if I were quite sure Rishan wouldn't look upon it as a species of chicken and eat it...

To H.B., Bagdad, June 27, 1920

...I haven't made any plans for myself yet. Frank is going in July to be married. It will leave us rather short-handed here. Things are quieting down and there's a promising scheme in the wind...In this flux there's no doubt that they turn to us. The old brick of a mayor constantly drops in while I'm having breakfast just to talk things over with the Khatun! There's no particular point in it except that he likes it. Yesterday he said that he much regretted Frank's going on leave. "But after all, you'll be here to tell Major Bullard who people are and what they're worth." That sort of remark makes it rather difficult to go away, doesn't it. Meantime I'm very well, though the temp. is up to its summer 115...

We've come to the conclusion that my report must be got out as soon as possible and Sir Percy has taken the first half home with him. He shall have a lot more this week, and there's now only half an administration chapter and the last political chapter to finish. The last I should like to keep by me for another month, by which time I may have got something satisfactory to end on. But we must publish something to show what the work here has been, and please will you do as much propaganda as you can.

Don't forget to go on loving me.

To H.B., Bagdad, Sunday, June 14th, 1920

The political tide ebbs and flows and we don't get much further. The mayor dropped in while I was breakfasting a few days ago, as his habit is, and told me that several of the leaders had approached him and asked whether if they accepted the mandate they could be sure that we really meant to set up an Arab Govt. He replied that they might be certain of it and that he was ready to go further into the matter with them at any time, but so far they have done nothing more...

This morning I rode out before breakfast to see H. Naji and found a large party of people with him. We talked long about the Political situation, they pointing out a good many of our errors, more of omission than of commission. They were extremely reasonable and had my full sympathy. We all agreed that there was no reason why the mandate shouldn't work with goodwill on both sides. Haji Naji, who is heart and soul with us, took a wise part in this conversation...

I'm quite well and it's not particularly hot, seldom up to 110. As long as I don't have fever or something silly I shall be all right, and I see no reason why I should have anything...

To H.B., Bagdad, Sunday, July 11th, 1920

A.T. has got permission from home to begin active preparation for the calling of a constituent assembly. All ex-deputies are going to be invited to meet in counsel and discuss the electoral basis and the method of election. It is, I think, rather a brilliant idea--we owe it to Mr. Forbes, the judge...

I dined last night with the Bowmans--they had an Arab dinner party, very pleasant...

I went to tea at the Civil Hospital with the French nuns in order to make arrangements with Capt. Braham for the opening of a small private hospital for better-class women. I have collected something over Rs. 20,000 towards it and though that isn't enough to build with it will suffice to put into order and furnish a little detached building which already exists. We shall have 4 rooms each with one bed and that will make a beginning...

To H.B., Bagdad, July 20th, 1920

Aurelia dined with me ...Still not very well. My household has been enlarged by the gift (from the Mayor's son) of a very young mongoose. It's a most attractive little beast. It sat in my hand this morning and ate fried eggs like a Christian.

The weather is fortunately mild, only about 106.

To H.B., Bagdad, July 26th, 1920

...Soon after I got to the office to-day I was visited by two distinguished Sunni magnates, fathers of turbans, one of them an advanced nationalist. I made them welcome and said it was long since I had had the pleasure of seeing them.

"Yes," they said, " we've come to you because you're beloved. Everyone in Bagdad praises you." This prelude indicated that there was something in the wind so I put a few tactful questions and discovered that they had come to find out if anything would be done to pacify the tribes. The upshot of it was that we sketched out a scheme for a joint Sunni and Shiah commission to go to Karbala and Najaf, and I took it to A.T... The two are coming to-morrow to give a final decision, but I'm rather afraid they'll say they can't take it on...

Well, if the British evacuate Mesopotamia, I shall stay peacefully here and see what happens...

Darling Father, I do hope you enjoy my letters as much as I enjoy writing them! If they seem to you rather mad, I can only offer as excuse that I'm living in a perfectly mad world. Added to which the heat makes one a little light-headed. One just accepts what happens, from day to day, without any amazement...

To H.B., Bagdad, August 2nd, 1920

My world hasn't grown any saner since I last wrote...My view of the matter is in a nutshell this : whatever our future Policy is to be we cannot now leave the country in the state of chaos which we have created, no one can master it if we can't. If we decided to withdraw at once we should have to send at least two divisions from India to extricate the troops and personnel we have here. Those 2 divisions or less might Just as well be employed in bringing the country back to order. When that is done we can begin talking...

I would give the Arabs a very long rope, as I've often said before, in the assurance that it is only if they want our help that we can help them, and in the certainty that if they are assured of the honesty of our intentions they will want our help...

Capt. Clayton, Major Bullard and I, Major Bowman and others went to a patriotic play which was got up by ardent young nationalists... Whenever the word independence occurred--which it did often--they clapped to the echo. I met on the most friendly terms everyone who had been doing his damnedest against us and we all shook hands in the greatest amity. While one of those who sit studiously on the fence whispered to me in anxiety "When in God's name are you going to release us from the terror of the tribes?" ...

It is touch and go--I'm quite unable to predict what will happen. Another episode like that of the Manchesters would bring the Tigris tribes out immediately below Bagdad. We are living from hand to mouth--I know it--and the situation is serious and might become very grave with any little swing in the scale.

Meantime I shall not go to India...

The waste it all means and the inevitable bitterness it must engender, the difficulty in pulling anything straight after this terrific upheaval--well, it's no good thinking of it.

At least it's more profitable to think of how to find immediate palliatives.

Goodbye, dearest family.

To H.B., August 8th, 1920

The political situation is improving. The military position is growing more stable with the arrival of fresh troops from India. The Euphrates tribes are still in full rebellion but they have had one or two nasty knocks and they are said to be getting a little tired of jihad. If only they would throw their hands in before we are in a position to take extreme measures it would be an immense relief. Order must be restored but it's a very doubtful triumph to restore it at the expense of many Arab lives...

To H.B., Bagdad, August 16th, 1920

It's dawn of Monday morning. I've got to go to a prizegiving at the native Church at 7:30 and I'll put in the time before I need dress in writing to you. Sunday is generally letter day but I was very busy yesterday getting ahead with a précis of the revolutionary movement which A.T. has asked me to write. It is a very difficult business to write history at such close quarters and it's complicated by the fact that one is so often interrupted in the morning at the office that there's seldom a good clear hour...

The Bowmans left for Egypt yesterday--as much regretted by their Arab as by their English colleagues. Personally I shall miss them dreadfully.

And now I'll tell you about the revolution. The committee of ex-deputies co-opted at the beginning of the week a number of people among whom were 4 of the leading extremists. On Wed. these 4 all refused the invitation and at the same time the police gave warning that there was to be a monster meeting in the big mosque next day,

434

after which a procession through the town was to be organized. It would undoubtedly have led to disturbances and that was the object desired. For the extremists have seen the ground cut under their feet by the formation of a moderate constitutional party round the committee of ex-deputies and they have no card left but an appeal to the mob. The police were therefore ordered to arrest the 4 leaders. I think they must have bungled the matter for they only got one, the others got away to Kadhimain and are now, I hear, in Najaf. Orders were then issued forbidding the holding of meetings in Mosques, together with a curfew-- no one to be out in the streets after 10 p.m. The combined effect has been excellent as far as Bagdad is concerned. The town has returned to its normal life and I think there is scarcely anyone who doesn't breathe a sigh of relief. Most of them asked why it wasn't done sooner but I think that A.T. has behaved with great wisdom in the matter. He has waited until it was clear that if the agitation was allowed to continue the town would be given over to rioters--most of those who attended the mosque meetings were riffraff of the worst sort--and there he has struck for the protection Of public security. And everyone knows that it isn't an attempt on his part to suppress Arab nationalist sentiment.

The worst news is that Col. Leachman has been ambushed and killed on his way from Bagdad to Ramadi. He was holding the whole Euphrates up to Anak single handed by means of the tribes, troops having all been withdrawn, and we don't know what will happen in those regions...

[Mr. Humphrey Bowman was Director of Education in Iraq. He sends me the following striking account of Gertrude as seen in the midst of an Arab circle, not in the desert, but in Bagdad:

"Sir Edgar Bonham Carter was giving an At Home to a number of Arab notables in Bagdad in 1919. Only one or two British were there, Cooke and myself, possibly another. We were all sitting on chairs round the room as we do in the East, getting up whenever some special guest entered. At last the door opened and Gertrude came in. She was beautifully dressed, as always, and looked very queenly. Everyone rose, and then she walked round the room, shaking hands with each Arab in turn and then saying a few appropriate words to each. Not only did she know them all by name--there must have been 40 or 50 in the room--but she knew what to say to each ..."]

To H.B., August 23rd, 1920

We have also had the staunchest adherence from Fahad Bey of the Anazeh-- the donor of my dogs. He wrote to A.T. and me last week saying that nothing would make him budge from his firm allegiance. From first to last he has never wavered and has given us all the help he can.

It has been rather cooler this week--enough cooler to make me catch cold, which doesn't however mean much as I do it easily. It's very difficult not to, for you go to bed in a temp. which makes a sheet too heavy a covering and wake at dawn chilled to the bone by a sudden drop of many degrees. We are sending away the wives of P.O.'s in the Provinces. I think it is the only thing to do. They have nearly all come in to Bagdad, where we haven't room for them, and the future is so uncertain that it's doubtful whether they will ever be able to go back-- or their husbands either in many cases. I don't anticipate that we shall reinstall the political service in the Euphrates area, though what will take its place we don't foresee. It's a sad business to see the whole organisation crumble.

To H.B., Bagdad, August 30th, 1920
[Gertrude visits the Naqib.]

While I was sitting with him this morning listening to his explanation of his neutral attitude throughout Ramadhan I was overcome--as I not infrequently am--with the sense of being as much an Asiatic as a European. For if I'm not too Asiatic to form a clear opinion, he made a pretty good case...

To be able to exchange the frankest views with the Ancient East, as I do with the Naqib, is both amazing and delightful.

To F.B., Bagdad, September 5, 1920

The truth is I'm very tired of being so hot. One always feels in September as if one could not bear it any longer. We had some bad days this week with a blazing wind, but really it's beginning to cool off a little. One doesn't need a fan till about 10 a.m., but fan or not my office nears 100 every afternoon...

The problem is the future. The tribes don't want to form part of a unified state; the towns can't do without it. How are we going to support and protect the elements of stability and at the same time conform to the just demand for economy from home? For you can't have a central government if no One will pay taxes and the bulk of the population won't pay taxes unless they are constrained to do so. Nor will they Preserve a sufficient amount of order to permit of trade...

We are now in the middle of a full-blown jihad, that is to say we have against us the fiercest prejudices of a people in a primeval state of civilisation. Which means that it's no longer a question of reason. And it has on its side the tendency to anarchy which is all over the world, I think, the salient result of the war. When one considers it, it's very comprehensible that the thinking people should revolt at an organisation of the universe which could produce anything so destructive to civilization as the war. The unthinking people, who form the great mass of the world, follow suit in a blind revolt against the accepted order. They don't know how to substitute anything better, but it's clear that few things can be worse. We're near to a complete collapse of society-- the end of the Roman empire is a very close historical parallel. We've practically come to the collapse of society here and there's little on which you can depend for its reconstruction. The credit of European civilisation is gone. Over and over again people have said to me that it has been a shock and a surprise to them to see Europe relapse into barbarism. I had no reply--what else can you call the war? How can we, who have managed our own affairs so badly, claim to teach others to manage theirs better? It may be that the world has need to sink back into the dark ages of chaos, out of which it will evolve something, perhaps no better than what it had.

To H.B., Bagdad, September 12th, 1920

It's getting a little cooler, thank Heaven; but Sep. is a disagreeable month. The air is very still and rather sticky--where it gets its stickiness from I can't think--and the dust hangs in long low lines over the world. This morning I was out riding just after sunrise--it was difficult to decide whether the earth or the air was the more solid. The dust bars hanging over the horizon were like slabs of desert in the sky, and in the uncertain light of sunrays dust and damp, when I turned round to look for my dogs I couldn't see anything tangible, but I marked each one by the little golden dust cloud that it made as it ran.

437

My dogs are very well. So's the parrot. But the mongoose has run away.

To H.B., Bagdad, September 19th, 1920

...Sir Percy knows what complete confidence there is between us and that I should always tell you exactly what I think or do. That I should be able to do so is to me the foundation of existence and it is entirely owing to you that you are to me not only a father but also the closest and most intimate friend. You have been the only person to whom I have related fully the ups and downs of these extremely difficult months and as far as anyone can relate without prejudice circumstances in which they have played a part, I have done so to you. You will therefore believe me when I tell you that it is only quite recently that I have realized how prominent a place I have occupied in the public mind here as the pro-Arab member of the administration. Over and over again lately I have heard from the frequenters of the coffee shops, my own servants and casual people up and down the bazaars, that I am always quoted in the coffee shop talk as the upholder of the rights of the Arabs. I have invariably replied that the talk is incorrect; it is H.M.G. which upholds the rights of the Arabs and we are all of us the servants of H.M.G.

To H.B., Bagdad, September 27th, 1920

The most remarkable feature this week has been the weather. On the 21st, it rained quite hard enough to lay all the dust. There hasn't been anything like it since 1907, they say, and then not quite so early. Then we had two days of South wind and cloud, very hot and stuffy and finally the most terrific dust storm lasting many hours and followed by violent thunder storms...

A. T. is going to India, Egypt and C'ple on his way home-- that's his scheme. He wants to get a comprehensive view of the Eastern question. I told him you would be very glad to see him in London...

What I hope Sir Percy will do is to give a very wide responsibility to natives of this country. It is the only way of teaching them how hard the task of government is. I think we must now wade through a long period of uncertainty and mistakes which, if they are wise enough and we patient enough may result in a more equable division of our respective spheres of activity. Up to now we've done it all. I should stand by and let them do it all for a bit and then see if a better adjustment is not possible...

To H.B., October 3rd, 1920

This morning being Sunday I rode out before breakfast to see Haji Naji. He had a party of guests sitting in his arbor and he was showing off the 'sécateur' you senthim. "The first," he said, "that has been seen in the Iraq," and he proudly snipped off the branches of an adjacent mulberry tree to show how well it worked. I wished you had been there to see. I've been very agricultural this week. I attended a demonstration at the cotton farm where experiments are being made in various kinds of cotton and various treatments. About a dozen Bagdad landowners were present and were deeply interested. So was I. On an average Of 3 years, a certain long-stapled American variety seems to be the most promising. There seems every reason to believe that we shall produce as good cotton as is grown anywhere in the world, and their yield is very large...

There is one other party I didn't tell you about. Capt. Clayton and I went to tea with one of the leading Agail of Bagdad. The Agail are nearly all central Arabians; they invariably speak of themselves as subjects of Ibn Saud. They are the merchants and caravan leaders of the desert. I had an Agaili with me when I went to Hayil. They live in the right bank part of Bagdad--Karkh is its name--and they have a famous coffee shop of their own. I'm in intimate relations with them for they are the people from whom I get news. I do them a good turn whenever I can and they respond by coming in to see me whenever they return from Syria or Arabia and telling me what they've heard and seen...The tea party was delightful. The walls of the diwan are mellow with decades of tobacco smoke, the only furniture, benches round the room and one table for us at the upper end. In order to do us honour he had provided a tinned plum pudding for our special benefit. We scooped it out of the tin and eat it cold. A large and distinguished party of Agaili had been invited to meet us--all frequenters of my office-- and we talked Arabian politics with great gusto for an hour and a half. During all that time Suliman stood in front of us and talked. It was a miracle of grace and poise. Incidentally, he has, like all Najdis, the most slender hands with long fingers and nails an American beauty might envy. Their hands are their most characteristic feature. They are seldom shaved but as a rule their beards are scanty--it is rare to see a full thick beard. Some are Wahabis, i.e., they do not smoke, but most of the frequenters of cities abandon the stricter rules of the desert creed. I do like them so much. They are to me an endless romance. They come and go through the wilderness as if it were a high road, and they all, most politely, treat me as a colleague, because I too have been in Arcadia. When they talk of tribes or sheikhs or watering places I don't need to ask who and where they are. I know; and as they talk I see again the wide Arabian horizon. ...

To H.B. and F.B., Bagdad, October 10th, 1920

I don't know what I should do without your weekly letters, they are the only link I have with the outer world. I do sometimes feel dreadfully isolated.

The Coxes were to have arrived yesterday but they've stayed an extra day in Amarah and Kut and don't get here until to-morrow. The delay was a godsend as far as I was concerned for I was prostrated with a violent cold yesterday and did not go out of the house. I'm better to-day and I hope I may be all right, to-morrow...

I had a long talk with Sasun Eff the other day--I went to Call On his sister-in-law and found all the men there eager to embark on talk. Sasun Eff said he felt sure that no local man would be acceptable as head of the state because every other local Man would be jealous of him. He went on to throw out feelers in different directions--one might think of a son of the Sharif, or a member of the family of the Sultan of Egypt, if there was a suitable individual, or of the family of the Sultan of Turkey? I said that I for my part felt sure that Sir Percy didn't and couldn't mind whom they selected except that I thought the Turkish family was ruled out--it ought to be an Arab Prince...Any one they think we are backing they will agree to, and then intrigue against him without intermission. It is not an easy furrow to plough! These reflections will throw an illumination on what is being said in the English papers, from which it would appear that Sir Percy has only to say "Hey Presto" for an Arab Government to leap on to the stage, with another Athene springing from the forehead of Zeus. You may say if you like that Sir Percy will play the role of Zeus but his Athene will find the stage encumbered by such trifles as the Shiah problem, the tribal problem and other matters, over which even a goddess might easily stumble. But if he's not a Zeus he is a very skilful physician and one in whom his patient has implicit confidence. That last item is our chief asset and it's clear to me that whatever line he may decide to pursue, it's up to us to follow him with all the strength and ability we may individually possess. The underlying truth of all criticism is however- and its what makes the critics so difficult to answer--that we had promised selfgoverning institutions, and not only made no step towards them but were busily setting up something entirely different. One of the papers says, quite rightly, that we had promised an Arab Government with British Advisers, and had set up a British Government with Arab Advisers. That's a perfectly fair statement...

As to expenses, you realize that my living expenses here don't include what I get from England, clothes, books, etc. The price of everything is really appalling but the best way to remedy that is to get nothing more. Meantime as far as I'm concerned that's the course which providence has marked out for nothing has come though I've got bills for tricotine and things which Elsa kindly bought for me. I shan't pay them till the things arrive.

Tuesday, 12th October. A word to say that Sir Percy arrived yesterday, thank Heaven. The Office is in rather a turmoil with no one knowing exactly what they ought to do next, so I can't write at length about his reception--I will next week. I'm taking on a sort of temporary Oriental Secretary job till people find their feet.

[I include here two historical summaries, written by Sir Percy Cox and Sir Henry Dobbs, respectively, of the years during which Gertrude worked under them in the East. I am most grateful to them for this very valuable help.]

By MAJOR-GENERAL SIR PERCY COX, G.C.M.G. etc.:

Lady Bell, having decided to publish a series of letters written from the Middle East by her distinguished and lamented daughter, has requested me and my successor as High Commissioner, Sir Henry Dobbs, to write, each of us, a background to those letters, a sketch of

441

events for the period during which her daughter was associated with us in the responsible and absorbing task of establishing national Government in Iraq under the guidance of Great Britain.

I cordially welcome the opportunity thus afforded me of paying a small tribute to the memory of a dear friend and most loyal and devoted comrade through eight years of strenuous service.

I first met Gertrude Bell at the house of mutual friends, the late Sir Richmond and Lady Ritchie, during the winter of 1909, which found me at home for a few weeks on duty from the Persian Gulf Residency. Sir Richmond had arranged for us to meet in order that Miss Bell might have an opportunity of discussing with me the possibility of carrying out during the coming year her long cherished ambition to penetrate into Central Arabia. Her particular objective at the time was Northern Nejd, the principality of Ibn Rashid, whose forbears, with their capital at Hayil, figured so prominently in the immortal pages of Charles Doughty. She was anxious to enter from one of the ports of the Arab coast of the Persian Gulf, lying within my sphere as British Resident. Unfortunately at that particular juncture inter-tribal relations between the principalities of Eastern Arabia were so disturbed that an expedition from that side would have been foredoomed to failure and I was obliged to advise her to wait for a more favourable opportunity. She accordingly turned her attention once more to the western borderlands and the early spring of 1910 found her back again in Syria embarking on a five months expedition from Aleppo to Bagdad and thence onwards through northern Mesopotamia to Konia, a journey which she described on her return in a second book of travels, "Amurath to Amurath," published in 1911.

It was not until four years after our meeting, that she found herself, in December 1913, once more in camp near Damascus, and this time she succeeded in giving the slip to tiresome Turkish officialdom and made a bid for northern Nejd. After an eventful and venturesome journey she returned safely from her wanderings in March 1914, with her object accomplished, but tired out with the trying conditions of desert travel and badly in need of repose; and hardly had she time to recover normal health, much less to devote herself to any account of her experiences, when the Great War broke out and claimed her for other service. There is little doubt that if she had been spared to return once again from Bagdad for a spell of leisure at home,

442

her first task would have been to work up her notes for publication; but as, alas, this was not to be, it is some consolation to know that her old friend Dr. David Hogarth, our great authority on Arabia has prepared from her notes a Paper which he will have read before the Royal Geographical Society ere this volume is in print; so that, at any rate, the results of the expedition have not been lost to geography.

After the brief intercourse of 1909-1910 above referred to, I did not meet Gertrude Bell again until the spring of 1916, when after a period of some months spent in our Arab Intelligence Bureau at Cairo, working up Arab questions and more particularly inter-tribal relations, she was sent on deputation to G.H.Q. Intelligence in Mesopotamia and reported herself at General Sir Percy Lake's Headquarters at Basrah. The intention was that having thoroughly mastered on the record the intricacies of Arab politics in the Hejaz she should now work up tribal questions from the Iraq side and maintain liaison in regard to these matters with her late comrades of the Arab Bureau at Cairo. After she had spent some weeks at her task, the military authorities decided that the particular service for which she had been deputed to Basrah had been completed as far as it could be for the time being, and finding a member of her sex a little difficult to place as a permanency in a military G.H.Q. in the field, they offered her services to me in my capacity of Chief Political Officer,--services which were gladly accepted. Thus began the 10 years of devoted service to myself and my successors, which were only terminated by her untimely death in harness on 11th of July 1926.

My duties as Chief Political Officer to the G.O.C.-in-Chief at the period when she joined me were partly military and partly civil. In the first place I was the medium of communication between the Military Commander and the civil population, and his adviser in his political dealings with them. For this purpose I worked as a member of his G.H.Q. Intelligence and was always in close touch with that branch, assisting in the examination of prisoners and spies, the sifting of information, the provision of informers and interpreters and so on. On the purely civil side it devolved on me, under the G.O. C.'s supreme control, to implement as far as the fluctuating tide of war allowed, the assurances which we had given to the Arabs at the beginning of the campaign, both in the Persian Gulf and in lower Mesopotamia,--assurances which it may be well to emphasise here.

As regards the Persian Gulf, our self-imposed task of main-taining Pax Britannica, had inevitably created for us in the course of several generations a series of treaties and obligations of responsibility towards the Arab rulers on its shores which there could now be no question of our disregarding. We had treaties of old standing with the Sultan of Muscat; with the Sheikhs of the Pirate (now the Trucial) Coast of Oman, with Bahrein, and with the Sheikh of Qatar. We were on intimate terms with Ibn Saud, the Wahabi chieftain of southern Nejd, who in 1913 had succeeded in extending his independent author-ity to the Coast of the Persian Gulf, and whose future prosperity and success depended mainly on our recognition and sympathetic co-operation in his plans of progress and reform. At the head of the Gulf the Sheikh of Koweit had been assured of our support against any Turkish encroachment on his independence; and finally, on the banks of the Shatt-el-Arab was the Sheikh of Moharnmerah, Arab by race though subject to Persia, who looked to us in view of the commercial stake we enjoyed in his territory to secure fair play for him in his rela-tions alike with Persia and with Turkey.

These close connections of treaty and friendship were an in-valuable asset to us when the time came to contemplate the lively probability of Turkey's entry into the War against us; but if an advan-tage was to be taken of them, it was clearly of primary importance that we should demonstrate to our friends at the outset the circumstances in which war had been forced upon us and should take such prompt ac-tion as would convince them that we were alive to the danger in which they would be placed, as friends of ours, and intended to take adequate steps to safe guard their interests as well as our own. Accordingly, the moment news of the outbreak of war with Turkey was received I was instructed to issue a proclamation in the above sense, assuring our Arab friends at the same time that their liberty and religion would be scrupulously respected, and that all we asked of them was that they should preserve order in their own territories and ensure that their sub-jects indulged in no action calculated to injure British interests. This was followed by a further proclamation guaranteeing to them and to Islam in general that so far as we were concerned, the Holy Places in the area of war should have complete immunity from molestation. With these assurances the Arab potentates were fully satisfied and thus it was that the benevolent Policy pursued by us for many Years past in our dealings with them now found its reward in an unwavering friend-ship, which was of incalculable value to us throughout the campaign.

It 'was in the same spirit that a few days later when the British Expeditionary Force first set foot on Turkish soil at Fao, I issued a similar announcement to the riverain Arabs, assuring them that it was with the Turks only that we were at war and not with the inhabitants of the country and that so long as the Arabs showed themselves friendly and refrained from going about armed or harbouring Turkish troops, they had nothing to fear from us.

In furtherance of this policy it was our duty as far as military exigencies permitted, to enable the peaceable inhabitants of the territory gradually falling under our occupation, to carry on their normal vocations; but the initial difficulties involved in setting up a civil administration with war in lively progress were naturally considerable and were greatly enhanced in this case by the fact that the Turkish régime having been almost entirely alien, all Turkish officials and those non-Turks who had been employed in the administration, fled with the retreating armies as each centre was evacuated, and we found no local material whatever with which to replace them. Consequently for the time being, and indeed for the whole duration of the war, personnel for the administration had either to be recruited from the British and the British Indian material serving with the Army, or to be borrowed from India. Nevertheless, as soon as we had settled down in Basrah a beginning was made towards the establishment of a system of government which would be consonant with the spirit of our announcements. For this branch of my duties I had separate Offices and Staff and divided my working hours between the Army G.H.Q., whether at the Base or in the Field, and my Civil Headquarters at Basrah. It was here that Gertrude Bell joined me in the circumstances above described, as also did Captain Arnold Wilson, (now Lieut. Colonel Sir Arnold Wilson, K.C.I.E., etc.). The latter had been serving with me for some years before the War, first in the Persian Gulf Residency and later at Mohammerah, but for the past year he had been on deputation as one of the British representatives on the TurkoPersian Boundary Commission, a body which had been surprisingly successful in its labours and had fortunately completed them just in time for its members to disperse before hostilities commenced. About the same time too I received a valuable reinforcement of Officers from the Government of India, including Mr. Henry Dobbs, who later on, as Sir Henry Dobbs, was to succeed me as High Commissioner in Mesopotamia--a senior official of the Indian Civil Service, with mature experience in revenue and fiscal matters, who at once set himself to get the revenue administration on to an effective working basis. Other senior members of the Political Department of the Government of India placed at my disposal about the same time were Colonel S. G. Knox, afterwards judicial Commissioner and Colonel R. E. A. Hamilton, now Lord Belhaven and Stenton, who became Political Agent at Koweit, in succession to Major W. H. L. Shakespear. The latter had been deputed to the court of His Highness Ibn Saud on the outbreak of war and his tragic death in a desert battle between Ibn Saud and his rival Ibn Rashid deprived his country of a most gallant and capable officer whose services could ill be spared at the time. Another new comer was Mr. H. St. J. Philby of the Indian Civil Service, afterwards to earn distinction as a traveller in Central Arabia. Other good men and true came and went according to the needs of my working staff which had to be augmented or modified as the tide mark of war advanced in our favour and left a continually expanding tract of country under our administration.

In this brief sketch it is not possible or necessary for me to deal with the military aspects of the campaign and I must pass over the eventful winter Of 1915 and the spring of 1916, which witnessed Townshend's victorious advance up the Tigris, culminating in the battle of Ctesiphon; his retirement to Kut, with its siege and final surrender; and the terrible trials of our troops in their gallant attempts to relieve the beleaguered garrison, the moving story of which has been told so graphically by the official "Eye-witness," the late Umund Candler, in his "Long Road to Bagdad."

During this period steady progress continued to be made with the creation of administrative machinery in all its branches throughout the Basrah Vilayet, and Gertrude Bell worked devotedly as Oriental Secretary to myself or my deputy, Captain Wilson, in the Bastah Secretariat. During the late summer of 1915, I had arranged to rendezvous at Oj air with the Sultan of Nejd for the purpose of concluding the Treaty negotiations, which had been interrupted by His Highness' abortive campaign above referred to, and a year later after the final signing of the documents, His Highness was invited first to a durbar at Koweit to meet the Sheikhs of Koweit and Mohammerah and other important tribal Sheikhs with whom we were now in touch; and afterwards to Basrah for a short visit, in the belief that it would be of interest and value to him to see the working, and the immense proportions, of a great military base and port such as Basrah had now become, and would also be a useful means of demonstrating to the inhabitants of the Basrah Vilayet the very close relations existing between us and the great Arab Chiefs of the principalities on their borders. I remember well with what delight and enthusiasm Gertrude Bell entered at this time into all the arrangements for Sultan Ibn Saud's visit, looking forward keenly as she did to making the acquaintance of this great and attractive actor on the Arabian stage; alike for the immediate interest of the prospect and also, I cannot help thinking, in the latent hope that it might lead to an s expedition to his capital when the clouds of war had dispersed. Ibn Saud, who had heard me speak of Gertrude Bell and of her pre-war expedition to Hayil, had never before come in contact with any European woman and the phenomenon of one of the gentler sex occupying an official position with a British Expeditionary Force was one quite outside his bedouin comprehension; nevertheless when the time came he met Miss Bell with complete frankness and sangfroid as if he had been associated with European ladies all his life.

Except for the interruption of this " royal visit " and an occasional week end trip to Basrah to enable me to keep in touch with passing events in the sphere of the civil administration and to see to the welfare of my wife, who at this time was engaged in good works among the troops in Basrah, I was able to remain with Sir Stanley Maude's Headquarters on the Tigris front throughout the winter campaign, which saw the recovery of Kut, the sudden crossing of the Tigris at Shimran and the subsequent advance on Bagdad, ending in its occupation on the 11th of March 1917.

The fall of Bagdad was an event full of significance and pregnant with possibilities both for ourselves and for the enemy. Throughout the Empire and among our allies the brilliant success of General Maude's campaign aroused the utmost enthusiasm, so that the tragedy of Kut seemed almost effaced in the public mind; while for the Turks the loss of Bagdad not only deprived them of their base of operations in Mesopotamia but laid them open to an Anglo-Russian offensive in the Mosul Vilayet. The prospect of joining up with our Russian allies as a prelude to concerted operations in northern Mesopotamia had always been one to conjure with in Force "D." A year previous a Russian Cossack patrol from General Baratoff's force, then at Kermanshah, had reached our lines at Ali Gharbi on the Tigris after a daring ride of 200 miles through the mountains of Pusht-i-kuh. They were naturally welcomed by us with great cordiality, and during the few days that they remained in our Camp to rest their horses before starting back their Officers were decorated by the G.O.C.-in-Chief with the British Military Cross " in recognition of this exploit and on this, the first meeting of British and Russian troops, as allies in the field, for 100 years." The meeting of the two armies later on was consequently looked forward to with great expectations, destined unfortunately to be grievously disappointed. Though we knew it not at the time, the date of our victorious entry into Bagdad coincided almost exactly with the abdication of the Tzar and the Bolshevik upheaval, and the Russian Troops on the Persian line had already been impregnated with the virus of bolshevism and were getting out of control. It was consequently the more unfortunate that military exigencies not only precluded our extending our occupation up to the frontier of Iraq near Khanikin, but obliged us to acquiesce in the occupation of that town by General Batatoff's troops. Whatever its Military aspect might be this phenomenon greatly upset the political situation at the time. The inhabitants of Khanikin Had had bitter experience of a hostile Russian occupation in 1916, but now decided to refrain from all opposition, because on this occasion the Russians came as our allies and with our consent, if not at our request. A great revulsion of feeling, however, was caused by their behaviour and in the process we ourselves rapidly lost prestige and sympathy among a race which had always been friendly to us. Military considerations were of course paramount but this Russian occupation left us a legacy which gave trouble for a long time to come. After a couple of months the Russian force withdrew and their ravages in the district were completed by the Turks who forthwith reoccupied it and it was not until December 1918 that we were in a position to assume control ourselves. When we did so we found the town in a state of acute misery, for the Turks when they retired had left it in the joint clutches of starvation and disease and it was with these formidable adversaries that the work of administration was confronted. Major E. B. Soane, the remarkable character to whom the charge was entrusted and who in addition to a very strong personality possessed the then rare accomplishment of a fluent knowledge of the Kurdish language, laboured devotedly for months at his task, which grew in direct ratio to the success achieved, for no sooner did the Kurds on either side of the frontier hear that help was to be had from the British Authorities at Suleimaniyeh than they poured down from the mountains starving and typhus stricken, to be brought slowly back to health or else to die in our camps and hospitals. Nevertheless by the early summer of 1918 when Major Soane, worn out by incessant toil, was compelled to take a year's rest, the battle was won and his successor Major Goldsmith, found the crops springing up and repeopled villages arising from the ruins which had been wrought.

But I am straying too wide from the track and will return for a few moments to the days of our entry into Bagdad. We found the pre-war British Residency in use as a Hospital, in which the Turks had left us an unwelcome legacy in the shape of their worst cases of wounds and disease. Its sanitary condition was indescribable, but other hospitable accommodation was gradually found for the inmates and the Residency after a thorough cleansing and overhaul was fitted up as Army Headquarters, a function which it still fills for the Royal Air Force to-day: but whereas the military Staff was already in being, my civil Staff for the Bagdad Vilayet was nonexistent and had to be created. I was allotted a house on the river bank below the Residency which had before our entry been the Austrian Consulate and there I began to form a Secretariat. My first act on arrival had been to seek out any of the old local employees of the pre-war Residency Staff, both because I was anxious to learn what might have happened to them at the hands of the enemy and also because, if forthcoming, I knew they could be very useful to me at this period, with their knowledge of the communities and individual inhabitants of Bagdad. To my great regret I found the family of Narcessian, the faithful Armenian Dragoman of the Residency, in the depth of despair; their father had been sent for by the Turkish Police shortly before our arrival and had not returned. He was never heard of again nor was I able to obtain any evidence as to the precise fate which had befallen him, but he was a man who had doubtless made enemies in the course of his duties as British Dragoman, quite apart from any grudge the Turkish Police might have had against him, and there seemed little doubt that he had met with a violent death during the period of uproar which intervened between the Turkish retreat and our arrival. My next act was to visit His Reverence Saiyid Abdurrahman Effendi, the Naqib, or Chief Noble, of Bagdad; head of the Sunni community and custodian of the shrine of Abdul Qadir Gilani, upon whose attitude towards us and influence with the people of Bagdad a good deal depended. Under the old régime of Sultan Abdul Hamid the Naqib had enjoyed a position of great dignity and stood high in public esteem and no doubt owed a considerable debt of obligation to the former Government; but under the Young Turk régime he had become of less account and indeed had little to thank them for. At this time his position was obviously a deli-

cate one and his attitude had naturally to be one of reserve, yet I enjoyed his frank and wise co-operation in all measures affecting the
welfare of his countrymen and likely to mitigate as far as might be the
rigours and inconveniences of a military occupation. I saw a great deal
of him in the course of my duties and the feelings of mutual confidence which were established between us at this time were to stand me
in good stead later on, and are now a grateful memory.

Directly the news of our occupation of Bagdad got abroad I
was perforce overwhelmed with visitors; first the notables of Bagdad
and then the tribal Sheikhs from near and far, many of whom had
never submitted to the authority of the Turkish Government and were
complete strangers to Bagdad. Some attempt had to be made to determine and record from whence these visitors came, what their relations
were to one another and what was their relative importance among
themselves, matters not at all easy for new comers to diagnose. It was
in connection with this task that I began to feel the want of Gertrude
Bell's indefatigable assistance and decided to bring her and one or two
others up from the Basrah Office to form a nucleus for my Secretariat
at Bagdad. All sheikhly visitors from the countryside had to be interviewed, entertained, given small presents and sent back to their homes
with injunctions to keep the peace and get busy with their agriculture;
so that a great proportion of my time during daylight was spent in
these interviews and Miss Bell acted as the strainer through which the
individuals filtered through to me, accompanied by a brief note as to
what their tribe was, where they came from and what they wanted. I
was thus saved endless time in getting to the point. I remember that
when I told him that some of my office staff were coming up from
Basrah, including Miss Bell, the G.O.C.-in-Chief expressed considerable misgiving at the news, as he feared her arrival might form an
inconvenient precedent for appeals from other ladies, but I reminded
him that her services had been specifically offered to me by his prede-
cessor as an ordinary member of my Secretariat; that I regarded and
treated her no differently from any male officer of my Staff, and that
her particular abilities could be very useful to me at the present moment. In due course she arrived and was not long in establishing happy
personal relations with Sir Stanley Maude and it is a sad memory to
me now that she and I were both members of his party at the entertainment in Bagdad City a few months later which proved to be his last
appearance in public, before his tragic death from cholera a few days
later, at the height of his success.

These first six months of our occupation of Bagdad were indeed no easy period for the Civil Administration. The Army was fully occupied consolidating its position round Bagdad and needed to husband its strength to the utmost for the coming winter campaign and so detachments for outlying places could not be spared; nor, for fear of inconvenient incidents, could civil officers be allowed to go far afield. In these circumstances it was naturally difficult for tribesmen to believe, especially in the face of the violent Turko-German propaganda which was rife at the time, that the existing régime at Bagdad was at all secure or that the Turks would not eventually return. Even in Bagdad itself great uncertainty prevailed as to the intentions of the Allies, even if they did win the war; in fact up to the time of our successful offensive in the Autumn of 19 18 it was the general impression that the Central Powers would be victorious or at any rate that nothing more than a stalemate would result.

Those who prided themselves on their intimate acquaintance with world politics declared that Iraq would undoubtedly be handed back to Turkey in exchange for the liberation of Belgium. Such rumours found their echo among the Sheikhs in general, causing many of our firmest friends to waver, or at least to wait on events. Altogether, in view of the actual political situation and the fact that with our Occupation of the Bagdad Vilayet the military régime found itself confronted with many difficult problems of a nonmilitary aspect, H.M's Government came to the conclusion that some development of my status as Chief Political Officer to the G.O.C.-in-Chief was now called for. Accordingly, from the beginning Of July 1917, my designation was altered to that of " Civil Commissioner," and while I still, of course, remained subject to the supreme authority of the Army Commander I was given the right henceforth of direct communication with the Secretary of State for India, in whose name the instructions of H.M's Government, in other than military matters, were thereafter issued; and sound advice and judicious support from that Department of State never failed the head of the Civil administration during the three difficult years which were to pass until 1921, when in connection with a new and significant development of policy the direction of affairs in Iraq was transferred to the Colonial Office. But of this more anon.

During the period of which I am speaking, the summer of 1917, the limits of our occupation beyond Bagdad were roughly; on the right flank, Baquba, on the river Diyala; in the centre, Samarra, on

451

the Tigris line; and on the Euphrates west of Bagdad, Falluja; and thence back to the Hindiyeh barrage on the same river.

On the Diyala the process of consolidation was necessarily slow, for not only had the country suffered greatly from long devastation by Turkish troops, but until the autumn Of 1917 the canal-heads were still in the enemy's control.

The Tigris gave us no further trouble; those tribal leaders who had joined the Turks again on our retirement from Ctesiphon had thought it safest to remain with them when they in turn retreated towards Mosul; meanwhile their sons, or other suitable kinsmen, had been installed for the time being in their holdings along the river and were now occupied in the cultivation of their lands, much as in time of peace. A most favourable impression was created at this time in the Tigris area by our decision to rebuild Kut-al-Amara, a task which was undertaken partly from expediency and partly in the way of a memorial to those among the beleaguered garrison and friendly Arab inhabitants who had given their lives in the defence of the town. Kut, since the Turks evacuated it in their hurried flight before General Maude had been left completely deserted; a tottering ruin among the palm groves; its streets choked with mud or blocked with barricades; its houses riddled with shells or undermined with dug-outs. The work of reconstruction was supervised with much skill and judgment by the District Political Officer and the country-side saw in the regeneration of the town not only profit and advantage to themselves but also some pledge that a new order of things SO solidly established must have come to stay.

On the Euphrates west of Bagdad there was little to be done for the moment and it was not until Sir Harry Brooking's successful push in November 1917 had brought about the capture of Ramadi that the tribal Sheikhs of that area began to come in.

On the middle Euphrates, from the Hindiyeh barrage to Samawa, the position was a curious one. Not a single British soldier was located south of the barrage until December 1917; nevertheless that area being the centre of an important grain growing district, irrigated by the Euphrates canals, could not in the interests of the Army be altogether neglected and a political Officer had accordingly been sent to Hillah in May 1917. His authority however did not extend to Diwaniyeh and southward thereof, where the local Sheikhs, after their visit to me on our first entry into Bagdad, had to be left pretty much to their own devices. It was typical of our slender hold on the middle Euphrates during this first summer that a small Turkish detachment which on our occupation at Bagdad had found itself isolated at Diwaniyeh and unable to get away with the retreating army, held out there until the end of August. It was commanded by a fire-eating Circassian, who, having shot His superior officers when they showed a disposition to surrender, had barricaded himself and his party in a caravan-serai on the river bank and completely terrorised the inhabitants, who regarded their unwelcome guest and his bomb-throwing men with no little dismay and made several attempts to oust them lest their presence should involve the town in hostilities with us. It was only when a visitation from some air-craft convinced him that the game was up that he surrendered with the 30 odd men who had stood by him to the end. On his arrival at Bagdad I had occasion to interview this gentleman and learnt that he considered that the Turks having forgotten him and left him completely in the lurch., he was now free to offer himself for service either with us or with the Arab Army in Hejaz. His artless overture could not however be accepted and as an officer-prisoner he spent the remainder of the war in the less exciting atmosphere of a prisoner's camp in India. He was a stout- hearted, attractive fellow; I trust fortune has since smiled on him.

But the most thorny problem on the Euphrates at that time was not so much the tribes as the Holy Cities of Islam, Karbala and Najaf. As in other cases on the lower Euphrates the Sheikhs of these towns, after their visit to me at Bagdad, had been sent back to their homes with pious instructions from me to maintain law and order themselves; and in order to strengthen their hands and give them some official recognition, small monthly allowances were provided for them; but before many weeks had passed it became evident that the arrangement was working unsatisfactorily both for the towns and for us. On the one hand the Sheikhs were found to be abusing their positions and making hay while the sun shone; while, worse still, the existence of a brisk trade in supplies to the enemy, both on the Iraq front and in Syria, was brought to light. If further trouble was to be avoided closer control had clearly become essential, and British Political Officers were accordingly posted at Karbala, and at Kufa in the Shamiyeh district on the border of which lies Najaf. These officers for the time being had to rely entirely on their own judgment and force of character and were often placed in positions of great difficulty and no little personal risk. Karbala it is true gave no serious trouble, but Najaf, where the town was in the hands of a lawless crew of local Sheikhs, remained a thorn in our side for some time to come. Fortunately, while the urgent need of food supplies for the population no less than for the army endowed the Euphrates basin with an ever increasing importance, military stringency had been somewhat eased as the danger of any serious attempt on the part of the enemy to move against Bagdad was diminishing, and so it was considered that troops could now be spared to complete the effective occupation of the area behind our fighting line. I accordingly made a tour of the district in December 1917 in order to be in a position to advise the G.O.C.-in-Chief as to the various points where, from the administrative point of view, detachments could advisably be placed. It was of course undesirable, and indeed incompatible with our previous announcements, to place troops in the Holy places themselves, and this made it especially difficult to exercise full control at Najaf, where the lawless elements in the town were being excited by persistent Turko-German propaganda, clear evidence of which was found a little later among enemy papers captured by our troops at Ramadi and Hit. Unfortunately affairs here culminated in the murder of a most promising young officer, Captain W. L. Marshall, who after serving with much credit in a similar post in the Holy City of Kadhimain was selected for the difficult charge at Najaf on account of his special qualifications and experience.

At the time of this tragedy I myself was on my way to Cairo to attend a conference regarding Arab affairs, but thanks to effective handling of the matter by the Commander-in-Chief and my deputy Colonel Arnold Wilson, heavy retribution was meted out to those concerned, 12 persons suffering the death penalty, while five were transported for life and two for a shorter period.

At Cairo under the hospitable roof and wise direction of the High Commissioner, Sir Reginald Wingate, I found a gathering of distinguished officers immediately concerned with the Arab problems of the moment; David Hogarth, once "A Wandering Scholar in the Levant" now, as I write, President of the Royal Geographical Society, at that time (as Commander Hogarth, R.N.V.R.) Director of the Arab Bureau: Ronald Storrs, Oriental Secretary at the Residency, the "Perfect Storrs" of King Hussein's despatches, since knighted and now

454

Governor of Cyprus : Gilbert Clayton, Director of Intelligence at Cairo, now Sir Gilbert Clayton and (1927) on an important mission to King Ibn Saud: George Lloyd, now Lord Lloyd, our High Commissioner in Egypt: and last but not least T. E. Lawrence, soon to win lasting fame for his exploits with the Arab contingent and later for his wonderful story of "The Revolt in the Desert." A truly brilliant constellation!

Our deliberations ranged over all the problems in which we in Mesopotamia and they in the Hejaz were mutually interested. I was chiefly concerned with the difficult one with which both alike were confronted in the bitter personal relations existing between our two Arab allies King Hussein and the Sultan of Nejd; relations which made it hard to decide how most advantage could be derived from their co-operation, either in combination or independently. I should mention that during the preceding winter an important Mission, consisting of Mr. H. St. J. Philby, on my behalf, Colonel R. E. A. Hamilton, Political Agent at Koweit, representing Koweit interests, and Colonel F. Cunliffe-Owen, on behalf of the military authorities at Bagdad, had proceeded to the capital of the latter potentate at Riyadh, to report on the situation in Central Arabia generally and in particular on the possibilities of a renewed campaign against Hayil, where Ibn Rashid was still active in Turkish interests and a difficult factor in the situation. Their report had been received shortly before I left for Cairo.

While there I received a summons to proceed on to London for the discussion of various current questions connected with Mesopotamia, and again, while en route back to Bagdad, I was directed to make a further diversion to Simla to confer with the Government of India. On arrival there I learnt that His Majesty's Minister at Teheran, Sir Charles Marling, who for months past had been having an extremely harassing time in the endeavour to combat Turko-German activities in Persia and the lively pressure which they were exercising upon the Persian Government, had been ordered home on sick leave and that it was desired that I should relieve him. I ventured to urge that having been with the Army in Mesopotamia from the commencement of the War I would much prefer to see the campaign through in my present post, but as it was considered that with British troops on the Bagdad-Enzeli line and questions for discussion continually arising between His Majesty's Minister and the G.O.C. in Mesopotamia, it was of great importance that the incumbent of the British Legation for the time being should be an officer with war- time experience of events and conditions in Mesopotamia and Persia, I did not feel justified in pressing my objections and left forthwith for Bagdad and Teheran. I halted at Bagdad only long enough to collect a convoy of cars for the conveyance of my wife and myself and our meagre war-scale belongings and we proceeded with all despatch to Teheran. At the moment of our passage the question of Persia's entry into the war against us was hanging by the slenderest of threads, her idea apparently being that as the Central Powers were evidently going to win, it would be profitable for Persia to be in with them at the finish. I even received a telegram at Hamadan, en route, suggesting that I was too late for the fair and had better not come further, but we pushed on without incident and I relieved Sir Charles Marling on the 15th September 1918, he returning by the same convoy next day.

During the20-odd months that I spent as British representative at Teheran events had continued to move apace in Mesopotamia. In fact at the time I left Bagdad both General Allenby and General Marshall were on the point of launching their respective autumn campaigns. In Palestine the former's forces were concentrating in the coastal plain and on September 19th commenced those brilliant operations which resulted in the destruction of the Turkish army, and the occupation of Damascus and Aleppo. On October 1st the desert mounted corps and the Arab army entered Damascus amidst scenes of great enthusiasm.

In Iraq, Sir William Marshall opened his campaign on the 23rd October, determining to combine a frontal attack on the Turkish position across the Tigris at the Fatha Gorge, with the advance of a column simultaneously from Kifti, with the object of threatening the Turkish communications. With such Success were his plans crowned that by the 30th October the greater part of the opposing force had surrendered and the Pursuit of the remainder was in active progress; we were within 12 miles of Mosul the following day when news of the Armistice reached the Commander-in-Chief. Two days later Mosul itself was occupied.

As I have explained in an earlier paragraph, the Turkish Administration in Mesopotamia having been almost entirely an exotic one and the personnel having disappeared with the retreating troops as we advanced, we had no alternative, if we were to fulfil our promises to the inhabitants, but to create a provisional administration from the only sources available to us during the war, namely British and British Indian personnel drawn from the Army or borrowed from India. No other course was possible either for myself, in so far as there was any personal element in the matter, or for my locum tenens, when I proceeded on deputation to Persia. There has been a disposition in some quarters to suggest that having regard to the pronouncement made to the inhabitants by Sir Stanley Maude on our entry into Bagdad, under instructions from home, and to the Anglo-French declaration promulgated by his successor Sir William Marshall in November 19 18, alluding respectively to the realization of the "natural aspirations of the noble Arabs" and "the establishment of national government" that, on the conclusion of the Armistice some prompt nationalization of the administration should have been attempted. This argument is plausible in theory and had the settlement of the Peace terms followed closely on the heels of the Armistice it might have been feasible in practice; but the actual course of events was far otherwise.

The work of peace proceeded very slowly; six months had already elapsed before the Terms to be imposed on Turkey were even discussed. It was not until May 1920 that, as the result of the San Remo Conference, the allocation of the Mandate for Mesopotamia to Great Britain was made known and even this announcement remained inoperative until confirmed in August 1920 by the Treaty of Sèvres, destined in turn never to be ratified. Meanwhile the spirit of President Wilson's 14 Points, with their potent element of " self determination," was gradually permeating the East--not only Mesopotamia but Islam in general--while at the same time our military position in the conquered territory was rapidly being weakened by the reduction of the army in Iraq to the irreducible minimum. A vast tract of country from Mosul to the Persian Gulf now lay under our civil administration and it would have been nothing short of dangerous, apart from the mere loss of efficiency involved, to embark upon any drastic change in the structure of that administration while the situation was so fluid. I emphasise this aspect of the question because when disturbances arose later, there was a disposition, as is so often the case when arrangements do not work quite according to plan, to confuse incidental phases of the unrest with its fundamental causes.

By the end of the war the people of Mesopotamia had come to accept the fact of our occupation and were resigned to the prospect of a permanent British administration; some, especially in Basrah and the neighbourhood, even looked forward with satisfaction to a future in which they would be able to pursue their commerce and agriculture with a strong central authority to preserve peace and order. Throughout the country there was a conviction, which frequently found open expression, that the British meant well by the Arabs, and this was accompanied by a frank appreciation of the increased prosperity which had followed in the track of our armies and, no doubt, by a lively sense of favours to come, in the way of progress and reform. But with the Armistice, and the Anglo French declaration by which it was immediately followed, a new turn was given to the native mind. In Bagdad, where political ambitions are more highly developed than elsewhere in Iraq, within a week of the publication of the Declaration the idea of an Arab Amir for Iraq was everywhere being discussed and in Mohammedan circles met with universal approval, though there was no consensus of opinion as to who should fill the rôle. At first the choice hovered between a son of Hussein, Sherif of Mecca, (later become King of the Hejaz); a member of the family of the Sultan of Egypt; and a magnate of Mosul. The venerable Naqib of Bagdad was also mentioned, and in some quarters a preference for a republic was expressed; but the latter idea was repugnant to most Moslems, while the Naqib showed no disposition to abandon his dignified religious seclusion in exchange for high Office of State.

Meanwhile Colonel Wilson, Acting Civil Commissioner, received instructions from H.M's Government to endeavour to elicit the views of the population of the occupied territories on the following points:-

(1) Were they in favour of a single Arab State under British guidance extending from the northern boundary of the Mosul Vilayet to the Persian Gulf?

(2) If so, did they consider that the new State should be placed under an Arab Amir?

(3) In that case, whom they would suggest?

On the first point there proved to be unanimous agreement. On the other two points the replies forthcoming were so divergent that they afforded little indication to H.M's Government as to the general feeling of the country and for the moment the solution of the problem remained in abeyance; I am speaking of the winter of 1918-19. During the ensuing year considerable progress was made with the introduction of natives of the country into the administration in subordinate positions, but not always with happy results. Meanwhile uncertainty as to the policy and precise intentions of H.M's Government still prevailed and the local situation was much complicated by the course of events in Syria. There an Arab Government assisted by several British advisers had been set up, from Aleppo to Damascus, immediately after General Allenby's entry in October 1918. At its head was the Amir Faisal, and it was practically independent as far as administration was concerned, though under the supreme control of the British Commander-in-Chief and upheld by the presence of his troops. During the campaign of the previous year the leading officers of Faisal's army had been nearly all of Iraqi origin, many of them Bagdadis, and they avowedly aimed at a federated Arab state of Syria and Iraq under an Arab prince; accordingly when in March 1920 Faisal was proclaimed King of Syria the Iraqis responded by proclaiming his brother the Amir Abdullah, King of Iraq. Hardly had this incident occurred when on the 5th May the assignment of the Iraq mandate to Great Britain was publicly announced, and of course set all tongues awagging.

Meanwhile, as acting Minister in Persia, I was naturally absorbed in the heavy duties of my own sphere and had not fully realised the turn which matters were taking in Iraq. I was the more surprised therefore to receive a telegram one morning from H.M's Foreign Office, informing me that it was desired that I should return to my post in Mesopotamia; but that on handing over to my successor in H.M's Legation I was to come first to London. The particular juncture from the point of view of our Persian interests seemed to me the worst possible one for a change of horses, but there were obvious limits to which I could press that point of view without danger of being misunderstood and having with due deference submitted my own opinion I resigned myself to the final instructions of H.M's Government and began to prepare for early departure. In due course my relief arrived and on 10th June my wife and I left Teheran, reaching Bagdad 4 days later. There we stayed with Colonel Wilson for 2 days while arrangements were being made for our onward journey, and I was able to learn from him and from Gertrude Bell the latest developments of the situation. A few days previously, on the 2nd June, Colonel Wilson had interviewed a selfappointed Committee Of 15 Bagdadis, which had been formed to voice opposition to the Mandate and had asked to be allowed to lay their views before the Civil Commissioner. After hearing what they had to say Colonel Wilson had undertaken to urge H.M's Government to expedite to the utmost a definite pronouncement of policy and in communicating the purport of the interview to London, he suggested abandonment of the idea of a provisional Government, recommending in the alternative that as soon as the terms of the Mandate had been settled a Constituent Assembly should at once be convened to deliberate upon the future form of Government. An announcement was accordingly drafted in the terms of which, just before leaving Bagdad, I concurred so far as concerned myself, and with the approval of H.M's Government this was sent to the leading delegates a few days later, on the 20th June. It stated that Mesopotamia was to be constituted an independent state under the guarantee of the League of Nations and subject to the Mandate of Great Britain, and that Sir Percy Cox was to return in the autumn to establish a provisional Arab government, pending preparation of a permanent organic law, to be framed with due regard to the rights, wishes, and interests of all communities of the country. But, alas, by now the fuse of disaffection had burnt too close to the powder, and probably nothing could have prevented the explosion. On 2nd July the tribesmen at Rumaithah, in the Lower Euphrates area, broke into open revolt.

By the time I reached London a few days later, the public at home were thoroughly disturbed at the turn things were taking in Iraq and a strong agitation was at work in a certain section of the Press which demanded that we should cut our losses and evacuate the country.

H.M's Government too were greatly exercised by the disquieting telegrams now coming in from Bagdad and there was considerable divergence of view as to what was the wisest course to pursue. But in any case it was clear that the rising must be suppressed before any other course of action was possible and the question at issue really was as to whether, after the restoration of law and order, we should cut our losses, abandon the Mandate and evacuate the country, or immediately set up a national Government, if that was really a practical alternative with reasonable chances of success. Asked for my opinion as the officer on the spot, I replied that to my mind evacuation was unthinkable; it would mean the abandonment of the Mandate and of the seven or eight millions worth of capital assets which we had in the country; the complete violation of all the promises we had made to the Arabs during the war, and their inevitable re-subjection to chaos and the hated yoke of the Turk as soon as we left; and lastly that an evacuation, which would arouse the active resentment of the betrayed inhabitants, could only be carried out without bloodshed if at least another division were sent to see it safely through. As to whether the alternative policy of establishing forthwith a national Government had a reasonable chance of success, I replied that without being too confident, I thought it had, and that the risk was at any rate worth taking if regarded as the only alternative to evacuation. Considerable discussion followed but ultimately I was asked whether if this course was decided upon I was prepared to undertake the task. I replied in the affirmative and left for Bagdad with my instructions by the next mail. It is no little satisfaction to me, six years later, to know that the ship thus launched on a somewhat tempestuous sea has safely reached port, and that so far as we are concerned the venture may be regarded on the whole as an imperial success. The Kingdom of Iraq has been placed on its feet, and its frontiers defined its future prosperity and progress rest with the Iraqis themselves.

But come what may, I can imagine no case in which H.M's Government have implemented their promises and obligations and pursued their settled policy with more complete good faith and resolution; dismayed neither by persistent and organised newspaper campaigns, nor by the interminable delays and difficulties which marked our peace negotiations with Turkey.

While these deliberations were going on in London, the rising in the Bagdad Vilayet was gathering force and reinforcements had to be drafted in from India for its suppression, so that by the time I reached Basrah on 1st October 1920, though active disaffection still smouldered in some places, the main centres of disturbances were under control, and the general situation no longer gave much cause for alarm.

I reached Bagdad on 5th October and a day or so later took over charge from Sir Arnold Wilson, who proceeded on leave. The task before me was by no means an easy or attractive one. The new line of policy which I had come to inaugurate involved a complete and necessarily rapid transformation of the facade of the existing administration from British to Arab and, in the process, a wholesale reduction in the numbers of British and British-Indian personnel employed. Many of the individuals affected had served with the utmost devotion during most difficult times and some had even abandoned all idea of returning to their pre-war posts in the hope Of making a career in Iraq., Added to that not a few of the British element were sceptical--and one could not blame them for their misgivings--as to the likelihood of the new enterprise succeeding, and did not disguise their feelings. But fortifying myself with the conviction that the project had at least an even chance of success, and was at any rate the only alternative to evacuation, I took heart of grace. My position however, was a very solitary one to begin with and the presence of Gertrude Bell and of Mr. Philby and Mr. C. C. Garbett both of the I.C.S. whom I had brought out with me from home was a great asset to me at this time. Except for a short spell of leave in England and a sojourn in Paris in the summer of 1919, the former had been in Bagdad with Sir Arnold Wilson throughout the two years of my absence at Teheran and had all the personnel and politics of the local communities at her fingers end, while I knew that her own ideas and those of the two Indian Civilians on the subject of Arab aspirations were such that I could be sure that at any rate in principle they were heart and soul in sympathy with the present policy of government. A year later I had to part company with Mr. Philby because at the stage of development at which we had then arrived his conception of the policy of H.M's Government began to diverge too much from mine, but I none the less readily recognise the great value he was to me in the early days. As regards the others, many of whom were strangers to me, it necessarily needed a little time for me to get my bearings; but whatever the primary feelings of many of my comrades may have, indeed must have been, most of them gradually came round to the view that as an alternative to the bag and baggage policy the new experiment was worth trying and was not necessarily doomed to failure. At any rate they rendered devoted service notwithstanding that for a long time to come the question of their future careers continued to hang in the balance, pending conclusion of peace with Turkey.

Though, as I have said above, the back of the rebellion was practically broken by the time I reached Basrah, a good many sections of the tribes in the Bagdad Vilayet were still "out," and it was not until February that the rising could be said to have been finally cleared up. Meanwhile, it did not take me long after my arrival at Bagdad to realise that I was being confronted at every turn with questions of policy

462

affecting the future of Iraq which I did not feel justified in disposing of myself without consultation with the representatives of the people. As an immediate expedient therefore, I determined to institute at once a Provisional Government which, under my control and supervision, should be responsible for the administration and political guidance of the country until the general situation had returned to normal and a start could be made with the creation of national institutions. It was here that I felt that my venerable friend the Naqib, who had given me such friendly co-operation on our first occupation of Bagdad, could now--if he would--render great and patriotic service, and I decided to appeal to him to preside over the proposed Council of State. Age and failing health might well have excused him from emerging from the studious seclusion of a Darwish in which he had preferred to spend the latter years of his life, but on October 23rd when I appealed to him, in the interests of his country, to shoulder the task, he courageously rose to the occasion, though with no little hesitation, and agreed to undertake the formation of a Cabinet. The high religious and social position of the Naqib and the universal respect he inspired placed his motives above all suspicion and endowed the Council of State with the necessary dignity and I shudder to think how my early efforts would have fared had he failed me at this time. For one of his venerable age and retired habits, it was a signal act of patriotism for which I could not be too grateful. The Council comprised 8 portfolios, Interior, Finance, justice, Defence, Public Works, Education and Health, Commerce, and Religious Bequests, and included, Saiyad Talib Pasha, eldest son of the Naqib of Basrah; Sassun Effendi Heskail who commanded universal respect and confidence as a leading representative of the Jewish Community in Baghdad; General jaafar Pasha el Askeri who had served with much distinction both during the war and afterwards in King Faisal's regime in Syria; and Abdul Latif Pasha Mandil a native of Nejd and one of the leading notables and merchants of Basrah.

The principal questions to which the Council had to give attention were the return from internment on Henjam Island of a number of the leaders of the late revolt; the repatriation, at the expense of the Government, of Iraqi Officers who had been serving in the Hejaz Army or in the Arab régime at Damascus, and who were left stranded on its collapse; the organization of a Civil Administration under Iraqi officials; the drafting of the electoral law; and a scheme for the formation of an Iraq Army. Under the Naqib's wise direction the Council carried on their work with surprising efficiency and absence of friction; and in the meanwhile many other Iraqis of experience and education who had held civil or military appointments under the Turks, as well as private individuals, were streaming back to their country and becoming available for employment under the new régime. It was in fact the advent of this contingent from Syria, who had mostly been enthusiastic adherents of Amir Faisal's cause, which started, or revived, the demand for him in Iraq, and of course at this time the question of the new ruler and the character of the permanent government which was to succeed the present provisional régime was being discussed in every coffee-shop.

In the meanwhile, in connection with the new departure of policy in Iraq the control of its destinies had been transferred from the India Office to the Colonial Office, of which Mr. Winston Churchill had now assumed the portfolio on transfer from the War Office. In order speedily to acquaint himself with the strings of his sphere and to consider the various aspects of the future of the Middle East, he determined to summon a conference at Cairo early in March, which I, among other British representatives in this region, was bidden to attend. Thanks to the satisfactory working of the provisional Government, I was able to leave Bagdad at the end of February in H.I.M.S. "Hardinge" in company with Sir Aylmer Haldane, G.O.C. in Mesopotamia, taking with me Sasun Effendi, Minister of Finance, and Jaafar Pasha, Minister of Defence in the Provisional Iraq Government; and among the British Staff, Major General E. H. Atkinson, Adviser to the Ministry of Works; Lieut. Col. S. Slater, I.C. S., Financial Adviser; and Miss Gertrude Bell, Oriental Secretary. Major General Sir Edmund Ironside, Commanding the troops in Persia was also a member of the party, while Sir Edgar Bonham Carter, judicial Adviser, held charge during my absence.

Apart from the incidental advantage of achieving personal touch with our new Ministerial Chief, who had been Secretary of State for War when I had last met him in the council chamber, and of being able to discuss with him Mesopotamian problems in general, it was clear that the main questions which would have to be threshed out at the Conference would be, the reduction of the present heavy expenditure; the qualifications of the various possible candidates for the throne of Iraq; the treatment of the Kurdish provinces; and the nature and composition of the force to be created for the defence of the new State in the future.

As regards the question of expenditure, if my memory serves me right the figure for the past year had been 37 millions sterling, whereas the Commander-in-Chief and I had come prepared with a draft scheme providing for reduction forthwith to 20 millions, with a progressive annual reduction thereafter, until the irreducible minimum should be reached.

The Secretary of State seemed no little relieved at the receipt of this preliminary news on our arrival.

As to the second question, it was easiest to arrive at a result by the process of elimination. My experience of public feeling on the question in Iraq had convinced me that among the several local candidates whose names had been suggested from time to time there was no individual who would be accepted or even tolerated by all parties in Iraq, while among the non-Iraqi possibilities there was no doubt whatever that one of the family of the Sherif of Mecca (King Hussein of the Hejaz) would command the most general if not the universal support of the inhabitants. I myself knew none of the family except from hearsay, but in the absence of any fresh candidate who might be suggested at the Conference, I went to Cairo prepared to recommend that that one of King Hussein's 4 sons whom a consensus of opinion should decide to be the most likely to fit the part, should be allowed to take his chance with the people of Iraq. It is common knowledge that the Amir Faisal won the ballot.

The other important question discussed was the treatment to be accorded to the Kurdish districts in the mandated territory and in this connection it was decided to make an attempt to ascertain the wishes of the Kurdish communities as to the degree of their prospective inclusion in, or separation from, the Iraq State.

But before the results could be made public it was incumbent on the Secretary of State on his return home to lay before the Cabinet the conclusions reached at the Conference, and unfortunately owing to the pre-occupation of H.M's Government with matters of grave importance at home, the much needed announcement on the subject by the Secretary of State was delayed until June.

On the 13th June, on the strength of telegrams received by Iraqis from the Hejaz, news was published in Bagdad that the Amir Faisal was leaving for Iraq. Friendly telegrams passed a day or two later between King Hussein and His Highness the Naqib and on 22nd Amir Faisal sent a personal wireless greeting to the Naqib announcing his early arrival at Basrah. Meanwhile the publication of the Secretary of State's pronouncement of policy had given to the bulk of the population that for which they had been asking, namely guidance from the Government whose obligation it was to offer advice. The express exclusion of a republican form of Government was recognised to be in accord with the traditions of Islam while the assurance of H.M's Government that they would regard the Amir Faisal as a suitable ruler should he be chosen by the people of Iraq dissipated apprehensions born of previous misunderstandings. But the Amir himself was his own best advocate. It was as the result of the popular tributes that he received during the first fortnight of his presence in Iraq that His Highness the Naqib, without any consultation with me, proposed to the Council on July 11th a resolution, which was unanimously approved, that the Amir Faisal should be declared King, on condition that his government should be a constitutional, representative and democratic one. On receiving a copy of the resolution according to the usual routine, I replied that before concurring in or confirming it I felt it necessary to fortify myself with direct evidence of the choice of the people by means of a referendum and the task of carrying out the measure was at once put in hand. The people of the Sulaimaniyeh District of Southern Kurdistan decided to abstain, as they were at liberty to do, from taking any part in the election of a King for the Iraq; with this exception the referendum was applied throughout the country and the results showed 96 per cent. of the votes to be in favour of the Amir Faisal's election, the remaining 4 Per cent. coming mainly from the Turcoman and Kurdish communities of Kirkuk. On 18th August the Ministry of the Interior informed His Highness the Naqib, as President of the Council, that an overwhelming majority of the people supported the Amir Faisal's election and accordingly on 23rd August in the presence of representatives of all local communities and deputations from every Liwa and Iraq, except Sulaimaniyeh and Kirkuk, I proclaimed His Highness the Amir Faisal to have been duly elected King of Iraq and at the same time announced his recognition as King by His Britannic Majesty's Government.

Careful to tread with dignity and in conformity with the constitutional practice usual on the accession of a Sovereign, His Highness The Naqib and the Provisional Government formally tendered their resignation to the King, who while thanking them for their services requested them to continue in Office until a new Cabinet should be formed. It was then my grateful duty to intimate to the Naqib that His Majesty George in recognition of his services to his country had pleased to confer on him the high distinction of Knight Grand Commander of the Order of the British Empire. King Faisal followed with a speech in which he stated the principle by which his Government would be guided, insisting on the maintenance of the alliance between Great Britain and Iraq which he said should be embodied in an instrument to be confirmed by the National Congress as soon as convened.

But it was an insecure and troubled heritage on which the new King of Iraq had entered. On the North the Turks, though theoretically the position was one of prolonged armistice, pending conclusion of peace, were in fact clearly hostile. Turkish garrisons and posts along the frontier were increased and the Kurds incited to rise. In June 1921 a Turkish Official reached Rowanduz within the Iraq frontier, with a small party of irregulars, stirred up all the tribes in the neighbourhood and intermittently kept the whole of Kurdistan in a ferment until finally expelled in the spring Of 1923. In June 1922 an able Commander of Turkish Irregulars, bearing the sobriquet of " Yuzdemir," arrived in Kurdistan and embarked on an intensive campaign among the tribes, some of their contingents advancing as far as Rania. Disaffection soon spread to the tribes of Sulaimaniyeh; the Harnavand revolted and a general cry arose from Sulaimaniyeh that the only way to compose the situation was to allow back Sheikh Mahmud who had been deported by us in 1919. As we were not disposed to reoccupy the district for the present nothing was to be lost by giving Sheikh Mahmud another trial and he was installed after giving the most binding assurances. Similarly, on the desert frontier of Iraq to the south-west, the bedouin tribes had since the early part of 1921 been in a continual state of unrest as the result of the operations of the Sultan of Nejd against his enemy Ibn Rashid and the Shammar tribes of Hayil. In consequence a large influx into Iraq of fugitive Shammar went on throughout the year 1921 and naturally had a deplorable effect on the relations between Iraq and Nejd, which was aggravated, when, exalted by his capture of Hayil in November, Ibn Saud claimed allegiance from the eastern Anizah tribe which had always been attached to Iraq. In the following March a serious attack took place by a strong raiding party of Ibn Saud's "Akhwan," as the Wahabis now style themselves, upon a harmless encampment of pastoral nomads guarded by a detachment of the Iraq Camel Corps, some 30 miles south of the railway line and near the provisional frontier. It could be taken for granted that the Sultan, at his distant capital, would repudiate the hostile action of his hot-headed tribesmen, and for us to have taken measures of retaliation without first communicating with the responsible Ruler, might have resulted in a state of war between the Sultan of Nejd and Iraq, which would have been a calamity from all points of view; nevertheless some aeroplanes which were sent to obtain news, having been fired on, were obliged to reply and a grave warning was immediately addressed by me to Ibn Saud remonstrating with him for this unprovoked raid by his tribesmen; reminding him of the provisional frontier which had been agreed upon and urging him to concert with me arrangements for its formal settlement.

Ever since King Faisal's advent to Iraq I had left no stone unturned in the difficult endeavour to promote cordial relations between the two potentates, both allies of H.M's Government and regarded with affection by myself, and it would have been a bitter personal as well as official disappointment to me, had a serious breach occurred. But the position of H.M's High Commissioner was a most delicate one at this time. The news of the raid had created profound indignation in certain quarters in Bagdad and immediate reprisals were demanded without any reflection as to whether means existed for carrying them out. It was even suggested quite seriously that the raid had been instigated by the British authorities as a means of making Iraq realise the extent of her dependence upon us! Unfortunately the episode took place at a moment when a serious divergence of view already existed between the British and the Iraq Governments as to the precise nature of their relations with one another. It was extraordinary with what aversion the mandatory idea had always been regarded in Iraq. The mere terms "Mandatory" and "Mandate" were anathema to them from the first, for the simple reason, I am convinced, that the words translate badly into Arabic, or rather were wrongly rendered in the Arabic press when they first emerged from the Peace Conference. I assume the term mandatory to have been introduced by its sponsor, President Wilson, in the particular and recognised sense of "one who undertakes to do service for another with regard to property placed in his hands by the other";

"the other" in this case being the League of Nations, while the "mandate" is the contract under which service is performed. But it was taken in Iraq in its other sense, "of an authoritative requirement, as by a sovereign"; and the "mandatory " as one who exercised the authority. Two widely different conceptions. Misunderstanding their meaning, as they did, there was always intense eagerness on the part of those in authority in Iraq, to get rid of the hated expressions, as defining their relations with us, and much needless controversy was the result.

H.M's Government had indeed agreed on my recommendation, that the terms of our mandatory relations with Iraq should be set out in the form of a treaty, instead of as first drafted, but King Faisal and his Ministers now went further and pressed for the complete abrogation of the mandatory relation, as being incompatible with the country's independence, and its replacement by a simple treaty of alliance; whereas the British Government had in mind a treaty within the scope of the mandate. It was as I have said unfortunate that this acute difference should have been synchronous with the incident of the desert raid. The anti-mandate agitation gained impetus and continued throughout the summer. In June, a vigorous campaign started in the Arab Press; symptoms of disorder again began to appear on the Euphrates, while the collection of revenue dropped to vanishing point, and though at the end of June the Council of Ministers accepted the treaty, it was with the characteristic reservation that it should not be ratified until agreed to by the forthcoming Constituent Assembly. The month of August was marked by the formation of two extremist political parties, and on the 16th of that month the whole of the existing moderate Cabinet, unable to keep the extremist elements within bounds, resigned, with the exception of the Naqib,who retained his post as Prime Minister in the hope of preventing a land-slide.

Meanwhile the extremist elements proclaimed that a new Cabinet was to be formed out of their number, under the presidency of a certain religious firebrand and a joint manifesto was published in the vernacular papers demanding that the British element in the administration should be entirely eliminated.

It was in such a highly charged atmosphere that on a stifling day in August, the 23rd to be precise, I proceeded officially to the Palace to offer my congratulations to His Majesty on this the first anniversary of his accession, and just before entering the building was treated to an anti-mandate demonstration by what proved to be a small packed crowd. I took immediate steps to demand an apology, which was accorded, but at the same moment it was announced that King Faisal had been struck down by a sudden and dangerous attack of appendicitis, necessitating an immediate operation and involving his complete insulation from the affairs of state for some time to come. I was thus faced with a unique if critical situation. The cabinet had resigned; the King was incapacitated; the Bagdad Vilayet and the Euphrates tribes were on the verge of rebellion to all appearances likely to be not less serious than that of 1926 and organised by the same elements. The Turks at the same moment, with their prestige greatly increased by their defeat of the Greeks, were in Rowanduz and Rania and were threatening Sulaimaniyeh. No authority was in fact left in the country except my own as High Commissioner and I felt bound to use it to the full. Accordingly a proclamation was at once issued explaining the situation and stating that the emergent measures which were being taken did not portend any change in the settled policy of H.M's Government. At the same time all friendly and moderate persons who had the welfare of their country at heart were called upon to rally to the side of the High Commissioner and resist irresponsible agitators. The ringleaders were forthwith arrested; the two new extremist parties closed down and certain mischievous papers suppressed. At the same time the two Persian divines who had been responsible for the anti-Foreign manifestoes were advised to repair to their own homeland for the benefit of their health, while some of the Arab officials on the Lower Euphrates who by their intrigues had fostered the disaffection, were dismissed or transferred.

The effect of these measures was instantaneous; and except for a few isolated acts of defiance, and the chronic unrest in the Kurdish districts which continued for some time to respond to Turkish propaganda and incitement, the whole of Iraq proper was quiet by September 10th. On that date King Faisal was reported strong enough to give me an interview, whereat he thanked me cordially for the action taken during the interregnum.

But the north-eastern frontier continued to give cause for anxiety. A Levy force from Sulaimaniyeh, pursuing a band of Kurdish rebels having become involved too far from their base, an Indian regiment was sent to reinforce them; the combined force getting into difficult country suffered a reverse near Rania in 1st September 1922 and was with difficulty extricated; in consequence it was decided to withdraw all British personnel from Sulaimaniyeh and the withdrawal was carried out by air in the course of a day without the slightest hitch--a remarkable example of the utility and efficiency of the air-method in such circumstances. It was undoubtedly a disappointing setback, but with Sheikh Mahmud in control of the town effective administration from Bagdad east of Erbil, Kifri and Kirkuk had become impossible.

Fortunately at this stage the face of the picture was transformed by the execution of a measure decided upon in principle at the Cairo Conference eighteen months before, namely the placing of all the Imperial Forces in Iraq, Ground Troops, Levies and Royal Air Force, under the Command of the Air Officer Commanding. It had not been intended to bring the change into force until a settlement had been reached with Turkey and the northern boundary determined, but Air Marshal Sir John Salmond assumed charge from 1st October 1922, and the vigorous air action taken from that date against the Turks and their adherents whenever they showed their heads had the effect 4 months later of forcing them to withdraw entirely from the Rania district and to concentrate in Rowanduz, whence they were finally ejected in April 1923. With the restoration of the King's health the moment had come for the instalment of a new Cabinet, which the Naqib had succeeded in forming by the end of September 1922. Difficulties with regard to the Treaty and the Mandate had by now been cleared away in correspondence with the Secretary of State and on October 10th His Highness the Naqib and I signed the Treaty of Alliance between Great Britain and Iraq, which was published on 13th October, together with a Proclamation by His Majesty King Faisal to his people expressing his profound satisfaction with the event. The period for which this, the original Treaty, was to run was 20 years, and during the long negotiations which led up to it nothing less than 15 years was ever discussed, but, as the sequel shows, the period was destined to be considerably curtailed.

With the near approach of the first Lausanne Conference Turkish propaganda, suggesting the intended restoration of Iraq to Turkey, grew stronger and stronger and had considerable effect both on the Sheikhs of the Euphrates and the inhabitants of northern Iraq. The King's Irade on 21st October ordering elections for the Constituent Assembly, which was to accept the Treaty and pass an Organic Law laying down the Constitution was countered by a "fatwah" or religious decree countersigned by some disaffected divines of Karbala and Kadhimain, forbidding participation in the elections.

It was now realised that a more vigorous line of action on the part of the Iraq Government was needed to cote with these adverse forces, and the venerable Naqib who had remained at the helm of affairs so gallantly through so many changes of weather felt that the time had come when he could resign the ship of state to the command of a younger man, and he was succeeded by Abdul Muhsin Bey, who reconstructed the Cabinet.

At this juncture a change of Government took place in England which profoundly affected the future in Iraq. The Coalition Government under which the Iraq Treaty had been framed and signed had resigned on 23rd October, 10 days after its signature, and the question of Iraq became a prominent plank in the course of the general election which followed; a fierce newspaper campaign being conducted against the expenditure of British money in the country and several members of the new House of Commons pledging themselves to work for its evacuation by the British at the earliest moment. As a consequence, a Cabinet Committee was set up in London in December 1922 to decide upon the future of Iraq. Meanwhile the Treaty lately signed, with its 20 years duration clause, had not been ratified, while at the first Lausanne Conference the Turkish delegates had resolutely refused to entertain any idea of the Mosul Vilayet remaining with Iraq, or to refer the Turco-Iraq frontier question to the League.

It was of course open to Great Britain to refuse to ratify the Treaty and thus for 4 months Iraq remained in dire suspense (flooded all the time with Turkish propaganda) as to whether she would not after all be handed back to Turkey. I was called home to attend the deliberations of this Conference and Sir Henry Dobbs having in the meanwhile arrived, on appointment as Counsellor to the High Commission, with the prospect of succeeding me at the end of my term, I left for London on 19th January 1923, leaving him in charge, and though he was no stranger to the country, having served with me for 2 years, early in the war, the situation which he had to take over was full of awkward possibilities.

I returned from my mission on 31st March bringing with me the results of the deliberations of H.M's new Government. They were in the shape of a draft Protocol to the Treaty of Alliance, reducing the duration of the treaty from 20 years to 4 (the period to commence on the date of the ratification of the Treaty of Peace by Turkey) but concluding with a consoling provision that "Nothing in this Protocol shall prevent a fresh agreement from being concluded, with a view to regulate the subsequent relations between the High Contracting Parties; and negotiations shall be entered into between them before the expiration of the above period." This document was signed by the Prime Minister of Iraq and myself on the 20th April 1923, and may be said to have been my last official act as High Commissioner; for being due for leave before the advent of the hot- weather pending retirement from the service and having many things to see to before my departure, I was content to leave the direction of current affairs in the experienced hands of my Counsellor and successor, Sir Henry Dobbs.

In compiling this condensed narrative of the period of our association, it has not been possible for me to allude repeatedly to the great degree to which Gertrude Bell enjoyed my confidence and I her devoted co- operation, a co-operation which I know from my successor she rendered with the same singleness of purpose to him. Her letters will tell their own story.

P. Z. C.

By H.E. SIR HENRY DOBBS, K.C.S.I., etc.,
High Commissioner for Iraq

On 22nd December, 1922, I arrived in Bagdad to take up the newly created post of Counsellor to the High Commissioner, with the prospect of succeeding Sir Percy Cox when, as was understood, he retired in the ensuing year. The prospect was not a firm one, since it was possible that, as a result of the deliberations of the British Cabinet, there might shortly be no High Commissioner to succeed. Almost immediately on my arrival, Sir Percy Cox was summoned to London to assist in those deliberations, and he left Bagdad by air on 19th January, 1923. He did not again take an active part in the general work of the High Commissioner, returning only to announce the new policy of the

British Government, to sign the Protocol of the Treaty necessitated by the change, and to prepare for his final departure on leave, which took place on 3rd May, 1923.

On taking up the work of High Commissioner in January, 1923, I found that all hope of holding an early election for the Constituent Assembly had vanished, while the Turkish threat on the north was growing more insistent. The first Lausanne Conference was on the verge of collapse. In Sulaimaniya the newly restored Sheikh Mahmud was already showing signs of revolt. The mass of the people of Iraq were silent, showing that strange and admirable restraint with which Oriental peoples await the fulfilment of the purposes of God; but unshakeable through all had been their belief (dimmed only for a time in the murk of the years succeeding the war) in the generosity and high purpose of Great Britain towards weaker peoples.

Sir Percy Cox returned on the 31st March, 1923, bringing with him the result of the deliberations of the British Government in the shape of a draft Protocol to the Treaty of Alliance. The Protocol cut down the period of the Treaty from twenty years to a maximum of four years from the date of ratification of peace with Turkey, and provided that, if before the lapse of that maximum period, Iraq became a member of the League of Nations, the Treaty should terminate immediately. The Protocol was signed on 30th April 1923. The more farseeing people feared that the reduced period was too short to enable Iraq to stand upon her own feet, and the so-called pro-British sections of the populations, especially some of the Euphrates tribes, the inhabitants of Basra and the Assyrians of Mosul, professed to regard this reduction as a betrayal of their interests. But the politicians of Bagdad and Mosul welcomed it with enthusiasm, and even King Faisal and his Ministers, while expressing constant gratitude for the support and favours received in the past, were undisguisedly delighted that a near term had been put to authoritative control by Great Britain of their affairs.

Sir Percy Cox left Iraq at the beginning of May, 1923, amid spontaneous demonstrations of affection and regret from all classes of the population. During his absence in London I had in January, 1923, taken steps to restore general confidence in the face of the Turkish threats. For this purpose a force, composed partly of British and partly of Iraq troops, moved up to Mosul, and His Highness the Amir Zaid,

474

the brother of King Faisal, who had arrived in Iraq in November, 1922, took up his residence at Mosul to initiate political measures for winning over Kurdish sentiment to the Iraq side. He also superintended the formation of a force of Arab tribal irregulars to operate, if need be, against invaders of the plains to the west of Mosul. This demonstration, combined with the firm stand of the British representatives at Lausanne, had an immediate effect on the whole country. But Turkish irregulars remained at Ruwanduz, and plans for a Kurdish rising with the co- operation of Sheikh Mahmud of Sulaimaniya came to light. To forestall such a combination, Sheikh Mahmud's headquarters were bombed from the air and he took to the mountains. It was now time to complete the pacification of the frontier by the reoccupation of Ruwanduz. Two columns of troops advanced on the town, which the Turkish irregulars and their leader, Euz Demir, evacuated without fighting on 22nd April, 1923, two days before the second conference of Lausanne began its sittings.

The district of Ruwanduz was placed under the Arbil Division and the Kurdish leader, Saiyad Taha, the hereditary chieftain of Neri, who was at that time a refugee in Iraq, was appointed Qaimmaqam. He was a man of strong character and of great reputation among the Kurds, and his appointment was an earnest of the wish of the British and Iraq Governments to administer the Kurdish districts through Kurdish officials. Helped by the presence of a battalion of Assyrian Levies, he succeeded in excluding Turkish influence from the important strategic centre of Ruwanduz.

A few weeks after the reoccupation of Ruwanduz, Sulaimaniya was temporarily occupied and Sheikh Mahmud fled across the Persian border. it had been hoped to set up some form of autonomous administration there with the help of friendly Kurdish leaders, but it proved impossible to lock up a large number of troops which might still be needed on the northern frontier, and no Kurdish chief could be found strong enough to resist the influence of Sheikh Mahmud without such backing. Sulaimaniya was accordingly evacuated on 20th June, 1923, and Sheikh Mahmud allowed to return there for a time and to resume his domination of the centre of the division, while the outlying parts were detached and placed under the Iraq administration.

The frontiers having thus been strengthened and the Turkish menace for the time staved off, the field was free to deal with the agitation of the reactionary Shiah divines against the elections for the Constituent Assembly. By July, 1923, their demeanour towards King Faisal and towards the Iraq Government had become intolerably arrogant, and King Faisal saw no other way than to authorise the deportation of their leader, Sheikh Mahdi al Khalisi. The deportation was arranged and carried out exclusively by Arab agency, and was followed by the voluntary exodus to Persia of several other prominent Persian divines as a public protest. The Iraq Government decided that it would be unsafe to permit any of these personages to return before the conclusion of the elections and the ratification by the Constituent Assembly of the Treaty of Alliance with Great Britain. This decision, although it caused agitation in Persia, was accepted as wise throughout Iraq. King Faisal had during this period made a progress throughout the whole country for the purpose of explaining his policy and exhorting the people to take part in the elections, and I followed shortly afterwards in his steps, so that the people were left in no doubt as to the identity of purpose of the British and Iraq Governments. Having thus prepared the ground, the Iraq Government ordered that the elections should begin again, and the completion of the registration of primary electors, which had before been found impracticable, was everywhere carried through with success, the most distant tribesmen of the Euphrates and of the Kurdish hills enrolling themselves with astonishing alacrity. The political atmosphere had, in fact, cleared as if by magic and the progress of the elections, notwithstanding the complications of the Electoral Law, threatened to be so swift that it was necessary to delay it, for fear that the Constituent Assembly should sit before the various agreements subsidiary to the Treaty of Alliance with Great Britain were ready for its consideration. The registration of primary electors was finally completed by 16th December, 1923, secondary elections began on 25th February, 1924, and all results were declared by the middle of March, 1924.

Apart from the labours of the Iraq Government and myself over the provisions of the "subsidiary agreements," the late summer and autumn Of 1923 were marked only by the growing tension between Iraq and Ibn Saud consequent partly on raids carried out upon Nejd territory by the Shammar who had taken refuge in Iraq when Ibn Saud took Hail in 1921. Finally a conference was arranged at Kuwait under the presidency of Colonel Knox, lately Acting Resident in the

Persian Gulf, to decide outstanding questions not only between Nejd and Iraq but also between Nejd and Hejaz and Trans Jordan. It met on 17th December, 1923, and was in a fair way to achieve some settlement, at all events between Iraq and Nejd, when on 14th March, 1924, a very serious raid by Akhwan, not less than 2,000 strong, was carried out upon the Iraq frontier nomads, 186 persons, men, women and children being killed, and 26,000 sheep and 3,700 donkeys captured. This aroused such indignation in Iraq that the conference had to be abandoned.

In the meantime the Cabinet of Abdul Muhsin Beg had resigned on 16th November, 1923, as a consequence of differences of opinion with His Majesty King Faisal, leaving the subsidiary agreements incomplete. Jafar Pasha succeeded him as Prime Minister and concluded the discussion of the Agreements subsidiary to the Treaty. They were signed on the 25th March, 1924. The whole Instrument of Alliance was thus ready for submission to the Constituent Assembly, which was opened by His Majesty King Faisal on 27th March, 1924. The month had already been made eventful by the declaration of King Husain as Khalifa, which enhanced the prestige of the Hashimite house.

The debates on the Treaty and Agreements in the Constituent Assembly lasted until 10th June, 1924, the issue growing more and more doubtful as the country deputies fell under the influence of certain extremist lawyers and coffee-house politicians of Bagdad. There was much misrepresentation and some solid ground for dissatisfaction in the heavy burdens imposed on Iraq by the obligation simultaneously to expand the Army, redeem the capital cost of the railway and shoulder a large share of the Ottoman Debt. This difficult position had been brought about mainly by the cutting down of the Treaty period from twenty to four years. For whereas, under the arrangements contemplated in the original Treaty, Iraq would have been able to expand her army very gradually, she was now forced into a feverish and most expensive programme, with little real hope of being able in so short a time to produce an army fit for external defence. Moreover, at the Cairo Conference of 1921, which laid down the original policy, the future revenues of Iraq had been gravely overestimated on the basis of the momentary prosperity succeeding the war. With shrunken revenues and increased obligations, it was feared that the conditions of the Financial Agreement must, if Iraq attempted to fulfil them, drive her to

477

bankruptcy. Another great objection felt to the Treaty was that it contained no definite undertaking that the economic and judicial capitulations, formerly enjoyed in the old Turkish Empire by certain European Powers and by the United States of America, should be abrogated. There was merely a clause laying down that in consequence of the "non-application" of these immunities, effect would be given to reasonable provisions to safeguard the interests of foreigners in judicial matters.

On 20th April, 1924, the Committee of the Assembly, appointed to study the Treaty and Agreements, presented a report containing some able criticism, the work of Yasin Pasha, President of the Committee. Agitation against the Treaty, which had already led to the attempted assassination of two pro-Treaty deputies, increased and it became clear that, without some assurance regarding future financial treatment, there was little hope of passing the Treaty. On the other hand it was not feasible to accept any amendments in the Treaty and Agreements before ratification, as this would have thrown all the relations between Great Britain and Iraq back into the melting-pot and have created difficulties both in England and in Iraq. Finally, His Britannic Majesty's Government gave an undertaking that, after ratification, they would reconsider the financial obligations of Iraq. This somewhat eased the situation, but also in some quarters increased the expectation of further British concessions and the anti-Treaty agitation continued. His Britannic Majesty's Government therefore resolved to put an end to a tension which was becoming dangerous, by bringing the Iraq Mandate before the League of Nations at the session of June, 1924, and announced that, if the Iraq Assembly had reached no decision by 10th June, this would be taken as a rejection of the Treaty. As a result, the Constituent Assembly accepted the Treaty and Agreements shortly before midnight on 10th June, stating in a rider to their resolution that they did so in reliance on the assurance that, after ratification, the British Government would "amend with all possible speed the Financial Agreement in the spirit of generosity and sympathy for which the British people are famous."

The acceptance of the Treaty was a notable landmark, for it has been the only instance since the close of the war of a complete and voluntary agreement to define future relations between Great Britain and an Arabic speaking community, made under freely elected representative institutions on both sides. That the nation on the whole was satisfied with the decision was testified by the number of congratulations which I received from all parts of the country.

The Treaty and agreements were placed before the Council of the League of Nations on 20th September, 1924. The League took note of these documents and, on 27th September, 1924, accepted them as giving effect to the provisions of Article 22 of the Covenant of the League for the regulation of the relations between Iraq and the Mandatory Power. The Treaty and Agreements were ratified by His Britannic Majesty King George V on 10th November, 1924, and by His Majesty King Faisal on 12th December, 1924.

After disposing of the Treaty the Constituent Assembly proceeded to the consideration of the Organic Law and the Electoral Law, which were passed, the first on 10th July and the second on 2nd August, 1924. The programme laid down for Iraq in Mr. Winston Churchill's announcement of 12th October, 1922, as a necessary preliminary to the admission of Iraq to the League of Nations and the termination of mandatory relations, had been the ratification of the Treaty and subsidiary Agreements, the bringing into effect of the Organic Law and the delimitation of the frontiers. Iraq had now fulfilled her part of the programme. The delimitation of the frontiers depended on Great Britain and Turkey. Jafar Pasha and his Cabinet, exhausted with their efforts, resigned office, the Constituent Assembly was dissolved, and Yasin Pasha al Hashimi was made Prime Minister.

The northern frontier and the Kurdish mountains had been fairly peaceful during the latter part Of 1923, and the first half of 1924. In Sulaimaniya, however, Sheikh Mahmud had persisted in overstepping the boundaries laid down for him when allowed to return after the withdrawal of the troops in July, 1923, and he had to be continually threatened from the air, his headquarters being occasionally bombed. In the middle of May, 1924, exaggerated reports of the agitation in Bagdad against the Treaty had encouraged him to more active rebellion. The adjoining division of Kirkuk became affected and intensive air action was taken against Sheikh Mahmud, with the result that he abandoned Sulaimaniya, which was occupied in July, 1924, by a column of Iraq Army Cavalry, supported by Assyrian Levies. Sheikh Mahmud again fled over the Persian frontier and the remaining portions of the Sulaimaniya Division were placed under a very loose form of civil administration on behalf of the Iraq Government. This has not secured complete tranquillity from the local depredations of outlaws, but the town of Sulaimaniya is now again flourishing and the prosperity of the district is gradually returning. The zone of disorder has, at all events, been pushed far back from the borders of the settled districts of Kirkuk and Arbil. Sulaimaniya itself, like the Indo-Afghan border, has never from the remotest times been completely pacified, and it is too much to expect that this will now be accomplished in the twinkling of an eye.

In Article 3 of the Treaty of Lausanne it had been provided that the frontier between Turkey and Iraq should be laid down in friendly arrangement to be concluded between Turkey and Great Britain within nine months, and that, in the event of no agreement being reached, the dispute should be referred to the Council of the League of Nations. Pending the decision, the two Governments had undertaken that no military or other movement should take place which might modify in any way the present state of the territories in question. During May and the first week of June, 1924, Sir Percy Cox had carried on in Constantinople fruitless negotiations with the Turkish Government on the frontier question. The Turks had been adamant in their demand for the whole Mosul Vilayat, and their intransigence had probably been encouraged by the reports from Bagdad that the Iraq Constituent Assembly was about to reject the Treaty with Great Britain. On 9th June, 1924, the day before the Iraq Assembly accepted the Anglo-Iraq Treaty, the Constantinople negotiations had broken down. There was now nothing left but a reference of the frontier dispute to the League of Nations, and, in the meanwhile the Turks became active on the frontiers. They sent the Wali of julamerk with a small escort to visit Chal, which they had been informed in October, 1923, was claimed by the British Government to lie within the sphere of the Iraq Administration, and in the course of his progress he was ambushed by some Assyrian Christians and taken captive, but released. At the beginning of September, 1924, the Turks concentrated troops for the invasion of the Assyrian area, and on the 14th they crossed the River Haizil into what was undoubtedly Iraq territory. They were met by an attack from the air and driven back and thereafter diverted their march to the north through the territory of the Sindi Guli Kurds (still Iraq territory), through which they moved and laid waste the Assyrian country, driving the Assyrians, some 8,000 in number, down into the valley of Amadia, where they had to be supported by the Iraq Government. It was a remarkable testimony to the success of the Iraq

480

Administration and to the good relations maintained with the Kurds that this incursion by the Turks did not lead to a general rising on the Mosul frontier against Iraq, which would have been unfortunate, as the League of Nations was at that moment sitting at Geneva to determine the delimitation of the Turco-Iraq frontier. Ultimately, the Turks agreed before the League to preserve the status quo until the frontier was decided. A preliminary dispute as to the line of the status quo was settled by a special meeting of the League at Brussels in October, 1924, and this provisional line has since been known as the "Brussels Line."

The Frontier Commission, consisting of three Commissioners, eminent subjects of Sweden, Belgium and Hungary, reached Bagdad in January, 1925, and spent three months in examining the frontier. They were accompanied by General Jawad Pasha, who had recently commanded the Turkish forces on the Iraq frontier, as Turkish assessor, and Mr. Jardine, a British Administrative Inspector in the service of Iraq, as British assessor. The Turks had, in the preceding negotiations, demanded a plebiscite of the inhabitants of the Mosul Vilayat, but this had been resisted by the British on the grounds that the circumstances of the population made a plebiscite impracticable. The League of Nations had left the methods of enquiry entirely to the discretion of the Commissioners, who went a long way towards satisfying the Turkish demand and besides undertaking a detailed study of the racial, geographical and economic factors of the problem, made secret enquiries from representatives of all sections of the inhabitants in the territories under dispute, as to which government they would prefer, that of Turkey or Iraq.

QUESTION OF THE CHRISTIANS OF MOSUL AND OF THE NESTORIAN OR ASSYRIAN MOUNTAINEERS.

One of the chief matters of concern to the Frontier Commission appeared to be the future of the Christians of Mosul, and especially of the Nestorians or Assyrians, who, as narrated above, were at the time of the visit of the Commission refugees in Iraq territory. They numbered altogether about 20,000 souls, some from regions lying considerably beyond the northernmost frontier claimed by Iraq and some from the Hakkiari mountains north of Amadia, which were included in the Iraq claim. They had revolted against Turkey in 1916 at the instigation of Russia, and then, being deserted by the Russians after the revolution, had fought their way through Persian territory to a junction with the British troops, losing two-thirds of their number in the process. The British had brought them into Iraq and maintained them there for three years, after which some were temporarily settled on vacant Iraq lands near Amadia and some encouraged to filter back to their deserted homes to the north. There they had stayed, repairing the damage as best they might, until once more expelled by the Turkish incursion of September, 1924. Numbers of them had, from 1921 onwards, entered the British service as Levies and had displayed magnificent fighting qualities, helping in the suppression of sporadic Kurdish insurrections and in the expulsion from Ruwanduz in 1923 of the Turkish irregulars. They were united in a determination never again to submit themselves to Turkish rule. In order to reassure them as to their future, two successive Iraq Cabinets, those of Jafar Pasha and of Yasin Pasha, officially pledged the Government of Iraq to provide lands in Iraq for those Assyrians who might be dispossessed of their original homes by the decision of the League of Nations and to devise a system of administration for them which should ensure to them the utmost possible freedom from interference. It can hardly be doubted that this liberal attitude on the part of the Government of Iraq had its influence on the deliberations of the Frontier Commission. The Commission terminated its labours in the third week of March, 1925. Its report could not be prepared in time for the June session of the League, and was held over till September..

POLITICAL EVENTS AFTER THE DEPARTURE OF THE FRONTIER COMMISSION.

It had not been thought advisable to proceed with elections for the first regular Iraq Parliament until the Frontier Commission had completed its labours. The promulgation of the Organic Law passed by the Constituent Assembly in July, 1924, had consequently been delayed, so as to avoid an interregnum between the close of arbitrary Cabinet Government and the introduction of a Parliamentary régime.

On 21st March, 1925, on the eve of the departure of the Commission, the Organic Law was officially promulgated amid widespread rejoicings, and orders were given for the completion of the new lists of primary electors and for the commencement of the parliamentary elections. The Cabinet of Yasin Pasha had, shortly before taking these steps, passed four notable measures vital for the future prosperity and stability of Iraq. The first was the signature of an agreement with the Anglo-Persian Oil Company for the dredging of the bar at the mouth of the Shatt al Arab, so as to allow vessels of heavy draught to enter the Port of Basra. The second was the signature of a trade transit convention with Syria. The third was the grant to the Turkish Petroleum Company of a concession for the development of oil throughout the Bagdad and Mosul Wilayats, and the fourth was the signature of long term contracts with some hundred British advisers and officials, whose experience and devoted industry were thus secured for Iraq throughout the first and most difficult stage of her career as an independent State.

While the elections were in progress the Secretary of State for the Colonies despatched to Iraq a Financial Mission to enquire into the financial position and prospects of Iraq, so that the British Government might be able to carry out their promise to reconsider the provisions of the Financial Agreement after its ratification. The report of the Mission, which was completed by 25th April, 1925, partially justified many of the criticisms of the Financial Agreement made in the Constituent Assembly Of 1924, as throwing upon Iraq burdens greater than she could bear. Its recommendations for the alleviation of these burdens were, when published, the cause of much public satisfaction in Iraq, and contributed to the election to the first Iraq Parliament of a majority of deputies actuated by the friendliest sentiments towards the British Alliance.

Another factor in this favourable situation was the visit to Iraq in the first half of April, 1925, of the Right Honourable L. S. Amery, Secretary of State for the Colonies, and of the Right Honourable Sir Samuel Hoare, Secretary of State for Air. The visit cheered and encouraged those whose minds had been upset by the inquisitions of the Frontier Commission and convinced the Government and people of Iraq of the steadfastness of the interest of Great Britain in their affairs. It gave an unique opportunity to His Majesty King Faisal and the leading personages in Iraq to bring their various difficulties and anxieties fully and frankly before the British Government, and the substitution of personal discussion for paper impersonalities had the happiest effect. Particularly valuable were the discussions which took place between Mr. Amery and King Faisal and his Prime Minister as to the prerogatives and duties of the King under the newly promulgated Constitution, a question which urgently needed discussion, since His Majesty King Faisal had been inclined to withdraw more than was desirable from influencing the conduct of affairs of State after the coming into force of the Organic Law. The main preoccupation of the two Secretaries of State was, however, the more rapid improvement and training of the Iraq Army. Many conferences were held on this subject, and, before the Secretaries of State left, a scheme had been accepted which should enable the Iraq Army in a short time to take the principal part in the maintenance of internal security and the control of the Iraq frontiers, and should relieve the British Exchequer of its burden on this account.

After the departure of the Secretaries of State, the elections were pushed on and were completed by 23rd June, 1925. There was no sign of any definite party activity, the various political parties which had been constituted in former years having died of inanition. On completion of the elections, the Cabinet of Yasin Pasha resigned as, owing to differences of opinion between the Prime Minister and the Minister of the Interior (Abdul Muhsin Beg), they felt they could not face the Parliament as a united Cabinet. The King invited Yasin Pasha to form a new Cabinet, and on his failing, invited Abdul Muhsin Beg to do so. The Cabinet of the latter took office on 26th June, 1925.

The first Iraq Parliament met on 16th July, 1925, and was opened by King Faisal. Its first session has been devoted to the discussion of its own rules of procedure, to certain necessary amendments to the Organic Law, and to the consideration of the Budget for 1925-26 in the light of the recommendations of the Finance Commission. Its debates have, so far, been characterised by earnestness and good sense.

Thus Iraq had in July, 1925, attained the first stage of her development. She had accepted, through her representatives, a Treaty of Alliance with Great Britain; she had passed an Organic Law and set up a stable and constitutional government under it. It only remained for her frontiers to be fixed according to the decision of the League of Nations, before she could apply for admission to the League of Nations and take on the full status of an independent State.

In August, 1925, King Faisal's state of health necessitated his departure for England to undergo medical treatment. His Majesty appointed his younger brother, the Amir Zaid, as Regent left Bagdad on the 5th August, returning on the 15th November.

Meantime, in August, 1925, the report of the Frontier Commission had been published. Before it could be translated in extenso the Prime Minister explained to the Chamber that it was proposed, if all the Mosul Wilayat were to be retained, that the relation of Iraq to Great Britain should be prolonged for a period of about twenty-five years. He added that there was no one who did not recognise the value of the existing relations with Great Britain and the advantages to the country which had accrued there from. There was a striking unanimity in both Houses in favour of prolonging these relations and when the Council of the League met in September and Mr. Amery accepted on the part of the British Government the terms proposed by the Commission, both Chambers telegraphed to thank him for his defence of the rights of Iraq. It had indeed alarmed the ultra-nationalist party to find a section of the British press averse from the extension of the alliance. It was even suggested as a possible explanation that these British papers were in the pay of the Turkish Government. Though the settlement which had been hoped for was not reached at the September meeting, owing to the reference Of certain legal points to the Permanent Court of International Justice at the Hague, the speeches of Mr. Amery and Mr. Baldwin had a most reassuring effect on public opinion and it was never doubted by the large majority of Iraqis that Great Britain would support their rights.

In January, 1925, a protest had been lodged with the Turkish Government, through His Britannic Majesty's Representative in Constantinople, against violation of the status quo boundary. In May, a police patrol was ambushed south of the " Brussels " line by a band under Turkish instigation and, in June, enquiries were addressed by His Majesty's Government to the Turkish Government as to the reason for the large concentration of troops in the area north of the Iraq frontier, since it had been officially declared that the Kurdish rebellion had been suppressed. At the same time reports began to come in that the Turks were taking vengeance on the Christians and Kurds of Goyan, who had testified to the Frontier Commission their desire to be included in Iraq, and some 500 refugees arrived at Zakho. Early in September, reports began to be received of atrocities committed on Chaldean villages north and also south of the provisional frontier. The villagers, though they had never taken part against Turkey during the war, were being systematically removed from the neighbourhood of the frontier and transported into the interior, but many escaped, in a pitiable state of destitution, and reached Zakho with tales of massacre and violence. The Iraq Ministry of Interior placed a sum of money at the disposal of the Mutasarrif of Mosul for the relief of these unfortunate people. Mr. Amery brought the matter in strong terms before the Council of the League at the meeting in September, 1925, the Turkish delegate equally hotly denied the accusations : and the Secretary of State requested the Council to send an impartial commission to report on the matter and also on charges and counter-charges as to the violation of the provisional frontier. The Council entrusted the task to a distinguished Esthonian, General Laidoner, and the Commission arrived on 26th October. The Turkish Government refused to allow General Laidoner to pursue enquiries north of the " Brussels " line, so that the Commission had access to such evidence only as could be gathered within Iraq territory. Immediately before its arrival the refugee camps were visited by the General Secretary of the Friends of Armenia Society, who satisfied himself that the Iraq authorities were diligent in their efforts to succour the refugees, but that owing to their number and their desperate plight, help from outside was required.. He sent telegrams to various Christian societies and communities, and a committee was formed in London to collect funds which were despatched to the High Commission and distributed through a committee of three British officers well acquainted with conditions on the frontier. In December, Colonel Fergusson, a member of the King's Bodyguard, was sent out by the British committee to administer all monies collected.

General Laidoner and his colleagues made a careful examination of the frontier and the relief camps, at the close of which the General telegraphed to the League, stating that the Turks had undoubtedly deported Christians from south of the "Brussels" line, that the deportees deposed that they had been removed by force and violence, and that the Turks had committed crimes, atrocities and massacres. He added that without means of enquiry on the Turkish side of the frontier, it was impossible to define the true reasons for the deportations of Christians, but that these deportations might well have results deserving the attention of the Council.

General Laidoner and part of the Commission left Iraq On 23rd November, but two members remained at Mosul to examine any further complaints which might arise. The full reports of the mission were presented to the Council of the League during the meeting in December, 1925.

The opinion of the Hague Court was received on 25th November, 1925. It was to the effect that the "decision to be taken" by the League Council would be in the nature of an arbitral award binding on both parties, that this decision must be unanimous, and that though both Great Britain and Turkey had the right to be represented and to vote, such votes, if adverse to the otherwise unanimous opinion of the Council of the League, would not be taken into count. This opinion was formally adopted by the League Council On 8th December. In this decision, which was published in Bagdad on 17th December, the Council unanimously held that the Turco- Iraq frontier should be the Brussels line on condition that Great Britain undertook by means of a new treaty with Iraq to continue her present relations with Iraq for a period Of 25 years, unless before the expiry of that period Iraq were admitted to membership of the League. The Turkish delegate refused to recognize the arbitral authority of the League Council and was not present at the meeting. At its close, Sir Austen Chamberlain expressed the hope that the situation between Great Britain and Turkey would be regulated by friendly agreement between the two governments.

King Faisal telegraphed to King George his sincere thanks and gratitude. The Prime Minister telegraphed to Mr. Baldwin and to the Secretary- General of the League, and Mr. Amery was the recipient of many grateful messages. All through Iraq there was a general sense of deep relief, and of hope that the stability thus attained would be reflected in the prosperity which the country would now be able to achieve.

Conversations with regard to the new treaty were begun before the end of the year. The King and the Cabinet showed the utmost willingness to comply with the request of Mr. Amery that the terms of the alliance should be accepted by Iraq before the re-assembling of the British Parliament in the beginning of February, 1926. On the part of the Opposition, now definitely constituted under the name of the People's Party, with Yasin Pasha as leader, doubts were expressed as to the advantage to Iraq of the extension of the 1922 Treaty for 25 years, and more particularly of the similar extension of the subsidiary Agreements; but it was clear from the first that the majority, both inside the Iraq Parliament and outside, agreed that the permanent welfare of Iraq was bound up with her connection with her ally. To this was added the consideration that the period of the new instrument of alliance might, and most probably would, as Mr. Amery had stated, be reduced by the entrance of Iraq into the League of Nations, a step which the British Government would be as anxious as that of Iraq to bring about, since it would relieve Great Britain of the responsibilities imposed by the treaty.

After considerable discussion the text of the new Treaty as approved by the British Government reached Bagdad on 27th December, 1925. The Cabinet was anxious that some specific allusion should be made to the early amendment of the Military and Financial Agreements and that provision should be made for the periodic review of the situation in order to determine whether Iraq were fit to enter into the League and whether the change in the general situation admitted of further alteration in the Agreements. The Secretary of State saw no objection to these requests and the treaty was accepted by the Cabinet on 10th January and signed on 13th January. It was laid before Parliament on 18th January. Yasin Pasha, heading the Opposition, asked that it should be referred to a Committee. The Prime Minister replied that 42 members of the Hizb al Taqaddam, the Government party, had signed a petition that discussion should take place at once in the House; he asked that the public should be excluded and the debate continued in secret. The Opposition headed by Yasin Pasha, numbering 19 members, then walked out. The public was excluded and, after a debate lasting one and a half hours, re-admitted. The President took the vote by calling on each member by name to express agreement or disagreement. Agreement was unanimous.

The House is composed of 88 Deputies. Of these 58 voted for the Treaty. 9 were absent (including 3 of the Opposition). 19 walked out in protest. 1 seat is vacant. 1 is held by the President.

The Senate passed the Treaty on 19th January, 17 members voted in favour, 1 against, 2 were absent.

The most notable events following the passage of the new Treaty were the formation of a new Kurdish independence Movement which spread rapidly along the eastern borders, and the influx into Iraq of large numbers of Kurdish refugees as a result of Turkish operations against the Kurdish tribes.

In May, 1926, Sir Ronald Lindsay, His Britannic Majesty's Ambassador at Constantinople, entered on negotiations with the Turkish Government necessitated by its refusal to recognise the arbitral authority of the Council of the League of Nations regarding the Iraq frontier. Turkey showed a most welcome readiness for friendly discussion, and negotiations advanced so rapidly that a tripartite Treaty was signed at Angora on the 5th June, 1926, between Great Britain, Iraq and Turkey, and Nuri Pasha, the representative of the Iraq Government in the negotiations, reached Bagdad with the Treaty on the 13th June. By this Treaty Turkey recognised the existing frontier or "Brussels" line, subject to one very slight variation, and Turkey and Iraq entered into mutual obligations of "bon voisinage." On the 14th June the two Chambers of the Iraq Parliament accepted the Treaty, and King Faisal immediately ratified it. On the 25th June the King gave a State banquet to celebrate the signing of the Treaty at which His Majesty expressed his profound thanks to the British Government and its representatives for all that they had done for Iraq. Miss Gertrude Bell was one of the most prominent of the guests at this banquet and shared conspicuously in the general atmosphere of congratulation which marked the close of the first stage in the existence of Iraq. It was the last State function which she attended.

CHAPTER XIX

1920 - BAGDAD

To H.B., Sunday, 17th Oct., 1920

I must try and give you an account of this remarkable week. Sir Percy arrived on Monday, 11th, at Bagdad West. When we got to the station, about 4:30, his train being due at 5:30, we found a sort of reception room, flagged and carpeted, with the railed off approach to the line ...I was told to go into the reception room, where gradually there collected some 20 Or 30 Magnates of Bagdad ...the C. in C. with his staff, the heads of the departments and officers of Sir Percy's H.Q. here. The salute Of 17 guns was fired outside the town, and the wind being contrary we didn't hear it, so that quite suddenly we were told the train was in sight, and we hurriedly took up our positions in the railed off space; on the right Sir Edgar with the heads of departments and me, next to us the consuls, then the religious heads, on the left the C. in C. with his staff, Saiyid Tahb and the deputies, the mayor and one or two magnates, such as the eldest son of the Naqib. Outside the enclosure was a crowd of people, British officers and their wives and a lot of others whom I couldn't distinguish--more of these later. It was near sunset when the train drew up and the C. in C. went forward to greet Sir Percy. He came out dressed in white uniform, and after shaking hands with the C. in C. stood at the salute while the band played "God save the King." I thought as he stood there in his white and gold lace, with his air of fine and simple dignity that there had never been an arrival more momentous--never anyone on whom more conflicting emotions were centred, hopes and doubts and fears, but above all confidence in his personal integrity and wisdom ...When he came into the enclosure Sir Edgar presented me, while I made my curtsey, it was all I could do not to cry.

As soon as the presentations were over Jamil Zahawi the famous Bagdad orator read him an address of welcome, to which Sir Percy replied in Arabic that he had come by order of H.M.G. to enter into counsel with the people of the Iraq for the purpose of setting up an Arab Govt. under the guidance--the word he used was " nidharah," which means exactly "supervision"--of Great Britain, and he asked the people to co-operate with him in the establishment of settled conditions so that he might proceed at once with his task. His words were interrupted by expressions of assent and agreement on the part of his audience.

Lady Cox, Mr. Philby and Captain Cheesman (the latter is Sir Percy's private secretary) had got out of the train by this time, and we had all exchanged warm greetings. Lady Cox stepped out after ten hours of dusty journey, looking as if she had emerged from the finest bandbox--a miracle, as we told her. Then we all drove to Sir Percy's house... Lady Cox, after giving us tea, disappeared with Capt. Cheesman to look at their new house above the bridge which isn't ready yet for them, while Sir Percy, Mr. Philby and I sat down to talk. From the first moment I saw that all was well. He said he intended to set up an Arab Ministry at once as a temporary expedient without waiting for the complete pacification of the country. His scheme was to call on someone to form a cabinet and he himself would appoint British Advisors to the Ministers. We all agreed that the difficulty was to hit on the right person to summon in the capacity of Prime Minister. His first idea had been Saiyid Talib but it was a matter which needed consideration. I said I thought he had better see people here and form his opinion; whatever he decided upon we would do our utmost to further; the main thing being to decide on something and get it done.

It is quite impossible to tell you the relief and comfort it is to serve under somebody in whose judgment one has complete confidence. To the extraordinarily difficult task which lies before him he brings a single-eyed desire to act in the interests of the people of the country...

With that we all dined with the C. in C. I sat by Sir Percy and had a most enjoyable dinner in spite of the fact that I was sitting in a raging draught. I forget if I told you that I've got bronchitis. Well, I have, and I don't see much chance of curing it. However, that's a minor consideration.

Next morning I went early to the office. Sir Percy called me up at once and we talked over some telegrams--I trying to conceal the fact that it was a wholly novel experience to be taken into confidence on matters of importance! No sooner had I got to my office than I began to receive letters and visitors., each more indignant than the last, saying that the whole town was in an uproar over the reception ceremony because the notables who had been invited were herded together, all but a very small number, in the dust outside the enclosure and hadn't not even had the opportunity of shaking Sir Percy by the hand. "We came in love and obedience," said a really furious old sheikh of distinction, "and when we tried to get near His Excellency we were pushed away." Even the brothers of the Naqib had been treated with this same lack of ceremony...

So I decided at once to invest myself with the duties of Oriental secretary, there being no one else in the office who knows Bagdad, and calling in Mr. Philby for help we drafted a form of invitation to all the notables of Bagdad for the following morning. It was almost lunch time before we got hold of Sir Percy, but meantime I had prepared the list of names--over 100--and drawn up also a small list of people to whom he ought to give private interviews. He approved everything and gave me a free hand ...and we had the invitations out that evening. It still makes me hot and cold to think what would have happened if we hadn't tackled the situation promptly, for there wasn't a single person in authority who was thinking of the Arab side of the matter and of how supremely important it was that Sir Percy should be put into immediate personal touch with the town. That night Mr. Philby dined with me and we had a long and profitable talk. He had been to tea with me also and I had Sasun Eff. to meet him, which was most valuable, for Sasun is one of the sanest people here and he reviewed the whole situation with his usual wisdom and moderation.

Next morning we had our reception--a huge success. The space in Sir Percy's room being rather limited I had sent out the invitations in 3 batches, leaving half an hour between each batch. We seated about 30 people at a time in Sir Percy's room and had them in 4 relays; those who were waiting were entertained by Mr. Philby and me in the waiting room next door to Sir Percy. But I went in with one of the batches and saw how well it was going with all the people sitting round and being properly served with coffee and cigarettes, while Sir Percy explained his programme and asked their opinions. It is the kind of thing Sir Percy is extremely good at, and everyone went away delighted. I got Abdul Majid Shawi, the mayor, for a private interview in the afternoon; next morning Sasun Eff. and others, and another batch on Friday morning. What with getting the right people to come and keeping the small fry of unworthy place-hunters off, I've had my hands full. Capt. Cheesman and I keep Sir Percy's list of engagements between us, for the moment. I, the Arabs and he the English, and the scheme works beautifully.

On Thursday afternoon Sir Percy called me in to discuss some advice Sasun Eff. had given him about the pacification of the Baqubah area to the effect that the big people of Bagdad who own estates there should be asked to send for some of their tribal tenants, explain Sir Percy's intentions and ask them what in the name of wonder they are now fighting for. Sir Percy at once saw this was a step in the right direction, because it calls on the Bagdadis to take a hand in what is after all their own game ...I told Sir Percy who were the people to ask and undertook to write the letters. He then dictated to me a Proclamation in the same sense and told me to get it out at once in Arabic, consulting with Mr. Philby. I must tell you in the morning important news had come in from the Euphrates saying that we had occupied Tuwairij and that Karbala was ready to make submission. On this Sir Percy held a Council consisting of Evelyn [Howell], Mr. Philby and me in which it was decided that the provisional govt. at Karbala set up by the insurgents should be told that they must make unconditional surrender and come in under guarantee to see Sir Percy. The Euphrates news has made a deep impression in the town.

To finish the Diala story, all the landlords have acquiesced with satisfaction in Sir Percy's suggestion. The Naqib is sending out his son Saiyid Safa-al-Din who came to see me this morning and told me all he was going to do. Close on his heels came Fakhri bringing telegrams to his tenants. So that's a success.

On Thursday evening after Sir Percy had laid his definite selection of A and B Ministers before Mr. Philby and me, I got him to meet the rest of our group--Major Murray, Major Yetts and Capt. Clayton, and we had a most satisfactory talk. I wanted him to realise that these were the men who would work heart and soul with him, and it didn't take him long to find it out. At the end he told Mr. Philby to submit to him a scheme for his own secretariat. This is the most thorny of all questions, because it is the personal one. We think he ought to have a complete secretariat at the Residency, Civil Secretary, Political Secretary, Military Secretary and Private Secretary...

I have kept religiously out of the controversy, the more readily because I feel perfectly certain that Sir Percy will go his own way. They were as bitterly opposed to an Arab Cabinet, but Sir Percy had gone straight through. He knows there is no alternative, and having made up his mind, nothing moves him. His direct simplicity is beyond all wonder ...it's still like a dream to find all things one has thought ought to be done, being done without question. I feel equally sure that when it comes to the difficult point of dealing with the tribal insurgents on the Euphrates he will drop all the silly ideas of revenge and punishment which have been current ...and be guided only by consideration for the future peace of the country under an Arab Govt. The first question is whom to call on to form a Cabinet? Most of the people he has seen have suggested the Naqib, and I think he will make an attempt in that direction to-morrow. I am convinced not only that the Naqib will refuse for himself, but that he will also refuse to recommend anyone...

If the Naqib refuses to step into the breach the only alternative that I see is for Sir Percy himself to summon and appoint the members of the provisional cabinet. The moderates are themselves taking up the idea; Fakhri jamil suggested it to me this morning. I need not say that I greeted it with the greatest show of surprise and interest, because I want everything to come from them and not from us. But if they do urge this scheme upon Sir Percy, what a striking proof it will be of my favourite maxim that if you thrust responsibility on them they are bound to turn to you for help.

The object of the provisional cabinet is merely that it should prepare for and hold the first general election. As soon as you get an elective body, that body chooses its own official representatives and the provisional govt. vanishes. While a good third of the country is still in open rebellion, it's obvious that you can't hold a general election, yet it's equally obvious, as Sir Percy sees, that you can't delay in setting up some form of native institutions. They all expect that he will do something at once, and if he doesn't the golden opportunity will be lost and confidence shaken.

I stayed at home all to-day except for half an hour with Sir Percy in the office this afternoon. He asked me if I would come on to his personal staff as Oriental Secretary or anything he decided, and I said I would love to serve with him in any capacity he chose ...I found him in talk with the editor of the Nationalist paper here, an ardent Nationalist, on whom he was making the most favourable impression...

I'm now going to be very sensible and perhaps stay at home to-morrow so as to get quite well.

To H.B., Bagdad, Oct. 24th, 1920

I mentioned bronchitis last week--well, it's won and I've spent the last six days in my house and partly in bed. As a result of which I'm now very nearly all right. In a way I'm not sorry, tiresome as it was to be laid up, to have been removed from the fierce personal controversies of which the echoes have reached me, and the inhabitants of Bagdad have seen to it that I've not been removed from the political crisis. For they have been at all hours by my side ...On the plea of enquiring after my health they have sat on my sofa--the big Persian sofa in my dining-room which has arrived since you left--and poured out their hopes and fears. I made an attempt to close my doors up to 11 a.m. but it wasn't very successful. When the Mayor of Bagdad rolled up at 9 or the Naqib sent his son Saiyid Mahmud I was obliged to 'endosser' dressing gown and go out to see them. The worrying thing was that we were not getting a move on. Sir Percy as being submerged in details which left him no leisure to consider the big issues, and there seemed to be no one in the office who had sufficient presence of mind to stand in his doorway and block their passage. So all I could do was to send in a daily report of the gossip, the rumour and the impatience with which the town was seething and point that nothing but a quick decision could end them. He had already come to the decision that his first step would be to invite the Naqib to form a provisional Council but day after day passed and could not get time to take it.

On Wednesday I had the Euphrates Sheikhs fresh from the interviews with Sir Percy, first Fahad Bey of the Anazeh, looking younger than ever (he's not far short of eighty) and proudly informing me that he has recently married two new wives. After which he expounded to me his simple scheme for the future, which was that in all

495

Tribal matters Sir Percy should rely upon the advice of Fahad and as for the rest he should seek counsel with the Naqib and two other old turbaned worthies. Then came Ali Sulaiman the head Sheikh of the Dulaim a very able man with plans better suited to modern conditions than those of Fahad--and after him various smaller fry, none of them fools.

On Thursday Sir Percy sent round a message to say that he had called a council of state for that afternoon in my house, since I couldn't come to the office. They assembled at three o'clock, Sir Percy, Evelyn Howell, Mr. Philby, Mr. Bullard, Sir Edgar and Col. Slater. Then followed three hours of poignantly interesting discussion for Sir Percy produced his scheme for a provisional cabinet, Arab Ministers and British Advisors ...Finally he carried his scheme through with un-important alterations, and announced that he was now going to lay it before the Naqib.

On Friday nothing further happened. I had innumerable visi-tors and all the restlessness of Bagdad seemed to eddy round my garden. In the evening came the Tods with the same story. "Make haste, make haste." And on this note I sent my daily report to Sir Percy.

Saturday began with a notable visit from Jafar Pasha. He is the Major General of distinguished service first with the Turks and then with Faisal. I saw him in Damascus last year, and he had repeatedly written to me. During the winter he came to me hot-foot from an inter-view with Sir Percy ...I told him it was his duty as an individual and a Nationalist to assist in establishing Arab institutions of whatever form and that if he and others went boldly forward relying on our support, they would silence criticism. Whether he believed me or not I don't know ...Jafar is the first of the Mesopotamians to return from Syria, and on his attitude much will depend...

Saiyid Hussain Afhan came in. I had just embarked on a heart to heart talk with Saiyid Hussain about some leading articles which he proposed to publish in his paper, when in came Mr. Philby and others, and on top of them Sir Percy. Everyone but Mr. Philby melted away, and we two turned to Sir Percy, breathless with excitement. "Well," he said, "he has accepted." He had come straight from the Naqib who had agreed to undertake the formation of the provisional govt. So the first success is scored and no one but Sir Percy could have done it. Indeed, that even he should have induced the Naqib to take a hand in public affairs is nothing short of a miracle. Sir Percy's delight and satisfaction was only equal to ours and we all sat for half an hour bubbling over with joy and alternatively glorifying the Naqib and the High Commissioner.

I woke this Sunday morning with an infinite sense of relief., and sent a note to Sir Percy begging him to follow historic precedent with regard to the Seventh Day ...The Naqib's invitations to the members of the future Cabinet will be out to-morrow ...I believe the thing will go through. And this first and most difficult beginning will have been made.

I've just had my carpets all put down after having them up all summer. They do look nice.

To H.B., Bagdad, November 1st, 1920

We have had a very critical week, but on the whole things are going as well as could be hoped. On Monday night the Naqib's letters and telegrams to the 18 people whom he invited to form the Council of State were prepared. That night I dined with Capt. Clayton and Major Murray to meet Jafar Pasha. It was an amazing evening ...I said complete independence was what we ultimately wished to give. "My Lady," he answered--we were speaking Arabic--"complete independence is never given; it is always taken"--a profound saying...

The man is an idealist with a high purpose, animated by fervour for his race and country ...When we parted that evening I did not think he would refuse the Naqib's invitation to join the Cabinet as Minister of Defence. Nor did he...That day a number of acceptances came in. In the afternoon I gave a great tea-party in my garden to Fahad Bey and the Agail ...It was really splendid. Fahad Bey sat and told tales of the desert and ended by opening his robes and showing me a huge hole in his breast formed by a lance thrust into his back in a youthful raid. " And I looked down and saw the head of the lance sticking out here." No one but an Arab of the desert could have recovered ...On Wednesday morning all seemed to be going well. In the afternoon Major Yetts dropped in to tea with the Tods. Mr. Tod sprang upon us that he had called on Sasun Eff. to congratulate his becoming Minister of Finance, and found him with Ramdi Pasha Baban (who had been offered a seat in the Cabinet without portfolio) both in the act of refusing ...I left my cup of tea undrunk and rushed back to the office to tell Mr. Philby. He wasn't there, but there was a light in Sir Percy's room. I went in and told him. He bade me go at once to Sasun Eff. and charged me to make him change his mind. I set off, feeling as if I carried the future of all Iraq in my hands, but when I got to Sasun's house, to my immense relief, I found Mr. Philby and Capt. Clayton already there. The Naqib had got Sasun's letter and had sent Mr. Philby off post haste. I arrived, however, in the nick of time. They had exhausted all their arguments, and Sasun still adhered to his decision. I think my immense anxiety must have inspired me, for after an hour of concentrated argument he was visibly shaken, in spite of the fact that his brother Shaul (whom also I admire and respect) came in and did his best against us ...We got Sasun Eff. to consent to think it over and see Sir Percy next day. I had an inner conviction that the game was won-- partly, thank heaven, to the relations of trust and confidence which I had personally already established with Sasun--but we none of us could feel sure. I didn't sleep much that night. I turned and turned in my mind the arguments that I had used and wondered if I could not have done better.

Next morning, Thursday, Sasun Eff. came in at ten; I took him straight to Sir Percy and left them. Half an hour later he returned and told me that he had accepted. He asked me what he could now do to help and I sent him straight to the Naqib. The leading Sheikh of Bagdad had also refused to join the Council, and it was essential to get him to. In the midst of this talk Sir Percy sent for me. I left Sasun to Mr. Philby and went to consult with Sir Percy. We agreed that I should send at once for Jafar, tell him what had happened and bid him bestir himself. It was past one o'clock before I caught Jafar. We had the most interesting conversation. He told me the misgivings and motives with which he had accepted the invitation to come into the Cabinet...

We then discussed how to win over the extremists. assured him that that was Sir Percy's chief desire, and, taking heart, he asked if he might talk to Sir Percy. I took him at once to Sir Percy and left them together, with the assured conviction that Sir Percy was the best exponent of his own policy.

On Saturday morning Mr. Philby and I went to the Naqib ...Mr. Philby has been Sir Percy's go-between with him, and most excellently he has done it. We found the Naqib radiant, not only full of good sense but also full of the determination to run the show himself. His one wish is to work hand in hand with Sir Percy, but he doesn't intend to let any other member of the cabinet be Prime Minister, and I'm heartily glad of it. He sent a message to Sir Percy to say that whenever Mr. Philby couldn't come he would like me to be Sir Percy's agent.

Long Life to the Arab Government. Give them responsibility and make them settle their own affairs and they'll do it every time a thousand times better than we can.

I ended the day by giving a dinner party to Sasun Eff., Jafar Pasha and Abdul Maji Shawi with Mr. Philby, Capt. Clayton and Major Murray to help. For I wanted to bring the first named three into touch with one another. It was immensely interesting; Abdul Majid told Jafar the whole story of the origins of tribal rebellion. Jafar with great eloquence, pleaded the need of an immediate settlement with the insurgents. "The peasant must return to his plough, the shepherd to his flock. The blood of our people must cease to flow and the land must once more be rich with crops. Shall our tribes be wasted in battle and our towns die of starvation?"

Jafir is right and the first great work of the Council must be to bring about pacification. To this end, as Sasun justly observed, it would be well for the Naqib to summon to the Council a leading man from Karbela and Najaf. One of the difficulties is that all or nearly all the leading men of the Shiah towns are Persian subjects and must be made to adopt Mesopotamian nationality before they can take official positions in the Mesopotamian State.

In the evening we talked of the Arab Army. Under the terms of the Mandate conscription may not be applied, and Jafar is beginning to wonder how he will get recruits--a difficult problem. Jafar also described his efforts to get into touch with the holy element in Kadhimain. He had been to the great people and tried to prove to them that the sole object of the Provisional Council summoned by the Naqib was to lay the foundations of National Institutions. But they would reply only that they wanted a govt. elected by the people, and that nothing else was of any use. "But you can't hold a general election in a day," said Jafar, "and we want to get to work at once." They offered no suggestion and remained obdurately hostile. "What did you say next," I asked. "I was silent," he answered. That's the Shiah attitude, and it's only countrymen--so far as Arabs can be called the countrymen of Persian divines--who will be able very gradually to bring them into line. Finally I hope a section will become definitely Arab and take a hand in the State...

Mr. Philby, Capt. Clayton and I went to tea with Shukri Alusi who is the most learned of the learned and a great recluse. It's an immense source of pride to me that I may go to his house whenever I like.

Oh, if we can pull this thing off; rope together the young hotheads and the Shiah obscurantists, and enthusiasts like Jafar, polished old statesmen like Sasun, and scholars like Shukri--if we can make them work together and find their own salvation for themselves, what a fine thing it would be. I see visions and dream dreams. I omitted to mention that the Council of State of the first Arab Govt. in Mesopotamia since the Abbassids meets to-morrow.

To H.B., Bagdad, November 7th, 1920

This week has been comparatively uneventful. The Cabinet met for the first time on Tuesday, but it doesn't seem to have done much except discuss what would be the relations between the Ministers and their advisors, and finally to resolve to ask Sir Percy to explain. He has gone into the whole matter very carefully with the Naqib, on the basis of an excellent memorandum drawn up by Mr. Philby, and I believe he meets the Cabinet to-morrow.

After the Cabinet Meeting the Naqib sent for Fahad Bey and asked whether he would be prepared to take a message from the Cabinet to the Insurgent Tribes. Fahad came hotfoot in to me. "Khatun," he said, "you I know and Kokus I know, but of Arab Governments I have no knowledge. Never will I give any answer to the Naqib till I'm assured that Kokus would approve." I brought in Mr. Philby and together we assured him. "Oh, Khatun," said he, " Oh, Veelbi, on your heads you tell me that Kokus would approve."

And he was so much perturbed that he came in the following day and said he hadn't been able to sleep for fear of doing anything contrary to the policy of Kokus. I couldn't help feeling that with such staunch allies as Fahad there was little fear that the influence of Kokus would not avail!

But if we had been setting up native institutions in the midst of order instead of disorder the task would have been incomparably easier...

Apart from the Pro-Turks, the Naqib's Council has against it almost the whole body of Shiahs, first because it's looked upon as of British parentage, but also because it contains considerably less Shiahs than Sunnis. The Shiahs, as I've often observed, are one of the greatest problems ...and their leading people the learned divines and their families are all Persian subjects. I find that the best argument when people Come to me and complain that So-and-So has not been included in the Cabinet, "Effendim, may I ask whether he is a subject of the Mesopotamian State?" "Effendim, No; he is a subject of Persia." Then I point out that in that case he can't hold office in a Mesopotamian Government. And none of my interlocutors have found an answer.

I attempt to give you the picture so that you may realise the problem; it's true that few are pleased, but they wouldn't have been pleased with any line whatever. I honestly believe that Sir Percy has chosen the best possible path. But it won't lead to immediate peace and contentment. That's not possible.

As soon as we can we must proceed to the election of an Assembly. And I shall be very much mistaken (but then I often am) if they don't ask for the son of the Sharif as an Amir. I regard that as the only solution. ...

To H.B., November 14th, 1920

Things are getting on. The Cabinet have accepted practically without alteration Sir Percy's scheme for the working of Ministers and their advisors. It was admirably drafted by Mr. Philby, and I think it is a real feather in his cap. Tomorrow the Ministry of the Interior gets into its new quarters in the Sarai--the old Turkish offices. They were turned, last year, into billets for officers and their wives, and it is a real dispensation that the W.O. ordered all the wives home otherwise we should have had great difficulty in recovering them ...There was no other possible place to put the Arab Govt. and people made a great point of having the old offices to which they were accustomed. To get the Ministries installed there is the only way of demonstrating that the Arab Govt. is a real thing. The Shiahs remain hostile, their chief grievance being that there is not a Shiah with a portfolio, I think there's going to be a shuffle in the Cabinet so as to admit one of them. There is also a pretty definite pro-Turkish party, consisting mainly of ex-Turkish officials, civil and military. They don't want an Arab Govt. and declare that they won't come in to it because the Turks must certainly and inevitably return.

Sir Percy preserves a calm and equitable judgment which is the most encouraging part of the whole business. Meantime, without waiting for further developments, I'm beginning to shape my branch of the Secretariat on the principle that the main thing is to get going. This week I shall bring out my first fortnightly intelligence Report--which is to be our official (and very confidential) contribution to the news of the world ...It's great fun, I need not tell you, to be creating a new office with Sir Percy's unfailing help and approval. This last week it has made a good step forward out of Chaos.

To H.B. and F.B., Bagdad, November 22nd, 1920

Man for man we may say without fear that the. British adviser is better than the Turkish and we want to give this country the best chance we can. The thing is to induce the Arabs to accept the chance. I believe we can if events beyond our control don't unseat us. If we had done 18 months ago what we are doing now the problem would have been infinitely more simple.

My garden is a mass of chrysanthemums--brown and yellow and white and pink. It's very cold--the cold has come early--and the dogs have been obliged to wear last year's coats till Marie has time to

502

make new ones., that will be after she has made a gown for me. They are disgracefully ragged and look like beggar dogs...

To H.B., Bagdad, November 29th, 1920

We are greatly hampered by the tribal rising which has delayed the work of handing over to the Arab Govt. Sir Percy, I think rightly, decided that the tribes must be made to submit to force. In no other way was it possible to make them surrender their arms or teach them that you mustn't lightly engage in revolution, even when your holy men tell you to do so ...Without the lesson and without drawing their teeth by fines of arms (impossible to obtain except by force) we should have left an impossible task to the Arab Govt. Nevertheless, it's difficult to be burning villages at one end of the country by means of a British Army, and assuring people at the other end that we really have handed over responsibility to native Ministers...Meantime, Sir Percy has held strictly to his doctrine that a general amnesty must wait on submission. The Ulama have done their best to make him accept them as intermediaries; the tribes have repeatedly asked that negotiations should be conducted through the premier Mujtahid, at whose orders they would lay down arms. Sir Percy has stoutly refused--more power to him! The claim of the Ulama to loose and bind is one of the most formidable problems of the Arab State; the refusal to recognise their political authority is unmitigatedly to the good ...And it's done with such skill, with such courtesy, the letters to the Ulama are such as Sir Percy alone knows how to write.

Finally I'm summing up our difficulties--there is the fact that Govt. can't be passed from one hand to another in the twinkle of an eye...

A momentous Cabinet meeting took place this afternoon but I've not heard yet what happened ...The number of heart to heart talks which take place in my office would surprise you! All the busybodies come in to say what they're busybodying and have to be listened to with sympathetic interest and given advice which it's little likely they'll follow. I sometimes wonder whether 'au fond' I'm not a busybody myself.

Sir Percy generally sends for me towards the end of the morning and we exchange experiences. I then lunch with him and Lady Cox and Capt. Cheesman, and though we don't as a rule talk of Mesopotamia, we tell each other stories, relate comic episodes and generally keep in touch. Therefore though an hour in the middle of the day is very difficult to spare, I feel that the constant unofficial intercourse is very valuable. Also we often have a Sunday outing. Yesterday Sir P. and I and Capt. Cheesman and Capt. Pedder (my host of last Sunday) went out shooting on the river bank opposite Ctesiphon ...We had about 20 Arab beaters. There were little encampments in the heart of what we call here the forest and the people were cutting liquorice and poplar for fuel to send to Bagdad and digging up the liquorice roots.

I love walking with the beaters and hearing what they say to each other in the broadest Iraq dialect which I'm proud to understand. Their clothes are amazingly unfitted for any job they're likely to undertake, especially struggling through thorns. They treat me with constant solicitous politeness, beat down the thorns with their bare feet so as to let me pass and bustle out of the way to give me the easiest place. You're not an Oriental for nothing...

To H.B., Bagdad, December 4th, 1920

I wish I kept a diary. My only record of this time is my letters to you...

Yesterday afternoon I rode out to Kadhimain to see an old Persian Princess. Banu Ozma is her title, and she is a daughter of Nasr al Din Shah...

She has come to Kadhimain on a visit and has hired a small house. There I found her in a little room opening on to the Courtyard, carpeted cushioned and curtained to keep out the cold. A charcoal brazier and a parrot in a cage completed the furniture. She was lying on a mattress on the floor, leaning against cushions and covered with a padded quilt. What you could see of her was swathed in black, down to her eyebrows and up to her chin. All that was visible were voluble hands and finely cut face with enormous eyes behind spectacles. She must at one time have been very beautiful; the Kajar women are famous for their looks. She lay there and talked the most exquisite

Persian, quick and sweet and faint like the shadow of a wonderful voice. These Kajar Princesses who turn up from time to time, mostly on pilgrimages, are extraordinarily interesting--they are such great ladies--but Banu Ozma is the one we liked far the best. I never saw greater native distinction than in that little old Persian lady lying on the floor.

To H.B., Bagdad, December 11th, 1920

It is exactly three weeks since the last Mail came in. Do my letters arrive with any regularity? I write as you do every week. But this week there's not much to write about for I've been rather a poor thing with a chill. I stayed at home two days and then couldn't bear it any longer so I went back to the office.

The idea is to have 30 Tribal members in the election assembly, 20 being representatives of the 20 biggest tribes and the other ten one apiece for the small tribes grouped together in each of the new ten divisions. I have supplied the data to the Electoral Law Committee and selected the 20 Tribes. I don't think the Council will quarrel with my selection.

All the big landowners on the Council will try to keep the tribes out, I expect the tribes will vote through a committee of their chief Sheikhs who will select one of themselves ...As I write a mail at last with delightful long letters. As for what you and Mother say about my letters, I can't tell you what it is to me to be able to write to you so fully and to know that you're both interested. Of course it makes it infinitely easier to write in such detail that you, Father, should have been actually here and seen the people and conditions ...I should not keep a record of all this time if it wasn't that I wanted to send it to you, and very often I feel that in writing to you I'm clearing my own mind...It helps me enormously.

To H.B., Bagdad, December 18th, 1920

The Council is aware and Sir Percy has constantly impressed upon them, the vital need of getting down to the formation of a native army to relieve ours. Incidentally, Jafar Pasha doesn't think that without conscription in some form they can raise an army which won't be

505

prohibitively expensive. If they have to compete in the labour market they must reckon on paying their men at least Rs 60 a month... However, that's a question which could only be settled by an elective assembly. Meantime Jafar has a committee of experts from G.H.Q. (at his request) and they're considering what steps should be taken. Roughly speaking, they think we might have a brigade by the autumn of 1921, and an Arab Division by the Autumn of 1922, which means that by that date we can reduce our force here to 1 Division, keeping it up to 2 Divisions till then...No Govt. in this country whether ours or an Arab administration, can carry on without force behind it. The Arab Government has no force till its army is organised, therefore it can't exist unless we lend it troops ...The bedrock on which this argument rests is that no administration can exist without force behind it. I think you have seen enough of the country to know that it's correct. Mesopotamia is not a civilised state, it is largely composed of wild tribes who do not wish to shoulder the burden and expense of citizenship. In setting up an Arab state we are acting in the interests of the urban and village population which expects and rightly expects that it will ultimately leaven the mass. Till the leavening has gone a good bit further than it has at present, this citizen population must control the mass, constrain it. That is why it needs force for the maintenance of internal order.

Meantime we've been busy with other matters. The early part of the week was devoted to the electoral law about which I wrote you last week. It was presented to the Council on Monday and with 5 exceptions they were all dead against making any special arrangement for tribal representation, and in favour of letting the tribes register and vote like the rest of the population. That would have meant that the tribes would have taken no part, for as Abdul Majid Shawi rightly pointed out, whereas the population of Iraq is mainly tribal and Shiah, in the. course of four general elections held under the Turks no tribesman or Shiah has been returned. Next morning Sasun Eff. and Daud Yusafani (of Mosul) came into my office to talk the matter over. We were all agreed that it would be disastrous if the tribesman were to swamp the townsmen, but I pressed upon them the consideration that whatever may have happened in Turkish times, an Arab National Govt. could not hope to succeed unless it ultimately contrived to associate the tribesmen with its endeavours. They raised good objections against providing for representatives from selected big tribes, but we also agreed that that might be got over by providing for a fixed number of tribal representatives for each division to be selected by all the tribes of that Division, i.e., by the Sheikhs. The ordinary tribesmen won't take part. It was clear that there was a good deal of misunderstanding as to what Sir Percy's views were and why he looked on adequate representation of the tribes as essential and I reported the whole conversation to him, with the result that he sent an admirable letter to the Council saying that in the election assembly which was to decide on the future of the Iraq every section of the community must be represented and that he must be able to assure his Govt. that this was the case. Jafar Pasha propounded the possible alternative of securing representation by divisions not by specified tribes. I said I thought that would meet the case excellently. Next morning, he and Sasun returned with a revised scheme--2 tribal representatives for each Division, but any tribesman who liked to register could vote in the ordinary way--first- rate proposal, for while it secures a minimum of ten tribal members in the assembly, it does not preclude tribesmen from taking part in elections like other registered electors--if they like.

This was finally carried in the afternoon's sitting, no doubt Sir Percy's letter helping to the desired result...

In the course of the week I had long visits from the two tribal chiefs on the Council. Both are satisfied with the turn the Electoral law has taken ...I said the matter was entirely in their hands, we didn't care whom they put up as Amir or what kind of Govt. they selected to have, provided we felt sure the choice was freely and fairly made without pressure or intimidation...

To sum my impression of the week, I feel more and more how anxious the people are here with whom we're dealing to work in with us and follow our advice. On big matters and on little matters they are always dropping in to my office to consult me as to Sir Percy's views. So and So is suggested as Mutasarrif of Hillah--will that be all right? Yes, I say firmly, that's all right. My interlocutor breathes a sigh of relief and goes off to vote for him...So with the electoral law--from Sasun downwards they all want to know how they had best meet our views. I never lose an opportunity of saying that our view is guided only by a desire to do the best by them and the country--they know the country best, how do they think this end is to be attained? and on that basis we discuss the matter, whether it's a law or an invitation to dinner! and unless I'm very much mistaken we have got the confidence of the people we're working with...

Oh dear ! I wonder what they'll decide on, and what we'll decide on, and all! What an interminable letter this is--do you mind? ...

To H.B., Bagdad, December 25th, 1920

I must tell you a silly story, to understand which you must learn a little Turkish. There's an amusing idiom in Turkish by which you say "such like" by repeating the original word, only changing its initial letter to "M"...We got recently an account of the conversation between the Sharif and an Arab of these parts--the latter told us the story. The Sharif was fuming against all and sundry: "Who" he cried "is this Kokus Mokus and this Philby Milby Sir Percy was delighted...

I've been feeling a good deal lately how much the Arabs who are our friends, want us to give them lead. They constantly come to me, not only for advice on immediate conduct but in order to ask about the future: "But what do you think, Khatun?...I feel quite clear in my own mind that there is only one workable solution, a son of the Sharif and for choice Faisal: very very much the first choice ...

CHAPTER XX

1921 - BAGDAD

To H.B., Bagdad, January 3rd, 1921

The big Dulaim Chiefs who live in tents all the winter (only Ali Sulaiman lives in a house outside Ramadi) inhabit during the summer dwellings which are unknown elsewhere. They are called Mahrab and they are, as you might say, the mud counterpart of a tent-- a long narrow room with very thin mud walls, windowless, but low down in the North wall just where your head comes when you are sitting on the floor a line of little openings made in patterns by the omission of mud bricks at regular intervals, so that the north wind blows in to cool you. Some square openings at the top of the wall takes off the hot air and they say the room keeps wonderfully fresh. In the men's room the East end is left open and terminates in an open--air diwan, a mud floor with a low wall round it, where they sit at night; but by day it can't be as cool as the women's room which is closed on all sides. No one builds these Mahrab but the Dulaim.

Hit on its ancient mound with the pitch wells bubbling up around it, is like nothing else in Mesopotamia, but to me its too full of the memories of rollicking journeys, of ghosts, riding about on camels before the world which was my world cracked together and foundered. I don't think I'll go there again, I don't like the look of those ghosts-- they are too happy and confident. It's I who feel a ghost beside them.

We walked round the town in the afternoon and amused ourselves by getting one of the pitch wells alight. The gas laden water came bubbling up, carrying with it writhing black snakes of pitch which form a crust on the pool. We threw in a lighted newspaper and the gas flamed and flickered over the bubbling pool, as if the water burned; then suddenly, after we had watched this devil's miracle for a long time, a thick pitch snake struggled up, and choked for a moment the bubbling water and gas, and the flame went out. Two boys were drawing off the pitch crust, twisting and breaking it off like toffee (a very difficult trick though it looks easy enough in their skilled hands-- from father to son they've been at the job some 5,000 years) and throwing it up to where a donkey stood waiting for his load...

North of Hit is No Man's Land. Since we withdrew, the tribes rob and loot all passers by and each man's hand is against his neighbour. Emissaries of Mustafa Kemal drift down through this chaos and Hit has the whole unrest of Asia at its doors...

Upon my soul I'm glad I don't know what this year is going to bring, I don't think I ever woke on a first of January with such feelings of apprehension. You can struggle through misfortune and failure, when they approach you slowly--you see them coming and gradually make up your mind to the inevitable. But if the future opened suddenly and you knew when you woke on the first of January all that lay before you it would be overwhelming. For the truth is there's little that Promises well...

Perceive that I'm not your daughter for nothing for the only fitting end to this tirade is a "God bless my soul--how any sane," etc.! I do write long letters don't I father ...aren't fools damnable.

To H.B., Bagdad, January 22nd, 1921

I've just got Mother's letter of December 15th saying there s a fandango about my report. The general line taken by, the Press seems to be that it's most remarkable that a dog Should be able to stand up on it's hind legs at all--i.e., a female write a white paper. I hope they'll drop that source of wonder and pay attention to the report itself, if it will help them to understand what Mesopotamia is like...

Talib seems to me to be doing very well. He put up to the Council the other day a long list of proposals for administration appointments in the provinces, Mutasarrifs and Kaimakams. It is very essential to get these appointments made so that people in the provinces may see Arab officials stepping in and realise that there is an Arab Government...

I've a feeling that we're making good progress. There's a greater sense of stability, the Arab Government is gaining ground and people begin to see that we really intend to do by it all we say. Poor human kind that has to spend so much of its time in trying to convince its fellows of the loyalty of its motives! ...Our task has been complicated by the fact that there was so much suspicion to get over. I know most of the people we are now working with trust us and that's a beginning...

We had to go to the funeral of the woman who was Matron in chief during the war and had come back here to help up with the organisation of our civil hospital...But as Matron in chief she was a tower of strength and I personally loved her for all her kindness to me, beginning from the time when I had jaundice in Basrah and not a soul to look after me. She was an angel of goodness, poor Miss Jones ...and they gave her a military funeral with the bugle call of the last Post and the salute of rifles into the empty air. And I hoped as I walked behind the Union Jack that covered her coffin that when people walked behind my coffin it would be with thoughts even dimly resembling those that I gave to her...

To H.B., Bagdad, January. 22nd, 1921

We have had a distracted week on account of the races. I didn't intend to go more than one day, but the first day Thursday, Aurelia telephoned and said I must come, so I went with them. There was a pretty good sprinkling of Bagdad Magnates and I thought it fairly amusing, so I went again to-day and was very much amused ...It was Cup Day, I must tell you; we didn't go till after lunch but the Coxes went in state at 11 a.m. and stayed the whole day. Sir Percy wore a frock coat and a grey top hat to the admiration of all beholders. I may mention that I was also very smart in a Paris hat and gown--it's really quite nice to dress up for once, a thing I haven't done for months...

I hear rumours that the Sunnis of Bagdad are considering whether it wouldn't suit their book best to have a Turkish prince as King. They are afraid of being swamped by the Shiahs, against whom a Turk might be a better bulwark than a son of the Sharif. The present Government which is predominantly Sunni isn't doing anything to conciliate the Shiahs. They are now considering a number of administrative appointments for the provinces; almost all the names they put up are Sunnis, even for the wholly Shiah province on the Euphrates, with the exception of Karbala and Nejd where even they haven't the face to propose Sunnis...

Sir Percy will have to intervene when the names come up to him for sanction, for if anything is certain it is that the Euphrates won't put up with Sunni officials. They must make up their minds that they can't have it both ways. If they want popular native institutions, the Shiahs, who are in a large majority, must take their share. There are a number of leading Shiahs on the Euphrates who would prefer British administration (which they can't have) to an Arab Sunni administration or a Turkish Sunni. But when it comes to the point the Moslem never dares to raise his voice against the Moslem, even if it's a kind of Moslem he hates. I believe if we could put up a son of the Sharif at once, he might yet sweep the board; if we hesitate, the tide of public opinion may turn overwhelmingly to the Turks...

To H.B., Bagdad, January. 30th, 1921

Do you know this is the eighth Xmas I've been away--1913 Arabia, 1914 Boulogne, 1915 Egypt, 1916 Bastah and the rest Bagdad. Extraordinary isn't it...

To H.B., Bagdad, February. 7th, 1921

We've had a rather stormy week owing to heated disagreement between two of the Advisors ...over the question of how to dispose of the Arab Levies (sort of Gendarmerie). They excited their respective ministers...to such a pitch that it was a question whether Sasun wouldn't resign when the decision of the Council went against his voice and the Levies were placed under the Interior instead of under Defence. The decision was a wrong one, I think, but it didn't very much matter, so long as they were placed under some Arab Ministry at once for we want them to take over in the middle Euphrates when British troops are withdrawn from there, as they will be in a fortnight or so...

The Council has made a number of appointments to administrative posts in the provinces--Mutasarrifs and Kaimmakams. Most of them are pretty good, some of them pretty bad. Sir Percy gives way when the Naqib insists. I think he is quite right. We have got to sit by and see them make mistakes. The appointments all originate in the Interior.

To H.B., Bagdad, February. 13th, 1921

I write you such long letters because it's the only form of Diary I keep. ...

It has been an interesting week marked first by the return of some twenty or more of the deportees whom A.T. sent to the Henjam including one of the ringleaders from Bagdad. And the very next day his son was arrested with a batch of other agitators who owned, wrote or inspired the Istiqlal--of which I sent you extracts last week. The suppression of the paper had been for some time under discussion but Sir Percy said rightly that it was for the Ministry of Interior to take action. It seems to have been entirely successful...

The present Government has got no hold in the Provinces but I think it is gaining ground here...

I don't know what hanky panky the Allies are up to about the mandates, but I'm all on the side of the League of Nations in protesting that they must be made public. That's the essence of them, publicity...

I'm often wrong in prophecy but I believe if we were to refuse the mandate we should have a clamour through the country begging us to accept it...

Meantime the Shiah question is a very burning one. Everyone from the Euphrates provinces says the people there won't accept Sunni officials and the Council goes on blandly appointing them...A Shiah of Karbala has at last accepted the ministry of Education which the Naqib was induced to offer him...

Another burning question is that of general amnesty. I feel sure the time has come, or is very near, when we must proceed to this. It will be bitterly opposed by the Military authorities.

...I want to have the kudos of taking the steps ourselves and not to look like one who gives way to pressure from the Arabs. We never do things in time. Sir Percy is very stiffly determined to do what he thinks right, no matter how many soldiers protest, more power to him. For as he rightly says its he who is responsible...

Anyway Sir Percy is standing out firmly about the Shiah appointments...

The other event of the week besides the suppressing of the Istiqlal, is the arrival of an emissary from Ibn Saud. Ahmad Thanayan is a relation of the Imam and was with his son Faisal in England in 1919. He was brought up in Constantinople and even knows a little French. A very delicate ailing man of about 30, with the fine drawn Najd face, full of intelligence and drawn yet finer by ill health. He has with him Ibn Saud's doctor, Abdullah Ibn Said, a Mosuli by origin, educated in Constantinople... They have come to discuss the interminable Question of Ibn Saud's quarrel with the Sharif--for which I think there's no solution; we can only hold it in suspense...and I had them to dinner tonight. It was the most interesting and curious dinner party I ever gave. Besides the two Najdis I had Major Eadie, Saiyid Muhi ud Din and Shakri Eff. al Arusi. The latter is one of the finest figures in Bagdad. An old scholar who comprises in himself all knowledge as such is understood by Islam--he teaches Mechanics, using the Hadith (traditions of the prophet) as text book and other sciences by like methods--a true Wahhabi, he neither drinks nor smokes, and he is the only known Mohammadan who has never married...He found in Wahhabi, Central Arabia the land of his dreams and looks upon it as the true source of all inspiration and learning. When he came in he fell on Ahmad Thanayan's neck while the latter fished among his beautiful embroidered cashmiri robes and produced from them a letter from Ibn Saud to Shukri. And to crown the cordiality of the gathering, Muhi ud Din discovered in the Doctor a former Constantinople acquaintance, and the embracing began afresh on their part. So we sat down to table--as queer a gathering as you could well see; Shukri, the unworldly old scholar, hanging on Ahmad Thanayan's words while the latter described the immense progress of the extreme Wahhabi sect, the Akhwan, (brotherhood) in Najd; Muhi ud Din, the smooth politician and divine,...and Abmad with his long sunken face lighted up by the purest spirit of fanatical Islam. "The Imam, God preserve him, under God has guided the tribes in the right way,"- "Praise be to God," ejaculated Shukri--"They are learning wisdom and religion under the rules of the Brotherhood,"--Shukri Eff: "God is great ...Not that they show violence,"--Ahmad Effend. "God forbid,"--"No such things happen among us as happened in Europe with the Inquisition and with Calvins"--(I must tell you incidentally that the Akhwan when they do battle kill all wounded and then put the women and children of their enemies, who are also infidels else they wouldn't fight the Ahkwan, to death ...) After dinner my four Arab guests carried on a brisk conversation among themselves. They discussed medicines and the properties of herbs, the doctor, incidentally, stating that incense was a capital disinfectant, they discussed the climate and customs of Najd and other matters of importance. Major Eadie and I sat listening and I felt as if we were disembodied spirits playing audience to an Oriental symposium, so entirely did our presence fail to impede the flow of talk which the learned men of the East are accustomed to hold with one another. Muhi ud Din played the game with the perfection of courtesy, but when they all went away, he last, I whispered in his ear "For all that I shall not join the brotherhood," "Nor I," he whispered back fervently. It's an interesting world I'm living in isn't it? ...

To H.B., on the way to Cairo, February 24th, 1921
On the Tigris boat and continued on the Hardinge

We're off and I've put off writing this week till I got on to the ship as any way I shall carry a letter myself quicker than the post would carry it...

The last week has seen the first arrival of a new element, the Mesopotamian officers who were in Syria are beginning to return, the first to come being Nuri Pasha Said, Jafar's brother-in-law. He came last week...The day after his arrival Jafar telephoned to me and asked when Nuri could see Sir Percy. Sir Percy asked them to come at once and stay to lunch. They came at 12 and sat for an hour with me. I called up Capt. Clayton, who knew and liked Nuri in Syria; Major Murray dropped in and we had a momentous talk. The moment I saw him I realised that we had before us a strong and supple force with which we must either use or engage in difficult combat. We began very gently feeling the ground as we went; my first questions he answered very warily; then as I persisted, he took his line and in a few sentences developed his Programme--the summoning of the constituent assembly which was to perform four tasks: (1) to appoint a

Cabinet, (2) to select a ruler, (3) to pass a law authorising some form of conscription for the Arab Army, (4) to design a flag. "That's all right," said we, and proceeded to discuss the points in detail...

[There are no letters from Gertrude during the Conference-- Her father joined her in Cairo for a while.]

To H.B., Bagdad, April 12th, 1921

I spent the whole of next day, Sunday, getting through Papers in the office and came back to tea, and a number of visitors, mostly European. Yesterday and to-day have been very busy days with a great deal of work and a great many callers. Faisal arrives at Suez to-morrow so that in a week or ten days we ought to be receiving the telegrams he is to address to his supporters announcing his candidature. By that time Sir Percy ought to be able to make a fuller pronouncement for he will have received permission from Mr. Churchill who will have consulted the Cabinet at home. Things should therefore begin to move pretty quickly. ...

To F.B., Bagdad, April 16th, 1921

Will you send me some thick woollen tricotine of a blue as near as may be to the enclosed colour, enough for Marie to make me a winter everyday gown, jumper and skirt. Also some soft blue silk on which to mount the skirt, the same colour. Further will you give a pattern of the blue to my hat maker, Anne Marie in Sloane Street, and tell her to send me by parcel post a blue felt hat--she knows the kind of shape like the green felt she made for me last year trimmed with reddish brown wings, pheasant would do or a red brown feather trimming of some kind. Not ostrich feathers, that's too dear.

To H.B., Bagdad, April 17th, 1921

...There was a rumour--that on the way down to Basrah when we went away, I had said to persons not named that the object of the conference was to declare Faisal King ...it was entirely untrue, but no doubt he knows that formerly when people pressed me to give my own opinion I have always said that Faisal would I thought be the best choice. I am therefore identified as a Sharifian, which I don't mind at all, but I have always been careful to say that the choice must rest with the people, and I am now careful to keep my private opinion for the present to myself...

Meantime telegrams are going daily to the King of the Hijaz begging him to send one of his sons. The functions of the Arab Ministers will be carried on by the Advisors (British). We have not yet received the telegram promised by Mr. Churchill after he had consulted with the Cabinet; we are not therefore at liberty to make public that Faisal has H.M.G's consent to run as a candidate, but I felt sure that some announcement about the conference could not be delayed and I got Sir Percy to publish a preliminary statement. It contains nothing about the elections but it says that a general amnesty will be declared very shortly and this has been received with acclamation...In a very short time therefore important new factors should have entered into the game : Faisal himself with his declared candidature, the pardoned leaders of last year's revolt, the Sharifian paper and the suspension of the Arab ministers ...

Meantime the general attitude of the country with regard to ourselves has immensely improved. There's a consensus of opinion that whatever happens they can't do without our guidance and help. Being Sunday, I rode down early this morning to Haji Naji and had breakfast with him on native bread, fresh unsalted butter, sugared apples and coffee. He is hand in glove with the Sharifians, thinks Naji, Nuri, Jafar and Co., the best Mesopotamians he knows and is convinced that the overwhelming majority in the country is for Faisal. Said he with his customary wisdom, "Let the people do it themselves; the British Government need not interfere." It is so restful and delicious sitting with him under his fruit trees which were in flower when I left and are now loaded with green fruit. It was a heavenly morning and hot sun and a cool little north wind...I'm happy in helping to forward what I Profoundly believe to be the best thing for this country and the wish of the best of its people...

To H.B., Bagdad, April. 25th, 1921

Capt. Thomas who is a musician, carried up a piano with him to Shatrah and invited his Sheikhs to come and listen to the Pathétique sonata. At the end he asked what they thought of it. "Wallahi," said one "khosh daqqah." By God a good thumping.

To her parents, Bagdad, May 2nd, 1921

Yesterday, Sunday, their Excellencies took a party to Babylon with me as guide. We left at 7 a.m. and arrived by motor about 11, saw the Palace and Ishtar gate and had an excellent lunch--need I say since it was provided by Lady Cox in the German Expeditions-Haus...

I've just had about 30 ladies to tea, quite a nice party in the garden, so that's that.

The office hours are now 7 a.m. till 1, which means breakfasting at 6:30. I think I shall rather like it. Later in the summer I shall come back for lunch and then have a rest in my house, but as yet it's not at all hot, an exceptionally cool pleasant spring...

Good-bye my dearest beloved Father and Mother, I'm happy and interested in my work and very happy in the confidence of my chief. When I think of this time last year...

To H.B., Bagdad, May 5th, 1921

Your weekly letters are the greatest joy, I don't know what I should do without them...

We are not having a very easy time. Persia is a doubtful quantity but so far remains quiescent.

In Angora, I think I told you, the extremists have got the upper hand, which from our point of view means that Turkish agitation continues on our northern frontier...

My young Nationalist friends are alarmed at the activity of the Turks on the frontier and the existence of a large body of pro-Turkish feeling in this country. Their fear is that the return of the Turks would kill or indefinitely postpone their dearest hopes--namely the setting up of an independent Arab State. This is the sentiment which we want to foster, and as it is held exclusively by Sharifians, they are the people for us to back, as we decided at Cairo. Unfortunately there must have been many delays and Faisal who should have been here in the middle of May has not yet left Mecca. The League of Nations is holding up the mandate in deference to American prejudice and Mr. Churchill's statement in the House which ought to have taken place on June 2nd is again postponed. Sir Percy has urged that we should drop the mandate altogether and go for a treaty with the Arab State when it is constituted. It would be a magnificent move if we're bold enough to do it. It isn't the mandate which bothers us here--no Nationalist wants to shake loose from British help and control --but the word mandate isn't popular and a freely negotiated treaty would be infinitely better liked, besides giving us a much freer hand. We have always known that Faisal would ultimately insist on a treaty in place of a mandate--now we have the opportunity of making a 'beau geste' and giving of our own accord what we should certainly have had to give later at his request.

Meantime the amnesty is out and my friends are busying themselves in the constitution of a moderate Sharifian party with a definite programme- the latter was submitted to me...Sir Percy has told them through me to go ahead and rely on his support...

Captain Smith and I (you know he's the son of the Master of Balliol) went to another school function this week. It was a Prodigious affair. 'Le tout' Bagdad was there---the Arab world. We were the only English- and it lasted the usual three hours. We sat in rows and listened to speeches, songs and poems and I really believe the audience liked it. There were parts of it which were quite remarkably long speeches (no speech lasted less than 15 minutes) about the light of education being the sole ray that illumines the world; but I must confess that there were also interesting moments. one was an ode by a half paralysed old poet, Jamil Zuhawi--there was 35 minutes of it, which is long for an ode, but nevertheless it was worth sitting through. He is not only a great poet but he is a very great 'diseur.) He began by tumbling off the estrade and having to be poked and pushed back on to it while everyone murmured "Allah!" Then he embarked on an invocation of some 20 couplets to the skies of the Iraq. He began very quietly with great throbbing lines which pulsed on to a glowing volume of sound. The whole audience took fire; they leant forward with their faces illuminated and time after time the falling couplet was revivified with a "Repeat! Repeat!"...jamil Zuhawi was followed by another and rival poet, a man called Maruf. He is said to be one of the greatest Arabists living. I didn't understand the poem which was immensely applauded but I did understand the speech with which he prefaced it and I thought it first rate, very bold and liberal and full of good sense...

We all had to get up at 5 next morning to go to the King's birthday parade which was held in the desert quite near my house. All the Arab magnates came and there were an astonishing number of troops; but this was a deception--we happened to have in Bagdad the regiments which have just come down from Persia and are going to India or England. It ended with a flight Of 30 aeroplanes which was really splendid. The Coxes gave a dinner that night...It was very well done. After dinner we sat on the terrace over the river. The trees were hung with coloured lamps and the lights of the town glittered across the river. It's a great asset having your river running through the heart of your city...

To F.B., Bagdad, May 8th, 1921

On Friday there was an immense tea party at the Persian Consul's in honour of the Shah's birthday--I wonder how many more birthdays the Shah will celebrate on his throne! Persian affairs seem fairly stable but there's a great pressure of opinion against the rich landlord class, most of whom are indeed in prison, the Shah only, who is the greatest landlord of them all, being spared...

I was feeling so tired of sitting up and behaving that this morning, Sunday, I rode out early to Karradah and breakfasted with Haji Naji who is the salt of the earth. We gossiped pleasantly of all that was happening--he is eminently sensible--and walked about under the fruit trees where the apricots are just ripening. I ate the first to-day. This week, Ramadhan begins, which will put an end to tea parties, a thing I shan't regret. I go into the office at 7 a.m. come away about 3:30, and if there's a tea party to follow I haven't a minute all day in which to ride or rest or look about me.

Our politics are rather hanging fire...A bewildered little Saiyid from Najaf way came to see me one day, and told me his hopes and fears. He was very shy...He left me feeling that it wasn't astonishing that they don't know what we're up to. First we imprison them for saying they want Abdullah and then we encourage them to ask for Faisal! One of my best informants about affairs in Bagdad, when he relates the conversation with people who inquire what he thinks the British Government wants, generally gives as his share in the conversation, this answer: "Wallahi, my brother! Who knows what is in their minds."

To H.B., Bagdad, May 15th, 1921

Your letters have an almost too acute interest...You speak of a possible settlement, but more than a month has passed without one. It is most interesting about the Defence Force and the miners joining it. It doesn't sound as if there were much bitterness in our part of the world...I think of all our countryside at this beautiful time and wish I were there, nevertheless I'm happy in the work here and it ought to develop very soon in various directions. We haven't even yet got the amnesty out. It has been held up first by having to consult the French, then the Government of India, nor has there yet been a pronouncement about the elections, but that is because we had to find out first what parts of the Kurdish provinces would come in to the Arab State. I hope that we shall know this week that most of them will. Answers are beginning to flow in from the Sharif in reply to the first telegram sent to him asking him to send one of his sons here. The answers are characteristically vague...

Basrah opinion will carry a good deal of weight. They are trying to draw up a programme for the election which will be wide enough to embrace the greatest number of opinions. I've got the draft and it seems quite good. If one leaves them alone, giving them only the sympathetic encouragement they ask, they come to an agreement with one another, and that's the best...

It strikes me that not many people of the upper classes are fasting this year. Even the Naqib, for the first time in his life, is not keeping the fast--for reasons of health. He would have died of it...I wonder how long the fast will hold Islam--like the veiling of women it might disappear, as a universal institution, pretty fast. The women who have come back from Syria or Constantinople find the Bagdad social observances very trying. They have been accustomed to much greater freedom. As soon as we get our local institutions firmly established they will be bolder. They and their husbands are afraid that any steps taken now would set all the prejudiced old tongues wagging and jeopardise their future. Nevertheless these new men bring their wives to see me, which is an unexpected departure from Bagdad customs according to which a man would never go about with his wife, I welcome everything that tends in this direction, but, again one can do so little but give sympathetic welcome to the women. They must work out their own salvation and it wouldn't help them to be actively backed by an infidel, even if the infidel were I who am permitted many things here...

Maurice must be having a time with his Territorials and the Defence Force, bless him.

To H.B., Bagdad, May 22nd, 1921

I anticipated that things would happen much more quickly. But they haven't happened. They are, I may say, just beginning now, for the telegrams from Mecca ...are making an appreciable effect. People are inclined to think ...that they are more or less inspired by H.M.G. or at rate imply a leaning in a Sharifian direction on the part of H.M.G. They are the natural result of our saying that a son of the Sharif would be regarded as a suitable candidate and might be approached as to whether he would stand...

Naji Suwaidi has drawn up and submitted to me a programme for a moderate Sharifian party--which I showed to Sir Percy who thought it all right. I'm very grateful to Naji for keeping me so closely in touch...I've found Naji very sensible and capable as well as very patient under the prolonged delay. All this promises well for the future...

We're debating what we can do to strengthen the foundation of Ctesiphon so as to save the great façade wall. There's no immediate prospect of its falling but it has a very marked list outwards. We have dug some holes down to the foundations and I went out early on Saturday morning with Major Wilson (the architect, you remember) to look at them. He proposes to put a big wad of concrete against the foundations underground, and I'm afraid we shall have to slope it off against the wall for about 10 feet of its height above ground, which won't be pretty, but ought to make the wall as safe as we can make it.

To H.B., Bagdad, May 29th, 1921

It's too soon for a forecast but probably this turn of the wheel will mean that North Persia will fall once more under Russian domination- under the new Russia whose foreign policy differs not a whit from that of the old...

From Anatolia the news is not good. The extremists have got the upper hand at Angora, they will accept no compromise over Smyrna or Thrace; they are in for a prolonged struggle with the Greeks during the whole of which they will be bitterly anti-European. Our chief hope there is that if we get Faisal he may come to some settlement with them on our northern frontier.

The amnesty is out tomorrow, Heaven be praised. It will set free the hands of our Nationalists and they will get to work in earnest. Mr. Churchill's statement to the House ought to clear the air further, for he must, I take it, say something about Faisal's being a candidate acceptable to H.M.G. which will be widely regarded as indicating that he is the most acceptable.

I'm thinking of going to Sulaimaniyah at the end of the week for a few days--to Kirkuk for a couple of nights and so on by motor. Sulaimaniya has refused, on a plebiscite, to come in under the Arab Govt. and is going for the present to be a little Kurdish enclave administered directly under Sir Percy...The population is wholly Kurdish and they say they don't want to be part of an Arab State. I've never been there and as we shall hear a good deal about it in the High Commissioner's Office I should like to get the colour and sentiment of it at first hand, so I spend my evenings rubbing up my rusty Persian.

To H.B., Bagdad, June 12th, 1921

Things are at last beginning to move. Telegrams have come from King Hussain saying that Faisal leaves for the Iraq this week.

What everybody wants to know is our wishes and as soon as they get any kind of lead they will all, I think, come into line. Meantime, I receive many agitated visits from my young Sharifian friends asking for reassurances and for guidance, which I give to the best of my ability and according to Sir Percy's directions. He is a master hand at the game of politics; it's an education to watch him playing it ...

I've just had this Sunday morning a long visit from two big Sheikhs, Fahad Bey of the Anazeh and Ali Sulaiman, of the Dulaim. Both came down from Ramadi to see Sir Percy and find out his views... So they have been told to stay here for a day or two when H.M.G. will make pronouncements.

I don't for a moment hesitate about the rightness of our policy. We can't continue direct British control though the country would be better governed by it, but its rather a comic position to be telling people over and over again that whether they like it or not they must have Arab not British Govt...

To H.B., Bagdad June 19th, 1921

We here are now launched on our perilous way. On Monday my old friend the Mayor came to my office and said that since Faisal was coming it was up to the notables of Bagdad to make a proper reception for him and not to leave it all to the young extremists. Faisal was a famous Arab and the son of a King and must be treated as such. I said I thought that view perfectly proper, he as the Mayor of the town, should make the arrangements.

The younger men have frequented my office this week. We had to settle on a temporary flag--I suppose the Constituent Assembly will have the final word there--and then there was the difficult question as to where Faisal should be lodged. If only we had got the official communiqué from home earlier everything would have been much easier ... I believe Faisal is statesman enough to realise that he must capture the older more steady going people while at the same time not chilling over much the enthusiasm of his more ardent supporters.

Well, to continue my tale ...Here was Faisal arriving at Basrah on the 23rd and we still without any communiqué from home...Meanwhile his partisans were growing naturally impatient and anxious to get busy. Sir Percy realised this and unofficially approved the project presented through me that they should summon the town to a big meeting on Friday, 6 days before Faisal's arrival. As soon as the invitations were out, in the name of Naji Suwaidi, clerics and others dropped in to my office to sound me as to whether they ought to go "Oh yes." said I "why not?" the meeting has the approval of H.E." On Thursday afternoon the Naqib... made a sound move. He informed the Council of Ministers that Faisal was coming and that they must make preparations to receive him properly and see that he was suitably lodged. Therefore they appointed a reception committee of 5 Ministers. I had been out after tea and on the way home I met the Secretary to the Council, who stopped me and told me this excellent news. I rode on much cheered and when I got home I found a letter from Sir Percy enclosing the long expected communiqué which he told me to get through to Jafar or Naji Suwaidi before the meeting which was to take place at 8 next morning. By good luck Jafar with his wife and sister were dining so I translated the communiqué to them and gave it to Jafar for the meeting. They were all delighted with it and indeed it was just what we wanted.

Next day Naji Suwaidi and the Mutasarrif, came to my office after the meeting to report. It had been a great success, everyone had been present and 60 people had been chosen to go down to Basrah to welcome Faisal--would I kindly make arrangements with the Railway. There remained the question of his lodging here which they proposed to solve by putting him into some rooms in the Sarai (the Government offices) which were now under repair, ...if they could be got ready in time. Public Works declared that it couldn't be done. Jafar telephoned to me in despair on Saturday morning; I telephoned to Public Works, made suggestions for covering bare walls with hangings and finally the thing was arranged.

In the evening I went to the Naqib, whom I found receiving the report of the Reception Committee. Directly I got in he showed me a telegram which had just come to him from King Hussain couched in very suitable terms and announcing that he was sending his son Faisal to him...

This morning, being Sunday, Mr. Tod and I rode before break-fast to Haji Naji ...Haji Naji presently drew me aside and told me he thought of going with the party to Basrah only he was rather afraid of being lost in the ruck. I said I would give him a letter of introduction to Mr. Cornwallis, who is coming with Faisal, so that he might be treated with consideration...

To H.B., June 23rd, 1921

Faisal arrives in Bastah to-day. His adherents anticipate that his coming will be the sign for a great popular ovation. Heaven send it may be so for it will immensely simplify matters for us. Meantime there can be no question that it is regarded with anxiety by the Magnates. On Monday we had a strong deputation from Basrah bringing a petition in which they asked for separate treatment for the Basrah area. They were ready to accept a common King but they asked that Basrah might have a separate Legislative Assembly, a separate Army, police service and raise and spend its own taxes, making a suitable contribution to the central administration. They came to me on their way to Sir Percy and asked me to support their request. I said No; whatever H.M.G. decided would have my loyal support as a Government servant, but until that decision was given I must exercise my private opinion which was that what they asked was not in the interests of the country as a whole and would not prove to be permanently in their own interests... With that they went to Sir Percy who gave them a sympathetic hearing but said in general terms that he would not conceal from them that H.M.G. wanted to see a United Iraq. However a large degree of local autonomy would be consistent with that end and a compromise on these lines should be considered ...I have been elected President of the Bagdad Public Library...

The Reception Committee got their programme through the Council on Monday. Mutasarrif Rashid Bey, a strong Sharifian, brought it in to us for Sir Percy's approval on Tuesday. What they wanted to know was what part Sir Percy was going to take and above all whether he would provide a guard of honour. I promised to get the reply as soon as possible. But things don't go as quickly as that and yesterday morning, Wed., Rashid Bey turned up again and said they had no answer. Later in the morning I arranged that he and Majid Bey al Shawi should come in and have a personal interview. Meantime Nuri Said, who had been in Basrah, had seen me the previous evening and told me about the popular demonstration. He thought it might result in an immediate acclamation of Faisal as King, and asked me anxiously whether we should mind that. I answered in suitable terms that we only wanted to know the opinion of the country...All this I reported to Sir Percy that night at a ball given by Lady Cox and it may have partly influenced his answer to Rashid Bey next morning. Anyway Faisal is to have his guard of honour both at Basrah and here...

I expect Faisal will come to terms with the Basrah magnates and satisfy them that Basrah will receive full consideration. Mr. Cornwallis is with him, a tower of strength and wisdom, I've sent him a letter explaining how the wind blows throughout the Iraq and as soon as he comes up here I shall be able to keep him posted in local politics...

Already the whole town is flying the Sharifian flag. I saw it today flying on every other shop in the Bazaar. The intention is good but the flag heraldically bad. I don't know if you know it. The red triangle colour comes over the black and green colour on colour, and therefore wrong isn't it...

Yesterday we had news of Faisal's arrival in Basrah and an excellent reception, heaven be praised...Faisal has now gone off to Najaf and Karbala and gets here on Wednesday 29th. Half of my mornings have been spent in receiving visits from the Mutasarrif or exchanging messages with him on the telephone about the reception and festivities here. We have got it right at last I think. Mosul also is coming forward. A large deputation of all the leading people came down here last night and Nuri Said, whom I saw this morning, tells me that their line of argument is that they can't think why there's such division of opinion here and that far the best course is to proclaim Faisal King at once ...and said that if they hadn't had my constant help they could not have carried on, and I replied that I stood fast all the time in Sir Percy's unswerving purpose. But I have been useful to them all the same, these last weeks and I'm glad I've been here.

I'm told that Naji Suwaidi is in favour of a mandate rather than the proposed treaty, because a mandate gives us more authority! Faisal wants a treaty I know, so probably that's the way it will work out, and for my part I think its quite immaterial. You can't run a mandate without the goodwill of the people, and if you've got that it doesn't matter whether its a mandate or a treaty, but what rejoices me is the fulfilment of my dream that we should sit by in an attitude of repose and have them coming up our front door steps to beg us to be more active...

NOTICE TO ALL AUTHORS, PUBLISHERS AND BOOKSELLERS

The Salam Library, Bagdad, intends to issue a periodical publication--in Arabic and English--the object of which is to review books published in Oriental languages, Arabic, Persian, Turkish, Hebrew, Syriac, Hindustani, etc.; and also books published in European languages, English, French and German, etc.

This publication will deal only with books presented to the library with a request from the publisher or author asking for a review or notice of the book.

It will also give an account of such manuscripts as may be found in the library or are to be found in local bookshops. Thus the Salam Library's periodical publication will be the best means for introducing European books to Orientals and Oriental books to Europeans and will serve as a means to facilitate the sale of books.

The Committee of the Salam Library is composed of Arab and British members who will undertake the publication of the periodical.

(Signed) Gertrude Bell, President,
Salam Library. Bagdad

[Gertrude sent copies of this notice to be distributed in England, together with a circular, addressed to English publishers, asking if they would care to send books to the Salam Library].

CHAPTER XXI

1921 - BAGDAD

To H.B., Bagdad, June 30th, 1921

It's being so frightfully interesting--there! There! Let me begin at the beginning. Where was I? It was Monday's vernacular paper which gave the first full account of Faisal's arrival at Basrah and the quite admirable speech which he made at a big function they had for him. Tumbling in on this came an agent whom I had sent down to Basrah to bring me a report of the temper of his reception and gave a very glowing account of the effort made by this speech which he said inclined all hearts towards Faisal. This was cheering and in the evening Naji Suwaidi and Nuri dropped in after tea; Naji back from Basrah with a rosy tale. Then we fell to talking of the next steps and agreed that we could not leave him here not knowing what his position would be for 6 or 8 weeks till the elections were over. Somehow or other the country must be got to declare itself. Sir Percy and I had already discussed this but I didn't feel at liberty to mention the fact to my two friends, so I only gave them comforting reassurances. But we don't want Faisal to come in by a coup d'état of the extremists--we must have something much more constitutional than that...On Wednesday Faisal was to arrive at 7 a.m. Col. Joyce and I motored to the station together, going all the way up the big street to the upper bridge. The whole town was decorated, triumphal arches, Arab flags, and packed with people, in the streets, on the housetops, everywhere. At the station immense crowds. It was very well arranged with seats for the magnates all round, and all filled with magnates. Sir Percy and Sir Aylmer and a guard of honour and all. But we learnt there had been an 'éboulement' on the line--a telegram had been received to say he was coming by motor and hoped to arrive at the appointed hour. We waited, we talked, we shook hands all round--at least I did--we looked at the Arab levies and towards 8, paf! Came a message down the line that he was in the train after all, couldn't get through and might be here at mid-day! Sir Percy quickly took command. Noon at the end of June is not an hour at which you can hold a great reception out of doors... He was accordingly asked to spend the day in the train and get in at 6 p.m. And so we all went home. I to the office where presently Nuri came in and assured me that the evening's reception would be better even than that of the morning. Then Haji Naji, up from Basrah, full of delight. Thanks to the letter I had given him to Mr. Cornwallis he had spoken to Faisal and he was the being they wanted and that was all right! ...And so behold me at 5:30 again setting off for the station ...And this time the train arrived.

Sidi Faisal stood at the carriage door looking very splendid in full Arab dress, saluting the guard of honour. Sir Percy and Sir Aylmer went up to him as he got out and gave him a fine ceremonious greeting, and all the people clapped. He went down the line of the guard of honour, inspecting it ...Sir Percy began to present the Arab Magnates, representatives of the Naqib, etc. I hid behind Mr. Cornwallis, but Faisal saw me and stepped across to shake hands with me. He looked excited and anxious--you're not a king on approbation without any tension of the spirit--but it only gave his natural dignity a more human charm. Then he was lost in the crowd and Col. Joyce and I stayed talking to Mr. Cornwallis who, poor dear, was so dried up with thirst that he could scarcely talk at all. But what he said was that up to now things hadn't gone well. The people were standing back...

All the way up the story they had heard was, the High Commissioner is neutral, the Khatun and Mr. Garbett want Faisal and Mr. Philby wants a republic...Naturally Faisal was bewildered--was the High Commissioner with him and if so why did his officers adopt a different attitude? All the more was he bewildered because he was told with equal frequency that if the local officers would lift a finger all the people would follow their lead. Why wasn't the finger lifted if that was the official policy? We explained all that had happened, and the long delay in getting the pronouncement from England, and that Sir Percy was absolutely sound and determined to carry the thing through...

This morning on my way to the office I went to the Sarai and gave my card to Faisal's A.D.C. He said would I wait a minute, the Amir would like to see me; it was a little past seven, rather early for a morning call. I waited, talking to the A.D.C. and presently Faisal sent for me. They showed me into a big room and he came quickly across in his long white robes, took me by both hands and said "I couldn't have believed that you could have given me so much help as you have given me." So we sat down on a sofa. I assured him that Sir Percy was absolutely with him...

Mr. Cornwallis came into the office later and I told him I had called on Faisal. He said (I must tell you because it pleased me so much) "That was quite right. All the way up he had been hearing your praise and he gave me a message for you in case he didn't see you to speak to to-day. I was to tell you how grateful he was. And my private spy the man I sent to Basrah tells me the people constantly say, "Is the Khatun satisfied. ..."

The next event was that evening's banquet in the Maude gardens. It was really beautifully done. The place lighted with electric lights looked lovely.

Faisal carried on a little conversation in French with Sir Aylmer, but mostly he and I and Sir Percy, and Abdul Majid and I talked across the table. Faisal looked very happy and I felt very happy and so did Sir Percy...

Then got up our great poet, of whom I've often told you, jamil Zahawi, and recited a tremendous ode in which he repeatedly alluded to Faisal as King of the Iraq and everyone clapped and cheered. And then there stepped forward into the grassy space between the tables a Shiah in white robes and a black cloak and big black turban and chanted a poem of which I didn't understand a word. It was far too long and as I say quite unintelligible but nevertheless it was wonderful. The tall robed figure chanting and marking time with an uplifted hand, the darkness in the palm trees beyond the illuminated circle--it hypnotised you...

But its not all smooth yet. We get reports about the lower Euphrates tribes preparing monstrous petitions in favour of a republic and of Shiah Alim Mujtahids being all against Faisal. I don't believe half of them are true but they keep one in anxiety. To-day I sent for one of the principal Euphrates Sheikhs...He is a strong Sharifian and we talked the whole matter over. Before him I had had an influential group of Bagdadis saying that we must finish the business, we couldn't wait for elections. Somehow or other Faisal must be proclaimed King. I referred them to Faisal himself, knowing that he has discussed it with Sir Percy, and told them to take Faisal's orders. In the afternoon Faisal sent for me and told me his ideas which were very sound. I also gave him a few suggestions to bring before Sir Percy...With that Faisal went off to see Sir Percy, so I should think things will happen. I'm beginning to feel as if I couldn't stand it much longer! One is straining every nerve all the time to pull the matter forward; talking, persuading, writing, I find myself carrying on the argument even in my sleep. But anyway Faisal's antechamber contains a good many of the right people and it's comforting to think that he can do the talking so well himself. We've got Bagdad and I'm pretty certain we've got Mosul the rest will fall into line.

To H.B., Bagdad, Thursday, July 7th, 1921

On Monday morning I was having a crucial interview. The leading Christian here, came in with the Mutasarrif and Naji Suwaidi to urge that once Faisal had come we couldn't afford to wait for election and must resort to referendum to place him on the throne. We were all fully aware of this, indeed Faisal had talked of it when I saw him on Saturday, but he added that the one thing he feared was a coup d'état, and we must continue to make the proceedings as constitutional as we could ...Accordingly Sir Percy saw the Naqib and it was arranged that the Council shall consider how soon the elections can take place, since there is obviously urgent need to come to a settlement. Sir Percy has ascertained that we can't get the registration of electors through under two months...The local press has already began to talk about a referendum, without an inspiration... I read the four local papers every morning and if there's anything I think unsuitable I intimate the fact to the editors, directly or indirectly. To-day I had to do it directly; one enthusiast had published a violent attack on the French in Syria. I sent for him and proved to his satisfaction that they had better leave the Syrians to take care of themselves...

What helps everything is that Faisal's personality goes three quarters of the way. He has been roping in adherents; they most of them come round to me to be patted on the back at which I'm getting to be an adept. It's a little more delicate when they are trembling on the brink but I then bring in the overwhelming argument that Sir Percy and Faisal are working hand in hand--it's really remarkable how completely satisfied they are if they know that Sir Percy approves. He has an extraordinary hold on the country.

Most of the towns--I think I told you--have sent deputations to greet Faisal. With these I exchange visits.

It's rather a complication in all these festivities that the temperature is 120--at least that's what it goes up to by day.

One by one all the leaders of the rebellion are coming in to pay their respects. One came on Tuesday and got a fine dressing down first from me and then from Sir Percy. However he took it in good part and went away saying that he was delighted with Sir Percy! All the Sheikhs and Saiyids who fought against us are turning up also. I need not say that Sir Percy's handling of them is perfect...This morning an opportunity presented itself in which I could both do the right thing and the thing that pleased me--a rare combination. There came in one of the leaders of the revolt, a horrid worthless man ...and I was more icily rude to him than I've ever been to anyone. He had evidently hoped to climb back into some sort of esteem by being allowed to see Sir Percy; I gave him firstly clearly to understand that Sir Percy could not receive him and he retired in disorder. It was a great satisfaction.

Friday, July 8th. Last night the Naqib gave a dinner to Faisal in his house opposite his own mosque. The English guests were Sir Percy and his staff. All the rest were the Ministers and Notables of Bagdad. Sir Percy took me. The streets were crowded with people as we drove up; the Naqib's family received us at the door and we climbed up two flights of stairs into a roof overlooking the mosque, a sort of wide balcony. It was carpeted and lighted; the mosque door opposite was hung with lamps and the minarets ringed with them. The Naqib was sitting with the Ministers; he got up and faltered forward to meet Sir Percy, a touching and dignified figure. The rest of the guests some 100 I should think, sat below us on the open gallery which runs round two sides of the courtyard on the first story of the house. A burning wind blew on us while we drank coffee and talked till the clapping of hands in the street announced the arrival of Faisal. The Naqib got up and helped by his personal physician walked across the whole of the carpeted space and reached the head of the stairs just as

Faisal's white-robed figure appeared. They embraced formally on both cheeks and walked back hand in hand to the end of the balcony where we were all standing up. Faisal sat down between the Naqib and Sir Percy and after a few minutes dinner was announced. Faisal, Sir Percy, the C. in C. and I went down: then the Naqib with a servant on each side of him to help him. The long dinner- table stood on the open gallery. Faisal sat in the place of honour opposite the Naqib with the C. in C. on one side of him and I on the other...It was a wonderful sight that dinner party. The robes and their uniforms and the crowds of servants, all brought up in the Naqib's household, the ordered dignity, the real solid magnificence, the tension of spirit which one felt all round one, as we felt the burning heat of the night. For, after all, to the best of our ability, we were making history.

[The Naqib, so much honoured and esteemed, died in May 1927.)

But you may rely upon one thing--I'll never engage in creating kings again; it's too great a strain...

Sir Percy and I, as we drove home, felt we had jumped another hedge, but we agreed that we were in a very stiff country.

Again to-day the same sort of morning in the office--it's a morning which lasts from 7 to 1:30! Faisal was there interviewing Sir Percy even before I got there...After lunch Sir Percy, Mr. Garbett and I drafted the crucial letter to the Council, and soon after 3 I came home and got to Faisal's house at four o'clock with all the tribal maps, to give him a lesson in tribal geography. Mr. Cornwallis turned up too. There it was cool for we sat in a big vaulted room, half underground, and for an hour we studied tribes and drank iced lemonade, after which we spent another hour discussing the formation of Faisal's first Cabinet and his very excellent idea of creating a sort of Privy Council of laymen and notables ...Came Izzat Pasha with a request for an interview with Sir Percy which I got him at once... He had come to tell Sir Percy that he had seen Faisal and could bring in to him the Kurdish chiefs any time Sir Percy wished..."Khatun," said he, "I've seen Walis and Sultans and Generals but I've never yet seen anyone like Sir Percy, and as long as he is guiding us I am satisfied." It is true that Sir Percy may easily be considered better than the average Wali, but Izzat's conviction that he was better than anyone was unmistakable. Isn't it an extraordinary position for any man to hold? The whole country waits for his word. What should we have done without him?...

I confidently expect that the Hindiyah tribes will roll up this week. That's what it's all like, they won't take a step till they asked the advice of some one of us whom they know...

To H.B., Bagdad, July 16th, 1921

The heat is terrific, day after day over 121 and the nights hot too... Sir Percy and I think we ought to put at end of difficult telegrams home: N.B. temp. 121.8. On the other hand, politics are running on wheels greased with extremely well melted grease and Sir Percy and Faisal are scoring great triumphs. On Monday the 11th the Council, at the instance of the Naqib ...unanimously declared Faisal King, and charged the Ministry of the Interior with the necessary arrangements. I was dining alone that night and feeling anxious--the heat makes one not quite normal, I think. You may fancy what it was like to get to the office next morning and hear this news from Sir Percy, the moment I arrived. He added that he felt, good as this was, that it wasn't enough and that we must have an election by Referendum to be able to prove that Faisal really had the voice of the people. With that, one of Faisal's A.D.C.'s telephoned to me and asked me to go round. I found him radiant- very different from my first early morning visit the day after he arrived! but eagerly insisting on the need of a referendum through the machinery of the Ministry of the Interior which I was able to assure him was exactly what Sir Percy wanted too... His ante-chamber was a sight to gladden one--full of Bagdad nobles and sheikhs from all parts of the Iraq. I went back to Sir Percy to report. The thing we have been looking for seems to be in a fair way to fulfilment. Sir Percy and Faisal between them are making a new Sharifian party composed of all the solid moderate people... Faisal has played his part; he has handled his over- zealous adherents with admirable discretion...

The office of a morning is flooded with tribal sheikhs. Today they were sitting in rows on the ground under the awning of the courtyard. They come up to see Faisal and pay their respects to Sir Percy and incidentally to me. What they come to learn is whether Faisal has our support. They hear it first from me and then from Sir Percy and I think they go away satisfied. This week it has been the Euphrates; next week it will be the Tigris. To-night Faisal has fifty of them to dinner. Dinners! in this weather they really are a trial. The Coxes gave one to Faisal on Wednesday. I was well off for I sat by Air Marshal Sir John M. Salmond who has flown over from Cairo in 9 hours and says he never suffered so much as he has in being transplanted so rapidly from the temperate climate of Egypt to our torrid zone...

To H.B., Wednesday, July 20th, 1921

Really these days are so packed with incident that I must quickly record them before one impression overlays another. In an atmosphere which has been uninterruptedly at a maximum of over 120 for the last three weeks-- I may mention that for the first time in my life I've got prickly heat- not very bad however. Well--on Monday the Jewish community gave a great reception to Faisal in the Grand Rabbi's official house. The Garbetts and I represented the Residency and Mr. Cornwallis came with the Amir. The function took place at 7:30 a.m. in the big courtyard of the house-- a square court round which the two storied house stands. It was filled with rows of seats, with rows of notables sitting in them, the Jewish Rabbis in their turbans or twisted shawls, the leading Christians, all the Arab Ministers and practically all the leading Moslems with a sprinkling of white-robed, black-cloaked Ulama. The Court was roofed over with an awning, the gallery hung with flags and streamers of the Arab colours. The Jewish school children filled it and the women looked out from the upper windows. They put me on the right hand of the chair prepared for Faisal--you know the absurd fuss they make about me, bless them. Faisal was clapped to the echo when we came and we all sat down to a programme Of 13 speeches and songs interspersed with iced lemonade, coffee, tea and cakes and ices! It took two hours by the clock, in sweltering heat...The Rabbi is a wonderful figure, stepped straight out of a picture by Gentile Bellini. The speeches on this occasion are all set speeches...But yet they were interesting because one knew the tensions which underlay them, the anxiety of the Jews lest an Arab government should mean chaos, and their gradual reassurance, by reason of Faisal's obviously enlightened attitude. Presently they brought the Rolls of the Law in their gold cylinders, they were kissed by the Grand Rabbi, and then by Faisal, and they presented him with a small gold facsimile of the tables of the law and a beautifully bound Talmud. I whispered to him that I hoped he would make a speech. He said he hadn't meant to say much but he thought he must, and added "You know I don't speak like they do. I just say what is in my thoughts." Towards the end he got up and spoke really beautifully; it was straight and good and eloquent...He made an immense impression.

The Jews were delighted at his insistence on their being of one race with the Arabs, and all our friends ...were equally delighted with his allusion to British support ...

To H.B., Bagdad, July 27th, 1921

I'm immensely happy over the way this thing is going. I feel as if I were in a dream...On our guarantee all the solid people are coming in to Faisal and there is a general feeling that we made the right choice in recommending him. If we can bring some kind of order out of chaos, what a thing worth doing it will be!

Our great heat is over, the temp. has fallen to about 115 more or less which is quite bearable, and I'm very well.

To H.B., Bagdad, July 31st, 1921

I must now give you an account of our doings. Overshadowing all else was the display at Ramadi. Fakhri jamil Zadah and I left at 4 a.m. but Faisal was a little in front of us. We caught him up at Naqtah, half way to the Euphrates and asked leave to go ahead so that I might photograph his arrival at Fallujah. Outside that village a couple of big tents were pitched in the desert and for several miles crowds of tribal horsemen gathered in and stood along the track as he Passed...Then we drove through Fallujah which was all decorated and packed with people. The tribesmen lined the road to the ferry some 6 miles--rode round, after and beside the cars (I was immediately behind Faisal) amid incredible clouds of dust...

Under the steep edge of the Syrian desert were drawn up the fighting men of the Anazeh, horsemen and camel riders, bearing the huge standard of the tribe. We stopped to salute it as we passed. Ali Sulaiman the Chief of the Dulaim, and one of the most remarkable men in Iraq came out of the Ramadi to meet us. He has been strongly and consistently pro- British...

We drove to the Euphrates bank where Ali Sulaiman had pitched a huge tent about 200 ft. long with a dais at the upper end and roofed with tent cloth and walled with fresh green boughs. Outside were drawn up the camel riders of the Dulaim, their horsemen and their standard carried by a negro mounted on a gigantic white camel; inside the tribesmen lined the tent 5 or 6 deep from the dais to the very end. Faisal sat on the high diwan with Fahad on his right while Major Yetts and I brought up people to sit on his left--those we thought he ought to speak to. He was supremely happy, a great tribesman amongst famous tribes and, as I couldn't help feeling, a great Sunni among Sunnis...Faisal was in his own country with the people he knew. I never saw him look so splendid. He wore his usual white robes with a fine black abba over them, flowing white headdress and silver bound Aqal. Then he began to speak, leaning forward over the small table in front of him, sitting with his hand raised and bringing it down on the table to emphasize his sentences. The people at the end of the tent were too far off to hear; he called them all up and they sat on the ground below the dais rows and rows of them, 400 or 500 men. He spoke in the great tongue of the desert, sonorous, magnificent--no language like it. He spoke as a tribal chief to his feudatories. "For four years," he said "I have not found myself in a place like this or in such company"--you could see how he was loving it. Then he told them how Iraq was to rise to their endeavours with himself at their head. "Oh Arabs are you at peace with one another?" They shouted "Yes, yes, we are at peace." "From this day-- what is the date? and what is the hour?" Someone answered him. "From this day the 25th July (only he gave the Mohammedan date) and the hour of the morning (it was 11 o'clock) any tribesman who lifts his hand against a tribesman is responsible to me-- I will judge between you calling your Sheikhs in council. I have my rights over you as your Lord." A grey bearded man interrupted, "And our rights" "And you have your rights as subjects which it is my business to guard." So it went on, the tribesmen interrupting him with shouts, "Yes, yes," "We agree . ...Yes, by God." It was the descriptions of great tribal gatherings in the days of ignorance, before the prophet, when the poets recited verse which has come down to this day and the people shouted at the end of each phrase, "The truth, by God the truth."

When it was over Fahad and Ali Sulaiman stood up on either side of him and said, "We swear allegiance to you because you are acceptable to the British Government." Faisal was a little surprised. He looked quickly round to me smiling and then he said, "No one can doubt what my relations are to the British, but we must settle our affairs ourselves." He looked at me again, and I held out my two hands clasped as a symbol of the Union of the Arab and British Governments. It was a tremendous moment, those two really big men who have played their part in the history of their time, and Faisal between them the finest living representative of his race--and the link ourselves. One after another Bali Sulaiman brought up his sheikhs, some 40 or 50 of them. They laid their hands in Faisal's and swore allegiance...The afternoon's ceremony was the swearing of allegiance on the part of the towns. From Fallujah to Qaim, the northern frontier, all the Mayors, Qazis and notables had come in. The place was a palace garden. There was a high dais built up against a blank house wall which was hung with carpets. On this Faisal and the rest of us sat while the elders and notables, sitting in rows under the trees, got up, stepped to the dais and laid their hands in his...The beauty of the Setting, the variety of dress and colour, the grave faces of the Village elders, white turbaned or draped in the red Arab kerchief and the fine dignity with which Faisal accepted the homage offered to him made the scene almost as striking as that of the morning...

We are now waiting for the Mosul and Hillah papers to come in to declare Faisal King. He may possibly be crowned next week. Isn't that very remarkable! 5 weeks work.

To H.B., Bagdad, August 6th, 1921

We have had a great week. The plébiscite is nearly finished throughout the country. Many districts, Ramadi, Basrah, the Euphrates, Amarah, have added a rider to the papers, swearing allegiance to Faisal "on condition that he accept British guidance."...

I had a terrific day on Tuesday. I got up at 4:45 motored at 5:45 with Mr. Cornwallis to Ctesiphon--we took Faisal there--office 10:30 to 3:30, with an interval for lunch, home to wash and change; visit to the Naqib 4:30 to 6, library Committee 6 to 7, visit to Sasun's sister-in-law 7 to 7:30. Hamid Khan to dinner 8 to 10. It was too much; I felt tired all next day--however it was worth it.

The Ctesiphon expedition was an immense success. I invited Faisal and two of his A.D.C's, the Garbetts, Fakhri jamil and Mr. Cornwallis, and I took Zaya, with an excellent breakfast of eggs, tongues, sardines and melons. It was wonderfully interesting showing that splendid place to Faisal. He is an inspiring tourist. After we had re-constructed the palace and seen Khosroes sitting in it, I took him into the high windows to the South, when we could see the Tigris, and told him the story of the Arab conquest as Tabari records it, the fording of the river and the rest of the magnificent tale. It was the tale of his own people. You can imagine what it was like reciting it to him. I don't know which of us was the more thrilled. I had a good audience too in one of his A.D.Cs.

Faisal has promised me a regiment of the Arab Army--the Khatun's Own." I shall presently ask you to have their colours embroidered. Nuri proposes that I should have an Army Corps!

Oh Father, isn't it wonderful. I sometimes think I must be in a dream.

Sorry to say that it's desperately hot again. As regards climate this is being the devil's own summer.

To H.B., Bagdad, August. 14th, 1921

The referendum is finished and we are only waiting for the last of the signed papers to come in from the Provinces, after which Faisal will be proclaimed King without delay. With one exception he has been elected unanimously...

The difficulty this week has been the climate. Not that it has been so very hot--never over 119 I think--but it has been quite still with a lightly coloured sky. When you get up in the Morning and see a cloud your heart sinks, for it means a close oppressive day like the half hour before a thunderstorm carried to the Nth. There were a couple of days at the beginning of the week when I seriously considered whether I could bear it. Now it is better...

The other day a young gentleman from Mosul who designs to start a paper there asked me to draw him up some directions for the guidance of the press. I did it with a will, and produced a minor masterpiece--with the more pleasure because I sent a copy to Faisal who was delighted.

I swam the Tigris--not much of a feat you will rightly observe, but the current is very strong in places. Sorry to Say there are sharks in the Tigris; they haven't yet been reported higher than the mouth of the Diala where one bit an Arab boy this week.

To H.B., Bagdad, August 21, 1921

There's no post in this week. I'm not only without letters but also without papers and books. However, thank God, I've got plenty to say. Wherein, as you'll note, I differ from My chief I heard a delightful saying about him the other day, quoted from the lips of one of the leading notables of Basrah. "Wallahi," he observed, "Sir Percy Cox has forty ears and only one tongue." I must tell you another nice tale about the Coxes. You know he is a great naturalist. He is making a collection of Mesopotamian birds--sometimes they arrive dead and sometimes alive. The last one was alive. It's a huge eagle, not yet in its grown up plumage but for all that the largest fowl I've ever set eyes on. It lives on a perch on the shady side of the house and it eats bats, mainly. These bats are netted for it in the dusk when they obligingly fly across the river and over Sir Percy's garden wall. But the eagle likes to catch them in the morning, so the long suffering Lady Cox keeps them in a tin in her ice chest, and if ever you've heard before of an eagle that lives on iced bat you'll please inform me.

And since I'm telling you stories, I must tell you one about the Naqib. It hangs on what I was relating to you last week on the subject of al Damakratiyah. It was the Naqib, to his huge delight--he's by every instinct an aristocrat, and an autocrat if ever there was one--who gave currency to the word, by announcing in the Council that Faisal should be King of a constitutional democratic state...The other day a Shammar Sheikh up from Hail, drops in to call. "Are you a Damakrati?" says the Naqib. "Wallahi, No!" says the Shammari, slightly offended. "I'm not a Magrati. What is it?" "Well," says the Naqib enjoying himself thoroughly, "I'm Sheikh of the Damakratiyah" (the Democrats). "I take refuge in God!" replied the Sheikh, feeling he had gone wrong somewhere. "If you are the sheikh of the Magratiyah, then I must be one of them, for I'm altogether in your service. But what is it?" "Damakratiyah," say the Naqib, "is equality. There's no big man and no little, all are alike and equal." With which the bewildered Shammari plumped on to solid ground. "God is my witness," said he, seeing his tribal authority slipping from him, "if that's it I'm not a Magrati."

Well now to the History of the Iraq.

Last Monday was the first day of the Id al Fitr, The Feast of Sacrifice, which is the great occasion of the Moslem year. It lasts four mortal days. At 7 a.m. on Monday, Mr. Cornwallis and I set out on a round of calls...

That afternoon Faisal called on the Naqib to form his first Cabinet--a very very wise move. He's embarking on a promising political career at the age Of 77. Good, isn't it.

That evening I had got so tired of sitting in the office that in spite of the heat I went out riding, and coming home along the river bank for coolness, I passed Faisal's new house, up-stream,, a house they have rented for him which is being done up. I saw his motor at the door so I left my pony with one of his slaves and went up on to the roof where I found him sitting with his A.D.Cs. It was wonderful, the sun just set, the softly luminous curves of the river below us, the belt of palm trees, and then the desert, with Agar Quf standing up against the fading red of the sky. We all ate and talked. Faisal uses no honorifics: "Enti, thou" he says to me--it's so refreshing after the endless "honours," and "excellencies"--Enti Iraqiyah, enti badawiyah--you're a Mesopotamian, a Bedouin."...

The Colonial Office has sent us a cable saying Faisal in his Coronation speech must announce that the ultimate authority in the land is the High Commissioner...Faisal urged that from the first he is an independent sovereign in treaty with us, otherwise he can't hold his extremists...

It is I suppose difficult for them to realise that we are not building. here with lifeless stones; we're encouraging the living thing to grow and we feel it pulsing in our hands. We can direct it, to a great extent, but we can't prevent it growing upwards. That is, indeed, what we have invited it to do...

To H.B., Bagdad, August 28th, 1921

We have had a terrific week but we've got our King crowned and Sir Percy and I agree that we're now half seas over,, the remaining half is the Congress and the Organic Law...

The enthronement took place at 6 a.m. on Tuesday, admirably arranged. A dais about 2ft. 6in. high was set up in the middle of the big Sarai courtyard; behind it are the quarters Faisal is Occupying, the big Government reception rooms; in front were seated in blocks, English, Arab Officials townsmen, Ministers, local deputations, to the number of 1,500.

Exactly at 6 we saw Faisal in uniform, Sir Percy in white diplomatic uniform with all his ribbons and stars Sir Aylmer, Cornwallis and a following of A.D.Cs descend the Serai steps from Faisals lodging an come pacing down the long path Of carpets, past the guard of honour (the Dorsets, they looked magnificent) and so to the dais... We all stood up while they came in and sat when they had taken their places on the dais. Faisal looked very dignified but much strung up--it was an agitating moment. He looked along the front row and caught my eye and I gave him a tiny salute. Then Saiyid Hussain stood up and read Sir Percy's proclamation in which he announced that Faisal had been elected King by 96 per cent of the people of Mesopotamia, long live the King! with that we stood up and saluted him. The national flag was broken on the flagstaff by his side and the band played "God save the King"--they have no national anthem yet. There followed a salute of 21 guns...It was an amazing thing to see all Iraq, from North to South gathered together. It is the first time it has happened in history...

Sir Percy had been unwell but on the day of the Coronation he began to recover and is now quite fit again, so I who had kept all people off him for a week quietly arranged for the deputations to pay their respects to him. We had two days of it Friday and Saturday morning. It would be difficult to tell you how many people there are in the office one and the same time. It was immensely interesting seeing them-- there were people I had never seen before and a great great many who had never seen Bagdad before. Basrah and Amarah came on Friday, Hillah and Mosul on Saturday; they were the big deputations, of these Mosul was the most wonderful. I divided it into three sections--first the Mosul town magnates, my guests and their colleagues, next the Christian Archbishops and Bishops--Mosul abounds in them--and the Jewish Grand Rabbi... The third group was more exciting than all the others; it was the Kurdish chiefs of the frontier who have elected to come into the Iraq state until they see whether an independent Kurdistan develops which will be still better to their liking...

After they had had their quarter of an hour with Sir Percy all in turn came down to me. The Kurds came last and stayed longest. The Mayor... said that they hadn't had an opportunity to discuss with Sir Percy the future of Kurdistan, what did I think about it? I said that my opinion was that the districts they came from were economically dependent on Mosul and always would be however many Kurdistans were created. They agreed but, they must have Kurdish officials. I said I saw no difficulty there. And the children must be taught in Kurdish schools. I pointed out that there would be some difficulty about that as there wasn't a single school book--nor any other--written in Kurdish. This gave them pain and after consideration they said they thought the teaching might as well be in Arabic, but what about local administrative autonomy ...I said "Have you talked it over with Saiyidna Faisal-- our Lord Faisal?" "No," they said. "Well you had better go and do it at once." I suggested. "Shall I arrange an appointment for you?" "Yes," they said. So I telephoned to Rustam Haidar and made an appointment for yesterday afternoon--I'm longing to hear from Faisal what came of it. Fun isn't it? Faisal ...asked me to tea.

We spent a happy hour discussing (a) our desert frontier to South and West and (b) the National Flag and Faisal's personal flag. For the latter we arranged provisionally this, i.e., the Hijaz flag with a gold crown on the red triangle. The red I must tell you is the colour of his house so he bears his Own crown on it. Father, do for heaven's sake tell me whether the Hijaz flag is heraldically right. You might telegraph. Its a very good flag and we could differentiate it for the Iraq by putting a gold star on the black stripe or on the red triangle. The Congress will settle it directly it meets. Do let me know in time, Also whether you have a better suggestion for Faisal's standard...

544

There's no doubt that this is the most absorbing job that I've ever taken a hand in...

To H.B., Bagdad, September. 11th, 1921

Faisal's first Cabinet is formed. On the whole we are well satisfied. Out of the 9 Ministers, 6 are eminently capable men, well-fitted for their job...

Faisal has got into his new house, on the river above Bagdad, it's small but it's really very nice. On Wednesday one of the A.D.C's telephoned to me to ask me to dinner--I went up by launch. Have I ever told you what the river is like on a hot summer night? At dusk the mist hangs in long white bands over the water; the twilight fades and the lights of the town shine out on either bank, with the river, dark and smooth and full of mysterious reflections, like a road of triumph through the mist. Silently a boat with a winking headlight slips down the stream, then a company of quffahs, each with his tiny lamp, loaded to the brim with water melons from Samarra. "Slowly, slowly," the voices of the Quffahijs drift across the water. "Don't ruffle the river lest we sink--see how we're loaded." And we slow down the launch so that the wash may not disturb them. The waves of our passage don't even extinguish the floating votive candle each burning on its minute boat made out of the swathe of a date cluster, which anxious hands launched above the town- if they reach the last town yet burning, the sick man will recover, the baby will be born safely into this world of hot darkness and glittering lights and bewildering reflections. Now I've brought you out to where the palm trees stand marshalled along the banks. The water is so still that you can see the Scorpion in it, star by star; we'll go gently past these quffahs--and here are Faisal's steps.

And you still can't form the remotest conception of how marvellously beautiful it is...I also rode with Nuri on Friday morning; we went down to breakfast with Haji Naji.

As we rode back through the gardens of the Karradah suburb where all the people know me and salute me as I pass, Nuri said "one of the reasons you stand out so is because you're a woman. There's only one Khatun. It is like when Sidi Faisal was in London and always wore Arab dress, there was no one like him. So for a hundred years they'll talk of the Khatun riding by."

I think they very likely will.

It may have escaped your notice that we are in the middle of Muharram. From the first to the fifteenth the Shiahs mourn for Hussain, the Prophet's grandson, who was invited over from Mecca by the Iraqis to be Khalif, and when he arrived got no support from them, was opposed by the army of his rival Muawiyah at the place where Karbala stands now, saw his followers die of thirst and wounds and was killed himself on the 15th. One small son escaped and from him Faisal is descended (so is the Naqib for that matter).

Incidentally when Faisal came, that story of his ancestor was in my mind. The parallel was so complete, the invitation, from Iraq, the journey from Mecca, the arrival with nothing but his formal following. If the end has proved different it's because I said "Absit omen" so often.

Well the Shiahs are mourning hard. It takes the form of processions every night, lighted torches, drums and beating of breasts. Some of the young men in our office invited me to dinner on Friday to see the processions...Presently the wild drums drew near, the glare of torches filled the sky and the processions turned into the courtyards. Torches, and men leading horses in gorgeous trappings, and men carrying large banners, and men with trays of lights on their heads. And then a black-robed company which spread out in two rows across the court, and they were swinging chains, with which they beat their backs--the black robes were open to the waist at the back so that the chains might fall on their bare skins. They swing them very skilfully with a little jerk at the top of the swing so that the chains barely touched the skin, but the effect was wonderful--the black figures in the glaring torch light, swinging rhythmically from side to side with the swing of the chains and the drums marking time. Next came the breast beaters, naked to the waist; and they stood in companies and beat their breasts in unison to a different rhythm of drums. Each procession surged through the courtyards, swung their chains, beat their breasts and surged out into the street; and another followed it interminably...

THE LETTERS OF GERTRUDE BELL

To F.B., Bagdad, September 17th, 1921

I'm glad you take an interest in my letters, bless you. It's not at all true that I have determined the fortunes of Iraq, but it's true that with an Arab Government I've come to my own. It's a delicate position to be so much in their confidence. I'm very careful about not obtruding myself on them, I let all the "come hither " emanate from them. When they want to come and ask my advice I'm always there; when they're busy with other things I go about affairs of my own...

Last Tuesday was the fifteenth of Muharram, the "Ashurah." It's the culminating day of mourning for Hussain, the anniversary of his death...They enact the whole history of Hussain's death, the attack of Muawiyah's hosts, the little band killed one by one, the burning of their tents and the cutting off of the heads of the dead to send to Muawiyah...

To H.B., Bagdad, September 25th, 1921

We've had a hot week--temp. up again to 108--but suddenly it dropped yesterday to 92 and to-day, for the first time for five months, I'm sitting in my little sitting-room with doors and windows open and no fan. It was so heavenly this morning when I went out riding at 6 (it being Sunday) that I rode right across the desert to Fahamah, close on 2 hours away and breakfasted with my friend Faiq Bey. We sat in his garden, full of roses just breaking into their second flower, while I ate hard boiled eggs, native bread and butter like cream, and Faiq Bey talked. His face ...grew quite perturbed while he related to me the difficulties of cultivators nowadays--the labourers all gone off to better paid jobs in town, or taking up land of their own on the near canals; they think they do you a service for working for ten times their former hire and even so, Yallah, you're lucky if they come an hour after dawn, don't knock off more than four hours at noon, nor leave earlier than an hour before sunset. Poor Faiq Bey! It's progress of course; the country is getting richer and the inhabitants expect more, but it's very awkward for the old society, when progress steps in to dislocate it. And in the end it won't produce anything better than Faiq Bey; straight out of Arcady he steps, with his rosy apple face, his personal rectitude and his industrious days among his palms and orange trees and barley fields...

To H.B., September. 29th, 1921

Sir Percy who is a very keen sportsman, has got two hawks which are being trained. Every morning there is a hawk party at the office. Our hawks invite their friends and when I come in of a morning I find two or three falconers each with a couple of hawks on his wrist waiting for Sir Percy to appear.

One of my daily jobs is to read and summarise the local papers. I have as assistant a capital little Soudanese as merry as a cricket. The more work you give him the merrier he grows. His Arabic is excellent and his English far from bad but very colloquial. His comments on the newspaper tosh, are a perpetual joy. Yesterday there was a literary piece by one of our local poets:

MAKKI: Oh, Lord! this fellow! This is a silly fellow. He talks to the moon. G.L.B. (severely): It's frequently done. Go on Makki, see if there's anything political in it. MAKKI (reading): My sorrows thou see'st, oh moon--Oh, Lord this fellow! No, its all general, nothing serious. G.L.B. : Hurry up then, what's next? etc., etc.

To H.B., Bagdad, Oct. 2nd, 1921

...I shall have to keep a sort of diary to you now for with fortnightly letters the intervals are too long...

We send an immense amount of dispatches home by every Air Mail and the 14th and the 30th of each month are days of feverish finishing off of work. Added to which they are the days when my fortnightly report has to be finished, so that Sir Percy may see it on the 15th and 1st, before it goes to the press--I am doing little less than writing a history of Mesopotamia in fortnightly parts. I myself find it an invaluable record, but I've not heard what they think of it at home. The 1st of October saw the 22nd number. Each number is divided into the following parts : (1.) Proceedings of the Council of Ministers (as you might say Hansard compressed). (2.) Public Opinion--all significant events, or propaganda or newspaper campaigns. (3.) Notes on Provincial affairs, the actual history of the provinces, tribal unrest, irrigation. (4.) Frontiers.

It's a great work, it really is. It goes to all our provincial officers as well as to India, Aden, Jaffa, Constantinople, Jerusalem and London, also Teheran. If they don't know everything they ought to know about us it is not my fault...

To F.B., Bagdad, Oct. 17th, 1921

They really are wonderful, these young Englishmen, who are thrown out into the provinces and left entirely to their own resources. They so completely identify themselves with their surroundings that nothing else has any significance for them, but if they think you're interested they open out like a flower and reveal quite unconsciously, wisdom, tact, and patience which you would have thought to be incompatible with their years...

My blue gown and cloak have arrived they are very nice indeed. I am so infinitely grateful for the trouble my kind family have taken about them. Lennox Gardens papers please copy...

I've suggested to Sir Percy that it would be a pleasant change for me to set up as uncrowned Queen of Kurdistan. I don't want to stand in his way if he has a fancy for the job--we might perhaps toss for it...

Yesterday, Sunday, I shook myself free and motored with Fakhri Eff: to his gardens above Baqubah. We started about 8 on a close hot morning ...and a more beautiful sight I don't think I ever saw. The dates are late in ripening this year and are still hanging in great golden crowns on the palms; below them the pomegranate bushes are weighed down with the immense rosy globes of their fruit and the orange trees laden with the pale green and yellow of ripening oranges- it was a paradise of loveliness; I walked about in a bewilderment of admiration. There was also a big stretch of vineyard where the last of the grapes were hanging on the vines--gigantic bunches of white grapes each sheltered from the sun by a little roof of liquorice stalks. Our lunch was cooked in the open air--excellent rice and chicken and stewed meats, with strained pomegranate juice to drink, and served to Us in an arbour made of a woven roof of boughs...

To H.B., Bagdad, Oct. 31st, 1921

what an excessive amount of trouble you take about your children and we accept it all as a matter of course--more shame to us. At
any rate I do realise from time to time what it is to have someone always watching and caring for one without the care having any relation
to the worth of the object it's expended on. The object is worth less
than you can guess. I think I may have been of some use here but I
suspect I've come very near the end of it...

To HB. Bagdad, Nov. 25th, 1921

I left Bagdad on the 22nd by train for Kirkuk.

Next morning I got off by motor at about 11, eastward to Sulaiman. The road ran at first through a broken country of little mud
hills, confused and ugly because they lack all mountain architecture.
Gradually the hillocks gathered themselves together and coalesced into
an upland down country with broad gracious curves and grassy hollows where a tiny spring would rise cradled in purple-flowered mint.
Before long we reached the summit and saw below us the Chemchemal valley with a range of real mountains beyond it, barren and rock
built, and beyond that, range behind range, the Kurdish highlands up
to the Persian frontier and further still to the N.E. the great massif of
Kandil Dagh lifted its snowy flanks against the sky. Hills and valleys
were almost alike, unpeopled and uncultivated; the sere grasses spread
their white gold carpet to the rock, the rock rose stark to heaven and
there was nothing else in the landscape except at our feet the tiny villages of Chemchemal, flat mud roofs clustered below an ancient
Median mound. It is the country of the fierce Hamawand tribe, a living
terror to the government and the scattered villages (which from their
protective colouring and their site among the hill folds I could not
see...) In the pass we met a buxom rosy Kurdish girl with a baby
strapped on to her back and a loaded cow walking sedately in front of
her--a strange pack animal. As soon as it saw us it took fright and attempted to scramble up the stony bank when, cow-like, it collapsed
hopelessly under its load. The baby began to cry, the woman beat the
cow and the cow struggled effetely till I thought it would break its
legs--such a pother we had made in Kurdistan with our motor! So we
flew to the rescue, unloaded the cow, set it on its feet, held the baby

till the mother had tied up the loads again and went happily on our several ways...

To H.B., Bagdad, December. 4th, 1921

Faisal privately doesn't want the Congress to be convened (it's duty is to draw up the Organic law) until he has got the terms of the treaty satisfactorily settled and respective responsibilities of the British and Arab Governments defined. It's this question of responsibility which perturbs everyone; on it the position of the Advisors and indeed most other things rests. Roughly the skeleton of the problem is whether we can assume responsibility for defence if the country is attacked from without...We must be able to satisfy the League of Nations that we can fulfil the international obligations with which the mandate entrusts us, and even if we drop the mandate and call it a treaty, that treaty must make certain reservations which the Arabs must accept...

The word Mandate produces much the same effect here as the word Protectorate did in Egypt...

But you mustn't think for a moment I have any part in settling these problems. I know about them because Sir Percy tells me about them in outline but I'm merely an onlooker and although Faisal is very friendly and agreeable he doesn't, quite rightly, consult me. I hadn't seen him for nearly 5 weeks what with his being away and my being away, and I very carefully abstain from offering advice in matters the delicate manipulation of which had much better be left to Sir Percy. All I can do and all I try to do, is to give as accurate an impression as I can of what people are saying and thinking.

I had a well spent morning at the office making out the Southern desert frontier of the Iraq with the help of a gentleman from Hayil and of Fahad Bey the paramount chief of the Anazeh. The latter's belief in my knowledge of the desert makes me blush. When he was asked by Mr. Cornwallis to define his tribal boundaries all he said was "You ask the Khatun. She knows." In order to keep up this reputation of omniscience, I've been careful to find out from Fahad all the Wells claimed by the Shammar. One way and another, I think I've succeeded in compiling a reasonable frontier. The importance of the matter lies in the fact that Ibn Saud has captured Hayil and at the earliest possible opportunity Sir Percy wants to have a conference between him and Faisal to state definitely what tribes and lands belong to the Iraq and what to Ibn Saud...

Did I tell you that Sir Percy is building an extra room on to my house? It's causing me acute discomfort at the moment but it will be a great blessing when finished.

One of the joys of my new sitting-room will be that it has a fireplace...To-day Percy Loraine arrived on his way to Persia. After lunch he and I retired to my office and had a real talk. I came home at tea-time to prepare for my own dinner party, the foundation of which was three of the Kirkuk delagates. I had just had time to get my room into some sort of order when at 5:30 (the time of the dinner party being 7:30) the first of my guests arrived...

CHAPTER XXII

1922-23 - BAGDAD

To H.B., January 2, 1922

I've been having an exceptionally horrid Christmas, as I will
now recount. Captain Clayton, Saiyid Hussain and I intended to go to
Baqubah on Dec. 23. The day looked very threatening, however we
decided by telephone that we would start. In the afternoon the weather
looked so bad that we gave up our scheme altogether. So there I was
landed with Christmas holidays with nothing to do and nowhere to go,
disgustingly cold and wet weather and an increasing cold which
gradually developed into the worst I've ever had. It's still very bad. Mr.
Tod and Major Wilkinson came to lunch with me on Saturday, which
was cheerful, and Nuri Said on Christmas day, after which I went to
tea with the King--he lives a long way outside the town, up river, and
the road was indescribable; however, I succeeded in getting there and
we had the usual delightful talk ... On Wednesday the damnable holidays were over-- but not my cold. I went to the office and made it so
much worse that I had to spend Thursday indoors ...I went to the office
Friday morning and came back to lunch feeling unutterably ill...

It is so uncheerful sitting by one's self on New Year's Eve.
They had an immense party for a Fancy Dress Ball to which I didn't go
nor was I in fancy dress--unless to dine in one's fur coat is fancy dress.
I didn't enjoy it very much because I was feeling so miserable, and
when they went to the ball I went home. However, I can't complain of
any loneliness of New Year's Day. My first callers arrived at 7:30 a.m.
while I was still in bed. They were Haji Naji and a sheikh of the Dulaim. Accordingly I invited them to breakfast ...I wish you could have
observed even for a minute my breakfast party--I wrapped up in furs
and they in their brown cloaks ...After that I had an uninterrupted
stream of visitors whom I regaled on coffee and chocolates until 1:15

when the last of them fortunately left, and I went out to lunch with the Joyces, feeling more dead than alive. After I came back the throng set in again till 6 o'clock when I closed my doors for a moment's breathing space before dinner. I dined with Sir Aylmer who had asked the King and the eldest son of the Naqib and Hadoud Pasha, Mr. Tod and some of the G.H.Q. staff and Sir John Davidson, a retired Major General and M.P.

He is coming to have a heart to heart talk with me one of these days. The dinner was a huge success. Faisal took me in and I must say I enjoyed myself mightily too. It is so pleasant and friendly at the General's house--everyone is at their ease and he is such a kind and delightful host.

Jan. 6th., I am a trifle better and though far from well I begin to think I may ultimately recover.

To H.B., Bagdad, January. 30th, 1922

During the last fortnight I've taken my health seriously in hand. I really was dreadfully run down and nearly expired Of fatigue at the end of a morning in the office so I've firmly Come away at 1 p.m. or thereabouts, lunched at home or with Mr. Cornwallis, the Joyces or any one else I wanted to see and then gone out riding till tea time. The weather has been delicious and this programme has been just what I wanted for it has got me out every afternoon into the sun and air. Never in my experience of Iraq has there been such a spring ...To-day I rode through the Dairy Farm and back by the gardens bordering the Tigris. Man and beast were rejoicing in the abundance of green--"By God, I've never seen the like!" I stopped to say to the shepherds. And they, "It is the mercy of God and your presence Khatun."

How I love their darling phrases: you know, Father, it's shocking how the East has wound itself round my heart till I don't know which is me and which is it. I never lose the sense of it. I'm acutely conscious always of its charm and grace which do not seem to wear thin with familiarity. I'm more a citizen of Bagdad than many a Bagdadi born, and I'll wager that no Bagdadi cares more, or half so much, for the beauty of the river or the palm gardens, or clings more closely to the rights of citizenship which I have acquired...

An excellent Municipal Council has been returned at Basrah but what pleases me almost most is that at Kirkuk the former Mayor who is a great ally of mine, had an immense majority, though the Turkish party pulled every possible string against him, including an appeal to pan-Islamic sentiment ...It will be very interesting to see what the Shah makes of it ...

My new room is so nice. It's also an indescribable blessing to have a real fireplace with a fire burning in it. My house has a wonderful feeling of spaciousness in a modest way. Rishan loves the fire even more than I do. You know, Father, I shall never be content till you come out again--I want you to see the King and my new room and everything. I think your next visit should be in the spring Of 1923--I'll come to Aleppo to meet you, and take you here by motor...

To H.B., Bagdad, February. 16th, 1922

I want to tell you, just you, who know and understand everything, that I'm acutely conscious of how much life has given me. I've gone back now to the wild feeling of joy in existence--I'm happy in feeling that I've got the love and confidence of a whole nation, a very wonderful and absorbing thing--almost too absorbing perhaps. You must forgive me if it seems to preoccupy me too much--it doesn't really divide me from you, for one of the greatest pleasures is to tell you all about it, in the certainty that you will sympathise. I don't for a moment suppose that I can make much difference to our ultimate relations with the Arabs and with Asia, but for the time I'm one of the factors in the game. I can't think why all these people here turn to me for comfort and encouragement; if I weren't here they would find someone else, of course, but being accustomed to come to me, they come. And in their comfort I find my own. I remember your saying to me once that the older one grows the more one lives in other people's lives. Well, I've got plenty of lives to live in, haven't I? And perhaps after all, it has been best this way. At any rate, as it had to be this way, I don't now regret it.

THE LETTERS OF GERTRUDE BELL

To H.B., Bagdad, February. 16th, 1922

The day after I wrote to you I went out with Mr. Thomson to see the Yusufiyah canal. We had a delightful day. We motored to Mahmudivah, half way to Hillah where we found our horses. Then with a local sheikh and a few outsiders we rode up the canal. It was an enchanting ride for this wonderful spring has covered the world with verdure ...I must tell you the Yusufiyah is one of the oldest canals in the world. It was the Babylonian Nahr Malka, Julian sailed down it to Ctesiphon and the Abbassids re-dug it. Consequently there are great early Babylonian mounds all along it. Where we crossed by the bridge we were four miles from Tel Abn Habbah, which was Sippa and as we came back we rode up on to a wonderful mound called Tel Dair. It was completely covered with potsherds and bits of brick and I picked up a half brick with an inscription in early Babylonian characters--which was rather interesting because so far as I know nothing earlier than Nebuchadnezzar has been noted there...

Faisal sent for me that day, but as I was out I telephoned a day or two later to ask if I might come to tea. We had a tremendous talk. He is most delightful and certainly often most amazing. I caught myself up in the middle of discussion and said to him that it was almost impossible to believe that while he had been born in Mecca and educated at Constantinople and I in England and educated at Oxford there was no difference whatever in our points of view.

Already the country is finding its feet. The stable people, the big sheikhs and nobles relying on our support of Faisal, are rallying round him and are combined. They are going to stand no nonsense from extremists and tub-thumpers...

To H.B., Bagdad, February. 26, 1922

I took the King to see the apricot blossom in Karradah. I hadn't warned Haji Naji beforehand and he unfortunately wasn't there, but the King and all his court were much impressed by the beautiful way the gardens were kept and very envious of the seedling fruit trees. One of Haji Naji's sons was there and said he would send him anything he wanted. The King's need for fruit trees is that he has bought a large bit of the Dairy Farm which he intends to make into a park...

I'm very glad. First of all because it's evidence of his taking root and secondly because it brings him up against different sorts of people.

Mr. Cooke and I sat long talking over the fire and we agreed that there couldn't be anything in the world more absorbing than to be in the very heart of intellectual Asia--to be watching and encouraging the effort to overmaster secular prejudices. Heaven knows their wits are acute enough; it's moral courage that's lacking to throw off the long domination of the theocratic ordinance in human affairs which from a valuable referent has become a cord of strangulation. After all it has taken us Europeans centuries to win through...

To turn to matters of minor importance, I'm largely living on delicious truffles. One usually gets them in from the desert at this time of the year but I've never known them in such abundance as in this extraordinarily beautiful spring. Daffodils, marigolds and wall-flowers are blooming in my garden and the rose trees coming into bud.

To H.B., Bagdad, March 12th, 1922

I spent Tuesday afternoon with the King and we had an immense talk, partly owing to the nearness of general elections, about the formation of political parties. He was anxious--I really think that in this country it would be best--that people of different opinions should find a platform of agreement and start a single party with a combined policy for the election. I've unexpectedly been thrown into the thick of it during the last few days. On Thursday the extremists petitioned the interior for permission to form a party...

It is pretty clear that the extremists are alarmed by the determined attitude of the moderates and I fancy they have every reason for being so...

Sir Percy has just been in to give his advice on the question of the parties, namely that if the two parties can't come to an agreement the moderates are bound to go ahead on their own lines ...It is deeply interesting but rather agonizing to be taking so decisive a share in all this. One feels that a wrong step may do a great deal of harm...

It is just on the cards that I may have to come back here after our time together in Palestine, but I don't think it is very likely. You see my feeling is that I can't very well leave my friends here stranded at such a crucial moment, for at least I serve as a sort of clearing house for them. But in the course of the next few weeks things may have shaped themselves... [Same letter continued.]

March 14th. The party question is still undecided and I haven't heard anything about it to-day. Meantime the wind is up in another quarter. For some time past letters have been passing between Sir Percy and Ibn Saud. The conquest of Hayil by the latter in November makes his frontiers continuous with the Iraq. Sir Percy is anxious to arrange a treaty between him and Faisal--on the basis that the desert edges into which our shepherds go down with their flocks in the spring shall be included in Iraq--Ibn Saud wants to claim all the desert as his and has recently been exacting tribute from our shepherds.

Finally matters came to a head on the 11th when Ibn Saud's People attacked in immense force a camel corps recently organised by the King to protect our frontiers and routed them. To-day the Akhwan fired on an aeroplane reconnaissance and orders were issued that their camp was to be bombed. Ibn Saud may of course repudiate the action of his followers; that's the best that can happen, for otherwise we're practically at war with him. Life in this country is not lacking in incident ...

Thanks to your sending me the cutting from the Times by air mail, my letter was published in one of the vernacular papers to-day and was the subject of much rejoicing to-night at the palace. It has made a good effect and I hope will restore my credit a little with the extremists who, I hear, regard me as exceedingly severe. Well, if it's severity to try and stop them from pitching headlong into a gulf of wild nationalist ambition, I am.

To H.B., Bagdad, March 30th, 1922

During the last fortnight I have come definitely to the conclusion that I can't go on leave this summer. Things are too much in the melting pot ... I'm not going to telegraph to you because it might prevent you from coming out and I not only want dreadfully to see you but also the little holiday will be immensely to the good. I shall very likely fly over on the 29th April, but you are not to mention this to anyone. Also it's not certain. I may come by motor via Aleppo in which case I should make to be in Jerusalem a day before you so as to welcome you. If I fly back I should leave Ramleh On May 27th so that I should come down to Egypt with you and see you off. Since I made up my mind I've been feeling rather homesick but I haven't any doubt I'm doing what I ought to do. We've put our hand to this plough and at any rate Sir Percy thinks that I'm some help to him in his difficult furrow. I'm perfectly well and I shall go up to Sulaimani for a month in the middle of the summer. I might possibly come home for a bit in the autumn so that it would only be six months difference. I hope you and Mother and Maurice won't be much disappointed. I do love you so much and I hate staying away so long.

Well now we come to the sordid but serious question Of clothes--of course, I've made no provision for the summer. I've written to Marte (78 Grosvenor Street) by this mail ,telling her that if she is in time to catch you, she is to send out by you two washing gowns, an evening gown and a hat ...if, however, you have left before this letter arrives Mother will open it and will tell Marte to post things I've asked her to send me as quickly as she can so that I may find them here if possible when I get back. But please if you possibly can bring a hat. Elsa might choose it if the combination with Marte fails--she is on the telephone, by the way--a ribbon hat, black or mauvy blue and mushroom in shape. There! You'll do your best, I feel sure, and if you can't do anything I must just wear the topee I shall come over in...

I've received a lovely photograph of Hugo's wedding. I think that is partly what made me feel homesick. You all look such darlings and my two sisters so especially delightful.

[Hugo's marriage to Frances Morkill took place on November 24th, 1922, at Kirby Malham in the West Riding of Yorkshire.]

To F.B., Bagdad, April 28th, 1922

I have just telegraphed to Father at Jerusalem telling him that I'm coming over by air on the 29th and suggesting that he should meet me at Amman on that day...

[This meeting with her father took place most successfully, as arranged. He had arrived at Jerusalem, and then gone on to Amman, where he received a telephone message to say that the two official aeroplanes, in one of which Gertrude was flying, had left Bagdad at 9 a.m. and were due to arrive at Ziza between 11 and 12. He at once motored to Ziza and stood with the officials who were awaiting the aeroplanes, looking out into the Eastern sky. It was an exciting moment when two small specks first appeared on the horizon and then came to a pause over the heads of the expectant group. The planes landed beautifully, Gertrude alighted and fell into her father's arms. For a little while she was dizzy, and unable to hear, then in a short time she completely recovered. Her father then told her that he and she had been invited to dine with Abdullah King Faisal's brother, the Emir of Transjordania, who' was then encamped near Amman, but that he had declined as he did not suppose that she would feel able to do so after her long flight. But Gertrude entirely repudiated the idea of refusing, got out her evening clothes, and they went to dinner with the Emir and enjoyed themselves very much.]

To F.B., Jerusalem, May 10th, 1922

I can't tell you what a wonderful time we have had. The joy of being with Father in these surroundings and of having his amazingly acute and perceptive mind to help one in coming to conclusions! Was there ever anyone who combined as he does such wealth of experience with so fresh and vital an outlook on all and everything that he encounters? And isn't he the most delicious companion with his humanness and his charming humour and his appreciation of beauty and history and birds and flowers and all that ever was the biggest thing to the least. I shall so dreadfully miss him when we part and I do very much regret that I'm not coming home to you, Maurice and my sisters. It's an extraordinary sense of rest, peace and understanding that one gets when one is with one's own family and it's just that which I miss so much--the intimacy and confidence in our love for one another. But though I feel so much drawn to home and you, I know I couldn't have left Iraq happily at this moment. I should always have felt that I had left my job at a moment when I might and very likely would be needed if anything untoward had happened, though I know I couldn't have made much difference, I should have imagined that just the little I could have done might have helped to turn the scale...

Marte sent me the most excellent clothes, bless her--lovely embroidered muslin gowns to wear during the summer

To H.B., Bagdad, Thursday, May 18th, 1922

We did the journey in six hours, coming down at For amadi a quarter of an hour to refill. It wasn't really quite as comfortable as Vickers-Vimy though so much quicker...the wind being slightly in the North was very battering on the left side. Guided, however, by the gesticulation of my charming pilot, Mr. Brunton, I succeeded in following the motor track across the desert and keeping count of the landing grounds, so that I knew exactly where we were all the time...We flew very high, 6,000 to 7,000 feet and very fast, 100 to 110 miles an hour. Just before we reached Ramadi it rained a little, and when we got in we found it quite cool. Our whole journey was most agreeable and I fear I've become the confirmed aviator...

I went to tea with the King. I took him your letter with which he was very much pleased, and told him all about Abdullah and Palestine and Syria. He talked very delightfully about his feeling that as long as he had our confidence nothing mattered. I said that I had come back with the conviction that we were the only Arab province which was set in the right path, and that if we failed here, which I hoped was unthinkable, it would be the end of Arab aspirations.

If I'm not mistaken, public opinion is crystallizing hard in our favour and I believe if H.M.G. would put the issue openly and clearly the large majority would declare for us on any terms.

To H.B., Bagdad, June 2nd, 1922

Yes, there wasn't one moment of our fortnight in Palestine that was not perfect. Everything helped--the lovely country and the nice people, but they were only the setting of the picture, which was you. There's no doubt that being with you is the most enjoyable thing known. Haven't you got your niche in the East ...

The Minister of the Interior telephoned to tell me that a group of extremists were planning a big demonstration against the mandate for the afternoon. The King had ordered it to be stopped and did I know where Mr. Cornwallis was? With that, Mr. C. came in and I left him to deal with the Minister. At five Mr. Cooke and I went out on another round of visits and got through some ten notables or more. There was a good deal of talk about the attempted demonstration and very plain speaking as to how this kind of thing could not be tolerated.

It was a horrible day that Tuesday of the Id. A south wind which scorched you and even at night was extremely hot. It has been better since, but summer has set in and you can't mistake it. Yesterday there were races to which I went--rather late in the afternoon, sat in the King's box and had a most cheerful talk with him. He was rather pleased with himself and I hastened to assure him that he had every reason for gratification. The extremist papers have been outrageous, describing the Sunday business as an immense popular demonstration.

The High Commissioner gave a Garden Party for the King's birthday. I had prepared the Arab list--all officials and nobles quite apart from their political opinions. They all came--trust Lady Cox for that!--and we hobnobbed with most of the people who led the rebellion two years ago. Sir Percy told me to look after the King and wallahi I did it well! First of all I took him round all the groups of Arab officials and notables. He made the circle, saying the right thing to everyone-- he plays his part. Then we got him established in a corner of the lawn and I brought up all the wives of Advisors so far as I could catch them, and gave each one a short audience with him. Also the new French Consul and his wife, the eldest son of the Naqib and any one else whom I thought he ought to speak to...

Faisal has hitched his wagon to the stars...At the bottom of his mind he trusts us and believes that one or two Of us would go to the stake for him and that's the strongest hold We have of him...

Oh, darling, isn't the human equation immensely interesting. I feel as if I and all of us were playing the most magical tunes on their heart strings, drawn taut by the desperate case in which they find themselves. Can they succeed in setting Up a reasonable government? Can they save themselves from chaos? Their one cry is "Help us." And one sits there, in their eyes an epitome of human knowledge, and feel-ing oneself so very far from filling the bill! Poor children of Adam, they and we! I'm not sure (but perhaps that's because of my sex) that the emotional link between us isn't the better part of wisdom, but I wish I had a little more real wisdom to offer. However, Sir Percy has plenty...

To-day the vernacular press was full of Lord Apsley [who had come over as representing the Morning Post) gratitude for the part the Morning Post had played in the Palestine question and hope that he would now direct his attention to that of Iraq. The leaders of the people will meet the Lord and expound to him the position, in which no doubt he will be deeply interested.

At five I took the Lord to tea with the King. I told him all that there was in the papers and he replied that he was to meet all the extremists to-morrow at Kadhaimain. I gave him the lie of the land and I've no doubt he will do extremely well. For in conversation with the King he was quite admirable--I'm free to confess that I translated like an angel! ...We talked over the whole mandate question with complete amity. Lord A. developed the reasons for which we had to have recourse to a mandate--a means of obtaining the consent of the powers to our treaty and of persuading the British Nation that we had accepted a responsibility and were bound to fulfil it etc. The King asked whether he saw any objection to a combined protest on the part of ourselves and the Arabs to the League of Nations against the mandatory relation once the treaty was an accomplished fact. Lord A. said on the contrary the Morning Post would do all it could to help us, but they must get the treaty through first otherwise all our enemies would declare that the Arab nation did not want us. The King enthusiastically agreed.

At the en, Lord Apsley, who really is a diplomat of the highest order, said that now he wanted to come to something really serious. They all pricked their ears--"Yes," he said "a thing of real importance--when are you going to have a polo team?" They were delighted...

In that we took our leave and I'll wager that a very pleasant impression remained with us. It was one of the most useful talks I've ever heard at the palace and I'm infinitely grateful to Lord Apsley for the skill with which he conducted it. I confided to him that I had been a very good interpreter, to which he replied that the Mufti of Jerusalem had told him that he had never heard better Arabic than mine on the lips of a foreigner. I was gratified by this...

To H.B., Bagdad, June 22nd, 1922

On the Sunday after I last wrote (June 11th) Mr. Cornwallis, Captain Clayton, Major Murray, Captain Ashton and I went to swim in the Diala. It wasn't a very well chosen day. There was a tempestuous south wind and we, motoring in the teeth of it, felt as if we were motoring through Hell. We hit the Diala in the wrong place, found it full of people bathing and had to go hunting for a better. I don't remember to have yet performed my toilet so completely in the open, it was merely by the mercy of providence that cows and women were the only spectators--had our swim in the dark--the Diala was running very strong still--and then sat on the high bank very peacefully and ate our cold dinner oh, above all drank our cold drinks! The wind dropped, night hushed the chattering in some Arab tents close by, the river hurried below us and a late moon lifted its distorted shape out of the East and spread a soft light over the interminable miles of desert thorn. We lay there till past nine talking of the Iraq and the Arabs and the things we are doing...

Next day I went to tea with the King and had one of the most interesting talks I've ever had with him...

When if ever we come up to eternal judgment, you may be very sure that we shall ultimately be graded according to the very highest point we have been able to reach...Faisal on that day will come out very high. He surges up a long long way across the heavenly strand; the tide goes down again, but he has been there and left his little line of sea gold on the shore.

On Thursday I took Mrs. Wilkinson to tea with some Arab ladies--I'm always taking some of our nice Englishwomen out to tea like that; it's such a help.

In the evening I had an evening party in my garden 9/11:30. Coffee and ices and talk under my lanterns. I asked about ten Arabs and five Englishmen. It was quite brought off and I shall do it again and again...This afternoon there is a very important meeting of Council--the treaty will be laid before the Ministers. I've been getting at Ministers this morning in the interval of writing to you and I suppose nothing more can be done. If it doesn't come out quite straight it will be up to Sir Percy, that great weaver of destinies, to put it right again.

Elsa will be gratified to hear that the parasol has come and excites the deepest admiration at Court!

Perhaps someday you might send me a Bridge Box--I haven't one. Also possibly some patience cards?

To H.B., Bagdad, July 16th, 1922

I must begin by a really remarkable observation on the weather. They are repairing something to do with the electric current and in consequence it's off till 1 p.m. and no fans. Nevertheless on this mid July Sunday morning as I am sitting, in a thorough draught it's true, between door and window, but quite cool enough to write to you with comfort, the temperature can't be over 100 degrees. I don't think we've had it over 110 this year, and generally, as to-day, a jolly north wind. My office is unfortunately the worst spot in Bagdad; it's sheltered from every breeze and exposed to every ray of the sun. My house, on the other hand, is wonderfully cool.

The King and the Naqib have proclaimed to the listening Universe that they will never, so help them God, accept the Mandate. H.M.G. have replied that they can conclude no treaty except by reason of the right to do so given to them by the League of Nations--i.e., the mandate.

I think I've said before, but anyway I'll say right here, that I'm convinced that no country in the world can work a mandate...The Arabs won't submit to any diminution of their sovereign rights such as being placed in tutelage under the L. of N. They are ready to exercise those rights in such manner as to bind themselves by treaty to accept advice in return for help.

We had a great function later in the afternoon--the opening of our Anglo-Arab Club. Sir Percy was there and was perfectly delightful to everyone. It's a man's club but I was asked to the party though I'm not a member. And our dashing Euphrates sheikhs were there, half a dozen of them, all up here to see the treaty put through, if they can. It remains to be seen whether the club will be a success--it is designed to be a common meeting ground...

Oh, we're up against such problems--the formation of political parties is the first. The extremists are already in the field and I'm pushing and dragging the others into the open.

Here is an engaging picture of the General Staff of the Iraq Army having their new drill. Jafar Pasha appears saliently on the extreme left.

July 17th, Yesterday's experiences were as usual remarkable. Feeling very energetic for once, I got up at five and rode out to Karradah to breakfast with Haji Naji on scrumptious roasted fish. While I was sitting in his summer house a curious episode occurred. There strode in a youngish man in the dress of a Dervish who announced that he had come as a guest. Haji Naji replied that he was busy and bade him begone. The man blustered a little, looked sharply at me and said he had just as much right to be a guest as others and finally went out and sat down just outside a mat-walled summer house. Haji Naji called the servants and one of his sons and told them to send the man away. They failed to make him move. Presently he began to read out the Koran in a loud voice. This was more than I could bear and I went out and told him, by God, to clear out. He said "I am reading the Holy Book." I replied I know you are--get out or I shall send for the police." He replied irrelevantly "I rely on God." I said "God's a long way off and the police very near," and with that I picked up his iron staff and gently poked him up. He made up his mind that he was beaten and saying "Because you are here I shall go", picked up himself and his Koran and made off...If I hadn't sent the man away Haji would have been absolutely helpless. A man who sits down on your threshold to read the Koran can only be regarded, in theory, as a blessing--you can't lift him. Curious, wasn't it? I shall tell the police to keep an eye on any dervish wandering about in Karradah...

10 P.M. I've just heard by telephone that the Ministers passed the treaty at this afternoon's meeting...

We're having a heat wave--I think the temperature must have been up to 120 degrees to-day. One knows at once when the thermometer runs up by the intolerable hotness of everything one touches. Mr. Cooke, Major Wilson and I accepted the invitation of Sabih Bey, Minister of P.W.D., to bathe from his house in Muadhdham. It was an ideal place. A delightful house with two courtyards full of flowering oleanders; you undress like a lady in Sabih Bey's bedroom, climb down the wall of his house by a ladder and so by a steep sandy bank straight into deep water- -so swiftly deep that you can dive in off the bank. You swim lazily down in the soft warm water under the high fortress-like walls of Muadhdham river front, after which, if you're me, you come to shore and run up Ahe bank to your starting point, but if you're Mr. Cooke you swim gallantly up against the current. That over, we drank many glasses of grape juice and so motored home...

To-day the King ordered me to tea and we had two hours most excellent talk. First of all I got his assistance for my Law Of Excavations which I've compiled with the utmost care in consultation with the legal authorities. He has undertaken to push it through Council--he's perfectly sound about archaeology, having been trained by T. E. Lawrence--and has agreed to my suggestion that he should appoint me, if Sir Percy consents, provisional Director of Archaeology to his government, in addition to my other duties. I should then be able to run the whole thing in direct agreement with him, Which would be excellent.

To H.B., Bagdad, July 30th, 1922

I left off in the beginning of a heat wave which I trust is now nearly over. The day after I wrote to you, the 21st, I got so tired of being hot that I thought I would try and mend it by being hotter so I went out riding about. I didn't go very far but before I got home I felt more like having a heat-stroke than I've ever felt in my life and when I looked in the looking glass my face was scarlet all over. I put my head quickly into iced water and recovered at once. I had a party in my garden that night--it was far too hot and I'm having no more until it gets cooler...

THE LETTERS OF GERTRUDE BELL

To H.B., Bagdad, August 15th, 1922

We are having a very exhausting time, physically and politically. Physically because of the incredibly horrible weather. It's not very hot, never much over 110, but heavy and close beyond all belief. Every two or three days I get up in the morning wondering why, instead of getting up, I don't lie down and die. At the end of the day one feels absolutely dead beat. Then for a day or two one is better, for no special reason, and then again moribund. It's not only me; everyone is the same...

On Sunday 6th the King invited us to a picnic. I walked with the King through the wonderful palm gardens and out to the desert. For the sixth time I've watched the dates ripen. Six times I've seen the palms take on the likeness of huge Crown Imperials, with the yellow date clusters hanging like immense golden flowers below the feathery fronds...The King took us back in his launch and as we slipped past the palm groves he and I laid plans to write the history of the Arab revival from first to last, from his diaries and my knowledge. It would be a remarkable tale.

Father, you do realise, don't you, how the magic and the fascination of it all holds one prisoner? ...

Yesterday in a perfectly infernal climate and feeling fit to die I worked from 7 to 1:30 in the office, came home and lunched and worked uninterruptedly from 2:30 to six, after which I went to a Committee meeting and then to a dinner at the French consulate where we played Bridge till midnight. I came home feeling like a horrible spectre.

The High Commissioner has telegraphed home that he doesn't see any advantage in Faisal's going to England. He recommends that we should publish the treaty, say that we're all agreed upon it and that the sole point of difference is the mandate. On that point the electors of the Iraq must decide; if they decide against it we will evacuate tomorrow. The King is delighted with this proposed solution.

But will our Government accept this suggestion? That's what we want to know, for being all away grouse shooting we can get no answer to any telegrams however urgent...

August 16th. This was one of the moribund days, nevertheless I've been extremely busy. Any quantity of Sheikhs came in this morning...I really believe they are getting to work. They have parcelled out the whole country according to administrative divisions. There's a head branch in every divisional headquarter and sub-branches in every district; the sheikhs are going back to organise them. Their tails are up sky high. They declare they'll bring in the whole country...And the sheikhs from further afield are trooping in to register themselves as members. They are the people I love, I know every Tribal chief of any importance through the whole length and breadth of Iraq and I think them the backbone of the country.

One has to take one's courage in one's hands when a wrong decision may mean universal chaos.

Meantime all these internal hostilities that are so gravely Preoccupying us may well be obliterated by the growing menace of the Kamalists of our northern frontier...

Now I come to think of it I can't imagine how you can bear to wade through all these reams of Iraq politics--can you bear it

August 18th, 1922. As there's an immense cryptic telegram from home--not deciphered yet. No doubt it contains the answer which we think will decide our fate.

I can't see any prospect of getting away this autumn, unless the whole thing blows up--a possible contingency. If it doesn't we shall be in the thick of a general election and the Constituent Assembly should be meeting towards the end of the year. But Iraq and everything else may go to the dogs before I stay here another summer. I should not be telling the truth if I did not observe that my disappearance from the scene at the present juncture would fill the breasts of my tribal sheikhs with dismay...

THE LETTERS OF GERTRUDE BELL

To H.B., August 27th, 1922

On Sunday evening August 20th we escaped from politics for a happy hour or two. The King came out bathing and picnicking with us and we had the usual party. It was my picnic and I did it beautifully. We roasted great fishes on spits over a fire of palm fronds--the most delicious food in the world--I brought carpets and cushions and hung old Bagdad lanterns in the tamarisk bushes where we kept simple state in the rosy stillness of the sunset. "This is peace," said the King. We lay on our cushions for a couple of hours after dinner while he and Nuri and Mr. Cornwallis told stories of the Syrian campaign--I have seldom passed a more enchanting evening.

Next day we were back in the turmoil.

Wednesday was the anniversary of the accession, August 23rd. I rode with His Majesty before breakfast on Tuesday morning to see his cotton farm...It is a tremendous cavalcade when the King goes out riding-- A.D.C.'s behind us and four lancers of the body guard bringing up the rear...

With that we stopped talking and played bridge. So we came to August 23rd...We were due at the Levée at 9:45.

I went across to the Residency by boat, all in lace clothes and miniature orders, the first time I had worn the miniatures; they are the greatest comfort--and we started off in a procession of two motors for the levee, the High Commissioner and his staff. When we got to the s Palace the courtyard was packed with people, three or four hundred under the King's stair, and numbers of white-robed persons on the balcony, apparently addressing them. The police had to clear a way for the High Commissioner's car. As he walked up the stair, a very striking figure in his white uniform and orders, a voice in the crowd called out something which he did not hear and I did not catch, upon which came a storm of clapping. It was almost as though they were clapping his appearance, and much perplexed we went into the audience room. The King seemed rather nervous but the conversation quickly got into easy channels--the morning's review and so forth--and after a quarter of an hour we came away. The court was empty.

As soon as we were back in the office the High Commissioner told me to get on to it at once and find out what had happened. I did, and within an hour I had the information we wanted. It was a demonstration on the part of the two extremist political parties, no doubt arranged to take place at the hour of Sir Percy's audience.

It was now Sir Percy's turn to get busy. He waited until the anniversary was over and on the following morning (24th) sent the letter and received the answer...At noon on the 24th we heard that the King was down with appendicitis, in the evening his temperature was up, at 6 a.m. next day, five doctors, two English and three Arabs, were debating whether an immediate operation were necessary, at 8 they decided it was and at 11 it was successfully over

The King has made a rapid convalescence. On Sunday he was allowed to see a selected body of notables. This was thought advisable because a rumour had been spread that he was dead. On Monday the Officers of the Iraq army offered him their congratulations on his recovery. To-day Mr. Cornwallis saw him--in the presence of notables and the A.D.C.'s There was no mention of politics...

The extreme right is just as subversive of the policy of H.M.G. as the extreme left. The one is opposed to the King and the Arab Government, the other opposed to British assistance. How are we to combine the two sharply conflicting schools of thought? I myself believe that if the King refuses to accept Sir Percy's action the majority of the Iraq will request him to abdicate. You'll understand that immediate preoccupations block out the firmament. If I don't specifically answer your letters it's not because I don't like having them. They are like an escape to another world. But waking and sleeping I am absorbed by what lies to my hand and the countless interviews which I conduct daily with turbaned gentlemen and tribesmen and what you please, seem to me to matter more than anything else in the world...

To H.B., Bagdad, September 8th, 1922

I spent the afternoon with the Davidsons. She is going home next week to my great sorrow. I shall miss her dreadfully. I do hope Aurelia Tod will be back this winter--it's nice to have a female friend.

At the beginning of September we had an unusual drop in the temperature, a month earlier than usual. I promptly caught cold--but I've also promptly got rid of it. You can't think how difficult it is to tackle the first on-coming of cold. You would think it absurd to speak of it as cold. The thermometer often goes up to 110 in the afterday, but it drops to 70 before dawn. You're just too hot without a punkah when the temperature of your room is 90 and just too cold with it.

September 10th. This Sunday morning while I'm writing to you Sir Percy and Mr. Cornwallis are having a momentous interview with the King, at which Sir Percy is asking him to endorse all he has done, and to give certain undertakings for the future...

Sept. 14th. Now I must tell you that the King's momentous conversation with Sir Percy passed off very satisfactorily. He accepted and endorsed all that Sir Percy had done...

To H.B., Bagdad, September 24th, 1922

Our next excitement was the arrival of Amir Zaid, H.M.'s youngest brother to whom he is devoted. He arrived last Sunday the 17th. There was a great reception for him at the station to which we all went- notables and advisors and Arab Army and everyone you can think of...

The Mandate has been much softened for them since Mr. Churchill has agreed to announce that the moment Iraq enters the League of Nations it becomes a dead letter. Now one of the clauses of the treaty is an undertaking on our part to get Iraq admitted as quickly as possible... ...

September 28th. A new planet has arisen in the shape of Sir John Salmond, Air Marshal, who takes over command of all British Forces on October 1st...He is alert, forcible, amazingly quick in the uptake, a man who means to understand the Iraq and our dealings with its people. He dined with me last night to meet Mr. Cornwallis--just we three for I wanted him to get into instant touch with the Iraq government to which Mr. Cornwallis belongs. We had the most enchanting evening for Sir John is delightful to talk to on any subject.

THE LETTERS OF GERTRUDE BELL

To H.B., Bagdad, October 8th, 1922

As usual a great many things seem to have happened but for the most part we have had our eyes fixed on Chanak...We, however, seem to have found a man in General Harington.

I wrote to you on the 29th. The 30th was the first of their Autumn races. We began the day, the Joyces and I, by taking the Amir Zaid to Ctesiphon...He is so eager to find out and learn about everything-- as quick and appreciative as the King. I took our breakfast which we ate under the shadow of the great walls, while I told Zaid of all the battles that had been fought there, 637 and 1914. In the afternoon we went to the races as H.M. was going. I went to Sir Percy's box and he put me next the King. After we had talked a little Sir John Salmond strolled over from his box, so I took him into H.M.'s box and we three had an hour's talk, I interpreting. The King went straight to the heart of things, asking the A.V.M, what he could do to protect us from attack, how much he could do if at the worst we could ask for more help and so on. The Air Vice Marshal answered with as much directness and produced, as he does, a great feeling of confidence...

Major Noel lunched with me yesterday and returned to Sulaimani last night. He described a situation in which he is hourly risking his life as a very interesting experience. He is what would be called at Eton mad--an enchanting adventurer, an immense understanding of the Kurd, and flawless courage

The main thing is to get the extremists and moderates to work together. At present the one is always on the alert to break the head of the other--I use the Arab idiom. It's very much on the principle of 'ôte-toi que je m'y mette'--there's often nothing else behind it...

I've been getting at the moderate party telling them they are quite disgracefully inactive...

I hear the King is overjoyed at the signature of the treaty. I went up and wrote my name with respectful congratulations yesterday but I haven't yet seen him. To-day I've been translating his really beautiful proclamation which will be published in English and Arabic tomorrow together with the treaty. I wish I had more time to do it properly; it demanded better work than could be put into the twenty-five minutes allowed me...

To H.B., Bagdad, October 24th, 1922

As for you and Uncle Lyulph you are the most remarkable people I know. I love to think of his trundling off to Perth, and I long to hear of your visit to Frankfort. Yes, your railway negotiations are not unlike things of which I have intimate knowledge and after all human affairs seem to be much the same all the world over...

The Cabinet at the request of the King, has appointed me honorary Director of Archaeology--there didn't seem to be any other way of keeping the place warm till we could afford a proper Director. The department to my great satisfaction, has been placed in the Ministry of Public Works, so that I am directly under my friend Sabih Bey and shall have the help of the architect Major J. M. Wilson, whom you remember pupil of Lutyens. I went over to the Ministry on Tuesday morning to have my first conference with the Minister about the Law of Excavation, which I've drafted...

Now that the treaty is signed the King is out to defend every line of it from the slightest breach of criticism. His own proclamation and his telegram to King George accurately reflect his state of mind. The Iradah for the holding of elections has been issued; registration of Directors begins this week and will last about six weeks--what with the somewhat cumbrous system of electoral colleges we shan't have the Constituent Assembly sitting till about January...The King is determined that it shall be an Assembly which will ratify the treaty and I think it will be.

October 25th. The news of the Cabinet appointments reached us last night. I'm so enchanted to have the Duke [of Devonshire] as our Minister that I've written to tell him so...

Registration of primary electors began yesterday...When I got in at six o'clock I found an urgent message from the King bidding me to dinner. Jafar, Nuri and Zaid were the party. We had a very merry dinner, during the course of which H.M. described the glories of Chatsworth, and played a game of Bridge afterwards, I teaching the

574

Amir Zaid. I like him more and more--and I never met anyone with such exquisite manners. Incidentally, I was wearing a new gold and white gown ...so I had a modest triumph too...I've had a terribly busy day. I was out, as usual, at six, riding (I came in past the Iraq Army parade and receive the salute of the units which happen to be drilling there) and when I got into the office at 8:15 I found Sir Percy champing for a draft of a telegram he wanted to send home, pointing out the disastrous effect that would result from the re-cession of Mosul to the Turks. So I proceeded to write it for him while he was at breakfast. I've no doubt he'll improve it in detail but the general lines were, if I may say, masterly. Having got that done I had to write the report for the Secretary of State, which goes fortnightly by air mail ...our successes against the Turks on the Kurdish frontier, the reception of the treaty and the King's plans. With an interval for lunch it took me till four o'clock, when I walked home and at once addressed myself to letters for the mail. I won't say I'm as active as you but still I do take my part in the affairs of the world, don't I?

To H.B., Bagdad, November 1st, 1922

I'm beginning this letter very early and shall close it early because the day after to-morrow I'm going to Mosul for a few days. It's this way : there has long been a promise that I shall personally conduct Major J. M. Wilson to Hatra. Round this kernel have solidified Capt. Clayton and Major Murray (just back from leave and posted to Mosul, to the regret of Captain Clayton and me) and we will set out on Friday night. We sleep a night at Shagat with the Arab Army as hosts, motor next day to Hatra where we spend the night à la grâce de Dieu (we have camp beds with us and the Shammar of Ajil al Yawar are in that neighbourhood and will, we hope, provide us with a sheep roasted whole and coffee) and then motor back to Qaiyarah where if we arrive late we may spend another night...

I've been figuring in my capacity as Director of Archaeology. Mr. Woolley arrived on Sunday. He is a first-class digger and an archaeologist after my own heart--i.e., he entirely backs me up in the way I'm conducting the department. He has come out as head of a joint expedition organised by the British Museum and Pennsylvania University and they are going to dig Ur, no less, and are prepared to put in two years' work. After lunch Sabih Bey and I went to a meeting of the Cabinet which I attended for the first time to explain and defend the

Law of Excavations which I had drafted. The Naqib and the Ministers made me affectionately welcome.

We passed to my law through which we laboured, clause by clause, for two hours I got it passed in principle but certain verbal alterations are still to be made in the Arabic text. When we had done I bowed myself out and went to a committee meeting of the Salam Library where it was my agreeable duty to present to them some 40 pounds worth of books, the response to my appeal to Sir Frederick Macmillan. Isn't it generous of him! ...I confidently expect that the Salam Library will soon be one of the best institutions in the East...

A deputation is coming down from Sulaimani to discuss the Kurdish question with H.E. and H.M. It has missed its train, as it naturally would, but it may possibly arrive tomorrow...

November 2nd. The deputation has come, fourteen in all, including their followers, and all armed to the teeth. They've put up at one of the smaller Hotels, from which they promptly ejected all other occupants. The landlord wilted and vanished into the cellar. Yet according to Major Noel their views are quite reasonable--not that he is a great judge of reasonableness, bless him--they are explaining them to Sir Percy this evening.

To H.B., Mosul, November 10th, 1922

...We motored straight across a heavenly rolling desert, across which I had ridden in 19 11 to Hatra. As we drew near we saw the Arab flag flying from the high vaults of the ruined palace and in the huge courtyard where the Arab Prince, liegeman of the Parthian kings, had sheltered his flocks in times of stress...

Hatra twice makes its appearance in the history of the world, the first time in 116 when Trajan besieged it twice, capturing it the first time and failing to take it the second after it had revolted from him. Then in 196 Septimus Severus in his turn besieged it twice and it held out against him both times. From that date it disappears from the ken of historians until Layard revisited its amazing ruins last century... At sunset I lay On the highest wall under the shadow of the Arab flag. I'd watched the light fall and fade across the universe of desert. Below me the camels and horses of Ajil's bairak strayed through the court and beyond the city wall the blue smoke from among the tents of a Shammar camp. It was a scene in which past and present were so bewilderingly mingled that you might have looked down upon its like any evening for twenty centuries...We left about nine and motored across the desert to the Mosul road which we joined at Qaiyarah, and so on through clouds of dust to Mosul...

There came to dinner Col. Rogers, O.C. of the Rajputs stationed here, and his Major named Johnson, both very nice, and Major Maclean (Arab Army), a charming person whom I already knew.

Next day, November 6th, I went down with Captain Flaxman to the Sarai and called on the Mutasatrif...He was chiefly preoccupied with the news from Zakho, on the extreme northern frontier, whence the Kaimmakam had the day before been sending alarmist telegrams to say that a Turkish and tribal attack was imminent and if more soldiers were not sent immediately he begged to resign. We did not feel very anxious because we knew that the new Inspector General of Levies, Colonel Dobbin, had arrived at Zakho the previous evening and that if there had been anything very serious he would have telegraphed. However Major Murray, Major Wilson, Captain Slater and I determined to pull on our chain armour, shoulder our muskets and go out next day to reinforce the Kaimmakam. And who so pleased as I?

So on November 7th we made a fairly good start about eight...An hour or two out we met Colonel Dobbin with his A.D.C. Unfortunately he was the bringer of bad news--the battle was off! ...

The Kaimmakam was all of a twitter--obviously not the man for a frontier post. Major Murray promised guns for the levy camp above the town-- they've now gone and I trust the Zakho valley reverberates with the sound of their practice. I've urged on Sir Percy that we shouldn't allow the Turks the advantageous position of heads I win and tails you lose. The guns they've heard; the Levies are ready, and behind them aeroplanes enough to obscure the light of the sun.

It was near sunset when we reached the Levy Camp which lies in a cup on the top of the foothills with the British flag flying on it...I occupied the hut of our hoot Captain Merry, a simple, cheerful, self-reliant young officer...We were waited on by four Assyrian boys, in full native dress--striped embroidered trousers, scarlet and yellow tassels flung over their shoulders under the white felt zouave jacket, white peaked caps with a white or scarlet feather at the side...

Before we left next day I inspected many of the huts--spotlessly clean, the women all dressed up in their best in anticipation of a visit, but their feathers are not so fine as those of the men. I went away much impressed. Truly we are a remarkable people. We save from destruction remnants of oppressed nations, laboriously and expensively giving them sanitary accommodation, teaching their children, respecting their faiths, but all the time cursing at the trouble they are giving us-and they're cursing us, not infrequently, for the trouble we are giving them with our meticulous regulations. And then behold, when left to themselves they flock to our standards, our Captain Merrys for their chosen leaders, our regulations their decalogue...And on all this we gaze without amazement. It's the sort of thing that happens under the British flag-don't ask us why, we don't know...

On the 15th I caught the train at Qaraghan and reached Bagdad on the 16th without incident except that the train was some six hours late-you know our ways. I arrived to find a political crisis, for which I was partly prepared by letter. The Naqib has resigned. It has happened quite simply and without anyone's feelings being hurt-the Cabinet has just died of inanition. So now they are busy Cabinet making as hard as they can go and with luck I think they may have a much stronger lot than before...

To-night Sir Percy goes off to the Persian Gulf--a long postponed conference which I hope will end in the conclusion Of a satisfactory treaty between Nejd and Iraq but it's rather agitating to have Sir Percy away when so many things are happening. We've had, however,, very reassuring telegrams from home about the attitude they are going to take up with the Turks in defence of the Iraq frontiers...

November 23rd. The new Cabinet is formed and is, I think, very good. Yasin Pasha goes to Public Works so I shall do my Archaeological dept. with him which I shall like. H.M. and the Cabinet are determined to take a strong line. It's needed, for the Shiah mujtahids have issued fatwahs forbidding people to take part in the elections...

To H.B., Bagdad, December 4th, 1922

Do you know-apropos of nothing at all-that I've been four times mentioned in dispatches for my valuable and distinguished services in the field! It came to me as a surprise--indeed it is singularly preposterous--when I counted up the documents in order to fill up a Colonial Office Form. I hadn't realised there were so many. Apparently one of the fields I distinguished myself in was Palestine, for I was mentioned by Sir Reginald Wingate...

I sent you by post the yearly report to the S. of S., a very silly sort of Xmas present. I wrote all the first general chapter and the next on administration, then the chapters on refugees and foreign relations. The other bits came from the respective departments. Mr. Slater's financial chapter is interesting and Mr. Davidson's judicial chapter. It was a tidy job putting it all together, but interesting.

To F.B., Bagdad, December 5th, 1922

Isn't it a shocking thing that four years after the armistice we should still see the world in such confusion...

But I would not have done what I'm doing here. I often wonder whether it is very selfish of me to have gone on with it. Life here has drawbacks, of course; there are long moments when I feel very lonely, but the work has been so interesting that as far as I am concerned I couldn't have experienced better or even as good, a destiny. My present plans are to come home on leave in May, arriving towards the end of the month If Sir Henry Dobbs wants me to return I should probably like to do so for another winter at any rate, but of course that's for him to say.

I can't think what it would have been like not to have had you and father taking such an interest in our doings, but this I know that you have added immensely to the pleasure of them. To write to you about them has been half the battle and you never seem bored however much I write.

December 7th. Sir Percy is still dallying in the Persian Gulf, not without profit, however, for he has got the Nejd-Iraq treaty ratified which Ibn Saud had refused to do. I knew I.S. would come round directly Sir Percy put the matter to him. What an amazing influence has my chief.

A very happy Xmas and all good things. The love of your children is always with you and I can't think that any of them can love you more than your daughter, Gertrude.

To H.B., Bagdad, December 16th, 1922

Sir Percy came back on the 11th with treaties all signed and finished in his hands. Ibn Saud is coming to the Iraq in the Spring to visit the King under Sir Percy's auspices. Sabih Bey, ex-Minister of Works, who went with Sir Percy as the King's representative told me that the matter is finished, that Sir Percy was magnificent and that Ibn Saud is convinced that the future of himself and his country depends on our goodwill and that he will never break with us. In point of fact the treaty is on exactly the lines that Sir Percy stipulated. I was glad to see him. It makes an immense difference having him back...

To H.B., Bagdad, December 18th, 1922

Major Young asked me whether I would accept appointment as Oriental Secretary, with the rest of Sir Percy's staff, till Oct. 1923 (which is to be the date of Sir Percy's own appointment). I said I would. So that's how matters stand. I shall hold the appointment till Sir Percy leaves at any rate. Major Young suggested that his successor might like me to stay on for a bit so as not to make a complete change all at once. I said, other things being equal, I should probably be able to do that, but of course it would depend largely on who the successor might be, and at that we left it. It has turned out very much as I should have wished because it's they who have asked me to stay and not I who am clinging on. I made it very clear to Major Young that I wasn't clinging on if they did not want me. What a strange political career I've had, to be sure...Oh for peace--peace at any price, I could almost say. I wonder if any generation was so weary of strife as we are. Jafar Pasha dropped into the office this morning for a talk. I wish there were more people of his integrity and moderation...Jafar's fidelity and devotion to the King are really beautiful. I know the man in every aspect and he is equally delightful in his affectionate chivalry towards his womenfolk, his adoration of his children and his fervent loyalty to Faisal, whom he regards (as indeed, I do also) as the one man who can lead the Arab cause to success.

We've another problem looming on our Southern borders. You know that Ibn Saud has captured Hayil, thereby changing the balance of Arabian politics. His frontier now runs with that of the Iraq and it's as yet an undefined frontier. Sir Percy has invited him to come into conference with himself and Faisal at the earliest possible moment, and I've been laying out on the map what I think should be our desert boundaries. There's nothing I should like so much as to attend that conference of Kings but I don't suppose for a moment that Sir Percy will take me... ...

The conquest of Hayil will have far-reaching consequences. It will bring Ibn Saud into the theatre of trans-Jordanian politics and probably into the Franco-Syrian vista also--it's difficult as yet to see with what results. I should, however, feel much greater anxiety if I weren't so certain of Sir Percy" power to guide him. It's really amazing that anyone should exercise influence such as his...I don't think that any European in history has made a deeper impression on the Oriental mind...

To H.B., Bagdad, December 31st, 1922

[Gertrude gives an account of a shooting party consisting of Mr. Davidson, Mr. Cornwallis and Major Murray besides herself.)

Our destination, the Shamiyah channel of the Euphrates, which runs parallel to the Mishkhab ...We poled up the river, stopping at any likely place on the banks to get out and shoot.

The Shamiyah Channel is much more beautiful than the Mishkhab. Willows and Euphrates poplars fringe the river, their red gold and amber frothing round the stiff green palms. The little straw villages lie closely in these woods and the white sails glitter down the river. Over all was a glorious sun shining through fresh keen air and we, plunging through the willows and the russet scrub, jumping over or into innumerable water courses, felt again the vigorous enchantment of that delightful place, the world...

At 4 a.m. we were up again and after a hasty cup of tea jumped into our boats and paddled down to the Hor. It was wonderful in the still night. The only sound was the talking of the geese, whom we were out to kill. But we didn't kill them--they were a great deal too many for us. Dawn was just beginning to break as we reached the Hor, the flocks of geese Were rising with immense chatter and disturbances, stringing out in long beautiful patterns across the pale sky, but ever so far above our heads. In the cold dawn we jumped out of our boats on to a wide desolate island in the middle of the Hor. There we scattered and finding what cover we could, lay and Watched the geese flighting. They were never really within shot, but that didn't make any difference to the beauty of it and for my part I couldn't tire of seeing the kingfishers hunting for their breakfast in their delightful fashion...

Christmas day was perhaps the best day we had, weather and sport and good spirits. We went by boat down the river, shooting all the way, till we got to the mouth of a loop canal, the Abu Tibn (Father of Straw) on which lives the paramount Sheikh of the Khazail...What we wanted to do was to shoot duck on the Hor, not to speak of geese, and we went out in tiny canoes...It was a delicious Hor full of beautiful flowering reeds and alive with water-birds--not much less alive after our visit I'm sorry to say. We got to the other side after sunset. The geese and ducks were flighting in thousands but all in the top of the sky. Nevertheless it was enchanting coming back under the moon and stars across the quiet Hor. The reeds brushed your boat softly, a sleepy goose raised his voice, a coot bustled over the water with noisy awkward flight and you lay in your boat and listened and wondered...And at mid-day on Thursday 28th, we were back in Bagdad, disgracefully sun and wind burnt, cheerful, fat and healthy...

To H.B., Bagdad, January 16th, 1923

The chief news is that Sir Percy is going home by this air mail to help the Cabinet to come to a conclusion about Iraq policy...It is far more satisfactory that he in person should go and put the whole case to the authorities, for you see, even if they don't want to shoulder the burden they have got to learn that it's amazingly difficult to let it drop with a bump. Even the evacuation of Mosul would mean, I am convinced that we should be faced with the problem of sixty to seventy thousand Christian refugees...

It is almost impossible to believe that a few years ago the human race was more or less governed by reason and considered consequences, before it did things. I don't feel reasonable myself--how can one when political values are as fluctuating as the currency? ...At the back of my mind I have a feeling that we people of the war can never return to complete sanity. The shock has been too great; we're unbalanced. I am aware that I myself have much less control over my own emotions than I used to have. I don't really feel certain about what I might do next and I can only hope that the opportunity for doing impossibly reckless things won't arise, if it did I should probably do them; at least I can't be sure I shouldn't...

It will be dreadfully flat when I return to London, not to be consulted about all Cabinet appointments!

Next came Sir Henry Dobbs for a good talk for which we really hadn't yet had an opportunity and we discussed Mesopotamia and history since the early days of the Occupation.

On Tuesday 9th I went to Diwaniyah with Major J. M. Wilson and Major Jefferies. Our object was to see the mound of Niffar which we did on the following day...Niffar is by far the most striking site I've seen here. It's so enormously big and the temple pyramid soars so high above the plain. Moreover you get a very clear impression of the topography of the town, from the old Nil canal, the forerunner of the Dagharah, cut through it, and it's easy to picture the huge temple with its library and divinity school on one bank and the commercial city on the other...you see in section age after age of civilization extending over a period of three or four thousand years. It's amazing and rather horrible to be brought face to face with millenniums of human effort and then to consider what a mess we've made of it, as I remarked above...

I got back to my house feeling as if I had travelled in nightmare trains for 10,000 hours at least.

I've been pretty busy these last two days picking up threads, writing reports for the mail and preparing things which Sir Percy wants to take with him. It's always the greatest pleasure to work for him and the fact remains that whatever I may do in the future I shall never have a chief whom I serve more whole heartedly than I serve him. The sense that one has gained his confidence, is I think the thing that I'm more proud of than anything else. He has, you know, been an angel of kindness and consideration to me...

To-night as I was coming back from the office very dirty and tired, I met Sir John Salmond and Air Commodore Borton on their doorstep and they dragged me in to a very Merry tea...I'm much attached to the Air Force; they have the same sort of charm that sailors have, they are so keen and so busy with their job, and it's a job that they are always at, just as sailors are. And they are so amazingly gallant. The things that they've done in this country without anything said about them, might be a theme for epics.

To H.B., January 18th

...I'm very glad to gather from your letter of Dec. 27th that there's every prospect of my predeceasing you, which is what I should wish to do. The world would be a poor place without you. I must have a talk with Sir Henry one day about plans, As at present arranged I've engaged berths for Marie and me on a ship that leaves Bombay on May 5th. ...Meantime I must break to Sir Henry that I'm going on leave and find out whether he wants me to come back. I don't like going just as he takes over but apart from seeing my family I think three consecutive summers here is enough...

To H.B., Bagdad, January 30th, 1923

...Seven years I've been at this job of setting up an Arab State. If we fail it's little consolation to me personally that other generations may succeed, as I believe they must...

I've been rather busy with archaeology. First I had long reports about Ur to write for my Minister and for the local papers and next I've had to tackle the Oxford University expedition to Kish--I was promised a field worker and an epigraphist and on that agreed to ask my

Minister for a concession, and lo and behold, one solitary man turns up...

I feel convinced that no one, however good, can undertake single handed so big a work as the excavation of Kish, so I've held up the concession and telegraphed for the advice of the joint Committee which is the highest archaeological authority at home--for convenience, I'm a member of it...

To H.B., Bagdad, February 13th, 1923

The relations between the Arabs and the British General Staff are most satisfactory. In times of stress like the present, Sir John takes supreme command of all forces and they work together without the slightest friction...

It was a delicious soft spring day yesterday and I rode out. To-day it has poured steadily almost all day, the heaviest rain we have had this month and very welcome though I tremble to think of the mud to-morrow. The streets were lakes this afternoon. And I had to run round with the Committee of the Salain Library and put off a performance we were going to have at the Cinema to-morrow for the benefit of the Library, because we felt sure that in this mud no one would come...

To-day, the roads have at last recovered from the rain. I rode down to Karradah and found the first apricots in flower in Haji Naji's garden. I have a bunch of flowering branches in my room now...

To H.B., Bagdad, March 1, 1923

Will you please do something for me. The King (with whom I've just been having tea) is in perplexity as to how to furnish a big room in the little palace that has just been built--a reception room. It's an awkward shape for it was meant for a dining room--170 paces long by about 70 wide with a monumental fireplace on one of the long sides. I've suggested that it must be somehow broken up in furnishing it and that he ought to make a central sitting place in the middle, opposite the fireplace, with three big handsome sofas, the middle one the most imposing. In this dusty country it's better to have furniture rather simple in pattern as otherwise it's difficult to clean, and we think that if we had some good drawings or pictures we could make it here. So could you perhaps send us a selection of catalogues or drawings from some of the best London shops by next air mail? We could get chairs and tables out of them too and make something that would do for the present. ...

I went to Ur with Major Wilson. They are closing down for the season and we had to go in person and divide the finds between the diggers and the Iraq...

It took us the whole day to do the division but it was extremely interesting and Mr. Woolley was an angel. We had to claim the best things for ourselves but we did our best to make it up to him and I don't think he was very much dissatisfied. We, for our part, were well pleased. The best object is a hideous Sumerian statue of a King of Lagach, about three feet high but headless.

It has a long inscription across the shoulder in which they have read the King's name, but it will go back to London to be completely deciphered and then return to us...

To H.B., Bagdad, April 10th, 1923

Thank you a thousand times for all the trouble you took about the King's furniture. He is delighted with the pictures. Major Wilson and I are going to have a great talk with him to-morrow and decide what he shall order ...

Sir Percy arrived safely on the 31st ...We're satisfied he thinks Parliament will agree to the scheme of the Cabinet Committee and that we can pull through on that though the economic conditions will be very difficult for the first few years. It's also settled that I should come back in September. I hate going away while the thing is still so much in the melting pot, but apart from my wish to see my family, I don't think I ought to stay a fourth summer on end and I shall come back more competent, we'll hope, to carry on the job...

Talking of archaeologists, isn't it terrible about Lord Carnarvon. And so extraordinarily tiresome that people should be given an opportunity to say it's a curse...

The floods have gone down, but it will be months before the desert East of Bagdad is dry. It is still a great sea of muddy water. They are digging a great cutin to the Diala to drain it off...

April 11th. We had a terrific day yesterday beginning with a great rush of work in the office, then at 12:30 an enormous lunch given by the Iraq Army. There were sports afterwards, but I got away early following H.M. who had commissioned Major Wilson and me to come and talk about the furniture...

To F.B., Bagdad, April 24th, 1923

I went to Hillah for the night on the 14th with Major Wilson and Dr. Herzfeld. We stayed with the Longriggs that night and next morning motored out about an hour to the East to see the excavations at Kish--I was inspecting, you understand. We found that Mr. Mackay had done a great deal of work at one of the mounds--the one for which I had got him a permit--but it was almost certainly not the oldest part of Kish which lies under another mound about a mile away. This second mound is covered with very ancient plans--convex bricks and very ancient pottery. I'm getting permission for him to do some preliminary work there...

Haji Naji gave a luncheon party in his garden last Sunday to Sir Percy. In spite of its being Ramadhan several of the Ministers came--scarcely any of them are fasting. It was a very charming little function and Haji Naji's sorrow at parting with Sir Percy goes to my heart. But fortunately he has made great friends with Sir Henry.

The hot weather has come in with a burst the last two days. The entertainments to Sir Percy continue. Yesterday we had in immense tea party in a garden--it was given by the Indian Mercantile community...To-day there's a dinner Of 200 people given by the civil community of Bagdad of whom I'm one. I'm one of four who propose the health of Sir Percy, Sir Henry, the A.V.M. and Col. Slater being the other three. How he'll hate our all talking about him.

All this time rather tears the heart strings, you understand, it's very moving saying good-bye to Sir Percy...We had the annual election of members of the Library Committee this Week. I came out top.

Last year I was third. They never elect any other European. That's the sort of thing that makes it difficult to leave.

To F.B., Bagdad, May 9th, 1923

This is I fear going to be a very scrappy letter for I'm rather overcome with departure...

Last week Sir Percy left--a very moving farewell...What a position he has made for himself here. I think no Englishman has inspired more confidence in the East. He himself was dreadfully unhappy at going--40 years service is not a thing one lays down easily.

To F.B., Haifa, May 21st, 1923

The Samuels [Sir Herbert Samuel was High Commissioner in Palestine] were extraordinarily kind. I had some interesting talks with them and felt great admiration for his breadth of view and honesty.

CHAPTER XXIII

SEPTEMBER 1923 TO JUNE 1924 - BAGDAD

To F.B., Bagdad, September. 11, 1923

Here's an interesting experiment: I am going to post this to-morrow by the overland mail, i.e. by car to Damascus. Will you tell me how many days it is on the way, for if it proves a success I shall write to you weekly instead of fortnightly.

I'm suffering from a violent cold in the head which I've caught from everybody else--there's a plague of colds. Mine began two days ago and to-day I hope to have nearly settled it by staying in all day. That seems absurd with the temperature at 100, but if I had gone out at all I should have had to dine with the King and sit under a punkah all the evening. So I made my excuse and he has kindly put me off till Friday. I was sorry not to go to-day because I haven't yet had a real good talk with him, other people being there when I dined with him before. However it doesn't matter much since things are going quite reasonably well.

Captain Clayton came down from Mosul on Thursday, the day I posted my last letter, with the Amir Zaid. He and Mr. Thomson and I dined with Haji Naji on Friday. That was a very delightful occasion, an excellent dinner spread on his roof over which nodded the tops of the mulberry trees--such broiled fish and such a lamb roasted whole and such figs from our host's garden! We dined about 7 and getting back early, the other two spent the rest of the evening with me. I had had a dinner party the night before, the Lloyds (he is Mr. CornWallis's assistant in the Interior and I like both him and his wife) Mr. Jardine from Mosul, Assistant Inspector, and a nice man called Mackay in the A.P.O.C. I enjoy seeing them all again.

On Saturday I rode out to see the Arab Army play polo. Mr. Thomson plays with them and all their British officers; they are getting quite good. But it's sad to ride out over that great stretch of desert which had been converted first by our army into a wonderful farm and was then taken over by the King. The floods of last spring have sent it back to desert, the roads are blotted out, the irrigation channels half filled in and the young trees which the King planted in hundreds, all killed or uprooted. And all the desert which was under water is horrid to ride on, covered with a cracked mud surface and full of holes.

I've had a fearful brawl in my household--not the fault of my household fortunately. You remember Mr. Thomson dismissed my gardener, Mizhir, and installed a brother in his place. When I came back Mizhir turned up at once expecting to be reinstated. I refused and finding him a day or two ago making claims to draw water at my pipe I forbade him to come into my garden. Yesterday while I was at the office and Zaya and the new gardener, Jaji Marzuq, were out being inoculated for cholera (doubly inoculated to show 'bonne volonté') did Mizbir and two other brothers come in and beat Haji Ali, my inestimable cook, over the head. Haji Ali quite rightly hauled Mizhir off to the police station next door and I who was lunching at home because of the cold in my head telephoned to a British Inspector. And then I heard shouting and screaming in the street and behold there was Mizhir let out and one of his brothers struggling in the arms of some privates of the Levies with the evident intention of renewing their proceedings with me or any other victim. So I had the police up at once and clapped all three into the police station. So I hope that's happily concluded.

I've been spending such part of the day as was not taken up in telephonic communication with the police in writing an article about the Iraq for the Round Table. They don't want it in till the end of October however, so I shall have to let it lie for a bit till I can tell of the result of the elections and see how the preliminary negotiations with the Turks are going.

Sept. 12. I'm better and have come into office--now I must go to the Minister of Justice to discuss the law with Mr. Drower.

THE LETTERS OF GERTRUDE BELL

To H.B., Bagdad, September. 17, 1923

It's been rather hot since I wrote, temp. up to 110 daily and the heavy mugginess which we generally get in September. However, it's needed to ripen the dates which are very late this year and still hanging quite unripe on the trees. I love to see them, it's the nicest part of dates, the great yellow crown of bunches, and as far as I'm concerned they may remain unripe as long as they please.

It's been very touching the welcome I've had from the big tribal people. Several of them have come in from as far as Diwaniyah on purpose to see me and I don't think one could mistake the fact that they're glad of my return. I feel rather ashamed of the immense confidence they place in one when I consider how little any of us can do really. They trust us as they never trust their own people and they think we have behind us the concentrated force of Great Britain entirely at our disposal, in any matter connected with the Iraq...

To H.B., September. 25th, 1923

I'm again going to write by the overland mail... The Waring and Gillow furniture has come--it's rather lighter in build than I expected and some of our Iraqis are weighty people...

On Saturday there was a huge dinner party at the Palace in honour of Sir Henry's accession to the High Commissionership. I sat by Zaid who next morning sent me two guinea pigs as a present--I felt as if I had retired into my remotest childhood as I installed them in a cage in my garden. ...And last night, we spent a delicious evening. Saiyid Hashim, the Naqib's son, invited Mr. Thomson, Ken and me to dine in the Turjmaniyah garden--away towards the Diala. It was a full moon and we loved motoring down and arriving in the peaceful coolness of the garden. We dined on the roof with the famous eucalyptus trees towering over us, and the sweet silence broken only by the gentle ripple of talk...

We're having great dealings with the Ministry of Pious Bequests in the matter of our library. It's finances are in a bad way and I can't go on struggling to get money for it, so we've conceived the idea of offering ourselves bodily to Auqaf and are now in negotiation with the Minister who favours the suggestion. We discussed it at length at a Committee meeting yesterday, after which I went round to call on Mina Abdud, a wealthy Christian lady. And there dropped in an old Christian of high repute who is a member of the central electoral committee. With him came the Director of Health, and then Jafar Pasha, and we sat gossiping till it was time for me to go away.

You know I do enjoy myself here. I like being in the middle of this Arab world and on the terms I'm on with it, but I confess even now I have moments of amazement at finding how much we're in the middle of it--for instance when I looked round Sheikh Ali's luncheon table at all those turban-murbans on either side of me!

To H.B. and F.B., Bagdad, October 1st, 1923

All the R'ton doings sound very pleasant, it's curious to have been so lately part of them and now to be so rapt again in to the life of Iraq. But I am immensely happy here, there's no doubt of it...My work in the office grows more interesting--I've got all the tribal questions into my hands now...

J.M. is full of his furnishings and decorations and I send you separately a drawing of a bit of the King 's throne for which we want a bit of stamped leather. Would you be so very angelic Father or Mother, to order it for me?

I'm so very sorry to see the death of Aubrey in the telegrams, I feared he was spinning a bad cotton when I saw him in London.

Oct. 4th. We had a terrific orgy last night! The dinner was excellent, Marie having supplied her best sauces and afterwards we played a preposterous game of cards invented by Capt. Clayton with pistachios, for counters. Ken Cornwallis kept the score and so well that at the end everyone was proved to have won. Unfortunately no one could pocket his winnings as there was no one to pay, so we ate the pistachios and separated in peace.

The temp. is rapidly falling--it's been down to a maximum of 95, very pleasant.

To H.B., Bagdad, October 13th, 1923

My article for the Round Table has also been approved by Sir Henry so it goes to Sir Percy by this mail. It's rather lifeless, I think, but at any rate it puts our case and it's a very encouraging story. On Friday I had a perfectly charming dinner with the Prime Minister en famille. The Minister of justice and his wife were also there. All the women are Turks of C'ple. They scarcely talk Arabic--Muhsin's wife talks none but his sister-in-law and her pretty daughter have learnt some. N.'s wife was very prettily dressed in a blue crêpe de chine gown. It was very agreeable and friendly...

I had to work 8 solid hours that day on a despatch Sir Henry had asked me to draft for him no less than a comprehensive statement of the whole Iraq case for the frontier negotiations. I was very glad H.E. asked me to do it and it interested me immensely. Moreover he is pleased with it. It will now have to be shown to the King and the P.M...

I've been spending most of the morning at the Ministry of Works where we are starting--what do you think? the Iraq Museum! It will be a modest beginning, but it is a beginning...

To H.B., Oct. 30th, 1923

The Naqib, the last time I saw him, expressed the hope that You had observed in what superior Arabic his letter was written. Few, he said, would have produced one like it. I replied that I had called your attention to the fact. There was a glorious stormy sunset and the tallest rainbow I've ever seen. It went on long after the sun was below the horizon, lifting itself higher and higher above the earth till it nearly touched the zenith. Light rains now are very beneficent. The weather has become delightful, a temperature rarely above 89 and cold dawns...

My household is in a great jig about the King's coming to dinner and Marie has quickly made a complete new set of lovely shades for the electric lights! ...It has begun to rain--it has been showery for the last two days. It's nice and early for rain; all the desert tribes will go out to pasture and keep quiet...

THE LETTERS OF GERTRUDE BELL

To H.B., Bagdad, Nov. 7th, 1923

I seem to have been socially very busy. On Friday morning we had the formal inauguration of the American School of Archaeology. There's no concrete school as yet because there's no money and no Director and no nothing. But I made the acquaintance of a charming man, Dr. Hewett, head of the American school in Mexico. He and his wife came to see me in the evening...On Sunday, the weather being heavenly, I got on to a pony at 10 o'clock and rode off to Fakhamah, 10 miles above Bagdad to see an old friend of mine, Faiq Eff. He greeted me with open arms and insisted on giving me lunch; very good it was, a ragout, sour curds and burghul, a sort of crushed wheat. While it was being prepared we walked in his date gardens and he told me of his recent journey to Syria to see a boy of his who was at the American College at Beyrout and has now gone to England to study. I've written to Professor Denison Ross about him...

Did I tell you that Rishan has been missing for nearly a fortnight? He turned up to-day, very thin and very explanatory. But he doesn't say where he has been.

To H.B., Bagdad, Nov. 14th, 1923

On Sunday I had Ken to dinner to meet Dr. and Mrs. Hewett. He's head of the American school in Mexico and told us most interesting things about American archaeology and anthropology. I expect you know--I didn't-- that while they have all the ancient beasts they haven't ancient man. He didn't develop there and America was peopled from Asia via Behring Straits--at quite a comparatively late period.

The Hewetts have now gone to Mosul. They're charming people, both of them. When they come back I'm going to take her to see an Arab family. She has never been in the East before and is deeply interested in everything.

Thank you both a thousand times for your kind shoppings and writings. In reply to Mother, I'm afraid the brocades will be too expensive but I long for the patterns to arrive.

THE LETTERS OF GERTRUDE BELL

To H.B., Bagdad, Nov. 21st, 1923

The Hewetts left. He wants me to come and lecture in America, but I shall not; think of the newspaper interviews!...

Sir Henry is in Basrah, meeting Lady Dobbs; I'm looking forward very much to her coming. It will be very amusing to have someone so alert and intelligent.

Nov. 22nd. Major Maclean tells us there's a new race game which everyone in London is playing. That would be the very thing When I have sticky dinner parties with people who don't play Bridge. Would you be very kind and send me this apparatus if it's not expensive...

To H.B., Bagdad, Nov. 29th, 1923

My chief news is the arrival of Lady Dobbs. We all went to meet them at the station on Friday and found that Sabih Bey had spontaneously arranged an elegant reception, carpets on the ground and a police guard, the King's chief A.D.C. and all the officials. Poor Lady Dobbs was rather taken aback.

She has with her a little cousin, Miss Miller, very bright-eyed and alert; she is learning Arabic for all she is worth. The meeting over I hurried home--it was 2 p.m. and found the magnates of the wilderness waiting in my garden by appointment--I had arranged to photograph them. Audah Abu Tai, Nuri al Shalan who is Fahad Bey's opposite number in Damascus--head of the western--and Ali Sulaiman of the Dulaim, our Dularn of the Euphrates.

I shall now stop photographing for I have done my masterpiece with Audah and I shall not be able to approach it. I'll send you a copy next week-- it's a magnificent engraving. But then he's a fine subject, the old eagle.

On Saturday afternoon we all went to the races, H.M. and Their Exs. It was Lady Dobbs' introduction to our world and she was much entertained. Lady D. is an angel to me.

We were all rather beaming on Saturday because the Cabinet had just been finally settled quite satisfactorily...Things are going almost incredibly well...

To H.B., December 6th 1923

I was having tea with H.M., it was the loveliest oriental scene. He was sitting in his garden near a fountain in full Arab dress, the white and gold of the Mecca princes. And by him, sitting on the stone lip of the fountain, were three of the great chiefs of the desert...Every where round them, tossed over the fountain edge, lying in swathes in the garden beds, gold and orange marigolds--waves and waves of them, with the white and yellow of chrysanthemums above them, echoing the King's white and gold. And the low sun sending long soft beams between the willow birches and the palms, brushing the gold and the orange the white and yellow into a brighter glow. Such a talk we had, too, of the desert and its secular strife...

To H.B., Bagdad, December. 11th, 1923

I've made a new friend, the Director of Operations at the W.O. General Burnett Stuart, who has been out to have a look at us. I sat by him at dinner at the Air Marshal's on Thursday and told him things a General ought to know--all through dinner from beginning to end...

The new railway crosses Euphrates by the Barraya and runs through the lovely gardens that gird Karbala. We got in about noon, glorious weather and an enthusiastic reception. I send you a picture of H.M. after he had cut the ribbons across the track, waiting for the trains to steam into the stations. Next to him is Sir Henry, then Col. Tainsh, Director of Railways, then H.M.'s chief A.D.C. then me. The Iraq flag flies from the engine. Then we went under a tent awning, gaily embroidered with carpets spread beneath, where the King received all the notables and sheikhs--he did it with a charming grace. So we sat down in rows, I between H.E. and the Mutasarrif on H.M's right hand and all the sheikhs in their brown robes and the turbaned gentlemen in their black and white; and a cinched, black-visaged Shiah got up and made a speech about the hope of Arab union resting in the King and his family... Next a boy scout read a poem in honour of the King and at the end coupled "Long live the King" with "Long live the

High Commissioner." And after another poem from a school boy, H.M. got up with a fine reply in thanks, his best manner, ending with a great phrase in which he expressed his assurance of success "because we walk hand in hand with the mightiest Power in the world."

To H.B., Bagdad, December. 31st, 1923

[They go for a shooting party.]

We collected beaters in the little village at bridge head and walked down the right bank of the arm of the Euphrates called Abu Shorah for 3 hours. It was glorious. The sun grew hotter and hotter as we walked through the poplar thickets and the green tamarisk scrub and thorns where the partridge lie. We got 55 brace to three guns-- Rasim is nothing of a shot and that day didn't hit a bird. At the last we reluctantly decided that we must turn back, crossed the river and shot a gorgeous island, at the end of which the birds rose in great coveys. Unfortunately we had neglected to take any food with us, so having shot 3 hours down we shot 3 hours up and were rather hungry and thirsty before we got back to the cars. Not that it mattered; we had had such tremendous fun that nothing mattered. Also Mr. Yapp deserves a testimonial, for he had made me such a fine pair of boots, lacing up to the knees, that though, as a rule, my skin comes off if you so much as look at it, after 6 hours hard walking I wasn't even rubbed. My costume, I must tell you, was a most successful creation--brown boots up to the knees and a brown tweed tunic down to them. We got back to Babylon an hour after sunset, washed, dined and went to bed. The whole 6 days we were there we never saw Babylon by daylight. We were off an hour before sunrise--aided by a full moon, and home after nightfall.

We shot for another hour after lunch and then motored home. It was a good Xmas Day spent with friends. Altogether I think no more delightful expedition has ever been made in Iraq.

Now everyone but me has gone to a fancy dress ball and I'm ending the year by writing to you,

I must tell you a curious problem that arose--I hope you'll think I decided rightly. To-morrow Sir Henry gives an official dinner to the King, Cabinet and Advisors, a male dinner. He told me about it before I went to Babylon and I made no comment except approval. When I came back I found an invitation to myself and I went to him and asked him, as man to man, whether he wanted me to come. He said "yes of course if you won't feel smothered." I said I thought, as a high official in his office, I was sexless and that I ought to come and would. Sir Percy, on these occasions (levees and so on) always treated me simply as an official and I don't think there's any other way. So I'm going,

Jan. 3, 1924. I spent New Year's Day from 10 a.m. to 5 p.m. receiving visitors. It was fatiguing but I felt rewarded when one of MY guests observed with satisfaction "the habits of the Khatut, are like ours--she sits at home on the Id to receive congratulations."

The dinner party at the Residency was a very small affair. I wore my best gown, our diamond tiara, Mother, and all my orders. Don't wish me back too much, life is being so interesting.

To H.B., Bagdad, Jam 9th, 1924

...I don't think I quite agree as to the possibility of submerging civilization. We're too self-conscious, too analytical and we've got too many means of exposing our views. We've broadcasted civilization in a way the Romans couldn't--I think it has sown too many seeds. Nevertheless your letter was very interesting. I'm not the least sorry that Labour should come in. They'll learn that it's not an easy thing to govern a large empire and they'll learn, I hope, that they don't know the nature of team work and that govt. as far as the individual is concerned is always a compromise. No one permanently has things exactly his own way of thinking except the dictator or the tyrant, who is 'ex- hypothesi' excluded. But is he?

To H.B., Bagdad, January. 9th, 1924

...I am planning on my way down to Ur a two days' jaunt by myself in the desert. I hope the scheme will come off. I want to feel savage and independent again for two days instead of being a Secretary in a High Commissioner's Office.

Mr. Woolley at Ur has been making wonderful finds and has written urgently to me to go down. So I'm going next Sunday, taking Kish en route--And I've a great scheme for visiting some mounds this side of Nasiriyah which I hope will come off.

To H.B., Bagdad, January. 22nd, 1924

I'll tell you the human details of my tour of inspection. I left Bagdad on Sunday 13th with J. M. Wilson and we went by train to Hillah. It was grey stormy weather and there had been rain in the night. We arrived at Hillah about 2 p.m. and found a taxi to take us the 12 miles into the desert to Kish.

We began our adventures by falling into the first canal, just outside the railway station--at least our front wheel was well over the narrow bridge. However, I called up support from the station and we pushed the car over. As we went on it behaved in a fashion madder and madder. Finally when the car in the open plain, began to spin round like a teetotum J.M. declared that he would not risk his precious life any longer. On examination it was proved that the sole connection between the steerage and the front wheels was a wire which had snapped; I wandered off to look for help. Sure enough I found a boy walking from Hillah to Kish. I bade him go back to Hillah, tell the Administration Advisor or the Mutasarrif to send us a relief car, gave him an eye glass case to serve as an identification badge and relieved him of his cloak and kerchief full of pomegranates which he was carrying so that he might run quicker. He set off at a fast trot and I returned to J.M. We walked for an hour and a half through rain and mud, to Kish where we were welcomed by Professor Langdon and Mr. Mackay. No car subsequently turned up and consequently no baggage. We spent the time before dinner in looking at their wonderful finds, and after dinner in discussing ancient Babylon sites with Professor Langdon. And then we went to bed in tents and slept soundly--at least I did anyway.

Next morning there was a thick white mist which gradually cleared into bright sunshine. The boy turned up and said the Mutasarrif would send out no car until he heard further from me and he reclaimed his cloak and pomegranates. Accordingly I despatched another boy with a letter. We spent 3 hours walking over the site and examining

599

the excavations. When we got back to the tents at 11 o'clock there was no car, so I climbed to the top of the zigurrat, hailed in 4 horsemen and requisitioned their horses, on two of which J.M. and I mounted and prepared to ride into s Hillah. But we hadn't gone ten minutes when we espied two cars, in one of which was the baggage. J.M. had by this time missed his train to Bagdad, but I had time to catch mine; so I jumped into the car and arrived without accident at Hillah.

Next day Tuesday 15th, my carriage was slipped at Khidhr Station before dawn. After an early breakfast I went down to the river, crossed in a ferry to Khidhr village and presented myself at the house of the Mudir, who provided me with a horse and escort to ride to Warka, which is Erah, the great Babylonian capital of the South. When we reached the mound we found quantities of people digging and rounded them up. They all screamed and cried when they saw me, but I gave them the salute and they were comforted. I said "Have you any anticas?" "No," they answered, "by God no." I observed, "What are those spades and picks for? I'll give you backsheesh for anything you have." At that a change came over the scene and one after another fumbled in his breast and produced a cylinder or a seal which I bought for the museum at a few annas. The people came from a little village, Hasyah, about a mile away and I sent them off to bring all that was there while I examined the mounds. They 'returned while I was lunching on the zigurrat and I bought a quantity of terra cottas. I rode to the village and then back to Khidhr and back to my carriage.

In the night I was carried down to Ur junction where I arrived at dawn on Thursday and walked out to Ur mound in the bitter cold of the early morning, to meet Mr. Woolley just coming back from the excavations to breakfast--a meal of which I partook heartily.

We spent the morning looking at their finds and at the excavations and the afternoon examining the Tall al Ubair site which gave me the greatest sensation, I think, which in archaeology I have ever experienced.

I left Ur on Friday night, got to Bagdad on Saturday afternoon and spent the whole evening up to 1 a.m. in writing my report.

On Sunday J. M. took me to the Ministry, where I deposited all that I had brought in the Museum.

Then I went to the house of Madame Jafar Pasha to attend a meeting of a women's club which is just coming into being. I am wholly in favour of it--it's the first step in female emancipation here.

Lionel Smith came to dinner to pour out his woes and be comforted by my tales of what happened to mankind 6,000 years ago. When you see their immensely old things your own troubles don't seem to matter.

We're longing to know who is to be S. of S. But already I find myself writing to him shadow-cast-before reports and despatches quite different from those I used to write to His Grace. It is curious--one insensibly finds oneself wanting to bring out different points, better ones often. I believe I shall feel at home with a Labour Government. I have written quite a good despatch to-day about Anglo-French relations I do hope Sir Henry will approve of it.

To H.B., February, 1924

This time Mother's letter has missed and I have yours of Jan. 22. Very interesting about the rly strike; I long to hear what you think of the settlement. Also a delightful analysis of your children, only the second thing that I am I can't read, so I remain only an Imperialist. Well, if I am, I contend that it's in the best sense for I've directed all my efforts to detaching a large kingdom--for the good of the Empire! Anyhow, you're sorely tried, to be sure, but I'm glad you're fond of us.

On Sunday I spent the morning at my museum editing the labels. This sort of thing: I pick up a little marble fragment of a horse's neck and mane and find it labelled thus "This is a portion of a man's shoulder, marble object."

"But," say I "does a man grow a mane on his shoulder?" "True, by God," murmurs the Chalabi.

I forget what day it was that I was overtaken by an idea, but it came about this way. Col. Tainsh, Director of Rlys, came one morning to ask me who could possibly write a little account of all the places of interest you could get to by his railways--in view of the tourists who will come by car from Damascus, you understand. So I said I could, which was what he wanted. And thinking over it, I said (to myself) damn it all! Why shouldn't I write Murray's Guide for the Iraq. I began it that day, but I haven't so far gone on, except to write to john Murray about it. It's a good idea but I'm now rather taken aback to think of the amount of writing and writing that it will mean. What do you think?

Oh dear, I wish I weren't so cold.

To H.B., February. 13th, 1924

On Tuesday afternoon I pursued my explorations round Kadhimain. This time I was looking for a house described by Herzfeld with an Assyrian statue on its roof. I found the house, standing outside the town, but nothing on the roof. But as I rode round it I espied half an elephant planted on the top of the courtyard wall over the door. It's unusual to see half an elephant standing on a wall--it may be a hippopotamus; I don't think I can distinguish between the hindquarters of an elephant and a hippopotamus except by the size and this one was only 3 feet high--so I rode into the court and asked who lived there. It was a very tumbledown place and the proprietor, or rather caretaker, was to match; but when he appeared he greeted me with joy and announced that he had been the servant of Miss Cheesman and had often seen me before. He evidently thought that I had come to ask if I could do anything for him. I asked if there were an idol in the house. "Oh, yes," he said, and taking me into the inner court, lifted up a mat, and there was the Assyrian statue. It's very roughly blocked out but so like a statue of Semiramis that was found at Assam that Herzfeld thinks it may be no other than she. It is said to have been brought from Babylon. Only the upper part remains, down to about the waist. It seems to have bobbed hair; Sir Henry says it must be Semiramis as a flapper. But I must have it for my museum. This may be easy for the house belonged to the late Sir Iqbal al Daulah, a British subject, and I understand that we administer his property.

(I shall have the elephant; it was brought from India 60 Years ago by Sir Iqbal).

I rode home by the river through the gardens of Kadhimain.% over the ground on which stood the palace of Harun al Rashid, but I wasn't thinking so much of him as of the fact that spring had come (Haji Naji sent me apricot flowers last week) the grass growing so beautifully green along the water channels and the buds showing on the pomegranates. And this naturally made me want to grow and open too, things almost impossible to do in an office.

So that evening, I being at dinner with the King--the party Ken and me, the Joyces and Col. Vincent and Yasin Pasha--Zaid began arranging to go out shooting tomorrow, I said I would come too. We go in the afternoon by car to a place near Baquba where Zaid sends out tents, shoot the evening flight of ducks and the morning flight at dawn next day, and then anything we can get all day long and the evening flight at night; sleep in net tents again and motor back at dawn. Doesn't it sound nice.

It's rather warmer today. When I came in at 4 from the office I found Marie sitting in the garden looking like a female St. Jerome, with a needle for a book, a slughi dog for a lion and a tame red-legged partridge standing solemnly beside her instead of a quail.

To H.B., Bagdad, February. 20th, 1924

On Sat. I had a hard day in the office--8:30 to 6 as hard as I could go. But you know, Father, I really am glad I'm not one of the unemployed. I can hold up my head and tell people that I do an 8-9 hours' day. That's what I have been doing these days--there has been a fearful amount of work.

Unfortunately, as soon as I got out of the sun, the cold came back. I stayed in all Sunday and did a lot of work...A very cheerful evening only I felt rather ill...

However, Monday was the day for writing the report to the Sec. of State, so I had to be early and late in the office...Yesterday again there was a terrific rush at the office.

Today I felt really ill--I'm better this evening so don't be anxious. I spent the morning at the office writing eloquent memos and came home after lunch to write to you. Now I've got to draft before dinner H.E.'s despatch to General ---

Goodbye, I lead a life almost as full as yours and I can't say better than that.

To H.B., Bagdad, February 27th, 1924

The sensation of the week is the elections, the results of which are coming out daily. Bagdad was declared on Monday. On the whole very good and such other reports as are in are good too...

I went with my minister to see the Bagdad orphanage. It's a very touching place, 85 boys from 6 to about 14 whom they've picked up in the streets. And there they all are, dressed as boy scouts, clean and tidy and being taught. The subscription lists are really wonderful.

Not money only is given--a bag of rice, a plate of cakes, people give what they can. And it's the first time it has ever occurred to any one in Bagdad to support a public institution of this kind and not to expect that dim entity, the Govt., to do it for him. They made a tremendous fuss about our coming, of course.

There were perturbations about my Sunday dinner party. I had asked a perfectly charming French traveller, Laurent-Vibert, a Lyonnais, He is going to translate Amurath into French--so he says.

To F.B., Bagdad, February, 28th, 1924

Would you be so obliging as to buy me a sun helmet. It's not as easy as you think because I'm very fussy about them. I scarcely feel the sun and only use a helmet for riding and I like it exceptionally small and light. I've now found the place to go for it, Woodrow, 46 Piccadilly. It's to be covered with cream-coloured tussore--I hate drill...

My guide book is becoming so exciting. The part I shall not like is writing the introduction about the coinage being rupees and annas, and that kind of thing. However I haven't got to that yet.

Confidential. This is what Sir Henry has written to the Col. Office about me in his annual report on his officers:

'It is difficult to write of Miss Bell's services both to the British and Iraq Govts., without seeming to exaggerate. Her remarkable knowledge of this country and its people and her sympathy with them enable her to penetrate into their minds, while her inextinguishable faith prevents her from being discouraged by what she sometimes finds there. Her long acquaintance with the tribes and sheikhs makes her advice in the recurring crises in tribal affairs invaluable and her vitality and width of culture make her house a focus of all that is best worth having in both European and Arab society in Bagdad. She is in fact a connecting link between the British and Arab races without which there would be dislocation both of public business and of private amenities.'

To H.B., Bagdad, March 6th, 1924

Oh dear, I've been so busy that I haven't written any letters and to- morrow is the mail. On Friday after lunch J. M. Wilson and I took the so-called express and went to Ur to do the division. We arrived at 5:10 a.m. on Sat. and Zaya having omitted to wake me, I had a bare half hour to get up and pack my bed and things. So I jumped up and put on my clothes, neither washed nor did my hair, and J.M. and I, with old Abdul Qadir, my curator walked out to Ur in the still dawn. It's about a mile. We arrived before sunrise, found no one up and went off to the Zigurrat to see the uncovered stair. It's amazing and unexpected, a triple stair laid against the Zigurrat with blocks of masonry between the stairways. It's latest Babylonian--Nabonidus, after Nebuchadnezzar--and must cover an Ur 3rd dynasty stair of which as yet we know nothing. We climbed up it to the top and watched the sun rise over the desert which was green with grass and covered with flocks and tents. By this time the workmen began to arrive, saluting us as Pasha (I'm going up in rank); and next Mr. Woolley, so we marvelled at the stair and all the rest and I went back to the house to wash, summarily and do my hair. By 8.15 when breakfast was ready I felt rather as if I had been up since the creation of the world, or at least since the time of Nabonidus. However that wasn't what we had to think about. Before 9 we started the division (it began by my winning the gold scarab on the toss of a rupee) and we carried on till 12:30, when I struck. It's a difficult and rather agonizing job, you know. We sat with our catalogues and ticked the things off. But the really agonizing part was after lunch when I had to tell them that I must take the milking scene. I can't do otherwise. It's unique and it depicts the life of the country at an immensely early date. In my capacity as Director of Antiquities I'm an Iraqi official and bound by the terms on which we gave the permit for excavation. J.M. backed me but it broke Mr. Woolley's heart, though he expected the decision. I've written to Sir F. Kenyon explaining.

I took very little of the bronze; we can't preserve it properly, and I gave them their choice with the door post stones.

By this time it was 3 P.M. J.M., poor dear, retired to bed with fever, and Mr. Woolley and I, undaunted, went on alone. We finished after 5 p.m. and I went to tea feeling so broken that all I could do afterwards was to play Patience with Mr. Newton till 7 when I left to catch my train...

On Sunday I spent the whole day in the train writing the guide book to Bagdad, which I finished. I wrote 11 foolscap pages and then for the last 2 hours buried myself in a novel. We got in at 6:15, only 11 hours late.

On Monday I had to write the fortnightly report for the Sec. of State which took from 8: 15 till 5. So that was that.

I had a dinner party in the evening to meet a Mrs. Harrison, an American traveller and writer and an exceptionally brilliant woman.

[The following extract from a long article written by Mrs. Marguerite Harrison in the New York Times, shows, on the other hand, the impression made on her by Gertrude.

"When I was first in Bagdad in 1923 I had the privilege of seeing Gertrude Bell on many occasions and of having several long talks with her. The first time I met her was by appointment at her office in the Administration building of the High Commission near the British Residency--across the Tigris from the present City of Bagdad...

"After waiting for a few moments I was ushered into a small room with a high ceiling and long French windows facing the river. It was the untidiest room I had ever seen, chairs, tables and sofas being littered with documents, maps, pamphlets and papers in English, French and Arabic. At a desk piled high with documents that had over-flowed on to the carpet sat a slender woman in a smart sports frock of knitted silk, pale tan in colour. As she rose I noticed that her figure was still willowy and graceful. Her delicate oval face with its firm mouth and chin and steel-blue eyes and with its aureole of soft grey hair, was the face of a'grande dame.' There was nothing of the weather-beaten hardened explorer in her looks or bearing. 'Paris frock, Mayfair manners.' And this was the woman who had made Sheikhs tremble at the thought of the Anglez!

"Her smile was completely disarming as was the gesture with which she swept all the papers from the sofa to the floor to make room for me ..."]

To H.B., Bagdad, March 12th, 1924

...Saturday the 15th was the anniversary of the Nahdhah, the Arab Awakening, i.e. of their joining in the war in 1916, and the cere-monies fixed for it were (a) a review of Iraq troops, (b) the laying of the foundation stone of the central building of the University of Al al Bait, (c) the opening of the Divinity School of that University, Faisal having laid the first brick two years ago.

Mr. Cooke dashed in on Thursday evening and asked me to write the leader for the papers about it. So I jumped up at 5:30 a.m. on Friday and complied. It was very important to get the right note. The functions were wonderful; for the first time I felt that we really had wakened up and become a nation. The review was at 9 on the Arab polo ground. Ken and I drove out and as we went saw the boy scouts marching along to line the roads. The whole town turned out, and the King taking the salute and looking so happy, Sir Henry, Sir John Sal-mond and all their staffs and all the notables, and Fahad Bey our great nomad sheikh, standing as close as possible to the King and Zaid. The troops were wonderful--as smart as could be, and all our soldiers said that they had accomplished a miracle in the last year.

When that was over, we went on to the Al al Bait. It's in a charming spot, barley growing under palms and nabk trees--thick evergreen trees- and the road running through the middle to the great dome of your imagination...

Then the King came, walking down on the carpeted path under the palm trees, between rows of clapping people. Presently they went up onto the platform and I slipped after them and not only got my photograph but heard what was said. And it was memorable, for after H.M. had laid the stone, Saiyid Mahmud, the Naqib's son, read a prayer in the name of King Faisal son of H.M. King Hussain ibn Ali Amiral Muminin and Khalifat al Muslimin. I must say my heart gave a jump--the Khalifat back to the Arabs!

Next came the opening of the Divinity School; the police were wonderful; the place was packed with cars and carriages and we all got away without any difficulty at all. Ken's chauffeur was on the look out for me, caught me and packed me into the car. We drove back together rejoicing, oh rejoicing so much. We agreed the time hadn't quite come to say our Nunc Dimittis, but we thought it would be appropriate to embark on the opening verse of some song of thanksgiving or other.

What do you think, we spent a riotous evening being taught Mah Jong by Capt. C.! We loved it and mean to go on with it when we've time. Wasn't it lucky I had it.

On Sunday Ken took us with him to the Sarai, for I was going to my museum, and there I fell into one of the worst passions I've ever been in. I found old--- mending the flowers from Ur with huge blobs of plaster of Paris so that the stone petals quite disappeared in them. I told him he was never to mend anything again and sent for a friend of mine, an antiquity dealer to repair the damage which he has done.

After that, feeling rather upset, I came home and arranged flowers and played in my garden...

Next day, March 17th, was St. Patrick's day and the Enniskillings gave a splendid show, trooping the colour. We all went. They kept murmuring "Beautiful, beautiful! Habu, habu!" And "This is an army," they said. I reminded them that we had been at it a long time and the Iraq army 3 years and suggested, to cheer them, that we might smarten the latter up by putting the big-drummer into a leopard skin. "Yes," said Zaid, delighted, "we'll kill the King's leopard and dress him up in it."

I did like that morning--and what fine folk we are, to be sure...

I didn't get back from the trooping of the colour till 11:30 and had a terrific day's work writing the Intelligence Report for the mail. It was finished about 5 by dint of letting no one interrupt me.

To F.B., Bagdad, March 18th, 1924

Send me out some mules (not for riding, for wearing on the feet). You get them at the Galerie Lafayette in Regent St. Black and gold, red and gold and blue and gold brocade are what I should like, one pair of each.

To H.B., March 27th, 1924

Well, my doings are not without moment. First Kish. We found an atmosphere of electric gloom and learnt afterwards that they had expected to find us such that in the first half hour Prof. Langdon would close down the excavations and Mr. Mackay would find himself without a job. So I, unknowing, while eating a scrap of lunch, explained that my object was to leave, as far as possible, the tablets to them for they should be at the disposition of students. On the other hand, they would have to make up by parting with some other fine objects. "Who decides," said the Professor, "if we disagree?" I replied that I did, but he needn't be afraid for he would find me eager to oblige. I said "Come on, Professor, you'll see how it works out." So we went to his tent where all the tablets were exposed. There was one unique object, a stone tablet inscribed with what is probably the oldest known human script. The Professor positively pressed it on me; he said he had copied it and read it and didn't mind what happened. So I took it. Then we went to a little room where all the other objects were, and began on the beads and jewels. There was a lovely pomegranate bud earring, found in the grave of a girl, time of Nebuchadnezzar, and he set against it a wonderful copper stag, early Babylonian and falling into dust. It was obvious that we here could not preserve the latter, as I explained. I took the pomegranate bud and he was pleased. So we turned to the necklaces, and we picked, turn and turn about. And thus with all the rest. The Professor grew more and more excited. It is very amusing to do I must say. And isn't it fantastic to be seeing pots and things four to six thousand years old! I got a marvellous stone inlay of a Sumerian king leading captives and not being at all nice to them, and a mother of pearl inlay of a king and his wives--inscribed with his name. The Professor got, what he longed for, a mother of pearl inlay representing a milking scene--you see I have my milking scene in the great plaque from Ur.

We worked from 1:30 to 10:30, with brief intervals for tea and dinner, choosing and packing, till I felt absolutely broken with fatigue--so tired that I couldn't sleep and when I slept dreamt restlessly. I was up at 7 and out to see the zigurrat where I met J.M. We began work again at 8 and went On till 11, by which time all was finished and packed except 3 huge Hamurabi pots which J.M. and I carried home on our knees. We went out, before we left, to see the palace--amazing! a niched and columned court (it's 4000 B.C. or thereabouts) with a stair leading up to an audience hall, unexcavated as yet...

(Oh dear, I've just seen the first mosquito of the season

The deputies are all pouring in and most of them pour through my office...

Out in the afternoon to see Haji Naji M.P. and had a very con-soling and soothing talk with him. He's a fund Of loyal good sense. And, Father, he wants another pair of pruning scissors. Will you get one for me? Not too big. Oh, but the really important thing I forgot--in the morning J.M. telephoned to me that Professor Sayce was "loafer-ing" about the Museum and would I come at once. So I rushed up in a launch and there he was, looking exactly the same as when I lunched with him in Edinburgh 10 years ago. He had arrived from Damascus the day before by car, and he is80. But he is not nearly as young as you physically though for wits he is bad to beat. I fell into his arms and showed him our treasures with which he was unspeakably thrilled.

I had tea with A.V.M. Higgins who had just arrived. I hap-pened in the course of conversation to quote Herbert [Richmond] and he mentioned that in all the three services there was no one whose opinion he valued so highly. That was nice, wasn't it.

I'm writing in the middle of the night, being unable to sleep.

To H.B., Bagdad, April 1, 1924

Well, the Assembly. The King came in looking very wonderful in full Arab dress. The Ministers followed him and sat down on either side, he sitting on the dais. He was tremendously clapped. Then he read his speech from the throne, a very fine bit of oratory and most moving. I think I have never seen him so much agitated; his voice shook. After it his procession reformed and he left.

Then they elected their President--a moment of breathless excitement. They all wrote their choice on bits of paper and dropped them into a box.

The annual lunch and sports of the Iraq army, a spring festival in the Maude gardens, this year swelled by all the deputies. It was really great fun, H.M. and Zaid, H.E., the Air Marshals and all the male world, and me in my official capacity. Such an atmosphere of goodwill and gratification too. At lunch I sat between two ministers with the President of the Assembly opposite. They do their lunch very well it is quite simple and good Arab food, sheep roasted whole, with rice, and a sweet and fruit, and it's quite short. The reports were very amusing, full of 'entrain,' and they only lasted an hour. H.M. gave the prizes and we all got away by 3 p.m.

I'll give you an outline of the next few days: tomorrow a garden party at the Residency to meet the deputies; Friday a lunch at Kadhimain to say goodbye to J. M. Wilson who is going on leave, and an official dinner at the Palace to Sir John. Saturday I'm going to see H.M. cut the first sod (if u can call it a sod) of a new canal at Najaf. And on Sunday Ramadhan begins, thank goodness. At 6:30 Ken and I were = at the station, prepared to travel in the Royal train to Karbala. We got to Karbala at 10:30 and found a crowd at the station. H.M. was most enthusiastically received.

This over we hustled into motors, Ken and I and Col. Tainsh together-- we were the only Europeans there. And motored through dust and a high hot wind, just like summer, for an hour and a quarter down the Najaf road. We alighted in an arid wilderness where the King lifted the first spadeful of sand of the first canal which is to supply Najaf with water.

To H.B., Bagdad, April 9th, 1924

... So we motored back to Karbala and while the King went to make a pilgrimage in the two mosques, we repaired to the bazaar where I bought shoes with turned up toes, yellow, red and blue.

To F.B., Bagdad, April 10th, 1924

...And will you please do a commission for me next time you are in London--no other than to buy me a new every morning hat. The one I have has faded so dreadfully. I enclose a Picture of a Woolland hat which seems to me nice, together with the approximate colour of the straw--the trimming should be a shade darker...

Summer has begun lamentably early this year. I like the present temperature--80 to 90--but it has come a month too soon. I expect we're in for a scorching time.

I must tell you something which has pleased me. I sent Mr. Scott, of the Manchester Guardian, my article about the Al al Bait university and he telegraphs asking for plans and photographs which I'm despatching this week. I hope he intends to put a very friendly article into his paper.

I woke up this morning at 3 a.m.--it's now 4 and I have just heard the gun which announces the beginning of the day's fast. The Muezzin next door to me is chanting the call to prayer in his tiny mosque.

To H.B., Bagdad, April 15th, 1924

...Yes, of course I think that there is a rationalizing spirit abroad in the East just as much as in the West, and do you know I think it will go much quicker here than it did with us because we have broken down the barriers and set the example which they will be eager to follow.

[She tells that she had a dinner party where one of the guests was a somewhat enterprising storyteller.)

One of the stories I will tell you--I laughed at it too. "How would you punctuate this sentence--Mary ran out into the garden naked?" Ken said: "with a full stop, I hope." "No," said Sir - "a dash after Mary."

On Sunday morning I went to my Museum where I had various visitors including Ken. It really is fun showing people over the museum; there are such wonderful things to be seen in it.

I've never had so many roses in my garden before--it blushes with them. And lovely carnations, stock, larkspur and things as well.

To H.B., Bagdad, April 21st, 1924

When I left the office I motored out to Kadhimain to see a very interesting woman, who is the mother of the Agha Khan and manages all his vast businesses, secular and religious, while he is in Europe. She is on pilgrimage here and is going on to Mashhad in Persia and so back to India via Seistan!--something of a journey, but she seems to take it in her stride...

...I dined with Nigel Davidson to meet the very nice Colonel of the Inniskillings, Col. Ridings...

In this phantasmagoria of a week we all went off to the circus.

It was a Belgian circus. Now I don't think I've been to a circus since the age of 6 but I shall never lose an opportunity of going to every one I can. It was delicious, so funny and so clever and so amazing. It was composed of every race under the sun; there were Japanese and Indians and Sudanese and Belgians who spoke broken English and yet more broken Arabic. But the nicest thing of all was the elephants on a seesaw. The elephant bumped the see-saw down and jumped the acrobat into the air, so high that he alighted on the elephant's head and slipped down his back and his tail. Then the audience were invited to participate and a lot of Arab coolie boys ran into the arena. Some were white with fear at being confronted with so large an animal; but the elephant loved it. He bumped them up and they fell all ways some onto the plank and some on to the ground, till at last one, more by good luck than by any skill, succeeded in falling on to the elephant's head. And we rocked with laughter--all except the Kurdish deputies who sat together in a box and never moved a muscle the whole evening. I suppose they thought it beneath their Kurdish dignity to laugh at elephants and coolie boys...

After lunch I rode up to the hospital to visit the Sheikhs. It wrung my heart. Addai whom I adore looked so white and tired. Salman with two compound fractures in the arms and a bullet through his leg declaring roundly that it was of no consequence. I sat with them not more than five minutes and they sent a boy running after me to beg me to hurry on the work. It is their blood which has hurried on the work!

Darling, I tell you all these things about my sheikhs and people and I daresay you think them very silly. I know I'm not seeing to scale, but my heart is in it--I live and die for it. Nothing else matters...

To H.B., April 29th, 1924

...In the evening I dined alone, and had dined early--by luck, when at 8 p.m. came a telephone message to say the King wanted me. I motored up to the Palace--he sent me a car. The little Palace in the garden. It was a strange sight in Ramadhan. In the lighted rooms of the Pavilion I caught a glimpse of long robed figures saying their prayers. ...

In the long saloon I found the King in full Arab dress, white and gold and black. There may be (I don't say there are not) more momentous affairs elsewhere, but there is nowhere I'll be bound where they are presented to you in such a setting. That night was unforgettable. The praying tribesmen, the King in white robes, the riot of flowers around the pavilion, and the sandflies goading you to distraction, while you try to think straight.

Your letter of April 15th: I'm not one of those whom Iraq keeps or sends away. I'm on the High Com.'s staff as long as there is a High Com. and a British Government servant. All you say on wages and economics is most interesting and most sound--but hard for general understanding.

To F.B., Bagdad, April 30th, 1924

...Summer has come and I find I want another lace gown to wear in the evenings. I would like a black one for I have a silver 'fourreau' which it will go with. so will you please send me four and a half yards of black filet lace two and a half inches wide. And the great thing is to get a lace covered with pattern as much as possible, not with a big stretch of blank net at the top if You understand me.

I forgot to tell Father that my picture for the King has come, in a gorgeous frame. I sent it to him yesterday but have not yet heard from him.

I had a very nice dinner party on Friday. The Colonel of the Inniskillings, Col. Ridings, (he knows the eldest Dorman and has stayed with him). He brought a charming Captain Vaughan, very keen about antiquities. There were also delightful Major and Mrs. Gore, such nice people, and Captain Braham, my beloved doctor. We sat in the garden after dinner for the first time, with Bagdad lanterns hanging in the trees and they thought it a half acre cut out of Paradise. It did indeed look lovely.

To-day I went to the Museum in the morning where Sir Henry, Esme and Captain Vaughan visited us. I burst with pride when I show people over the Museum. It is becoming such a wonderful place. It was a great morning because there were 6 boxes from Kish to be unpacked--the remainder of our share. Such copper instruments as have never before been handed down from antiquity; the shelves shout with them

To F.B., May 5th, 1924

Could you please send me a bit of lace like the enclosed to renovate a muslin gown. This is exactly the quantity I want and it must be very good otherwise it washes to a rag. This was very good but you see how it is worn out. I think this kind is best.

To H.B., Bagdad, May 14th, 1924

I'm waiting for two old Turbans. I hope they'll come soon for I want to ride before dinner.--They came, nice old things.

In the matter of the hat I'm most grateful. The mules have come and are exactly what I want.

To H.B., Bagdad, May 20th, 1924

Your letters are almost always delivered on Saturday after-noon--9 days post--and I've now made an arrangement with the office by which they send them over. So you may think of me happily read-ing them on Saturday evening when I come in from riding or what not. And indeed they are a great solace.

Meantime, I've ceased to worry. I tell all who come to see me that I'm thinking how nice it will be to go back to live at home.

To H.B., Bagdad, June 11th, 1924

We beat Cinderella by half an hour--the Treaty was ratified last night at 11:30.

To H.B. [who was in Australia], Bagdad, June 25th, 1924

I suppose it's the reaction from the unholy excitement in which we have lived for the last few months, but whatever may be the reason, I'm feeling shockingly dull and depressed. So I'm afraid this letter won't be up to standard.

First a little bit of business--since you say that the quickest way of writing to Ceylon is via London, I don't see why I shouldn't send my letters to you to mother, for her to read and forward. It will be a great simplification for me, for I shall not have to write the general news twice over--which I really cannot do--and I can write her a little extra note about the things I generally confide to her private ear. So, unless you raise objections, that is the course I shall pursue. And in order that I may not be deterred from keeping you informed as to the history of the Iraq and of your daughter, would you think it worth while to present me with some more writing paper like this? What you gave me four or three years ago has lasted till now, but it is very nearly finished. I think, as far as you are concerned, I've put it to good use-- don't you agree?

At present we really are the happy nation which has no history. The Assembly is passing the Organic Law...Now there is a solid block in the Assembly--the upholders of the treaty--who, having learnt wisdom from the vagaries of the only representative body they have known, are determined not to weaken the powers of the throne. There's a fund of good sense in the Arab, of real value.

I have not done much this week. I swim a good deal and every Sunday the usual party of us goes up by launch to near Muadhdham where we swim and dive on the river bank. I have a little reed mat hut there to undress in and another at the swimming place, opposite the King's palace, where we go when we want to be back for dinner. Yesterday the King and Zaid joined us--and I'm now going to let them know whenever we go up so that they can come across and swim with us.

To F.B., Bagdad, June 25th, 1924

I have been swimming so vigorously that my bathing costume is wearing out and already has to be darned. Will you please get me another? The kind I like is in two pieces, drawers and jumper, and I like it black with a coloured border of some kind round all the edges. I prefer silk tricotine to silk and I like best a square or V-shaped opening at the neck. As to colour if you see something nice in a variegated tricotine (vide enclosed--but this particular one is in silk not tricotine and I don't like that so much) it might be a pleasant change from black. But the colours should show a general tendency to dark blue or green if you understand me.

Bathing clothes are so exiguous that I think it might be sent by letter post by overland mail--they don't normally take parcels.

Ever your very affectionate (but tiresome) daughter,

Gertrude.

[This particular order for clothes certainly was tiresome, for it was completely baffling. There were no bathing costumes to be found in two pieces, there were none to be found in tricotine, variegated or otherwise: there were very few in black or dark blue, or green, and of these none had a coloured border. Most of the costumes obtainable were in one piece, usually of bright coloured silk, with a design in gaudy embroidery on back or front, sometimes on both.

One of the least impossible of these garments was finally despatched to Gertrude. It did not give entire satisfaction, as will be seen from a subsequent letter.]

CHAPTER XXIV

BAGDAD - JULY 1924-DECEMBER 1924

To H.B., Bagdad, July 2nd, 1924

As for my annals, they are now becoming very tame, I'm glad to say! The Assembly is duly passing the Organic Law: which ought to be through before Sir Henry goes on leave on the 14th. Did I tell you he was going on leave? He will be away for about 2 months, leaving Nigel Davidson in command. I think it is a good plan. He needs a little rest and also it will be an advantage his seeing the authorities in London and impressing his views upon them. I entirely agree with Lord Cromer who used to say that a big official should take leave every year if possible as much for the sake of H.M.G. AS for his own sake. And so far as I can see we shall be very peaceful for the next two months.

The most interesting thing which happened during this week was a performance by the R.A.F., a bombing demonstration. It was even more remarkable than the one we saw last year at the Air Force show because it was much more real. They had made an imaginary village about a quarter of a Mile from where we sat on the Diala dyke and the two first bombs dropped from 3000 feet, went straight into the middle of it and set it alight. It was wonderful and horrible. Then they dropped bombs all round it, as if to catch the fugitives and finally fire bombs which even in the brightest sunlight made flues of bright flame in the desert. They burn through metal and water won't extinguish them. At the end the armoured cars went out to round up the fugitives with machine guns.

I was tremendously impressed. It's an amazingly relentless and terrible thing war from the air...

THE LETTERS OF GERTRUDE BELL

To F.B., Bagdad, July 2nd, 1924

(She writes of her father who had gone to Ceylon to see the Richmonds. Vice-Admiral Richmond was now Naval Commander-in-Chief, East Indies.]

Isn't it really a good thing that he should be so full of vitality and the power of enjoyment. How delightful it will be for Elsa and Herbert to have him! He is, we may admit to one another, like no one else in the world. I can't think how other daughters can bear not having him for a father.

I have been reading a bunch of modern plays published by Benn. Some of them seem to me to be very good and to strike a very real and human note. What do you think of The Fanatics? It took me by the throat as an expression of what, in general terms, I also think. I'm not sure that it is a play, in the sense that it could be good on the stage. I have sent for two new plays by O'Neill--if there's anything else you think remarkable, you might tell me. One is apt to miss even outstanding things when one is guided only by reviews.

I read when I come home after lunch. I've had six and a half steady hours of work and I'm tired, and besides it's too hot to do much. So I read myself to sleep, if I can, for an hour, and then go on reading till it's time to swim. On Saturday evening I get my mail, just before dinner--that's an exciting and delightful evening.

To F.B., Bagdad, July 9th, 1924

...We picnic every Sunday on the river bank after swimming and that is unfailingly delightful. We take a great fish which the servants roast over a wood fire, excellent food, a cold chicken and joint, and we don't get back till after 10. I look forward to Sunday evenings. Besides that I swim two or three times a week between tea and dinner. The water is quite warm now with the temperature up to 116. You can stay in as long as you like. I love it. Otherwise I do very little. Office 7 to 1.30, lunch with Sir Henry and then home. On Sunday I have an advisor or a minister to lunch as a rule. Not an eventful life--one estimates, you can't do anything else--with the heat closed down round

620

you like a wall. I'm quite well though. But I would give no small thing for a fortnight at Rounton.

Saturday evenings I look forward to also for its then the mail comes in and the delightful letters of my family, I dine alone and read them several times over. They're not wasted I assure you...

To H.B., Bagdad, July 9th, 1924

This is a very cleverly conceived letter designed to catch you at Port Said...

Do you know, I have a great admiration for Sir Henry. He is extremely good at his job; I admire his despatches home immensely-- they are very courageous and very illuminating. He is a considerable administrator. He goes on leave next week and will be away 2 months.

To H.B., Bagdad, July 16th, 1924

I can't say I had a nice Birthday, indeed it was one of the most infernal days I ever remember. The temperature had jumped up to 121 with a raging furnace wind. It was so bad that Sir Henry, who was to have started off for Ramadi by air, on his way home, failed to get off at 6 and again at 10 and came back sadly to lunch. Finally he left at 5 and with considerable difficulty landed safely at Ramadi after dark. To-day I hope he is in Egypt. To-day the temperature has dropped again to something reasonable, round about 110 and I'm hoping that you won't be too hot in the Red Sea.

Nigel Davidson is left in charge and is living at the Residency, where I lunch with him. We're hoping that no 'orrible crisis will occur while the H.C. is away.

To F.B., Bagdad, July 16th, 1924

...I think I told you in one of my letters what I do every day. I get up at 5:30, do exercises till 5:45 and walk in the garden till 6 or a little after cutting flowers. All that grows now is a beautiful double jasmin of which I have bowls full every day, and zinnias, ugly and useful. I breakfast at 6:40 on an egg and some fruit, interview my old cook Haji Ali at 6:45 when I order any meal I want and pay the daily books. Leave for the office by car at 6:55, get there at 7. I'm there till 1:30 when I lunch with the High Commissioner--now with Nigel.

The first thing I do in the office is to look through the three vernacular papers and translate anything that ought to be brought to the notice of the authorities. These translations are typed and circulated to the H.C., the Advisers in the Arab offices, and finally as an appendix of the fortnightly reports to the Secretary of State. By the time I've done that, papers are beginning to come in, intelligence reports from all the Near East and India, local reports, petitions, etc. The petitions I generally dispose of myself; the local reports I note on, suggesting if necessary memoranda to the Ministries of Interior or Finance (mostly Interior which is the Ministry I'm most concerned with) or despatches and letters. Sometimes I write a draft at once, sometimes I propose the general outlines and wait for approval or correction. In and out of all this people come in to see me, sheikhs, and Arab Officials or just people who want to give some bit of information or ask for advice, if there's anything important in what they have to say I inform the H.C. At intervals in the daily routine, I'm now busy writing the Annual Report for the League of Nations. I usually get a clear hour or two before lunch.

I get home about 2:30 and do nothing till 5. I don't often sleep, but I lie on a big sofa under a fan and read novels or papers. All the windows are shut and the room is comparatively cool. After 5 I go out swimming or I take a little walk or people come to see me. I very seldom ride in the summer, it's too hot in the evening and I haven't time before going to office. I dine about 7:30 on some iced soup or a bit of fish or some fruit and sometimes if I'm feeling unusually energetic I do an hour's work or I write letters. Generally I read again till about ten and then go to bed on the roof, and that's the hot weather life. And now it's time to go and have my bath before dinner. Now I come to think of it, it seems rather a hermit programme. It is. I hate dining out or having people to dinner in the hot weather.

To F.B., Bagdad, July 23rd, 1924

About the bathing dress. It was my fault. I ought to have left you carte blanche about the material. Probably no one wears tricotinc now- something else is the vogue. The one you sent is rather baggy but I shall be very glad of it when my present one goes into holes.

Nigel and I are getting on famously. Of course I'm rather a Person now that we are so short handed. I hope I shall not make any dreadful mistakes--but there's always Nigel to stop me. He is very cautious.

I've been bathing and it's now after dinner and I have two despatches to draft so I must turn to them.

To H.B., Bagdad, July 30th, 1924

I have had a good deal of work this week. And there have been two or three very complicated and important administrative propositions which I have had to study and prepare for Nigel Davidson's decision. We are so shorthanded in the office, you see, that at this moment the greater part of the two other people's work comes to me. It's very interesting, however; I don't mind doing it. And in the summer it's well to be pretty fully employed. It keeps you from brooding on being a dog.

For once in my life I really am almost indispensable, someone has to do the routine work in the office and there literally isn't anyone but me to devil for Nigel the political and administrative things ...

To F.B., August. 5th, 1924

It is deadly hot and I'm as thin as a lathe--I can't eat anything in the heat. But I have a glass of iced soup at 11 a.m. and find that it makes all the difference. There is another month of extreme heat and then it begins to tail off.

M--- made a malady last week--fortunately she's well again. Do you remember Richmond Ritchie writing "My wife and family have influenza. The cook, thank God, is spared." I felt I knew what he meant.

There is really a great deal of work in the office; to-day I spent from 9 to 1 just over routine work--memoranda to write to the Ministries, office notes explaining papers and proposing action for Nigel, translating the papers, dealing with petitions. I didn't get down to my own work, reports, etc. till the morning was nearly over.

But I like having plenty of work; it keeps one alive. However as I began life at 5:30 and have been ceaselessly at it and it's now 10 p.m. I shall end this letter.

To H.B., Bagdad, August. 13th, 1924

We have come to the end of Muharram without incident, yesterday was the last day. I'm glad it's over. Every night for the last 10 days the air has been uneasy with the wailings of the processions mourning for Hussain, their cries and the dull throb of the chains with which they beat their breasts. It is savage even from far off and it makes one feel disturbed. There is a little Shiah mosque a few hundred yards away behind my house and on the first nights of the month, when the moon was young, the glare of the torch flickered through my windows. The people work themselves up into such a state of frenzy that it's amazing some outburst of fanaticism doesn't occur, but it never does here.

To F.B., Bagdad, August. 13, 1924

Thank you for the two books--The Adding Machine and Men and Masses. Modern literature is very queer isn't it, but it's also extremely interesting. One has to get oneself accustomed to entirely new forms- that which they embody is as old as the world because it is a variant of the human story! thought both those books--I can't call them plays--very striking and I'm so grateful because that is just the kind of thing I miss, not knowing about them. Yes, I've read St. Joan, this week. I thought it wonderful; I wish I had seen it on the stage. It is so clever of him to have made her a bluff--not to say rough--country girl. Of course so she was, with the mysticism threaded separately through her.

To H.B., Bagdad, August. 20, 1924

I dined with Haji Naji on his roof It was a nice cool evening for once and we sat on the roof with the full moon so bright that we wanted no other light and the tops of the mulberry trees waving round us. Presently I glanced up and saw the moon looking a very odd shape and found that it was a total eclipse! You saw it too I expect. It's a sinister thing, an eclipse, isn't it. As we motored back the shadow spread over the moon, deepened and left the world in a threatening darkness. The people in the houses were beating pans and firing off revolvers to frighten the whale which was devouring the moon. This they ultimately succeeded in doing, but not without great trouble. It was a very long eclipse.

...Bathing in our favourite pool opposite the King's palace. To us a party of shining ones, the King, Zaid, Jafar, Nuri ...all the King's pals. They had come, some of them to bathe and all of them to picnic on the bank. Do you know it's difficult to make a curtsey with grace when you're wet in a bathing dress.

On Sunday morning I went to the Museum which I had promised to show to some teachers from Mosul. They were very much impressed and said many complimentary things about the service I was rendering to the Iraq. But what pleases me still more--since I'm blowing my own trumpet so loud--is that I have a letter from Sir F. Kenyon saying that he holds up the Iraq Department of Antiquities as the model for the manner in which the division of finds is made between excavators and the local Government and that as long as things remain in my hands he will be perfectly satisfied. I am very much relieved for I feared they would never forgive me for taking the milking plaque which was by far the best thing they found. I could do no other and I am so glad they recognized it. They have been most reasonable.

To H.B., Bagdad, September. 17th, 1924

And what do you think I was doing this morning? I was taking a friend of yours to Babylon, Mr. Tom Griffiths. This is how it came about. Two Labour members and a Unionist, Mr. Griffiths, Dr. Williamson and Mr. Davies are here for three days on their way to Muhammarah and on to India. It is a tour arranged by the A.P.O.C., whose guests they are--a bit of propaganda. Lionel Smith and I took them to Babylon. We started, I may mention, by trolley on the railway, at 5:20 a.m. Mr. Griffiths conceived a high opinion of me when I told him I was your daughter and it wasn't diminished when he heard that I was sister-in-law to Charles. "We call him Charlie" he observed affectionately; "Our Charlie." I hope you like Mr. Griffiths; I think him such a nice man (like Mr. Terrapin) and certainly I never had a better audience at Babylon than I had to- day.

...It was quite cold going down in the early morning and not too hot at Babylon, but coming back, from 10 to 1, it was infernal. There was a wind that scorched you. I had to take refuge on the floor to get out of that blast. I still feel like a cinder...

To H.B., Bagdad, September. 30, 1924

...The evening he arrived (Thursday) there was an official dinner at the Residency. He at once greeted me as sister and after dinner he came and talked. Lord Thomson is certainly very pleasant socially. Next day the King asked me to tea to interpret for him, but there was a circle of Ministers sitting round and the talk was quite on the surface. On Saturday Lord T. flew to Mosul, Sunday all round the N. frontier, Arbil and Kirkuk where he spent the night. On Monday he flew to Sulaimani, had two hours there, flew back to Bagdad and was at the Residency at lunch. Wonderful isn't it! In the evening there was a staff banquet at the Palace --it was amusing, as much as such things can be. The King had his talk afterwards in the garden; Sasun interpreted. Sir Henry told me that Lord T. had been very sympathetic...Lord T. had a tremendous reception at Sulaimani. All the Kurdish chiefs came in to see him with hundreds of followers, sheeted in ammunition belts with revolvers and daggers sticking out from them. The procession was so long that before they had finished the round of the town they were treading on their own tail--a difficult question of precedence arose! Lord T. said he felt like a minor Roman emperor and was conscious that there should have been a man riding by his side to remind him that he must some day die. He flew away this morning.

The King has acquired an estate near Khanaqin and he invited me to motor up with him today as he wanted to choose a site for a shooting cottage. I have arranged with Sir Henry to go up by tonight's train, arriving about 6 a.m., spend the day with H.M. and return by tomorrow night's train, getting back to the office on Thursday morning. I shall like having a day out of doors--H.M. is in tents--and today for the first time for a month there's a little north wind. I really think the weather may be going to cool down. It has been a very hot, still September... ...

I've reverted now to a regular Sunday dinner party and bridge. I expect I shall be able to get away very little. But George I shall send up to Mosul with Lionel Smith the week before the Richmonds come. The A.V.M *is going to fly Herbert all round the frontiers and I shall show Elsa and George, and Herbert when he is here, the local sights.

I'm very much engrossed in the Cambridge Ancient History which certainly is a very remarkable achievement. Its first two volumes have got down to 1000 B.C. It gives one a wonderfully universal idea of the beginnings of history a fascinating book. I'm writing the Mosul part of my guide book, in and out of my work. I wish I had time to go steadily at it. I've wholly failed to discover who now publishes Murray's Guides--could you find out for me and put me into touch with the publishers? It is not either Murray or Stanford, so don't try those blind avenues.

To H.B., Bagdad, Oct. 15th, 1924

I have letters from you and Mother of October 1, all about your Free Traders. You are thick in the election and I'm longing to know your views, Upon my soul, I think I would vote Labour if I were in England. The turning out of the Government at a time when the peace of Europe is still on such thin ice seems to me to be such a mean party trick. And the programmes of the Conservatives and Liberals are poor, hackneyed stuff, don't you think?

[In October of this year Gertrude had the great pleasure of a visit from the Richmonds, Elsa and her husband Vice-Admital Herbert Richmond and their daughter Mary. They were on board the flagship Chatham on one of its official cruises and came up to the Persian Gulf to Basrah and then to Bagdad. This coincided with a visit from George Trevelyan, Molly's elder son who was on his way to stay with the Richmonds in Ceylon and spent a week at Bagdad on the way. His arrival was a great joy to Gertrude. It is worth including some extracts from her letters for the interest of seeing that she who had cared so much for her younger sisters when they were children was ready to welcome their children as if they had been her own.]

To H.B., Bagdad, Oct. 29, 1924

I have been a very poor thing this week with a touch of bronchitis- entirely my own fault for going out to dinner when I had a bad cold. However, at last, thank goodness, I'm better and have been doing short hours in the office for the last three days. The disappointment was that I was still in bed when George arrived and could not have him here. I was really crumpled up and Sinbad said I wasn't fit for company, so George went to the Residency, coming to see me every evening after tea. I have written to Moll about him. He is the most enchanting creature. He went off with Lionel Smith to Mosul on Monday night and will be away about a week. The Richmonds arrive next Monday, by which time I hope I shall be quite well.

There was a heavy fall of rain on Monday night, heavy for the time of year, for we scarcely ever have rain till November. It has cleaned the world wonderfully and made the temperature drop to a reasonable autumn level. To-night, for the first time since February, I have a fire in my sitting room. Summer has passed so rapidly into winter this year that I never wore any intermediate clothes but passed straight out of the thinnest muslin gowns into heavy woollens. It is a difficult climate to tackle. You can't at first believe that you really feel cold.

The excavations at Kish and Ur are opening--Kish has already begun and Mr. Woolley arrived last Saturday and goes down to Ur to-morrow. We are all frightfully thrilled by the discovery in India by Sir John Marshall of seals which are exactly like Sumerian seals here. I have written to Sir John Marshall asking him for impressions of his seals. I do hope they will have a good season at Ur this year.

I've so little to write about because I have been seeing so few people. But oh I'm thankful to be getting well again! I do get so dreadfully bored when I'm ill.

To her sister, Bagdad, October 28th, 1924

DARLING MOLL,

George arrived safely on Saturday at 1:30. I was delighted to see him. We sat hand in hand talking breathlessly.

He is immensely eager to know and understand and so intelligent and quick in the uptake. He went off after dinner with Lionel Smith to Mosul.

He is so outgoing and so eager, besides being so charming to look at. I am very proud of having him for a nephew. it was a great disappointment not being able to take him about myself, but next week when he comes back I hope I shall be all right again and we will go about with the Richmonds.

To the same, Bagdad, November 12th, 1924

We had the most delicious days all together when George joined us after his Northern tour ...

He is wildly interested in everything. He used to sit and listen when Herbert talked of India and I of the Iraq asking us now and then of things he had not understood. He is not going to waste his time on this journey, he will come back full of new impressions and experiences and now the East looms so very large it is worth while to know something about it...

Well, I hope I have made a new friend with him. I should always like to be in close touch. Last year in England I made a new friend in Pauline and now I've got George. Isn't it nice. Kitty must be next... [Pauline and Kitty Trevelyan.]

The Chatham sailed from Basrah this morning at ten. I do feel rather flat without them. All my servants adored them and one of them wept when they left.

THE LETTERS OF GERTRUDE BELL

To Charles Trevelyan, Bagdad, December 3, 1924

MY DEAR CHARLIE,

...He may be too young to appreciate to the full all that he is seeing but I do not doubt that you and Moll have done well to let him make this journey. He may miss a good deal but he will understand a good deal more especially with such a guide as Herbert.

I do love him very much and I think he has got the makings of a fine and generous creature...

To H.B., Bagdad, Nov. 5, 1924

As you may imagine, we have been having rather a rushing time, complicated by the fat that I had only just got out of bed. But I'm really beginning to feel well now.

The Richmonds all arrived on Saturday. My car broke down on the way to the station so that I didn't succeed in meeting them, but after telephonic communications, they all turned up in my office at 10:30. I took them to the Sarai, showed them the Museum, at which Herbert was thrilled; after which we called on several of the Ministers. We all lunched together at my house, and Elsa and I spent the afternoon lying in the garden and talking while Mr. Cooke took Herbert and Mary on some wild round, which they appear to have loved. I had the Prime Minister to dinner, Sasun Eff. and J. M. Wilson--most successful. Elsa and Herbert are universally loved.

On Sunday we sat about in the sun in my garden till noon, when I took them for a little sightseeing in the town and out to Kadhimain to lunch with the Mayor, Saiyid Jafar--you had tea with him--a nine course lunch. We saw as much of the mosque as one can see. The Sinbads were also of the party and came home to tea. Jafar dined and my Minister, Muzahim, and my ex-Minister, Sabih Bey.

On Monday morning they went to Ctesiphon and I to the office. We all lunched at the Residency. Esme is back and is being kindness itself, putting her car at our disposal and so forth. After a tea party with the King, the Richmond family dined with the A.O.M., where Herbert is staying, but I didn't go as I felt still rather shaky.

On Tuesday Herbert flew to Kut and back. Elsa and Mary went shopping carpets with Elsie Sinbad and Mr. Cooke, and we all lunched with the Sinbads. Then I gave a tea--party attended by 10 ladies and two of their daughters, at which Elsa and Mary shone. I hear it is likely to be the talk of the town for the next month. They dined with Jafar--I didn't go.

This afternoon Elsa, Mary, the King, the Amir Ghazi, Sabih Bey and I all had tea with Haji Naji and walked about his garden--a delicious entertainment. Saiyid Hussain Afnan and his wife are coming to dinner to play Mahjong. Herbert has flown to Mosul and won't be back till Friday. George arrives from his northern tour to-morrow morning and is being put up at the Residency.

I feel as I did when you were here that it is almost incredible that they should actually be in Bafdad. It is also incredibly delightful. Elsa is so delicious always. She is picking up Arabic and delights everyone with her efforts to talk it. isn't she wonderfully quick and intelligent! And it has been so endlessly enjoyable to have her to talk to. I feel as if I had got things off my mind that had lain on it for months and months. She is amazingly well--never tired, eats enormously and is amused by everything.

Now I must go and dress for dinner.

Ever your very affectionate daughter,

Gertrude.

To F.B., Bagdad, Nov. 12, 1924

...To act The Verge [acted by Sybil Thorndike in London] really does seem to me to be a supreme adventure. All these modern plays are eagerly borrowed by my colleagues so that I scarcely have time to read them myself...

I continue to think Elsa perhaps the nicest person in the world--don't you?

THE LETTERS OF GERTRUDE BELL

To H.B., Bagdad, December. 3, 1924

...After lunch, while I was sitting in my garden, there rolled up an American, adviser or ex-adviser to the U.S.A. on the subject of irrigation engineering and he had just been the guest of the Australian and Indian Governments! As he shook hands with me on the garden path, he observed: "I greet the first citizen of Iraq." Gratifying, wasn't it. He then proceeded to talk as ceaselessly as Americans do, but I got a word or two in edgeways. Finally, he said that J.M. (who had sent him to me) had told him I was going to see the King and might he come and present his respects! I was going on my way to a Library Committee so I took him there (it was conducted in Arabic which must have left him cold) and then on to H.M. who received him very graciously and gave him tea, after which he left.

...I wonder who he really is. He was all superlatives he had the deepest admiration for and confidence in my great nation; he was convinced that the future of the Iraq as one of the leading cotton growing countries was assured; he could scarcely believe that he was really having the honour of spending an hour with me, etc., etc.

On Monday--Forget what did, as we used to put in our diaries when we were small...

To F.B., Bagdad, December. 14, 1924

I'm going to try to get a letter through by the special Xmas mail though I doubt whether I shall succeed, for it's raining hard this evening and I don't think cars will run to-morrow. Anyhow, if it does get through, this is to wish you all a merry Xmas.

I've just had the little Amir Ghazi to tea, with his tutor and governess. The train and soldiers I had ordered for him from Harrod's had arrived last mail and were presented, with great success. Especially the train. He loves all kinds of machinery and in fact was much cleverer about the engine than any of us--found out where the brake was and how to Make the engine go backwards or forwards. We all sat on the floor and watched it running along the rails, following it with shouts of joy. Fancy a little Mecca child introduced to the most lovely modern toys! . ...

THE LETTERS OF GERTRUDE BELL

To H.B., Bagdad, December. 10th 1924

Your most beloved letter of Nov. 26th--I was glad to have it--it made me feel quite warm inside. I'm perfectly aware that I don't merit so much love, but the nicest thing about love is that you can have it without merit. You mustn't bother, darling, about my health. You are not reckoning with the immense elasticity which comes of being everywhere sound. I shall always be thin--an inherited characteristic; and I would rather anyhow. I don't like fat people. I really did have a very hard and lonely summer and I suppose it temporarily sapped my powers of withstanding heat. But now all my own friends are back it's very different and if we get out shooting at Xmas I shall walk eight hours a day without turning a hair.

[I am told that Lionel Smith after one of the said shooting parties in which Gertrude was included said that she had outlasted them all in the matter of walking, and was as fresh at the end of the day as when she started.]

To H.B., Bagdad, December. 23rd, 1924

Yesterday a very interesting thing happened--I went to see the Queen. She's charming, I'm so happy to say. She has the delicate, sensitive Hashimi face (she's his first cousin, you know) and the same winning manner that he has. She had on a very nice, long tunicked brown gown made by the nuns, a long long string of pearls, and a splendid aquamarine pendant. I saw the two eldest girls who are just like her, rather shy but eager to be outgoing, one could see.

Will you tell Geoffrey Dawson next time you see him that it was a great pleasure to meet Mr. Peterson whom I thought singularly level and unprejudiced. I've no doubt you will see some articles from him in the Times. They will be worth reading.

Oh dear! isn't it a difficult world.

I've a growing conviction, Father, that I shall not come on leave next year. Don't be disappointed.

[The following are two of the annual testimonials about Gertrude's work sent to the Colonial Office in 1925.]

'To describe Miss Bell as a complete and accurate encyclopaedia on all matters concerning this country would be true--but inadequate. Her extensive and detailed knowledge of past happenings and existing personalities is sufficient in itself to make her an invaluable colleague. But beyond all this, her keen intellect and her unfailing sympathy for the struggles of the infant Iraq state enable her to play a part that could not be played by anyone else, in ensuring not only the closeness but also the cordiality of the relations between this High Commission (the officials, be they Iraqi or British) and the Iraq Government. I cannot adequately express my gratitude for the assistance I receive from her.'

- B. BOURDILLON.

'Miss Bell's extraordinary abilities and sympathies need no further testimony from me. But I realise them even better than I did last year and am still most grateful to her for all that she has done during the critical time through which we have been passing.'

- H. DOBBS.

CHAPTER XXV

1925 - BAGDAD-ENGLAND

To F.B., Bagdad, January, 1925

...I'm turning over in my mind whether I will or I won't write the Iraq book for Benn's Modern World Series. In a wild moment I promised Herbert Fisher nine months ago to do the volume of the Arab States. A month ago I wrote and said I wouldn't...Whereat far from being discouraged they replied that that was all right and wouldn't I write a book about the Iraq only. So I'm rather caught for they have already advertised me ...and I feel some reluctance as to letting them down entirely--though far greater reluctance to write the book. Lionel is urging me to do it, and I'm feeling that I haven't enough time energy or knowledge. I'm postponing decision for a week.

To H.B., Bagdad, January. 7th, 1925

I've had a week with the Queen and her court, culminating in her first reception to-day. On Saturday morning I went up to talk to her about it and on Saturday afternoon I took Esme to see her.

What with this and with preparing reports for the League of Nations delegation, I've been busy. But I did have a holiday last Friday--the only one of the season. We all went out shooting, Baqubah way--Bernard and Ken and I, Col. Joyce and Major Maclean. We started at 6:30 in freezing bitter cold and when we got out into the country it was still colder, the whole world white with hoar frost and all the waters frozen. But we enjoyed it tremendously--it looked so lovely, the green palm gardens against the white frost. We ran to the beats to keep ourselves warm and we returned 12 hours later with a bag Of 150, geese, duck and snipe.

On New Year's Day, in the intervals of receiving the visits of Ministers, I made a little account of the year's expenditure. I have spent in all some 560 pounds over and above my salary. Of this, 230 (in round figures) is the cost of living here above my salary and another 79 is goods from England--also cost of living, therefore. 90 for books, papers, seeds and bulbs for my garden and various little odds and ends of that sort, and 160 for clothes--that is to say, gloves, shoes, hats, silks or stuffs for Marie to make up, for I have had no new clothes from home. On the whole I don't think it has been an extravagant year--do you?

In the afternoon Iltyd Clayton and I went to call on two Syrian families, friends of his, one Christian and one Moslem, but they all live together. It is very interesting, the little group of Syrians here. They are almost all in Govt. employment, like Hussain Afhan--a good many of them are teachers in the schools. They are making a little social revolution of their own, for the women, even if they are Moslems, are educated and behave as far as they can like European women. It is the thin edge of the wedge and I need not say that I am all in its favour.

I feel at this moment that I am a little tempted of discouragement, as the monk said of St. Francis.

I shall love to hear about your Xmas party which was just assembling when you wrote.

It is still dreadfully cold and freezing at nights. My office is icy and I sit and work in a fur coat, which doesn't keep my feet warm.

To F.B., Bagdad, January. 15th, 1925

...But you know, though I love hearing of it, I don't feel that I should fit into an Xmas party. I've grown too much of a recluse. After all such years and years as I have had of being alone are bound to alter one's character. Not for the better, I admit and fear.

But there it is; if you have children and grandchildren growing up round you it is very different. I haven't had that, more's the pity...

To H.B., Bagdad, January 15th, 1925

I have had rather an unsatisfactory week, the icy cold of the reception added to the daily freezing cold of my office having been finally too much. So I stayed indoors solidly for 4 days, bored to tears, and am now practically all right. There's a great deal too much doing to have anything the matter with one at this moment...

The Frontier Commission arrives to-morrow...

To H.B., Bagdad, January. 21st, 1925

This is going to be a very scrappy letter I fear, for I have too much to say and too little time to say it in. It's the Commission which is running us all to death. They arrived on Friday...

On Saturday Sir Henry sent for me, he sent me straight up to the King. I found H.M. in the charming domed room he uses as an office, sitting in full Arab dress before a blazing fire (it's still very cold). I gave my message to which he listened attentively...

As I motored back I found the Kotah bridge cut and stood in the crowd to watch the big launch pass up with Sir Henry and the Commission...

I dined at the Residency--a biggish party and a tail--all English. The Dobbses are being admirable, they are always cheerful and apparently amused, and all their arrangements go beautifully. They had an enormous reception on Saturday afternoon for the Bagdadis to meet the Commission ...

January 22nd We were 58 at dinner last night! All the Iraqis appeared without a fez, the first time I had ever seen many of them bareheaded. It was a protest against the Turkish head dress--I wonder if they now intend to abandon it altogether.

To F.B., Bagdad, January. 28th, 1925

...We are still having an amazing bout of cold weather. It has frozen almost every night since Xmas and for the last three nights the temp. has been down to 18. By day it's little above freezing point with an excruciating north wind which cuts you like a knife. The sheep are dying like flies, the benyon trees and sweet limes are all killed (I shan't wear mourning for the latter) and all the young orange trees are dead. The people suffer horribly; the price of food has doubled and trebled, and they are not clad or lodged in a manner to resist cold. Lots of people in the desert and the villages have died. In the north we hear that there is deep snow. They say there has not been such prolonged cold for 40 Of 50 years. Anyhow, I hope it won't happen again in my time for it is extremely disagreeable even if it is salutary for those who have furs and fires like me. I live in a fur coat except when I'm sitting before the fire in my sitting room. It's rare in this country to be longing for a little sun and warmth.

We are living through a very agitating time, feeling all of us that our destinies are in the melting pot. If good comes out of the Frontier Commission it will be mainly due to Sir Henry's extraordinarily tactful handling and the charming courtesy with which he and Esme treated them. ...

The Bagdadis played up splendidly. On Thursday there was a great Boy Scout function to which I went. We were in the teeth of an almost unendurable north wind. There were 1500 Iraqi Scouts and all the Scout Masters were Iraqis. It was in the Sarai, the old Turkish military head- quarters. All the balconies were crowded with people and the great open square too--there were some 5000 spectators. Besides the ordinary Scout exercises and tent pitchings--which they did extremely well--they took the opportunity of introducing a little nationalist propaganda. They made the Iraq flag in living boys dressed in the national colours, and they drew in chalk over the square a huge map of the Iraq, with frontiers formed by a line of boys--stretching north, I need not say, far beyond the present boundary!--and boys with Iraq flags indicating the three towns, Basrah, Bagdad and Mosul.

At the end they hoisted the Iraq flag on a tall standard. It was wonderfully moving. Some boys ran forward with the flag staff and set it up; then all the boys who carried the various scout flags ran up and formed a circle round it, while the other boys crowded in in a huge semi-circle, with the spectators crowding in behind them. When the chief Scout Master broke the flag a huge roar went up from the boys and the crowd and after it had died down the Scout Master cried out

"Three cheers for King Faisal the First!" Even out of doors they made a great sound...

To H.B., Bagdad February. 4th 1925

It is a trifle less cold. It no longer freezes at night and the sun is hot in the middle of the day, but the wind is still bitter. I walked out this afternoon, fetched a round outside the town and finally called on my dear Mistress of the Ceremonies to discuss a mourning party which the Queen is to give. It appears that you ought to be given the opportunity to express your sympathy and ask how she is. As soon as the French nuns have made her a plain white gown--white is Hijazi mourning--we're to issue the invitations.

To H.B., Bagdad February. 11th 1925

This isn't going to be a very bright letter for I am suffering under the shock of a domestic tragedy with which I feel sure you will sympathise- the death of my darling little spaniel, Peter, and of his mother, Sally, who was Ken's dog. I don't know which of them I loved most, for Sally was with me all the summer while Ken was on leave. But I shall now miss Peter most--he was always with us, in the office and everywhere, and he adored me, and I him. Sally had a cold a few days ago and as Ken was going out shooting with the King I offered to take her--we neither of us, nor the vet, had any idea that it was distemper which it really was, the very worst kind that ends in pneumonia. Peter caught it and died after agonies of stifled breathing at 4 a.m. this morning--I had been up with him all night--and Sally died after the same agonies at 5 p.m. Ken and I were both with her. So you will understand that I am rather shattered. My whole household was affected to tears--they all loved them. One should not make trouble for oneself by unnecessary affections, should one, but without affections what would life be? It is difficult to know where to draw the line.

Well, that's that. They are both buried in my garden...

I hope you are feeling a sense of relief at getting out of the rush. Your time on the sea will be very good for you, and how nice it will be seeing Elsa--my dear love to her. Tell her about Sally and Peter; she will be sorry for me, I know.

To F.B., Bagdad February. 18th, 1925

Thank you so much for the Cross Puzzle book. I have cracked my brain over it a little, with much amusement, and I'm going to bring it out on some suitable occasion at my parties...

We have had very heavy rain and on Friday afternoon I came home to find my sitting room more like a shower bath than anything else. You who live in solid houses don't know what the vicissitudes of the weather really mean. However, the sun came out on Saturday and the world has dried up wonderfully fast. It is beginning to feel like spring though it is still very cold at night...

To H.B., Bagdad February. 18th 1925

...It did rain! On Friday my roof, having been opened up by the frosts, gave up the game and I came home after lunch to find my sitting room more like a shower bath than anything else. However, fortunately the rain ceased about 5 and next day there was sun in which to dry the carpets. The world has dried up wonderfully fast...

I have been feeling dreadfully mopish about my poor little dogs, specially Peter, because I miss him dancing round me all day. Everyone has been most kind and sympathetic...

To H.B., Bagdad, February. 25th, 1925

...Even though I have been a govt. servant for 9 years I continue to be disappointed by the slowness with which official wheels grind...

To F.B., Bagdad, February. 25th, 1925

...I went to the Palace and first of all we looked at the children- Ghazi in a fearful jig because he had his first lesson in developing photographs in the developing box I had given him. He really is a nice little boy. He rushed and brought me a chair and said in English "Please sit down." The two girls were having a music lesson. And then we went to see Ghazi having a writing lesson in his own little house. He is making a garden, digging and planting in it himself and much pleased with it. Altogether I had a very pleasant impression...

Sunday was a delicious spring day. We lunched in the sun on the river bank. The peasants were all planting their summer vegetables. The whole family turns out for the day; the babies lie in the furrows and the dogs sit by. [A dinner followed by Bridge.] I introduced the Cross Puzzle book and Iltyd became so wrapped in it that he could scarcely remember what was trumps. It is very entertaining.

To H.B., Bagdad, March 4th, 1925

I got in from Ur at 6 a.m. this morning and not having slept in the train, I slept all this afternoon till 6...

Our excavations this year, without being so sensationally exciting as they were last year, have been extremely good and there were some wonderful objects to divide. The division was rather difficult but I think J.M. and I were very fair and reasonable--I hope Mr. Woolley thinks the same.

I do miss my Peter so. I longed for his little cheerful presence when I went to Ur. He would have loved that boring journey--so many dogs to look at out of the window...

H.M.G. has appointed the Financial Commission to enquire into the finance of Iraq--Hilton Young and Mr. Vernon (the latter financial adviser to the Col. Office). They arrive on March 15th. Excellent, we think, and it really looks like business. Our spirits are all going up.

To F.B., Bagdad, March 4th, 1925

...It has been a good season, though not so sensational as last year, but still there were some wonderful finds, rather more difficult than usual to divide. This year I left the great piece to them--it is a huge stele with amazingly interesting reliefs, but as it was all in fragments and needed a great deal of careful reconstruction, which we can't do here, I thought it was in the interests of science to let it go to

641

some big museum --the British Museum or Pennsylvania--where it can be properly treated...

To H.B., Bagdad, March 11th, 1925

...Upon my soul I almost wish there weren't a desert route--it brings silly females, all with introductions to me...

To F.B., Bagdad, March 12th, 1925

...I spent Sunday morning rearranging the Museum in a horrible dust storm which prevented J.M. and me from making a brief archaeological expedition by train that night. It was lucky we decided not to go as the train was held up by floods which wrecked the line and it never got anywhere...

Esme leaves next week to my great regret--she does make such a difference. We all love her. Sir Henry and she and I went for a little walk yesterday along the river bank where it was not too muddy, and it was so nice. It's a great pity that Esme won't be here to entertain the secretaries of state.

To H.B., Bagdad, March 18th, 1925

...Hilton Young has come bringing me a letter from Moll. He was to have dined with me the day after his arrival, but the High Commissioner pinched him. He is coming next Sunday. Everyone likes him, I hear, but he is gravelled to invent any way to make our budget balance for the next few years...

To H.B., Bagdad, March 25th, 1925

Uncle Lyulph's death came in Reuters yesterday--I feel very sad about it. It makes a great hole in the family, doesn't it...[This was Lord Sheffield.]

J.M. and I had a pleasant night at Kish, did our work and got safely back without motor accidents, contrary to our habit. The digging this year has been rather disappointing---nothing but grave finds, good of their kind but not specially important. One gets blasée about small Sumerian objects which were once so exciting and I do wish the ancients hadn't used so many copper pins. They are very dull in a museum. I spent most of Sunday morning arranging them, with Madame La Caze to help me...

On Sunday afternoon Ken and I took Hilton Young out to some marshes near the Baquba road to see birds. That was very nice. The birds played up and I brought out tea--partly in your thermos which is still one of the mainstays of existence--and Hilton Young was delighted and delightful.

Chiefly we are busy preparing for the Secretaries of State who arrive to-morrow. There are to be no end of functions for them.

To F.B., Bagdad, March 25th, 1925

...The Secretaries of State arrive to-morrow and we seem to spend our time in the office making arrangements for their parties and sightseeings. I hope they will be as nice as Mr. Hilton Young, who is charming. We all loved him. Tell Molly...

J.M. and I had a pleasant night at Kish. The finds aren't very good, at least, they are good of their kind but it's rather a boring kind, nothing of any great importance. I have a feeling that Kish is not going to yield much and I am sorry for the excavator, Mr. Mackay, who is looking very well and carefully without much to reward him...

Yes, I'm sure the snapdragons will be nice [at Rounton] if the peacocks don't sit on them.

To H.B., Bagdad, April 1st, 1925

I feel that I have been addressing myself to the winds and waves for a long time; I wonder when I shall get your first letter from Australia.

We have been remarkably busy with secretaries of state. They arrived last Thursday and I met them at lunch on Friday and carried off Mr. Amery in the afternoon to look at birds...They are all very sympathetic and I do like Sir John Shuckburgh so much...

On Monday we began again with an official dinner at the Residency to meet the Secretaries of State and the Cabinet...And on Tuesday everyone flew away to Mosul except Sir John who has stayed to study our difficulties and see what he can do to help...

To F.B., Bagdad, April 1st, 1925

...The description of Uncle Lyulph's funeral was so touching and beautiful. I can't yet picture the difference that his death makes in the family--I did care for him so much.

I have had rather a rushing week. The Ministerial party came back from their northern tour on Saturday. The Prime Minister gave an official dinner for them that night. I had a dinner for Sir John Shuckburgh on Sunday and another for Mr. Amery on Monday...

To-morrow we go off for a three days' Easter jaunt, Ken and Lionel and I, to Ukhaidhir. J.M. was to have come but can't get away. Mr. Cooke is coming in his place. I haven't been to Ukhaidhir since 1911.

The Secretaries of State flew down to Basrah to-day. I feel sure that their visit has been very useful and advantageous, but I shan't be sorry to relapse into a more humdrum existence when they go next week... Naturally, I have had nothing to do with their conferences; I have only heard the hopes and fears which they evoked in subsequent echoes.

There was a terrific dust storm last week after which the temperature fell to lower than it should normally be and we all shivered.

What a tale about Father's nearly missing his boat at Ceylon! Haven't heard from him yet from Australia--it's a terrific way off, isn't it.

To H.B., Bagdad, April 8th, 1925

I seem to be much busier outside the office than in it and I'm going to write to you this morning while I'm waiting for more files to turn up. The Secretaries of State were to have come back from their northern flights last Friday, but the whole country was wrapped in the most terrific dust stormlike a yellow London fog, we worked in the morning by electric light--and they were delayed in Kirkuk...

Mr. Amery's knowledge is encyclopaedic--he acquires it with extraordinary speed and never forgets what he has once acquired. He is not the least a pedant; what he knows, he knows quite naturally and simply...

To H.B., Bagdad, April 15th, 1925

[The "Easter jaunt" to Ukhaidir to which she had been looking forward.] It made me feel rather ghostlike to be in these places again, with such years between, and I was glad I wasn't there alone. Next day we motored back to Bagdad, lunching on the bank of the Euphrates under willow trees.

The Secretaries of State also returned from Bastah that day but I did not see them on Sunday, which I spent partly at the Museum in the morning and riding after tea, with the usual Bridge party at night.

Yesterday morning the Secretaries of State flew away in clouds of dust and glory and we all went down to the aerodrome to bid them farewell. And then, though relieved, we felt a little flat! But there's no doubt that their visit has done good. I love Sir John and Mr. Amery. The latter distinguished himself by conversing in Turkish which he hadn't done since 1898

To F.B., Bagdad, April 16th, 1925

The Secretaries of State left on Tuesday. I went with Mr. Amery to the Museum on Monday morning and on the way back he said very satisfactory things. He said he had been much struck by the admirable relations between the British officials and the Arabs, and thought the former had done wonderful work and that the whole administration was much better than he expected. I was very glad because I felt that he was giving praise where it was due...

I really am surprised that The Verge was a success on the stage--I should have thought it would have been too bewildering...

THE LETTERS OF GERTRUDE BELL

To H.B., Bagdad, April 22, 1925

I am very much interested by your accounts of the fifth continent and its inhabitants, but what you say confirms my feeling that I should never want to go there or to see them at home. But I like hearing about them from you. It must be horrid to have to cook one's own dinner always--it would be horrider to eat always the one I should cook, I'm bound to say.

As for my plans, I'm thinking of coming home for a couple of months towards the end of July, so as to have two peaceful months at Rounton. If I drop into the end of a London season, I rush about so and it's not very restful. So barring accidents, that is what is in my mind...

In the evening we were mainly engaged in canvassing the merits of a little black and white puppy which Col. Prescott had offered me. She ought to have been a spaniel but she has got mixed up with an Airedale and has the oddest little ugly pathetic face and very apologetic manners. I've got her so far on appro. She is singularly intelligent and already has a passion for me. The servants all call her Peter so I've called her Petra--my poor Peter!

We have been having odd weather--violent dust storms at the end of last week and on Sunday night a terrific thunderstorm and heavy rain which sent the temperature down with a bump. Very nice that was. J.M. and I had got permission from the AN.M. to go up to Kirkuk by air mail in order to see a little excavation which is being done there under the auspices of the Museum. We went yesterday morning and came back this morning--two and a half hours up and two hours down, with a following wind. I like flying. The only 'contretemps' was that they forgot to put my little valise into the plane and I arrived with nothing. However, my hostess, Mrs. Miller (Capt. Miller is Administrative Inspector) lent me brushes and combs and things, and once you have made up your mind that you have no luggage, it is rather an exhilarating feeling.

We got in about 10:30, saw some things in the town that we wanted to see and after lunch went out to the dig which is being very well done by a certain Dr. Chiera, an Italian professor of Assyriology at an American University. It's a villa, a house belonging to some wealthy private person who lived about 800 B.C. Chiera has found masses of tablets from which we hope that we shall ultimately piece together the story of the family. It's a comfortable house with a bathroom, hot and cold water laid on, so to speak (we found and traced the drain while we were there), nice big reception rooms, a paved court and all you could wish. It was very interesting and the country round Kirkuk looked so agreeable with scarlet ranunculus on the edges of the green barley fields. It was delightfully cold too...

The King has asked me to go out to his farm near Khanaqin for a couple of days during the holidays at the end of Ramadhan. They begin on Friday or Saturday but as H.M. wants to leave on Friday afternoon I expect they will continue to see the new moon on Thursday. I shall go, I think; a couple of days out of doors would be good and it doesn't look as if it would be too hot.

To H.B., Bagdad, April 29th, 1925

We had some emotions as to the beginning of the Id. on Thursday night no one knew whether the moon had been seen nor whether there was an Id and a levee and a departure to the King's farm (for me) next day. At 11 p.m. the guns announced the Id, for they had managed to get the moon seen at sunset but it had taken the Qadhi all those hours to make sure that the witnesses had spoken true.

I hopped up at 6 to get Zaya and my baggage off to the station and at 8 behold me at the King's levee. I then in the course of an hour visited all the Ministers and the Naqib, went home and got into country clothes and at 10 was picked up by H.M. at the station near my house. We went up by trolley--the party was H.M., Naji Suwaidi, a Chamberlain and an A.D.C. The King's farm is a little to the N.W. of Khanaqin. We got to the nearest point to his tents at 2, having had an excellent lunch in the trolley, found horses waiting and rode up through the fields to the tents, about 20 minutes away. It was so heavenly to be riding through grass and flowers--gardens of purple salvia and blue borage and golden mullein, with scarlet ranunculus in between. After tea we went out for a walk through the crops, H.M. rejoicing over his splendid hemp and barley and wheat--they were splendid, I must say. And then we sat in the pleasant dark till dinner, after which we all went to bed. Zaya had arrived by this time and I had all my camp furniture in an enormous tent--unfortunately I shared it with innumerable sand flies. Petra had come with me; she enjoyed herself enormously and behaved not too badly for one so young. She is going to be a nice little dog...

We left after dinner, Iltyd, J.M. and I riding for half an hour to the station through black night on a path which played in and out of the irrigation canals. I had Petra on my saddle bow--she proved an excellent rider but it was fright rather than pleasure which kept her quiet I think. We succeeded in catching the train after missing our way several times and got safely to Bagdad next morning. It was a very nice Id.

Hilton Young has presented his report and gone. I read the report this morning. It's admirable. There are no miracles, just good sense --and helpful advice to both Governments, but if it is followed we ought to get on to our feet in a year or two...

To F.B., Bagdad, April 29th, 1925

Your visit to Newtimber sounds delightful but it wasn't nicer than my visit to the King's farm last week...It was so delicious, grass and wild flowers everywhere; you can't think what that was like after the arid desert round Bagdad. The farm is just under the Persian hills with lovely views in all directions. On Saturday morning Iltyd Clayton arrived by train and on Sunday J. M Wilson, so we made a regular house- party. We walked and rode and motored, looked at all the crops, settled where the house is to be built (he is still in tents) and where the roads are to be made and we were very peaceful and happy. It is very delightful being with the King up there: he is a perfect host and he puts politics out of his head and becomes the country gentleman very contentedly. It is excellent for him that he should have a place of his own to go to and when the little house is built it will be even better. For though it is very pleasant to be in tents at this moment, in another week or so it will be too hot. Even to-day I had a fan in my office for the first time. We got back on Monday morning and were very sorry that it was over...

Now I must go up and see the Queen about her washing silk dresses. Those sent by Moll are a great success. I've written a long rambling letter to Father about the visit to the farm thinking it would beguile him on the ship and that's why this one to you is rather scrappy. I shall be glad when my parents are happily reunited! I daresay they will too.

To F.B., Bagdad, May 6th, 1925

...Yes, I think clothes are frightful, or at least they offer vast opportunities for frightfulness...

To F.B., Bagdad, May 13th, 1925

...There has been a nice, very young Guardsman here, Mr. Codrington. I have just been showing him some of the sights of the town...

To F.B., Bagdad, May 13th, 1925

We have had a week of very disagreeable weather, not hot--not for us; it's rarely 100--but south wind and cloud and heaviness and dust. It takes all the stiffening out of you. On Saturday night it suddenly became wonderful fresh for a few hours and we made the most of them by going out to the Karradah gardens and dining on Haji Naji's roof, Ken and Iltyd and Lionel and I. He gave us a very good dinner--roast fish and chicken and rice and all the different kinds of vegetables he grows on his farm, and fruit. After dinner we lay on his cushioned benches under the moon and talked to one another while Haji Naji and a friend bubbled with narghilehs...

To F.B., Bagdad, May 20th, 1925

The chief news this week is that which you already know, namely that the Council of the League will not receive the report of the Frontier Commission till the Autumn session...

Last night just as night fell we were enveloped in a raging dust storm; the subsequent night was disgusting, the wind so hot that one couldn't sleep out of doors and the house so stuffy that one could scarcely sleep inside. Weather of this kind cannot be described; it must be experienced.

649

So far as heat goes, it has not been bad--only once over 100 I think- but south wind and dust storms have been unusually frequent and they take the stiffening out of you more than heat...

I'm not writing to father this week. It is a comfort he is coming nearer. Australia is dreadfully far away isn't it. Thank heaven, I hear that Cook is opening an office here so that I shall no longer be the sole agent for tourists...

To H.B., Bagdad, June 10th, 1925

We are in the thick of elections and so far the results are more than reasonably good. The electors choosing decent, solid men. I don't think the House will meet till the autumn; the budget is not ready and cannot be prepared until a decision on the Hilton Young report has been taken by both governments, so there's nothing for it to meet about...

Now I'm going to swim. Petra is a great swimming dog and loves it. She is a clever little thing but not as nice as Peter. Are you glad to be home and to see so many of your family?

You didn't say whether you saw Elsa in Ceylon this time.

To H.B., Bagdad, June 17th, 1925

...On Monday the Queen asked me to come and take a stroll on the bank opposite the palace. I arrived about 5:15 and we spent half an hour in desultory talk. Then I suggested that we should cross over the river, but their launch was out of order so at 6 I insisted on going over in a boat. Mme. Jaudat, the Mistress of the Ceremonies had meantime arrived with her little boy, and we all went over, the two girls, Ghazi, Miss Fairley, H.M. and I. On the other bank I found that leisurely preparations for a large meal were going on, including a pile of fish waiting to be roasted ...and finally about 7 a sort of high tea was ready, sandwiches and roast fish and cakes. And as it was a very pleasantly cool evening it was agreeable to sit there and eat...

To H.B., Bagdad, June 24th, 1925

It was very nice to get your letter home of June 11th and Mother's of June 10th in which she says she is suffering so from the heat. I know what will happen--by the time I get home it will be icy and will remain so for the two months of my leave. And probably rain all the time. However perhaps that will be a pleasant change.

I was cut to the heart about Anthony. [Brig. Gen. Hon. Anthony Henley, who had died suddenly in Roumania.] I hope you will give me some news of Sylvia.

An interesting man came to see me on Monday, one Pernot. He is editor of the Revue des Deux Mondes and is making an exhaustive enquiry for it and for the Débats into the state of Moslem feeling towards the West ...

Politically we are in full crisis ...On the whole the country is all in favour of stability. It's a pity that here as elsewhere the economic stringency presses ...so greatly. Trade is at a low ebb and a bad harvest has made things especially difficult.

Goodbye, dearest. There's a despatch waiting to be written for Sir Henry.

[Gertrude came on leave this year and arrived in London on July 17th. She was in a condition of great nervous fatigue, and appeared exhausted mentally and physically. Sir Thomas Parkinson, M.D., our old and valued friend as well as our doctor said that she was in a condition which required a great deal of care and that she ought not to return to the climate of Bagdad. Dr. Thomas Body, M.D., of Middlesbrough who saw her when she went north took the same view. On Gertrude's way through London she saw Mrs. W. L. Courtney, who came to dine one night at 95 Sloane Street with her and her father. She had a few minutes private talk with Mrs. Courtney and asked her to suggest something that she could do if she remained in England. Mrs. Courtney wrote a few days later suggesting that Gertrude should stand for Parliament. The following letter is the reply.]

THE LETTERS OF GERTRUDE BELL

To Mrs. W. L. Courtney, Rounton Grange, Northallerton, August 4

YOU DEAR AND BELOVED JANET,

No, I'm afraid you will never see me in the House. I have an invincible hatred of that kind of politics and if you knew how little I should be fitted for it you would not give it another thought--though it is delightful of you, all the same, to think of it. I have not, and I have never had the quickness of thought and speech which could fit the clash of parliament. I can do my own job in a way and explain why I think that the right way of doing it, but I don't cover a wide enough field and my natural desire is to slip back into the comfortable arena of archaeology and history and to take only an onlooker's interest in the contest over actual affairs. I know I could not enter the lists, apart from the fact that it would make me supremely miserable.

I shall hope to see you in London before I leave--that will be about the end of September. For I think I must certainly go back for this winter, though I privately very much doubt whether it won't be the last.

Goodbye, my dear,

and don't forget that I'm ever your very affectionate,

Gertrude.

[Gertrude came to Rounton, for a while, much enjoying her own gardens, and grew gradually better there. She then went to stay in Scotland with Mr. and Mrs. Lionel Dugdale at their shooting box, where the affectionate solicitude with which they surrounded her went far to complete her cure.

We all felt after this last visit of Gertrude to England that she had never seemed more glad to be with us all, never more affectionate and delightful to all her Yorkshire surroundings. It was a solace to her when the time came for her return to Bagdad at the beginning of October to have the company of her cousin Sylvia (Hon. Mrs. Anthony Henley) for whom she cared very much.]

THE LETTERS OF GERTRUDE BELL

To F.D. October 2nd, 1925

...You must think of us as very happy together--I can't be too glad that I've got Sylvia. She is an enchanting traveling companion. I read the Great Pandolfo in the train yesterday and began Black Oxen-- both very good...

To H.B., Monday. Oct. 5th, 1925

...Sylvia's delight in everything has been such an added zest-- she has never been on a sea voyage before and her interest culminated when Captain S. took us on to the bridge last night and showed us the stars through a sextant...

To H.B., Haifa, October 9th, 1925

Here we are nearly at the end of a rather tiresome slow jour- ney which would have been more than tiresome if it had not been for Sylvia's delight in all the places we touched at...

[They go on shore at Jaffa].

...We went on shore after breakfast and drove out to the new Jewish suburb, the inhabitants of which subsist I understand on taking in one another's washing. It looked a poorish place--on the outskirts gaunt new houses were being run up on the sand. These are let out room by room, at exorbitant rates, to Jewish immigrants. Gladly we drove back to Jaffa which is however, also submerged by Jews. At last we got out of them to a delightful little Palestinian hotel by the sea at the extreme southern end of the town--is to the north. We lunched happily on a balcony and on our way back walked through the old Arab town, a tiny medieval place with narrow streets, half arched over, climbing up and down a hill. It was the first really Eastern place which Sylvia had seen and she loved it. So did I. That night we played bridge with a brother and sister called Kennedy--he is in Posts and Telegraphs here. Before parting we arranged to meet on shore at 3 p.m. to-day so that he should take us in his car on to Mount Carmel. Accordingly we stayed on board till after lunch, but when we proposed to go on shore we found that we had not got the necessary documents for landing, the Customs Officer having disappeared before we were up. The policeman left in charge doggedly refused to allow our boat to put off--we were a long way from the shore. However, I cajoled the Arab boatmen and they took us away under the very eyes of the indignant policeman. On the pier we met the Kennedys and between us persuaded the English Customs House man to give us our permits and forgive our boatmen. We had a delightful drive on Carmel and from the top saw the heights of Gilead, across Jordan. On the way back we stopped at the Monastery and at that moment a Carmelite monk came out of the door. "That's Father Lamb," said Mr. Kennedy, "the Father-Superior." With that I went boldly up and said who I was--of course he had heard of me from the Carmelites at Bagdad. Our success was complete when Sylvia announced herself to be the niece of Monsignor Algernon [Stanley]. Nothing would satisfy Father Lamb but to take us all about himself, into Elijah's cave, into the garden (where Sylvia made him pose for a picture with the monastery behind him) and finally up to the guest rooms to give us a glass of Carmel liqueur. We parted in warm friendship and the Kennedys drove us back to the port where we found our boatmen waiting...

[They finally land at Beyrout].

BEYROUT, Oct. 10th. 1925. The French C.G.S., Commandant Deutz, has telephoned to ask if he may come and see me. I met him at Bagdad, a very intelligent, liberal-minded man...

We went to the American College--exquisite place. The Dodges were out, but I introduced myself to one of the professors and we ran to ground Sabah son of Nuri Pasha, who rushed to greet me as soon as he saw me and asked me to take a letter to his father. While I was waiting for the letter to be written Sylvia went to see the hospital. Several other Iraq boys came and greeted me--one the nephew of the Naqib. They all came over ten days ago and the road is quite safe.

Then we went to the Museum where I sent in my card to the Director. He came and showed us over and opened for us the safe which contains the famous golden treasure of Byblos --about 1300 B.C. Most interesting, but what interested me more were the sarcophagi with Phoenician inscriptions said to date from the 4th millennium B.C. That's as early as our earliest inscriptions from Ur...

654

Oh it's fun to be me when one gets to Asia--there's no doubt of it...

...Got to Bagdad at 1:30, in thick winter clothes with a temperature of 90. S. went straight off to the Residency and I home where I was greeted rapturously by my servants. Marie performed prodigies of unpacking and by one o'clock I had had a bath and got into a cotton gown...

This is very much potted news I have no time for more except to say that the Iraq and its government are being models of orderliness and wisdom and that Sir H. still hopes to get home on leave at Xmas.

To H.B., Bagdad, October 14th, 1925

It has been so wonderful coming back here. For the first two days I could not do any work at all in the office, because of the uninterrupted streams of people who came to see me. "Light of our eyes," they said, "Light of our eyes," as they kissed my hands and made almost absurd demonstrations of delight and affection. It goes a little to the head, you know--I almost began to think I were a Person.

Sylvia also came to dine ...On Friday she moved over to me. She has Marie's room which we have made very comfortable and Marie sleeps in the garden room--the sitting room when you were here. My household are thrilled to have her and put themselves in four to serve her...

On Saturday afternoon we annexed Mr. Warner (our travelling companion who is on his way to the Teheran Legation) and took him off to call on Haji Naji. Haji Naji took us through all the orange gardens, loaded us with fruit and flowers and gave us tea and coffee. It was so delicious- Sylvia loved it...

I called on all the Ministers, found them all in their offices and had a most satisfactory talk with each one of them : they are worn to a shadow what with having to sit in Parliament all the morning, get through their office work between12and 4 and then attend a meeting of the Government party to settle the line which is to be taken next day in the house. But the system is working excellently...

They have almost got through the work of the preliminary session (the budget) and hope to adjourn next week. The new session meets on November 1 but their scheme is to open it formally and then prorogue for a month or 6 weeks. I devoutly hope they will for I find the compilation of the parliamentary reports from the very bad reports in the vernacular papers a most exhausting business. One begins by reading all the papers through and then one compiles a composite report drawn from all four.

On Sunday afternoon Sylvia and I went to the races. It was excessively hot--it has been over 90 every day since we came back--and S. wasn't feeling very fit, though she would not hear of not going...

She was looking quite enchanting in a black and white muslin gown. She creates a sensation in Bagdad society whenever she appears. H.E. brought us back and sat talking for a bit. Sylvia then went to tea and read while I tackled some of my gradually diminishing pile of papers. At 7:30 I went in and found her very unwell and in great pain. I sent at once for a Doctor; Sinbad is still away but I got hold of Woodman whom we both like very much. Her temperature was 104

To H.B., Bagdad, October 14th, 1925

On Monday morning S. was better. I saw her Doctor before I went to the office and heard that he considered her malady to be nothing but the usual sort of internal upset that almost every newcomer goes through before they settle down to Bagdad. I've no doubt the unaccustomed heat had something to do with it ...

[After this, Sylvia had ups and downs of health, although able at intervals to join in seeing the people and the sights of Bagdad all of which she enjoyed very much. It was finally decided that she ought not to remain in the East, and she returned to England in November, 1925, to Gertrude's great disappointment.]

Sir Henry has written a quite admirable report on the history of the country since 1920--taking it up where my white paper left it. The C.O. is going to publish it and you must read it at once. There is a really beautiful page about Sir Percy with a very graceful mention of me at the end. For once in my life I have liked being mentioned by name as part of Sir Percy's material...

...no, railway discussions can't be very cheerful at this juncture. I do wish you hadn't such horrid things to do--I feel a real compunction at having such nice ones to do myself.

...On Sunday morning I didn't go out--far from it. I had breakfast in bed and tried to make believe that I wasn't an overworked Oriental secretary. I wrote a remarkable memo. on tribal customs, the second. I had spent all Saturday morning over the first at the office.

...In spite of all I have said of my activities in the office you must please remember that I am not a Person...

To H.B., Bagdad, Nov. 17th, 1925

On Sunday the King at last arrived. Ken took Sylvia and me to the aerodrome where all high dignitaries and notables were assembled. We waited there for about three-quarters of an hour but it was very amusing talking to all the people. At 11 H.M.'s great plane came in sight, convoyed by 9 little planes, a most beautiful spectacle, and made a perfect landing, drawing up exactly opposite the reception tents. H.E., Zaid and Ghazi went forward to greet him as he stepped out, the Ministers, Advisers and I followed, and out he came looking very well and very much pleased while the British guard of honour played the Arab national tune. It was immensely effective and has made a deep impression here on the Arab mind.

Having made my curtsey I retired into the background while H.M. sat in his tent and received the notables. S. and I drove behind his procession with Ken to the end of the town to see the decorations and the crowd. There is no doubt he has come back with a large and shining halo...

To H.B., Bagdad, Nov. 25th, 1925

...The two Americans dined with Mr. Edwards who is a very eager amateur. After dinner we three examined pottery which they had picked up on the tells near Khabu, a northern tributary of the Euphra-

657

tes. I'm going to bore you by telling you that a lot of it was our oldest Sumerian stuff which we have got both in the Southern Delta and round Kirkuk, all of which means that the earliest Sumerian civilization (circa 3300 B.C. a date well within the margin) covered the whole area of the two rivers. Some other pottery they had obviously much later, which they could not place. I had a vague idea that I knew it. I got down one of the Hertzfeld's great Euphrat-Tigris Gebiet volumes and there it was! exactly, exactly the same in his pictures late classical or early Byzantine. I may add that the Americans jumped (too hastily) to the conclusion that they had met in me the first authority on Mesopotamian pottery...

...My hat what a social asylum bridge is

...Next day Sunday, I went to the Museum where I had an assignation with the two Americans. We spent a glorious hour over early pottery and all of us learnt a good deal--I know I did. On the way home I showed them a couple of mediaeval buildings and an 8th century marble mahrab, the oldest monument in Bagdad. They were thrilled and so was I. We went to the Diala and walked along the bank in palm groves, most lovely hough why a bit of desert and a stretch of and a few palms and a sunset should have been so lovely I don't know. It was only God's bright and intricate device I suppose...

To H.B., Bagdad, December. 9th, 1925

To-day I have worked like a beaver all the morning--Bernard being away I had to do a lot of his work...I have a terrific amount to do--the annual report and an article for the Encyclopaedia and I don't know what more.

To H.B., Bagdad, December 30th, 1925

I've had some adventures myself. Following the example of everyone in Bagdad--nearly--I had a terrific cold in the head last week and when I wrote to you I had been indoors for two days, but I didn't tell you "not wishing to trouble you." Bernard was in bed with a cold too so it was all most inconvenient...

On Sunday I put on more clothes than I have ever worn before, and with a hot water bottle on my knees, went up with the King
and Ken and Iltyd in a closed trolley to Khanaqin. We got to the farm
about sunset, found some of the new furniture arrived and spent a
happy time arranging it, the King and I began then to feel very tired
and went to bed immediately after dinner. Next morning I felt rather
bad; they all came in to see if I wanted things and were in favour Of
not going out shooting. However I shoo'd them off and Zaya looked
after me till 5 when they came in. I felt rather better and had them in
before dinner to play a game of Bridge with me in bed. But the next
day I was pretty bad so Ken sent for the very good local doctor only to
find that he was spending Xmas away and immediately, without telling
me, telegraphed to Bagdad for a doctor. By that time I wasn't taking
much notice, except that I had a general feeling that I was slipping into
great gulfs ...Finally at 6 arrived Dr. Spencer. He brought with him a
charming nurse, Miss Hannifan, who sat up with me all night. They
were both of them convinced that I had got pneumonia, but not a bit
Of it. Next morning it was clear that it was no worse than pleurisy and
a pretty general congestion. So they delayed the departure of the morning train by an hour, thus do we behave with our railway management,
and took me down to Bagdad ... They sat a good deal in my compartment and amused me, I had a very comfortable journey. An ambulance
met me at the station and took me straight to hospital, I told Ken to go
and sit on my letters for I didn't think I could bear them while I felt so
weak, but he did far better, for he found your telegram of the 24th in
my house and sent it straight down to me. So by the 27th I was feeling
that acute anxiety was over--I hope I am right.

[This refers to Hugo. See last paragraph of this chapter.]

I have spent two very quiet days in bed. Marie comes in the
morning and Ken and Iltyd to tea. The Prime Minister paid me a visit
this morning and Sayad Afhan came the morning before, and Elsie
Sinbad to-day before lunch. Sinbad came in yesterday coming as soon
as he got back to see how I was going on. Otherwise, --with the strong
backing up of Dr. Spencer, I've refused to be flooded with visitors after the Arab fashion, and I'm quickly getting well. I have had a night
nurse up to now, but I feel sure I shall not need her after to-night--Miss
Isherwood, I like her very much too, but Miss Hannifan is a nurse who
almost makes it worth while to be ill. And lest you may think that I'm
tottering about on edges of graves, I may tell you that Drs. Spencer,

Woodman and Dunlop all declare that if I hadn't the most remarkable constitution I should certainly have now been dangerously ill with pneumonia.

[This December and January were overshadowed for Gertrude by the deep anxiety which she shared with us about her much-loved brother Hugo. He contracted typhoid on his voyage home from South Africa with his wife and children in the autumn of 1925, and when they arrived in England on December 11th, he was desperately ill. Hope was almost abandoned. In the third week of December, however, his condition improved, and at Christmas and the New Year the cloud seemed to be lifting. Then he had a relapse. He died on February 2nd, 1926.]

CHAPTER XXVI

1925-1926 - BAGDAD

To Hon. Mrs. Henley., Bagdad, December. 9th, 1925

...I am anxious about Hugo. My parents write me that they hear by wireless that he has pneumonia on board ship coming home and I know no more. If anything happened to him it would be such a terrible blow...

To the same, Bagdad, December. 23rd, 1925

...You can't think what a memory you have left with me, of courage and delicious companionship, and of distinguished wit and high character. I often think about you and I always think how fortunate I am to have you for a cousin and a friend.

You will realise that I am terribly unhappy about Hugo...My heart aches for my darling mother and father and for his poor wife. Isn't it all tragic. If it weren't for love and friendship the world would be a bitter place, but thank God for them, and I will try to make my corner warmer and kinder. I feel I have so much more than I deserve.

To the same, Bagdad, January. 15th, 1926

...I don't suppose you can imagine how often I have missed you and how much. Not only to talk to for myself...we seem to have left such a lot of things untalked about, we Must have wasted our time--but also when there are other people here, to throw the ball so that we may catch it and throw it back. Mr. Cooke says "she woke us all up" and that's perfectly true, but being awake to what companionship can be like it is hard to have it snatched from me. I keep seeing in imagination all your darling ways and your charming grace and hearing echoes of your delicious voice--but there it is...

To H.B., Bagdad, January 6th, 1926

I can't tell you how I've enjoyed reading the "Confessions of a Capitalist." It's a book everyone should read and I'm now going to lend it to all my friends. It contains as much good sound sense as there are sentences to the page. I did rejoice over it--things like the fallacy involved in profit sharing, you remember. I can't say that any of it is exactly new to me (except Pareto's law which I hadn't heard of before) for I have been brought up so well that I could hear you saying most of the things I was reading in the book. But he has put it well together and in fact what I really meant to say was "God bless my soul! how any" etc. That's what I feel. I hope it will be widely read, that book, and that it will cause a storm of controversy over which its author will sail joyously with his good heavy facts for a keel. Anyhow, you see you gave me a most successful present and I've been talking about it to everyone who comes to see me ... are all scrambling for it and I'm only wondering which of them will read it quickest so that I may get it on to more people still.

That and the 3rd vol. of the Cambridge Ancient History which has just come out, have been the staples of my days, but if you want to laugh feebly I can tell you a silly ass book which will help you--"Bill the Conqueror"; I forget the name of the talented author, but he nearly gave me a relapse and I'm sure you would feel that way too. Lionel is now seeking round Bagdad for the rest of his books. "Bill the Conqueror" was supplied by Ken. For good simple nonsense he is not easy to beat.

To F.B., Bagdad, January 6th, 1926

I've been having a little quiet illness of my own but it's nearly gone. I was quite bad for a day or two, but now they all saying that they really wouldn't have bothered if they had known the kind of person they were dealing with. For three nights I had the most preposterous sort of nightmares, mostly about Iraq and the treaty and so on, but I'm pleased to remember that one was about flints, which I've been hearing about lately. You'll scarcely believe me but someone (in the nightmare) gave me a flint which had a fossil shell in it and I was so fearfully angry at anyone being such an idiot as to think that a flint could have a fossil shell in it, that I had to wake myself up and say what I thought about it. I found myself saying it and afterwards thought that, 'mutatis mutandis,' it was just the kind of thing that Father would do when he was ill...

To H.B., Bagdad, January 13th, 1926

My convalescence has been happily spent reading a great deal of archaeology and writing an article for the Encyclopaedia on the Iraq. The article would have been better if I had not been forced to compress so fearfully. Even as it is, I don't think it is so bad, but it has to be vetted by the Colonial office and perhaps they will take the spark of life out of it. I'm now embarked on the Annual Report for the League and am (if the truth were known) postponing my return to the office in order to break the back of it. For it is a terrific effort to get through a big piece of work while one is involved in the daily drudgery. I am, however, quite well, sleep, eat and go out walking daily. Indeed I think that the ten days of enforced idleness has done me a great deal of good.

The Iraq Cabinet has accepted the new treaty and I don't think there will be any difficulty about it in our Parliament...

...You need not be alarmed about our 25 years' mandate. If we go on as fast as we've gone for the last two years, Iraq will be a member of the League before five or six years have Passed, and our direct responsibility will have ceased. It's almost incredible how the country is settling down. I look back to 1921 or 1922 and can scarcely believe that so great a change has taken place...It's all being so interesting. Archaeology and my museum are taking a bigger and bigger place. I do hope this year to get the Museum properly lodged and arranged. It's such fun isn't it, to make things new from the beginning...

Did I tell you I was now started off on flints, the most enthralling study. We have nothing as yet in the Iraq earlier than historic times (4000 B.C. downwards, roughly) but I'm going to set the oil geologists to find the oldest iron terraces and see if we can't pick up palaeolithic flints on them. If you could send me any short and handy treatise on flints I should be much obliged. I gather that, as a mineral, they are not very old, not what geologists call old...

To H.B., Bagdad, January 20th, 1926

I'm afraid that this will be a short and dull letter for the truth is that I'm being overworked! I have the rather tedious 'corvée' of the annual report upon me and to fit it into the ordinary office routine and take a little necessary exercise is about all I can do. I hope to get through it in the next fortnight and then to go to see the excavations at Ur and Kish which will be very refreshing...

You will please note that the Iraq is the only eastern country which pulls together with Great Britain and the reason is that we have honestly tried out here to do the task that we said we were going to do, i.e., create an independent Arab state...

Your letter and Mother's of Jan. 6th gave such a satisfactory account of Hugo and I also had a most delightful letter from Frances. It is to me more and more miraculous that he should be alive, isn't it to you? To have been so terribly ill under such unfavourable conditions and to have recovered is almost incredible. It is so comforting to think that now every circumstance is favourable...

What a good plan that Herbert should go with you to Italy. He will be the most delightful addition to the party.

I did so love Mother's letter of Jan. 6 with the account of Xmas doings and I'm only not writing to her this week because, as I told you, my fingers are worn to the bone!

To H.B., Bagdad, January 27th, 1926

...It has been bad weather and I have done very little but work. The horrible annual report can't make the League of Nations yawn more than I have over it. It's the dullest thing I've ever written. It's so much more interesting to write about wicked people than good ones, and the same applies to states. The better we get the duller we shall be.

Incidentally I have read the enchanting volume of Page's "Letters to President Wilson." Do you remember when Lichnowsky accuses the U.S.A. of putting off the evil day in Mexico, and Page replies "What better can you do with an evil day than put it off?"

Now do you know, that is what I feel about leaving here. I simply can't bear to think of it, and I don't...

To F.B., Bagdad, 3rd March, 1926

I feel sure you will be glad to hear that I have got the building I wanted of all others for my museum. After addressing the Prime Minister in exalted terms, His Excellency came hurrying into my office, replete with promises. He advised me to get hold of Ken whose Ministry disposes of Government buildings. What could be easier! I hauled Ken off to the place and found him the more easy to convince because it was he who first gave me a secret hint that it might be obtainable and be is now full of satisfaction that his idea has turned out so well. So we settled it all in half an hour and to-day its former occupants have almost all turned out, and I have been settling about repairs, etc. Ken observes with complacency that the Ministry of Interior, when it once gets going, sticks at nothing and indeed I am amazed at the promptness with which it has been done. Government offices don't usually move fast I am going to lodge the Library of the American School, which will be a great advantage to us, besides being very gratifying to them, and have heaps and heaps of room to show off all our things. At present you must tumble over one in order to have a glimpse of another. Oh dear, how much I should like you to see it! It will be a real Museum, rather like the British Museum only a little smaller. I am ordering long shallow drawers in chests to hold the pottery fragments, so that you will pull out a drawer and look at Sumerian bits, and then another and look at Parthian glaze, and another for early incised, then Arab incised (which I can pick up in quantities a quarter of an hour from my door) and Arab glaze and all. Won't it be nice? It is also nice to think that I shall clear the cupboards of my house of a mass of biscuit tins full of dusty fragments...

THE LETTERS OF GERTRUDE BELL

To H.B., Bagdad, March 3rd, 1926

...My chief concern, at present, is that I have got the place I wanted for a museum and to-day I have been round it with the Civil Engineer of Bagdad and arranged about needful whitewashings and repairs. It is an excellent building which will give me ample space and allow me an office for the curator and an office for myself, which I ought to have, room to house duplicates till I can dispose of them and a big, fine room for large exhibits. When I come back from Ur, where I am going next week for the division of the objects found this year, I shall be able to begin getting in to it, I hope. I shall take great pride in making it something like a real museum. I always feel, when I'm back to archaeology, that I am nothing better than an antiquarian at heart.

I had Vita Nicolson [Hon. Mrs. Harold Nicolson] with me for two days. She arrived on Saturday morning for breakfast and left on Sunday night after an early dinner...She was most agreeable.

[I reproduce here, by Mrs. Nicolson's permission, a chapter from A Passage to Teheran describing her brief visit to Gertrude.]

Gertrude Bell in Bagdad, by V. Sackville-West.

"...Anyone who goes to Bagdad in search of romance will be disappointed. It is a dusty jumble of mean buildings connected by atrocious streets, quagmires of mud in rainy weather, and in dry weather a series of pits and holes over which an English farmer might well hesitate to drive a waggon. I confess that I was startled by the roads of Bagdad, especially after we had turned out of the main street and drove between high, blank walls along a track still studded with the stumps of palm-trees recently felled; the mud was not dry here, and we skidded and slithered, hitting a tree-stump and getting straightened on our course again, racketing along, tilting occasionally at an angle which defied all the laws of balance, and which in England would certainly have overturned the more conventionally minded motor.

"Then: a door in the blank wall, a jerky stop, a creaking of hinges, a broadly smiling servant, a rush of dogs, a vista of garden-path edged with carnations in pots, a little verandah and a little low house at the end of the path, an English voice--Gertrude Bell.

"I had known her first in Constantinople, where she had arrived straight out of the desert, with all the evening dresses and cutlery and napery that she insisted on taking with her on her wanderings; and then in England; but here she was in her right place, in Iraq, in her own house, with her office in the city, and her white pony in a corner of the garden, and her Arab servants, and her English books, and her Babylonian shards on the mantelpiece, and her long thin nose, and her irrepressible vitality. I felt all my loneliness and despair lifted from me in a second. Had it been very hot in the Gulf? got fever, had I? but quinine would put that right; and a sprained ankle--too bad!--and would I like breakfast first, or a bath? and I would like to see her museum, wouldn't I? did I know she was Director of Antiquities in Iraq? wasn't that a joke? and would I like to come to tea with the king? and yes, there were lots of letters for me. I limped after her as she led me down the path, talking all the time, now in English to me, now in Arabic to the eager servants. She had the gift of making everyone feel suddenly eager; of making you feel that life was full and rich and exciting. I found myself laughing for the first time in ten days. The garden was small, but cool and friendly; her spaniel wagged not only his tail but his whole little body; the pony looked over the loose-box door and whinnied gently; a tame partridge hopped about the verandah; some native babies who were playing in a corner stopped playing to stare and grin. A tall, grey sloughi came out of the house, beating his tail against the posts of the verandah; 'I want one like that,' I said, 'to take up into Persia.' I did want one but I had reckoned without Gertrude's promptness. She rushed to the telephone, and as I poured cream over my porridge I heard her explaining--a friend of hers had arrived--must have a sloughi at once--was leaving for Persia next day-- a selection of sloughis must be sent round that morning. Then she was back in her chair, pouring out information: the state of Iraq, the excavations at Ur, the need for a decent museum, what new books had come out? what was happening in England? The doctors had told her she ought not to go through another summer in Bagdad, but what should she do in England, eating out her heart for Iraq? next year, perhaps ...but I couldn't say she looked ill, could I? I could, and did. She laughed and brushed that aside. Then, jumping up--for all her movements were quick and impatient--if I had finished my breakfast wouldn't I like my bath? and she must go to her office, but would be back for luncheon. Oh yes, and there were people to luncheon; and so, still talking, still laughing, she pinned on a hat without looking in the glass, and took her departure.

"I had my bath--her house was extremely simple, and the bath just a tin saucer on the floor--and then the sloughis began to arrive. They slouched in, led on strings by Arabs in white woollen robes, sheepishly smiling. Left in command, I was somewhat taken aback, so I had them all tied up to the posts of the verandah, till Gertrude should return, an array of desert dogs, yellow, white, grey, elegant, but black with fleas and lumpy with ticks. I dared not go near them, but they curled up contentedly and went to sleep in the shade, and the partridge prinked round them on her dainty pink legs, investigating. At one o'clock Gertrude returned, just as my spirits were beginning to flag again; laughed heartily at this collection of dogs which her telephone message (miraculously, as it seemed to me) had called into being, shouted to the servants, ordered a bath to be prepared for the dog I should choose, unpinned her hat, set down some pansies on her luncheon-table, closed the shutters, and gave me a rapid biography of her guests.

"She was a wonderful hostess, and I felt that her personality held together and made a centre for all those exiled Englishmen whose other common bond was their service for Iraq. They all seemed to be informed by the same spirit of constructive enthusiasm; but I could not help feeling that their mission there would have been more in the nature of drudgery than of zeal, but for the radiant ardour of Gertrude Bell. Whatever subject she touched, she lit up; such vitality was irresistible. We laid plans, alas! for when I should return to Bagdad in the autumn: we would go to Babylon, we would go to Ctesiphon, she would have got her new museum by then. When she went back to England, if, indeed, she was compelled to go, she would write another book...So we sat talking, as friends talk who have not seen one another for a long time, until the shadows lengthened and she said it was time to go and see the king..."

To H.B., Bagdad, March 10th, 1926

Last Thursday night I went up to Khanaqin to spend Friday with the King ...In the morning, a carpenter and I were busy laying down linoleum and arranging furniture...

We lunched early, went a few miles down the line on a trolley to a place in the farm where we found horses waiting, and spent the afternoon riding about...

When we got back, the drawing room and two of the bed-rooms were finished. I whipped the furniture into place and the drawing room looked like a nice comfy room in an English country house. Not all the furniture is covered yet--I have now bought supplementary chintzes and silks in the bazaar to finish it off.

After dinner I left, an A.D.C. taking me to the train. The motor car, characteristically, hadn't enough petrol to reach the station, so we had to get out and walk. But there was no danger of missing the train which would have been kept waiting for me, till I turned up, unlike the North Eastern...

To H.B., Bagdad, March 16th, 1926

...We got to Ur in the early morning, after about 18 hours' journey and left at five in the evening, catching the mail and getting into Bagdad at 7 a.m. So I had a very busy day dividing the things. Nor was it very easy. I had to take the best thing they have got, a small but very perfect statue of the goddess Ban who presided over the farm-yard and has two geese by her throne and two under her feet. As we walked up to Ur from the train, the sky was black with geese flighting north, and talking as hard as they flew. I felt the goddess had been well supplied with them in her time.

I relinquished the lovely little head of the Moon goddess which was published in "The Times," and very reluctantly I relinquished two very early plaques showing sacrificial scenes...

I'm getting much more knowing with practice. I now can place cylindrical and other seals at more or less their comparative date and value, so that I don't choose wildly according to prettiness.

The goddess Ban is worth a great deal of money. Lionel was so anxious lest we should be robbed of her that he carried her about in his 'rucksack' and I fancy used her as a pillow, like a crossed Foreign

Office Bag. I took her away when we reached Bagdad, kept her in my house for a day and on Sunday deposited her in a safe.

To F.B., Bagdad, March 23rd, 1926

...I went to tea with the Queen on Sunday to say goodbye to the little Ghazi heir apparent who is going to England to be educated. I was so sorry for her. It must be hard to send your only little boy far away into conditions of which you haven't an inkling.

I have been spending the afternoon to-day trying to learn a little about arranging a museum. Oh dear! there's such a lot to be learnt that my heart sinks. However, I know what I shall do. I shall concentrate on exhibiting the best objects properly and get the others done little by little. Meantime the new museum building has to be re-roofed, for the present mud and beams could be cut through almost by a penknife held by a determined thief. So it will be some time before I get in to the upper floor, but I shall shortly be able to begin on two downstairs rooms...

To F.B., Bagdad, April 6th, 1926

...In 30 years I don't suppose there has been such a spring--slopes and rivers of scarlet ranunculus, meadows of purple stock and wild mignonette, blue lilies, black arums and once a bank of yellow tulips. These and commoner things made the world look like a brilliant piece of enamel...

...I went to Public Works and saw the measured drawings for my museum cases. Mr. Woolley and I (chiefly Mr. Woolley) have standardized wall cases and table cases so that one drawing does for all and the size suits the new building. But there were a good many points which hadn't been understood and the drawings needed careful revision. In the museum afterwards I found Squadron Leader Harnett who takes a deep interest in archaeology and will be very helpful when it comes to arranging the things in the cases. We sat each On a Sumerian gate socket and drew up a scheme for numbering. You see, every object must have a running museum number besides its number in its particular room--the latter for making a catalogue easily usable by the public. As yet we have only the excavators' numbers, Ur 1 to 4000, say, and Kish ditto; while objects that don't come from an excavation have no number at all. The new arrangement will be chronological not geographical, except in the downstairs rooms where all the big, heavy stone objects too heavy to carry upstairs, will stand--a Babylonian room, an Assyrian room and an Arab room are what I shall begin on downstairs when the necessary fittings are made. I foresee that I shall be very boring about Museums for some time to come! Also that I shall make innumerable mistakes...

To F.B., Bagdad, April 14th, 1926

Our chief preoccupation during the past week has been water. The two days of south wind, of which I spoke with disgust in my last letter, were being more disgusting than I knew. They were melting the snows in the northern mountains and on Thursday we were in for a terrific flood. The river was already so high that no cars or cabs were allowed to cross the bridges and one walked to office hoping devoutly that one would also be able to walk back. In fact the bridges have stood. On Thursday evening the river was almost lapping over its left bank and everybody was busy sandbagging his garden terrace lest the water should come in. After dinner, I sent my gardener round to Ken's house to help and went there myself for a better look at the flood. It was rumbling and sulking past; as we stood on the terrace it sounded as though it were pushing into the foundations under our feet. On Friday the Tigris dyke broke on the left bank--my bank--above the King's palace which it flooded. He was away at Khanaqin and his family had to be moved hastily into a house in the town. The water rushed over the eastern desert, lapping along the torn dyke and from then until now we have never been sure that it would not break through and flood the low lying parts of the town, which include my quarter! I think that risk is over now, unless the Tigris again does something very perverse, but the possibility of having 6ft. of water in one's house hasn't been pleasant. How dreadfully annoyed I should have been, to be sure. It has been difficult to think of anything else. They have brought in thousands of peasants and propped the banks with reed mats and sand bags, but the worst is when the water begins to drip in through rotten places in the lower parts of the dyke. They have electric light all along and people watching and looking night, and day. The big railway station on the east bank is under water and enormous quantities of merchandize waiting to go up to Persia spoilt...

The Arabs are so incurably careless; they won't shut their channels when the flood is coming down and then it finds a way in and breaks through. ...

This is a country of extremes. It's either dying of thirst or it's dying of being drowned. Bagdad can never be made really safe, it lies in such low ground; but I expect that after this experience, following on that Of 1923, they will do a great deal to make it safer. The whole desert to the east is under water for miles and miles; now the Euphrates is beginning and it's to be hoped that it won't lay under water the whole desert to the west! Anyhow it can't destroy my house, which is something.

This is only a flood letter I'm afraid.

I'm so sorry for the King--his nice house all spoilt. And poor Iltyd, who is in Mosul...

To H.B., Bagdad, April 21st, 1926

I ought to have told you about it and also to look for the Arabic graffiti on the columns, in the doorways of St. Mark's. I could not read them but they obviously must have been written before the columns were carried off from the east. I liked the general aspect of St. Mark's less when I saw it again, and some of the details more...

We are now safe from floods--as safe as we can be, for as Mr. Bury observes, Bagdad cannot ever be safe unless it is rebuilt in another place. Fortunately the Diala did not rise too high so that the Tigris water began to flow off into it. But the Baquba road is for two miles under water--they have managed to get a temporary road open across the desert three or four miles to the south. The breach in the Tigris was closed on Friday by throwing sandbags between rows of wooden piles. It did not look very solid but they are now building a strong earth dyke behind. The King's palace is not so bad. They got all the furniture out, though most of it will have to be recovered, and the water has now run off. But the big house on the river bank where the Queen and the family live is cracking and probably means to fall into the Tigris. The bank is undermined...The King means to get back by day into his own little palace and offices as soon as he can. Isn't it horribly boring for him.

I also find it boring, for all the desert where I used to ride and walk is a lake...

The Prime Minister, I can't think why, has asked me to serve on the Government Committee for distributing relief to the peasants who were washed out above Bagdad. There's a meeting to-morrow...

Iltyd is away in Mosul where he received a telegram thus worded "On approach of the water your house fell down" from one of his Arab officers. His house has in fact collapsed into the flood but he had moved all his clothes and things into the brick barracks nearby before he left, and these are safe. All his furniture was washed away and lost.

The only other thing I have done was to dine with Ken on Monday to meet the King, who was very cheerful considering all his troubles. But as we were six we had to play Vingt et Un (a very dull game I think) instead of bridge.

I was exceedingly sorry to hear of Will Pease's death--it was in the papers. I've written to Ernest.

We have all been imprisoned by very heavy rain. It's over now. On Saturday there wasn't a room in the office through the ceiling of which the rain wasn't dripping. On Sunday morning I went to the Sarai and did a lot of work in the Museum and then had a long gossip with the police about Bolsheviks, etc. An American came to lunch, he is the representative of the American school this year. We looked at pottery and flints collected by him on the southern mounds; we looked at them till four, I learnt something, I think, but he learnt more, for he knows much less about pottery than I do, which is saying that he knows very little. However, he had found some interesting inscribed bricks and these he did know about. The net result of his labours is that we don't yet know the site of an ancient Babylonian city called Isin, for he has got Isin bricks out of another mound. It's negative but it's better not to think we know when we don't.

This afternoon I went into the desert which was fairly dry and now I'm going to pack for I go to Ur to-morrow.

Iltyd and I are going to a little music party given by the Vernons to- night. I like the Vernons.

To H.B., Bagdad, May 5th, 1926

[This is during the Strike in England.] Everything else is swallowed up in the thought of what is happening to you. The scanty news in Reuter gives one some impression of the terrible upheaval. One peers into the future much as one did at the beginning of August, 1914--absit omen! ...

On Saturday night I had a bridge party to while away the time before my train left which wasn't till 11:30...It was rather a hot journey down to Ur, just hot enough to do nothing but laze and read a novel, but I restored the balance by unusual activity on arrival. There was a lot of pottery belonging to us left at the Expeditions Haus. I had brought 4 cases to pack it in and my museum clerk--to help--the capable station master provided us with men to carry the cases out across the desert and soon after 6 o'clock we were busy packing up by the light of a lantern and with the willing assistance of the Arab guards. It took us about two hours, after which we walked back in the night over the deliciously cool desert...

The King arrived from Basrah about 5:30 a.m. on Monday. We were all ready to receive him, the Mutasarrif, Administrative Inspector, sheikhs, I, etc. When he had finished with salutations we decided to go off at once to the excavations and come back to breakfast after. H.M. and I stepped into the Mutasarrif's car and the others followed in taxis, a Minister and a varied lot of officials who were with H.M. It was a most successful visit; the King was much interested--we got through before 8, when the sun was just beginning to be a little hot, having seen all that Kings need see. Then breakfast in the King's car with a couple of Ministers and nice Mr. Bury (irrigation). Subsequently I returned to my own compartment. It was a special train and we stopped nowhere but at Diwaniyah where we moved into a restaurant car for lunch (I lunched with a Minister and two Saiyids, one a Senator, one a Deputy) and again at Hillah where the King sent for me to have tea with him. It was now cool again and H.M. and I, a Minister and a courtier played bridge till we reached Bagdad at 6:45 p.m. on April 3rd. There I learnt that the strike had begun--Ken came in before dinner with the news. Since when we have all talked of little else.

Telegrams continue to come from the Colonial Office we suppose that Sir John Shuckburgh is transported thither in a government lorry.

We suppose and we wonder and we wish we knew more. Incidentally I don't know whether letters will reach you or how long they will be delayed, so I shall not write any other than this.

To H.B., Bagdad, May 11th, 1926

Your letter of April 28th, written on the eve of the strike reached me by last mail; I wonder whether letters will have got through in the first week and fear that the next letter may be delayed. We have no news but Reuter and you may imagine how eagerly we await it. Indeed anxiety is never out of my mind; there has been word of disturbances at Middlesbrough and to-day there are railway accidents. These things don't make one feel easier. s You ask about my plans for the summer. This doesn't seem to be the moment to make any plans which involve expenditure, for I don't know whether I shall have any income or whether any of us will. My duty to the museum is of the first importance. I can't go away and leave all those valuable things half transferred and the work goes very slowly. It will take months and months, I think. I have made a little headway this week. The alterations in the building itself are finished and a few simple fittings in one of the lower rooms were ready so on Sunday morning I called on Squadron Leader Harnett to help and we placed all the big gate sockets (dull things but valuable) on the bench along the wall that had been made for them, or rather we superintended the placing of them by porters. In the middle of the wall I had had a solid cement pedestal set up and onto this we hauled (I didn't) a great roughly blocked out Babylonian statue. When we had done, we were quite pleased with the look of it, but we have not got any further for we are waiting for a wooden pedestal for a statue which is to stand in the middle of the room and some shallow boxes in which to set some broken bits of relief in cement. In one corner I am going to reconstruct the tomb of a deified king of Ur which was found this year, and as that is about all which the room will hold for the present (I mean, I have nothing more for that room), it ought not to take very long to get it finished. It will look, no doubt, rather home-made, but even now it is beginning to look like a museum. When it is ready, I want quickly to make a catalogue of it-- no great task--and then get the King to open it so as to show people that we are doing something...

To F.B., Bagdad, May 13th, 1926

I don't see how I can possibly make any plans for the moment so of course keep the pageant where you like. I think it is extremely unlikely that I can afford to come back and out again this summer--it's a very expensive business. It would be worse to finish the museum and then be told not to come back here if I thought that the best course which I probably shall. Bernard is going on leave in about 3 weeks and when he is away Sir Henry rather leans on me, not so much to do things as to talk them over. He is full of plans for big administrative work, which doesn't in fact touch me. They interest me very much, his schemes and I think them on the whole very good.

Oh dear, I wonder what it is all like with you--what it will be like after, if there's any sort of an "after." ...

To H.B., Bagdad, May 18th, 1926

I had scarcely posted my letter last week, when we got news of the ending of the general strike, but that doesn't mean the ending of difficulties and you are still in the thick of them. Indeed, I don't know whether your worst difficulties are not just about to begin...

I have been very busy with my museum, but it has not got far yet. I go in at 7 a.m. and spend a couple of hours there before I go to office. On Sunday we can work until it gets too hot and fortunately it is being remarkably cool weather. In a day or two I shall have my own workroom with an electric fan which will make things easier...As for cases, tables and things, they have not begun to materialize yet and for the moment I am occupied with the big stone objects which do not need to be behind glass.

I forget if you know Sir John Cadman. He is, or is going to be, Chairman of the A.P.O.C. He was here a year and a half ago and brought a letter to me from Willie Tyrrell. He passed through again last week on his way back from Persia, where he had been to represent the A.P.O.C. at the coronation of the Shah. During the 4 days he spent here he succeeded in getting through the agreement with the Iraq Government for the working of the oil at Khanaqin which has been hanging fire for three years or more. I met him every day, lunching with Sir Henry, and was thrilled to hear his account of the way matters were proceeding. If all goes well- and there's no reason why it should not--the Iraq ought to begin to draw royalties next year and to have cheap oil from the Khanaqin refinery. On Sunday, the night before Sir John left, Sir Henry gave a large dinner party to meet the King. Sir John was sitting between H.M. and me and they spent most of the dinner in exchanging sentiments of gratitude and hopeful anticipation. As they had no common tongue, it fell to me to interpret for them. I felt I earned my dinner.

Sir John had with him as secretary a young Bridgeman, son of the First Lord of the Admiralty, a nice boy. He, and a very attractive and intelligent young soldier in the Iraq army, Captain Edwells, came to tea with me on Saturday, after which I took them sight seeing.

Iltyd is going to Mosul for a month, which is very tiresome. He dined with me on Tuesday and we played piquet afterwards. He is such a pleasant companion--I miss him very much when he is away. Lionel is also a great stand by. He comes in frequently to tea on his way back from office and we walk together to his house at Alwiyah about a mile away, through what you might almost call fields. But now that the barley is being cut they are gradually relapsing from fields into desert... Ken and I dined with him last night and had an agreeable evening. We caught some huge hawk moths. Lionel is rather good at lepidoptera. and Ken is an expert. Between us we are getting quite a collection. It is an amusing way of passing the time.

I lunch always with Sir Henry and we discuss the affairs of the day, public and private, and then, if I have been early at the Museum, I go to sleep for a bit when I get home; in the evening if I am alone I read Babylonian history or books about seals and things so that I may know a little better how to arrange the Museum. It sounds rather a monotonous existence, but it is inexpensive and peaceful which, I am afraid, is more than can be said for yours.

To F.B., Bagdad, May 26th, 1926

Your letter of May 11th was the very first news I had of your doings during the general strike. You don't sound as if you were living in a strike at all, but it is wonderful how little difference it made, even in London, I gather from Elsa. But if the coal strike drags on and on, it will be very dreadful and it must end in dislocating life. Molly hasn't written since just after she was ill.

I am sure that Maurice must have been admirable at Middles-brough but there were anxious moments, weren't there. Oh dear, isn't it a horrid world.

I hope you won't think I'm wrong in saying that I can't go away yet and leave all my antiquities unarranged and unguarded. I have been writing to father about it. I'll see later how things go on, but it's so very expensive to return home and then come back here that I think I would rather finish and then go away. It isn't because I don't immensely want to see you and father, but I know you will understand that it means a very great deal to leave everything that I have been do-ing here and find myself really rather loose on the world. I don't see at all clearly what I shall do, but of course I can't stay here forever; al-ready I feel that when Bernard is here, and Sir Henry, I'm not at all necessary in the office.

I would have liked to stay in the Department of Antiquities if I could come home every year, but I don't feel justified in asking the Iraq Government to give me anything like a permanent post. The Di-rector here should know cuneiform and be a trained museum official. What I can do is just to tide them over...

All the same I feel very much torn. Tell me what you think, will you please.

THE LETTERS OF GERTRUDE BELL

To H.B., Bagdad, May 26th, 1926

I received by last mail your letters of May 5th and 11th and
read them with the deepest interest. Also letters from mother and Elsa,
of May 11th, so that I had a good all round view of what things were
like. Your forecast as to the duration of the general strike was very
good and I was particularly glad that you gave me a resumé of dealings with the colliers because Sir Henry is always asking me about it
and your outline was so clear. I am going to have it typed for distribution to my colleagues...Anyhow, I take it that we shall have very little
income this year.

That is not the only reason, though it's a very good one, for my
wanting to stay here this summer. I hope you won't be very much disappointed. What I vaguely think of doing (but don't talk about it) is to
stay with the High Commissioner till Bernard comes back in the autumn; then to resign and ask the Iraq Government to take me on as
Director of Antiquities for six months or so. (I'm only Hon. Director
now, you know.) I should not in any case stay much longer with the
H.C.; it has really ceased to be my job. Politics are dropping out and
giving place to big administrative questions in which I'm not concerned and at which I'm no good. On the other hand, the Department
of Antiquities is now a full time job. I am trying to get the Cabinet to
let me deal with all the things the Germans left at Babylon as I should
deal with a new excavation. Privately, I have put up the Deutch Orient
Gesellschaft to make the proposal and they have suggested sending out
Andrae, who dug at Shergat, to arrange and catalogue the objects, after
which I would make a division. I know Andrae very well and like him;
the fact that I was working with him would make everything go
smoothly and the Iraq Government has complete confidence in me as
Director and would not question anything I did. But all this would
mean far too much work to be treated as a secondary employment.
Yale is nibbling at the biggest mound in the Iraq, and if I have three
excavations on my hands besides Babylon and the Museum it is very
certain that I cannot do anything else. I am waiting to see how all this
turns out, but already I know that I ought to have all my time for the
Museum. As it is I now go there from 7 to 8:30 or SO every morning
and get to the office about 9. That has meant a pretty strenuous four
and a half hours but I find that I can just get through the work, sometimes taking papers home to read in the evening. The weather has been
beautifully cool. On Sunday (Whit Sunday) I worked from 7 to 1 in

679

the Museum without any fans. Monday was a holiday in the office though I could not take it all as I had a report to write, but by doing some of it on Sunday afternoon I got from 7 to 1 in the Museum. One big room downstairs, the Babylonian Stone Room, is now finished and I am only waiting for the catalogue, which I have written, to be translated and printed, to ask the King to open it--just to show them that we are doing something. But this is the easiest of all the rooms, big objects not under glass, it is when I come to the upstairs rooms and all the little objects that the difficulties begin. The mere cataloguing and numbering of them is terrific. The cataloguing of things from Ur and Kish for the past three years has been done and I have now nearly finished the things of this year. But the serial number of the Bagdad Museum has to be put onto everything and until each object is in the catalogue we can't number it. There are a mass of things from other places than Ur and Kish which we have not begun on. Then will come the arrangement in cases--none of which have begun to come in yet. I have moved about half the things from the old room into the new Museum and they are lying about, some on tables, some on the floor, a desolating spectacle. In the course of the next ten days it will be even worse, for by that time I hope I may have got almost everything moved over. I don't think I could possibly leave it like this. If in the middle of the summer I felt tired or seedy, I might have got things into enough order to come away for a bit, but it's very expensive to come as far as England as I have Marie to take too. I'll see later.

The afternoons, after tea, hang rather heavy on my hands...We can't swim yet because the river is so high and the current so strong. This last week I have sometimes gone into the Museum at 5, but it will soon be too hot to do that with any comfort and it is not really a good plan because one gets no exercise. I did it in order to finish cataloguing the Ur and Kish things of this year...

To F.B., Bagdad, June 2nd, 1926

...Lionel and I yesterday were busy discussing the programme he is drawing up for a university curriculum. Sir Henry is pressing for a faculty of Fine Arts. Lionel's idea is to combine languages and literature--at least French and English--with history, political economy, all in a three years' course...

I suggested that, in special historic subjects Babylonia and Assyria should be included. I should like to lecture on that myself, but I don't think the scheme will materialize for a long time ...

Nevertheless, Sir Henry does put a great deal of vitality into things and I always stand amazed at his general capacity.

To H.B., Bagdad, June 2nd, 1926

I can't refer to the Times because I have had no papers since the general strike. I can't think why they didn't come last week. Anyway the last Times I received was that of April 28th while your letter from Mt. Grace was dated May 18th. The 'sécateur' for Haji Naji has arrived, however. I have not taken it to him yet because I have been so busy in the Museum. Profiting by remarkably cool weather I've been there between tea and dinner as well as in the early morning. I know he will love it. I will try to take it down to him on Sunday. There is a little basket of fruit from him on my dining room table most mornings.

To-morrow we have a holiday for the King's birthday and I shall have a whole day for my Museum. That enthusiast, Squadron Leader Harnett, is coming too. We have been engaged in taking down a beautiful late Abbassid inscription (not brick) which was dropping out of the ruined building in which it stood...It is coming out very well and Squadron Leader Harnett is now going to clean it and build it up against the wall of the big Arab room. We spent a long peaceful morning on Sunday cataloguing cylinder seals...He is certainly a great asset and he seems to be amused with what some people might consider a very tedious job. I don't, for there is an indescribable attraction about these fine little things. The worst of it is that I can't extract the furniture out of the railway people so we don't get to anything final.

I haven't told you about the floods for a long time. The Euphrates, after threatening to cover the country up to the embankment of the Hillah railway, thought better of it. The Tigris is definitely going down, but one of the deputies told me the other day that the cellars of his house in the middle of Bagdad, a good deal below the river level, are 4ft. deep in water...

THE LETTERS OF GERTRUDE BELL

To F.B., Bagdad, June 9th, 1926

I unfortunately overslept myself this afternoon and the King is coming to dinner. I hope you will like the picture postcards I sent to Father of two of the exhibits in the Museum. They do rather fill me with pride. I haven't got any of my cases or tables yet for the upper rooms and I don't know when they will begin to come in. Meantime, with the help of S/L Harnett and occasionally Mr. Cooke, I am getting on with the numbering of all the objects. This year's finds have all been catalogued and numbered and all the cylinder seals are done--we could arrange them at once if we had the cases. That will be an absorbingly interesting task.

I have an extremely nice Indian foreman who is deputed to do all the odds and ends of jobs that arise--such as building up Bur Sin's shrine. He is so capable and so pleasant. And I shall be very much interested to see what the Arab bigwigs think of the lower room which the King opens next week. The one or two who have dropped in to see us at work have been much impressed.

To H.B., Bagdad, June 9th, 1926

...I am enclosing the catalogue of the Babylonian Stone Room of the Museum and two picture postcards of the exhibits. No. 7 is the thing I am proudest of--there is nothing like it in any museum in the world. I forgot to mention in the catalogue that the bricks which form the pedestal of the statue (No. 1) are blue glazed bricks from the top of the Ziggurrat at Ur, remains of an upper chamber built or restored by Nabonidus the last king of Babylon. We brought away a lot of fragments and built them up into a pedestal--it is most effective. The King is going to open this room on Monday. it is the easiest of all to arrange because it consists only of a few large objects but it looks extremely well and I hope it will impress the Ministers! It has indeed all the appearance of a Museum...

Thursday was a very nice day for I had the whole morning there (in the Museum) and came back to lunch and a good rest. There was a state dinner party for the King's birthday and a reception of about 500 people in the garden afterwards. The party was very interesting. All the deputies and senators and everyone one had ever known

682

in Bagdad were there, the Ministers and most of the Arab civil servants in ordinary European evening dress and hatless and the religious leaders in robes and turbans. There was a wonderful diversity...

On Sunday S/L Harnett and I had a good morning in the Museum. After tea Ken and I went out to Karradah and caught four exquisite swallow tail butterflies, the first we had seen. We were much elated.

Haji Naji is delighted with his knife and sends you a thousand messages of thanks.

To-night the King comes to dine and play bridge...

To H.B., Bagdad, June 16th, 1926

My principal news you have seen in the papers--the Turkish treaty. It is almost too good to be true...

I had a nice little ceremony on Monday when the King opened the first room of the Museum. It was open to the public for the first time to-day and as I came away at 8:30 this morning, I saw some 15 or 20 ordinary Bagdadis going round it under the guidance of the Arab curator--very gratifying. Everyone agrees that it looks like a Museum. All the other rooms are still chaos, but S/L Harnett and I are forging ahead with the numbering and cataloguing and I actually hope to add a couple of small cases this week. But it is such a stupendous job that without the support of the admirable S/L Harnett I should certainly succumb. Fortunately it is being quite comparatively cool.

To F.B., Bagdad, June 16th, 1926

...Decidedly a pageant is a much bigger undertaking than a Museum. I wonder if you sometimes think, as I do, that you Will never get through with it! But it was a great satisfaction this morning to see the public actually looking at the room which the King opened on Monday. It is only open two days a week for a couple of hours because all my staff (an old Arab curator, a very intelligent Jew clerk and an odd man) is so busy. We are now beginning to see daylight through the preliminary task of numbering the objects--between three and four thousand of them.

It is being a very grim world, isn't it. I feel often that I don't know how I should face it but for the work I'm doing and I know you must feel the same. I think of you month after month as the time passes since that awful sorrow, and realize all the time that the passage of the months can make little difference. I wish I were coming home this summer but I feel sure that when I leave I shall not want to come back here and I would like to finish this job first--indeed, I feel that I must finish it, there being no one else. But it is too lonely, my existence here; one can't go on for ever being alone. At least, I don't feel I can...

To H.B., Bagdad, June 23rd, 1926

We are labouring under the difficulties presented by the four days' holiday of the big Id when all the Arab offices are closed and one can't get anything through. A holiday at this time of year is no good as far as holiday making goes, for it is too hot to go out on any expedition. By luck--and the vagaries of the moon--it didn't begin till Monday, so that I had Sunday morning in the Museum. I have to give my staff a holiday and I shall not be able to work there again till Saturday which is a bore. However, I brought back some cases of cylinder seals at which I have been working of an evening...

We had a terrific day on Monday. It began with a levee at the palace at 6:10. I was in an ace of going without orders, but I discovered their absence as I was waiting for the High Commissioner at the end of the Maude Bridge and dispatched a Kavass hotfoot to fetch them. The H.C. being fortunately late, they arrived in the nick of time.

I then came home, breakfasted and did an hour's work, after which I set out again on visits. First the Naqib, then the Ministers, then selected notables and finally the Queen and Ali and his family...

It has been extremely mild for Bagdad, rarely over a hundred and the nights quite cold; but after dinner my house is stuffy and I am glad when it is time to go to bed on the roof. We are going to begin swimming which is the only agreeable form of exercise at this time of year...

I am being much enthralled by the study of seals. In the scenes of worship and domestic life depicted on those tiny cylinders I constantly find pots and things which I have actually got in the Museum. Then I suddenly place them with a much greater sense of reality. just as I placed the mace heads in the shrine of Bur Sin--I have found them on quantities of seals standing in the shrines of other gods. That is rather thrilling, isn't it...

To H.B., Bagdad, June 30th, 1926

...What an enormous waste and loss two months' coal strike must mean. It's so amazing that the world seems to go on just the same--Ascot and balls and parties are what I read of in the Times--or, rather, I see they are there--and extraordinarily little about things that really matter.

We are now well into the hot weather--temperature at 113--but I am feeling it scarcely at all. Partly, I think, because we have begun bathing though the river is still very high and the current strong: It makes such a difference. We go up by launch to a place above the town where I have a little hut to undress in and get back after seven feeling both exercised and refreshed...It is too hot now to dine indoors and play bridge and much pleasanter to lie out on the river bank and come home by launch about 10.

I often wonder how the old Babylonians with whom I now feel such a close connection, passed their summer. Much as we do, I daresay, but without our ice and electric fans which add immensely to the amenities of existence. The moment of the day I don't like is going home after lunch at the hottest moment, but there is no way out of it.

In the Museum S/L Harnett and I are engaged in classifying seals. I have read books and books about them. The really important ones are usually plain sailing; one is pretty certain of their period, but there are dreadful backwaters of decadence when one is never sure whether the thing is very early or just very bad late work. Also the authorities are not in entire agreement and one has to make up one's mind whom one will follow. Still on the whole, I don't think I shall be very much out...Next week I hope to have my seal case and by that time we shall have got all the seals fairly well grouped and ready to be put in...

Faisal has given me a bronze bust of himself by Feo Gleichen to put in the Museum. I shall set it up in the big Arab room. There, now I must go to lunch. My letters are extremely dull, but there is really nothing to recount.

To H.B., 2nd July, 1926

...I don't see for the moment what I can do. You see I have undertaken this very grave responsibility of the museum--I have been writing about it ad nauseam for months. I had been protesting for more than a year that I must have a proper building; this winter one fell vacant and they gave it to me together with a very large sum of money for fittings, etc. Then first I had to re-roof it and next I was held up at least two months by the floods and the work they entailed which prevented work being done for me. Now all the very valuable objects-they run into tens of thousands of pounds and incidentally they would never have been taken out of the ground if I had not been here to guarantee that they would be properly protected, have been transferred pell-mell into the new building and there is absolutely no one but I who knows anything about them, since J. M. Wilson left. It isn't merely a responsibility to the Iraq but to archaeology in general. I could not possibly leave things in this state except for the gravest reasons. I work at it as hard as I can, but it's a gigantic task--of course I love it and am ready to give all my spare time to it. But I can't resign from my post as Oriental Secretary. And as I am a civil servant, I have only about 2 months' leave owing to me, which means a little over 9 weeks in England.

That is the whole position. In a couple of months or so I may be beginning to see daylight in the museum or at any rate a condition in which I could safely leave it for a little. Let us wait for a bit, don't you think, and see how things look.

You do realise, don't you, that I feel bound to fulfil the undertakings I gave when, at my instance the Iraq Government allowed

686

excavations to be begun 4 years ago. The thing has grown and grown--it can't do otherwise--and whereas until last autumn I had J.M. to help me, I now have no one. All the plans that were begun before Hugo was ill even, are now bearing fruit and I'm rather overwhelmed by them. Anyhow, father, give me a little time to get things into some kind of order and then if you want me to take what leave I can I will do so. But in that case I think I should have to come back for next winter or part of it.

Except for the Museum work, life is very dull.

To H.B., Bagdad, July 7th, 1926

...It had been very hot in the morning in the Museum but we have now changed into a north room and had a fan put into it which makes it comparatively luxurious. We can work there quite comfortably without a fan on week days when we leave at 8:30, but on Sundays when we stay until 1, it is essential to have a cool room. I have got a few standard cases and hope to have the seal case this week. But there is so much to learn; one constantly finds that the things don't exactly serve one's purpose and they have to be modified. However both we and the carpenters are learning gradually.

I have been having very busy mornings, lots of dispatches to write and long things to do. Sir Henry is delightful to work with, but he is most careful of detail and one has to pay great attention to what one is doing.

Darling I must stop now; summer does not conduce to the writing of very long letters.

To F.B., Bagdad, July 7, 1926

...photograph of you and the little boys. They are darlings. Is not the eldest one like Hugo? In this photograph I see a great likeness... ...

I am so glad you like the pictures of my museum, and when in return will you give me the text of the Pageant? I want so much to read it. I wish I were at the point of having photographs of the upper rooms

687

taken, but they are still in chaos--not so chaotic as they were, however for most of the objects are roughly classified and ready to be put into cases. But I find arranging cases very difficult. Even the two tiny ones which I have done so far take an enormous amount of thought and re-arrangement till one puts them approximately right. And then the writing of labels! Fortunately my Arab clerk writes them beautifully so I only have to give him a list of what has to go on each one and leave him to do it during the rest of the morning while I am in the office...

[These two letters of July 2nd and July 7th were the last she wrote home. They reached England after her death.

Her strenuous self-imposed work in the museum, in the terrible heat of a Bagdad summer, added to the daily round of her duties in the office, proved too much for her slender stock of physical energy. She had never really recovered from her illness in the winter.

She died quite peacefully in her sleep, in the early morning hours of Monday July 12th, 1926.

CHAPTER XXVII

CONCLUSION

The tidings brought an overwhelming manifestation of sorrow and sympathy from all parts of the earth, and we realised afresh that her name was known in every continent, her story had crossed every sea. There had clustered round her in her lifetime so many fantastic tales of adventure, based on fact and embroidered by fiction, tales of the Mystery Woman of the East, the uncrowned Queen, the Diana of the Desert, that a kind of legendary personality had emerged which represented Gertrude in the imagination of the general public, to the day of her death.

When the crowning sequel came to those times of desert adventure, when she saw her dreams of the Arab resurgence turn into reality, she was one of those who helped to achieve it. She was at the throbbing centre of the events which lead to the dramatic leap into history of the Kingdom of Iraq with an Arab prince on the throne.

During the years that followed, when she became a servant of the State, her abilities were again conspicuously displayed in what was to her the entirely new field of official life. But her officialdom was always tinged with ardour and romance, and it was an unceasing interest to her that her congenial Post as Oriental Secretary to the High Commissioner enabled her still to keep in close touch with the Arabs of the desert as well as with the increasing number of their kinsmen in the town.

At the news of her death messages were received at the High Commissioner's office from all parts of Iraq, from Bagdad, from the desert, from officials and representatives--and most of them seem to be no mere formal condolences, but to have in them a note of real sorrow.

I quote here a sentence from a moving letter from Haji Naji, for whom Gertrude felt such warm friendship, and whose garden was always her delight:

"It was my faith always to send Miss Bell the first of my fruits and vegetables and I know not now where I shall send them."

I wish I had space enough to reproduce here many other letters from Gertrude's Arab friends.

In her own country there was a widespread expression of regret. Telegrams and letters, all seeming to convey a sense Of personal loss, poured in from every layer of the social scale. They came from the highest in the land, they came from people of distinction in the world of letters, the world of art, the political world, the social world, from the villages of her Yorkshire countryside, who were so proud of her, from the Works where she had so many friends; and her family felt that however different the senders might be from one another, and however differently they expressed themselves, they were all saying and meaning the same thing--they all really cared.

Their Majesties sent the following message:

"The Queen and I are grieved to hear of the death of your distinguished and gifted daughter whom we held in high regard.

"The nation will with us mourn the loss of one who by her intellectual powers, force of character and personal courage rendered important and what I trust will prove lasting benefit to the country and to those regions where she worked with such devotion and self-sacrifice. We truly sympathise with you in your sorrow.

"(Signed) GEORGE R. I."

The Colonial Secretary, Mr. Amery, paid her the grate tribute of a statement in the House of Commons, recapitulating her devoted service, in answer to a question from Mr. Runciman.

Sir Valentine Chirol, who, as shown so often in the letters, was one of her closest friends, wrote an obituary notice of her which

690

appeared in the Times the day after she died. It was a striking portrait, written with the most profound sympathy and understanding. Sir Arnold Wilson, the " A.T." of her letters, under whom she served, wrote in the Times a generous appreciation of her work; so did Mr. Woolley, who shared her work in archaeology, so did also Dr. David Hogarth, her friend and counsellor, whose wide and learned experience of the East, added to his steadfast friendship, was always to Gertrude such a support. So did M. Salomon Reinach (writing in the Revue Archéologique) from whom Gertrude learned so very much.

Some of the letters we received were written by people who went to her house once, perhaps, as they passed through Bagdad, and record the vivid and ineffaceable impression she made on them.

The High Commissioner wrote the following letter to Gertrude's father about the Museum she founded in Bagdad, now called the Iraq Museum--how she would have preferred that name to any other!

6th June, 1927, High Commissioner's Office, Bagdad

My Dear Sir Hugh,

King Faisal some time ago wrote to the Prime Minister of Iraq suggesting that one of the principal rooms in the Bagdad Museum should be named the "Gertrude Bell Room," and I understand that this has been accepted by the Iraq Cabinet.

A meeting of Gertrude's friends later decided to associate her name with the whole Museum by putting in a prominent position a brass plaque with a suitable inscription, which was to be submitted to you for approval. After you had approved it they thought of asking J. M. Wilson to design the plaque...

Yours very sincerely,
H. DOBBS.

THE LETTERS OF GERTRUDE BELL

Gertrude Bell, whose memory the Arabs will ever hold in reverence and affection, created this Museum in 1923, being then Honorary Director of Antiquities for the Iraq. With wonderful knowledge and devotion she assembled the most precious objects in it and through the heat of the Summer worked on them until the day of her death on 12th July, 1926.

King Faisal and the Government of Iraq, in gratitude for her great deeds in this country, have ordered that the Principal Wing shall bear her name and with their permission her friends have erected this tablet.

It is a source of deep satisfaction to Gertrude's family that King Faisal, who honoured her with his friendship and to whom she was so loyally devoted, should have suggested that her name should be associated with the Museum and should have consented to the placing of the beautifully worded plaque.

Gertrude was buried in the afternoon of July 12th, in the cemetery outside Bagdad, with the honours of a military funeral. "A huge concourse of Iraqis and British," we were told "were present. The High Commissioner and the whole of the British Staff, civil, military and Air Force, the Prime Minister of Iraq and the members of the Cabinet, and a great number of Arab sheikhs from the desert. The troops of the Iraq army lined the road, and an enormous crowd paid a last homage to one who was honoured throughout the length and breadth of the land."

Her coffin was borne from the gate of the cemetery to the graveside by the group of young men on the High Commissioner's staff, whose names recur so often in her letters, her intimate friends and comrades, to whom her house was always a beloved centre, a meeting place and haven. Her death had come to them as an unbelievable catastrophe.

The High Commissioner, Gertrude's chief, issued an official notification of her death, in which a sense of acute grief is felt to underlie the dignified and restrained wording. I quote from it two sentences which seem to me to sum up all that can be said about her services in the East.

"She had for the last ten years of her life consecrated all the indomitable fervour of her spirit and all the astounding gifts of her mind to the service of the Arab cause, and especially to Iraq. At last her body, always frail, was broken by the energy of her soul."

"Her bones rest where she had wished them to rest, in the soil of Iraq. Her friends are left desolate."

But let us not mourn, those who are left, even those who were nearest to her, that the end came to her so swiftly and so soon. Life would inexorably have led her down the slope--Death stayed her at the summit.

IMAGES

Gertrude from a drawing by Sargent

Gertrude's house in Bagdad

At Bagdad

Sir Hugh Bell in Gertrude's sitting-room at Bagdad

H. M. King Faisal of Iraq

The Conference at Cairo

Sheikhs of the Desert
Kamadi--the Standard of the Dulaim

Gertrude at the age of fifty-three

Gertrude beside her aeroplane

A picnic with King Faisal

Opening of the railway by King Faisal

Auda

Dividing the finds (top image)
Gertrude looking out at the Desert (bottom image)

Also from Benediction Books ...

Wandering Between Two Worlds: Essays on Faith and Art
Anita Mathias
Benediction Books, 2007
152 pages
ISBN: 0955373700

Available from www.amazon.com, www.amazon.co.uk
www.wanderingbetweentwoworlds.com

In these wide-ranging lyrical essays, Anita Mathias writes, in lush, lovely prose, of her naughty Catholic childhood in Jamshedpur, India; her large, eccentric family in Mangalore, a sea-coast town converted by the Portuguese in the sixteenth century; her rebellion and atheism as a teenager in her Himalayan boarding school, run by German missionary nuns, St. Mary's Convent, Nainital; and her abrupt religious conversion after which she entered Mother Teresa's convent in Calcutta as a novice. Later rich, elegant essays explore the dualities of her life as a writer, mother, and Christian in the United States-- Domesticity and Art, Writing and Prayer, and the experience of being "an alien and stranger" as an immigrant in America, sensing the need for roots.

About the Author

Anita Mathias was born in India, has a B.A. and M.A. in English from Somerville College, Oxford University and an M.A. in Creative Writing from the Ohio State University. Her essays have been published in The Washington Post, The London Magazine, The Virginia Quarterly Review, Commonweal, Notre Dame Magazine, America, The Christian Century, Religion Online, The Southwest Review, Contemporary Literary Criticism, New Letters, The Journal, and two of HarperSanFrancisco's The Best Spiritual Writing anthologies. Her non-fiction has won fellowships from The National Endowment for the Arts; The Minnesota State Arts Board; The Jerome Foundation, The Vermont Studio Center; The Virginia Centre for the Creative Arts, and the First Prize for the Best General Interest Article from the Catholic Press Association of the United States and Canada. Anita has taught Creative Writing at the College of William and Mary, and now lives and writes in Oxford, England.